PATTERNS OF PSYCHOLOGICAL THOUGHT

THE SERIES IN CLINICAL AND COMMUNITY PSYCHOLOGY

CONSULTING EDITORS:

CHARLES D. SPIELBERGER and IRWIN G. SARASON

IN PREPARATION

PATTERNS OF PSYCHOLOGICAL THOUGHT

Readings in Historical and Contemporary Texts

James R. Averill
University of Massachusetts

HEMISPHERE PUBLISHING CORPORATION
Washington   London

A HALSTED PRESS BOOK
JOHN WILEY & SONS
New York   London   Sydney   Toronto

Hemisphere Publishing Corporation
1025 Vermont Ave., N.W., Washington, D.C. 20005

Distributed solely by Halsted Press, a Division of John Wiley & Sons, Inc., New York.

1 2 3 4 5 6 7 8 9 0   D O D O   7 8 3 2 1 0 9 8 7 6

Library of Congress Cataloging in Publication Data

Main entry under title:

Patterns of psychological thought.

    (The Series in clinical and community psychology)
    Includes index.
    1. Psychology—History—Addresses, essays, lectures.
2. Psychology—Methodology—Addresses, essays, lectures.
I. Averill, James R.
BF81.P3 1976   150'.19   76-4901
ISBN 0-470-15070-X

Printed in the United States of America

Contents

XI. THE INSTITUTIONALIZATION OF BEHAVIOR

Preface

In the oft-quoted words of Ebbinghaus, "Psychology has a long past, but only a short history." This volume is concerned primarily with psychology's long past (from the ancient Greeks to the middle of the 19th century), and with the relevance of that past for contemporary issues. Until recently, most courses and textbooks in the history of psychology have concentrated on relatively recent developments—from about the mid-19th century on. From a disciplinary standpoint, there is good reason for this emphasis; as an independent discipline, psychology is not quite 100 years old. But if psychology is conceived as the study of behavior (in the broad sense), then it did not begin with the founding of the first experimental laboratory in 1879, nor with the establishment of university departments specifically labeled "Psychology." Therefore, if we are to understand contemporary problems and debates, we must look beyond psychology's short history to the traditions that gave it birth.

The importance of psychology's long past is being increasingly recognized in the university curriculum and in textbooks on the history of psychology. Such recent texts as Esper's *A History of Psychology*, Kantor's *The Scientific Evolution of Psychology*, Klein's *A History of Psychology*, and Watson's *The Great Psychologists* all devote considerable space to pre-19th century thought. However, authors who attempt to survey psychology's long past are faced with an almost insurmountable problem. With more than 20 centuries to cover, no more than a chapter, and typically less, may be devoted to the work of any one thinker.

The result is necessarily a caricature. A student may learn, for example, that Plato postulated the real existence of ideal Forms; that Aristotle conceived of the *psyche* as the "first grade of actuality" of a potentially living body; that Descartes believed that the soul—a mental substance—interacted with the body at the pineal gland; that Berkeley argued against the existence of material objects; and so forth. But what relevance could these ideas have for contemporary psychology? Simply to point out, say, that Berkeley's position led him to make important contributions to the theory of space perception is not enough. The student can rightfully respond: "So what? Few ideas are ever completely novel. To know that an idea was 'anticipated' by another may be interesting but not especially important. After all, if I wanted to learn about atomic physics, I would not read the Greek atomists. Similarly, if I want to know about depth perception, I will read the latest research, and not Bishop Berkeley."

This response ignores the fact that the kinds of observations theorists make and the structures of the arguments they use are often more important than the specific conclusions they reach. Yet these observations and arguments defy summary and secondhand reportage. It is thus not sufficient to abstract and explain a historical figure's thought, and to point out its relevance to contemporary problems. There is no real alternative to reading the original sources.

Probably few persons would disagree with this assertion in principle; in practice, however, there are major difficulties. To begin with, the wealth of historical material is so great that only a small fraction of it can be covered within the scope of any single volume. Most anthologies of primary sources therefore sample broadly, attempting to include important figures from different eras and to cover a variety of topics. The result is a series of brief excerpts from many different authors. Thus, Herrnstein and Boring's *A Sourcebook in the History of Psychology*, one of the best historical anthologies available, contains 116 excerpts. Sahakian's *History of Psychology* covers 133 different authors, with about 4 pages being devoted to each. Diamond's *Psychology Re-Collected*, is even more wide ranging, with excerpts from 225 authors.

Sourcebooks such as these are perhaps of greater value to the person already familiar with the history of psychology than they are to the student just beginning historical studies. Indeed, such anthologies may even discourage the student from further historical inquiry. They are a mosaic of strange language and arcane concepts, and from the student's point of view the result is more often discouragement than enlightenment.

The problem is compounded by the fact that most present-day students are not particularly disposed to historical inquiry in the first place. Not only is the Weltanschauung of the youth culture rather ahistorical, but the typical undergraduate curriculum in psychology militates against a historical attitude. Almost from their very first encounter with psychology, students are warned against the dangers of armchair (philosophical) speculation, and the struggle of psychology to free itself from the shackles of philosophy is recounted in dramatic terms. In more advanced courses, the importance of being aware of the latest research findings is impressed on the student, and any textbook with a three-year-old copyright may not be considered worth reading. Is it any wonder, then, that when junior and senior students enroll in a history of psychology course (often as a departmental requirement) they display resistance and even incredulity when asked to study Plato, Aristotle, and other ancient and not-so-ancient thinkers?

This anthology differs from previous ones in two ways. First, it attempts to sample relatively few historical figures (10), each at sufficient length to allow the student to become involved in the author's work. Second, each historical excerpt is paired with the writings of a contemporary theorist. The purpose is not to demonstrate how the historical figure "anticipated" a modern counterpart; rather, it is to show how both have something to say about an issue of contemporary concern. In other words, it is hoped that the student will learn from these selections the value of reading historical sources, not just for their historical interest, but for the insights they can provide with regard to contemporary problems.

The volume is divided into 11 sections, each containing two chapters. The first section consists of two introductory chapters, one written specifically for this book and one on the nature of science by Thomas Kuhn. The remaining 10 sections consist of two chapters each, one by a historical and one by a contemporary figure. Each chapter begins with a brief introduction outlining its historical and contemporary relevance.

Three main criteria guided the selection of historical material included in the volume. First, an attempt was made to sample important historical epochs in a chronological sequence. Thus, from Classical Greece, there are excerpts from Plato and Aristotle; from the Roman and Patristic periods, Plotinus and Augustine; from the late Middle Ages, Aquinas; and from the start of the modern period, Descartes. Hume was chosen to represent British empiricism, and Kant represents the reaction to Hume. Finally, from the mid-19th century, there are Darwin and Marx.

The second criterion was that the historical selections should be of relevance to contemporary issues. Among the issues considered are: the logic of explanation, particularly the notion of causality; the organization of thought processes, including states of consciousness; the relationship between thought and reality; the validation of scientific theories; the concept of self, personality change, and emotion; and the evolution of behavior. From this list, it should be obvious that the book is intended to be more than just a history of psychology. The intent is, rather, to use history as a vehicle to examine the philosophical foundations of some of the more important issues in contemporary psychology.

The third criterion for the selection of historical material was that the pieces should be understandable by students of psychology with little or no formal training in philosophy. Where this was not possible, and yet the material was deemed important, the necessary background is included in the editor's introduction introduction to each chapter.

With regard to the selection of contemporary readings, the major criterion was that the author should address the same problem raised by the historical counterpart. Within this limitation, an attempt was also made to include persons who are prominent in their own right, i.e., who might be included in some future history of psychology.

I. INTRODUCTORY ESSAYS

1. Patterns of Psychological Thought: a general introduction

The greatest drawback to any anthology is that it be little more than a collection of disconnected parts. The risk is especially acute when an attempt is made to sample broadly from both historical and contemporary sources. To help overcome this difficulty, the present readings were chosen not only for their historical interest, but also because they bear on one or more of the following themes: (I) patterns of explanation; (II) the self and human nature; (III) the nature of emotion; and (IV) the logic of evolution. The primary purpose of this general introduction is to provide a brief overview of these issues; a second purpose is to introduce certain concepts that may aid in the understanding of the readings, but that may not be familiar to the typical student of psychology.

I. PATTERNS OF EXPLANATION

Most people would probably agree that the task of science is explanation. There is little agreement, however, on what constitutes a scientific explanation. The type of questions scientists ask obviously depends on the type of answers they regard as explanatory. To understand the history of science, therefore, it is necessary to examine the ways explanation has been viewed during different historical periods. This task is made easier because there are certain recurrent patterns of explanation, around which much of the history of psychological thought can be organized. In this section, we shall attempt to sketch these patterns of explanation in terms of a matrix of underlying presuppositions regarding the nature of reality and of knowledge. We also shall examine certain problems associated with the validation of scientific theories.

The Nature of Explanation

Let us begin with a few observations regarding the nature of explanation in general. In everyday affairs, an event is considered explained when it is related to some familiar or accepted frame of reference. A similar process characterizes scientific explanation. For example, the orbit of a planet might be explained by showing that it is consistent with (in this case, deducible from) the basic assumptions of Newtonian mechanics; or, the appearance of a neurotic symptom might be explained by showing that it is consistent with the assumptions of Freudian psychodynamics. Of course, the frames of reference used by scientists to explain phenomena are not the same as everyday frames of reference, and so it is helpful to have a special name for the former. Since the middle of the 18th century, the term *paradigm* has been used for this purpose.[1] In spite of this long usage, however, there is still little agreement on what exactly constitutes a scientific paradigm. The present introductory remarks are limited to the views of Thomas Kuhn, whose ideas are set forth in greater detail in Chapter 2.

Kuhn defines a paradigm as a fundamental scientific achievement that attracts and guides the work of an enduring number of adherents. A paradigm is manifested in certain key theoretical assumptions, methodological procedures, and model experiments that its adherents accept without question. A prime example of a scientific paradigm, as noted previously, is Newtonian mechanics. One must be careful, however, not to identify a paradigm too closely with a specific theory. A theory can be made explicit in a set of theorems, etc., but a paradigm is largely implicit in the way a scientist approaches the subject matter. In some respects, the paradigm of a science can be likened to the grammar of a language. The latter is an implicit set of rules for the production and comprehension of speech; similarly, a paradigm is an implicit set of rules for the production and comprehension of scientific research.

It may not be evident from this description, but Kuhn's analysis of paradigms marks a sharp break with the empiricist philosophy of science that has dominated American psychology for the past half century. According to the empiricist philosophy,

---

[1] S. Toulmin, *Human understanding.* Oxford: Clarendon Press, 1972, pp. 106 ff.

empirical facts are largely independent of the interpretive framework in which they are placed. According to Kuhn, on the other hand, facts are paradigm dependent. This means that disputes among adherents of competing paradigms cannot be settled simply by an appeal to empirical evidence; what is accepted as a fact under one paradigm may be dismissed as an artifact under another. The situation might be compared to disputes between people of different religious persuasions. Rational arguments may be used in such disputes, but ultimately the conversion from one religion to another involves the acceptance of certain fundamental assumptions or beliefs that cannot be justified on strictly logical grounds. Or, to use another analogy, the acceptance or rejection of a scientific paradigm may be likened to a switch in a reversible figure. Consider, for example, the woman depicted in Figure 1. Is she a beautiful young girl or an ugly old hag? The answer depends on one's orientation (paradigm). If two people viewing the figure both see a young girl, then they may argue about how beautiful she actually is; but if one sees a young woman and the other an old hag, then any meaningful debate about her "beauty" is impossible.

A Matrix of Presuppositions

It is evident that scientific paradigms are quite complex. However, there are certain presuppositions that can be used to distinguish among general classes of paradigms. These presuppositions are of three types; and each can be further divided into three subcategories. The matrix of presuppositions thus formed is depicted in Figure 2.

Each cell of Figure 2 represents a different pattern of explanation formed by the stance taken with regard to an appropriate model of explanation (formalistic, mechanistic, or organismic), an accepted source of knowledge (rationalism, empiricism, or mysticism), and the type of inference accepted as valid (deductive, inductive, or intuitive). Once a scientist's stance is known with respect to each of these presuppositions, the *type* of theory developed (though not its content) can often be predicted with some precision. Therefore, let us examine each of these presuppositions in more detail.

Model of explanation By model of explanation we mean the basic analogy one uses to make the operation of nature meaningful. For example, the person who adopts a formalistic model typically views the world in mathematical terms; for the person who prefers a mechanistic model, on the other hand, the

FIGURE 1   Portrait of a woman.

world is essentially a vast machine; and, finally, the theorist who adopts an organismic model tends to use the living organism as an analogue. These models are seldom explicitly stated as such, and it is often difficult to determine exactly which model a theorist is actually using. Fortunately, for our purposes, models of explanation are closely linked to notions of causality, and most of the historical figures we will be dealing with have had something explicit to say on this subject. Therefore, it will be convenient to begin this discussion by tracing the history of ideas regarding

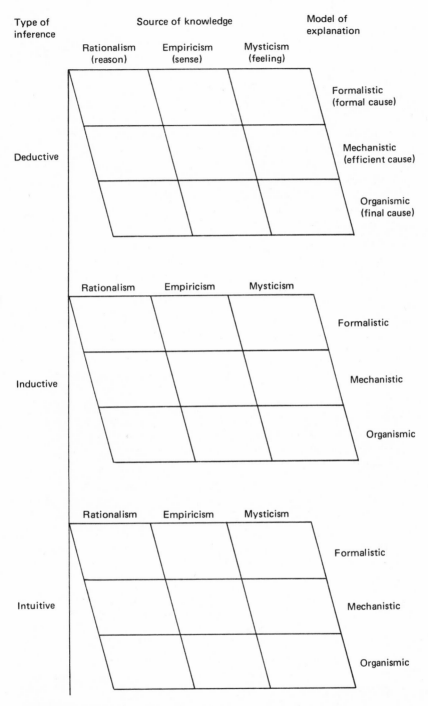

FIGURE 2 A matrix of presuppositions regarding the nature of explanation.

causality from Plato to Kant. In the process, the relationship between causality and models of explanation will be clarified.

In Chapter 3, Plato considers several types of causes that might explain why Socrates remained in prison and accepted execution when he (Socrates) could easily have fled into exile. Plato rejects any explanation that relies solely on physiological mechanisms, e.g., the contraction of muscles. Socrates remained in prison, Plato argues, because he believed it was the just and honorable thing to do. And justice and honor are not the kinds of things that can be explained in strictly mechanical terms. Plato asserts that the only notion of cause that he can understand is one that refers to some formal property, e.g., an ideal of beauty or justice, or a mathematical formula. For example, an object is beautiful because it reflects, to a greater or lesser extent, an ideal of beauty; similarly, a just act is one that corresponds to an ideal of justice, and a circular figure is one that corresponds to the mathematical formula for a circle. In short, explanation for Plato is the identification of the formal properties of an object or event that make the object what it is.

Aristotle's view of explanation was more complex than Plato's. In Chapter 5, he outlines four ways to answer the question, Why? We may state the material cause (that out of which a thing is made), the efficient cause (the antecedent event that produces a change), the formal cause (the essential characteristic of an event), and the final cause (that for which something is done).

The notions of efficient, formal, and final cause are related to the three models of explanation outlined earlier. Specifically, theorists who emphasize efficient causes generally view nature as a vast machine, with one object (the efficient cause) impinging on another, thus producing an effect. (A machine may be conceived of as an arrangement of objects, e.g., gears and levers, so that efficient causes are constrained to produce useful effects.) Theorists who emphasize formal causes often adopt what is called a formalistic model of explanation. That is, an event is explained when its underlying formula is enunciated. This, as we have seen, was Plato's view. Finally, theorists who emphasize final causes typically take the living organism as their basic model. Organisms show a developmental sequence—the acorn grows into an oak tree and the infant grows into an adult. According to an organismic model, the occurrence of an event is explained when it is placed at the appropriate stage in a developmental sequence.

Aristotle believed that psychological explanations, i.e., explanations that invoke the notion of *psyche*, entail the specification of efficient, formal, and final causes. His emphasis, however, was on final causes, and his basic model of explanation was thus organismic.

In one form or another, an organismic model remained fundamental to most conceptions of explanation throughout the Middle Ages. This proved disastrous for the development of the physical sciences and, during the course of the Scientific Revolution, final (and also formal) causes came to be viewed as explanatory fictions. The opinion grew that "proper" scientific explanations could refer only to efficient causes, and hence the mechanistic model became the new orthodoxy. This trend was given considerable impetus, even for the life sciences, by René Descartes (Chapt. 13), who argued that animals and the human body, as well as the physical universe, are nothing but complex machines. Descartes did not believe, however, that all mental activity could be explained in strictly mechanistic terms. Therein lies one of the major features of Cartesian dualism: the postulation of two different models of explanation, one for the body and another for the mind.

Most scientists after the Scientific Revolution believed that efficient causes are in some sense "real." That is, one event (the cause) has the power or force to produce another event (the effect); and, moreover, every effect has its antecedent cause. But what does it mean to say that one event has the power or force to produce another event? This is the question posed by David Hume (Chapt. 15). The cause–effect relationship is, according to Hume, simply a habit of thought built up through past experience. Efficient causes, like formal and final causes, are "in the mind of the beholder," so to speak. However, if the impression of causality is simply a habit of thought (whether built up through past associations or due to some other psychological mechanism), doesn't this make scientific explanations relative to the individual scientist's psychological history and/or makeup? And if so, in what sense can science offer a true representation of reality?

Two schools of thought developed in order to avoid the relativistic implications of Hume's analysis. Immanuel Kant (Chapt. 17) reasoned that if scientific propositions are universally and necessarily true, it must be because there are certain universal and necessary ways of ordering experience. Kant referred to these *a priori* ways of perceiving and thinking as "forms of intuition" and "categories of judgment." Causality is one of the categories of judgment. The meaning of Kant's analysis can perhaps be clarified by comparing his category of judgment with Kuhn's paradigm. The categories are implicit rules by which experience is organized and interpreted. Kant believed them to be universal and necessary (a priori) modes of cognition, discoverable in the laws of Newtonian physics and Aristotelian logic. In other words, Kant took the scientific paradigms prevalent in his day as representing the structure of human thought in general. The consequences of this thesis will be examined in more detail shortly.

The second school of thought that developed from Hume's analysis is known as *positivism*. If causation is only a habit of thought, then the whole notion of cause has little relevance to science. The task of science, according to this view, is to describe events, not to explain them. Or perhaps more accurately, explanation *is* description (albeit very precise description, preferably expressed in mathematical terms). This view of scientific explanation has exerted considerable influence on American psychology, especially behaviorism.

A third implication can be drawn from Hume's analysis. If the three types of causes emphasized by Aristotle (i.e., efficient, formal, and final) are equally subjective, then by the same token they are also equally real. Recognizing this helps eliminate one of the major prejudices against explanations that invoke formal and final causes. For example, saying that an acorn grows into an oak tree is just as valid a description of events as saying that water and sunlight "stimulate" the acorn to grow. The question, then, is not whether teleological explanations (i.e., explanations that invoke final causes) are valid in a descriptive sense, but whether they can be reduced to more "fundamental" types of explanation, e.g., those that refer only to antecedent conditions (efficient causes). Aristotle did not think it was possible, and neither does Charles Taylor (Chapt. 6), who argues that teleological explanations may be more fundamental than mechanistic explanations when it comes to psychological phenomena. Noam Chomsky makes a similar point (Chapt. 14) in his discussion of Cartesian linguistics. Chomsky argues that Descartes was essentially correct in recognizing that complex psychological processes—particularly language—cannot *in principle* be explained by the same set of concepts that has been developed so successfully to explain the movement of inanimate objects. (Chomsky, however, places greater emphasis on the formal than on the functional properties of language, and hence belongs more to the Platonic than to the Aristotelian tradition.)

Of course, neither Taylor nor Chomsky argues that purposeful behavior and higher mental activity are irreducibly different from other phenomena studied by the natural sciences. Both believe that someday machines will be built that can simulate human thought processes in a meaningful way. When such machines are built, however, the principles of their operation may well be explained in terms fundamentally different from those used to explain the operation of the simpler machines of today.

Source of knowledge Theorists differ not only on presuppositions regarding causality, but also on what they consider to be the ultimate source of knowledge or, perhaps more accurately, the kind of data they consider fundamental to the verification of scientific theories. This second set of presuppositions can be introduced with a paradox posed by Plato in the *Meno* (Chapt. 3). How can we hope to discover something without already knowing the object of our inquiry, i.e., what we are searching for? But if we already know what we are searching for, then we do not have to discover it. Plato's solution to this dilemma is contained in his doctrine of innate ideas. The acquisition of knowledge is not a matter of learning or discovery; instead, it is the recollection of dimly perceived truths that the soul knew before its incarnation at birth. This might seem to be a fanciful notion, but it does not sound so absurd if one substitutes "genetically determined" for "incarnation." Also, consider the rather similar problem addressed by Chomsky in Chapter 14. Children of a young age and limited intellectual ability are capable of acquiring a remarkable amount of linguistic knowledge in a very few years. How is this possible? According to Chomsky, the human mind must have certain formal properties—a "deep structure"—that are actualized when children hear the "surface structure" of the language spoken around them. In a sense, children do not simply acquire linguistic knowledge; rather, experience actualizes a linguistic competence that they already possess.

The position represented by Plato and Chomsky is known as *rationalism.* Its antithesis is *empiricism*, which maintains that the mind is essentially a blank slate upon which external reality can impress its seal with relative fidelity. Of course, not even the most extreme rationalist can deny the assistance of sense experience in the acquisition of knowledge; and, conversely, a critical reading of empiricist philosophers such as Locke and Hume invariably reveals the postulation of innate propensities or ways of organizing thought. Nevertheless, the distinction between rationalism and empiricism is important historically, and the influence of these traditions is still readily discernable in contemporary psychology, e.g., in the contrast between Gestalt and behaviorist schools of psychology.

Rationalism, with its emphasis on reason or the inherent structure of thought, and empiricism, with its emphasis on sense experience, do not exhaust the presuppositions regarding sources of knowledge. Claims of knowledge can also be based on an inner feeling or conviction, a kind of "sixth sense" that transcends both rational thought and empirical evidence. This position, called *mysticism*, is exemplified historically by such thinkers as Plotinus (Chapt. 7); in contemporary psychology, its influence can be seen most clearly in certain existentialist schools of thought.

Type of inference Before an explanatory principle is accepted as valid, it must conform to certain assumptions regarding the nature of causality and the source of knowledge, and it must also be based on a proper chain of reasoning or inference. For example, one of the earliest—and still prevalent—criticisms of Charles Darwin's theory of evolution is that its central tenet, the principle of natural selection, is tautological (true by definition) and that the arguments adduced by Darwin in support of this principle are actually irrelevant. It is not necessary to enter into the details of this debate[2]; suffice it to say that if the charge were true, then many scientists would disallow the claim that Darwin had explained the origin of species.

Of course, we are not concerned here with the specifics of any particular inference, but with presuppositions regarding broad classes of inference. Three types of scientific inference are often recognized: deduction, induction, and intuition. In deduction, a particular conclusion is drawn from general principles according to rules of logic, as in the case of a mathematical proof. The essential feature of a valid deductive inference is that if the premises are true, then the conclusion must also be true. Induction in some respects is the reverse of deduction. That is, an inductive inference proceeds from the observation of singular facts to the formulation of general principles. This type of inference does not entail logical necessity, because a future observation could always disconfirm the generalization.

Theorists who favor a deductive type of inference often maintain that induction by itself—sometimes called the "true Baconian method"—may lead to a collection of facts and low-level generalizations (as may be found in a nautical ephemeris) but that it can never lead to the construction of true scientific theory. Theorists who favor an inductive type of inference contend that deductive arguments often turn out to be little more than intellectual playthings, devoid of empirical content. Of course, few people have ever utilized completely deductive or inductive

---

[2] M. Ruse, Natural selection in the origin of species. *Studies in History and Philosophy of Science*, 1971, *1*, 311-351.

inferences in their theorizing; nevertheless, opinions on this issue may be so strongly held that antithetical schools of thought are dismissed or ignored as being too theoretical, on the one hand, or too immersed in data, on the other.

This debate may be joined by intuitionists who respond with, "a plague on both your houses." They ask the deductive theorists: "How do you recognize the truth of first principles?" Such truths cannot be deduced from other principles, because then they would not be "first." And the advocate of induction is asked, "How do you know the truth of simple observations?" Not by induction, certainly, for then they would not be "simple." The answer in both cases is intuition. But this is only a beginning. There may be whole classes of phenomena, from the mundane (e.g., historical events, the feelings of others) to the preternatural (e.g., spirits and deities), that—so the argument goes—cannot be known by ordinary discursive (deductive and inductive) reasoning.

There is no doubt that intuitive inferences play a role in science as well as in everyday affairs. There is little agreement, however, on how intuition should be regarded. Some argue that it is important only in the context of discovery, but has little relevance for the validation or acceptance of scientific theory. But there are others[3] who argue that intuition is a fundamental type of scientific inference, one that has its own "logic." Indeed, there is a loosely knit school of psychological thought, sometimes called *Verstehende* ("understanding") psychology,[4] that emphasizes a form of intuition or empathy as the primary type of inference.

Earlier, we used the terms rationalism, empiricism, and mysticism to describe the stance taken regarding the source of knowledge. The reader may sometimes find these terms used in a broader sense to describe the type of inference as well as the source of knowledge. This is because, in general, the rationalist prefers a deductive method of inquiry, where the main criterion of validity is the logical consistency of one's argument; the empiricist prefers an inductive method of inquiry, where the main criterion of validity is empirical observation; and the mystic prefers an intuitive method of inquiry, where the main criterion of validity is an empathic understanding of, or even union with, the object known. This correspondence is not complete, however, and hence it is advisable to treat these two sets of presuppositions separately. Thus, a person may adopt an empiricist stance with regard to the

---

[3] For example, M. Polanyi, *Personal knowledge.* New York: Harper and Row, 1964.
[4] For an illustration of this line of thought, see K. Jaspers, *General psychopathology.* Chicago: University of Chicago Press, 1963.

source of knowledge and then rely primarily on deductive arguments to explore the consequences of this stance, as did Thomas Aquinas (Chapt. 11) and Hume (Chapt. 15). It might also be added, if it is not already obvious, that the stance taken regarding the source of knowledge (rationalism, empiricism, or mysticism) and the type of inference (deduction, induction, or intuition) is logically independent of the preferred model of explanation (formalistic, mechanistic, and organismic).

Let us now return to Figure 2, which depicts the patterns of explanation made possible by various combinations of sources of knowledge, types of inference, and models of explanation. It must be emphasized that these patterns are very general. They represent the different ways people can attempt to understand the world around them, independently of the specific subject matter under investigation. For this reason, Figure 2 is a convenient heuristic device for comparing authors from different historical periods, and of different disciplinary interests. For example, the Greek atomists of antiquity (cf. Democritus), the British empiricists of the 17th and 18th centuries (cf. Hobbes), and certain modern behaviorists (cf. Clark Hull), all illustrate the pattern of explanation characterized by the presuppositions of an empiricist epistemology, a largely deductive method of inquiry, and a mechanistic model of explanation.

In using Figure 2 for comparative purposes, two facts must be recognized. First, not all the patterns depicted are equally common; indeed, some are practically unheard of (e.g., a mystical, inductive, mechanistic pattern). Second, it would be unrealistic to expect a historical or contemporary figure to fit without contortion into any of the cells of Figure 2. Also, some thinkers (such as Descartes) might actually be placed in several different cells depending on whether they are attempting to explain psychological or physical phenomena.

The Validation of Scientific Theories

Having considered the nature of explanation in general, and some of the presuppositions that determine various patterns of explanation, we now turn to the problem of validation. What factors influence the acceptance or rejection of a scientific paradigm, or even a whole pattern of explanation? For purposes of the present discussion it will be convenient to treat a scientific paradigm, not just as a set of logical propositions, but as a kind of cognitive structure or organized pattern of thought.

Thought and reality We have seen how, from Plato to Hume, there was considerable disagreement over the nature of causality, the source of knowledge, and the proper type of scientific inference. Prior to Kant, however, all philosophers agreed on one point: True knowledge must somehow reflect the way things actually are; or, stated differently, the structure of thought must somehow correspond to the structure of reality. There was, of course, dispute about what reality *really* is (e.g., ideal forms, material atoms, or even ideas in the mind of God); but no major philosopher argued that reality as we know it is dependent on, or structured by, human thought. The latter contention is what Kant called his "Copernican revolution" in epistemology (Chapt. 17), and its implications are the major concern of this section.

As explained in the discussion of causality, Kant was concerned with how the laws of mathematics and science could be a priori, i.e., universally and necessarily true, and yet refer to matters of fact. Hume had argued that empirical facts are always subject to doubt. One implication of his thesis is that causal relationships do not entail logical necessity, but are, rather, habits of thought. If such were the case, then scientific laws, to the extent that they imply causal relationships, would be mere summaries of past experience that need not hold true in the future. In an attempt to refute Hume, Kant conceded that scientific judgments, including judgments regarding causal relationships, must be attributable to mental rather than physical processes. But such judgments are not, Kant argued, simply habits of thought built up through experience. Quite the contrary: if the mind were not able to make certain judgments on an a priori basis, there would be no possibility for experience in the first place. That is, the mind structures phenomenal reality according to its own a priori principles. Scientific laws are thus universal and necessary because they presuppose cognitive processes that are themselves universal and necessary.

At this point, an analogy may help clarify the meaning of Kant's argument. Picture the mind as a complex computer for the processing of information. The programs (and/or design characteristics) that govern the flow of information through this mind/computer would be its "cognitive structures." Similarly, "reality" for the computer would be the type of data it had to deal with; and "knowledge" would be the product of the computer's operations on appropriate data. Obviously, any data incompatible with the computer's programs could not be processed, and hence could not become an object of knowledge.

By the same token, if all computers were built alike and were equipped with the same programs, then any knowledge they possessed would, in a sense, be universally and necessarily true.

Kant wished to rescue science from the relativism that seemed implicit in Hume's analysis. His victory, however, contained the seeds of its own destruction. If phenomenal reality depends on cognitive processes, then knowledge is relative to the perceiving organism. This implication of Kant's analysis did not seem too important in his own day. Euclidean geometry, Aristotelian logic, and Newtonian physics were generally accepted as universally true, although, many details remained to be worked out. The situation changed dramatically shortly after Kant's death in 1804. Modern symbolic logic and non-Euclidean geometries were developed, and the limitations of Newtonian physics became increasingly recognized. In short, the foundations of Kant's philosophical edifice were soon undermined by advances in science and mathematics. But this did not destroy the core feature of Kant's "Copernican revolution," namely, that in some sense reality is determined by the structure of thought rather than vice versa.

If there are underlying cognitive structures that give meaning to reality, and if these are not a priori in Kant's sense, then what are their origins? Following Darwin, it was natural to interpret a priori as meaning not universally and necessarily true, but biologically innate. Thus, in Chapter 18, Lorenz argues that each animal species possesses its own "apparatus of thought" for structuring phenomenal reality. Lorenz asks: "Would not the laws of reason necessary for *a priori* thought be entirely different if they had undergone an entirely different historical mode of origin, and if consequently we had been equipped with an entirely different kind of nervous system?" He answers his own question with the observation: "Many aspects of the thing-in-itself which completely escaped being experienced by our present-day apparatus of thought and perception may lie within the boundaries of possible experience in the near future, geologically speaking."

In the case of humans, cultural as well as biological evolution helps shape cognitive structures. Hence, a priori can also refer to socially determined ways of perceiving and thinking. This sense of a priori is best exemplified by Marx's contention (Chapt. 21) that the consciousness of man is determined by his social existence. Pursuing this theme, the Soviet psychologist Luria (Chapt. 22) illustrates how presumably "fundamental" psychological processes, such as deductive reasoning, may vary as a function of social conditions.

It should be noted that the line of argument we have been

considering arises primarily within the rationalist tradition of thought. For the empiricist, the notion that reality is dependent on human thought hardly arises. To use a common empiricist metaphor, a blank slate (the mind) does not determine what is written on it. As we shall see in the case of Hume (Chapt. 13), empiricism leads to skepticism about the possibility of knowledge in general; Kantian "constructivism" is the rationalist answer to Humean skepticism. And how does the mystical tradition fit into this debate? The mystic seems to suggest that it is possible (e.g., through meditation, drugs, etc.) to transcend standard patterns of thought and thereby achieve an intuitive insight into the true nature of reality. But, as might be expected if the mystical experience involves a breakdown of customary patterns of thought, the mystic often perceives reality as ineffable and lacking in structure (Plotinus, Chapt. 7). This does not mean, however, that the altered states of consciousness experienced by the mystic are necessarily devoid of scientific insight. Tart (Chapt. 8) discusses some of the problems associated with the validation of such insights.

The self-validation of psychological theories These considerations bring us back to a problem that was mentioned earlier in connection with Kuhn's analysis of scientific paradigms. Given several different patterns of explanation for the same phenomena, by what criteria can we choose among them? For example, how might one decide whether a formalistic, mechanistic, or organismic model is the most appropriate for psychology; or whether rationalism, empiricism, or mysticism provides a more adequate picture of reality? At first, the answer might seem quite straightforward: test the various presuppositions against the facts. But this answer begs the question, for it already assumes an empiricist theory of knowledge, i.e., that there are facts independent of theory.

From the preceding discussion, it is obvious that the relationship between fact and theory is a complex issue even in the physical sciences. And when we turn to the social sciences, the complexity increases by another order of magnitude. Even Kant recognized a sense in which physical reality (the "thing-in-itself") remains independent of the way it is conceptualized. But a person is not like an inert physical object. People who accept psychoanalytic theory may relive their oedipal conflicts; people who believe in Skinnerian operant conditioning may respond to reinforcement in the appropriate manner; and people who believe in witchcraft may die a voodoo death. In other words, beliefs about human beings can be self-validating—sometimes in dramatic ways. This fact, if no other, should demand of any serious student of psychology a thorough examination of the historical and philosophical foundations of his discipline.

If a person is not like a physical object, impervious to the ways he is conceptualized, neither is he a completely plastic being without a nature of his own. This brings us to the second theme that runs through most of the selections contained in this volume.

II. THE SELF AND HUMAN NATURE

When we speculate about the causes of behavior, we are inevitably led to ask about the referent of the pronoun *I*. "I did it because I wanted to." To what does the "I" in such a statement refer? The answer psychologists give to this question is likely to influence many aspects of their research and professional endeavors. Or perhaps it would be more accurate to say that the way a psychologist views the self is likely to reflect more general theoretical, social, and personal factors.

In the following section, we shall sketch briefly the vicissitudes that the concept of self has undergone during the course of history. We shall also comment briefly on certain personal or temperamental factors that may influence one's view of the self and external reality.

The Concept of Self

Before beginning our historical survey, several ambiguities in the concept of self must be noted. First, it is somewhat misleading even to speak of the "self" as though it were a single concept. In the discussion that follows, four related concepts will be considered: psyche, soul, self, and personality. *Psyche* is the Greek term for the principle of life, only certain aspects of which are peculiar to man; *soul* stands for the spiritual element of man, conceived within the framework of Judeo-Christian religious traditions; *self*, in a strict sense, refers to the *I* and *Me* of experience; and *personality* stands for the assemblage of relatively enduring traits and qualities that makes a person what he is. Different as these various concepts are, there is a common strand that unites them. In one sense or another, they all concern what it means to be a person as opposed, say, to being an animal or even a machine. For simplicity in this discussion, the term *self* will be used to refer to this common strand, as well as to the *I* and *Me* of experience.

A second ambiguity in the concept of self is that it may be used (often by the same author in the same context) to refer both to man in particular and man in general. For example, the opening paragraph of Section II began with a question regarding the referent of the pronoun *I*, but it concluded with statements regarding human nature. This distinction between the self of personal identity and the self of human nature corresponds roughly to the distinction between idiographic and nomothetic approaches in contemporary personality theory. The idiographic approach attempts to understand the uniqueness of each individual, while the nomothetic approach attempts to discover the laws that apply to all mankind. While these approaches may be treated separately in the abstract, like the concave and convex sides of an arc, in practice they are inextricably intertwined. The individual (whether a human or any other object) can be understood only within a general framework. A unique phenomenon could not even be discussed. Therefore, any theory of personal identity assumes a theory of human nature, implicitly if not explicitly.

A third ambiguity in the concept of self concerns the substantive nature of its referent. Is the self a spiritual or a material entity, or can it be given some other meaning? At first, this question might seem anachronistic. However, the stand taken with regard to the substantive nature of the self is closely related to another question that is obviously relevant to contemporary psychology: Are the principles that regulate human behavior of the same nature as (although perhaps much more complex than) the principles that regulate the behavior of inanimate objects? One who answers in the negative, will strongly tend to postulate a substratum for behavior that is distinct from the material substratum of inanimate objects. This tendency may be reinforced by broader theological and cultural beliefs, as in the case of the Christian notion of a soul. But the important point to remember is that, historically, debates regarding the substantive nature of the self (psyche or soul) have typically included arguments about the kind of mechanisms or principles that must be postulated to explain behavior; it is for this reason that such debates are relevant to contemporary psychology.

The Evolution of Concepts Regarding the Self

With these potential sources of ambiguity in mind, let us turn now to a brief survey of the concept of the self as it has evolved during the course of Western history.

The discovery of the self It will be helpful to begin our historical survey with the Homeric Greeks (ca. the 9th century B.C.), who apparently had no unitary concept of the self. Analyses of epic poems such as the *Iliad* and the *Odyssey* reveal a variety of terms for psychological and physiological functions, but no word for the self as a whole.[5] The term *psyche*, which later accrued many of the connotations of the concept of self, referred at that time to a "life principle," and it was given a quasiphysiological interpretation. The psyche had little to do with psychological processes such as thinking or feeling.

The Homeric Greeks also had no unitary concept for the living body, but as in the case of psychological activities, they used a variety of terms to refer independently to various bodily functions. This does not mean, of course, that the ancient Greeks had no sense of personal identity. But to them the individual was not the autonomous inner being that came to play such an important role in the subsequent history of Western thought; rather, the individual was a concatenation of parts and functions, strongly under immediate stimulus control and subject to direct intervention by the gods.

The Homeric Greeks' conception of man can be understood in terms of their harsh living conditions and social organization.[6] Success in acquiring goods and protecting one's family and group was of paramount importance. Good intentions meant little if they did not bring success, and the meanest of motives could be justified as long as the outcome was favorable. This emphasis on results led to a model of man that was intellectual and calculative, rather than volitional, and that placed little emphasis on the self as a determinant of behavior. Remnants of these attitudes can be found in later Greek thought, including Plato and Aristotle. However, by the time of classical Greek antiquity (ca. the 5th and 4th centuries B.C.), the concept of psyche had expanded to encompass not only the principle of life, but the various psychological functions as well. And, with the development of a unitary concept for psychological functions, developed a corresponding concept—*soma*—for the living body in its entirety. The relationship between psyche and soma has been a topic of lively debate ever since.

In the *Phaedo* (Chapt. 3), Plato summarizes his views on the nature of the psyche and its relationship to the body. As previously noted, the setting for this dialogue is Socrates' last day in prison. Socrates takes this opportunity to examine the nature of his true self (psyche) and its potential fate following execution.

---

[5] B. Snell, *The discovery of the mind.* Cambridge, Mass.: Harvard University Press, 1953.

[6] A. W. H. Adkins, *From the many to the one.* London: Constable, 1970.

The view of the psyche presented by Socrates is simple. He argues that all genuinely human functions can ultimately be reduced to questions of knowledge. For example, virtue is a matter of knowledge, and wrongdoing is basically an error in judgment. Moreover, if a person knows what is good, he cannot help but do good; hence, all wrongdoing is involuntary. It follows that anything that hinders the acquisition of knowledge is to be forsaken, including the body. The true philosopher does not fear death, he welcomes it.

These remarks pertain primarily to the nature of man in general. What about the individual man, i.e., the psyche that is Socrates? The Platonic dialogues are like small dramas, offering vivid descriptions of the vanity, pomposity, foolishness, courage, and wisdom of individual protagonists. Yet Plato did not attempt to give a systematic account of the individual differences that he dramatized, except to indicate that some people are better suited "by nature" (*physis*) to certain stations in life (e.g., philosopher, warrior, or merchant) than to others. Individual differences presented more of a practical than a theoretical problem for Plato. In general, he took a rather dim view of human nature insofar as it is "human." This is not surprising, considering Plato's general theory of knowledge. The true objects of knowledge—the Forms—are universal and immutable. And, to the extent that an individual psyche achieves knowledge of the Forms, there is little need to consider the vagaries of human nature.

The *Phaedo*, it should be noted, was one of Plato's earlier dialogues. His mature views of the psyche were psychologically more sophisticated than the model just described. In later dialogues (not included in this volume) Plato made a tripartite division of the psyche into thinking, spirited, and appetitive aspects, each with its own motivations and each in potential conflict with the others. In fact, Plato's final model of mental functioning was remarkably close to that developed by Freud.[7] However, the spirited (superego) and appetitive (id) functions of the psyche are not, for Plato, on the same plane with the rational (ego) functions. The former are closely associated with the body and hence are transitory, while the latter belong to the immortal aspect of the psyche. It is thus fair to say that the essential characteristic of Platonic man is disembodied rationality.

Aristotle criticized Plato, and others among his predecessors, for attempting to comprehend human nature without paying

[7] B. Simon, Models of mind and mental illness in ancient Greece: II. The platonic model. *Journal of the History of the Behavioral Sciences*, 1972, *8*, 389–404; 1973, *9*, 3–17.

sufficient attention to the body. Plato, for example, had spoken of the psyche as though it could occupy any body (transmigration), as a person might occupy any house. But this is absurd, according to Aristotle. Every object or particular thing is a composite of form and matter, and the psyche is simply the form of a potentially living body.

Aristotle's meaning of *form* and *matter* is considered in greater detail in the introduction to Chapter 5. However, a few remarks are in order at this point. In one sense, form is the essence or defining characteristic of an object, i.e., those attributes that make it the kind of thing it is—a stone, a tree, a horse, or a person. Matter is what distinguishes one member of a class from another (e.g., this tree from that tree). When used to refer to essential characteristics, the Aristotelian and Platonic notions of form have an obvious affinity. But, where Plato saw the Forms as ideal archetypes capable of independent existence, Aristotle saw the forms as principles of organization inherent within the body.

Aristotle also used the notion of form to connote actuality, as opposed to potentiality. Matter can take on form, and hence has the potential to become one kind of thing or another. But when matter has form, it is actualized as an object of a specific kind. According to Aristotle, all matter tends toward actualization. More will be said about this sense of form and matter in the next section on models of evolution.

Still a third sense in which Aristotle used the notion of form was as the capacity or disposition of an object to behave in certain ways. For example, the form of an ax is to cut, that of an eye is to see, etc.

We may now relate these meanings of *form* to Aristotle's definition of *psyche* as the form of a potentially living body. First, psyche comprises those essential characteristics that distinguish living from nonliving objects. Second, psyche is the actualization of potentially living bodies; or, stated differently, psyche is the cause of life (in the sense of efficient, formal, and final cause—see Chapt. 5). Finally, psyche is the capacity of naturally organized bodies to carry out the functions characteristic of living organisms (e.g., growth, reproduction, sensation, movement, and—in the case of man—rational thought).

Applying the three aspects of psyche to man, it may be said that the human psyche represents the essential features and capacities of man in general (particularly, rational thought, but including as well all the lower functions of life). The human psyche is also that which all people strive to actualize, but which few achieve, either because of their material make-up or because of faulty habits acquired through experience. Finally, the human psyche consists of all those functions (e.g., perception, memory, imagination, rational thought, etc.) of which humans are capable.

In many ways, Aristotle's conception of the self and human nature is similar to that of modern psychology, provided that psychology is defined as the study of living organisms and not just as the study of conscious experience. This does not mean that Aristotle was a behaviorist in the contemporary sense. As we shall see, the modern notion of "behavior" derives much of its meaning from its contrast with the notion of "mental," especially as the latter has come to be conceptualized following Descartes. For Aristotle, the relevant distinction was between the living and the nonliving, not between the mental and the physical. And, of course, Aristotle's basic model of man (as of nature in general) was organismic, not mechanistic.

The self as microcosm   It is evident that there is often a close relationship between one's concept of external reality and one's concept of self. Plato's view of man was, for example, closely related to his theory of Forms. It will be recalled that Plato made a sharp distinction between intellectual knowledge (of the Forms) and sensory knowledge (of material objects) and a corresponding distinction between psyche (which mediates intellectual knowledge) and the body (which mediates sensory knowledge). By contrast, Aristotle considered the forms to be inseparable from material objects. He therefore derived intellectual knowledge from sense experience by attributing the power of abstraction to the psyche; and, accordingly, he found little need to make the psyche independent of the body.

Because Plato's and Aristotle's theories of the self and human nature were based primarily on their theories of the external world, their psychology is sometimes referred to as "naturalistic." But the primary direction of inference can also be reversed, i.e., from internal experience to external reality, a position sometimes known as *personalism*. Two early representatives of personalism were Plotinus (Chapt. 7) and Augustine (Chapt. 9).

Plotinus was the first major philosopher to use the self (as opposed to external reality) as the basis for a comprehensive world view. Plotinus saw man as a kind of microcosm, the epitome of the universe in general. To obtain ultimate knowledge, therefore, man must turn inward and contemplate the world within. This can be done only by withdrawing from the world of sense experience, and even from the world of rational thought. In Plotinus' mystical language, the self alone, stripped of ordinary discursive thought, turns inward, and there glimpses—indeed, becomes one with—true reality.

Mystical experiences, such as the one described by Plotinus, raise important questions regarding the nature of the self. But before turning to these questions, it will be helpful to carry our historical survey one step further and to consider a related kind of experience, religious conversion, as described by Augustine.

Augustine was much influenced by Plotinus and other Neoplatonic sources. (His last recorded dying words were a quotation from Plotinus: "He is not great who thinks it wonderful [worthy of note] that wood and stones fall and mortals die."[8]) But Augustine differed from his predecessors in many fundamental respects. For example, the classical Greek thinkers used the world (*Kosmos*) as the fundamental analogy upon which to build a system of knowledge. This was true even for Plotinus, although he viewed the self as a kind of microcosmos. Augustine, by contrast, took man (or "person") as the model of reality. In part, this substitution of man for *Kosmos* was due to the challenge of Christian theology. As stated in the book of Genesis, man is created in the image and likeness of God; moreover, in Christ, God took human form. In other words, the God of Christianity (unlike the Plotinian One) is a *person*—indeed, he is three persons in one (as defined by the Councils of Nicaea and Constantinople in the 4th century). But what, then, is a person, whether divine or human? Augustine sought to answer that question, using himself as an object of analysis. His *Confessions* is probably the first and, from a psychological point of view, one of the greatest autobiographies in literature.

Augustine differed from earlier thought not only in his emphasis on, but also in his conception of, the person. The Greeks, including Plotinus, viewed man as an essentially rational being. For Augustine, the highest human faculty is the will, and under his influence issues related to motivation (intention, choice, etc.) displaced the problem of knowledge as the major concern of psychology. Augustine's conception of man as a volitional rather than a rational being also stemmed in part from theological considerations. It would be blasphemy in Augustine's view, to claim that man—with his finite reason—could ever know God, or literally be one with him; nevertheless, man must will to serve God, and to do the right thing regardless of consequences, or face eternal damnation.

Augustine's focus on the will raises an issue of central importance for subsequent theories of personality: What is the source of the will, and to what extent is it "free"? Augustine

---

[8] Cited by P. Henry, *Saint Augustine on personality*. New York: Macmillan, 1960.

rightfully saw the will as a function of the whole man, an expression of character. A person cannot will to be what he is not, i.e., a man of good will cannot intentionally perform an evil act, or vice versa. But this just leads to another question: From whence do individual differences in character arise? Augustine was not able to answer this question except by appeal to theology (e.g., the notions of sin and grace). But in the account of his own conversion to Christianity (Chapt. 9), he posed the issue in a very dramatic form.

These are, in brief outline, some of the contributions of Plotinus and Augustine to the history of psychology. However, selections from these individuals are not included in the present anthology simply because of their historical interest. (Indeed, some would argue that personalism was a detriment, rather than a contribution, to psychology.) Plotinus and Augustine are perhaps more important for the problems they pose than for the answers they offer. How, for example, is one to explain the type of mystical experience described by Plotinus (Chapt. 7), or the radical transformation of the self (religious conversion) experienced by Augustine (Chapt. 9)? This question obviously requires a reexamination of the concept of self.

In Chapter 10 (the companion selection to Augustine), Theodore R. Sarbin and Nathan Adler define the self as a "set of knowings or beliefs that accumulate as the result of efforts actively to locate oneself with reference to differentiated habitats or ecologies"; or, more simply, as "the inferences the person makes about the predicates for 'I.' " This definition of the self is very similar to the definition of a scientific theory or paradigm; that is, the self is a way of conceptualizing, making meaningful, and hence gaining control over a certain range of phenomena (that concerning one's own behavior).[9] Pursuing this analogy between the concept of self and a scientific paradigm further, we might ask: What would happen if one's self-concept were temporarily suspended or disrupted? Probably, there would be a sense of meaninglessness, dread, and acute anxiety. However, if one were sufficiently prepared for the experience and had some residual frame of reference (e.g., religious or philosophical) through which to interpret what was happening, then he might have the kind of undifferentiated and ineffable, but very pleasant, experience described by Plotinus.

It is often said that a scientific theory or paradigm is never

[9] For a detailed exploration of the analogy between the self-concept and a scientific theory, see S. Epstein, The self concept revisited, or a theory of a theory. *American Psychologist*, 1973, 28, 404–416.

simply abandoned; it will be given up only in favor of another paradigm. And the same is true of a person's concept of self; but in the case of the self the difficulty of change is even greater, for one's self-concept was acquired earlier and is more ingrained than one's theory of external reality. This fact is well illustrated by Augustine's conversion to Christianity. Augustine wanted to become a Christian, having already adopted a Christian world view on an intellectual level. But changing his own self-concept, so that *he* was a Christian, proved more difficult. And when the change did occur, it was sudden and dramatic.

In a previous section on the nature of explanation, we compared the shift in a scientific paradigm to a religious conversion. But the analogy obviously works both ways: A religious conversion (or any other transformation of the self) can be likened to a change in scientific paradigm.

The self as conscious experience   We shall not discuss here the views of Aquinas on the self, for these are largely a synthesis of Aristotelian and Augustinian conceptions (see Chapt. 16, p. 434). Rather, we will turn directly to a conception of man that has proven to be one of the biggest bugaboos in the history of psychology—Cartesian dualism.

Descartes was a major contributor to the Scientific Revolution of the 17th century, and he attempted to develop a philosophy of man that would incorporate the insights of the new science. Such a philosophy, he believed, should be based on a system of principles that are beyond doubt. Descartes found, however, that he could doubt almost everything. He could conceive, for example, that he had no body, and that there was no physical world; but he could not conceive that he himself did not exist, for the proof of his own existence was contained in his very act of doubting. From this fact, Descartes concluded that the whole essence or nature of the self is to think; and, moreover, that the self is entirely distinct from, and is even more easily known than, the body.

By *thinking*, Descartes meant any kind of conscious experience, not just doubting or discursive thought. But what of unconscious thought processes? As Descartes states in Chapter 13, "It might possibly be the case if I ceased entirely to think, that I should likewise cease altogether to exist." In other words, in the Cartesian scheme of things, the notion of unconscious thought seems to imply a literal self-contradiction. Before Descartes, there was no question that mental activity could occur outside of conscious awareness. Plotinus, for example, spoke of feelings and desires that occur in the body, only subsequently to be detected by the soul; and Augustine likened his memory to a large and infinite roominess, which made it impossible for him to fathom all that he was. Going back even further, Aristotle considered consciousness to be simply one attribute of certain grades of psyche; and Plato recognized not only multiple levels of consciousness, but also the existence of intrapsychic conflicts. It is sometimes said today that Freud "discovered" the unconscious. If this assertion has meaning, it is only in light of the Cartesian conception of the self as conscious experience. Freud and his forerunners reintroduced into psychology what Descartes had temporarily hidden from view.

Most discussions of Cartesian dualism emphasize Descartes' complete separation of the self from the material body. But this point can easily be overemphasized. After all, most philosophies prior to Descartes also were dualistic. Descartes' originality and importance lies more in his conception of the body as a complex machine than in his conception of the self as an independent spiritual substance. From this perspective, the Cartesian self may be viewed as the hypostasis of those human functions (particularly language and intellectual behavior) that cannot be explained in strictly mechanistic (i.e., bodily) terms.

As noted in the previous section on patterns of explanation, it is still an open question whether Descartes was correct in maintaining that certain psychological functions cannot be explained in mechanistic terms. But when it comes to his conception of the self as entirely distinct from the body, there is little disagreement. As William James observed in his famous chapter on the self: "Metaphysics or theology may prove the Soul to exist, but for psychology the hypothesis of such a substantial principle of unity is superfluous."[10] If James were writing today, he would have no grounds for revising that statement.

The self as fiction James' assertion notwithstanding, the tendency to identify the self with a substantive entity (e.g., a soul or psyche) is obviously very powerful. One manifestation of this tendency, especially since the time of Plotinus and Augustine, has been to accept the existence of the self as intuitively obvious and then to postulate a psyche or soul as its substratum. But the opposite—and equally fallacious—chain of reasoning is also common. That is, for metaphysical or other reasons, a theorist may deny the existence of a substantive soul and therefore conclude that the notion of the self also is devoid of meaning. This is illustrated in the selection on personal identity by Hume (Chapt. 15). According to Hume, the "self" is essentially a fiction, a name we apply to a phantasmagoria of fleeting perceptions.

---

[10] W. James, *Psychology: The briefer course.* New York: Henry Holt & Co., 1910, p. 203.

In certain respects, Hume's conception of the self resembles that of the Homeric Greeks described earlier. But the resemblance is only superficial. The Homeric Greeks had little need for a notion such as the self, since in their culture rewards and punishments were based on outcomes, not on intentions or other sources of "personal" causation. Hume's denial of the self, on the other hand, was an outgrowth of his empiricist philosophy, a philosophy that reduced most psychological phenomena, including the self, to simple sensations and their combinations.

If "responses" are substituted for "sensations" in the Humean analysis of the self, one has the S-R (stimulus-response) model of man that has dominated American psychology for the past half-century. According to this model, the person is essentially a passive mechanism for transmission of S-R relationships, without any real capacity for spontaneity or self-generated behavior. The fact that the same stimulus does not always produce the same response in different people is generally attributed to structural changes in the mechanism induced by past learning experiences.

Hume's arguments regarding personal identity raise many issues that are central to psychology. What, for example, should be the basic units of analysis be for the study of behavior—simple elements, such as sensations or S-R connections, or more complex structural units, such as dispositions and traits? And if we choose simple elements as the units of analysis, then how do we account for the obvious consistency and meaningfulness of most behavior? These are some of the issues taken up by Gordon Allport in Chapter 16 on pattern and growth in personality. Allport attempts to bridge the gap between extreme empiricism, as exemplified by Hume, and more rationalist approaches common among continental European (especially German) psychologists.

The self as social construction The last conception of the self and human nature that we will consider here is that of Karl Marx (Chapt. 21). As an introduction to Marx, however, it will be helpful to review briefly the position of Kant with regard to the self. Kant subjected Hume's analysis of the self to the same kind of criticism as he did Hume's analysis of causation. It will be recalled that, according to Kant, causality is not observable in experience because it is presupposed by experience. Similarly, the mere fact that there is no "self" observable within consciousness—only individual sensations and their combinations—is no argument against the existence of the self as a precondition for experience. Without a unitary self, Kant argued, there could be no unity of experience, which there obviously is.

Stripped of its universalistic (a priori) features, Kant's conception of a transcendental self has had considerable influence on subsequent thought. And, as with Kant's categories of judgment, a major question has been the origin of the self, not as a substantive or spiritual entity, but as a principle of organization, or as a human potential to be actualized. Our present concern is the answer to this question offered by Marx (Chapt. 21), as illustrated in his notion of self-alienation.

Marx never developed a thoroughgoing philosophy of the individual person. His interest was in man as a "species being," by which he meant man as both the creator and the product of society. But, while not particularly interested in the individual man, Marx also wanted to dissociate himself from the idea of an unchanging human nature, an idea that had been popular among philosophers of the Enlightenment, including Kant. Thus, although in his earlier writings Marx frequently spoke of the "essence" and "nature" of man, he later dissociated himself from such "philosophical" phraseology because it seemed to imply a too-static view of human nature. But Marx also was loath to adopt the view of cultural relativism when it came to the nature of man. His compromise was to postulate an ideal human nature, i.e., man's true potential, and an actual human nature as it is realized in any historical epoch. The disjunction between man's ideal and actual natures is "self-alienation."

Marx considered self-alienation to be an objective not a subjective state, i.e., the self-alienated person does not necessarily *feel* alienated. To take a specific example, the devoutly religious man may be quite contented, even blissful (cf. Plotinus) in his beliefs. But, according to Marx, he has created an alien spirit—God, by whatever name—that he fails to recognize as his own creation and, even worse, before which he falls down and worships. To use the current argot, a certain amount of "consciousness raising" is often required before a person realizes his or her own alienation. Moreover, as the example of the religious man might indicate, Marx believed self-alienation was the common state of man historically. Only when the conditions of society are right can man achieve his true potential and eliminate self-alienation. In short, it is society that makes a man what he is, and that allows him to achieve, more or less, his own true potential.

It should be obvious that if the concept of self-alienation is to have scientific meaning, then the true potential of man must be objectively specifiable. That is, of course, a valid task for an empirical psychology. However, if we accept the notion of self-alienation as formulated by Marx, that task is given a nonempirical twist. For example, man's true potential cannot be discerned by the simple observation of existing men and women, because the most contented and happy among us may also be the most alienated. On the other hand, the most discontented among us hardly provide the best basis for building a psychology of man's true potential. It can thus be seen that the notion of self-alienation implies the acceptance of a value system that stipulates what man should be; it further assumes that the way man *should be* is the way man actually *would be* under ideal conditions. From Plato and Aristotle to Marx, we have in a sense come full circle.

Temperamental Factors Associated with Theory Construction

We have noted how the concept of self, as a theory of internal reality, stands in a dialectical relationship with theories of external reality, each influencing the other. But the situation is, of course, much more complex than this assertion would indicate. There are many other factors—sociological, psychological, and perhaps even physiological—that might predispose a person to theorize in a particular manner, whether the actual theory constructed is about the self or about external reality. Since our main concern in this book is with the history of ideas, and not with the sociology or psychology of knowledge, we cannot take the time to examine these other factors in any detail. It will be helpful, however, to note some of the personal characteristics often associated with rationalism and empiricism, for these two patterns of thought represent rough guideposts around which a great deal of historical material can be organized.

We have seen in an earlier section how rationalists seek abstract principles and immutable truths, and regard reason as their principle ally. Empiricists, on the other hand, find comfort in concrete facts, and rely on sense experience. We have also seen how rationalists and empiricists typically differ in the stance they take regarding the organization of thought processes, the former emphasizing innate structures and the latter emphasizing the role of learning. But these are not the only issues on which rationalists and empiricists differ. According to William James[11] these two philosophical traditions reflect a basic clash of human temperaments, which he called "tender-minded" and "tough-minded," respectively. In addition to being rationalistic, the tender-minded philosopher or scientist also tends to be intellectualistic, idealistic,

[11] W. James, *Pragmatism*. Cleveland: World Publishing Co., 1955.

optimistic, monistic (holistic), free-willist, religious, and dogmatic. Tough-minded thinkers possess the opposite set of traits; that is, they tend to be sensationistic, materialistic, pessimistic, irreligious, fatalistic, pluralistic (atomistic), and skeptical.

In some respects, James' choice of the terms *tender-minded* and *tough-minded* was unfortunate. They seem to imply that the rationalist viewpoint is somehow less scientific than the empiricist. It is true that rationalism can degenerate into intolerant dogmatism, on the one hand, or romantic mysticism, on the other. But empiricism, if carried to an extreme, has its own pitfalls—a "know-nothing" skepticism, for example, or a crass pragmatism. Because most contemporary American psychology falls within the empiricist tradition, the pitfalls of empiricism have often been downplayed and the dangers of rationalism emphasized. But this one-sidedness is a mistake. In the history of science, rationalism has been just as important as empiricism, if not more so.

In the introductions to the various chapters, we shall refer frequently to the rationalist and empiricist traditions. In so doing, the terms *rationalism* and *empiricism* may be used in a broad sense (more or less synonymous with what James meant by tender- and tough-minded), rather than in the strict epistemological sense outlined earlier (see Fig. 2). The context should make the meaning clear. Of the historical figures included in this volume, Plato, Augustine, and Descartes could be considered rationalists in a rather strict sense, while Aristotle, Aquinas, and Hume are generally classified as empiricists. Kant and Marx were rationalists by temperament, although they advocated a limited empiricist epistemology. Darwin, by contrast, was an empiricist by temperament who came to champion the innate determinants of behavior. Plotinus was both a rationalist and a mystic, which is not surprising since both of these traditions fall within James' general rubric of "tender-minded."

III. THE NATURE OF EMOTION

The major preoccupation of Western philosophy has been epistemology, i.e., the problem of knowledge. Reflecting this philosophical heritage, modern psychology also has been concerned primarily with such issues as perception, learning, memory and thinking. By contrast, the problem of emotion has been relatively neglected. In view of this imbalance, I have attempted to include in the present volume selections that deal with emotional as well as epistemological issues. Thus, in Chapter 3 Socrates engages Laches in a dialogue on courage; in Chapter 5 Aristotle examines the causes of anger; in Chapter 7 Plotinus attempts to express in words the mystical experience; in Chapter 9 Augustine recounts the anguish and despair that often accompany a radical transformation of the self; and in Chapter 21 Marx considers the problem of alienation. Two more general approaches to emotion are also found in the selections by Aquinas (Chapt. 11) and Descartes (Chapt. 13).

Some of these selections (by Plotinus, Augustine, and Marx) have been discussed in the previous section on the self, while others (by Plato and Aristotle) were mentioned in connection with the causes and explanation of behavior (Sect. I). Therefore, the present remarks will be limited to a few comments on the concept of emotion as it appears in the works of Aquinas and Descartes.

The term *emotion* is derived from the Latin *e + movere*, which originally meant to migrate or to transfer from one place to another. It also was used in a somewhat metaphorical sense to refer to states of agitation, physical (e.g., stormy weather) or psychological. It is in the latter sense that the term ultimately was applied to affective states. But this was a rather recent development. For over 2,000 years, at least from the time of Plato and Aristotle to the middle of the 18th century, the emotions were commonly referred to as *passions*. It is therefore the meaning of *passion* that must be considered if we are to understand the historical development of emotional concepts.

In Chapter 11, Aquinas presents a succinct analysis of the various meanings of *passion*. The term is derived from the Latin verb, *pati* (to suffer), which in turn is related to the Greek, *pathos*. Also derived from *pati* are such terms as *passive* and *patient*. At the root of these concepts is the idea that an individual (or physical object) is undergoing or suffering some change, as opposed to doing or initiating change. Historically, *passivity* has been the generic term used to express this idea. In less formal and archaic terminology, the passivity of emotion may be expressed in many ways. It is often said, for example, that a person is gripped, seized, or possessed by emotion. On the other hand, it is almost a logical contradiction to say that a person deliberately performed an emotional reaction, for a deliberate response is by definition an action and not a passion.

Aquinas not only examines the notion of passivity as it applies to emotional behavior, he also relates the emotions to sensory (cognitive) processes; and, finally, he enumerates criteria for distinguishing among the so-called fundamental emotions. Aquinas was very aware of the fine nuances of language used to express psychological concepts, and his classification of the emotions bears comparison with the type of componential analysis currently popular among psycholinguists. The contemporary influence of Aquinas can be seen most directly in the work of Magda Arnold (Chapt. 12), one of the theorists most responsible for the recent upsurge of interest in the cognitive mediation of emotion.

A quite different approach to the nature of emotion is found in the selection by Descartes (Chapt. 13). As previously described, Descartes did not believe that *self*-initiated behavior (i.e., behavior that requires deliberate choice) is amenable to a mechanistic type of explanation. This was one of the primary reasons he made such a sharp distinction between the self (a thinking substance) and the body (a physiological machine). From the discussion of passivity, however, it will be noted that emotional concepts are based on a distinction between things we do (actions) and things that happen to us (passions). Uniting these parallel distinctions, Descartes concluded that the emotions are a function of the body, not of the mind. More specifically, the experience of emotion is the perception by the soul of certain bodily changes, which were aroused in a strictly mechanical fashion by external stimulation. The lingering influence of Descartes on this matter can be found in many modern theories of emotion, especially those that treat the emotions as noncognitive, instinctive, and/or closely linked to physiological change (compare, for example, the James-Lange theory of emotion).

The selections by Aquinas and Descartes also illustrate that any comprehensive analysis of emotion presupposes a theory of the self, just as any comprehensive theory of the self presupposes a general view of nature. In an age of scientific specialization, it is easy to lose sight of the broader patterns of thought that help guide even our most specific and well-circumscribed inquiries.

IV. THE LOGIC OF EVOLUTION

As the last remark indicates, the three themes discussed thus far form a rough progression from the general to the specific. Thus, the first section examined the relationship between thought and reality; the second section was devoted to one aspect of reality, namely, the self and human nature; and the third section considered one aspect of the self, namely, the emotions. Now, in this final section, we return to more general considerations with an examination of the process and mechanism of evolutionary development. Our concern here is not so much with particular theories of evolution as with the "logic" of an evolutionary point of view.

Today it is commonplace to adopt an evolutionary point of view when attempting to explain phenomena. This is true whether the topic under consideration is cosmology (the origin of stellar systems), biology (the origin of species), sociology (the origins of cultures), or psychology (the origin of individual behavior patterns). Indeed, the present volume is an expression of the belief that a thorough understanding of contemporary psychological theory must include some insight into the evolution of psychology. The widespread adoption of an evolutionary perspective, however, is of relatively recent origin. It hardly occurred to the thinkers of the Enlightenment, for example, that an understanding of the past is necessary in order to explain the present. The idea of evolution is largely a 19th-century development. It is the product of many people working in diverse fields, but two individuals stand out as most prominent—Darwin, in biology, and Marx, in sociology. It would be misleading, however, to imply that the idea of evolution was new to the 19th century. Quite the contrary, an evolutionary perspective can be found in Aristotle's philosophy, although this aspect of his thought has been largely ignored until recently.

Two aspects of evolution will be discussed in these introductory remarks: first, the general features that distinguish an evolutionary process from other types of change; and, second, the mechanisms or means by which evolution occurs.

The Process of Evolution

Evolution may be defined as the alteration of a system or organized structure (whether physical, biological, psychological, or social), such that the alteration is (1) adaptive, (2) sequential, (3) irreversible, and (4) dialectical. Any process that exhibits these four features may be called "evolutionary." Let us illustrate what is meant by each feature with some examples from biology, where the "system" under consideration is the population of individuals that comprises a species.

1. To say that an alteration in a species is *adaptive* means that the species as a whole is brought into better functional relationship with its environment, and hence better able to maintain itself. It is important to note that adaptation is a relative concept, and that what is adaptive in one environment may be maladaptive in another.

2. To say that an alteration in a species is *sequential* means that a species that exists at one stage of development becomes transformed into something related to, but different from, a

species that existed earlier. This implies that no stage in an evolutionary sequence can be skipped without consequences for later stages of development. For example, mammalian species (as we know them) could not have evolved directly from fish without having gone through amphibian and reptilian stages of development.

3. To say that an alteration in a species is *irreversible* means that earlier stages of development cannot be recaptured. A biological species may become extinct, or evolve in new directions, but it cannot simply retrogress to an earlier stage. This follows from the sequential nature of an evolutionary sequence, where each stage of development incorporates elements from prior stages. Thus, the mammal that returns to the sea does not become a fish, but an aquatic mammal.

4. Finally, to say that an alteration is *dialectical* means that as a species changes in response to the environment, the environment is changed in turn, thereby creating conditions for further evolutionary change. The evolution of a predator species, for example, creates the condition for the evolution of defensive measures among the prey, which in turn requires further adaptive change in the predator, etc.

From this description, it should be obvious that an explanation of change in terms of evolutionary processes involves much more than knowing the historical antecedents of an event; rather an evolutionary perspective involves a particular way of interpreting history. A basic assumption underlying the present volume is that scientific development must also be viewed from an evolutionary perspective. To illustrate this, let us apply the four aspects of evolution just described to alterations in scientific theory. If changes in the system of ideas that constitute a theory are to endure, they must first of all be *adaptive*. But, as just noted, it is meaningless to speak of adaptation in the abstract; a system must be adapted *to* something. In the case of scientific theories, the environment of adaptation includes, most importantly, the phenomena that the theory purports to explain. However, as was emphasized earlier, much more is involved in the acceptance and rejection of a scientific theory than how well it "fits the facts." For example, the scientific environment also includes the general cultural matrix (competing ideas and supporting institutions) in which a theory is supposed to function. What this means in a concrete sense is that the type of theory best suited to one range of phenomena, and to one cultural context, is not necessarily the best suited in another environment. This may seem like a rather trivial and self-evident observation, but it often has been ignored and even denied. For example, a common practice today is to judge past theories by how well they suit the present scientific environment. But in order to understand the scientific insights of past thinkers, they must be examined on their own grounds, not ours. Or, to take another example, psychologists often have assumed that the type of theory developed to explain simple physical systems (e.g., celestial mechanics) is *mutatis mutandis* applicable to the more complex behavior of organisms. As Taylor points out in Chapter 4, we may be making the same mistake (but in reverse) that the Greeks made when they assumed that a basically biological (teleological) model of explanation could be applied to the motion of inanimate objects.

The development of scientific theories is also *sequential*. That is, the form a scientific theory takes depends, in part, on the kinds of theories that preceded it. The observation is sometimes made that what psychology needs is a Galileo or a Newton who will somehow transform it from a "young" to a "mature" science (the meaning of youth and maturity seldom being defined). Such a hope must be viewed with considerable skepticism. No stage in an evolutionary sequence can be skipped without consequences for later stages of development, and any attempt to model psychology directly on so-called mature or advanced sciences is bound to meet with difficulties, if it is indeed even meaningful.

Scientific evolution is *irreversible*, as well as sequential. To be sure, once-discarded theories may be resurrected at a later date, but the resurrected form is never precisely the same as the original. This fact is illustrated in nearly every pair of readings contained in this volume (i.e., each historical source and its contemporary counterpart). Suffice it to note that one should not expect to find in historical sources ideas that are *directly* relevant or "pre-adapted" to the present-day environment. It takes a certain amount of insight and originality, as well as a good deal of effort, to see how the ideas of a historical thinker can be transformed and made relevant to current problems.

The fourth feature of scientific evolution is its *dialectical* nature. Not only does the environment help shape scientific theories, but science, by providing us with greater understanding and control, can in turn shape our environment. This is obviously true with respect to that aspect of the scientific environment determined by cultural factors. One need only consider the reciprocal influence of scientific and economic factors. However, even when the scientific environment is interpreted in the more narrow sense as the phenomena under investigation, a dialectical relationship between theory and fact still obtains. This is perhaps not too important in the case of physical sciences, where phenomena have some objective existence independent of the way they are conceptualized (although in recent years, advances in technology threaten to alter in a significant way even the physical environment). But it is perhaps worth repeating what already has been stated in a previous section: Human behavior is not independent of the interpretive framework in which it is placed. The possibility thus exists for a thoroughgoing dialectic between psychological theory and behavior, each helping to constitute the other.

Mechanisms of Evolution

Having described various features that characterize evolutionary changes in a system, let us consider briefly the kinds of mechanisms that might account for such changes. These mechanisms can be grouped into two general classes, depending on whether they follow a "growth" model or a "variation and selective-retention" model. The growth model can be traced to Aristotle. It postulates some inner necessity or self-actualizing tendency that directs change toward a predetermined end. The variation and selective-retention model is Darwin's contribution. As its name implies, this model postulates a twofold mechanism: a source of variation among the elements of a system and a method for the selective retention of certain variations.

Growth models of evolution Let us begin this discussion with Aristotle's analysis of change. For change to occur, two factors must be present: form and matter. We already have encountered these complex notions in the discussion of the psyche as the form of a potentially living body. To recapitulate briefly, form makes an object the kind of thing it is; matter can take on form, and hence has the potential to become one kind of thing or another. Stated differently, form is actuality, and matter is potentiality. Within this formulation, all change involves the actualization of a potential inherent in matter, and, conversely, all matter tends toward actualization.

There are two strains in Aristotle's analysis of change: one leads to an evolutionary perspective and the other—often referred to as "essentialism"—inhibits such a view. Let us consider the latter first. As previously described, the form of an object is its essence. For example, the essence of man is rationality and the form of man is the rational psyche. But essences, being the objects of true knowledge, are not subject to change. On this score, at least,

Aristotle was in basic agreement with his mentor, Plato (although the two differed on "where" the forms exist and how they are known). Applying this line of reasoning to biological species, the essence or form "horse," for instance, is not subject to change, although individual horses are born and perish.

> It is impossible that such a class of things as animals should be of an eternal nature, therefore that which comes into being is eternal in the only way possible. Now it is impossible for it to be eternal as an individual . . . but it is possible for it as a species. This is why there is always a class of men and animals and plants.[12]

However, if species are eternal, there obviously can be no transmutation of species, and hence no biological evolution.

But there is a contrary strain in Aristotle's thought, one that leads rather naturally to an evolutionary perspective. In Aristotle's scheme, matter and form are relative notions, so that lower forms may provide the matter for higher forms. This can be illustrated by referring again to the notion of the psyche. Plants are characterized by the vegetative psyche (i.e., the capacity to nourish themselves, grow, and reproduce). In the case of animals, the capacity for sensation (and, in most cases, movement) is also added. But an animal is not simply a plant that can sense. Rather, the animal psyche incorporates and transforms that which is available at a lower level. Similarly, in the case of humans the rational psyche incorporates and transforms those capacities present in animals. When we add this notion of a hierarchy of forms to the notion that all matter possesses an inner tendency toward self-actualization, then the idea of a dialectical progression or evolutionary sequence from lower to higher forms readily suggests itself. Aristotle evidently did not grasp this suggestion when it came to the evolution of species, but rather he confined his analysis to the ontogenetic development of members within a species. That is, the growing organism assumes a variety of intermediate forms (stages) until it reaches its adult species form.

The postulation of a self-actualizing tendency as an explanation of evolutionary processes may strike the reader as peculiarly antiquated and unscientific. However, under various guises, growth models are quite common in contemporary thought. For example, the Hegelian and Marxist views of history involve a growth model of cultural evolution (see Chapt. 21). On a more strictly psychological level, Maslow's self-actualizing tendencies and Freud's psychosexual stages illustrate growth models of development.

---

[12] Aristotle, *De generatione animalium* (II. 1, 731b 32–39). In *The works of Aristotle* (Vol. 5). Oxford: Clarendon Press, 1912.

Perhaps, too, Lawrence Kohlberg's analysis of moral development (Chapt. 4) should be included in this list.

Variation and selective-retention models of evolution It is over two millennia from Aristotle to Darwin; during that time there were few significant advances in evolutionary theory, at least as far as biological evolution is concerned. This state of affairs is perhaps best reflected by Darwin's observation that "Linnaeus and Cuvier have been my two gods . . . but they were mere schoolboys to old Aristotle."[13] It is true that in the century preceding Darwin, others had suggested the evolution of biological species. However, such suggestions were based primarily on a vague growth model, e.g., an inner tendency toward perfection, and hence met with little acceptance. Darwin's importance, then, is not that he advanced the idea of biological evolution but rather that he postulated a new type of mechanism to account for its occurrence. The mechanism that Darwin proposed (see Chapt. 19) contains two basic elements: (1) a source of variability among the members of a population; and (2) the selective retention of certain attributes within the population. With regard to the source of variability, Darwin had little to say of consequence. (The science of genetics is largely a product of the 20th century.) But he did observe and document the great variability—in size, strength, longevity, fertility, behavior, etc.—that does in fact exist within any natural population. Moreover, Darwin recognized that such variation was used by man in the selective breeding of animals and plants. His task, then, was to discover how selective breeding could occur naturally, thus leading to the evolution of species. He found the answer in the struggle for survival (natural selection) and in differential attractiveness to members of the opposite sex (sexual selection). Both types of selection result in greater reproductive success, and hence the retention and propagation within the population of the favored attributes.

Like many major scientific contributions, the idea of variability and selective retention appears quite simple. However, the postulation of such a mechanism required a major reorientation in biological thought. Specifically, the view that each species has its own essential nature, which had dominated Western thought since the time of Aristotle, had to be discarded. In its place was substituted the view that species are populations or systems of interbreeding individuals. The implications of this aspect of the Darwinian "revolution" are discussed more fully in the introduction to Chapter 19.

[13]Cited by E. A. Esper, *A history of psychology*. Philadelphia: W. B. Saunders, 1964, p. 155.

Although one who speaks of Darwin naturally thinks of biological evolution, it is important to remember that the variation and selective-retention model is not limited to the development of biological species. In fact, the logic behind Darwin's theory can be applied to a wide range of phenomena, including conditioning and learning,[14] personality development,[15] and even creative thinking.[16]

Relationship between the models Growth models and selective-retention models of evolution are not incompatible, provided they are not applied to the same phenomena at the same level of analysis. Consider again the case of an oak tree. The characteristics of an acorn or a sapling might be explained in terms of a growth model by reference to particular developmental stages and how these contribute to the ultimate form of the tree. There is nothing wrong or unscientific about such an explanation, as far as it goes. But one might wish to inquire further. Why, for example, does an oak tree take the form that it does, and why is this form reached by certain developmental stages and not by others? An appropriate answer to the last question would be in terms of a variation and selective-retention model. That is, through natural selection certain growth patterns and features are retained (encoded in the genetic material) while others are weeded out as maladaptive.

We can thus see that the Aristotelian and Darwinian conceptions of evolution complement rather than contradict each other. In fact, a teleological system in the Aristotelian sense may be viewed as the product of a selection process in the Darwinian sense.[17] In view of this, it is not surprising to find that the Aristotelian notion of form also has its analogue in contemporary biological theory, namely, the concept of genotype (i.e., the genetic factors that direct development). The biologist, Delbrück, has even suggested—only half in jest—that the Nobel Prize should be awarded to Aristotle for the discovery of the principle underlying DNA (the chemical substance that constitutes the genotype).[18] Aristotle postulated that semen contains the form

[14] J. E. R. Staddon & V. L. Simmelhag, The "superstition" experiment: A reexamination of its implications for the principles of adaptive behavior. *Psychological Review*, 1971, *78*, 3–43.

[15] R. A. LeVine, *Culture, behavior and personality.* Chicago: Aldine, 1973.

[16] D. T. Campbell, Evolutionary epistemology. In P. A. Schilpp (Ed.), *The philosophy of Karl R. Popper.* La Salle, Ill.: Open Court Publishing Co., 1973.

[17] W. C. Wimsatt, Teleology and the logical structure of function statements. *Studies in the History and Philosophy of Science*, 1972, *3*, 1–80.

[18] M. Delbrück, Aristotle-totle-totle. In J. Monad & E. Borek (Eds.), *Of microbes and life.* New York: Columbia University Press, 1971.

(genetic information) that directs the development of the organism and determines its species kind, but is not itself changed in the process. Delbrück also speculates that the lack of appreciation of Aristotle among modern biologists is due in part to a hangover from Newtonian mechanics, where every action must have a reaction. There is no room in such a scheme for Aristotle's unmoved mover (e.g., the psyche as form of the body) that creates change without itself undergoing change.

The Nature-Nurture Controversy

Thus far, we have considered evolution as a general perspective on historical development, including the development of science. As such, it represents a general orientation to this book as a whole. Two models of evolution, exemplified by Aristotle and Darwin, also have been discussed. But there is still a third way in which evolutionary considerations enter into the present set of readings. This concerns the controversy over the source of behavior—heredity (nature) or environment (nurture). Starting from very different background orientations, B. F. Skinner (American behaviorism), Konrad Lorenz (German rationalism), and Alexander R. Luria (Soviet Marxism) attempt to show in their respective chapters that there is no basic conflict between biological evolution, on the one hand, and individual or social development, on the other.

There is no need to discuss these chapters at this point. It should be pointed out, however, that the nature-nurture controversy is not just a contemporary issue. An early version of it can be found in Plato and Aristotle. As will be recalled from an earlier discussion (Sect. I), Plato argued that knowledge of the Forms is innate, and that learning is really a form of reminiscence; Aristotle, on the other hand, argued that all knowledge is based on sense experience, and hence is learned in the ordinary sense. This debate between Plato and Aristotle was primarily epistemological and not biological, but the ease with which it can be assimilated into the latter context is illustrated by the following remark from Darwin's notebooks: "Plato . . . says in *Phaedo* that our *'necessary ideas'* arise from the pre-existence of the soul, are not derived from experience.—read monkeys for preexistence."[19]

An analogous debate can be found between the continental rationalists (e.g., Descartes) and the British empiricists (e.g., Hume). And if a survey were made today, it is likely that those

[19] Cited by M. T. Ghiselin, Darwin and evolutionary psychology. *Science*, 1973, *179*, 964–968.

who champion heredity over environment would also lean toward philosophical rationalism, while those who champion environmental determinants of behavior would also favor an empiricist orientation. The relationship is not perfect, of course, as indicated by the fact that Darwin was basically an empiricist while Marx, who championed cultural as opposed to biological evolution, was more within the rationalist tradition. But these are issues that are better discussed in the specific introductions to the relevant selections. These observations are simply to alert the reader to the relevance of some of the early chapters to what might at first appear to be a strictly contemporary issue.

CONCLUSION

The four themes—patterns of explanation, the self and human nature, the nature of emotion, and the logic of evolution—should not be viewed as the four posts of a procrustean bed, into which all the reading must snugly fit. While each of the readings does illustrate one or more of these themes, each selection also has its own unique focus of interest. Moreover, other themes could have been developed that would have tied the readings together in a fashion differently than has been done in this general introduction. Some of the other themes will be discussed in the specific introductions to the various selections.

To change metaphors, the purpose of this chapter has not been to provide a detailed map of the material, but only a rough guide to some of the more salient features. The real task of exploration remains for the reader.

2. Thomas S. Kuhn

EDITOR'S INTRODUCTION

During the past several decades, a minor revolution in the philosophy of science has taken place. The traditional view of science was largely ahistorical. The most advanced theories, usually drawn from mathematics and physics, were examined for their logical properties, and these properties were then stipulated as the desiderata of any scientific theory. The logic of science thus reconstructed was coupled with a positivistic epistemology that maintained that if theories are to be considered meaningful, they must ultimately be verifiable by direct observation. One of the people most responsible for questioning the basic tenets of this empiricist-positivist view of science was Thomas Kuhn, whose own views on the nature of science are presented in this chapter.

By way of introduction, Kuhn's major thesis can be divided into three aspects: (1) Scientific activity—observation as well as theory construction—takes place within a certain intellectual framework or paradigm that is itself accepted without question. (2) There are two fundamentally different types of scientific activity—normal science, which occurs within a generally accepted paradigm, and extraordinary or revolutionary science, which involves a switch in paradigms. (3) Commitment to any particular paradigm is determined by personal and historical factors, as well as by rational considerations and empirical evidence. Let us consider each of these aspects in turn.

Fundamental to Kuhn's thesis is his notion of a paradigm. Yet this is a very ambiguous concept. One sympathetic critic,[1] for example, has noted 21 different uses of the term in Kuhn's classic

---

[1] M. Masterman, The nature of a paradigm. In I. Lakatos and A. Musgrave (Eds.), *Criticism and the growth of knowledge.* Cambridge University Press, 1970.

book, *The Structure of Scientific Revolutions*, of which the present chapter is a condensed version. In its broadest sense, Kuhn speaks of a paradigm as a kind of intellectual framework that commits one to a "particular way of viewing the world and of practicing science in it." In a narrow sense, the term refers to "concrete problem solutions that the profession has come to accept as paradigms." In other words, the notion of a paradigm can be stretched to cover an entire world view, or it can be restricted to something as specific as an experimental technique (e.g., operant conditioning).

In one sense or another, the concept of a paradigm covers nearly anything that allows a scientist to engage in theory or research. But when used so broadly, the thesis that scientific activity (i.e., observation and theory construction) is paradigm dependent becomes an empty tautology. Recognizing this criticism, Kuhn has more recently[2] suggested that the notion of a paradigm be limited to concrete scientific achievements as presented in standard textbooks and laboratory exercises. By studying these paradigm cases, and working out closely related problems on their own, students acquire an intuitive grasp of acceptable procedures and results. It is not clear that the notion of a paradigm can be so restricted without also destroying the argument that all scientific activity is paradigm dependent. But this issue need not concern us here. Suffice it to say that the ambiguity in Kuhn's original concept of a paradigm is not without merit. Science is a complex activity, and any concept that does justice to this complexity will necessarily contain ambiguities. Logical precision can sometimes be obtained only by sacrificing relevancy. And it is largely because practicing scientists have found relevance in Kuhn's analysis that his notion of a paradigm has become so popular.

A second aspect of Kuhn's argument is his distinction between normal and extraordinary science. Normal science proceeds within a paradigm, i.e., it follows accepted rules and works toward agreed upon goals. It is a kind of "mopping up" operation, where generally accepted theories and procedures are extended in scope and rigor. To use Kuhn's own analogy, normal scientific research is similar to trying to solve a puzzle, the solution to which may already be known. Extraordinary or revolutionary science, by contrast, involves a switch in paradigms. The change in this case is so profound that scientists working under old and new paradigms have little in common. They see and talk about the world differently, and hence there is little room for rational debate. With

---

[2] T. Kuhn, *The structure of scientific revolutions*, 2nd ed. Chicago: University of Chicago Press, 1970. Postscript.

the consolidation of the new paradigm, another period of normal science ensues. The old paradigm is now confined to history, for its problems and solutions have little relevance to the new order.

In order to avoid confusion, it should be noted that the term *revolution* is somewhat misleading when applied to scientific development. Consider, for example, the Copernican revolution, and the change from a geocentric to a heliocentric world view. This took approximately 150 years to complete, and it was accompanied by rational (as well as irrational) debate every step of the way. Viewed historically, 150 years is not a long time, but when viewed in terms of the productive lifetime of an individual scientist, the Copernican revolution was slow indeed. And this is true of most of the so-called revolutions in science; they do not represent the cataclysmic changes that the term *revolution* implies.

Moreover, on the other side of the coin, normal science is not as ordinary or routine as Kuhn's description might seem to imply. Most scientific progress, even during normal periods, involves minor conceptual innovations that are not subject to strict logical or deductive proof. If innovations accumulate rapidly, the result might appear revolutionary in historical perspective, but only because normal processes have been accelerated, not because there is any difference in underlying processes. In short, scientific change might better be characterized as evolutionary rather than revolutionary.

Although Kuhn's distinction between normal and extraordinary science has its limitations when applied to evolutionary changes within a paradigm, it does have considerable merit when applied to the analysis of contemporaneous but competing paradigms. Perhaps an analogy from biological evolution will help clarify this point. Biological species evolve through the selective retention of many small variations or genetic mutations. And although the beginning and end point of an evolutionary sequence may be radically different (as modern man—*homo sapiens*—is radically different from earlier hominid species), at no point along the line is there a revolutionary transition from one species to another. On the other hand, two closely related species may evolve from the same parent population, e.g., due to geographic isolation. If these species should again come into contact, cross-fertilization will be impossible, and in the struggle for survival, one species may completely displace the other. Applying this analogy to the clash of scientific paradigms, it is not uncommon for different schools of thought to evolve semiindependently, e.g., due to national or disciplinary boundaries, or to different foci of interest. There can then occur a clash of paradigms in much the way that Kuhn describes it. Such a situation is particularly common in psychology.

A third aspect of Kuhn's argument is that commitment to a particular paradigm is based on more than logical factors. There is, in fact, an element of dogmatism in science, just as there is in politics and religion. It is perhaps this aspect of Kuhn's thesis that has aroused the most controversy, for it seems to call into question science's most cherished image—objectivity.

Of course, the mere fact that the original acceptance of a paradigm cannot be justified on strictly rational grounds does not mean that commitment to a paradigm has to be dogmatic. Hypotheses and procedures are often accepted provisionally, tried out, and rejected if found wanting. However, the fundamental assumptions represented by a paradigm are not so easily accepted or rejected; and, as a matter of historical fact, Kuhn is on solid ground when he insists that strong emotional commitment plays a major, perhaps essential, role in science. The reasons for this "dogmatism" are not difficult to find. A scientist, to be productive, must pursue research within a generally accepted paradigm. Eclecticism in science is seldom very fruitful. To conduct research by drawing ideas and methods from various paradigms would be like trying to write a novel with words and grammatical constructions borrowed from English, German, French, and Chinese. A commitment has to be made as a matter of practical necessity. But even more important, perhaps, is the fact that scientific achievement is as much a product of passionate vision as of disinterested reason. The scientist must be willing to pursue an idea to its logical consequences, even when those consequences are highly unpopular and contrary to what many believe to be the "facts." Such passion is seldom born of eclecticism, but can be based only on a firm commitment to a particular paradigm.

Of course, passionate vision can deceive as well as enlighten. Scientists must therefore continually remind themselves (as others surely will) that even their most cherished insights may prove to be mere illusions. At the risk of overdramatizing the point, it may be said that practicing scientists must be intellectually schizophrenic—passionately committed to a vision and yet continually skeptical of its truth.

The Function of Dogma
in Scientific Research

At some point in his or her career every member of this Symposium has, I feel sure, been exposed to the image of the scientist as the uncommitted searcher after truth. He is the explorer of nature—the man who rejects prejudice at the threshold of his laboratory, who collects and examines the bare and objective facts, and whose allegiance is to such facts and to them alone. These are the characteristics which make the testimony of scientists so valuable when advertising proprietary products in the United States. Even for an international audience, they should require no further elaboration. To be scientific is, among other things, to be objective and open-minded.

Probably none of us believes that in practice the real-life scientist quite succeeds in fulfilling this ideal. Personal acquaintance, the novels of Sir Charles Snow, or a cursory reading of the history of science provides too much counter-evidence. Though the scientific enterprise may be open-minded, whatever this application of that phrase may mean, the individual scientist is very often not. Whether his work is predominantly theoretical or experimental, he usually seems to know, before his research project is even well under way, all but the most intimate details of the result which that project will achieve. If the result is quickly forthcoming, well and good. If not, he will struggle with his apparatus and with his equations until, if at all possible, they yield results which conform to the sort of pattern which he has foreseen from the start. Nor is

"The Function of Dogma in Scientific Research," by Thomas S. Kuhn from *Scientific Change: Historical Studies in the Intellectual, Social and Technical Conditions for Scientific Discovery and Technical Invention, From Antiquity to the Present*, Edited by A. C. Crombie, © Heinemann Educational Books Ltd. 1963, Basic Books, Inc., Publishers, New York.

The ideas developed in this paper have been abstracted, in a drastically condensed form, from the first third of my monograph, *The Structure of Scientific Revolutions*, Chicago: University of Chicago Press, 1962. Some of them were also partially developed in an earlier essay, "The essential tension: tradition and innovation in scientific research", which appeared in Calvin W. Taylor (ed.), *The Third (1959) University of Utah Research Conference on the Identification of Creative Scientific Talent* (Salt Lake City, 1959).

On this whole subject see also I. B. Cohen, "Orthodoxy and scientific progress", *Proceedings of the American Philosophical Society*, XCVI (1952) 505-12, and Bernard Barber, "Resistance by scientists to scientific discovery", *Science*, CXXXIV (1961) 596-602. I am indebted to Mr. Barber for an advance copy of that helpful paper. Above all, those concerned with the importance of quasi-dogmatic commitments as a requisite for productive scientific research should see the works of Michael Polanyi, particularly his *Personal Knowledge* (Chicago, 1958) and *The Logic of Liberty* (London, 1951). . . . Mr. Polanyi and I differ somewhat about what scientists are committed to, but that should not disguise the very great extent of our agreement about the issues discussed explicitly below.

it only through his own research that the scientist displays his firm convictions about the phenomena which nature can yield and about the ways in which these may be fitted to theory. Often the same convictions show even more clearly in his response to the work produced by others. From Galileo's reception of Kepler's research to Nägeli's reception of Mendel's, from Dalton's rejection of Gay Lussac's results to Kelvin's rejection of Maxwell's, unexpected novelties of fact and theory have characteristically been resisted and have often been rejected by many of the most creative members of the professional scientific community. The historian, at least, scarcely needs Planck to remind him that: "A new scientific truth is not usually presented in a way that convinces its opponents . . .; rather they gradually die off, and a rising generation is familiarized with the truth from the start."[1]

Familiar facts like these—and they could easily be multiplied— do not seem to bespeak an enterprise whose practitioners are notably open-minded. Can they at all be reconciled with our usual image of productive scientific research? If such a reconciliation has not seemed to present fundamental problems in the past, that is probably because resistance and preconception have usually been viewed as extraneous to science. They are, we have often been told, no more than the product of inevitable *human* limitations; a proper scientific method has no place for them; and that method is powerful enough so that no mere human idiosyncrasy can impede its success for very long. On this view, examples of a scientific *parti pris* are reduced to the status of anecdotes, and it is that evaluation of their significance that this essay aims to challenge. Verisimilitude, alone, suggests that such a challenge is required. Preconception and resistance seem the rule rather than the exception in mature scientific development. Furthermore, under normal circumstances they characterize the very best and most creative research as well as the more routine. Nor can there be much question where they come from. Rather than being characteristics of the aberrant individual, they are community characteristics with deep roots in the procedures through which scientists are trained for work in their profession. Strongly held convictions that are prior to research often seem to be a precondition for success in the sciences.

Obviously I am already ahead of my story, but in getting there I have perhaps indicated its principal theme. Though preconception and resistance to innovation could very easily choke off scientific progress, their omnipresence is nonetheless symptomatic of characteristics upon which the continuing vitality of research

---

[1] *Wissenschafiliche Selbstbiographie* (Leipzig, 1948) 22, my translation.

depends. Those characteristics I shall collectively call the dogmatism of mature science, and in the pages to come I shall try to make the following points about them. Scientific education inculcates what the scientific community had previously with difficulty gained—a deep commitment to a particular way of viewing the world and of practising science in it. That commitment can be, and from time to time is, replaced by another, but it cannot be merely given up. And, while it continues to characterize the community of professional practitioners, it proves in two respects fundamental to productive research. By defining for the individual scientist both the problems available for pursuit and the nature of acceptable solutions to them, the commitment is actually constitutive of research. Normally the scientist is a puzzle-solver like the chess player, and the commitment induced by education is what provides him with the rules of the game being played in his time. In its absence he would not be a physicist, chemist, or whatever he has been trained to be.

In addition, commitment has a second and largely incompatible research role. Its very strength and the unanimity with which the professional group subscribes to it provides the individual scientist with an immensely sensitive detector of the trouble spots from which significant innovations of fact and theory are almost inevitably educed. In the sciences most discoveries of unexpected fact and all fundamental innovations of theory are responses to a prior breakdown in the rules of the previously established game. Therefore, though a quasi-dogmatic commitment is, on the one hand, a source of resistance and controversy, it is also instrumental in making the sciences the most consistently revolutionary of all human activities. One need make neither resistance nor dogma a virtue to recognize that no mature science could exist without them.

Before examining further the nature and effects of scientific dogma, consider the pattern of education through which it is transmitted from one generation of practitioners to the next. Scientists are not, of course, the only professional community that acquires from education a set of standards, tools, and techniques which they later deploy in their own creative work. Yet even a cursory inspection of scientific pedagogy suggests that it is far more likely to induce professional rigidity than education in other fields, excepting, perhaps, systematic theology. Admittedly the following epitome is biased toward the American pattern, which I know best. The contrasts at which it aims must, however, be visible, if muted, in European and British education as well.

Perhaps the most striking feature of scientific education is that, to an extent quite unknown in other creative fields, it is conducted through textbooks, works written especially for students. Until he is ready, or very nearly ready, to begin his own dissertation, the student of chemistry, physics, astronomy, geology, or biology is seldom either asked to attempt trial research projects or exposed to the immediate products of research done by others—to, that is, the professional communications that scientists write for their peers. Collections of 'source readings' play a negligible role in *scientific* education. Nor is the science student encouraged to read the historical classics of his field—works in which he might encounter other ways of regarding the questions discussed in his text, but in which he would also meet problems, concepts, and standards of solution that his future profession had long-since discarded and replaced.[2] Whitehead somewhere caught this quite special feature of the sciences when he wrote, "A science that hesitates to forget its founders is lost."

An almost exclusive reliance on textbooks is not all that distinguishes scientific education. Students in other fields are, after all, also exposed to such books, though seldom beyond the second year of college and even in those early years not exclusively. But in the sciences different textbooks display different subject matters rather than, as in the humanities and many social sciences, exemplifying different approaches to a single problem field. Even books that compete for adoption in a single science course differ mainly in level and pedagogic detail, not in substance or conceptual structure. One can scarcely imagine a physicist's or chemist's saying that he had been forced to begin the education of his third-year class almost from first principles because its previous exposure to the field had been through books that consistently violated his conception of the discipline. Remarks of that sort are not by any means unprecedented in several of the social sciences. Apparently scientists agree about what it is that every student of the field must know. That is why, in the design of a pre-professional curriculum, they can use textbooks instead of eclectic samples of research.

Nor is the characteristic technique of textbook presentation altogether the same in the sciences as elsewhere. Except in the occasional introductions that students seldom read, science texts make little attempt to describe the *sorts* of problems that the professional may be asked to solve or to discuss the *variety* of techniques that experience has made available for their solution. Instead, these books exhibit, from the very start, concrete problem-solutions that the profession has come to accept as

[2] The individual sciences display some variation in these respects. Students in the newer and also in the less theoretical sciences—e.g. parts of biology, geology, and medical science—are more likely to encounter both contemporary and historical source materials than those in, say, astronomy, mathematics, or physics.

paradigms, and they then ask the student, either with a pencil and paper or in the laboratory, to solve for himself problems closely modelled in method and substance upon those through which the text has led him. Only in elementary language instruction or in training a musical instrumentalist is so large or essential a use made of 'finger exercises'. And those are just the fields in which the object of instruction is to produce with maximum rapidity strong 'mental sets' or *Einstellungen*. In the sciences, I suggest, the effect of these techniques is much the same. Though scientific development is particularly productive of consequential novelties, scientific education remains a relatively dogmatic initiation into a pre-established problem-solving tradition that the student is neither invited nor equipped to evaluate.

The pattern of systematic textbook education just described existed in no place and in no science (except perhaps elementary mathematics) until the early nineteenth century. But before that date a number of the more developed sciences clearly displayed the special characteristics indicated above, and in a few cases had done so for a very long time. Where there were no textbooks there had often been universally received paradigms for the practice of individual sciences. These were scientific achievements reported in books that all the practitioners of a given field knew intimately and admired, achievements upon which they modelled their own research and which provided them with a measure of their own accomplishment. Aristotle's *Physica*, Ptolemy's *Almagest*, Newton's *Principia* and *Opticks*, Franklin's *Electricity*, Lavoisier's *Chemistry*, and Lyell's *Geology*—these works and many others all served for a time implicitly to define the legitimate problems and methods of a research field for succeeding generations of practitioners. In their day each of these books, together with others modelled closely upon them, did for its field much of what textbooks now do for these same fields and for others besides.

All of the works named above are, of course, classics of science. As such their role may be thought to resemble that of the main classics in other creative fields, for example the works of a Shakespeare, a Rembrandt, or an Adam Smith. But by calling these works, or the achievements which lie behind them, paradigms rather than classics, I mean to suggest that there is something else special about them, something which sets them apart both from some other classics of science and from all the classics of other creative fields.

Part of this "something else" is what I shall call the exclusiveness of paradigms. At any time the practitioners of a given specialty may recognize numerous classics, some of them—like the works of Ptolemy and Copernicus or Newton and Descartes—quite incompatible one with the other. But that same group, if it has a paradigm at all, can have only one. Unlike the community of artists—which can draw simultaneous inspiration from the works of, say, Rembrandt *and* Cézanne and which therefore studies both—the community of astronomers had no alternative to choosing *between* the competing models of scientific activity supplied by Copernicus and Ptolemy. Furthermore, having made their choice, astronomers could thereafter neglect the work which they had rejected. Since the sixteenth century there have been only two full editions of the *Almagest*, both produced in the nineteenth century and directed exclusively to scholars. In the mature sciences there is no apparent function for the equivalent of an art museum or a library of classics. Scientists know when books, and even journals, are out of date. Though they do not then destroy them, they do, as any historian of science can testify, transfer them from the active departmental library to desuetude in the general university depository. Up-to-date works have taken their place, and they are all that the further progress of science requires.

This characteristic of paradigms is closely related to another, and one that has a particular relevance to my selection of the term. In receiving a paradigm the scientific community commits itself, consciously or not, to the view that the fundamental problems there resolved have, in fact, been solved once and for all. That is what Lagrange meant when he said of Newton: "There is but one universe, and it can happen to but one man in the world's history to be the interpreter of its laws."[3] The example of either Aristotle or Einstein proves Lagrange wrong, but that does not make the fact of his commitment less consequential to scientific development. Believing that what Newton had done need not be done again, Lagrange was not tempted to fundamental reinterpretations of nature. Instead, he could take up where the men who shared his Newtonian paradigm had left off, striving both for neater formulations of that paradigm and for an articulation that would bring it into closer and closer agreement with observations of nature. That sort of work is undertaken only by those who feel that the model they have chosen is entirely secure. There is nothing quite like it in the arts, and the parallels in the social sciences are at best partial. Paradigms determine a developmental pattern for the mature sciences that is unlike the one familiar in other fields.

That difference could be illustrated by comparing the development of a paradigm-based science with that of, say,

---

[3] Quoted in this form by S. F. Mason, *Main Currents of Scientific Thought* (New York, 1956) 254. The original, which is identical in spirit but not in words, seems to derive from Delambre's contemporary eloge, *Memoires de ... l'Institut ...*, *année 1812*, 2nd part (Paris, 1816) p. xlvi.

philosophy or literature. But the same effect can be achieved more economically by contrasting the early developmental pattern of almost any science with the pattern characteristic of the same field in its maturity. I cannot here avoid putting the point too starkly, but what I have in mind is this. Excepting in those fields which, like biochemistry, originated in the combination of existing specialties, paradigms are a relatively late acquisition in the course of scientific development. During its early years a science proceeds without them, or at least without any so unequivocal and so binding as those named illustratively above. Physical optics before Newton or the study of heat before Black and Lavoisier exemplifies the pre-paradigm developmental pattern that I shall immediately examine in the history of electricity. While it continues, until, that is, a first paradigm is reached, the development of a science resembles that of the arts and of most social sciences more closely than it resembles the pattern which astronomy, say, had already acquired in Antiquity and which all the natural sciences make familiar today.

To catch the difference between pre- and post-paradigm scientific development consider a single example. In the early eighteenth century, as in the seventeenth and earlier, there were almost as many views about the nature of electricity as there were important electrical experimenters, men like Hauksbee, Gray, Desaguliers, Du Fay, Nollet, Watson, and Franklin. All their numerous concepts of electricity had something in common—they were partially derived from experiment and observation and partially from one or another version of the mechanico-corpuscular philosophy that guided all scientific research of the day. Yet these common elements gave their work no more than a family resemblance. We are forced to recognize the existence of several competing schools and sub-schools, each deriving strength from its relation to a particular version (Cartesian or Newtonian) of the corpuscular metaphysics, and each emphasizing the particular cluster of electrical phenomena which its own theory could do most to explain. Other observations were dealt with by *ad hoc* elaborations or remained as outstanding problems for further research.[4]

One early group of electricians followed seventeenth-century practice, and thus took attraction and frictional generation as the

---

[4] Much documentation for this account of electrical development can be retrieved from Duane Roller and Duane H. D. Roller, *The Development of the Concept of Electric Charge: Electricity from the Greeks to Coulomb* (Harvard Case Histories in Experimental Science, VIII, Cambridge, Mass., 1954) and from I. B. Cohen, *Franklin and Newton: An Inquiry into Speculative Newtonian Experimental Science and Franklin's Work in Electricity as an Example Thereof* (Philadelphia, 1956). For analytic detail I am, however, very much indebted to a still unpublished paper by my student, John L. Heilbron, who has also assisted in the preparation of the three notes that follow.

fundamental electrical phenomena. They tended to treat repulsion as a secondary effect (in the seventeenth century it had been attributed to some sort of mechanical rebounding) and also to postpone for as long as possible both discussion and systematic research of Gray's newly discovered effect, electrical conduction. Another closely related group regarded repulsion as the fundamental effect, while still another took attraction and repulsion together to be equally elementary manifestations of electricity. Each of these groups modified its theory and research accordingly, but they then had as much difficulty as the first in accounting for any but the simplest conduction effects. Those effects provided the starting point for still a third group, one which tended to speak of electricity as a "fluid" that ran through conductors rather than as an "effluvium" that emanated from non-conductors. This group, in its turn, had difficulty reconciling its theory with a number of attractive and repulsive effects.[5]

At various times all these schools made significant contributions to the body of concepts, phenomena, and techniques from which Franklin drew the first paradigm for electrical science. Any definition of the scientist that excludes the members of these schools will exclude their modern successors as well. Yet anyone surveying the development of electricity before Franklin may well conclude that, though the field's practitioners were scientists, the immediate result of their activity was something less than science. Because the body of belief he could take for granted was very small, each electrical experimenter felt forced to begin by building his field anew from its foundations. In doing so his choice of supporting observation and experiment was relatively free, for the set of standard methods and phenomena that every electrician must employ and explain was extraordinarily small. As a result, throughout the first half of the century, electrical investigations tended to circle back over the same ground again and again. New effects were repeatedly discovered, but many of them were rapidly lost again. Among those lost were many effects due to what we should now describe as inductive charging and also Du Fay's famous discovery of the two sorts of electrification. Franklin and Kinnersley were surprised when, some fifteen years later, the latter

[5] This division into schools is still somewhat too simplistic. After 1720 the basic division is between the French school (Du Fay, Nollet, etc.) who base their theories on attraction-repulsion effects and the English school (Desaguliers, Watson, etc.) who concentrate on conduction effects. Each group had immense difficulty in explaining the phenomena that the other took to be basic. (See, for example, Needham's report of Lemonier's investigations, in *Philosophical Transactions*, XLIV, 1746, p. 247). Within each of these groups, and particularly the English, one can trace further subdivision depending upon whether attraction or repulsion is considered the more fundamental electrical effect.

discovered that a charged ball which was repelled by rubbed glass would be attracted by rubbed sealing-wax or amber.[6] In the absence of a well-articulated and widely received theory (a desideratum which no science possesses from its very beginning and which few if any of the social sciences have achieved today), the situation could hardly have been otherwise. During the first half of the eighteenth century there was no way for electricians to distinguish consistently between electrical and non-electrical effects, between laboratory accidents and essential novelties, or between striking demonstration and experiments which revealed the essential nature of electricity.

This is the state of affairs which Franklin changed.[7] His theory explained so many—though not all—of the electrical effects recognized by the various earlier schools that within a generation all electricians had been converted to some view very like it. Though it did not resolve quite all disagreements, Franklin's theory was electricity's first paradigm, and its existence gives a new tone and flavour to the electrical researches of the last decades of the eighteenth century. The end of inter-school debate ended the constant reiteration of fundamentals; confidence that they were on the right track encouraged electricians to undertake more precise, esoteric, and consuming sorts of work. Freed from concern with any and all electrical phenomena, the newly united group could pursue selected phenomena in far more detail, designing much special equipment for the task and employing it more stubbornly and systematically than electricians had ever done before. In the hands of a Cavendish, a Coulomb, or a Volta the collection of electrical facts and the articulation of electrical theory were, for the

---

[6] Du Fay's discovery that there are two sorts of electricity and that these are mutually attractive but self-repulsive is reported and documented in great experimental detail in the fourth of his famous memoirs on electricity: "De l'Attraction & Répulsion des Corps Electriques", *Memoires de ... l'Académie ... de l'année 1733* (Paris, 1735) 457–76. These memoirs were well known and widely cited, but Desaguliers seems to be the only electrician who, for almost two decades, even mentions that some charged bodies will attract each other (*Philosophical Transactions ...*, XLII, 1741–2, pp. 140–3). For Franklin's and Kinnersley's "surprise" see I. B. Cohen (ed.), *Benjamin Franklin's Experiments: A New Edition of Franklin's Experiments and Observations on Electricity*, (Cambridge, Mass., 1941) 250–5. Note also that, though Kinnersley had *produced* the effect, neither he nor Franklin seems ever to have *recognized* that two resinously charged bodies would repel each other, a phenomenon directly contrary to Franklin's theory.

[7] The change is not, of course, due to Franklin alone nor did it occur overnight. Other electricians, most notably William Watson, anticipated parts of Franklin's theory. More important, it was only after essential modifications, due principally to Aepinus, that Franklin's theory gained the general currency requisite for a paradigm. And even then there continued to be two formulations of the theory: the Franklin—Aepinus one-fluid form and a two-fluid form due principally to Symmer. Electricians soon reached the conclusion that no electrical test could possibly discriminate between the two theories. Until the discovery of the battery, when the choice between a one-fluid and two-fluid theory began to make an occasional difference in the design and analysis of experiments, the two were equivalent.

first time, highly directed activities. As a result the efficiency and effectiveness of electrical research increased immensely, providing evidence for a societal version of Francis Bacon's acute methodological dictum: "Truth emerges more readily from error than from confusion."

Obviously I exaggerate both the speed and the completeness with which the transition to a paradigm occurs. But that does not make the phenomenon itself less real. The maturation of electricity as a science is not coextensive with the entire development of the field. Writers on electricity during the first four decades of the eighteenth century possessed far more information about electrical phenomena than had their sixteenth- and seventeenth-century predecessors. During the half-century after 1745 very few new sorts of electrical phenomena were added to their lists. Nevertheless, in important respects the electrical writings of the last two decades of the century seemed further removed from those of Gray, Du Fay, and even Franklin than are the writings of these early eighteenth-century electricians from those of their predecessors a hundred years before. Some time between 1740 and 1780 electricians, as a group, gained what astronomers had achieved in Antiquity, students of motion in the Middle Ages, of physical optics in the late seventeenth century, and of historical geology in the early nineteenth. They had, that is, achieved a paradigm, possession of which enabled them to take the foundation of their field for granted and to push on to more concrete and recondite problems.[8] Except with the advantage of hindsight, it is hard to find another criterion that so clearly proclaims a field of science.

These remarks should begin to clarify what I take a paradigm to be. It is, in the first place, a fundamental scientific achievement and one which includes both a theory and some exemplary applications to the results of experiment and observation. More important, it is an open-ended achievement, one which leaves all sorts of research still to be done. And, finally, it is an accepted achievement in the sense that it is received by a group whose members no longer try to rival it or to create alternates for it. Instead, they attempt to extend and exploit it in a variety of ways to which I shall shortly turn. That discussion of the work that paradigms leave to be done will make both their role and the reasons for their special efficacy clearer still. But first there is one

---

[8] Note that this first electrical paradigm was fully effective only until 1800, when the discovery of the battery and the multiplication of electro-chemical effects initiated a revolution in electrical theory. Until a new paradigm emerged from that revolution, the literature of electricity, particularly in England, reverted in many respects to the tone characteristic of the first half of the eighteenth century.

rather different point to be made about them. Though the reception of a paradigm seems historically prerequisite to the most effective sorts of scientific research, the paradigms which enhance research effectiveness need not be and usually are not permanent. On the contrary, the developmental pattern of mature science is usually from paradigm to paradigm. It differs from the pattern characteristic of the early or pre-paradigm period not by the total elimination of debate over fundamentals, but by the drastic restriction of such debate to occasional periods of paradigm change.

Ptolemy's *Almagest* was not, for example, any less a paradigm because the research tradition that descended from it had ultimately to be replaced by an incompatible one derived from the work of Copernicus and Kepler. Nor was Newton's *Opticks* less a paradigm for eighteenth-century students of light because it was later replaced by the ether-wave theory of Young and Fresnel, a paradigm which in its turn gave way to the electromagnetic displacement theory that descends from Maxwell. Undoubtedly the research work that any given paradigm permits results in lasting contributions to the body of scientific knowledge and technique, but paradigms themselves are very often swept aside and replaced by others that are quite incompatible with them. We can have no recourse to notions like the 'truth' or 'validity' of paradigms in our attempt to understand the special efficacy of the research which their reception permits.

On the contrary, the historian can often recognize that in declaring an older paradigm out of date or in rejecting the approach of some one of the pre-paradigm schools a scientific community has rejected the embryo of an important scientific perception to which it would later be forced to return. But it is very far from clear that the profession delayed scientific development by doing so. Would quantum mechanics have been born sooner if nineteenth-century scientists had been more willing to admit that Newton's corpuscular view of light might still have something significant to teach them about nature? I think not, although in the arts, the humanities, and many social sciences that less doctrinaire view is very often adopted toward classic achievements of the past. Or would astronomy and dynamics have advanced more rapidly if scientists had recognized that Ptolemy and Copernicus had chosen equally legitimate means to describe the earth's position? That view was, in fact, suggested during the seventeenth century, and it has since been confirmed by relativity theory. But in the interim it was firmly rejected together with Ptolemaic astronomy, emerging again only in the very late nineteenth century when, for the first time, it had concrete relevance to unsolved problems generated by the continuing practice of nonrelativistic physics. One could argue, as indeed by implication I shall, that close eighteenth- and nineteenth-century attention either to the work of Ptolemy or to the relativistic views of Descartes, Huygens, and Leibniz would have delayed rather than accelerated the revolution in physics with which the twentieth century began. Advance from paradigm to paradigm rather than through the continuing competition between recognized classics may be a functional as well as a factual characteristic of mature scientific development.

Much that has been said so far is intended to indicate that—except during occasional extraordinary periods to be discussed in the last section of this paper—the practitioners of a mature scientific specialty are deeply committed to some one paradigm-based way of regarding and investigating nature. Their paradigm tells them about the sorts of entities with which the universe is populated and about the way the members of that population behave; in addition, it informs them of the questions that may legitimately be asked about nature and of the techniques that can properly be used in the search for answers to them. In fact, a paradigm tells scientists so much that the questions it leaves for research seldom have great intrinsic interest to those outside the profession. Though educated men as a group may be fascinated to hear about the spectrum of fundamental particles or about the processes of molecular replication, their interest is usually quickly exhausted by an account of the beliefs that already underlie research on these problems. The outcome of the individual research project is indifferent to them, and their interest is unlikely to awaken again until, as with parity nonconservation, research unexpectedly leads to paradigm-change and to a consequent alteration in the beliefs which guide research. That, no doubt, is why both historians and popularizers have devoted so much of their attention to the revolutionary episodes which result in change of paradigm and have so largely neglected the sort of work that even the greatest scientists necessarily do most of the time.

My point will become clearer if I now ask what it is that the existence of a paradigm leaves for the scientific community to do. The answer—as obvious as the related existence of resistance to innovation and as often brushed under the carpet—is that scientists, given a paradigm, strive with all their might and skill to bring it into closer and closer agreement with nature. Much of their effort, particularly in the early stages of a paradigm's development, is directed to articulating the paradigm, rendering it more precise in areas where the original formulation has inevitably been vague. For example, knowing that electricity was a fluid whose individual particles act upon one another at a distance, electricians after Franklin could attempt to determine the quantitative law of force between particles of electricity. Others could seek the mutual interdependence of spark length, electroscope deflection, quantity of electricity, and conductor-configuration. These were the sorts of problems upon which Coulomb, Cavendish, and Volta worked in the last decades of the eighteenth century, and they have many parallels in the development of every other mature science. Contemporary attempts to determine the quantum mechanical forces governing the interactions of nucleons fall precisely in this same catagory, paradigm-articulation.

That sort of problem is not the only challenge which a paradigm sets for the community that embraces it. There are always many areas in which a paradigm is assumed to work but to which it has not, in fact, yet been applied. Matching the paradigm to nature in these areas often engages much of the best scientific talent in any generation. The eighteenth-century attempts to develop a Newtonian theory of vibrating strings provide one significant example, and the current work on a quantum mechanical theory of solids provides another. In addition, there is always much fascinating work to be done in improving the match between a paradigm and nature in an area where at least limited agreement has already been demonstrated. Theoretical work on problems like these is illustrated by eighteenth-century research on the perturbations that cause planets to deviate from their Keplerian orbits as well as by the elaborate twentieth-century theory of the spectra of complex atoms and molecules. And accompanying all these problems and still others besides is a recurring series of instrumental hurdles. Special apparatus had to be invented and built to permit Coulomb's determination of the electrical force law. New sorts of telescopes were required for the observations that, when completed, demanded an improved Newtonian perturbation theory. The design and construction of more flexible and more powerful accelerators is a continuing desideratum in the attempt to articulate more powerful theories of nuclear forces. These are the sorts of work on which almost all scientists spend almost all of their time.[9]

Probably this epitome of normal scientific research requires no elaboration in this place, but there are two points that must now

[9] The discussion in this paragraph and the next is considerably elaborated in my paper, "The function of measurement in modern physical science", *Isis*, LII (1961) 161–93.

be made about it. First, all of the problems mentioned above were paradigm-dependent, often in several ways. Some—for example the derivation of perturbation terms in Newtonian planetary theory—could not even have been stated in the absence of an appropriate paradigm. With the transition from Newtonian to relativity theory a few of them became different problems and not all of these have yet been solved. Other problems—for example the attempt to determine a law of electric forces—could be and were at least vaguely stated before the emergence of the paradigm with which they were ultimately solved. But in that older form they proved intractable. The men who described electrical attractions and repulsions in terms of effluvia attempted to measure the resulting forces by placing a charged disc at a measured distance beneath one pan of a balance. Under those circumstances no consistent or interpretable results were obtained. The prerequisite for success proved to be a paradigm that reduced electrical action to a gravity-like action between point particles at a distance. After Franklin electricians thought of electrical action in those terms; both Coulomb and Cavendish designed their apparatus accordingly. Finally, in both these cases and in all the others as well a commitment to the paradigm was needed simply to provide adequate motivation. Who would design and build elaborate special-purpose apparatus, or who would spend months trying to solve a particular differential equation, without a quite firm guarantee that his effort, if successful, would yield the anticipated fruit?

This reference to the anticipated outcome of a research project points to the second striking characteristic of what I am now calling normal, or paradigm-based, research. The scientist engaged in it does not at all fit the prevalent image of the scientist as explorer or as inventor of brand new theories which permit striking and unexpected predictions. On the contrary, in all the problems discussed above everything but the detail of the outcome was known in advance. No scientist who accepted Franklin's paradigm could doubt that there was a law of attraction between small particles of electricity, and they could reasonably suppose that it would take a simple algebraic form. Some of them had even guessed that it would prove to be an inverse square law. Nor did Newtonian astronomers and physicists doubt that Newton's law of motion and of gravitation could ultimately be made to yield the observed motions of the moon and planets even though, for over a century, the complexity of the requisite mathematics prevented good agreement's being uniformly obtained. In all these problems, as in most others that scientists undertake, the challenge is not to uncover the unknown but to obtain the known. Their fascination lies not in what success may be expected to disclose but in the difficulty of obtaining success at all. Rather than resembling exploration, normal research seems like the effort to assemble a Chinese cube whose finished outline is known from the start.

Those are the characteristics of normal research that I had in mind when, at the start of this essay, I described the man engaged in it as a puzzle-solver, like the chess player. The paradigm he has acquired through prior training provides him with the rules of the game, describes the pieces with which it must be played, and indicates the nature of the required outcome. His task is to manipulate those pieces within the rules in such a way that the required outcome is produced. If he fails, as most scientists do in at least their first attacks upon any given problem, that failure speaks only to his lack of skill. It cannot call into question the rules which his paradigm has supplied, for without those rules there would have been no puzzle with which to wrestle in the first place. No wonder, then, that the problems (or puzzles) which the practitioner of a mature science normally undertakes presuppose a deep commitment to a paradigm. And how fortunate it is that that commitment is not lightly given up. Experience shows that, in almost all cases, the reiterated efforts, either of the individual or of the professional group, do at least succeed in producing within the paradigm a solution to even the most stubborn problems. That is one of the ways in which science advances. Under those circumstances can we be surprised that scientists resist paradigm-change? What they are defending is, after all, neither more nor less than the basis of their professional way of life.

By now one principal advantage of what I began by calling scientific dogmatism should be apparent. As a glance at any Baconian natural history or a survey of the pre-paradigm development of any science will show, nature is vastly too complex to be explored even approximately at random. Something must tell the scientist where to look and what to look for, and that something, though it may not last beyond his generation, is the paradigm with which his education as a scientist has supplied him. Given that paradigm and the requisite confidence in it, the scientist largely ceases to be an explorer at all, or at least to be an explorer of the unknown. Instead, he struggles to articulate and concretize the known, designing much special-purpose apparatus and many special-purpose adaptations of theory for that task. From those puzzles of design and adaptation he gets his pleasure. Unless he is extraordinarily lucky, it is upon his success with them that his reputation will depend. Inevitably the enterprise which engages him is characterized, at any one time, by drastically restricted vision. But within the region upon which vision is focused the continuing attempt to match paradigms to nature results in a knowledge and understanding of esoteric detail that could not have been achieved in any other way. From Copernicus and the problem of precession to Einstein and the photo-electric effect, the progress of science has again and again depended upon just such esoterica. One great virtue of commitment to paradigms is that it frees scientists to engage themselves with tiny puzzles.

Nevertheless, this image of scientific research as puzzle-solving or paradigm-matching must be, at the very least, thoroughly incomplete. Though the scientist may not be an explorer, scientists do again and again discover new and unexpected sorts of phenomena. Or again, though the scientist does not normally strive to invent new sorts of basic theories, such theories have repeatedly emerged from the continuing practice of research. But neither of these types of innovation would arise if the enterprise I have been calling normal science were always successful. In fact, the man engaged in puzzle-solving very often resists substantive novelty, and he does so for good reason. To him it is a change in the rules of the game and any change of rules is intrinsically subversive. That subversive element is, of course, most apparent in major theoretical innovations like those associated with the names of Copernicus, Lavoisier, or Einstein. But the discovery of an unanticipated phenomenon can have the same destructive effects although usually on a smaller group and for a far shorter time. Once he had performed his first follow-up experiments, Röntgen's glowing screen demonstrated that previously standard cathode ray equipment was behaving in ways for which no one had made allowance. There was an unanticipated variable to be controlled; earlier researches, already on their way to becoming paradigms, would require re-evaluation; old puzzles would have to be solved again under a somewhat different set of rules. Even so readily assimilable a discovery as that of X-rays can violate a paradigm that has previously guided research. It follows that, if the normal puzzle-solving activity were altogether successful, the development of science could lead to no fundamental innovations at all.

But of course normal science is not always successful, and in recognizing that fact we encounter what I take to be the second great advantage of paradigm-based research. Unlike many of the early electricians, the practitioner of a mature science knows with considerable precision what sort of result he should gain from his research. As a consequence he is in a particularly favourable position to recognize when a research problem has gone astray.

Perhaps, like Galvani or Röntgen, he encounters an effect that he knows ought not to occur. Or perhaps, like Copernicus, Planck, or Einstein, he concludes that the reiterated failures of his predecessors in matching a paradigm to nature is presumptive evidence of the need to change the rules under which a match is to be sought. Or perhaps, like Franklin or Lavoisier, he decides after repeated attempts that no existing theory can be articulated to account for some newly discovered effect. In all of these ways and in others besides the practice of normal puzzle-solving science can and inevitably does lead to the isolation and recognition of anomaly. That recognition proves, I think, prerequisite for almost all discoveries of new sorts of phenomena and for all fundamental innovations in scientific theory. After a first paradigm has been achieved, a breakdown in the rules of the pre-established game is the usual prelude to significant scientific innovation.

Examine the case of discoveries first. Many of them, like Coulomb's law or a new element to fill an empty spot in the periodic table, present no problem. They were not 'new sorts of phenomena' but discoveries anticipated through a paradigm and achieved by expert puzzle-solvers: that sort of discovery is a natural product of what I have been calling normal science. But not all discoveries are of that sort: many could not have been anticipated by any extrapolation from the known; in a sense they had to be made 'by accident'. On the other hand the accident through which they emerged could not ordinarily have occurred to a man just looking around. In the mature sciences discovery demands much special equipment, both conceptual and instrumental, and that special equipment has invariably been developed and deployed for the pursuit of the puzzles of normal research. Discovery results when that equipment fails to function as it should. Furthermore, since some sort of at least temporary failure occurs during almost every research project, discovery results only when the failure is particularly stubborn or striking and only when it seems to raise questions about accepted beliefs and procedures. Established paradigms are thus often doubly prerequisite to discoveries. Without them the project that goes astray would not have been undertaken. And even when the project has gone astray, as most do for a while, the paradigm can help to determine whether the failure is worth pursuing. The usual and proper response to a failure in puzzle-solving is to blame one's talents or one's tools and to turn next to another problem. If he is not to waste time, the scientist must be able to discriminate essential anomaly from mere failure.

That pattern—discovery through an anomaly that calls

established techniques and beliefs in doubt—has been repeated again and again in the course of scientific development. Newton discovered the composition of white light when he was unable to reconcile measured dispersion with that predicted by Snell's recently discovered law of refraction.[10] The electric battery was discovered when existing detectors of static charges failed to behave as Franklin's paradigm said they should.[11] The planet Neptune was discovered through an effort to account for recognized anomalies in the orbit of Uranus.[12] The element chlorine and the compound carbon monoxide emerged during attempts to reconcile Lavoisier's new chemistry with laboratory observations.[13] The so-called noble gases were the products of a long series of investigations initiated by a small but persistent anomaly in the measured density of atmospheric nitrogen.[14] The electron was posited to explain some anomalous properties of electrical conduction through gases, and its spin was suggested to account for other sorts of anomalies observed in atomic spectra.[15] Both the neutron and the neutrino provide other examples, and the list could be extended almost indefinitely.[16] In the mature sciences unexpected novelties are discovered principally after something has gone wrong.

If, however, anomaly is significant in preparing the way for new discoveries, it plays a still larger role in the invention of new theories. Contrary to a prevalent, though by no means universal, belief, new theories are not invented to account for observations that have not previously been ordered by theory at all. Rather, at almost all times in the development of any advanced science, all the facts whose relevance is admitted seem either to fit existing theory well or to be in the process of conforming. Making them conform better provides many of the standard problems of normal science. And almost always committed scientists succeed in solving them. But they do not always succeed, and when they fail

[10] See my "Newton's optical papers" in I. B. Cohen (ed.), *Isaac Newton's Papers & Letters on Natural Philosophy* (Cambridge, Mass., 1958) 27–45.

[11] Luigi Galvani, *Commentary on the Effects of Electricity on Muscular Motion*, trans. by M. G. Foley with notes and an introduction by I. B. Cohen (Norwalk, Conn., 1954) 27–9.

[12] Angus Armitage, *A Century of Astronomy* (London, 1950) 111–15.

[13] For chlorine see Ernst von Meyer, *A History of Chemistry from the Earliest Times to the Present Day*, trans. G. M'Gowan (London, 1891) 224–7. For carbon monoxide see Hermann Kopp, *Geschichte der Chemie* (Braunschweig, 1845) III, 294–6.

[14] William Ramsay, *The Gases of the Atmosphere: the History of their Discovery* (London, 1896) Chs. 4 and 5.

[15] J. J. Thomson, *Recollections and Reflections* (New York, 1937) 325–71; T. W. Chalmers, *Historic Researches: Chapters in the History of Physical and Chemical Discovery* (London, 1949) 187–217; and F. K. Richtmeyer, E. H. Kennard and T. Lauritsen, *Introduction to Modern Physics* (5th ed., New York, 1955) 212.

[16] Ibid. pp. 466–470; and Rogers D. Rusk, *Introduction to Atomic and Nuclear Physics* (New York, 1958) 328–30.

repeatedly and in increasing numbers, then their sector of the scientific community encounters what I am elsewhere calling 'crisis'. Recognizing that something is fundamentally wrong with the theory upon which their work is based, scientists will attempt more fundamental articulations of theory than those which were admissible before. (Characteristically, at times of crisis, one encounters numerous different versions of the paradigm theory.[17]) Simultaneously they will often begin more nearly random experimentation within the area of difficulty hoping to discover some effect that will suggest a way to set the situation right. Only under circumstances like these, I suggest, is a fundamental innovation in scientific theory both invented and accepted.

The state of Ptolemaic astronomy was, for example, a recognized scandal before Copernicus proposed a basic change in astronomical theory, and the preface in which Copernicus described his reasons for innovation provides a classic description of the crisis state.[18] Galileo's contributions to the study of motion took their point of departure from recognized difficulties with medieval theory, and Newton reconciled Galileo's mechanics with Copernicansim.[19] Lavoisier's new chemistry was a product of the anomalies created jointly by the proliferation of new gases and the first systematic studies of weight relations.[20] The wave theory of light was developed amid growing concern about anomalies in the relation of diffraction and polarization effects to Newton's corpuscular theory.[21] Thermodynamics, which later came to seem a superstructure for existing sciences, was established only at the price of rejecting the previously

[17] One classic example, for which see the reference cited below in the next note, is the proliferation of geocentric astronomical systems in the years before Copernicus's heliocentric reform. Another, for which see J. R. Partington and D. McKie, "Historical studies of the phlogiston theory", *Annals of Science*, II (1937) 361–404, III (1938) 1–58, 337–71, and IV (1939) 113–49, is the multiplicity of 'phlogiston theories' produced in response to the general recognition that weight is always gained on combustion and to the experimental discovery of many new gases after 1760. The same proliferation of versions of accepted theories occurred in mechanics and electromagnetism in the two decades preceding Einstein's special relativity theory. (E. T. Whittaker, *History of the Theories of Aether and Electricity*, 2nd ed., 2 vols., London, 1951–53, I, Ch. 12, and II, Ch. 2. I concur in the widespread judgment that this is a very biased account of the genesis of relativity theory, but it contains just the detail necessary to make the point here at issue.)

[18] T. S. Kuhn, *The Copernican Revolution: Planetary Astronomy in the Development of Western Thought* (Cambridge, Mass., 1957) 133–40.

[19] For Galileo see Alexandre Koyré, *Études Galiléennes* (3 vols., Paris, 1939); for Newton see Kuhn, op. cit. pp. 228–60 and 289–91.

[20] For the proliferation of gases see Partington, *A Short History of Chemistry* (2nd ed., London, 1948) Ch. 6; for the role of weight relations see Henry Guerlac, "The origin of Lavoisier's work on combustion", *Archives internationales d'histoire des sciences*, XII (1959) 113–35.

[21] Whittaker, *Aether and Electricity*, II, 94–109; William Whewell, *History of the Inductive Sciences* (revised ed., 3 vols., London, 1847) II, 213–71; and Kuhn, "Function of measurement", p. 181 n.

paradigmatic caloric theory.[22] Quantum mechanics was born from
a variety of difficulties surrounding black-body radiation, specific
heat, and the photo-electric effect.[23] Again the list could be
extended, but the point should already be clear. New theories arise
from work conducted under old ones, and they do so only when
something is observed to have gone wrong. Their prelude is widely
recognized anomaly, and that recognition can come only to a
group that knows very well what it would mean to have things go
right.

Because limitations of space and time force me to stop at this
point, my case for dogmatism must remain schematic. I shall not
here even attempt to deal with the fine-structure that scientific
development exhibits at all times. But there is another more positive
qualification of my thesis, and it requires one closing comment.
Though successful research demands a deep commitment to the
status quo, innovation remains at the heart of the enterprise.
Scientists are *trained* to operate as puzzle-solvers from established
rules, but they are also *taught* to regard themselves as explorers and
inventors who know no rules except those dictated by nature itself.
The result is an acquired tension, partly within the individual and
partly within the community, between professional skills on the one
hand and professional ideology on the other. Almost certainly that
tension and the ability to sustain it are important to science's
success. In so far as I have dealt exclusively with the dependence of
research upon tradition, my discussion is inevitably one-sided. On
this whole subject there is a great deal more to be said.

But to be one-sided is not necessarily to be wrong, and it may be
an essential preliminary to a more penetrating examination of the
requisites for successful scientific life. Almost no one, perhaps no
one at all, needs to be told that the vitality of science depends upon
the continuation of occasional tradition-shattering innovations. But
the apparently contrary dependence of research upon a deep commitment to established tools and beliefs receives the very minimum
of attention. I urge that it be given more. Until that is done, some of
the most striking characteristics of scientific education and development will remain extraordinarily difficult to understand.

[22] For a general account of the beginnings of thermodynamics (including much
relevant bibliography) see my "Energy conservation as an example of simultaneous
discovery" in Marshall Clagett (ed.), *Critical Problems in the History of Science* (Madison,
Wisc., 1959) 321–56. For the special problems presented to caloric theorists by energy
conservation see the Carnot papers, there cited in n. 2, and also S. P. Thompson, *The Life
of William Thomson, Baron Kelvin of Largs* (2 vols., London, 1910) Ch. 6.
[23] Richtmeyer et al., *Modern Physics*, pp. 89–94, 124–32, and 409–14; Gerald
Holton, *Introduction to Concepts and Theories in Physical Science* (Cambridge, Mass.,
1953) 528–45.

II. TRUTHS AND VALUES

3. Plato

EDITOR'S INTRODUCTION

According to Plato, the goal of philosophy and science is "the vision of truth." But what exactly is truth? And by what methods can a vision of it be obtained? The answers Plato offered to these questions are among the most enduring and influential contributions to Western thought. By way of preface, consider the rather commonplace assumption that there is something permanent and unchanging about truth. A mathematical axiom or moral principle, for example, cannot be true one day and false the next. But this raises a problem. If we observe the world about us, its most characteristic feature is change, not permanence. This might lead one to conclude, as did Plato, that the objects to which we attribute truth must somehow transcend the material world. Plato called these transcendent objects Ideas or Forms. True knowledge, then, is an apprehension of the Forms. Such apprehension can be achieved only through reason. Sense experience, i.e., the observation of material objects, can lead only to "opinions."

The difference between Plato's conception of knowledge as opposed to opinion is illustrated in the first selection. This passage is part of a dialogue between Socrates and Laches, a distinguished Athenian general, on the nature of courage. Laches has had considerable firsthand experience with acts of courage; yet, when he is pressed by Socrates to give a definition that would cover all courageous deeds, he is forced to admit that he "cannot get hold of her [courage] and tell her nature." Laches has only an opinion of what courage is, based on his observation of individual courageous acts. He cannot see behind these acts and discern the true characteristics of courage per se.

The dialogue between Socrates and Laches is not unlike a psychological "bull session," e.g., on the nature of anxiety, intelligence, motivation, etc. And like most bull sessions, the result is inconclusive. The reason for this inconclusiveness deserves brief comment. Suppose you asked someone "What is the cube root of 216?" and he said, "8." The answer would be incorrect. But what if he said, "Green." The answer in this case would still be wrong, but now in a different sense. In the latter instance, the person did not simply calculate the result incorrectly; his answer was not even *appropriate* to the question.

Normally, when we ask a question we know what kind of answer would be appropriate. In many philosophical and psychological discussions, however, it is not clear what type of answer is being sought. When a person asks, for example, "What is anxiety?" is he looking for an answer in terms of physiological changes, subjective experience, etc., or is he looking for a more fundamental ("underlying") mechanism? Unless there is some agreement on the type of answer being sought, discussion is bound to be inconclusive. Unfortunately, it is not always easy to recognize and make explicit the presuppositions behind a question.

Some of the presuppositions behind Plato's inquiries can be found in the dialogues, *Meno* and *Phaedo*, excerpts from which are also reprinted in this chapter. In the former, Meno asks: Can virtue be taught? Socrates replies that he cannot teach it, because he does not know what virtue is. The two therefore undertake to discover the essential nature of virtue. Socrates believes that this can be done because, as poets and priests have claimed, the soul (psyche) of man is subject to a continual cycle of birth and rebirth; and, with sufficient effort, we can recollect what our souls knew in former lives. Socrates demonstrates this by making one of Meno's slaves, an uneducated boy, give a complex geometrical proof. The boy was able to do so, Socrates maintains, because the soul had direct contact with truths in prior existence.

Before we consider the nature of the truths that, according to Plato, the soul recollects, let us comment briefly on the method Socrates used to assist Meno's slave in his recollection. In certain respects, Socrates' method resembles programmed instruction.[1] That is, behavior is "shaped" slowly, step by step, until the final response (in the case of Meno's slave, a geometrical solution) is achieved. Of course, the rationale behind Plato's use of this technique is diametrically opposed to the rationale underlying Skinner's operant conditioning. Plato believed that the slave boy's answer demonstrated the existence of innate knowledge, whereas Skinner emphasizes the role of the environment in determining

[1] Cf. B. F. Skinner. *The technology of teaching.* New York: Appleton, 1968.

knowledge (see Chapt. 20). If nothing else, this demonstrates the need for caution in accepting theoretical assumptions on the basis of successful technical applications.

In the *Phaedo* Plato examines the nature of the truths obtained by recollection. This dialogue describes Socrates' last day in prison. He has been condemned to death for corrupting the youth of Athens and for ignoring the city's gods. Phaedo, a devoted disciple, recounts the events of that day as Socrates awaits execution. Although the views expressed in the dialogue are undoubtedly more Plato's than Socrates', there is probably some historical accuracy to the events portrayed. In any case, the setting provides Plato with a dramatic opportunity to summarize some of the major points of his personal as well as intellectual philosophy. We are concerned here with his theory of Forms, the transcendental objects of true knowledge.

The existence of Forms seemed evident to Plato from facts such as the following: No one has ever observed exact equality among physical objects, for no two objects are exactly alike. Nevertheless, we do recognize degrees of equality, which indicates the existence of some standard against which particular instances of equality can be judged. This standard must be the Form, Idea, or underlying principle of equality. But the Forms are not simply static objects, they are the objects of *knowledge*, i.e., basic explanatory principles. To illustrate this logical function of the Forms, Plato considers why Socrates remained in prison and accepted execution when he could have fled into exile. It would be inappropriate, according to Plato, to answer such a question by referring to the state of Socrates' body, i.e., the contraction of his muscles, the relationship of one bone to another, etc. A physiological mechanism was a necessary condition for Socrates to remain in prison, but the *reason* he remained was his belief that it was the honorable thing to do. Stated more formally, remaining in prison partook of the Form, honor, and that is what "caused" Socrates to remain. To further clarify this point, Plato offers the example of beauty. An object is beautiful, he argues, to the extent that it approaches the standard or Form of absolute beauty. In this sense, we may say that the Form, beauty, causes an object to be beautiful.

In these examples, Plato is using the notion of cause in a rather unusual way, at least to modern ears. And even Plato was not entirely clear or consistent in his interpretation of causation. At times he spoke of the Form as a generative agent; at other times, he considered the Form to be a goal or end state toward which an action tended; his most consistent interpretation, however, was that the Form represents the underlying principle (*form*ula) that specifies the ideal of any class of objects or events (e.g., honor, beauty, etc.). And although Plato tended to hypostatize the Forms, e.g., to treat honor as though it were a distinct and separate *thing*, his ultimate view seems to have been that the Forms are like mathematical entities. Translated into modern terms, Plato's position was that a scientific theory should reveal the mathematical structure of phenomena. That such a view would have an important influence on the development of science is evident.

Having postulated the Forms as basic explanatory principles, Plato had to consider how a person can come to know the Forms. As previously noted, such knowledge cannot be obtained through sense experience, for the senses are in contact only with the changeable world of material objects. Reason, then, must be the primary source of knowledge. As we already have seen, Plato believed that the soul (psyche) existed before birth, during which time it had direct contact with the Forms. What we normally call learning is really recollection. Sense experience may serve as a goad to recollection, but it is an imperfect goad at best. In other words, Plato envisioned the *deduction* of all pure science from a few explanatory principles (the Forms), knowledge of which is in some sense inborn. We shall see a similar vision of truth in later thinkers, especially Descartes (Chapt. 13) and Kant (Chapt. 17).

The argument used by Plato for the existence of innate ideas, and the preexistence of the soul before birth, is somewhat different in the *Phaedo* than in the *Meno*. In the *Meno*, the demonstration rests on problems associated with the acquisition of knowledge, while in the *Phaedo* it rests on the justification of judgments. The latter argument runs somewhat as follows: We never do observe complete equality in material objects; nevertheless, we do recognize degrees of equality. But to say that two objects are more or less equal presupposes some idea of equality, i.e., the idea of equality is prior to any particular judgment of equality. Finally, since we begin to see and hear and make sensory judgments from birth, the idea of equality must have existed in the soul before birth.

This argument, as well as that in the *Meno*, illustrates a very seductive fallacy. It is true that before a person can make judgments regarding equality, he must have some idea of equality. However, the "before" in this sense is logical and not temporal. The fact that certain actions or statements logically precede others does not mean that at some prior time those presuppositions were, should, or even could be, known. The confusion of logical with temporal priority is quite common in psychology. It is, for example, one of the sources of the nature-nurture controversy discussed in Chapter 1. But the fallacy also intrudes into more mundane and practical issues. Thus, consider the frequent assertion that children should learn the assumptions underlying certain arithmetical operations (e.g., multiplication) before they learn those operations (e.g., by memorizing the multiplication table). Such may or may not be the case, depending on the type of operation. The important thing to note is the persuasiveness of the argument even in the absence of any empirical support.

Finally, with his emphasis on inborn potentialities as a source of knowledge, and on deductive argument as a method of inquiry, Plato is one of the first—and certainly one of the greatest—of the systematic rationalists. The temperamental traits often associated with rationalism (see Chapt. 1, p. 30) are also well exemplified by Plato in the *Phaedo*. It is generally maintained that scientific theories should be accepted or rejected on the basis of empirical evidence rather than on personal predelictions. As an ideal, that may be true. As a matter of historical fact, however, personality factors often play an important role in determining the *type* of theory and method of approach a particular scientist will adopt.

On Courage

Socrates

Tell me, if you can, what is courage.

Laches

Indeed, Socrates, I see no difficulty in answering; he is a man of courage who does not run away, but remains at his post and fights against the enemy; there can be no mistake about that.

Socrates

Very good, Laches; and yet I fear that I did not express myself clearly; and therefore you have answered not the question which I intended to ask, but another.

Laches

What do you mean, Socrates?

Socrates

I will endeavour to explain; you would call a man courageous who remains at his post, and fights with the enemy?

Laches

Certainly I should.

Socrates

And so should I; but what would you say of another man, who fights flying, instead of remaining?

Laches

How flying?

Socrates

Why, as the Scythians are said to fight, flying as well as pursuing; and as Homer says in praise of the horses of Aeneas, that they knew 'how to pursue, and fly quickly hither and thither'; and he passes an encomium on Aeneas himself, as having a knowledge of fear or flight, and calls him 'a deviser of fear or flight'.

Plato, *Laches* (B. Jowett, trans.) in *The dialogues of Plato*, Vol. 1 (4th ed., 1953), pp. 85–86, 87–88, 89–90, by permission of the Oxford University Press, Oxford.

Laches

Yes, Socrates, and there Homer is right: for he was speaking of chariots, as you were speaking of the Scythian calvary; now calvary have that way of fighting, but the heavy-armed soldier fights, as I say, remaining in his rank.

Socrates

And yet, Laches, you must except the Lacedaemonians at Plataea, who, when they came upon the light shields of the Persians, are said not to have been willing to stand and fight, and to have fled; but when the ranks of the Persians were broken, they turned upon them like cavalry, and won the battle of Plataea.

Laches

That is true.

Socrates

That was my meaning when I said that I was to blame in having put my question badly, and that this was the reason of your answering badly. For I meant to ask you not only about the courage of the heavy-armed soldiers, but about the courage of cavalry and every other style of soldier; and not only who are courageous in war, but who are courageous in perils by sea, and who in disease, or in poverty, or again in politics, are courageous; and not only who are courageous against pain or fear, but mighty to contend against desires and pleasures, either fixed in their rank or turning upon their enemy. There is this sort of courage—is there not, Laches?

Laches

Certainly, Socrates.

Socrates

And now, Laches, . . . what is that common quality which is called courage, and which includes all the various uses of the term when applied both to pleasure and pain, and in all the cases to which I was just now referring?

Laches

I should say that courage is a sort of endurance of the soul, if I am to speak of the universal nature which pervades them all.

Socrates

But that is what we must do if we are to answer our own question. And yet I cannot say that every kind of endurance is, in my opinion, to be deemed courage. Hear my reason: I am sure, Laches, that you would consider courage to be a very noble quality.

Laches

Most noble, certainly.

Socrates

And you would say that a wise endurance is also good and noble?

Laches

Very noble.

Socrates

But what would you say of a foolish endurance? Is not that, on the other hand, to be regarded as evil and hurtful?

Laches

True.

Socrates

And is anything noble which is evil and hurtful?

Laches

I ought not to say that, Socrates.

Socrates

Then you would not admit that sort of endurance to be courage—for it is not noble, but courage is noble?

Laches

You are right.

Socrates

Then, according to you, only the wise endurance is courage?

Laches

It seems so.

Socrates

But as to the epithet 'wise',—wise in what? In all things small as well as great? For example, if a man shows the quality of endurance in spending his money wisely, knowing that by spending he will acquire more in the end, do you call him courageous?

Laches

Assuredly not.

Socrates

Or, for example, if a man is a physician, and his son, or some patient of his, has inflammation of the lungs, and begs that he may be allowed to eat or drink something, and the other is inflexible and refuses; is that courage?

Laches

No; that is not courage at all, any more than the last.

Socrates

Again, take the case of one who endures in war, and is willing to fight, and wisely calculates and knows that others will help him, and that there will be fewer and inferior men against him than there with him; and suppose that he has also advantages in position;—would you say of such a one who endures with all this wisdom and preparation, that he or some man in the opposing army who is in the opposite circumstances to these and yet endures and remains at his post, is the braver?

Laches

I should say that the latter, Socrates, was the braver.

Socrates

But, surely, this is a foolish endurance in comparison with the other?

Laches

That is true. . . .

Socrates

But foolish boldness and endurance appeared before to be base and hurtful to us?

Laches

Quite true.

Socrates

Whereas courage was acknowledged to be a noble quality.

Laches

True.

Socrates

And now on the contrary we are saying that the foolish endurance, which was before held in dishonour, is courage.

Laches

So we are.

Socrates

And are we right in saying so?

Laches

Indeed, Socrates, I am sure that we are not right.

Socrates

Then according to your statement, you and I, Laches, are not attuned to the Dorian mode, which is a harmony of words and deeds; for our deeds are not in accordance with our words. Anyone would say that we had courage who saw us in action, but not, I imagine, he who heard us talking about courage just now.

Laches

That is most true.

Socrates

And is this condition of ours satisfactory?

Laches

Quite the reverse.

Socrates

Suppose, however, that we admit the principle of which we are speaking to a certain extent?

Laches

To what extent and what principle do you mean?

Socrates

The principle of endurance. If you agree, we too must endure and persevere in the inquiry, and then courage will not laugh at our faint-heartedness in searching for courage; which after all may frequently be endurance.

Laches

I am ready to go on, Socrates; and yet I am unused to investigations of this sort. But the spirit of controversy has been aroused in me by what has been said; and I am really grieved at being thus unable to express my meaning. For I fancy that I do know the nature of courage; but, somehow or other, she has slipped away from me, and I cannot get hold of her and tell her nature. . . .

Innate Ideas

Meno

Can you tell me Socrates—is virtue something that can be taught? Or does it come by practice? Or is it neither teaching nor practice that gives it to a man but natural aptitude or something else? . . .

Socrates

I don't know what [virtue] is. . . . Nevertheless I am ready to carry out, together with you, a joint investigation and inquiry into what it is.

Meno

But how will you look for something when you don't in the least know what it is? How on earth are you going to set up something you don't know as the object of your search? To put it another way, even if you come right up against it, how will you know that what you have found is the thing you didn't know?

Socrates

I know what you mean. Do you realize that what you are bringing up is the trick argument that a man cannot try to discover either what he knows or what he does not know? He would not seek what he knows, for since he knows it there is no need of the inquiry, nor what he does not know, for in that case he does not even know what he is to look for.

Meno

Well, do you think it a good argument?

Plato, *Meno*, in *Protagoras and Meno*, W. K. C. Guthrie, trans. (Penguin Classics, 1956), pp. 115, 128–129, 129–138. Copyright 1956, by W. K. C. Guthrie. Reprinted with permission.

Socrates

No.

Meno

Can you explain how it fails?

Socrates

I can. I have heard from men and women who understand the truths of religion ... that the soul of man is immortal: at one time it comes to an end—that which is called death—and at another is born again, but is never finally exterminated. ...

Thus the soul, since it is immortal and has been born many times, and has seen all things both here and in the other world, has learned everything that is. So we need not be surprised if it can recall the knowledge of virtue or anything else which, as we see, it once possessed. All nature is akin, and the soul has learned everything, so that when a man has recalled a single piece of knowledge—*learned* it, in ordinary language—there is no reason why he should not find out all the rest, if he keeps a stout heart and does not grow weary of the search; for seeking and learning are in fact nothing but recollection.

We ought not then to be led astray by the contentious argument you quoted. It would make us lazy, and is music in the ears of weaklings. The other doctrine produces energetic seekers after knowledge; and being convinced of its truth, I am ready, with your help, to inquire into the nature of virtue.

Meno

I see, Socrates. But what do you mean when you say that we don't learn anything, but that what we call learning is recollection? Can you teach me that it is so?

Socrates

I have just said that you're a rascal, and now you ask me if I can teach you, when I say there is no such thing as teaching, only recollection. Evidently you want to catch me contradicting myself straight away.

Meno

No, honestly, Socrates, I wasn't thinking of that. It was just habit. If you can in any way make clear to me, that what you say is true, please do.

Socrates

It isn't an easy thing, but still I should like to do what I can since you ask me. I see you have a large number of retainers here. Call one of them, anyone you like, and I will use him to demonstrate it to you.

Meno

Certainly. (*To a slave-boy.*) Come here.

Socrates

He is a Greek and speaks our language?

Meno

Indeed yes—born and bred in the house.

Socrates

Listen carefully then, and see whether it seems to you that he is learning from me or simply being reminded.

Meno

I will.

Socrates

Now, boy, you know that a square is a figure like this?
(*Socrates begins to draw figures in the sand at his feet. He points to the square* ABCD.)

Boy

Yes.

Socrates

It has all these four sides equal?

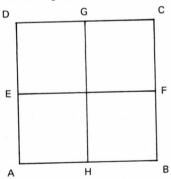

Boy

Yes.

Socrates

And these lines which go through the middle of it are also equal? (The lines EF, GH.)

Boy

Yes.

Socrates

Such a figure could be either larger or smaller, could it not?

Boy

Yes.

Socrates

Now if this side is two feet long, and this side the same, how many feet will the whole be? Put it this way. If it were two feet in this direction and only one in that, must not the area be two feet taken once?

Boy

Yes.

Socrates

But since it is two feet this way also, does it not become twice two feet?

Boy

Yes.

Socrates

And how many feet is twice two? Work it out and tell me.

Boy

Four.

Socrates

Now could one draw another figure double the size of this, but similar, that is, with all its sides equal like this one?

Boy

Yes.

Socrates

How many feet will its area be?

Boy

Eight.

Socrates

Now then, try to tell me how long each of its sides will be. The present figure has a side of two feet. What will be the side of the double-sized one?

Boy

It will be double, Socrates, obviously.

Socrates

You see, Meno, that I am not teaching him anything, only asking. Now he thinks he knows the length of the side of the eight-feet square.

Meno

Yes.

Socrates

But does he?

Meno

Certainly not.

Socrates

He thinks it is twice the length of the other.

Meno

Yes.

Socrates

Now watch how he recollects things in order—the proper way to recollect.

You say that the side of double length produces the double-sized figure? Like this I mean, not long this way and short that. It must be equal on all sides like the first figure, only twice its size, that is eight feet. Think a moment whether you still expect to get it from doubling the side.

Boy

Yes, I do.

Socrates

Well now, shall we have a line double the length of this (AB) if we add another the same length at this end (BJ)?

Boy

Yes.

Socrates

It is on this line then, according to you, that we shall make the eight-feet square, by taking four of the same length?

Boy

Yes.

Socrates

Let us draw in four equal lines (*i.e. counting* AJ, *and adding* JK, KL, *and* LA *made complete by drawing in its second half* LD), using the first as a base. Does this not give us what you call the eight-feet figure?

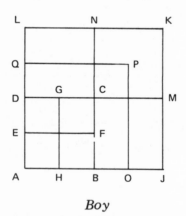

Boy

Certainly.

Socrates

But does it contain these four squares, each equal to the original four-feet one?

(*Socrates has drawn in the lines* CM, CN *to complete the squares that he wishes to point out.*)

Boy

Yes.

Socrates

How big is it then? Won't it be four times as big?

Boy

Of course.

Socrates

And is four times the same as twice?

Boy

Of course not.

Socrates

So doubling the side has given us not a double but a fourfold figure?

Boy

True.

Socrates

And four times four are sixteen, are they not?

Boy

Yes.

Socrates

Then how big is the side of the eight-feet figure? This one has given us four times the original area, hasn't it?

Boy

Yes.

Socrates

And a side half the length gave us a square of four feet?

Boy

Yes.

Socrates

Good. And isn't a square of eight feet double this one and half that?

Boy

Yes.

Socrates

Will it not have a side greater than this one but less than that?

Boy

I think it will.

Socrates

Right. Always answer what you think. Now tell me: was not this side two feet long, and this one four?

Boy

Yes.

Socrates

Then the side of the eight-feet figure must be longer than two feet but shorter than four?

Boy

It must.

Socrates

Try to say how long you think it is.

Boy

Three feet.

Socrates

If so, shall we add half of this bit (BO, *half of* BJ), and make it three feet? Here are two, and this is one, and on this side similarly we have two plus one; and here is the figure you want.

(*Socrates completes the square* AOPQ.)

Boy

Yes.

Socrates

If it is three feet this way and three that, will the whole area be three times three feet?

Boy

It looks like it.

Socrates

And that is how many?

Boy

Nine.

Socrates

Whereas the square double our first square had to be how many?

Boy

Eight.

Socrates

But we haven't yet got the square of eight feet even from a three-feet side?

Boy

No.

Socrates

Then what length will give it? Try to tell us exactly. If you don't want to count it up, just show us on the diagram.

Boy

It's no use, Socrates, I just don't know.

Socrates

Observe, Meno, the stage he has reached on the path of recollection. At the beginning he did not know the side of the square of eight feet. Nor indeed does he know it now, but then he thought he knew it and answered boldly, as was appropriate—he felt no perplexity. Now however he does feel perplexed. Not only does he not know the answer; he doesn't even think he knows.

Meno

Quite true.

Socrates

Isn't he in a better position now in relation to what he didn't know?

Meno

I admit that too.

Socrates

So in perplexing him and numbing him like the sting-ray, have we done him any harm?

Meno

I think not.

Socrates

In fact we have helped him to some extent towards finding out the right answer, for now not only is he ignorant of it but he will be quite glad to look for it. Up to now, he thought he could speak well and fluently, on many occasions and before large audiences, on the subject of a square double the size of a given square, maintaining that it must have a side of double the length.

Meno

No doubt.

Socrates

Do you suppose then that he would have attempted to look for, or learn, what he thought he knew (though he did not), before he was thrown into perplexity, became aware of his ignorance, and felt a desire to know?

Meno

No.

Socrates

Then the numbing process was good for him?

Meno

I agree.

Socrates

Now notice what, starting from this state of perplexity, he will discover by seeking the truth in company with me, though I simply ask him questions without teaching him. Be ready to catch me if I give him any instruction or explanation instead of simply interrogating him on his own opinions.

(*Socrates here rubs out the previous figures and starts again.*)

Tell me, boy, is not this our square of four feet? (ABCD.) You understand?

Boy

Yes.

Socrates

Now we can add another equal to it like this? (BCEF.)

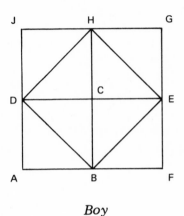

Boy

Yes.

Socrates

And a third here, equal to each of the others? (CEGH.)

Boy

Yes.

Socrates

And then we can fill in this one in the corner? (DCHJ.)

Boy

Yes.

Socrates

Then here we have four equal squares?

Boy

Yes.

Socrates

And how many times the size of the first square is the whole?

Boy

Four times.

Socrates

And we want one double the size. You remember?

Boy

Yes.

Socrates

Now does this line going from corner to corner cut each of these squares in half?

Boy

Yes.

Socrates

And these are four equal lines enclosing this area? (BEHD.)

Boy

They are.

Socrates

Now think. How big is this area?

Boy

I don't understand.

Socrates

Here are four squares. Has not each line cut off the inner half of each of them?

Boy

Yes.

Socrates

And how many such halves are there in this figure? (BEHD.)

Boy

Four.

Socrates

And how many in this one? (ABCD.)

Boy

Two.

Socrates

And what is the relation of four to two?

Boy

Double.

Socrates

How big is this figure then?

Boy

Eight feet.

Socrates

On what base?

Boy

This one.

Socrates

The line which goes from corner to corner of the square of four feet?

Boy

Yes.

Socrates

The technical name for it is 'diagonal'; so if we use that name, it is your personal opinion that the square on the diagonal of the original square is double its area.

Boy

That is so, Socrates.

Socrates

What do you think, Meno? Has he answered with any opinions that were not his own?

Meno

No, they were all his.

Socrates

Yet he did not know, as we agreed a few minutes ago.

Meno

True.

Socrates

But these opinions were somewhere in him, were they not?

Meno

Yes.

Socrates

So a man who does not know has in himself true opinions on a subject without having knowledge.

Meno

It would appear so.

Socrates

At present these opinions, being newly aroused, have a dream-like quality. But if the same questions are put to him on many occasions and in different ways, you can see that in the end he will have a knowledge on the subject as accurate as anybody's.

Meno

Probably.

Socrates

This knowledge will not come from teaching but from questioning. He will recover it for himself. . . .

A Rationalist Vision of Truth

'Socrates,' said Crito, 'that man who is to give you the poison has been asking me for a long time to tell you to talk as little as possible; he says that talking makes you heated, and that you ought not to do anything to affect the action of the poison. Otherwise it is sometimes necessary to take a second dose, or even a third.'

'That is his affair,' said Socrates. 'Let him make his own preparations for administering it twice or three times if necessary.'

'I was pretty sure you would say that,' said Crito, 'but he's been bothering me for a long time.'

'Never mind him,' said Socrates. 'Now for you, my jury. I want to explain to you how it seems to me natural that a man who has really devoted his life to philosophy should be cheerful in the face

Plato, *Phaedo*, in *The last days of Socrates*, Hugh Tredennick, trans. (Penguin Classics, 1959), pp. 107–113, 114–116, 120–122, 122–125, 127–128, 153–159 *passim*, 179–183. Copyright 1954, 1959 by Hugh Tredennick. Reprinted with permission.

of death, and confident of finding the greatest blessing in the next world when his life is finished. I will try to make clear to you, Simmias and Cebes, how this can be so.

'Ordinary people seem not to realize that those who really apply themselves in the right way to philosophy are directly and of their own accord preparing themselves for dying and death. If this is true, and they have actually been looking forward to death all their lives, it would of course be absurd to be troubled when the thing comes for which they have so long been preparing and looking forward.'

Simmias laughed and said 'Upon my word, Socrates, you have made me laugh, though I was not at all in the mood for it. I am sure that if they heard what you said, most people would think—and our fellow-countrymen would heartily agree—that it was a very good hit at the philosophers to say that they are half dead already, and that they, the normal people, are quite aware that death would serve the philosophers right.'

'And they would be quite correct, Simmias; except in thinking that they are "quite aware". They are not at all aware in what sense true philosophers are half dead, or in what sense they deserve death, or what sort of death they deserve. But let us dismiss them and talk among ourselves. Do we believe that there is such a thing as death?'

'Most certainly,' said Simmias, taking up the rôle of answering.

'Is it simply the release of the soul from the body? Is death nothing more or less than this, the separate condition of the body by itself when it is released from the soul, and the separate condition by itself of the soul when released from the body? Is death anything else than this?'

'No, just that.'

'Well then, my boy, see whether you agree with me; I fancy that this will help us to find out the answer to our problem. Do you think that it is right for a philosopher to concern himself with the so-called pleasures connected with food and drink?'

'Certainly not, Socrates,' said Simmias.

'What about sexual pleasures?'

'No, not at all.'

'And what about the other attentions that we pay to our bodies? do you think that a philosopher attaches any importance to them? I mean things like providing himself with smart clothes and shoes and other bodily ornaments; do you think that he values them or despises them—in so far as there is no real necessity for him to go in for that sort of thing?'

'I think the true philosopher despises them,' he said.

'Then it is your opinion in general that a man of this kind is not concerned with the body, but keeps his attention directed as much as he can away from it and towards the soul?'

'Yes, it is.'

'So it is clear first of all in the case of physical pleasures that the philosopher frees his soul from association with the body (so far as is possible) to a greater extent than other men?'

'It seems so.'

'And most people think, do they not, Simmias, that a man who finds no pleasure and takes no part in these things does not deserve to live, and that anyone who thinks nothing of physical pleasures has one foot in the grave?'

'That is perfectly true.'

'Now take the acquisition of knowledge; is the body a hindrance or not, if one takes it into partnership to share an investigation? What I mean is this: is there any certainty in human sight and hearing, or is it true, as the poets are always dinning into our ears, that we neither hear nor see anything accurately? Yet if these senses are not clear and accurate, the rest can hardly be so, because they are all inferior to the first two. Don't you agree?'

'Certainly.'

'Then when is it that the soul attains to truth? When it tries to investigate anything with the help of the body, it is obviously led astray.'

'Quite so.'

'Is it not in the course of reflection, if at all, that the soul gets a clear view of facts?'

'Yes.'

'Surely the soul can best reflect when it is free of all distractions such as hearing or sight or pain or pleasure of any kind—that is, when it ignores the body and becomes as far as possible independent, avoiding all physical contacts and associations as much as it can, in its search for reality.'

'That is so.'

'Then here too—in despising the body and avoiding it, and endeavouring to become independent—the philosopher's soul is ahead of all the rest.'

'It seems so.'

'Here are some more questions, Simmias. Do we recognize such a thing as absolute uprightness?'

'Indeed we do.'

'And absolute beauty and goodness too?'

'Of course.'

'Have you ever seen any of these things with your eyes?'

'Certainly not,' said he.

'Well, have you ever apprehended them with any other bodily sense? By "them" I mean not only absolute tallness or health or strength, but the real nature of any given thing—what it actually is. Is it through the body that we get the truest perception of them? Isn't it true that in any inquiry you are likely to attain more nearly to knowledge of your object in proportion to the care and accuracy with which you have prepared yourself to understand that object in itself?'

'Certainly.'

'Don't you think that the person who is likely to succeed in this attempt most perfectly is the one who approaches each object, as far as possible, with the unaided intellect, without taking account of any sense of sight in his thinking, or dragging any other sense into his reckoning—the man who pursues the truth by applying his pure and unadulterated thought to the pure and unadulterated object, cutting himself off as much as possible from his eyes and ears and virtually all the rest of his body, as an impediment which by its presence prevents the soul from attaining to truth and clear thinking? Is not this the person, Simmias, who will reach the goal of reality, if anybody can?'

'What you say is absolutely true, Socrates,' said Simmias.

'All these considerations,' said Socrates, 'must surely prompt serious philosophers to review the position in some such way as this. "It looks as though this were a bypath leading to the right track. So long as we keep to the body and our soul is contaminated with this imperfection, there is no chance of our ever attaining satisfactorily to our object, which we assert to be Truth. In the first place, the body provides us with innumerable distractions in the pursuit of our necessary sustenance; and any diseases which attack us hinder our quest for reality. Besides, the body fills us with loves and desires and fears and all sorts of fancies and a great deal of nonsense, with the result that we literally never get an opportunity to think at all about anything. Wars and revolutions and battles are due simply and solely to the body and its desires. All wars are undertaken for the acquisition of wealth; and the reason why we have to acquire wealth is the body, because we are slaves in its service. That is why, on all these accounts, we have so little time for philosophy. Worst of all, if we do obtain any leisure from the body's claims and turn to some line of inquiry, the body intrudes once more into our investigations, interrupting, disturbing, distracting, and preventing us from getting a glimpse of the truth. We are in fact convinced that if we are ever to have pure knowledge of anything, we must get rid of the body and contemplate things by themselves with the soul by itself. It seems, to judge from the argument, that the wisdom which we desire and upon which we profess to have set our hearts will be attainable only when we are dead, and not in our lifetime. If no pure knowledge is possible in the company of the body, then either it is totally impossible to acquire knowledge, or it is only possible after death, because it is only then that the soul will be separate and independent of the body. It seems that so long as we are alive, we shall continue closest to knowledge if we avoid as much as we can all contact and association with the body, except when they are absolutely necessary; and instead of allowing ourselves to become infected with its nature, purify ourselves from it until God himself gives us deliverance. In this way, by keeping ourselves uncontaminated by the follies of the body, we shall probably reach the company of others like ourselves and gain direct knowledge of all that is pure and uncontaminated—that is, presumably, of Truth. For one who is not pure himself to attain to the realm of purity would no doubt be a breach of universal justice." Something to this effect, Simmias, is what I imagine all real lovers of learning must think themselves and say to one another; don't you agree with me?'

'Most emphatically, Socrates.'

'Very well, then,' said Socrates; 'if this is true, there is good reason for anyone who reaches the end of this journey which lies before me to hope that there, if anywhere, he will attain the object to which all our efforts have been directed during my past life. So this journey which is now ordained for me carries a happy prospect for any other man also who believes that his mind has been prepared by purification.'

'It does indeed,' said Simmias.

'And purification, as we saw some time ago in our discussion, consists in separating the soul as much as possible from the body, and accustoming it to withdraw from all contact with the body and concentrate itself by itself; and to have its dwelling, so far as it can, both now and in the future, alone by itself, freed from the shackles of the body. Does not that follow?'

'Yes, it does,' said Simmias.

'Is not what we call death a freeing and separation of soul from body?'

'Certainly,' he said.

'And the desire to free the soul is found chiefly, or rather only, in the true philosopher; in fact the philosopher's occupation consists precisely in the freeing and separation of soul from body. Isn't that so?'

'Apparently.' . . .

'Doesn't it follow, Simmias,' he went on, 'that the virtue which we call courage belongs primarily to the philosophical disposition?'

'Yes, no doubt it does,' he said.

'Self-control, too, as it is understood even in the popular sense—not being carried away by the desires, but preserving a decent indifference towards them—: is not this appropriate only to those who regard the body with the greatest indifference and spend their lives in philosophy?'

'Certainly,' he said.

'If you care to consider courage and self-control as practised by other people,' said Socrates, 'you will find them illogical.'

'How so, Socrates?'

'You know, don't you, that everyone except the philosopher regards death as a great evil?'

'Yes, indeed.'

'Isn't it true that when a brave man faces death he does so through fear of something worse?'

'Yes, it is true.'

'So in everyone except the philosopher courage is due to fear and dread; although it is illogical that fear and cowardice should make a man brave.'

'Quite so.'

'What about temperate people? Is it not, in just the same way, a sort of self-indulgence that makes them self-controlled? We may say that this is impossible, but all the same those who practise this simple form of self-control are in much the same case as that which I have just described. They are afraid of losing other pleasures which they desire, so they refrain from one kind because they cannot resist the other. Although they define self-indulgence as the condition of being ruled by pleasure, it is really because they cannot resist some pleasures that they succeed in resisting others; which amounts to what I said just now—that they control themselves, in a sense, by self-indulgence.'

'Yes, that seems to be true.'

'I congratulate you on your perception, Simmias. No, I am afraid that, from the moral standpoint, it is not the right method to exchange one degree of pleasure or pain or fear for another, like coins of different values. There is only one currency for which all these tokens of ours should be exchanged, and that is wisdom. In fact, it is wisdom that makes possible courage and self-control and integrity or, in a word, true goodness, and the presence or absence of pleasures and fears and other such feelings makes no difference at all; whereas a system of morality which is based on relative emotional values is a mere illusion, a thoroughly vulgar conception which has nothing sound in it and nothing true. The true moral ideal, whether self-control or integrity or courage, is really a kind of purgation from all these emotions, and wisdom itself is a sort of purification. Perhaps these people who direct the religious initiations are not so far from the mark, and all the time there has been an allegorical meaning beneath their doctrine that he who enters the next world uninitiated and unenlightened shall lie in the mire, but he who arrives there purified and enlightened shall dwell among the gods. You know how the initiation-practitioners say:

"Many bear the emblems, but the devotees are few"?

Well, in my opinion these devotees are simply those who have lived the philosophic life in the right way; a company which, all through my life, I have done my best in every way to join, leaving nothing undone which I could do to attain this end. Whether I was right in this ambition, and whether we have achieved anything, we shall know for certain (if God wills) when we reach the other world; and that, I imagine, will be fairly soon.

'This is the defence which I offer you, Simmias and Cebes, to show that it is natural for me to leave you and my earthly rulers without any feeling of grief or bitterness, since I believe that I shall find there, no less than here, good rulers and good friends. If I am any more convincing in my defence to you than I was to my Athenian jury, I shall be satisfied.'

When Socrates had finished, Cebes made his reply. 'The rest of your statement, Socrates,' he said, 'seems excellent to me; but what you said about the soul leaves the average person with grave misgivings that when it is released from the body it may no longer exist anywhere, but may be dispersed and destroyed on the very day that the man himself dies, as soon as it is freed from the body; that as it emerges it may be dissipated like breath or smoke, and vanish away, so that nothing is left of it anywhere. Of course if it still existed as an independent unity, released from all the evils which you have just described, there would be a strong and glorious hope, Socrates, that what you say is true. But I fancy that it requires no little faith and assurance to believe that the soul exists after death and retains some active force and intelligence.'

'Quite true, Cebes,' said Socrates. 'But what are we to do about it? Is it your wish that we should go on speculating about the subject, to see whether this view is likely to be true or not?'

'For my part,' said Cebes, 'I should be very glad to hear what you think about it. . . . There is that theory which you have often described to us—that what we call learning is really just recollection. If that is true, then surely what we recollect now we must have learned at some time before; which is impossible unless our souls existed somewhere before they entered this human shape. . . .

'How did the proofs of that theory go, Cebes?' broke in Simmias. 'Remind me, because at the moment I can't quite remember.'

'One very good argument,' said Cebes, 'is that when people are asked questions, if the question is put in the right way they can give a perfectly correct answer, which they could not possibly do unless they had some knowledge and a proper grasp of the subject. And then if you confront people with a diagram or anything like that, the way in which they react is an unmistakeable proof that the theory is correct.'

'And if you don't find that convincing, Simmias,' said Socrates, 'see whether this appeals to you. I suppose that you find it hard to understand how what we call learning can be recollection?'

'Not at all,' said Simmias. 'All that I want is to be helped to do what we are talking about—to recollect. I can practically remember enough to satisfy me already, from Cebes' approach to the subject; but I should be none the less glad to hear how you meant to approach it.'

'I look at it in this way,' said Socrates. 'We are agreed, I suppose, that if a person is to be reminded of anything, he must first know it at some time or other?'

'Quite so.'

'Are we also agreed in calling it recollection when knowledge comes in a particular way? I will explain what I mean. Suppose that a person on seeing or hearing or otherwise noticing one thing not only becomes conscious of that thing but also thinks of something else which is an object of a different sort of knowledge; are we not justified in saying that he was reminded of the object which he thought of?'

'What do you mean?'

'Let me give you an example. A human being and a musical instrument, I suppose you will agree, are different objects of knowledge.'

'Yes, certainly.'

'Well, you know what happens to lovers when they see a musical instrument or a piece of clothing or any other private property of the person whom they love; when they recognize the thing, their minds conjure up a picture of its owner. That is recollection. In the same way the sight of Simmias often reminds one of Cebes; and of course there are thousands of other examples. . . . Does it not follow from all this that recollection may be caused either by similar or by dissimilar objects?'

'Yes, it does.'

'When you are reminded by similarity, surely you must also be conscious whether the similarity is perfect or only partial.'

'Yes, you must.'

'Here is a further step,' said Socrates. 'We admit, I suppose, that there is such a thing as equality—not the equality of stick to stick and stone to stone, and so on, but something beyond all that and distinct from it—absolute equality. Are we to admit this or not?'

'Yes indeed,' said Simmias, 'most emphatically.'

'And do we know what it is?'

'Certainly.'

'Where did we get our knowledge? Was it not from the particular examples that we mentioned just now? Was it not from seeing equal sticks or stones or other equal objects that we got the notion of equality, although it is something quite distinct from them? Look at it in this way. Is it not true that equal stones and sticks sometimes, without changing in themselves, appear equal to one person and unequal to another?'

'Certainly.'

'Well, now, have you ever thought that things which were absolutely equal were unequal, or that equality was inequality?'

'No, never, Socrates.'

'Then these equal things are not the same as absolute equality.'

'Not in the least, as I see it, Socrates.'

'And yet it is these equal things that have suggested and conveyed to you your knowledge of absolute equality, although they are distinct from it?'

'Perfectly true.'

'Whether it is similar to them or dissimilar?'

'Certainly.'

'It makes no difference,' said Socrates. 'So long as the sight of one thing suggests another to you, it must be a cause of recollection, whether the two things are alike or not.'

'Quite so.'

'Well, now,' he said, 'what do we find in the case of the equal sticks and other things of which we were speaking just now: do they seem to us to be equal in the sense of absolute equality, or do they fall short of it in so far as they only approximate to equality? Or don't they fall short at all?'

'They do,' said Simmias, 'a long way.'

'Suppose that when you see something you say to yourself "This thing which I can see has a tendency to be like something else, but it falls short and cannot be really like it, only a poor imitation"; don't you agree with me that anyone who receives that impression must in fact have previous knowledge of that thing which he says that the other resembles, but inadequately?'

'Certainly he must.'

'Very well, then; is that our position with regard to equal things and absolute equality?'

'Exactly.'

'Then we must have had some previous knowledge of equality before the time when we first saw equal things and realized that they were striving after equality, but fell short of it.'

'That is so.'

'And at the same time we are agreed also upon this point, that we have not and could not have acquired this notion of equality except by sight or touch or one of the other senses. I am treating them as being all the same.'

'They are the same, Socrates, for the purpose of our argument.'

'So it must be through the senses that we obtained the notion that all sensible equals are striving after absolute equality but falling short of it. Is that correct?'

'Yes, it is.'

'So before we began to see and hear and use our other senses we must somewhere have acquired the knowledge that there is such a thing as absolute equality; otherwise we could never have realized, by using it as a standard for comparison, that all equal objects of sense are desirous of being like it, but are only imperfect copies.'

'That is the logical conclusion, Socrates.'

'Did we not begin to see and hear and possess our other senses from the moment of birth?'

'Certainly.'

'But we admitted that we must have obtained our knowledge of equality before we obtained them.'

'Yes.'

'So we must have obtained it before birth.'

'So it seems.'

'Then if we obtained it before our birth, and possessed it when we were born, we had knowledge, both before and at the moment of birth, not only of equality and relative magnitudes, but of all absolute standards. Our present argument applies no more to equality than it does to absolute beauty, goodness, uprightness, holiness, and, as I maintain, all those characteristics which we designate in our discussions by the term "absolute". So we must have obtained knowledge of all these characteristics before our birth.'

'That is so.'

'And unless we invariably forget it after obtaining it, we must always be born *knowing* and continue to *know* all through our lives; because "to know" means simply to retain the knowledge which one has acquired, and not to lose it. Is not what we call "forgetting" simply the loss of knowledge, Simmias?'

'Most certainly, Socrates.'

'And if it is true that we acquired our knowledge before our birth, and lost it at the moment of birth, but afterwards by the exercise of our senses upon sensible objects, recover the knowledge which we had once before, I suppose that what we call learning will be the recovery of our own knowledge; and surely we should be right in calling this recollection.'

'Quite so.' . . .

'Well, how do we stand now, Simmias? If all these absolute realities, such as Beauty and Goodness, which we are always talking about, really exist; if it is to them, as we re-discover our own former knowledge of them, that we refer, as copies to their patterns, all the objects of our physical perception;—if these realities exist, does it not follow that our souls must exist too even before our birth, whereas if they do not exist, our discussion would seem to be a waste of time? Is this the position, that it is logically just as certain that our souls exist before our birth as it is that these realities exist, and that if the one is impossible, so is the other?'

'It is perfectly obvious to me, Socrates,' said Simmias, 'that the same logical necessity applies to both. It suits me very well that your argument should rely upon the point that our soul's existence before our birth stands or falls with the existence of your grade of reality. I cannot imagine anything more self-evident than the fact that absolute Beauty and Goodness and all the rest that you mentioned just now exist in the fullest possible sense. In my opinion the proof is quite satisfactory.'

'What about Cebes?' said Socrates. 'We must convince Cebes too.'

'To the best of my belief he is satisfied,' replied Simmias. 'It is true that he is the most obstinate person in the world at resisting an argument, but I should think that he needs nothing more to convince him that our souls existed before our birth. As for their existing after we are dead as well, even I don't feel that that has been proved, Socrates; Cebes' objection still holds: the common fear that a man's soul may be disintegrated at the very moment of his death, and that this may be the end of its existence. Supposing that it *is* born and constituted from some source or other, and exists before it enters a human body: after it has entered one, is

there any reason why, at the moment of release, it should not
come to an end and be destroyed itself?'

'Quite right, Simmias,' said Cebes. 'It seems that we have got
the proof of one half of what we wanted—that the soul existed
before birth—but now we need also to prove that it will exist after
death no less than before birth, if our proof is to be complete.' . . .

After spending some time in reflection Socrates said, 'What you
require is no light undertaking, Cebes. It involves a full treatment
of the causes of generation and destruction. If you like, I will
describe my own experiences in this connexion; and then, if you
find anything helpful in my account, you can use it to reassure
yourself about your own objections.'

'Yes, indeed,' said Cebes, 'I should like that very much.'

'Then listen, and I will tell you. When I was young, Cebes, I
had an extraordinary passion for that branch of learning which is
called natural science; I thought it would be marvellous to know
the causes for which each thing comes and ceases and continues to
be. I was constantly veering to and fro, puzzling primarily over this
sort of question "Is it when heat and cold produce fermentation,
as some have said, that living creatures are bred? Is it with the
blood that we think, or with the air or the fire that is in us? Or is
it none of these, but the brain that supplies our senses of hearing
and sight and smell; and from these that memory and opinion
arise, and from memory and opinion, when established, that
knowledge comes?" Then again I would consider how these
faculties are lost, and study celestial and terrestrial phenomena,
until at last I came to the conclusion that I was uniquely unfitted
for this form of inquiry. . . .

'However, I once heard someone reading from a book (as he
said) by Anaxagoras, and asserting that it is Mind that produces
order and is the cause of everything. This explanation pleased me.
Somehow it seemed right that Mind should be the cause of
everything; and I reflected that if this is so, Mind in producing
order sets everything in order and arranges each individual thing in
the way that is best for it. Therefore if anyone wished to discover
the reason why any given thing came or ceased or continued to be,
he must find out how it was best for that thing to be, or to
act or be acted upon in any other way. On this view there
was only one thing for a man to consider, with regard both to
himself and to anything else, namely the best and highest good;
although this would necessarily imply knowing what is less good,
since both were covered by the same knowledge.

'These reflections made me suppose, to my delight, that in
Anaxagoras I had found an authority on causation who was after

my own heart. I assumed that he would begin by informing us whether the earth is flat or round, and would then proceed to explain in detail the reason and logical necessity for this by stating how and why it was better that it should be so. I thought that if he asserted that the earth was in the centre, he would explain in detail that it was better for it to be there; and if he made this clear, I was prepared to give up hankering after any other kind of cause.' . . .

'It was a wonderful hope, my friend, but it was quickly dashed. As I read on I discovered that the fellow made no use of Mind and assigned to it no causality for the order of the world, but adduced causes like air and ether and water and many other absurdities. It seemed to me that he was just about as inconsistent as if someone were to say "The cause of everything that Socrates does is Mind" and then, in trying to account for my several actions, said first that the reason why I am lying here now is that my body is composed of bones and sinews, and that the bones are rigid and separated at the joints, but the sinews are capable of contraction and relaxation, and form an envelope for the bones with the help of the flesh and skin, the latter holding all together; and since the bones move freely in their joints the sinews by relaxing and contracting enable me somehow to bend my limbs; and that is the cause of my sitting here in a bent position. Or again, if he tried to account in the same way for my conversing with you, adducing causes such as sound and air and hearing and a thousand others, and never troubled to mention the real reasons; which are that since Athens has thought it better to condemn me, therefore I for my part have thought it better to sit here, and more right to stay and submit to whatever penalty she orders—because, by Dog! I fancy that these sinews and bones would have been in the neighbourhood of Megara or Boeotia long ago (impelled by a conviction of what is best!) if I did not think that it was more right and honourable to submit to whatever penalty my country orders rather than take to my heels and run away. But to call things like that causes is too absurd. If it were said that without such bones and sinews and all the rest of them I should not be able to do what I think is right, it would be true; but to say that it is because of them that I do what I am doing, and not through choice of what is best—although my actions are controlled by Mind—would be a very lax and inaccurate form of expression. Fancy being unable to distinguish between the cause of a thing, and the condition without which it could not be a cause! It is this latter, as it seems to me, that most people, groping in the dark, call a cause—attaching to it a name to which it has no right. That is why one person surrounds the earth with a vortex, and so keeps it in place by means of the heavens; and another props it up on a pedestal of air, as though it were a wide platter. As for a power which keeps things disposed at any given moment in the best possible way, they neither look for it nor believe that it has any supernatural force; they imagine that they will some day find a more mighty and immortal and all-sustaining Atlas; and they do not think that anything is really bound and held together by goodness or moral obligation. For my part, I should be delighted to learn about the workings of such a cause from anyone, but since I have been denied knowledge of it, and have been unable either to discover it myself or to learn about it from another, I have worked out my own makeshift approach to the problem of causation. Would you like me to give you a demonstration of it, Cebes?'

'I should like it very much indeed.'

'Well, after this,' said Socrates, 'when I was worn out with my physical investigations, it occurred to me that I must guard against the same sort of risk which people run when they watch and study an eclipse of the sun; they really do sometimes injure their eyes, unless they study its reflection in water or some other medium. I conceived of something like this happening to myself, and I was afraid that by observing objects with my eyes and trying to comprehend them with each of my other senses I might blind my soul altogether. So I decided that I must have recourse to theories, and use them in trying to discover the truth about things. Perhaps my illustration is not quite apt; because I do not at all admit that an inquiry by means of theory employs "images" any more than one which confines itself to facts. But however that may be, I started off in this way; and in every case I first lay down the theory which I judge to be soundest; and then whatever seems to agree with it—with regard either to causes or to anything else—I assume to be true, and whatever does not I assume not to be true. But I should like to express my meaning more clearly; because at present I don't think that you understand.'

'No, indeed I don't,' said Cebes, 'not a bit.'

'Well,' said Socrates, 'what I mean is this, and there is nothing new about it; I have always said it, in fact I have never stopped saying it, especially in the earlier part of this discussion. As I am going to try to explain to you the theory of causation which I have worked out myself, I propose to make a fresh start from those principles of mine which you know so well; that is, I am assuming the existence of absolute Beauty and Goodness and Magnitude and all the rest of them. If you grant my assumption and admit that they exist, I hope with their help to explain causation to you, and to find a proof that soul is immortal.'

'Certainly I grant it,' said Cebes; 'you need lose no time in drawing your conclusion.'

'Then consider the next step, and see whether you share my opinion. It seems to me that whatever else is beautiful apart from absolute Beauty is beautiful because it partakes of that absolute Beauty, and for no other reason. Do you accept this kind of causality?'

'Yes, I do.'

'Well, now, that is as far as my mind goes; I cannot understand these other ingenious theories of causation. If someone tells me that the reason why a given object is beautiful is that it has a gorgeous colour or shape or any other such attribute, I disregard all these other explanations—I find them all confusing—and I cling simply and straightforwardly and no doubt foolishly to the explanation that the one thing that makes that object beautiful is the presence in it or association with it (in whatever way the relation comes about) of absolute Beauty. I do not go so far as to insist upon the precise details; only upon the fact that it is by Beauty that beautiful things are beautiful. This, I feel, is the safest answer for me or for anyone else to give, and I believe that while I hold fast to this I cannot fall; it is safe for me or for anyone else to answer that it is by Beauty that beautiful things are beautiful. Don't you agree?'

'Yes, I do.' . . .

[*At this point, Socrates uses the supposed immutability and eternality of the Forms to argue for the survival of the soul after death. These arguments are skipped here, and we move directly to the conclusion of the dialogue.*]

When he had finished speaking, Crito said 'Very well, Socrates. But have you no directions for the others or myself about your children or anything else? What can we do to please you best?'

'Nothing new, Crito,' said Socrates; 'just what I am always telling you. If you look after yourselves, whatever you do will please me and mine and you too, even if you don't agree with me now. On the other hand, if you neglect yourselves and fail to follow the line of life as I have laid it down both now and in the past, however fervently you agree with me now, it will do no good at all.'

'We shall try our best to do as you say,' said Crito. 'But how shall we bury you?'

'Any way you like,' replied Socrates, 'that is, if you can catch me and I don't slip through your fingers.' He laughed gently as he spoke, and turning to us went on: 'I can't persuade Crito that I am this Socrates here who is talking to you now and marshalling all the arguments; he thinks that I am the one whom he will see presently lying dead; and he asks how he is to bury me! As for my long and elaborate explanation that when I have drunk the poison I shall remain with you no longer, but depart to a state of heavenly happiness, this attempt to console both you and myself seems to be wasted on him. You must give an assurance to Crito for me—the opposite of the one which he gave to the court which tried me. He undertook that I should stay; but you must assure him that when I am dead I shall not stay, but depart and be gone. That will help Crito to bear it more easily, and keep him from being distressed on my account when he sees my body being burned or buried, as if something dreadful were happening to me; or from saying at the funeral that it is Socrates whom he is laying out or carrying to the grave or burying. Believe me, my dear friend Crito: mis-statements are not merely jarring in their immediate context; they also have a bad effect upon the soul. No, you must keep up your spirits and say that it is only my body that you are burying; and you can bury it as you please, in whatever way you think is most proper.'

With these words he got up and went into another room to bathe; and Crito went after him, but told us to wait. So we waited, discussing and reviewing what had been said, or else dwelling upon the greatness of the calamity which had befallen us; for we felt just as though we were losing a father and should be orphans for the rest of our lives. Meanwhile, when Socrates had taken his bath, his children were brought to see him—he had two little sons and one big boy—and the women of his household—you know—arrived. He talked to them in Crito's presence and gave them directions about carrying out his wishes; then he told the women and children to go away, and came back himself to join us.

It was now nearly sunset, because he had spent a long time inside. He came and sat down, fresh from the bath; and he had only been talking for a few minutes when the prison officer came in, and walked up to him. 'Socrates,' he said, 'at any rate I shall not have to find fault with you, as I do with others, for getting angry with me and cursing when I tell them to drink the poison—carrying out Government orders. I have come to know during this time that you are the noblest and the gentlest and the bravest of all the men that have ever come here, and now especially I am sure that you are not angry with me, but with them; because you know who are responsible. So now—you know what I have come to say—goodbye, and try to bear what must be as easily as you can.' As he spoke he burst into tears, and turning round, went away.

Socrates looked up at him and said 'Goodbye to you, too; we will do as you say.' Then addressing us he went on 'What a charming person! All the time I have been here he has visited me, and sometimes had discussions with me, and shown me the greatest kindness; and how generous of him now to shed tears for me at parting! But come, Crito, let us do as he says. Someone had better bring in the poison, if it is ready prepared; if not, tell the man to prepare it.'

'But surely, Socrates,' said Crito, 'the sun is still upon the mountains; it has not gone down yet. Besides, I know that in other cases people have dinner and enjoy their wine, and sometimes the company of those whom they love, long after they receive the warning; and only drink the poison quite late at night. No need to hurry; there is still plenty of time.'

'It is natural that these people whom you speak of should act in that way, Crito,' said Socrates, 'because they think that they gain by it. And it is also natural that I should not; because I believe that I should gain nothing by drinking the poison a little later—I should only make myself ridiculous in my own eyes if I clung to life and hugged it when it has no more to offer. Come, do as I say and don't make difficulties.'

At this Crito made a sign to his servant, who was standing near by. The servant went out and after spending a considerable time returned with the man who was to administer the poison; he was carrying it ready prepared in a cup. When Socrates saw him he said 'Well, my good fellow, you understand these things; what ought I to do?'

'Just drink it,' he said, 'and then walk about until you feel a weight in your legs, and then lie down. Then it will act of its own accord.'

As he spoke he handed the cup to Socrates, who received it quite cheerfully, Echecrates, without a tremor, without any change of colour or expression, and said, looking up under his brows with his usual steady gaze, 'What do you say about pouring a libation from this drink? Is it permitted, or not?'

'We only prepare what we regard as the normal dose, Socrates,' he replied.

'I see,' said Socrates. 'But I suppose I am allowed, or rather bound, to pray the gods that my removal from this world to the other may be prosperous. This is my prayer, then; and I hope that it may be granted.' With these last words, quite calmly and with no sign of distaste, he drained the cup in one breath.

Up till this time most of us had been fairly successful in keeping back our tears; but when we saw that he was drinking, that he had actually drunk it, we could do so no longer; in spite of myself the tears came pouring out, so that I covered my face and wept broken-heartedly—not for him, but for my own calamity in losing such a friend. Crito had given up even before me, and had gone out when he could not restrain his tears. But Apollodorus, who had never stopped crying even before, now broke out into such a storm of passionate weeping that he made everyone in the room break down, except Socrates himself, who said:

'Really, my friends, what a way to behave! Why, that was my main reason for sending away the women, to prevent this sort of disturbance; because I am told that one should make one's end in a tranquil frame of mind. Calm yourselves and try to be brave.'

This made us feel ashamed, and we controlled our tears. Socrates walked about, and presently, saying that his legs were heavy, lay down on his back—that was what the man recommended. The man (he was the same one who had administered the poison) kept his hand upon Socrates, and after a little while examined his feet and legs; then pinched his foot hard and asked if he felt it. Socrates said no. Then he did the same to his legs; and moving gradually upwards in this way let us see that he was getting cold and numb. Presently he felt him again and said that when it reached the heart, Socrates would be gone.

The coldness was spreading about as far as his waist when Socrates uncovered his face—for he had covered it up—and said (they were his last words): 'Crito, we ought to offer a cock to Asclepius. See to it, and don't forget.'

'No, it shall be done,' said Crito. 'Are you sure that there is nothing else?'

Socrates made no reply to this question, but after a little while he stirred; and when the man uncovered him, his eyes were fixed. When Crito saw this, he closed the mouth and eyes.

Such, Echecrates, was the end of our comrade, who was, we may fairly say, of all those whom we knew in our time, the bravest and also the wisest and most upright man.

4. Lawrence Kohlberg

EDITOR'S INTRODUCTION

From the previous selections it is obvious that Plato was very concerned with questions involving value judgments, e.g., the nature of courage, honor, beauty, and the like. Modern science, on the other hand, prides itself on being objective or "value free." The task of science, so this argument goes, is to discover and explain the facts and not to judge whether those facts are right or wrong, good or bad. To a certain extent, this stance is laudable. Too often the progress of science has been hindered, and scientists themselves persecuted, because their findings threatened established political and moral beliefs. Less dramatically, but perhaps more important in the long run, there is much evidence that the biases and prejudices of individual scientists may have considerable influence on the way they interpret their data. The demand for objectivity and value-free judgments is thus based on hard-learned historical lessons. But what about psychologists who wish to investigate values per se? Can they remain value free? To a certain extent, yes. Psychologists can, for example, adopt the view that all value judgments are relative, i.e., that there is no such thing as "good" or "bad" in an absolute sense. Strategically, this point of view obviates many difficulties: If it is assumed that goodness is in the eye of the beholder, then the object of study becomes the beholder and the thorny question of what goodness actually is can be disregarded.

The view that value judgments are relative is based on more than just strategic considerations; it is also fostered by the empiricist philosophical tradition that, in its later historical developments at least, has divided reality into primary, secondary, and value qualities. Primary qualities (e.g., mass, size, shape, motion, etc.) are the fundamental properties of physical substance;

secondary qualities (colors, sounds, smell, etc.) are dependent on
the transaction of a sentient organism with an external object; and,
finally, value qualities (goodness, beauty, justice, etc.) are a matter
of individual judgment and taste. According to this philosophical
tradition, primary qualities comprise the basic facts of nature, and
hence are the proper subject of scientific inquiry.

Two trends, then, militate against the psychological investigation of values: (1) the very real and valid concern regarding
political and social interference in the pursuit of truth; and (2) a
questionable but widely held philosophical assumption that values
are not real facts. These two trends have tended to limit the
psychological investigation of values to normative studies of what
people do and think. While such studies can be extremely valuable,
and even controversial (e.g., the Kinsey reports), they tend to skirt
the touchy issue of what people *should* do. In order to address this
latter issue, while still maintaining the ideal of objectivity, one is
almost led to the assumption that values are real and not just
relative, i.e., that there are things people should do, and that it is
possible to discover and analyze such "things."

Obviously Plato believed that values are real. Indeed, it is a
mark of Platonism to treat a thing as real just to the extent that it
is valued. While probably no contemporary psychologist would
follow Plato unequivocally in this regard, there are signs of a
modest Platonic revival in such areas as aesthetics and moral
development. One of the people most responsible for this revival
(in the United States, at least) is Lawrence Kohlberg. In this
selection, Kohlberg relates his ideas directly to those of Plato,
arguing that there is such a thing as justice, that it can be studied
scientifically, and that it can and should be taught in the
classroom.

LAWRENCE KOHLBERG

Education for Justice:
a modern statement of the platonic view

When I called this essay a Platonic view I hoped it implied a paradox that was more than cute. It is surely a paradox that a modern psychologist should claim as his most relevant source not Freud, Skinner, or Piaget but the ancient believer in the ideal form of the good. Yet as I have tried to trace the stages of development of morality and to use these stages as the basis of a moral education program, I have realized more and more that its implication was the reassertion of the Platonic faith in the power of the rational good.

It is usually supposed that psychology contributes to moral education by telling us appropriate *methods* of moral teaching and learning. A Skinnerian will speak of proper schedules of reinforcement in moral learning, a Freudian will speak of the importance of the balance of parental love and firmness which will promote superego-identification, and so on. When Skinnerians or Freudians speak on the topic of moral education, then, they start by answering yes to Meno's question "Is virtue something that can be taught?" and go on to tell us how. In *Walden Two*, Skinner not only tells us that virtue comes by practice and reinforcement but designs an ideal republic which educates all of its children to be virtuous in this way.

My own response to these questions was more modest. When confronted by a group of parents who asked me "How can we help make our children virtuous?" I had to answer, as Socrates, "You must think I am very fortunate to know how virtue is acquired. The fact is that far from knowing whether it can be taught, I have no idea what virtue really is." Like most psychologists, I knew that science could teach me nothing as to what virtue is. Science could speak about causal relations, about the relations of means to ends, but it could not speak about ends or values themselves. If I could not define virtue or the ends of moral education, could I really offer advice as to the means by which virtue should be taught? Could it really be argued that the means for teaching obedience to authority are the same as the means for teaching freedom of moral opinion, that the means for

Reprinted by permission of the publishers from *Moral Education: Five Lectures*, (edited by J. M. Gustafson, pp. 57-66, 69-78, 80, 82, 135-136) Cambridge, Mass.: Harvard University Press, copyright © 1970 by the President and Fellows of Harvard College.

teaching altruism are the same as the means for teaching competitive striving, that the making of a good storm trooper involves the same procedures as the making of a philosopher-king?

It appears, then, that we must either be totally silent about moral education or speak to the nature of virtue. In this essay, I shall throw away my graduate school wisdom about the distinction of fact and value and elaborate a view of the nature of virtue like that of Socrates and Plato. Let me summarize some of the elements of this Platonic view.

First, virtue is ultimately one, not many, and it is always the same ideal form regardless of climate or culture.

Second, the name of this ideal form is justice.

Third, not only is the good one, but virtue is knowledge of the good. He who knows the good chooses the good.

Fourth, the kind of knowledge of the good which is virtue is philosophical knowledge or intuition of the ideal form of the good, not correct opinion or acceptance of conventional beliefs.

Fifth, the good can then be taught, but its teachers must in a certain sense be philosopher-kings.

Sixth, the reason the good can be taught is because we know it all along dimly or at a low level and its teaching is more a calling out than an instruction.

Seventh, the reason we think the good cannot be taught is because the same good is known differently at different levels and direct instruction cannot take place across levels.

Eighth, then the teaching of virtue is the asking of questions and the pointing of the way, not the giving of answers. Moral education is the leading of men upward, not the putting into the mind of knowledge that was not there before.

I will spend little time on my disagreements with Plato, except to point out that I conceive justice as equality instead of Plato's hierarchy. I should note, however, that I have earlier discussed my views within John Dewey's framework. In speaking of a Platonic view, I am not discarding my basic Deweyism, but I am challenging a brand of common sense first enunciated by Aristotle, with which Dewey partly agrees. According to Aristotle's *Ethics*, "virtue is of two kinds, intellectual and moral. While intellectual virtue owes its birth and growth to teaching, moral virtue comes about as a result of habit. The moral virtues we get by first exercising them; we become just by doing just acts, temperate by doing temperate acts, brave by doing brave acts."

Aristotle then is claiming that there are two spheres, the moral and the intellectual, and that learning by doing is the only real method in the moral sphere. Dewey, of course, does not distinguish the intellectual from the moral and objects to lists of virtues and vices in either area. Nevertheless, Deweyite thinking has lent itself to the Boy Scout approach to moral education which has dominated American practices in this field and which has its most direct affinities with Aristotle's views.

American educational psychology, like Aristotle, divides the personality up into cognitive abilities, passions or motives, and traits of character. Moral character, then, consists of a bag of virtues and vices. One of the earliest major American studies of moral character, that of Hartshorne and May, was conducted in the late twenties. Their bag of virtues included honesty, service, and self-control. A more recent major study by Havighurst and Taba added responsibility, friendliness, and moral courage to the Hartshorne and May bag. Aristotle's original bag included temperance, liberality, pride, good temper, truthfulness, and justice. The Boy Scout bag is well known, a Scout should be honest, loyal, reverent, clean, brave.

Given a bag of virtues, it is evident how we build character. Children should be exhorted to practice these virtues, should be told that happiness, fortune, and good repute will follow in their wake; adults around them should be living examples of these virtues; and children should be given daily opportunities to practice them. Daily chores will build responsibility; the opportunity to give to the Red Cross will build service or altruism, etc.

Let me quote a concrete program of moral education from Jonathan Kozol's book *Death at an Early Age. The Destruction of the Hearts and Minds of Negro Children in the Boston Public School*[1] Kozol says (pages 174–176):

> There is a booklet published by the Boston Public Schools bearing the title, "A Curriculum Guide in Character Education." This is the list of character traits which the teacher is encouraged to develop in a child: Obedience to duly constituted authority, self-control, responsibility, kindness, perseverance, loyalty, fair play.
>
> The section on obedience begins with the following selected memory gems. "We must do the thing we must before the thing we may; We are unfit for any trust til we can and do obey—Honor thy father and mother—True obedience is true liberty—The first law that ever God gave to man was a law of obedience."
>
> The section on self-control begins by the necessity for self-discipline by all people. The teacher is then advised to give examples of self-disciplined people, Abraham Lincoln, Charles Lindbergh, Robinson Crusoe, Florence Nightengale, Dwight D. Eisenhower.

[1] Boston, Houghton Mifflin, 1967.

It is hardly surprising that this approach to moral education doesn't work. Hartshorne and May found that participation in character education classes of this sort, in the Boy Scouts, in Sunday school did not lead to any improvement in moral character as measured by experimental tests of honesty, service, and self-control, and more recent research does not provide any more positive evidence as to the effects of character-building programs.

Let me point out, too, that while Kozol's example sounds both particularly systematic and particularly old fashioned, it is in principle pretty much that of enlightened public schools throughout the country. As long as teachers direct classroom groups, they must inevitably moralize about rules. They may choose to try to be value-neutral and treat all rules as traffic rules, that is, to assume that definition and maintenance of the rules is a matter of administrative convenience.

Let me cite an example from my observation of an enlightened and effective young fourth-grade teacher. The teacher was in the back of the room working with a project group, the rest of the class engaged with their workbooks. In the front row, a boy said something to his neighbor, who retaliated by quietly spitting in his face. The first boy equally quietly slugged the other without leaving his seat, by which time the teacher noted the disturbance. She said calmly, "Stop that and get back to your workbooks." The boy who had done the slugging said, "Teacher, I hit him because he spit in my face." The teacher replied, "That wasn't polite; it was rude. Now get back to work, you're supposed to be doing your workbooks." As they went back to work, the boy who had done the spitting said to his opponent with a grin, "I will grant you that; it was rude."

However, even teachers who prefer to keep moralizing oriented to traffic rules have to specify some moral goals. The teacher just mentioned had put together suggestions of the class in the form of a moral code, which was displayed in poster form at the back of the class. The code had the following commandments:

1. Be a good citizen
2. Be generous by helping our friends
3. Mind your own business
4. Work quietly
5. No fighting
6. Play nicely and fairly
7. Be neat and clean
8. Be prepared

9. Raise your hand
10. Be polite

While this code lacks a little in depth and completeness, a little more system and we would come up with one of the bags of virtues we have mentioned.

Let us try to systematize our objections to the bag of virtues, since it will start us on the road to a more Platonic view. Your reaction to the Boston program is likely to be similar to that of Kozol. He says (page 179), "You look in vain through this list for anything to do with an original child or an independent style, there is an emphasis on obedience characteristics. The whole concept of respect for unearned authority is bitter to children within these kinds of schools. I wonder whether anyone really thinks that you are going to teach character, or anything else by rattling off a list of all the people in America who have struggled to make good."

These comments don't themselves carry us very far, positively. They suggest a new bag of virtues centering on creativity instead of on obedience. They suggest substituting newer and more liberal models. Read Langston Hughes for Robinson Crusoe or Dwight Eisenhower.

Beyond a greater sympathy for the minds and hearts of Negro children, Kozol suggests no real solution. He does appear to suggest a solution in another setting, the Newton Junior High School described by him in a *New York Times Magazine* article (Oct. 29, 1967). There a modern moral education course is called "Man Alone" and is according to Kozol "a whirlwind tour of alienation, loneliness, dying and narcotics with writings from John Donne to Bruno Bettelheim." According to Kozol, in this class a picture of one of the Hell's Angels was projected on the wall in gory, swastika-painted vividness.

"Cool man, great," a voice shouted.
"That's sick," said another.
"He's honest anyway," chimed in another, "he's living out his own feelings."
"He's not faking."

Kozol goes on to say "the teacher then ventured the idea that an alienated person might not be able to be truly creative. A creative person is really alive and noncompulsive; alienation means the opposite."

In this seminar the class has turned the virtues around 180 degrees so that the Hell's Angels are truly honest and creative while the teacher uses psychological jargon about compulsivity and alienation to rotate the virtues back part way toward moral conformity. Clearly, this jazzing up of the bag of virtues has no more rational base than the program of the Boston public schools. There is no substitute for a good hard look at what virtue is.

Let us start at the beginning, then. The objection of the psychologist to the bag of virtues is that there are no such things. Virtues and vices are labels by which people award praise or blame to others, but the ways people use praise and blame toward others are not the ways in which they think when making moral decisions themselves. You or I may not find a Hell's Angel truly honest, but he may find himself so. Hartshorne and May found this out to their dismay forty years ago by their monumental experimental studies of children's cheating and stealing. In brief, they and others since have found:

1. You can't divide the world into honest and dishonest people. Almost everyone cheats some of the time; cheating is distributed in bell-curve fashion around a level of moderate cheating.

2. If a person cheats in one situation, it doesn't mean he will or won't in another. There is very little correlation between situational cheating tests. In other words, it is not a character trait of dishonesty which makes a child cheat in a given situation. If it were, you could predict he would cheat in a second situation if he did in the first.

3. People's verbal moral values about honesty have nothing to do with how they act. People who cheat express as much or more moral disapproval of cheating as those who don't cheat.

The fact that there are no traits of character corresponding to the virtues and vices of conventional language should comfort us. Those who would try to capture for themselves the bag of virtues prescribed by the culture find themselves in the plight described by the theme song of the show, "You're a Good Man, Charlie Brown." . . .

[*In this song by Clark Gesner, the comic-strip character, Charlie Brown, is described as having a great number of virtues, including humility, a sense of honor, kindness, courage, and courteousness, to name a few. The chorus concludes that with a heart so good Charlie Brown could open any door—if only he weren't so wishy-washy.*]

If, like Charlie Brown, we define our moral aims in terms of virtues and vices, we are defining them in terms of the praise and blame of others and are caught in the pull of being all things to all men and end up being wishy-washy. The attraction of the bag of virtues approach to moral education is that it encourages the assumption that everyone can be a moral educator. It assumes that any adult of middle-class respectability or virtue knows what virtue is and is qualified to teach it by dint of being adult and respectable. We all have to make these assumptions as parents, but perhaps they are not sound. Socrates asked "whether good men have known how to hand on to someone else the goodness that was in themselves" and goes on to cite one virtuous Greek leader after another who had nonvirtuous sons. Shortly, I will describe what I believe to be a valid measure of moral maturity. When this measure was given to a group of middle-class men in their twenties and also to their fathers, we found almost no correlation between the two. The morally mature father was no more likely to have a morally mature son than was a father low on moral development. So numbers now support Socrates' bitter observation that good fathers don't have good sons or don't qualify as teachers of virtue.

In the context of the school, the foolishness of assuming that any teacher is qualified to be a moral educator becomes evident if we ask "Would this assumption make sense if we were to think of moral education as something carried on between one adult and another?" A good third-grade teacher of the new math and a good math teacher of graduate students operate under much the same set of assumptions. How many moralizing schoolteachers, however, would wish to make the claim that Protagoras made to young graduate students, that "I am rather better than anyone else at helping a man to acquire a good and noble character, worthy of the fee I charge."

If we think of moral education as something carried on at the adult level, we recognize that the effective moral educator is something of a revolutionary rather than an instiller of virtues. Protagoras could safely collect his fees for improving character because he meant by moral education the teaching of the rhetorical skills for getting ahead. When Socrates really engaged in adult moral education, however, he was brought up on trial for corrupting the Athenian youth. Perhaps there is still nothing more dangerous than the serious teaching of virtue. Socrates was condemned to death, because, as he said in the *Apology*:

> I do nothing but go about persuading you all, old and young alike, not
> to take thought for your person or property, but for the improvement

of the soul. I tell you virtue is not given by money, but that from virtue comes money, and every other good of man, public as well as private. This is my teaching, and if this is the doctrine which corrupts the youth, my doctrines are mischievous indeed. Therefore, Men of Athens, either acquit me or not; but whichever you do, understand that I shall never alter my ways not even if I have to die many times.

I stress the revolutionary nature of moral education partly because at this time it is comforting to reach back into history and recall that it is not only America that kills its moral educators. Martin Luther King joins a long list of men who had the arrogance not only to teach justice but to live it in such a way that other men felt uncomfortable about their own goodness, their own justice. In the last weeks, one has frequently heard the question, "Why King, not Carmichael or Brown?" It is not the man who preaches power and hate who gets assassinated. He is not a threat; he is like the worst in others. It is the man who is too good for other men to take, who questions the basis on which men erect their paltry sense of goodness, who dies. . . .

My hope is to have stirred some feelings about the seriousness and the reality of that big word, that Platonic form, justice, because men like King were willing to die for it. I suppose there may have been men willing to die for honesty, responsibility, and the rest of the bag of virtues, but, if so, we have no empathy with them. I am going to argue now, like Plato, that virtue is not many, but one, and its name is justice. Let me point out first that justice is not a character trait in the usual sense. You cannot make up behavior tests of justice, as Hartshorne and May did for honesty, service, and self-control. One cannot conceive of a little set of behavior tests that would indicate that Martin Luther King or Socrates were high on a trait of justice. The reason for this is that justice is not a concrete rule of action, such as lies behind virtues like honesty.

To be honest means don't cheat, don't steal, don't lie. Justice is not a rule or a set of rules, it is a moral principle. By a moral principle we mean a mode of choosing which is universal, a rule of choosing which we want all people to adopt always in all situations. We know it is all right to be dishonest and steal to save a life because it is just, because a man's right to life comes before another man's right to property. We know it is sometimes right to kill, because it is sometimes just. The Germans who tried to kill Hitler were doing right because respect for the equal values of lives demands that we kill someone murdering others in order to save their lives. There are exceptions to rules, then, but no exception to principles. A moral obligation is an obligation to respect the right or claim of another person. A moral principle is a principle for resolving competing claims, you versus me, you versus a third person. There is only one principled basis for resolving claims: justice or equality. Treat every man's claim impartially regardless of the man. A moral principle is not only a rule of action but a reason for action. As a reason for action, justice is called respect for persons.

Because morally mature men are governed by the principle of justice rather than by a set of rules, there are not many moral virtues but one. Let us restate the argument in Plato's terms. Plato's argument is that what makes a virtuous action virtuous is that it is guided by knowledge of the good. A courageous action based on ignorance of danger is not courageous; a just act based on ignorance of justice is not just, etc. If virtuous action is action based on knowledge of the good, then virtue is one, because knowledge of the good is one. We have already claimed that knowledge of the good is one because the good is justice. Let me briefly document these lofty claims by some lowly research findings. Using hypothetical moral situations, we have interviewed children and adults about right and wrong in the United States, Britain, Turkey, Taiwan, and Yucatan. In all cultures we find the same forms of moral thinking. There are six forms of thinking and they constitute an invariant sequence of stages in each culture. These stages are summarized in the table on page 124.

Why do I say existence of culturally universal stages means that knowledge of the good is one? First, because it implies that concepts of the good are culturally universal. Second, because an individual at a given level is pretty much the same in his thinking regardless of the situation he is presented with and regardless of the particular aspect of morality being tapped. There is a general factor of maturity of moral judgment much like the general factor of intelligence in cognitive tasks. If he knows one aspect of the good at a certain level, he knows other aspects of the good at that level. Third, because at each stage there is a single principle of the good, which only approaches a moral principle at the higher levels. At all levels, for instance, there is some reason for regard for law and some reason for regard for rights. Only at the highest stage, however, is regard for law a regard for universal moral law and regard for rights a regard for universal human rights. At this point, both regard for law and regard for human rights are grounded on a clear criterion of justice which was present in confused and obscure form at earlier stages.

Levels and stages in moral development

Levels	Basis of moral judgment	Stages of development
I	Moral value resides in external, quasi-physical happenings, in bad acts, or in quasi-physical needs rather than in persons and standards	*Stage 1:* Obedience and punishment orientation. Egocentric deference to superior power or prestige, or a trouble-avoiding set. Objective responsibility *Stage 2:* Naively egoistic orientation. Right action is that instrumentally satisfying the self's needs and occasionally others'. Awareness of relativism of value to each actor's needs and perspective. Naive egalitarianism and orientation to exchange and reciprocity
II	Moral value resides in performing good or right roles, in maintaining the conventional order and the expectancies of others	*Stage 3:* Good-boy orientation. Orientation to approval and to pleasing and helping others. Conformity to stereotypical images of majority or natural role behavior, and judgment by intentions *Stage 4:* Authority and social-order maintaining orientation. Orientation to "doing duty" and to showing respect for authority and maintaining the given social order for its own sake. Regard for earned expectations of others
III	Moral value resides in conformity by the self to shared or shareable standards, rights, or duties	*Stage 5:* Contractual legalistic orientation. Recognition of an arbitrary element or starting point in rules or expectations for the sake of agreement. Duty defined in terms of contract, general avoidance of violation of the will or rights of others, and majority will and welfare *Stage 6:* Conscience or principle orientation. Orientation not only to actually ordained social rules but to principles of choice involving appeal to logical universality and consistency. Orientation to conscience as a directing agent and to mutual respect and trust

Let me describe the stages in terms of the civil disobedience issue in a way that may clarify the argument I have just made. Here's a question we have asked: Before the Civil War, we had laws that allowed slavery. According to the law if a slave escaped, he had to be returned to his owner like a runaway horse. Some people who didn't believe in slavery disobeyed the law and hid the runaway slaves and helped them to escape. Were they doing right or wrong?

A bright, middle-class boy, Johnny, answers the question this way when he is ten: "They were doing wrong because the slave ran away himself. They're being just like slaves themselves trying to keep 'em away." He is asked, "Is slavery right or wrong?" He answers, "Some wrong, but servants aren't so bad because they don't do all that heavy work."

Johnny's response is Stage 1: *Punishment and obedience orientation.* Breaking the law makes it wrong; indeed the badness of being a slave washes off on his rescuer.

Three years later he is asked the same question. His answer is mainly Stage 2 *instrumental relativism.* He says: "They would help them escape because they were all against slavery. The South was for slavery because they had big plantations and the North was against it because they had big factories and they needed people to work and they'd pay. So the Northerners would think it was right but the Southerners wouldn't."

So early comes Marxist relativism. He goes on: "If a person is against slavery and maybe likes the slave or maybe dislikes the owner, it's OK for him to break the law if he likes, provided he doesn't get caught. If the slaves were in misery and one was a friend he'd do it. It would probably be right if it was someone you really loved."

At the end, his orientation to sympathy and love indicates the same Stage 3, *orientation to approval, affection, and helpfulness* better suggested by Charlie Brown.

At age nineteen, in college, Johnny is Stage 4: *Orientation to maintaining a social order of rules and rights.* He says: "They were right in my point of view. I hate the actual aspect of slavery, the imprisonment of one man ruling over another. They drive them too hard and they don't get anything in return. It's not right to disobey the law, no. Laws are made by the people. But you might do it because you feel it's wrong. If 50,000 people break the law, can you put them all in jail? Can 50,000 people be wrong?"

Johnny here is oriented to the rightness and wrongness of slavery itself and of obedience to law. He doesn't see the wrongness of slavery in terms of equal human rights but in terms of an unfair economic relation, working hard and getting nothing in return. The same view of rights in terms of getting what you worked for leads Johnny to say about school integration: "A lot of colored people are now just living off of civil rights. You only get education as far as you want to learn, as far as you work for it, not being placed with someone else, you don't get it from someone else."

Johnny illustrates for us the distinction between virtue as the development of principles of justice and virtue as being unprejudiced. In one sense Johnny's development has involved increased recognition of the fellow-humanness of the slaves. From thinking of slaves as inferior and bad at age ten he thinks of them as having some sort of rights at age nineteen. He is still not just, however, because his only notions of right are that you should get what you earn, a conception easily used to justify a segregated society. In spite of a high school and college education, he has no real grasp of the conceptions of rights underlying the Constitution or the Supreme Court decisions involved. Johnny's lack of virtue is not that he doesn't want to associate with Negroes, it is that he is not capable of being a participating citizen of our society because he does not understand the principles on which our society is based. His failure to understand those principles cuts both ways. Not only does he fail to ground the rights of Negroes on principles but he fails to ground respect for law on this base. Respect for law is respect for the majority. But if 50,000 people break the law, can 50,000 be wrong? Whether the 50,000 people are breaking the law in the name of rights or of the Ku Klux Klan makes no difference in this line of thought.

It is to be hoped that Johnny may reach our next stage, Stage 5, *social contract legalism*, by his mid-twenties, since some of our subjects continue to develop up until this time. Instead of taking one of our research subjects, however, let us take some statements by Socrates as an example of Stage 5. Socrates is explaining to Crito why he refuses to save his life by taking advantage of the escape arrangements Crito has made:

Ought one to fulfill all one's agreements?, Socrates asks. Then consider the consequences. Suppose the laws and constitution of Athens were to confront us and ask, Socrates, can you deny that by this act you intend, so far as you have power, to destroy us. Do you imagine that a city can continue to exist if the legal judgments which are pronounced by it are nullified and destroyed by private persons? At an earlier time, you made a noble show of indifference to the possibility of dying. Now you show no respect for your earlier professions and no regard for us, the laws, trying to run away in spite of the contracts by which you agreed to live as a member of our state. Are we not speaking the truth when we say that you have undertaken in deed, if not in word, to live your life as a citizen in obedience to us? It is a fact, then, that you are breaking covenants made with us under no compulsion or misunderstanding. You had seventy years in which you could have left the country if you were not satisfied with us or felt that the agreements were unfair.[2]

As an example of Stage 6, *orientation to universal moral principles*, let me cite Martin Luther King's letter from a Birmingham jail.

There is a type of constructive non-violent tension which is necessary for growth. Just as Socrates felt it was necessary to create a tension in the mind so that individuals could rise from the bondage of half-truths, so must we see the need for nonviolent gadflies to create the kind of tension in society that will help men rise from the dark depths of prejudice and racism.

One may well ask, "How can you advocate breaking some laws and obeying others?" The answer lies in the fact that there are two types of laws, just and unjust. One has not only a legal but a moral responsibility to obey just laws. One has a moral responsibility to disobey unjust laws. An unjust law is a human law that is not rooted in eternal law and natural law. Any law that uplifts human personality is just, any law that degrades human personality is unjust. An unjust law is a code that a numerical or power majority group compels a minority group to obey but does not make binding on itself. This is difference made legal.

I do not advocate evading or defying the law as would the rabid segregationist. That would lead to anarchy. One who breaks an unjust law must do so openly, lovingly, and with a willingness to accept the penalty. An individual who breaks a law that conscience tells him is unjust, and willingly accepts the penalty of imprisonment in order to arouse the conscience of the community over its injustice, is in reality expressing the highest respect for law.

King makes it clear that moral disobedience of the law must spring from the same root as moral obedience to law, out of

[2] For a recent example of this line of thought, see a piece by William F. Buckley, Jr., in the *New York Times Magazine*, November 28, 1967, Symposium on Civil Disobedience and Vietnam, "For Some Deportment, Deportation." "It ought to be the individual's right to go along with his community, but the community not the individual should specify the consequences. For those who ask to retain a personal veto over every activity of their Government, whether it is a war in Vietnam or the social or educational policies of a municipal administration, are asking for the kind of latitude which breaks the bonds of civil society. The consequence for studied and aggravated civil disobedience seem to me obvious, deportation. Ideally of course, a citizen whose disagreements with his country are organic should take the initiative and seek out more compatible countries." Other statements by eminent people in this symposium are examples of Stages 4, 5, and 6.

respect for justice. We respect the law because it is based on rights, both in the sense that the law is designed to protect the rights of all and because the law is made by the principle of equal political rights. If civil disobedience is to be Stage 6, it must recognize the contractual respect for law of Stage 5, even to accepting imprisonment. That is why Stage 5 is a way of thinking about the laws which are imposed upon all, while a morality of justice which claims to judge the law can never be anything but a free, personal ideal. It must accept the idea of being put in jail by its enemies, not of putting its enemies in jail. While we classified Socrates' statements to Crito as Stage 5, his statement of his civilly disobedient role as a moral educator quoted earlier was Stage 6, at least in spirit.

Both logic and empirical study indicate there is no shortcut to autonomous morality, no Stage 6 without a previous Stage 5.

We have claimed that knowledge of the moral good is one. We now will try to show that virtue in action is knowledge of the good, as Plato claimed. We have already said that knowledge of the good in terms of what Plato calls opinion or conventional belief is not virtue. An individual may believe that cheating is very bad but that does not predict that he will resist cheating in real life. Espousal of unprejudiced attitudes toward Negroes does not predict action to assure civil rights in an atmosphere where others have some prejudice; however, true knowledge, knowledge of principles of justice, does predict virtuous action. With regard to cheating, the essential elements of justice are understood by both our Stage 5 and our Stage 6 subjects. In cheating, the critical issue is recognition of the element of contract and agreement implicit in the situation, and the recognition that while it doesn't seem so bad if one person cheats, what holds for all must hold for one. In a recent study, 100 sixth-grade children were given experimental cheating tests and our moral judgment interview. The majority of the children were below the principled level in moral judgment; they were at our first four moral stages. Seventy-five percent of these children cheated. In contrast, only 20 percent of the principled subjects, that is, Stage 5 or 6, cheated. In another study conducted at the college level, only 11 percent of the principled subjects cheated, in contrast to 42 percent of the students at lower levels of moral judgment. In the case of cheating, justice and the expecatations of conventional authority both dictate the same behavior. What happens when justice and authority are opposed?

An experimental study by Stanley Milgram[3] involved such an opposition. Under the guise of a learning experiment,

[3] S. Milgram, "Behavioral Study of Obedience," *Journal of Abnormal Social Psychology*, 67 (1963), 371–378.

undergraduate subjects were ordered by an experimenter to administer increasingly more severe electric shock punishment to a stooge victim. In this case, the principles of justice involved in the Stage 5 social contract orientation do not clearly prescribe a decision. The victim had voluntarily agreed to participate in the experiment, and the subject himself had contractually committed himself to perform the experiment. Only Stage 6 thinking clearly defined the situation as one in which the experimenter did not have the moral right to ask them to inflice pain on another person. Accordingly, 75 percent of those at Stage 6 quit or refused to shock the victim, as compared to only 13 percent of all the subjects at lower stages.

A study of Berkeley students carries the issue into political civil disobedience. Berkeley students were faced with a decision to sit in the Administration building in the name of political freedom of communication. Haan and Smith administered moral judgment interviews to over 200 of these students.[4] The situation was like that in Milgram's study. A Stage 5 social contract interpretation of justice, which was that held by the University administration, could take the position that a student who came to Berkeley came with foreknowledge of the rules and could go elsewhere if he did not like them. About 50 percent of the Stage 5 subjects sat in. For Stage 6 students, the issue was clear cut, and 80 percent of them sat in. For students at the conventional levels, Stages 3 and 4, the issue was also clear cut, and only 10 percent of them sat in. These results will sound very heartwarming to those who have engaged in protest activities. Protesting is a sure sign of being at the most mature moral level; however, there was another group who was almost as disposed to sit in as the Stage 6 students. These were our Stage 2 instrumental relativists, of whom about 60 percent sat in. From our longitudinal studies, we know that most Stage 2 college students are in a state of confusion. In high school most were at the conventional level, and in college they kick conventional morality, searching for their thing, for self-chosen values, but cannot tell an autonomous morality of justice from one of egoistic relativism, exchange, and revenge. Our longitudinal studies indicate that all of our middle-class Stage 2 college students grow out of it to become principled adults. If the pressures are greater and you are a Stokely Carmichael, things may take a different course. . . .

Having, I hope, shown the validity of the Platonic view of virtue, I will take the little time left to consider the sense in which it may be taught. The Platonic view implies that, in a sense,

[4] N. Haan, M. Smith, and J. Block, "The Moral Reasoning of Young Adults: Political-Social Behavior, Family Background and Personality Correlates." *Journal of Personality and Social Psychology*, 10 (1968), 183–201.

knowledge of the good is always within but needs to be drawn out like geometric knowledge in Meno's slave. In a series of experimental studies, we have found that children and adolescents rank as "best" the highest level of moral reasoning they can comprehend. Children comprehend all lower stages than their own, and often comprehend the stage one higher than their own and occasionally two stages higher, though they cannot actively express these higher stages of thought. If they comprehend the stage one higher than their own, they tend to prefer it to their own. This fact is basic to moral leadership in our society. While the majority of adults in American society are at a conventional level, Stages 3 and 4, leadership in our society has usually been expressed at the level of Stages 5 and 6, as our example of Martin Luther King suggests. While it may be felt as dangerous, the moral leadership of the Platonic philosopher-ruler is nonetheless naturally felt.

Returning to the teaching of virtue as a drawing out, the child's preference for the next level of thought shows that it is greeted as already familiar, that it is felt to be a more adequate expression of that already within, of that latent in the child's own thought. If the child were responding to fine words and external prestige he would not pick the next stage continuous with his own, but something else. . . .

The first step in teaching virtue, then, is the Socratic step of creating dissatisfaction in the student about his present knowledge of the good. This we do experimentally by exposing the student to moral conflict situations for which his principles have no ready solution. Second, we expose him to disagreement and argument about these situations with his peers. Our Platonic view holds that if we inspire cognitive conflict in the student and point the way to the next step up the divided line, he will tend to see things previously invisible to him.

In practice, then, our experimental efforts at moral education have involved getting students at one level, say Stage 2, to argue with those at the next level, say Stage 3. The teacher would support and clarify the Stage 3 arguments. Then he would pit the Stage 3 students against the Stage 4 students on a new dilemma. Initial results with this method with a junior high school group indicated that 50 percent of the students moved up one stage and 10 percent moved up two stages. In comparison, only 10 percent of a control group moved up one stage in the four-month period involved.[5] . . .

[5] M. Blatt and L. Kohlberg, "The Effects of Classroom Discussion on Moral Reasoning," in *Research on Moralization, The Cognitive-Developmental Approach*, ed. Kohlberg and Turiel (New York, Holt, Rinehart & Winston).

III. TYPES OF PSYCHOLOGICAL EXPLANATION

5. Aristotle

EDITOR'S INTRODUCTION

If Plato is considered the first systematic rationalist, then Aristotle may be regarded as the first systematic empiricist. In contrast to Plato, Aristotle believed that most, though perhaps not all, knowledge is ultimately based on sense experience, and in accordance with this belief, he engaged in a good deal of naturalistic observation to support his theories. But perhaps the greatest contribution of Aristotle (as of Plato) was not his substantive observations; but, rather, the manner in which he explored the logical advantages and limitations of various *types* of explanation. It is, therefore, the logic of explanation that is the primary concern of this chapter. Specifically, in the first selection, Aristotle distinguishes among four types of explanation, referring to material, formal, efficient, and final causes, respectively. In the second selection, he explains how psyche encompasses the last three of these four causes. And, finally, in the third selection, he examines a specific psychological phenomenon, namely, anger.

In order to understand Aristotle's approach to science, and to psychology in particular, one must have a clear conception of his distinction between *matter* and *form*. As was discussed in Chapter 1, these are logical constructs that have various, though related, meanings depending on the context in which they are used. To recapitulate briefly, matter is (in one sense) the substratum or "stuff" out of which an object is made; form is the essence of an object, i.e., what makes it the kind of object it is (a horse, say, as opposed to a cow). In another sense, matter is the potential to become something; form is the actualization of that potential. But a potential may be actualized in two ways: first, as a capacity to do something and, second, as the exercise of that capacity.

As an illustration of these various senses of matter and form, consider a set of electronic components—resistors, transistors, diodes, etc. They are the matter used to construct a computer, for example. Or, stated differently, the unassembled components have the potential to become a computer. When they are assembled, that potential is actualized, i.e., the components take the form of a computer. The form of a computer is not simply the shape or configuration of its parts; rather, it is the capacity to do calculations. This is the first grade of actuality, which the computer possesses whether or not it is in operation at the moment. The second grade of actuality involves the exercise of the computer's capabilities, e.g., in the actual solution of a problem.

To complicate things even further, the distinction between matter and form is relative; what is matter at one level of analysis may be considered form at another (lower) level of analysis. We have just seen, for example, how resistors, transistors, etc., may be treated as matter in the case of a computer. However, each of these components is itself an assemblage of more elementary parts. Thus, considered in its own right, the transistor has form (the capacity to amplify) and matter (the silicon used to make it). Generalizing from this simple example, it can be seen how the Aristotelian world view envisions a progression or heirarchy from lower to higher forms.

With these considerations in mind, it is easy to understand Aristotle's definition of psyche as the first grade of actuality (form) of a potentially living body (matter). Stated most simply, psyche is the capacity for life, the essential characteristic of animate objects. In plants, this capacity exists at a relatively low level, involving only nutrition, growth, and reproduction. This is the vegetative psyche. In infrahuman animals, sensation and related functions are added. These functions define the sensitive psyche. Finally, there also is the capacity for reason, the rational psyche, which is the essential characteristic of man.

Analyses in terms of matter and form can be applied to each part of the body, as well as to the organism as a whole. For example, the matter of the eye is its anatomical structure, while its form is the capacity for sight. Sight, in turn, provides the matter for rational thought, a higher level of psychic functioning.

As the last example illustrates, the notion of matter is not limited to a material substratum or structure, but refers also to processes and functions. Thus, with regard to a behavioral episode, "matter" would be the particular movements out of which a response is made, while "form" would be the object or goal around which the response is organized. To take a specific example, one rat in a Skinner box might press the lever with its foot while another might produce the same result with its snout. What allows us to call these two quite different responses (in terms of movement) the same *act* is that they achieve the same result (have the same form), namely, depression of the bar. (Note that the terms *act* and *actuality* are derived from the same root.) The response of bar pressing may, in turn, provide the matter for an act at a higher level of generality, e.g., the attainment of food or the avoidance of shock.

As explained thus far, the Aristotelian notion of psyche might be considered primarily a principle of classification, i.e., it provides the rationale for grouping objects (organisms, anatomical structures, behavioral episodes) into a hierarchical structure or taxonomy. But for Aristotle, psyche was a principle of explanation as well as classification. To introduce this aspect of psyche, we must consider briefly what Aristotle meant by explanation. In the *Phaedo* (Chapt. 3), we came across two suggestions regarding the explanation of behavior. The first, by Anaxagoras, was essentially mechanistic. A mechanistic type of explanation involves what Aristotle called an *efficient cause*. That is, one event is determined by some antecedent event, e.g., a response is elicited by a prior stimulus, neural impulse, or whatever. We shall have more to say about this notion of causation in subsequent chapters, for it underlies much of contemporary psychology. We also have seen how Plato rejected mechanistic types of explanations because they do not express the form or principle that makes an action "reasonable." This underlying principle is the *formal cause*. Aristotle's notion of a formal cause was both similar to and different from that of Plato. Like Plato, Aristotle viewed the form as the essential characteristic of an object; but unlike Plato, he considered the form to be a capacity inherent in the object, and not a mathematical principle or independently existing archetype. But there are still other ways to explain an event, in addition to the specification of efficient and formal causes. For example, one might specify the substance used to make an object (the *material cause*) and the function or goal that the object serves (the *final cause*). The latter was the type of cause most emphasized by Aristotle.

The notion of final cause will be considered in detail in the next chapter. Therefore, we shall conclude this brief introduction by pointing out some similarities between the Aristotelian view of nature and the contemporary approach to science known as *general systems theory*. Both illustrate what we have called the organismic model of explanation.

We have seen how Aristotle viewed nature as an organized whole consisting of a hierarchy of matter and form. This view may be compared with that of Bertalanffy, one of the most prominent advocates of systems reaserch:

> We presently "see" the universe as a tremendous hierarchy, from elementary particles to atomic nuclei, to atoms, molecules, high-molecular compounds, to the wealth of structures (electron and light microscopic) between molecules and cells . . . to cells, organisms, and beyond to supra-individual organizations.[1]

Moreover, Bertalanffy continues,

> A similar hierarchy is found both in "structures" and in "functions." In the last resort, structure (i.e., the order of parts) and function (order of processes) may be the very same thing: in the physical world matter dissolves into a play of energies, and in the biological world structures are the expression of a flow of processes.[2]

As conceived by Bertalanffy, general system theory is the study of organized wholes or systems (whether atoms, molecules, cells, organisms, or social institutions) and the elucidation of principles common to such systems. This approach, Bertalanffy argues, introduces a new paradigm or "philosophy of nature" into science. The old paradigm, epitomized by post-Newtonian physics, tended to be atomistic, reductionistic, and mechanistic. Within its framework, the goal of science was to analyze complex systems into elementary particles, on the assumption that when the particles were assembled again, the whole system would be intelligible. By contrast, general systems theory does not assume that organized wholes are simply the sum of their parts. Rather, through the interaction of elements within a system, new and different properties may emerge that are not reducible to any properties characteristic of the elementary particles. Life (psyche) is one example of such an emergent property; so, too, are such phenomena as consciousness and values.

In many fundamental respects, the "new" paradigm advocated by Bertalanffy represents a reintroduction of the Aristotelian perspective into science after an eclipse of nearly four centuries. This is not to imply that general systems theory is simply an

---

[1] L. von Bertalanffy, *General System Theory*. New York: George Braziller, Inc., 1968, p. 27, reprinted with permission of the publisher. Copyright © 1968 by Ludwig von Bertalanffy.

[2] *Ibid.*, p. 27.

updating of Aristotle. That would be as misleading as the assertion that modern atomic physics is simply an updating of Greek atomism. But no matter how much they differ in specifics, in terms of general patterns of thought there is an obvious affinity between Aristotle's and Bertalanffy's "philosophy of nature." And in this book, we are more concerned with general patterns of thought than with specific theoretical formulations.

Types of Causality

[L]et us now examine what and how many sorts of explanatory factors there are. All inquiry aims at knowledge; but we cannot claim to know a subject matter until we have grasped the "why" of it, that is, its fundamental explanation. It must clearly, therefore, be our aim in the present inquiry to get knowledge of the first principles to which we may refer any problem in our exploration of generation and destruction and of any natural transformation.

"An explanatory factor," then, means (1) from one point of view, the material constituent from which a thing comes; for example, the bronze of a statue, the silver of a cup, and their kinds. From another point of view, (2) the form or pattern of a thing, that is, the reason (and the kind of reason) which explains what it was to be that thing; for example, the factors in an octave are based on the ratio of two to one and, in general, on number. This kind of factor is found in the parts of a definition. Again, (3) the agent whereby a change or a state of rest is first produced; for example, an adviser is "responsible" for a plan, a father "causes" his child, and, in general, any maker "causes" what he makes, and any agent causes what it changes. Again, (4) the end or the where-for; so, when we take a walk for the sake of our health, and someone asks us why we are walking, we answer, "in order to be healthy," and thus we think we have explained our action. So any intermediate means to the end of a series of acts: for example, as means of health there are reducing, purging, drugs, instruments, and so forth; for all these are for an end, though they differ from one another in that some are instruments, and others are actions.

Since what we call an "explanatory factor" may be any one of these different aspects of a process, it follows not only that anything actually has several such factors which are not merely accidental differences of meaning (as both the sculptor's art and the bronze are needed to explain a statue as a statue, the bronze being its material, and the sculpturing, its agent), but it follows also that these factors are reciprocal: for example, exercise explains good health, and good health explains exercise; though they explain each other differently (good health as end, and exercise as means). And the same thing may explain contraries: for the same thing which by its presence explains a given fact is "blamed" by its

Reprinted from *Physics* by Aristotle (R. Hope, trans.) by permission of University of Nebraska Press. Copyright © 1961 by the University of Nebraska Press, 194^{b}18–195^{b}30.

absence for the contrary fact; for example, a shipwreck is "caused" by the absence of the pilot, whose presence is responsible for the ship's safety.

All the factors here mentioned clearly fall under four varieties. From letters come syllables; from building materials come buildings; from fire, earth, and so forth, come bodies; from parts come wholes; and from assumptions come conclusions. The first factor in each of these pairs is the subject matter or the parts; the second is what it meant to be that particular whole, or synthesis, or form. A "cause" in the sense illustrated by a seed, a physician, an adviser, and any agent generally, is the factor whereby a change or state of being is initiated. Finally, there are the ends or the good of the others; for all the others tend toward what is best as toward their end. It makes no difference now whether we say "their good" or "their apparent good."

These, then, are the kinds of explanatory factors. But they fall into many lesser varieties, which can also be summarized under a few heads. There are several ways in which explanatory factors explain, even when they are of the same general kind. Thus one factor is prior to another, which is posterior: for example, health is prior to both the physician and the technician; the octave is prior to the ratio of two to one and to number; and so always, the inclusive factor is prior to individual factors.

Then there are accidental factors of various kinds; for example, a statue is, we say, by Polyclitus, but it is also by a sculptor; the sculptor happens to be Polyclitus. And so the kind (sculptor) and the accidental (Polyclitus) it embraces are both factors in the statue; thus a man is responsible for the statue, and so is the more general species "animal"; for Polyclitus is a man, and man is an animal. These accidental factors are sometimes remote and sometimes proximate; for example, between Polyclitus in particular and man in general there would be such intermediate factors as "a white man" and "an artist."

Besides, any factor, whether essential or accidental, may be actually in operation or merely capable of acting: a house being built is the work of "builders," but more actually of the builder who is building it. The same is true of the things to which explanatory factors refer—they may be singled out or referred to more generally: for example, "this statue," or "a statue," or even more generally, "an image"; and "this bronze," or "of bronze," or, generally, "of matter"; and similarly with reference to the accidental factors.

Moreover, both accidental and essential factors may be combined: for example, instead of Polyclitus or the sculptor, we say "Polyclitus the sculptor." However, these varieties reduce to but six, each being taken either individually or collectively: the accidental factors (individual or collective); combined or separate factors; and actual or potential factors. There is another difference between them: the operating and individual causes exist and cease to exist simultaneously with their effects (for example, this man actually healing is correlative with this man who is now being healed, and this actual builder, with this thing-being-now-built); but potentially they do not exist together (for the house and the builder do not perish with the act of building).

We must, however, always seek the "highest" [or "principal"] explanatory factor of each case, as in any other investigations [of "reasons why"]; for example, a man builds only because he is a builder, and a builder, only because he has mastered the builder's art, which is therefore the more primary factor; and so in all such cases. Again, generic effects go with generic explanatory factors (for example, a statue with a sculptor), particular effects go with particular explanatory factors (for example, this statue, with this sculptor); so, too, potential effects correspond precisely to potential factors, and things actualized, to factors actually operating.

Let this suffice, then, concerning types of explanatory factors and the ways in which they operate.

Psyche as a Principle of Causality

[L]et us now ... make as it were a completely fresh start, endeavouring to give a precise answer to the question, What is soul? i.e. to formulate the most general possible definition of it.

We are in the habit of recognizing, as one determinate kind of what is, substance, and that in several senses, (a) in the sense of matter or that which in itself is not 'a this', and (b) in the sense of form or essence, which is that precisely in virtue of which a thing is called 'a this', and thirdly (c) in the sense of that which is compounded of both (a) and (b). Now matter is potentiality, form actuality; of the latter there are two grades related to one another as e.g. knowledge to the exercise of knowledge.

Among substances are by general consent reckoned bodies and especially natural bodies; for they are the principles of all other

Aristotle, *On the soul*, (J. A. Smith, trans.) in *The Works of Aristotle*, Vol. 3, W. D. Ross, ed., (1st ed., 1931), 412^{a}20–415^{b}26, by permission of the Oxford University Press, Oxford.

bodies. Of natural bodies some have life in them, others not; by life we mean self-nutrition and growth (with its correlative decay). It follows that every natural body which has life in it is a substance in the sense of a composite.[1]

But since it is also a *body* of such and such a kind, viz. having life, the *body* cannot be soul; the body is the subject or matter, not what is attributed to it. Hence the soul must be a substance in the sense of the form of a natural body having life potentially within it. But substance[2] is actuality, and thus soul is the actuality of a body as above characterized. Now the word actuality has two senses corresponding respectively to the possession of knowledge and the actual exercise of knowledge. It is obvious that the soul is actuality in the first sense, viz. that of knowledge as possessed, for both sleeping and waking presuppose the existence of soul, and of these waking corresponds to actual knowing, sleeping to knowledge possessed but not employed, and, in the history of the individual, knowledge comes before its employment or exercise.

That is why the soul is the first grade of actuality of a natural body having life potentially in it. The body so described is a body which is organized. The parts of plants in spite of their extreme simplicity are 'organs'; e.g. the leaf serves to shelter the pericarp, the pericarp to shelter the fruit, while the roots of plants are analogous to the mouth of animals, both serving for the absorption of food. If, then, we have to give a general formula applicable to all kinds of soul, we must describe it as the first grade of actuality of a natural organized body. That is why we can wholly dismiss as unnecessary the question whether the soul and the body are one: it is as meaningless as to ask whether the wax and the shape given to it by the stamp are one, or generally the matter of a thing and that of which it is the matter. Unity has many senses (as many as 'is' has), but the most proper and fundamental sense of both is the relation of an actuality to that of which it is the actuality.

We have now given an answer to the question, What is soul?—an answer which applies to it in its full extent. It is substance in the sense which corresponds to the definitive formula of a thing's essence. That means that it is 'the essential whatness' of a body of the character just assigned.[3] Suppose that what is literally an 'organ',[4] like an axe, were a *natural* body, its 'essential whatness', would have been its essence, and so its soul; if this disappeared from it, it would have ceased to be an axe, except in

---

[1] Sc. 'in a sense, i.e. so as to preserve its homogeneity in even its smallest part'.
[2] Sc. in the sense of form.
[3] Viz. organized, or possessed potentially of life.
[4] i.e. instrument.

name. As it is,[5] it is just an axe; it wants the character which is required to make its whatness or formulable essence a soul; for that, it would have had to be a *natural* body of a particular kind, viz. one having *in itself* the power of setting itself in movement and arresting itself. Next, apply this doctrine in the case of the 'parts' of the living body. Suppose that the eye were an animal—sight would have been its soul, for sight is the substance or essence of the eye which corresponds to the formula,[6] the eye being merely the matter of seeing; when seeing is removed the eye is no longer an eye, except in name—it is no more a real eye than the eye of a statue or of a painted figure. We must now extend our consideration from the 'parts' to the whole living body; for what the departmental sense is to the bodily part which is its organ, that the whole faculty of sense is to the whole sensitive body as such.

We must not understand by that which is 'potentially capable of living' what has lost the soul it had, but only what still retains it; but seeds and fruits are bodies which possess the qualification.[7] Consequently, while waking is actuality in a sense corresponding to the cutting and the seeing,[8] the soul is actuality in the sense corresponding to the power of sight and the power in the tool;[9] the body corresponds to what exists in potentiality; as the pupil *plus* the power of sight constitutes the eye, so the soul *plus* the body constitutes the animal.

From this it indubitably follows that the soul is inseparable from its body, or at any rate that certain parts of it are (if it has parts)—for the actuality of some of them is nothing but the actualities of their bodily parts. Yet some may be separable because they are not the actualities of any body at all. Further, we have no light on the problem whether the soul may not be the actuality of its body in the sense in which the sailor is the actuality[10] of the ship.

This must suffice as our sketch or outline determination of the nature of soul.

Since what is clear or logically more evident emerges from what in itself is confused but more observable by us, we must reconsider our results from this point of view. For it is not enough for a definitive formula to express as most now do the mere fact;

---

[5] Being an artificial, not a natural, body.
[6] i.e. which states what it is to be an eve.
[7] Though only potentially, i.e. they are at a further remove from actuality than the fully formed and organized body.
[8] i.e. to the second grade of actuality.
[9] i.e. to the first grade of actuality.
[10] i.e. actuator.

it must include and exhibit the ground also. At present definitions are given in a form analogous to the conclusion of a syllogism; e.g. What is squaring? The construction of an equilateral rectangle equal to a given oblong rectangle. Such a definition is in form equivalent to a conclusion. One that tells us that squaring is the discovery of a line which is a mean proportional between the two unequal sides of the given rectangle discloses the ground of what is defined.

We resume our inquiry from a fresh starting-point by calling attention to the fact that what has soul in it differs from what has not in that the former displays life. Now this word has more than one sense, and provided any one alone of these is found in a thing we say that thing is living. Living, that is, may mean thinking or perception or local movement and rest, or movement in the sense of nutrition, decay and growth. Hence we think of plants also as living, for they are observed to possess in themselves an originative power through which they increase or decrease in all spatial directions; they grow up *and* down, and everything that grows increases its bulk alike in both directions or indeed in all, and continues to live so long as it can absorb nutriment.

This power of self-nutrition can be isolated from the other powers mentioned, but not they from it—in mortal beings at least. The fact is obvious in plants; for it is the only psychic power they possess.

This is the originative power the possession of which leads us to speak of things as *living* at all, but it is the possession of sensation that leads us for the first time to speak of living things as animals; for even those beings which possess no power of local movement but do possess the power of sensation we call animals and not merely living things.

The primary form of sense is touch, which belongs to all animals. Just as the power of self-nutrition can be isolated from touch and sensation generally, so touch can be isolated from all other forms of sense. (By the power of self-nutrition we mean that departmental power of the soul which is common to plants and animals: all animals whatsoever are observed to have the sense of touch.) What the explanation of these two facts is, we must discuss later. At present we must confine ourselves to saying that soul is the source of these phenomena and is characterized by them, viz. by the powers of self-nutrition, sensation, thinking, and motivity.

Is each of these a soul or a part of a soul? And if a part, a part in what sense? A part merely distinguishable by definition or a part distinct in local situation as well? In the case of certain of these powers, the answers to these questions are easy, in the case of others we are puzzled what to say. Just as in the case of plants which when divided are observed to continue to live though removed to a distance from one another (thus showing that in *their* case the soul of each individual plant before division was actually one, potentially many), so we notice a similar result in other varieties of soul, i.e. in insects which have been cut in two; each of the segments possesses both sensation and local movement; and if sensation, necessarily also imagination and appetition; for, where there is sensation, there is also pleasure and pain, and, where these, necessarily also desire.

We have no evidence as yet about mind or the power to think; it seems to be a widely different kind of soul, differing as what is eternal from what is perishable; it alone is capable of existence in isolation from all other psychic powers. All the other parts of soul, it is evident from what we have said, are, in spite of certain statements to the contrary, incapable of separate existence though, of course, distinguishable by definition. If opining is distinct from perceiving, to be capable of opining and to be capable of perceiving must be distinct, and so with all the other forms of living above enumerated. Further, some animals possess all these parts of soul, some certain of them only, others one only (this is what enables us to classify animals); the cause must be considered later. A similar arrangement is found also within the field of the senses; some classes of animals have all the senses, some only certain of them, others only one, the most indispensable, touch.

Since the expression 'that whereby we live and perceive' has two meanings, just like the expression 'that whereby we know'—that may mean either (a) knowledge or (b) the soul, for we can speak of knowing *by* or *with* either, and similarly that whereby we are in health may be either (a) health or (b) the body or some part of the body; and since of the two terms thus contrasted knowledge or health is the name of a form, essence, or ratio, or if we so express it an actuality of a recipient matter—knowledge of what is capable of knowing, health of what is capable of being made healthy (for the operation of that which is capable of originating change terminates and has its seat in what is changed or altered); further, since it is the soul by or with which primarily we live, perceive, and think:—it follows that the soul must be a ratio or formulable essence, not a matter or subject. For, as we said, the word substance has three meanings—form, matter, and the complex of both—and of these three what is called matter is potentiality, what is called form actuality. Since then the complex here is the living thing, the body cannot be the actuality of the soul; it is the soul which is the actuality of a certain kind of body. Hence the rightness of the view that the soul cannot be without a body, while it cannot *be* a body; it is not a body but something relative to a body. That is why it is *in* a body, and a body of a definite kind. It was a mistake, therefore, to do as former thinkers did, merely to fit it into a body without adding a definite specification of the kind or character of that body. Reflection confirms the observed fact; the actuality of any given thing can only be realized in what is already potentially that thing, i.e. in a matter of its own appropriate to it. From all this it follows that soul is an actuality or formulable essence of something that possesses a potentiality of being besouled.

Of the psychic powers above enumerated some kinds of living things, as we have said, possess all, some less than all, others one only. Those we have mentioned are the nutritive, the appetitive, the sensory, the locomotive, and the power of thinking. Plants have none but the first, the nutritive, while another order of living things has this *plus* the sensory. If any order of living things has the sensory, it must also have the appetitive; for appetite is the genus of which desire, passion, and wish are the species; now all animals have one sense at least, viz. touch, and whatever has a sense has the capacity for pleasure and pain and therefore has pleasant and painful objects present to it, and wherever these are present, there is desire, for desire is just appetition of what is pleasant. Further, all animals have the sense for food (for touch is the sense for food); the food of all living things consists of what is dry, moist, hot, cold, and these are the qualities apprehended by touch; all other sensible qualities are apprehended by touch only indirectly. Sounds, colours, and odours contribute nothing to nutriment; flavours fall within the field of tangible qualities. Hunger and thirst are forms of desire, hunger a desire for what is dry and hot, thirst a desire for what is cold and moist; flavour is a sort of seasoning added to both. We must later clear up these points, but at present it may be enough to say that all animals that possess the sense of touch have also appetition. The case of imagination is obscure; we must examine it later. Certain kinds of animals possess in addition the power of locomotion, and still another order of animate beings, i.e. man and possibly another order like man or superior to him, the power of thinking, i.e. mind. It is now evident that a single definition can be given of soul only in the same sense as one can be given of figure. For, as in that case there is no figure distinguishable and apart from triangle, &c., so here there is no soul apart from the forms of soul just enumerated. It is true that a highly general definition can be given for figure which will fit all figures without expressing the peculiar nature of any figure. So here in the case of soul and its specific forms. Hence it is absurd in this and similar cases to demand an absolutely general definition which will fail to express the peculiar nature of anything that *is*, or again, omitting this, to look for separate definitions corresponding to each *infima species*. The cases of figure and soul are exactly parallel; for the particulars subsumed under the common name in both cases—figures and living beings—constitute a series, each successive term of which potentially contains its predecessor, e.g. the square the triangle, the sensory power the self-nutritive. Hence we must ask in the case of each order of living things, What is its soul, i.e. What is the soul of plant, animal, man? Why the terms are related in this serial way must form the subject of later examination. But the facts are that the power of perception is never found apart from the power of self-nutrition, while—in plants—the latter is found isolated from the former. Again, no sense is found apart from that of touch, while touch *is* found by itself; many animals have neither sight, hearing, nor smell. Again, among living things that possess sense some have the power of locomotion, some not. Lastly, certain living beings—a small minority—possess calculation and thought, for (among mortal beings) those which possess calculation have all the other powers above mentioned, while the converse does not hold—indeed some live by imagination alone, while others have not even imagination. The mind that knows with immediate intuition presents a different problem.

It is evident that the way to give the most adequate definition of soul is to seek in the case of *each* of its forms for the most appropriate definition.

It is necessary for the student of these forms of soul first to find a definition of each, expressive of what it is, and then to investigate its derivative properties, &c. But if we are to express what each is, viz. what the thinking power is, or the perceptive, or the nutritive, we must go farther back and first give an account of thinking or perceiving, for in the order of investigation the question of what an agent does precedes the question, what enables it to do what it does. If this is correct, we must on the same ground go yet another step farther back and have some clear view of the objects of each; thus we must *start* with these objects, e.g. with food, with what is perceptible, or with what is intelligible.

It follows that first of all we must treat of nutrition and reproduction[11] for the nutritive soul is found along with all the

---

[11] Sc. 'which we shall see to be inseparable from nutrition'.

others and is the most primitive and widely distributed power of soul, being indeed that one in virtue of which all are said to have life. The acts in which it manifests itself are reproduction and the use of food—reproduction, I say, because for any living thing that has reached its normal development and which is unmutilated, and whose mode of generation is not spontaneous, the most natural act is the production of another like itself, an animal producing an animal, a plant a plant, in order that, as far as its nature allows, it may partake in the eternal and divine. That is the goal towards which all things strive, that for the sake of which they do whatsoever their nature renders possible. The phrase 'for the sake of which' is ambiguous; it may mean either (a) the end to achieve which, or (b) the being in whose interest, the act is done. Since then no living thing is able to partake in what is eternal and divine by uninterrupted continuance (for nothing perishable can forever remain one and the same), it tries to achieve that end in the only way possible to it, and success is possible in varying degrees; so it remains not indeed as the self-same individual but continues its existence in something *like* itself—not numerically but specifically one.[12]

The soul is the cause or source of the living body. The terms cause and source have many senses. But the soul is the cause of its body alike in all three senses which we explicitly recognize. It is (a) the source or origin of movement, it is (b) the end, it is (c) the essence of the whole living body.

That it is the last, is clear; for in everything the essence is identical with the ground of its being, and here, in the case of living things, their being is to live, and of their being and their living the soul in them is the cause or source. Further, the actuality of whatever is potential is identical with its formulable essence.

It is manifest that the soul is also the final cause of its body. For Nature, like mind, always does whatever it does for the sake of something, which something is its end. To that something corresponds in the case of animals the soul and in this it follows the order of nature; all natural bodies are organs of the soul. This is true of those that enter into the constitution of plants as well as of those which enter into that of animals. This shows that that for the sake of which they are is soul. We must here recall the two senses of 'that for the sake of which', viz. (a) the end to achieve which, and (b) the being in whose interest, anything is or is done.

We must maintain, further, that the soul is also the cause of

---

[12] There is an unbroken current of the same specific life flowing through a discontinuous series of individual beings of the same species united by descent, [cf. The discussion of Aristotle's essentialism in relation to theories of evolution, Chapt. 1, p. 37 ff.]

the living body as the original source of local movement. The power of locomotion is not found, however, in all living things. But change of quality and change of quantity are also due to the soul. Sensation is held to be a qualitative alteration, and nothing except what has soul in it is capable of sensation. The same holds of the quantitative changes which constitute growth and decay; nothing grows or decays naturally[13] except what feeds itself, and nothing feeds itself except what has a share of soul in it.

[13]i.e. of itself.

The Causes of Anger

The Emotions are all those feelings that so change men as to affect their judgements, and that are also attended by pain or pleasure. Such are anger, pity, fear and the like, with their opposites. We must arrange what we have to say about each of them under three heads. Take, for instance, the emotion of anger: here we must discover (1) what the state of mind of angry people is, (2) who the people are with whom they usually get angry, and (3) on what grounds they get angry with them. It is not enough to know one or even two of these points; unless we know all three, we shall be unable to arouse anger in any one. The same is true of the other emotions. So just as earlier in this work we drew up a list of useful propositions for the orator, let us now proceed in the same way to analyse the subject before us.

Anger may be defined as an impulse, accompanied by pain, to a conspicuous revenge for a conspicuous slight directed without justification towards what concerns oneself or towards what concerns one's friends. If this is a proper definition of anger, it must always be felt towards some particular individual, e.g. Cleon, and not 'man' in general. It must be felt because the other has done or intended to do something to him or one of his friends. It must always be attended by a certain pleasure—that which arises from the expectation of revenge. For since nobody aims at what he thinks he cannot attain, the angry man is aiming at what he can attain, and the belief that you will attain your aim is pleasant. Hence it has been well said about wrath,

Aristotle, *Rhetoric* (W. R. Roberts, trans.), in *The works of Aristotle*, Vol. 11, W. D. Ross, ed. (1st ed., n.d., reprinted, 1966), $1378^a20-1380^b$, by permission of the Oxford University Press, Oxford.

Sweeter it is by far than the honeycomb dripping with sweetness,
And spreads through the hearts of men.

It is also attended by a certain pleasure because the thoughts dwell upon the act of vengeance, and the images then called up cause pleasure, like the images called up in dreams.

Now slighting is the actively entertained opinion of something as obviously of no importance. We think bad things, as well as good ones, have serious importance; and we think the same of anything that tends to produce such things, while those which have little or no such tendency we consider unimportant. There are three kinds of slighting—contempt, spite, and insolence. (1) Contempt is one kind of slighting: you feel contempt for what you consider unimportant, and it is just such things that you slight. (2) Spite is another kind; it is a thwarting another man's wishes, not to get something yourself but to prevent his getting it. The slight arises just from the fact that you do not aim at something for yourself: clearly you do not think that he can do you harm, for then you would be afraid of him instead of slighting him, nor yet that he can do you any good worth mentioning, for then you would be anxious to make friends with him. (3) Insolence is also a form of slighting, since it consists in doing and saying things that cause shame to the victim, not in order that anything may happen to yourself, or because anything has happened to yourself, but simply for the pleasure involved. (Retaliation is not 'insolence', but vengeance.) The cause of the pleasure thus enjoyed by the insolent man is that he thinks himself greatly superior to others when ill-treating them. That is why youths and rich men are insolent; they think themselves superior when they show insolence. One sort of insolence is to rob people of the honour due to them; you certainly slight them thus; for it is the unimportant, for good or evil, that has no honour paid to it. So Achilles says in anger:

He hath taken my prize for himself and hath done me dishonour,

and

Like an alien honored by none,

meaning that this is why he is angry. A man expects to be specially respected by his inferiors in birth, in capacity, in goodness, and generally in anything in which he is much their superior: as where money is concerned a wealthy man looks for respect from a poor man; where speaking is concerned, the man with a turn for oratory looks for respect from one who cannot speak; the ruler demands the respect of the ruled, and the man who thinks he ought to be a ruler demands the respect of the man whom he thinks he ought to be ruling. Hence it has been said

Great is the wrath of kings, whose father is Zeus almighty,

and

Yea, but his rancour abideth long afterward also,

their great resentment being due to their great superiority. Then again a man looks for respect from those who he thinks owe him good treatment, and these are the people whom he has treated or is treating well, or means or has meant to treat well, either himself, or through his friends, or through others at his request.

It will be plain by now, from what has been said, (1) in what frame of mind, (2) with what persons, and (3) on what grounds people grow angry. (1) The frame of mind is that in which any pain is being felt. In that condition, a man is always aiming at something. Whether, then, another man opposes him either directly in any way, as by preventing him from drinking when he is thirsty, or indirectly, the act appears to him just the same; whether some one works against him, or fails to work with him, or otherwise vexes him while he is in this mood, he is equally angry in all these cases. Hence people who are afflicted by sickness or poverty or love or thirst or any other unsatisfied desires are prone to anger and easily roused: especially against those who slight their present distress. Thus a sick man is angered by disregard of his illness, a poor man by disregard of his poverty, a man waging war by disregard of the war he is waging, a lover by disregard of his love, and so throughout, any other sort of slight being enough if special slights are wanting. Each man is predisposed, by the emotion now controlling him, to his own particular anger. Further, we are angered if we happen to be expecting a contrary result: for a quite unexpected evil is specially painful, just as the quite unexpected fulfilment of our wishes is specially pleasant. Hence it is plain what seasons, times, conditions, and periods of life tend to stir men easily to anger, and where and when this will happen; and it is plain that the more we are under these conditions the more easily we are stirred.

These, then, are the frames of mind in which men are easily stirred to anger. The persons with whom we get angry are those who laugh, mock, or jeer at us, for such conduct is insolent. Also those who inflict injuries upon us that are marks of insolence.

These injuries must be such as are neither retaliatory nor profitable to the doers: for only then will they be felt to be due to insolence. Also those who speak ill of us, and show contempt for us, in connexion with the things we ourselves most care about: thus those who are eager to win fame as philosophers get angry with those who show contempt for their philosophy; those who pride themselves upon their appearance get angry with those who show contempt for their appearance; and so on in other cases. We feel particularly angry on this account if we suspect that we are in fact, or that people think we are, lacking completely or to any effective extent in the qualities in question. For when we are convinced that we excel in the qualities for which we are jeered at, we can ignore the jeering. Again, we are angrier with our friends than with other people, since we feel that our friends ought to treat us well and not badly. We are angry with those who have usually treated us with honour or regard, if a change comes and they behave to us otherwise: for we think that they feel contempt for us, or they would still be behaving as they did before. And with those who do not return our kindnesses or fail to return them adequately, and with those who oppose us though they are our inferiors: for all such persons seem to feel contempt for us; those who oppose us seem to think us inferior to themselves, and those who do not return our kindnesses seem to think that those kindnesses were conferred by inferiors. And we feel particularly angry with men of no account at all, if they slight us. For, by our hypothesis, the anger caused by the slight is felt towards people who are not justified in slighting us, and our inferiors are not thus justified. Again, we feel angry with friends if they do not speak well of us or treat us well; and still more, if they do the contrary; or if they do not perceive our needs, which is why Plexippus is angry with Meleager in Antiphon's play; for this want of perception shows that they are slighting us—we do not fail to perceive the needs of those for whom we care. Again, we are angry with those who rejoice at our misfortunes or simply keep cheerful in the midst of our misfortunes, since this shows that they either hate us or are slighting us. Also with those who are indifferent to the pain they give us: this is why we get angry with bringers of bad news. And with those who listen to stories about us or keep on looking at our weaknesses; this seems like either slighting us or hating us; for those who love us share in all our distresses and it must distress any one to keep on looking at his own weaknesses. Further, with those who slight us before five classes of people: namely, (1) our rivals, (2) those whom we admire, (3) those whom we wish to admire us, (4) those for whom we feel reverence, (5) those who feel reverence for us: if any one slights us before such persons, we feel particularly angry. Again, we feel angry with those who slight us in connexion with what we are as honourable men bound to champion—our parents, children, wives, or subjects. And with those who do not return a favour, since such a slight is unjustifiable. Also with those who reply with humorous levity when we are speaking seriously, for such behaviour indicates contempt. And with those who treat us less well than they treat everybody else; it is another mark of contempt that they should think we do not deserve what every one else deserves. Forgetfulness, too, causes anger, as when our own names are forgotten, trifling as this may be; since forgetfulness is felt to be another sign that we are being slighted; it is due to negligence, and to neglect us is to slight us.

The persons with whom we feel anger, the frame of mind in which we feel it, and the reasons why we feel it, have now all been set forth. Clearly the orator will have to speak so as to bring his hearers into a frame of mind that will dispose them to anger, and to represent his adversaries as open to such charges and possessed of such qualities as do make people angry.

Since growing calm is the opposite of growing angry, and calmness the opposite of anger, we must ascertain in what frames of mind men are calm, towards whom they feel calm, and by what means they are made so. Growing calm may be defined as a settling down or quieting of anger. Now we get angry with those who slight us; and since slighting is a voluntary act, it is plain that we feel calm towards those who do nothing of the kind, or who do or seem to do it involuntarily. Also towards those who intended to do the opposite of what they did do. Also towards those who treat themselves as they have treated us: since no one can be supposed to slight himself. Also towards those who admit their fault and are sorry: since we accept their grief at what they have done as satisfaction, and cease to be angry. The punishment of servants shows this: those who contradict us and deny their offence we punish all the more, but we cease to be incensed against those who agree that they deserved their punishment. The reason is that it is shameless to deny what is obvious, and those who are shameless towards us slight us and show contempt for us: anyhow, we do not feel shame before those of whom we are thoroughly contemptuous. Also we feel calm towards those who humble themselves before us and do not gainsay us; we feel that they thus admit themselves our inferiors, and inferiors feel fear, and nobody can slight any one so long as he feels afraid of him. That our anger ceases towards those who humble themselves before us is shown even by dogs, who do not bite people when they sit down. We also feel calm towards those who are serious when we are serious, because then we feel that we are treated seriously and not contemptuously. Also towards those who have done us more kindnesses than we have done them. Also towards those who pray to us and beg for mercy, since they humble themselves by doing so. Also towards those who do not insult or mock at or slight any one at all, or not any worthy person or any one like ourselves. In general, the things that make us calm may be inferred by seeing what the opposites are of those that make us angry. We are not angry with people we fear or respect, as long as we fear or respect them; you cannot be afraid of a person and also at the same time angry with him. Again, we feel no anger, or comparatively little, with those who have done what they did through anger; we do not feel that they have done it from a wish to slight us, for no one slights people when angry with them, since slighting is painless, and anger is painful. Nor do we grow angry with those who reverence us.

As to the frame of mind that makes people calm, it is plainly the opposite to that which makes them angry, as when they are amusing themselves or laughing or feasting; when they are feeling prosperous or successful or satisfied; when, in fine, they are enjoying freedom from pain, or inoffensive pleasure, or justifiable hope. Also when time has passed and their anger is no longer fresh, for time puts an end to anger. And vengeance previously taken on one person puts an end to even greater anger felt against another person. Hence Philocrates, being asked by some one, at a time when the public was angry with him, 'Why don't you defend yourself?' did right to reply, 'The time is not yet.' 'Why, when *is* the time?' 'When I see some one else calumniated.' For men become calm when they have spent their anger on somebody else. This happened in the case of Ergophilus: though the people were more irritated against him than against Callisthenes, they acquitted him because they had condemned Callisthenes to death the day before. Again, men become calm if they have convicted the offender; or if he has already suffered worse things than they in their anger would have themselves inflicted upon him; for they feel as if they were already avenged. Or if they feel that they themselves are in the wrong and are suffering justly (for anger is not excited by what is just), since men no longer think then that they are suffering without justification; and anger, as we have seen, means this. Hence we ought always to inflict a preliminary punishment in words: if that is done, even slaves are less aggrieved by the actual punishment. We also feel calm if we think that the offender will not see that he is punished on our account and because of the way he has treated us. For anger has to do with individuals. This is plain from the definition. Hence the poet has well written:

Say that it was Odysseus, sacker of cities,

implying that Odysseus would not have considered himself avenged unless the Cyclops perceived both by whom and for what he had been blinded. Consequently we do not get angry with any one who cannot be aware of our anger, and in particular we cease to be angry with people once they are dead, for we feel that the worst has been done to them, and that they will neither feel pain nor anything else that we in our anger aim at making them feel. And therefore the poet has well made Apollo say, in order to put a stop to the anger of Achilles against the dead Hector,

For behold in his fury he doeth despite to the senseless clay.

It is now plain that when you wish to calm others you must draw upon these lines of argument; you must put your hearers into the corresponding frame of mind, and represent those with whom they are angry as formidable, or as worthy of reverence, or as benefactors, or as involuntary agents, or as much distressed at what they have done.

6. Charles Taylor

In this chapter, Charles Taylor examines in detail the nature of psychological explanation. By way of introduction, let us consider again the three major types of explanation or causality attributed by Aristotle to the psyche, and some current views regarding the validity or usefulness of each type. In order to have a concrete example before us, imagine the following situation. You and three companions are walking down the street and you see an acquaintance, John, angrily striking another person, Bill. You turn to your companions and ask them why John should do such a thing, and you receive the following answers:

1. John is a very hostile person.
2. John wants Bill to stop annoying him (in the future).
3. Bill has insulted John (in the past).

The first of these answers is called a dispositional explanation, because it refers to a disposition (hostility) on John's part to respond aggressively. In the Aristotelian scheme of causation, a dispositional explanation is one that appeals to formal causes. It will be recalled that Aristotle's concept of form includes not only the essential characteristic of an object—its "whatness"—but also the capacity or disposition to respond—its "first grade of actuality." The second answer explains John's behavior in teleological terms, i.e., it appeals to the goal or end result (final cause) that John wishes to achieve by striking Bill. Finally, the third answer refers to an efficient cause, namely, the stimulus (insult) that provoked John's aggressive response.

In an everyday context, any one (or all three) of these answers might be accepted as an explanation of John's behavior, depending on the situation and the background information already available to the inquirer. But are they all of equal value from a scientific point of view, or is one type of explanation basic to the others? Many contemporary psychologists reject dispositional and teleological explanations as scientifically unfruitful. With regard to dispositional explanations, for example, B. F. Skinner has argued:

> When we say that a man eats because he is hungry, smokes a great deal because he has the tobacco habit, fights because of the instinct of pugnacity, behaves brilliantly because of his intelligence, or plays the piano well because of his musical ability, we seem to be referring to causes. But on analysis these phrases prove to be merely redundant descriptions. A single set of facts is described by the two statements: "He eats" and "He is hungry." A single set of facts is described by the two statements: "He smokes a great deal" and "He has the smoking habit." A single set of facts is described by the two statements: "He plays well" and "He has musical ability." The practice of explaining one statement in terms of the other is dangerous because it suggests that we have found the cause and therefore need search no further. Moreover, such terms as "hunger," "habit," and "intelligence" convert what are essentially the properties of a process or relation into what appear to be things. Thus we are unprepared for the properties eventually to be discovered in the behavior itself and continue to look for something which may not exist.[1]

Teleological explanations have been even more frowned on than those that utilize dispositional variables. Clark Hull, perhaps the most influential American psychologist during the 1940s and 1950s, provides a good illustration of the attempt to derive purposeful behavior from principles that refer to nothing but efficient causes (prior movements within the body, or, in Hull's terms, "fractional anticipatory goal responses"). Hull has expressed his general position as follows:

> An ideally adequate theory even of so-called purposive behavior ought, therefore, to begin with colorless movement and mere receptor impulses as such, and from these build up step by step both adaptive behavior and maladaptive behavior. The present approach does not deny the molar reality of purposive acts (as opposed to movement), of intelligence, of insight, of goals, of intents, of striving, or of value: on the contrary, we insist upon the genuineness of these forms of behavior. We hope ultimately to show the logical right to the use of such concepts by deducing them as secondary principles from more elementary objective primary principles. Once they have been derived, we shall not

[1] B. F. Skinner, *Science and human behavior*. New York: Macmillan, 1953, p. 31, with permission.

only understand them better but be able to use them with more detailed effectiveness, particularly in the deduction of the movements which mediate (or fail to mediate) goal attainment, than would be the case if we had accepted teleological sequences at the outset as gross, unanalyzed (and unanalyzable) wholes.[2]

Aristotle obviously believed that explanations in terms of formal and final causes were not only scientifically valid, but also necessary for the explanation of behavior. Who was right on this issue, Aristotle or Skinner and Hull? This question cannot be answered easily. It requires an examination of what is meant by explanation in general, and scientific explanation in particular. In this selection, Charles Taylor undertakes such an examination. As Taylor points out, the view that efficient causes (and mechanistic types of explanations) are somehow scientifically more respectable than the others is based more on prejudice than on fact. The prejudice may ultimately turn out to be justified, but the issue can be decided only on the basis of empirical evidence and not by a priori pronouncements about what scientific explanation really is. And as the empirical evidence mounts, it is becoming increasingly likely that Aristotle may have been more right than wrong on this particular issue.

[2] C. L. Hull, *Principles of behavior.* New York: Appleton, 1943, pp. 25-26, with permission.

The Explanation of Purposive Behaviour

I

'Explanation' has many meanings, and there would seem to be no common ground between its use in some ordinary contexts, and its role in science. But the scientific sense is continuous with at least one common meaning in ordinary speech. Here 'explain' very often means 'to make what appears strange and outlandish understandable'. This is often done by relating what appears to stand outside the normal course of events to this course in another way. Thus, if someone does something which is strange or shocking, we 'explain' it by describing the context in a way which makes the action understandable given current conceptions of human motivation. Someone suddenly gets angry in the course of a discussion; we ask why? The event is explained when it is pointed out that a subject mentioned is taken as a reflection on the man's honour, or that his convictions are very strong on this subject and he cannot stand its being spoken about lightly, or something of the kind.

Explanation involves here, therefore, bringing the strange back to a place in the normal course of events. Something analogous holds of explanation in a scientific context. But here what corresponds to the 'normal course' is established by the explanation and not already received in ordinary conceptions. We usually claim to have explained an event when we give an antecedent from which it follows; not indeed *any* antecedent, but one which has a certain saliency: either because it is the one which we can alter most easily, or because it is the one which varies most often, the other conditions being standing conditions, or for some other reason. But in a scientific context, we have come to demand something more: we expect the antecedent condition to be singled out in concepts which show the connection between this outcome which we are explaining and a host of others. Typically, for instance, the antecedent conditions might be expressed in a statement attributing certain values to key variables, which had they had other values, would have determined other predictable outcomes. This element is perhaps always present, even in

From C. Taylor, The explanation of purposive behavior. In R. Boyer and F. Cioffi, Eds., *Explanations in the Behavioral Sciences*. Cambridge: The University Press, 1970, pp. 49–51, 53–75, 78–79. Reprinted with permission.

explanations of the most rudimentary kind. If we explain that a bridge has collapsed because of the weakness of one of its supports, we obviously understand that a stronger support would have kept it up, *ceteris paribus*. What the progress of science adds here is exactness, the ability to define the antecedent conditions of breakdown more exactly, and also to predict a great number of other outcomes more finely.

But what it also patently has added is explanation at greater depth. To pursue the above example, the progress of scientific enquiry not only adds exactness to the common sense explanation by giving a measure of strength, but also sheds light on the determinants of strength. This accomplishes more than simply adding to our criteria for measuring strength, though it certainly does that. It also *explains* why the original criteria are criteria of strength; that is, it accounts for the correlation between strength and the properties by which we originally assessed it. For instance, let us say that we start off estimating the strength of possible materials roughly as we go about building the bridge, by, say, the type of material: this alloy is stronger than that metal, and so on. When, however, we come to understand something about molecular structure, then we are in a position to explain the original rough correlations by which we operated. But, in line with what was said above, we consider this explanation a scientifically satisfactory one partly because it shows the connection between the outcomes we are explaining—here the correlations between certain materials and certain strengths—and a whole host of others. We know more than that material M has molecular structure S and therefore a certain degree of strength. We know also more exactly what modifications in it would alter its strength, more exactly therefore how it differs from other materials whose strength is different. And this means, of course, that we can go beyond the original repertoire of materials with which we were operating at first; for the new language of molecular structure enables us to give the formula for new materials as yet non-existent.

Scientific explanation therefore has two important properties: it gives the antecedent conditions of the explicandum in terms of a set of factors which make evident its connection with others, which makes clear with some exactitude what would need to be changed for other outcomes to eventuate; and it also is capable of building in tiers, that is the correlations which explain at one level can be taken as explicanda and explained at another. The result is that the progress of science sees more and more outcomes connected by the network of explanatory theory. For, as a set of connected correlations are themselves explained at a deeper level, they are connected with a wider class. Scientific theory thus becomes more wide-ranging as research progresses; it brings under the same framework widely separated phenomena; it homogenizes, one might say, what at first appears different.

Thus the laws of Kepler by which one can explain on one level certain aspects of planetary behaviour are explained in turn by Newton in terms of the law of attraction and certain initial velocities. In this way the regularities that Kepler charted are shown to be one case of a broader class of regularities to which Newton's laws also apply. Newton can be said to have explained Kepler's laws because he has shown the connection to a broader range of phenomena by singling out the factors alteration in which would alter the behaviour of the system in known ways; or, in other words, because he has singled out the variables such that, where they are found to have other values, a different sort of system is predictably found to be in operation. The same set of variables which enables us to account for the movement of the planets—mass, distance, velocity—enable us to account also for the revolutions of the moon, of artificial satellites, and so on. They also help us to account for the movements of bodies in systems of a quite different kind. Newton's account homogenizes, as it were, what at first appears different. . . .

This idea of a 'normal course' of events sometimes enables us to make a non-arbitrary distinction between necessary and sufficient conditions. As was mentioned above, this distinction is sometimes made in ordinary contexts: one condition is singled out as the 'cause' or explanation, and the others are seen as necessary conditions. The 'cause' or sufficient condition is singled out either because it is the one we can bring about, or because all the other conditions are considered to be part of the normal state of affairs, and only this one different (e.g. a bridge falls down because of a weak support; but it also falls because of a car going over it; this, however, is part of the 'normal' conditions for the bridge, and therefore counts as a necessary condition), or because the rest are standing conditions and the 'cause' is an event (from this point of view the cause of the bridge falling is the car that drove into it). But in the case of scientific explanation, we often have a less arbitrary criterion. The class of events which are explained by a given set of factors and thus connected may form a system or systems, in this sense that the set of correlations involved may hold only if certain boundary conditions are fulfilled. The boundary conditions may be simply the relative independence of the system from outside interference: thus Kepler's laws apply only in the absence of some large foreign body traversing our solar system, such as is regularly depicted in science fiction novels. Or they may be some positive state conditions, such as, for example, an organism's requiring such and such atmospheric, climatic, etc., conditions to function. But in either case the outcome concerned is contingent on the boundary conditions' holding as well as on the antecedent's being present. But we distinguish the antecedent here as cause or sufficient condition since it is what embodies the explanatory force; it connects the outcome concerned to others, and allows us to predict and create precise alterations in outcome. The boundary conditions, on the other hand, are connected indiscriminately with a whole host of outcomes, all those which are explained by variations in antecedent conditions within the system. We thus speak of these conditions as necessary. The title 'cause' or 'sufficient condition' of a given outcome is reserved for the antecedent which selectively explains this outcome, although within the bounds of the necessary conditions, which are, however, shared with others.

II

The search for a conceptual framework, for a concept of the 'normal' course, is no less vital in the sciences of behaviour than it is in the physical sciences. Only in the former field it seems to have met with much less success. One can describe the state of disarray and contention in which we find the sciences of man—whether in the field of political science, sociology, anthropology or psychology—as arising from deep disagreements over the conceptual frameworks which are appropriate. Each of the above fields is the scene of several rival 'approaches', no one of which seems to be able to establish itself to the satisfaction of all workers in the field as the definitive framework.

In psychology, one of the major questions concerns the validity for scientific purposes of the type of framework implicit in our ordinary concept of action, an explanation in terms of concepts of the range of 'purpose', 'goal', 'meaning'. Concepts of this range are central to some forms of explanation (e.g. psychoanalysis), but have been vigorously rejected by others (behaviourism).

The form of explanation which we can call explanation in terms of purpose can perhaps be more closely defined in terms of two principal features: (1) explanation of behaviour takes a teleological form, and (2) explanation is sometimes cast in terms of the way the agent sees himself and his situation, of 'the meaning' that they have for him. Let us examine each of these features in turn.

It is fairly obvious that our ordinary form of explanation of behaviour in terms of action is teleological in form. This is not to say that all ordinary explanations of behaviour as action point to some end at which the action is aimed, but that all such explanations carry the implication that acting for the sake of an end is a fundamental feature of human behaviour (for further discussion of this cf. Taylor, 1964, Chap. 2). Now a teleological form of explanation can be characterized in this way: where the behaviour is explained by the goal to which it is aimed, in other words, where it is explained by that 'for the sake of which' it occurs.

Now it seems to be a widespread belief among researchers in the field of academic psychology that this form of explanation is inherently non-empirical, that is, untestable; that it involves an absurdity, like explaining an event by another one subsequent to it (which would certainly make prediction rather difficult), or postulating an unobservable force. They have been encouraged in these beliefs by philosophers of science of the positivist persuasion. But a little reflection should show that this view is ill-founded. That behaviour is a function of what it serves to bring about, rather than some other unrelated factor, is a fact (if it is one) about the form of the antecedent; it is not a claim to dispense with an antecedent altogether or the invocation of an unobservable one. An explanation is teleological if the events to be explained are accounted for in this way: if G is the goal 'for the sake of which' events are said to occur, B the event to be explained, and S the state of affairs obtaining prior to B, then B is explained by the fact that S was such that it required B for G to come about. In other words, a teleological explanation is defined as such by the form of the antecedent, a form in which the occurrence of the event to be explained is made contingent on the situation's being such that this event would bring about the end in question.[1]

Now it is evident that an antecedent of this kind is both open to observation, and open to observation *ex ante* (thus permitting

[1] One can perhaps add: that this event *and this event only* would bring about the goal. This stronger expression is equivalent to the formulation above: a situation where B is *required* for G. But although the stronger form is usually appropriate, since we are dealing with beings with a limited repertoire (as we shall see below), the weak form must be mentioned as a possibility: if there are several possibile occurrences in a given situation which would bring about the goal, then the teleological explanation making reference to *this* goal cannot account for the fact that one is chosen rather than another. The teleological explanation can thus be only partial; it yields us a necessary but not sufficient condition. Of course, the selection among possible 'routes' to the goal may be accounted for by another goal which one serves more than the others (parsimony of effort, or custom, or dignity, or whatever). Because with animate beings, it can plausibly be claimed that a unique selection of this kind usually takes place, through limitation of repertoire, or through some norm, I shall go on using the strong formulation (that B is required for G) in what follows.

prediction). Of course, it makes *reference* to the end which will occur later, and reference, too, to the explicandum (and to a relation between it and the end). But this is not the same thing as making the end the antecedent, or defining the antecedent in terms of the consequent, or any other such vices of explanation. That the situation is such that B is required for G can be established independently of discovering whether B has occurred. It can be objected that, defined in this way, teleological explanation ceases to be a distinct form; for if the teleological antecedent is an observable state of affairs, that B is required for G, then surely it can also be described in other terms, terms which made no reference to the event explained or the end. Let us call this type of description an 'intrinsic' characterization. Then for any state of affairs which one can describe as requiring B for G an intrinsic characterization can be found. But if the situation so characterized is taken as the antecedent, then we no longer have a teleological explanation. Hence we cannot claim that this latter is a distinct form with a different empirical content.

But this objection is fallacious. The antecedent condition in any given causal sequence can be described in an indefinite number of ways. But that does not mean that we can indiscriminately characterize the situation described in any of these ways 'The antecedent'. First, and most obvious, there are descriptions which pick out the features of the situation which are causally irrelevant. An accident occurs because the driver is drunk. But the state of affairs where the driver is drunk is also that state of affairs where he is talking too much. But this does not mean that the state of affairs where he is talking too much is the antecedent of the accident. We could imagine a case in which we would call it the antecedent, where he was talking too much and thus not paying attention and thus didn't see the sign, and so on. But this is a separate case from that where his reaction time was impaired through drunkenness or where drinking too much made him foolhardy, and *this* is how the accident occurred, although his being drunk also had other results such as making him tell you his life story. In this case his loquaciousness, although causally linked to drunkenness as an effect, is not causally relevant to the accident.

But, of course, those who propose to translate out teleological antecedents undoubtedly have in mind to choose intrinsic characterizations which are causally relevant. But this is where a problem arises: not all characterizations of an antecedent which pick out its causally relevant aspects are on the same footing. For they differ in the degree to which they yield a functional relation valid in general or over a wide range of instances. Thus the state of affairs where the driver is drunk is also the state of affairs where he has imbibed the greater parts of the contents of a bottle with a label marked 'Canadian Club'. This latter description undoubtedly characterizes the antecedent in a causally relevant way, unlike the reference to loquaciousness above. But it is not as adequate as a description of the antecedent. For it describes this situation in a way which is not as widely generalizable as the original description in terms of drunkenness: in the next village housewives use old Canadian Club bottles to keep fruit juice in, other men get drunk and have accidents after drinking gin or scotch, some men can drink this much and not get drunk, and so on, and so on.

But what is important here is not the generality. This is the corollary of something else, namely that some descriptions offer a more basic explanation than others. An explanation A is more basic than another B, as we have seen in the previous section, when the correlations invoked in B can in turn be explained by those invoked in A together with certain initial conditions. The correlations of B are shown thus to be a special case of the correlations in A. Thus with the accident case above: the explanatory correlation involved in the description of the antecedent as 'his having drunk the contents of a bottle labelled "Canadian Club" ' must itself be explained by the explanatory correlation involved in the description of the cause as 'his being drunk'. In other words, his drinking the contents of this bottle led to his having the accident only because of his being drunk led to the accident (more basic correlation) and his drinking the contents etc., made him drunk (initial conditions).

Thus we can see that not all descriptions of a causal antecedent, among those which pick it out as causally relevant, are on the same footing; some are more basic than others, and we can say, for instance, that the event characterized as B (less basic characterization) is only an antecedent of the explicandum because in the circumstances its being B is also its being A (more basic characterization). Thus we can hardly claim that the two descriptions are interchangeable. The fact then that a teleological antecedent also bears an intrinsic description, even an intrinsic description which picks it out as causally relevant, proves nothing by itself. We still have to know which description is more basic. The intrinsic one may apply to the antecedent of a given event in one case, or even in a wide class of cases, but it may nevertheless be that this is only the case because in these circumstances having the intrinsic characterization amounts to having the teleological one. This may be the case, or it may be the other way around. But the important point is that this cannot be determined *a priori.* Thus although we might admit it to be true *a priori* that for any state of affairs which we can describe as requiring B for G an intrinsic characterization be found, this is utterly irrelevant to the point at issue. What is relevant is which explanation is more basic, and this can only be discovered empirically.

Which of the two is more basic is a matter of which yields a really general functional relation, one in terms of which the other can be explained as a special case. It may be possible to establish this by seeing that one applies to cases where the other does not. But even where the limits of experimentation make a discovery of this kind impossible, we may establish their relationship by seeing that the set of correlations to which one belongs and from which it can be derived can be used to account for (and perhaps also manipulate) the phenomenon over a wide range, whereas the set to which the other belongs yields only a random collection of *ad hoc* relations. In other words, the first is part of a system which can be used to account for variations in the phenomena which the second cannot explain; this is enough to show that the former offers the more basic explanation. For the set of *ad hoc* regularities parallel the individual correlations of the more basic system of laws. But since these latter should be seen as special cases of this system the former must as well.

After weighing this objection, we are in a better position to define what is at stake in the question about frameworks of explanation in psychology. The question whether we should use a framework based on explanation by purpose involves the question whether we should allow a teleological mode of explanation. But this means surely, whether we should allow that the most basic explanation is teleological. No one can quarrel with the thesis that out of human and animal behaviour we can abstract regularities at *some* level which are teleological in form. This is what we do all the time in ordinary speech and have been doing for some hundreds of thousands of years. The question is whether these regularities can in turn be accounted for by others of a non-teleological sort. And this turns on the question whether the teleological regularities can be explained by non-teleological laws which account for a wider range of phenomena, for instance by allowing us to predict similar outcomes even when the normal teleological antecedent isn't present, but the 'intrinsic' one is (e.g. a stimulus, or condition of the brain or nervous system), or else by offering a system permitting greater prediction and control, from which the teleological regularities can be derived as disconnected *ad hoc* connections. Or whether, on the contrary, the relations are not reversed, and the teleological laws provide a wider explanation.

Of course, in applying teleological explanation to animate beings account has to be taken of the fact that all species, even man, are limited in some way, that for each species there is a certain shape of the universe of possible behaviours which we can call its repertoire. Thus, in saying that B is required for G, account is implicitly taken of the limitations of the repertoire. In the abstract, there may be some more efficient way of getting G, but B is the way of getting it which lies within the capacities of the being in question. This cannot be made the ground for an objection against teleological explanation, that it inadequately characterizes the response. In an abstract sense this is true. But there is no incoherence in the claim that once the repertoire is given we can only account for the selection of the response which occurs by invoking an antecedent of teleological form. In terms of the distinction of the previous section we can see the behaviour of the animal in question as a system, where the limits of the repertoire constitute part of the boundary or necessary conditions, and where in consequence that B is required for G is a sufficient condition for B's occurring. And, indeed, we have no choice but to look at things this way, if no other law-like correlations can be found to account for the occurrence of B and other behaviours.

But there is a second and just as important restriction to be made in applying teleological explanation to animate beings, and that is that we have to take account of the way that the agent sees the situation. We come then to the second main feature of explanation by purpose. Plainly, explanations of human behaviour, for instance, can only be teleological if we interpret 'requiring B for G' as 'requiring B for G in the view of the agent'. That an action is required in fact for a given goal will not bring it about unless it is seen to be such; and many actions can be accounted for in terms of the goals of the agents concerned which in no wise really serve these goals. Thus an important part of our explanations of human behaviour consist in making actions intelligible by showing how the agent saw the situation, what meaning it had for him.

It is obvious that on a lower level an analogous principle holds for animal behaviour, or at least for that animal behaviour which is phylogenetically high enough for us to be tempted to account for it in teleological terms. But there is still a qualitative difference in the importance of this principle when we come to the human level. Men through language can differ in culture to the point that recognizable human goals, which are in a sense universal—not only hunger, sex, etc., but also the need for self-respect, human companionship, and so on—take on characteristic forms in different cultures. Their meaning is different for men from different backgrounds. Thus, the set of values which are important and in terms of which men see their situation and themselves are different and often untranslatable from one culture to another. Translating words from a foreign language as 'honour', 'integrity', 'sainthood' and so on may create more misunderstanding than comprehension of another people.

Explanation in terms of purpose therefore involves taking into account the conceptual forms through which agents understand and come to grips with their world. That people think of their environment in certain concepts, that is, use certain modes of classification, is an element in accounting for what they do. Indeed, it can be said to define what they do. For if we think of actions as defined by the purposes or intentions which inform them, then we cannot understand man's actions without knowing the concepts in which they frame their intentions.

This principle is valid whether or not we explain men's behaviour in concepts which they would understand or accept. We may show that much of what men think of their own behaviour is not only untrue, but the result of a powerful drive towards self-deception or repression. But this is to appeal from how men say that they see their situation to how they really see it; it is not to make this dimension irrelevant. From this point of view, therefore, psychoanalysis is a development of explanation by purpose. For recognizing that much thought and motivation is unconscious, it accounts for this in terms of goals; indeed, repression itself is accounted for teleologically; and thus a central aspect of psychoanalytic explanation concerns the meanings that events, situations, symbols, have for the agent, even if these are unconscious.

This accounts in part for the suspicion with which psychoanalysis is regarded among academic psychologists. For there is a strong resistance to explanation by purpose in these circles. This springs from a deep-lying complex of views about scientific method, observation and explanation, according to which only explanations by efficient causes can be accepted, and these must not make use of any intentional properties (properties of the way in which a reality is seen by a subject). This outlook thus rejects both teleological explanation and any reference to the meaning of the situation for the agent; it rejects explanation by purpose root and branch.

The historical roots of this view are complex; modern academic psychology draws its hostility to teleology partly from the scientific tradition of modern times. Behaviour theorists seem to be hypnotized by the victory of Galileo and Newton over the teleological physics of Aristotle, and seem to aspire to achieve the same thing in philosophy.[2] But they are also opposed to explanation by purpose because it seems to involve having recourse to the unobservable. Here we can see the influence of positivism and its ancestor empiricism. For empiricism backs up the rejection of explanation by purpose in two ways: the notion that all knowledge is based on impressions which come to the mind from outside leads first to a dualistic notion of body and mind as in causal interaction (for the body, too, is 'external' reality *qua* spatial), and second gives rise to a notion of observation according to which it is difficult to give a sense to observing an action as against observing the corresponding bodily movement (for they cannot be thought to cause distinct 'impressions' on the mind). In both these ways empiricism gave support to the view that the mental could not be directly observed; it could only be inferred from physical external behaviour.

This is the dichotomy from which behaviourism starts. Once we have a dualist notion of body–mind interaction, we only need to suppress one term and we have behaviorism. At this point, all the different sources of the behaviourist orientation give each other mutual support. How can we take account of intentional properties (how the agent sees things) if this involves taking account of totally unobservable entities? Moreover, entities whose only function can be to interfere with the only form of law-like regularity we can observe? 'There is no separate soul or life-force to stick a finger into the brain now and then and make neural cells do what they would not do otherwise' (Hebb, 1949, p. xiii). In short one cannot accept intentional properties because this would involve some strange interactionism. But if one cannot accept intentional qualities, then obviously one cannot accept teleological explanation, for this can only be applied to the goals and situation as envisaged by the agent, as we have seen above. Thus all causality is efficient. But then reciprocally, if all causality is efficient, any attempt to explain behaviour by purpose can only be interpreted as the introduction of another efficient cause, viz. 'purpose'. But

---

[2] But it may be that the lesson which the seventeenth century has to teach us is precisely the opposite: not to try to cram all reality into the same mould; then men learnt not to treat inanimate nature as though it was animate, now perhaps we have to learn the inverse. More generally, we can learn from the opposition to Galileo how readily men can fail to grasp empirical reality because their philosophical system hasn't allowed a place for it.

this is not among the efficient cause that we observe, therefore it must be unobservable; moreover, it must be operating in addition to the causes we observe so it must be in interaction with them. But this is necessarily an unverifiable hypothesis, and of no interest to science. If follows that scientific psychology cannot take account of purposes, and hence of the goals that agents seek and the ways that they envisage them; that is, it has no use for intentional properties. 'If one is to be consistent, there is no room . . . for a mysterious agent that is defined as not physical and yet has physical effects . . .' (Hebb, 1949). We are back where we started.

The behaviourist view of science is a kind of closed circle, a self-induced illusion of necessity. For there is no self-evidence to the proposition that the mental is the unobservable. In a perfectly valid sense I can be said to observe another man's anger, sadness, his eagerness to please, his sense of his own dignity, his uncertainty, love for his girl, or whatever. I can find out these things about another sometimes by just observing him in the common sense of that term, sometimes by listening to what he says. But, in this latter case, I am not leaning on the fruits of some dubious and uncheckable 'introspection' on his part. For what people say about themselves is never in principle and rarely in practice uncheckable. Nor, as we have seen, does any necessity attach to the proposition that teleological explanation is non-empirical, unverifiable or absurd. Quite the contrary. It follows that teleological explanation in terms of intentional properties requires no appeal to an interactionism involving the unobservable.

In fact the idea of interactionism is closely linked to behaviourism. It is the alibi, the only other ontological hypothesis which is admitted, which by its very absurdity gives behaviourism its unchallengeable metaphysical credentials. The hidden assumption of behaviourism is that only these two possibilities are open. But this cannot be accepted a priori. The premisses from which this assumption could be derived are far from self-evident, as we have seen. The choice lies rather between a form of explanation in terms of efficient causes and non-intentional properties, such as is exhibited by the different behaviourist theories, and some form of explanation by purpose as we see, e.g. with psychoanalysis. The issue between these two can only be decided by the evidence; it cannot be foreclosed by a priori considerations about scientific method, which are so reminiscent of the pleas of the schoolmen of the seventeenth century that the new physics just couldn't be right.

III

Let us examine more closely the debate between these two forms of explanation in modern psychology, and see at what stage it has arrived. As was said above, academic psychology, in Anglo-Saxon countries anyway, has largely been working on the hypothesis that explanation must be in terms of efficient causes and non-intentional properties (let us call this the 'mechanist' orientation, for short). This has been the case for at least the last half-century.

But this approach has taken a particular form, known generally as 'behaviourism', whose aim has been to establish such an explanation at the level of 'molar' phenomena, that is, gross elements of the environment and bodily movement. This may seem strange in that the original impulse for mechanism, in the seventeenth and eighteenth centuries, springs rather from seeing the human organism as a machine, and therefore tends naturally to a mechanistic physiology, an attempt to trace out the connections on the level of the nervous system. If behaviourism eschewed this path, it was partly because of the great difficulty of the enterprise since so little was known (and is known) about the finer workings of the nervous system and the brain. To which was added the additional incentive that what came to be known contradicted the simpler mechanistic models, like that of the 'reflex arc'. For instance, the work of Lashley (e.g. Lashley, 1929) seemed to show that for many functions the brain operated in a complex way which couldn't be reduced to the linking of an afferent to an efferent stimulation. Moreover, many functions couldn't be identified with a specific set of connections in the brain. In face of this, it was perhaps normal that psychologists should abandon the track of mechanistic physiology as premature, or at least as not likely to yield immediate results, and should attempt to establish a mechanistic behaviour theory on the gross observable level of environment and movement. It remained, of course, an article of faith that this would eventually be shown to be derived from a set of mechanistic laws on the physiological level, but meanwhile psychology would be getting on with the job of bringing behaviour into the domain of Science.

The enterprise was undertaken with a quite extraordinary lack of doubt as to its feasibility. There were, of course, differences of approach. Not all theorists went as far as Skinner in eschewing all reference to inner processes. Some preferred the line of Hull who allowed recourse to 'intervening variables', which, however, remained unrelated in any but the most incidental and speculative way to any physiological embodiment. But all were convinced that a mechanistic science of behaviour on the molar level was possible. I say that the lack of doubt was extraordinary, for a minute's reflection will show that even if we grant the behaviourists' *a priori* thesis concerning the rightness of mechanism (and we have seen in the last section that there is no reason to grant this), there is still no guarantee that the mechanistic laws can be discovered *at a specific level*. There is no rule in force in the universe which says that the laws governing a given range of things must be discoverable at any level of analysis, and using any range of concepts. Indeed, precisely the opposite is the case, and the crucial step in the development of any science is the discovery of the conceptual framework in terms of which explanatory laws can be discovered. It may well be that what we know about intentional properties can be fully accounted for in laws applying exclusively to non-intentional properties: but it may also be that this can only be done on the level of neurophysiology. Even the mechanist faith cannot assure us that it can be done just by watching rats in a maze.

And the sequel has shown this confidence in a molar mechanist science to be misplaced. The result can only be described as a failure. Whatever the ultimate truth of the mechanist thesis, it is now becoming pretty clear that it cannot be established on this level. The attempt was to link the environment, characterized non-intentionally as the 'stimulus', and behaviour, characterized non-intentionally in terms of movement as the 'response', in a series of law-like correlations. Since obviously the relation between stimuli and responses changes over time, notably with learning and with changes in motivation, stimulus-response connections were in turn to be shown as functions of behaviour history. In the case of learning this meant a function of the responses to stimuli the animal had emitted in the past (or a function of the responses to stimuli in a context of reward, according to the law of Effect). The motivational condition of the animal was held to be a function of his history of gratification and deprivation. In this way, all the different dimensions of behaviour could be coped with while remaining in the purview of efficient causation and non-intentional properties, as Hull put it, 'colourless movement and mere receptor impulses as such' (Hull, 1943, p. 25).

But the trouble was that this programme broke down at just about every point.

1. The phenomena of 'insight' as reported by Gestaltists, and also by a large number of other students of normal behaviour, and the phenomena of 'improvisation' in a new situation, as shown, e.g.

by the experiments of Tolman and his associates, make it just about impossible to exhibit the behaviour resulting from learning as a function of past responses to stimuli. Of course there are attempts to account for the element of adaptive novelty by means of *ad hoc* hypotheses, of which the best known are Hull's 'stimulus acts'. But apart from the fact that no consistent role was ever devised for these unobservable stimuli which could account for all the phenomena concerned,[3] the frequency with which recourse must be had to them begins to raise questions about the criteria for success and failure of molar science. For being without any known physiological basis, inner stimulus acts are fully as unobservable as the 'ideas' of introspectionist yesteryear, that is we come to know of their operation in exactly the way in which we ordinarily see that an animal has 'caught on' or 'learnt to get around the maze', and so on. The set of hypotheses about these inner stimuli add in no way to our ability to explain and predict the phenomena; indeed, the need to have recourse more and more to hypotheses of this kind is itself a symptom, as with the Ptolemaic system of old, that we are on the wrong track. 'Insight', that is the ability to see new relationships and behavioural possibilities in the situation, and some generalized knowledge of the environment seem to be irreducible facts of human and (higher) animal behaviour on the molar level.

2. The notion of 'stimulus' itself cannot fill the role for which it is cast. It is meant to be a physically defined feature of the environment, or perhaps a physiologically defined 'receptor discharge'; but in fact the matter cannot be left here. For, as one would suspect, animals can be trained to react differentially to all sorts of features of the environment, not only to its elements, but to its configuration, to the number of elements rather than their shape, size, etc.,[4] and even to complex relations.[5] Thus the animal's response to a given environment is not a function of the same elements all the time, but the way in which it is relevant to his behaviour can change. Or, as we would say in ordinary speech, the way the environment is seen by the animal changes. Of course, behaviour theorists have responded to these 'discoveries' by a set of hypotheses concerning the organization and selection of stimuli.[6] But these, too, raise questions concerning the viability of molar theory. Since even a casual inventory of the problem will

---

[3] For the confusions involved, cf. Deutsch, 1960, and also Taylor, 1964, Chap. 8.
[4] Cf. experiments of O. Koehler, reported in Thorpe, 1956.
[5] Such as the matching experiments of Nissen show, e.g. Nissen, 1953.
[6] Cf. Nissen's own comments, 1953; also Broadbent, 1958 and Deutsch & Deutsch, 1963.

show that the operation of selection and organization involved in perception is immensely complicated, and connected with so many other dimensions of mental function, motivation, interest, past experience, novelty, and so on, it is clear that some simple mechanism[7] will not do. Moreover, we are unlikely to unearth the mechanism (if there is one) by free invention, without careful study of perception itself, and some knowledge of the physiology involved. For we are unlikely to be able to account for the operation of this mechanism in molar terms as we could, for instance, a simple mechanism of selection between different elements. It is obvious that the problem of accounting for 'the way the animal sees the environment' goes way beyond the selection of different parts for saliency to the very structuring of the perceptual field into 'parts' in the first place, and this cannot be a simple function of the environment, but involves an important contribution of central processes. Besides, what we know of the operation of the brain confirms that 'sensory signals invade *ongoing activity*, which is capable of distorting these signals to favour or work against their further penetration of the central nervous system, all in accordance with the concurrent and antecedent events, taking place simultaneously in many regions of the nervous system (Livingston, 1962, p. 71). Thus it would seem clear that the hope for mechanism lies in some 'centralist' theory, the fruit of physiological enquiry, and that at a molar level, intentional language concerning the way the animal sees the situation is unavoidable.

3. Analogous problems arise for the 'response'. This, too, cannot be treated as a simple 'colourless movement'. On the contrary, we only derive a law-like relation when we define it in terms of its goal. It is obvious that animals have a more or less flexible repertoire, and that they can substitute one behaviour route for another to the same goal, if the first is inappropriate; so that to say that an animal has 'acquired a response' is often to say that he has learnt to bring about some outcome. This, together with the evidence on improvisation, points strongly to the conclusion that, on the molar level, we have to think of behaviour as directed to certain goals. The *ad hoc* hypotheses which have been devised to cope with this suffer from the same disabilities as those mentioned above,[8] and point again to the conclusion that the hope for mechanism must lie on the molecular physiological level.

[7] Like, e.g. Wyckoff's learned response of 'attention', cf. Wyckoff, 1952.
[8] Cf. MacCorquodale & Meehl, 1954 and in discussion in Taylor, 1964, Chaps. 8 and 9.

4. The field of motivation theory also raises insuperable problems for behaviourism. The aim of behaviourism is obviously to avoid the teleological notion of behaviour as directed to goals, and therefore the concept of 'drive' was devised as an activator of behaviour which was nevertheless 'directionless', that is, didn't give behaviour its direction and shape. This latter was thought to be the function of stimulus-response connections, either innate, or built up in learning history.

But this position is hard to maintain in face of the evidence (see 3 above) that behaviour on the molar level must be understood as purposive, as directed to certain goals. Some semblance of plausibility can perhaps be maintained for instrumental behaviour, such as finding the way through a maze to get food; this behaviour could be seen as the result of S—R connections 'stamped in' by previous training. But when it came to 'intrinsically' motivated activity, like exploration, exercise, not to mention more complex human ambitions, the scheme obviously breaks down. The attempt to put human desires, such as for money, esteem, power, etc. into the 'drive as directionless activator' mould[9] merely produces some ingenious verbal adaptations.

Behaviourism is being forced, therefore, more and more towards a 'molecular' or 'centralist' approach. For it becomes clearer and clearer that the operations of selection and organization which are crucial to behaviour cannot be accounted for (mechanistically) in terms of properties of the environment and gross skeletal behaviour alone; that reference has to be made to the properties of central processes in the brain and nervous system.

It would seem, in other words, that the molar level, the level in which we speak of human or animal acts and the features of their situation which provide their context, is irretrievably teleological and purposive. Indeed, it may be asked why so much effort has been spent arriving at this conclusion. Future generations may well look on molar behaviourism with the awe and wonder reserved for some incomprehensible cult of a previous epoch. For the facts of insight, improvisation, goal-direction, and intentionality are so obvious in human behaviour and that of the animals which are most similar to us, that it was only by special efforts that they could be overlooked or minimized to the point of appearing tractable to S—R approach. Behaviourists had to go some distance down the phylogenetic scale (not too far, though—the rat is still intelligent enough to refute the hypotheses of his tormentors) and

---

[9] Cf., e.g. Dollard & Miller, 1950 and discussion in Taylor, 1964, Chap. 10.

above all devise experiments of a certain rigidity (discrimination and maze experiments) to keep a semblance of plausibility to the ambition of a mechanistic molar science. Those who tried to track animals in their normal environment (ethologists, like, for example, Thorpe) soon revealed the real capacities of animals of different species. The S—R language then only remains appropriate for more rigid instinctual routines of animals lower on the scale,[10] and even there requires extensive changes.

The hope for mechanism thus lies on the neurophysiological level. But it might be thought that here its victory was assured; and this in virtue of another *a priori* argument. Either we admit that behaviour, thought, etc., can be accounted for in terms of physiology, or we have to claim that there is in addition some non-physical reality lying behind behaviour. But this latter hypothesis leads us back to the type of interactionism which we considered in the last section and which is an impossible basis for scientific advance, since it involves reference to a factor which cannot be observed. Besides this, interactionism is unplausible in itself: where exactly in the flow of physiological happenings is there an interruption from the mental? Where, indeed, is the mental? Can we really believe that there are states of the mind for which there is no expression (or, if this is preferred, correlate, or aspect) in neural terms, so that the change from mental state A to mental state B could occur without any alteration in neural state? We thus seem driven to adopt the other possibility, viz., that behaviour, thought, etc., can be accounted for in terms of physiology. Thus Hebb (1949, p. xiii): 'Modern psychology takes completely for granted that behaviour and neural function are perfectly correlated, that one is completely caused by the other. There is no separate soul or life-force to stick a finger into the brain now and then and make neural cells do what they would not otherwise.'

Now this conclusion doesn't follow, not, that is, unless we already assume in deriving it that all explanation is mechanistic.

For this assumption is needed to step from the thesis that all mental states have a neural expression to the thesis of mechanism. Let us call this first the expression thesis. According to it, any condition which we describe in intentional language, e.g., that a person is thinking, or desiring, or suffering, or purposing or intending, or enjoying something, and so on, must have (can only come to be if mediated by) a neural expression. The word 'expression' is chosen here in a perhaps vain attempt to preserve

---

[10] The kind of behaviours which, e.g. Tinbergen and Lorenz have uncovered.

neutrality between two views, one of which would use the term 'correlate' to mark the view that there are two separate entities here, the other which might use a term like 'aspect', 'facet' or description, thus underlining the identity of the two. Neutrality may be all the more desirable in that these two views may not jointly exhaust the possibilities, and may be both misleading, as we shall see below. To say that all thoughts, etc., must have a neural expression is not necessarily to say that a given thought has a characteristic neural expression which always pertains to it whenever it appears in the mind of any human being, or even whenever it appears in the mind of a given human being. The expression thesis need involve no guarantee that the criteria for identity of mental states will parallel the criteria of identity of brain states. What is required for the thesis, however, is that there be no disembodied thought. But if each thought doesn't have a characteristic neural expression, how can we verify whether a given thought is embodied or not in the neural events contemporary to it? How, in other words, can the thesis be given a content? We want to claim that no mental state can come to be unmediated by neural expression, without claiming anything about the nature of this expression (although empirical discovery *could* reveal regularities which would allow us to judge 'same thought' on neural criteria). The thesis then must be to the effect that no change can occur from mental state A to mental state B without there being a change in neural state which can be seen as its expression.[11]

Now this thesis in no way entails the thesis of mechanism. For it is quite compatible with the view that explanation by purpose is the appropriate model for human and animal behaviour. If the thesis of expression is true then we can certainly trace the pattern of mental life in the pattern of excitation in the brain, and we can establish laws and correlations governing the latter's function; but it does not follow that these correlations must make no reference to purpose, that is, that they be neither teleological in form, nor themselves susceptible to more basic explanation in terms of intentional properties. The expression thesis leaves the two possibilities open, and the issue between purpose and mechanism is untouched by it. We can only derive the thesis of mechanism, if like most theorists of the behaviourist persuasion, we assume it beforehand. Once more the *a priori* argument is shown to be bogus. There is just no substitute for examining the facts, that is,

[11] This last clause is there to rule out of consideration irrelevant neural changes which plainly have no relation to the mental state change in question, and also to give a place to those correlations between mental and neural states which can be established.

discovering the nature of the laws which hold in this field. Let us turn then to see if we can define more exactly what the issue is about in physiological psychology.

The trouble is that not enough is known about the workings of the brain and nervous system from this point of view. The simpler earlier views which saw the nervous system as a set of afferent-efferent connections, set up through changes in synaptic structure, have been shown to be inadequate. So have views which ascribed specific behaviours to definite anatomical pathways. Any normal function of animal or man in a waking condition involves a complex integration involving different parts of the nervous system. How exactly this comes about to produce the behaviour selected is as yet not clear.

But the dimensions of the problem can be clarified. An animal or man has a repertoire of possible behaviours, a set of capacities for action. Out of this repertoire, somehow the appropriate response is (often) selected. The question is, how does this come about? It cannot be by some connection 'stamped in' by past experience as was once thought, for behaviour shows improvisation and novelty. We are typically not dealing with a set of fixed movements, but with plastic capacities which can be deployed to many effects. The selection determines how they are to be deployed. Thus I am thirsty: I reach out my hand for a glass of water, or, I go to get a glass at the sink, or I go to a fountain or to a restaurant, or ring for room service, or call for the waiter, and so on, *ad infinitum*. I select somehow the behaviour which is appropriate (or which I believe is appropriate). It is not necessary that I should have done this particular act before in quenching my thirst. It is not even necessary that I have done this particular act before at all. It may be the deployment of a newly-acquired capacity in a novel way: it may be a motor capacity: I may have to execute some as yet unprecedented series of movements to get what I want (though this is not likely if all I want is a drink); or it may be another type of capacity: someone may have told me about phrase books, and I go to get one and look up the phrase for 'give me a drink' in the language of the country. But in spite of the element of novelty we are usually equal to the task.

The fact that much of our behaviour is the exercise of plastic capacities of this kind, motor or other, shows the inadequacy of much traditional learning theory. Learning seems to be much more the acquisition of a capacity of this kind, which is available then for a host of different accomplishments, than it is the mastering of specific performances and achievements. The child may learn to reach and grasp while trying to get a rattle to put in his mouth, but this motor capacity is then available the rest of his life for whatever other goals he has where reaching and grasping are appropriate.

The problem is thus to account for how the appropriate response gets selected. We must discover, that is, in virtue of what a response is chosen among many possible. We are looking for an antecedent condition of this form: a property of the response which earns its selection. Now a mechanistic solution to this problem must select a property which provides us with a non-teleological antecedent, that is, one which makes no mention of that property of the response which is its being appropriate, that is, required for the goal in question. Thus theorists of this persuasion generally look for some mechanism which would select the response in virtue of some anatomical or chemical or electrical property, the formula for which would already be encoded in the nervous system as a result of the need-state which the response relieves; so that as a result of the need-state, just this response is activated. Let us call this intrinsic property I. It would thus be the case that the appropriateness of the action would be explained on a mere basic level by the fact that the bahaviour having I is selected, and I is appropriate. And the fact that need-state N gives rise to appropriate action A is accounted for by the fact that N gives rise to a state of nervous system, RI, which is such as to activate behaviour the neural structure of which has the property I. Or A-N is explained by RI-I.

Some explanation of this kind may turn out to be the correct one. But it is an unjustifiable assumption that the true explanation *must* be of this form. It may be, that is, that we can only account for the selection of the response in terms of its appropriateness. In other words, it may be that there is no other property I which determines which behaviour is selected—the antecedent condition of its selection is just that a behaviour is A (within the limits of the repertoire); there is, in other words, no further explanation for A's occurring on the grounds that it is I. On this hypothesis, possessing a given capacity would just mean having a nervous system and cortex which within the limits of the capacity sets up the pattern of excitation required by the behaviour which is appropriate, which suits the agent's goals. If I am thirsty, and there is a glass of water to hand, and no reason not to drink it, etc., then I must reach for it, that is, the pattern of excitation in the 'sensory', 'motor' and 'association' cortex is set up which is involved in my reaching for the glass.

In this case, we are accounting for the neural developments in teleological terms. But the expression thesis still holds. I have the goal of reaching for the glass, and a pattern of excitation is set up which is involved in my reaching for the glass. But these are not two events in causal relation one with another. The second is the neural expression of the first. Of course, it may only be part of that expression. For human beings have many ways of having goals, besides the most direct primitive expression which is trying to encompass them. They can, for instance, contemplate them without acting. This is by means of another, more complex capacity, that of verbal thought; and the display of this is not without neural expression. Thus what is involved in my reaching may be only part of the neural expression of my having this goal. But it can be the whole of it, and often is in what we call unreflective action, and moreover, even where it is part, it can only be called the *result* of my having the goal if this latter is identified with something, e.g. thinking about the goal, which has another neural expression. That the pattern of excitation involved in reaching for the glass is the neural expression of the goal of reaching for the glass and thus not a fact to do with a supposedly ghostly inner cause, but rather the fact that we explain this event teleologically, that it arises when it is appropriate in the situation (as understood by the agent).

What is it for the situation to be appropriate? It can be a fact of body chemistry, as in the case of thirst.[12] Or it can be a much more complicated fact about the attitudes, outlook, fears, ambitions, etc., of the person. I am about to make a speech. I am nervous, am thinking over what I am going to say. I can sense that I am going to have a frog in my throat as soon as I start to talk, thus embarrassing me severely. I reach for the glass of water (or go through any of the other routines mentioned above). Here the goal being appropriate is something to do with the way I see my situation, with other goals and desires. The neural expression of this must be very complex indeed. But in either case the question is whether the link between chemical state or neural pattern on one hand and the appropriate behaviour (or the neural pattern involved) on the other can be explained by a nonteleological mechanism of selection, or whether what is crucial in the two cases is just the appropriateness of the goal.

But this last example brings us to a second point. A teleological approach of this kind would also make use of intentional properties in explanation. If I explain that the neural

---

[12] *This* is, of course, subject to manipulation on mechanistic principles, the question is whether the link between the chemical state of deficit and the appropriate behaviour can be explained mechanistically, through some non-teleological selection mechanism of the kind described above.

pattern expressive of nervous thoughts and rehearsings before the speech gives rise to the pattern involved in reaching for the glass in a teleological way, i.e. by making the behaviour of reaching for the glass appropriate, then the properties in terms of which the first makes the second appropriate become relevant for explanation. But in order to explain how the first condition makes the action of reaching for the glass appropriate, we have to make reference to how I see my situation, how I judge a certain possible outcome as embarrassing, and so on. In other words, on a teleological view, what makes the first neural condition an antecedent of the second is something to do with what it is a neural expression of, viz. a certain set of thoughts and feelings about my situation. And thus intentional properties also enter into the explanation on this view.

But once again we would be wrong to see this as a form of interaction. That the content of thoughts enters into the explanation even of neural events doesn't mean that we are making appeal to another sphere. The intentional content of thought is only in another sphere from its neural embodiment for us if we already accept a dualist hypothesis. But what we are saying is that the neurological level would be the wrong level on which to find an explanation of behaviour of this complexity, if this hypothesis is right; that for this range of behaviour, the key level of explanation is a psychological one, and that the shape of the developments in the cortex can themselves not be fully explained without reference to this level. In other words, for this range of behaviour, the most basic level of explanation is psychological.

This is not a striking or outlandish thesis. Nor is it in conflict with the thesis of expression. It was only thought to be because of a confusion between two theses: (1) that mental function is not a set of extra entities or a process taking place in another medium which could occur without neural function but is in interaction with it (thesis of expression); and (2) that mental function and the neural events which express it can be explained on the most basic level in terms of concepts of the neurophysiological level (which make, therefore, no mention of intentional properties), and mechanistically at that.[13] Now this second thesis is not self-evidently true, if it is true at all. On the contrary, there is no ontological guarantee, as we have seen, that a given range of phenomena are explicable in concepts of one level rather than another. The progress of science would, indeed, be much easier if there were; for we would be spared the difficult search for the right conceptual framework, the right notion of 'normalcy', in

---

[13] It is necessary to add this last clause because it cannot be held to be true *a priori* that all physiological explanations are non-teleological, although behaviour theorists generally assume them to be.

terms of which the phenomena can be presented as functions of the same set of factors. We cannot say *a priori*, therefore, what concepts will prove adequate for the most basic explanation of human behaviour; and there is no greater implausibility in the thesis that we shall have to account for the sequence of certain neural events by appeal to psychological laws governing intentional properties and purposes, than there is in its converse.

But nor does thesis (2) follow from thesis (1): that there is no disembodied mental life tells us nothing *per se* about the laws governing this life. The derivation can only be made if we assume the thesis of mechanism. The blithe way in which this assumption is made can be seen in the quote from Hebb above: 'Modern psychology takes completely for granted that behaviour and neural function are perfectly correlated, that one is completely caused by the other.' It seems that, for Hebb, the second half of the sentence is just another way of saying what is conveyed in the first half. But this is far from being the case. The first half can be taken as an assertion of the thesis of expression; but the second half, that behaviour is completely caused by neural function (we are safe in assuming that Hebb didn't mean the converse), amounts to *a priori* legislation about the type of concepts which will figure in an adequate explanation. Whether this is so can only be decided by the facts, by discovering what explanations actually succeed. The implied inference from (1) to (2) is therefore based on a *petitio principii*.

But it is the easier to make in that it introduces a certain simplicity. For explanation by purpose introduces a complexity not found in mechanism. For it marks a distinction between levels where mechanism sees none. Obviously some aspects of our behaviour must be accounted for in concepts appropriate to a neurological level of description. For one thing the limits of our repertoire must be, for another certain determinants of desire— hunger, thirst, sexual desire most notably—are under the control of our body chemistry, for a third, many forms of breakdown must be accounted for in neurological terms. Explaining our behaviour by purpose, therefore, involves a view of behaviour as existing on several levels. This poses the problem of the relations between them.[14]

[14] We can thus see the debate about the supposed identity of sensations and brain processes in a new light (cf. J. J. C. Smart, 1963; Hilary Putnam, 1961; and U. T. Place, 1956). The whole question is badly put because it involves a confusion between theses (1) and (2). We are asked to consider a given class of mental and a given class of neural states as entities and decide whether they are identical. Put in this way, we have to say, no; for there is no guarantee that a given mental state will always be expressed by the same (qualitatively) neural state. Indeed, there is some reason to believe that this is not the case, given the multi-functional nature of much of the brain. But that does not mean

I say 'several' levels, and not just two, because we are not dealing with the dualism of traditional Cartesianism or empiricism where the 'mind' can be thought to make use of a number of automatisms in order to encompass its ends. No instrumentalist view will do. In fact there is no clearcut demarcation between the levels, on any hypothesis which accepts the thesis of expression.

We can in fact see two types of relations between the levels. On one hand the 'higher' behaviours can obviously only exist if certain conditions, specifiable in neurological terms, are met. In this way the existence of the neural conditions necessary to capacity and normal function can be seen as boundary conditions in the sense discussed earlier. These conditions must hold for any normal function, but once this is assured sufficient conditions can only be discovered for behaviour in teleological terms.[15]

On the other hand, there is plainly a continuation between behaviours which are more 'automatic' and those which are more flexible. The 'automatic' behaviours are the ones which are more rigid, are set off by a limited set of releasing conditions and are performed in a more or less stereotyped way; this probably corresponds to a less complex and widely integrative neural pattern (something more closely approaching the classical theory of the 'arc'); in any case, automatic behaviours are those which can most plausibly be accounted for in mechanistic terms. These behaviours dominate low in the phylogenetic scale, as we can see from the rigid instinctual patterns described by ethologists (cf., e.g. Tinbergen, 1951), and also early in ontogeny. What is striking is how plasticity develops as we advance both phylo- and ontogenetically. More plastic behaviours are more adaptive, involve intelligence in judging their appropriateness and in adapting means to the end. Thus men, who start their lives with an automatic routine, sucking, as their only food-getting behaviour later develop an almost unlimited repertoire which can be directed to this end.

---

that mental states are separate entities from neural states. Given the thesis of expression, we can say that mental function is not some set of extra entities apart from neural function. But put this way, the thesis of identity loses all its interest. The really interesting question is whether mental function can be explained by laws whose concepts are drawn from descriptions only appropriate on the neurological (or more radically the physical level), or whether it must be explained by concepts of its own range. (In other words the question whether thesis (2) is true.) This is the question of 'reduction', and this is what materialists like Smart and Place appear really to want to establish. But to put it in terms of identity is to confuse the issue: because reducibility is not a question about, e.g. sensations and brain states an entities, but about the laws governing mental and neural functions in general. The question is not: are sensations and brain states identical; but, can we account for sensations in terms of laws mentioning only brain states and their appropriate description (that is, without any mention of psychic properties)? This, if I understand him, is the principal point of the interesting article by Richard Rorty, 1965, which restates the identity thesis in a defensible form.

[15] Cf. the distinction between 'necessary' and 'sufficient' conditions in Sec. I.

But in the case of man, and perhaps some of the higher animals, there is an interesting development in the other direction. Men are capable of learning and as it were entrenching routine behaviours. Indeed, this procedure even seems to be essential to their achievement. Because secondary functions can become 'second nature' to us, as we say, we can concentrate on other things and extend our scope. Those who know how to drive cars will slam their foot on the brake when the 'releasing stimulus' of something running across the road impinges on their receptors, very much as geese will fly from the shadow shaped like their species predator. And in either case, the reaction may happen where it is inappropriate, for instance on an icy highway.

But with man, the routine is potentially under higher control in the immediate situation, and is subject to training in or out in the long run. It is thus rightly called '*second* nature'. On this view, therefore, there can be no clearcut line of demarcation between 'higher' behaviours whose necessary conditions are psychological in form and 'lower' ones where an explanation may be adequate in exclusively neurological concepts.

Thus the question between the two modes of explanation can perhaps be put in this way: are there certain non-teleological neurophysiological mechanisms which can account entirely for the selection, integration of functions and organization necessary for behaviour, or must we explain some behaviour in terms of its appropriateness for the goals of the agent concerned? In the latter case, the 'higher' behaviour is subject to certain necessary conditions which are defined in purely neurophysiological terms, and is embedded in a complex of 'lower' behaviours which approach at the limit a degree of rigidity which makes mechanism plausible; but sufficient conditions for these higher behaviours cannot be given without using purposive and intentional concepts. The question is, in other words, whether all purposive behaviour can be explained on a more basic level mechanistically, or whether on the other hand, different aspects of the stream of behaviour must be seen as taking place at different levels, albeit not rigidly separated, for some of which the most basic explanation remains psycholgical and hence in terms of purpose.

It is impossible to say at this stage whether this latter thesis or the mechanist one offers the best hope for a science of behaviour. All that we can say is that what is known of the operation of the brain is compatible with explanation in terms of purpose. . . .

What is really needed is to throw open the doors, and examine the real world, take account not only of the more surprising performances of the white rat, but examine also what men can do.

What is needed is a reflection on behaviour in its own terms and a classification of its different varieties, a study of its structure, which will reveal the full range and limits of flexibility and intelligence. We need to see what has to be explained to get an idea of what it would mean to explain behaviour. We can no longer go on the behaviourist assumption that we can grasp the simple lower behaviours first, and then build from there to the higher ones. This assumes that there are no differences of level in behaviour between more rigid and more intelligent, and thus begs one of the most central questions of psychology. All it can lead to is an examination of those behaviours which have already been made to fit the theory. In order to make progress the science of behaviour has to knock down the walls of the maze and look afresh at the real world.

REFERENCES

Broadbent, D. E. 1958. *Perception and Communication*. London.
Deutsch, J. A. 1960. *The Structural Basis of Behaviour*. Cambridge.
Deutsch, J. A. & Deutsch, D. 1963. Attention: some theoretical considerations. *Psychol. Rev.* 70, 80-90.
Dollard, J. & Miller, N. E. 1950. *Personality and Psychotherapy*. New York.
Hebb, D. O. 1949. *The Organization of Behaviour*. New York.
Hull, C. L. 1943. *Principles of Behaviour*. New York.
Lashley, K. S. 1929. *Brain Mechanisms and Intelligence*. Chicago.
Livingston, R. B. 1962. Neurophysiology and psychology. *Psychology: A Study of a Science*, vol. 4. Ed. S. Koch. New York.
MacCorquodale, K. & Meehl, P. E. 1954. Study of E. C. Tolman. *Modern Learning Theory*. W. K. Estes *et al*. New York.
Nissen, H. W. 1953. Sensory patterning versus central organization. *J. Psychol.* 36, 271-87.
Place, U. T. 1956. Is consciousness a brain process? *Br. J. Psychol.* 47, 44-50.
Putnam, Hilary. 1961. Minds and machines. *Dimensions of Mind*. Ed. Sidney Hook. New York.
Rorty, Richard. 1965. Mind-body identity, privacy and categories. *Rev. Metaphysics*. 19, 24-54.
Smart, J. J. C. 1963. *Philosophy and Scientific Realism*. London.
Taylor, Charles. 1964. *The Explanation of Behaviour*. London.
Thorpe, W. H. 1956. *Learning and Instinct in Animals*. London.
Tinbergen, N. 1951. *The Study of Instinct*.
Wyckoff, L. B. 1952. The role of observing responses in discrimination learning. *Psychol. Rev.* 59, 431-42.

IV. STATES OF CONSCIOUSNESS

7. Plotinus

EDITOR'S INTRODUCTION

Classical Greek science did not end with Aristotle, but underwent a shift in both locale and emphasis. The Egyptian city of Alexandria (founded by Alexander the Great in 332 B.C.) replaced Athens as center of Greek science, and the emphasis in science tended to become both practical and empirical. This change in emphasis was not without its benefits, and some of the greatest discoveries of Greek science stem from the Alexandrian period. For example, there was Euclid, who systematized geometry; Archimedes, who founded the science of statics; and Aristarchus, who argued that the earth rotates daily on its axis and revolves yearly around the sun. The biological sciences also advanced at the hands of Alexandrian physicians, who buttressed their speculations with dissection and experimentation. But in spite of this apparent vigor, Greek science following Aristotle was on the wane. Research became increasingly specialized and fragmented. In terms of overall systems of thought, people's attention was turning more and more to moral and ethical issues and away from the naturalistic attitudes that form the foundation of scientific thought. Thus, the great philosophical systems of later Greek periods, such as Stoicism and Epicurianism, were concerned primarily with how people should live and not with the analysis of natural phenomena. What naturalistic speculation these systems do contain is largely an elaboration and systematization of earlier innovations (e.g., atomism in the case of the Epicurians).

The shift in emphasis from the theoretical to the practical, and from the natural to the ethical, is not surprising. The expansions of first the Alexandrian and later the Roman empires brought not only a need for technical proficiency, but also a disruption of established social life. Throughout the Mediterranean world, national boundaries were violated, indigenous political leaders displaced, caste systems disrupted, and local ties severed by the mass movement of people. Nor did the ascendance of the Roman impirium bring with it social stability. Too often the emperors were either debauched or insane, and they were routinely removed from office by treachery and murder. The rich became very rich, and were well provided with servants from conquered territories. The poor were desperate but powerless, especially the free farmers who had been displaced from their lands and crowded into the cities. This state of affairs has led some historians to characterize the first few centuries A.D. as an "Age of Anxiety," and epithet often applied to our own times.

It is within this context that the work of Plotinus, the last of the classical Greek philosophers, must be understood. Plotinus studied in Alexandria for almost 20 years before coming to Rome at the age of 40, in 244 A.D. He considered himself to be a follower and expositor of Plato, but he was much more than a mere expositor. A thinker of considerable originality, Plotinus exploited certain transcendental and mystical tendencies that were only latent in Plato.

We have seen how Plato postulated a distinct Form for each abstract notion such as justice or beauty. The Form embodies the essential characteristics shared by individual instances of the object or quality in question. For example, the Form of beauty embodies those features that all beautiful objects share, to the extent that they may be considered "beautiful." This was Plato's answer to the problem of "the one and the many," an issue that preoccupied most ancient philosophers. Simply stated, the problem is as follows: Is there anything permanent, real, and unitary (the one) in a world that appears to be multifaceted and in constant change (the many)? It will be noted that Plato's theory of Forms gives only a partial solution to this problem, for each of the Forms is itself an individual object, i.e., the Forms are actually many. A further question, therefore, presents itself: Is there a unity behind the Forms, a Form of Forms, so to speak, that contains within itself all the essential features of the individual Forms—perfection, immutability, nonmateriality, and the like? There is such a Form of Forms, Plato believed, and he called it the Good. In the *Republic*, Plato compared the Good with the sun; it illuminates the individual Forms and is the source of all knowledge. Plato did not pursue the implications of this analogy, but his formulation gave impetus to certain mystical tendencies in later Neoplatonic thought.

In Plotinus' system, the Good becomes identified with a transcendental intellect, itself beyond being and yet the source of all being. Appropriately, enough, Plotinus called this transcendental intellect, the One, and postulated a scale of being emanating from it. These emanations, or modes of existence, decrease in reality as their distance from the One increases. The first emanation is the Intelligence. From the Intelligence emanates the Soul, which contains within itself all individual souls. The Soul in turn creates Nature, the visible universe. Nature is composed of matter and is the point at which the creative powers of the One come to an end. Matter, it might also be noted, is the source of evil; or, more properly speaking, evil is a deficiency in reality (goodness).

Man is a complement of matter and soul, the latter being a particularization of Soul in general. The human soul is "in" the body, somewhat as light is "in" the air; that is, the soul permeates the body but is not a constituent of it.

The One is the goal as well as the source of being, and all things strive to return from lower to higher forms, culminating in reunion with the One. For man, this return may be accomplished in two ways. First, for those who live virtuously, successive emancipation from lower forms can be achieved through cycles of birth and death. Second, through meditation and contemplation, it is possible to experience mystical reunion with the One. The latter course is the topic of the following selection, in which Plotinus attempts to describe the mystical experience. The selection begins (Sects. 1 and 2) with a rather mundane inquiry into the source of unity. These sections contain Plotinus' solution to the problem of the one and the many. From what already has been said, the nature of his solution should be evident: the source of unity is the One.

In the remainder of the selection (Sects. 3-9), Plotinus offers a description of how the soul gains access to the One through contemplation and meditation. In order to understand Plotinus on this point, it is important to note that he conceived of man as a microcosm, a reflection of being in general. The lowest in man reflects material Nature, the last emanation of the One and the source of sense experience; the highest in man reflects the Intelligence, the first emanation of the One and the source of rational knowledge. The first step toward comprehension of the One therefore requires a withdrawal from the objects of sense experience. Turning inward, the higher aspect of the soul finds itself, and in itself, the Intelligence. Grasping what the Intelligence sees, the soul can contemplate the One independent of sense experience. But even the kind of knowledge afforded by the Intelligence must ultimately be transcended, for it implies a duality between the knower and the known. The One is absolute simplicity and transcends all duality. In order to truly comprehend the One, the soul must rise alone, carrying with it nothing that is alien to the One. Success in this endeavor can be described as love as well as knowledge, for it entails complete union with, and ecstatic respose in, the One.

And what has all this to do with psychology? Like Plato and Aristotle, Plotinus stands at the beginning of one of the major intellectual traditions of the West, namely, mysticism. In Chapter 1, the rationalist (Plato), empiricist (Aristotle), and mystical (Plotinus) traditions were related to certain presuppositions regarding the source of knowledge (i.e., reason, sense experience, and feeling), and hence to various patterns of explanation. Of course, not all people who emphasize feeling as a source of knowledge are true mystics in the sense of Plotinus. We could just as well have labeled this tradition *romanticism* or *existentialism*, but each of these terms has its own specialized usage which makes it no more appropriate than *mysticism*. We may therefore stick with the latter term in recognition of Plotinus' contribution to this tradition.

Still, in order to avoid misunderstanding, it is necessary to say a few words about the mystical experience and its relationship to knowledge. The mystical experience is often described as an emotional state (e.g., of ecstasy and love, or sometimes, of dread and anxiety). But for the mystic, the experience is primarily one of understanding and insight. In a recent study of mysticism, Greeley compared the mystical insight to the creative processes by which, say, a musician perceives an entire symphony before beginning to compose, or a novelist intuits a story before beginning to write. Greeley emphasizes that he is not describing something that goes on "inside" people, but something that people see in the world "out there." That is, the mystical experience is a means whereby people understand the world about them. But unlike other kinds of knowledge, it is more direct, immediate, and intuitive. The emotional experiences that often accompany such direct and intuitive knowledge are an analog of the satisfaction that comes from solving a complex intellectual problem, or the enjoyment that comes from contemplating a great work of art. Pursuing still another analogy, Greeley compares the mystical way of knowing to an act of faith:

> Is it possible that an act of faith calls into play the same dimensions of personality that are activated in the ecstatic interlude? Does the

ordinary believer see the same thing the ecstatic sees, though perhaps less clearly? Or, to put it the other way around, does the ecstatic see the same thing the believer does but much more dramatically? Both leap beyond discursive reasoning; both perceive love at work in the universe; both have confidence in peace and joy as the result of their insight; the convictions of both are totally inexplicable in the categories of positivist empiricism.[1]

By *faith*, Greeley is not referring to the blind acceptance of dogma. Rather, he is referring to the feeling that one has insight into, or comprehension of, some fundamental aspect of reality. This kind of faith is as common to scientists and artists as it is to religious thinkers. That, at least, would seem to be one implication of Kuhn's analysis of the role of "dogma" in science (cf. Chapt. 2). It would also agree with data collected by Maslow on the mysticlike experiences of creative scientists. According to Maslow, the creative scientist "lives for the moments of glory when a problem solves itself, when suddenly through a microscope he sees things in a very different way, the moments of revelation, of illumination, insight, understanding, ecstasy."[2] Maslow goes on to add, however, that "scientists are very, very shy and embarrassed about this." Such embarrassment, he believes, not only inhibits a true understanding of scientific activity, but also fosters a serious gap in the education of scientists, where feelings are viewed with some distrust.

In the next chapter (by Tart), the validity of mysticlike experiences as a source of knowledge will be examined in detail. In the meantime, let us turn to Plotinus' classic description of the mystical experience.

[1] A. M. Greeley, *Ecstasy: A way of knowing*, © 1974, p. 80. Reprinted by permission of Prentice-Hall, Inc., Englewood Cliffs, New Jersey.
[2] A. H. Maslow, *The farther reaches of human nature*. New York: Viking, 1971, p. 178.

The Flight of the Lone to the Alone:
a mystical journey

1.

It is by The One that all beings are beings.

This is equally true of those that are primarily beings and those that in some way are simply classed among beings, for what could exist were it not one? Not a one, a thing is not. No army, no choir, no flock exists except it be one. No house, even, or ship exists except as the unit, house, or the unit, ship; their unity gone, the house is no longer a house, the ship is no longer a ship. Similarly quantitative continua would not exist had they not an inner unity; divided, they forfeit existence along with unity. It is the same with plant and animal bodies; each of them is a unit; with disintegration, they lose their previous nature and are no longer what they were; they become new, different beings that in turn exist only as long as each of them is a unit. Health is contingent upon the body's being coordinated in unity; beauty, upon the mastery of parts by The One; the soul's virtue, upon unification into one sole coherence.

The Soul imparts unity to all things in producing, fashioning, forming, and disposing them. Ought we then to say that The Soul not only gives unity but is unity itself, The One? No. It bestows other qualities upon bodies without being what it bestows (shape, for instance, and Idea, which are different from it); so also this unity; The Soul makes each being one by looking upon The One, just as it makes man by contemplating the Idea, Man, effecting in the man the unity that belongs to Man.

Each thing that is called "one" has a unity proportionate to its nature, sharing in unity, either more or less, according to the degree of its being. The Soul, while distinct from The One, has greater unity because it has a higher degree of being. It is not The One. It is one, but its unity is contingent. Between The Soul and its unity there is the same difference as between body and body's unity. Looser aggregates, such as a choir, are furthest from unity; the more compact are the nearer; The Soul is nearer still, yet—as all the others—is only a participant in unity.

Reprinted by permission of Hackett Publishing Company, P.O. Box 55573, Indianapolis, Indiana 46205 from *The Essential Plotinus* (VI, 9 [9]) translated by Elmer O'Brien, New York: Mentor, 1964, pp. 73–88.

The fact that The Soul could not exist unless it was one should not, really, lead anyone to think it and The One identical. All other things exist only as units, and none of them is The One; body, for instance, and unity are not identical. Besides, The Soul is manifold as well as one even though it is not constituted of parts; it has various faculties—discursive reason, desire, perception—joined together in unity as by a bond. The Soul bestows unity because it has unity, but a unity received from another source.

2.

Granted that being is not identical with unity in each particular thing, might not the totality, Being, be identical with unity? Then upon grasping Being, we would hold The One, for they would be the same. Then, if Being is The Intelligence, The One would also be The Intelligence; The Intelligence, as Being and as The One, would impart to the rest of things both being and, in proportion, unity.

Is The One identical with Being as "man" and "one man" are identical? Or is it the number of each thing taken individually? (Just as one object and another joined to it are spoken of as "two," so an object taken singly is referred to as "one.") In the second case, if number belongs to the class of being, evidently The One will belong in that way, too, and we shall have to discover what kind of being it is. But if unity is no more than a numbering device of the soul, The One has no real existence; but this possibility is eliminated by our previous observation that each object upon losing unity loses existence as well.

Accordingly, we must determine whether being and unity are identical either in each individual object or in their totality.

As the being of each thing consists in multiplicity and The One cannot be multiplicity, The One must differ from Being. Man is animal, rational, and many things besides; and this multiplicity is held together by a bondlike unity. Thus there is a difference between man and unity: man is divisible, unity indivisible. Being, containing all beings, is still more multiple, thus differing from The One even though it is one by participation. Because being possesses life and intelligence, it is not dead. It must be multiple. If it is The Intelligence, it must be multiple—and the more so if it contains the Ideas, because Ideas, individually and in their totality, are a sort of number and are one only in the way in which the universe is one.

In general, then, The One is the first existent. But The Intelligence, the Ideas, and Being are not the first. Every form is multiple and composite, and consequently something derived because parts precede the composite they constitute.

That The Intelligence cannot be primary should be obvious as well from the following. The activity of The Intelligence consists necessarily in intellection. Intelligence, which does not turn to external objects, contemplates what is superior to it; in turning towards itself it turns towards its origin. Duality is implied if The Intelligence is both thinker and thought; it is not simple, therefore not The One. And if The Intelligence contemplates some object other than itself, then certainly there exists something superior to The Intelligence. Even if The Intelligence contemplate itself and at the same time that which is superior to it, it still is only of secondary rank. We must conceive The Intelligence as enjoying the presence of the Good and The One and contemplating it while it is also present to itself, thinks itself, and thinks itself as being all things. Constituting such a diversity, The Intelligence is far from being The One.

Thus The One is not all things because then it would no longer be one. It is not The Intelligence, because The Intelligence is all things, and The One would then be all things. It is not Being because Being is all things.

3.

What then is The One? What is its nature?

It is not surprising that it is difficult to say what it is when it is difficult to say even what being is or what form is, although there knowledge has some sort of approach through the forms. As the soul advances towards the formless, unable to grasp what is without contour or to receive the imprint of reality so diffuse, it fears it will encounter nothingness, and it slips away. Its state is distressing. It seeks solace in retreating down to the sense realm, there to rest as upon a sure and firm-set earth, just as the eye, wearied with looking at small objects, gladly turns to large ones. But when the soul seeks to know in its own way—by coalescence and unification—it is prevented by that very unification from recognizing it has found The One, for it is unable to distinguish knower and known. Nevertheless, a philosophical study of The One must follow this course.

Because what the soul seeks is The One and it would look upon the source of all reality, namely the Good and The One, it must not withdraw from the primal realm and sink down to the lowest realm. Rather must it withdraw from sense objects, of the lowest existence, and turn to those of the highest. It must free itself from all evil since it aspires to rise to the Good. It must rise to the principle possessed within itself; from the multiplicity that it was it must again become one. Only thus can it contemplate the supreme principle, The One.

Having become The Intelligence, having entrusted itself to it, committed itself to it, having confided and established itself in it so that by alert concentration the soul may grasp all The Intelligence sees, it will, by The Intelligence, contemplate The One without employing the senses, without mingling perception with the activity of The Intelligence. It must contemplate this purest of objects through the purest of The Intelligence, through that which is supreme in The Intelligence.

When, then, the soul applies itself to the contemplation of such an object and has the impression of extension or shape or mass, it is not The Intelligence that guides its seeing, for it is not the nature of The Intelligence to see such things. From sensation, rather, and from opinion, the associate of sensation, comes this activity. From The Intelligence must come the word of what its scope is. It contemplates its priors, its own content, and its issue. Purity and simplicity characterize its issue and, even more, its content and, most of all, its priors or Prior.

The One, then, is not The Intelligence but higher. The Intelligence is still a being, while The One is not a being because it is precedent to all being. Being has, you might say, the form of being; The One is without form, even intelligible form.

As The One begets all things, it cannot be any of them—neither thing, nor quality, nor quantity, nor intelligence, nor soul. Not in motion, nor at rest, not in space, nor in time, it is "the in itself uniform," or rather it is the "without-form" preceding form, movement, and rest, which are characteristics of Being and make Being multiple.

But if The One is not in motion, why is it not at rest? Because rest or motion, or both together, are characteristic of Being. Again, because what is at rest must be so on account of something distinct from it, rest as such. The One at rest would have the contingent attribute, "at rest," and would be simple no longer.

Let no one object that something contingent is attributed to The One when we call it the first cause. It is to ourselves that we are thereby attributing contingency because it is we who are receiving something from The One while The One remains self-enclosed. When we wish to speak with precision, we should not say that The One is this or that, but revolving, as it were, around it, try to express our own experience of it, now drawing nigh to it, now falling back from it as a result of the difficulties involved.

4.

The chief difficulty is this: awareness of The One comes to us neither by knowing nor by the pure thought that discovers the other intelligible things, but by a presence transcending knowledge. When the soul knows something, it loses its unity; it cannot remain simply one because knowledge implies discursive reason and discursive reason implies multiplicity. The soul then misses The One and falls into number and multiplicity.

Therefore we must go beyond knowledge and hold to unity. We must renounce knowing and knowable, every object of thought, even Beauty, because Beauty, too, is posterior to The One and is derived from it as, from the sun, the daylight. That is why Plato says of The One, "It can neither be spoken nor written about." If nevertheless we speak of it and write about it, we do so only to give direction, to urge towards that vision beyond discourse, to point out the road to one desirous of seeing. Instruction goes only as far as showing the road and the direction. To obtain the vision is solely the work of him who desires to obtain it. If he does not arrive at contemplation, if his soul does not achieve awareness of that life that is beyond, if the soul does not feel a rapture within it like that of the lover come to rest in his love, if, because of his closeness to The One, he receives its true light—his whole soul made luminous—but is still weighted down and his vision frustrated, if he does not rise alone but still carries within him something alien to The One, if he is not yet sufficiently unified, if he has not yet risen far but is still at a distance either because of the obstacles of which we have just spoken or because of the lack of such instruction as would have given him direction and faith in the existence of things beyond, he has no one to blame but himself and should try to become pure by detaching himself from everything.

The One is absent from nothing and from everything. It is present only to those who are prepared for it and are able to receive it, to enter into harmony with it, to grasp and to touch it by virtue of their likeness to it, by virtue of that inner power similar to and stemming from The One when it is in that state in which it was when it originated from The One. Thus will The One be "seen" as far as it can become an object of contemplation. Anyone who still lacks faith in these agruments should consider the following:

5.

Those who believe that the world of being is governed by luck or by chance and that it depends upon material causes are far removed from the divine and from the notion of The One. It is not such men as these that we address but such as admit the existence of a world other than the corporeal and at least acknowledge the existence of soul. These men should apply themselves to the study of soul, learning among other things that it proceeds from The Intelligence and attains virtue by participating in the reason that proceeds from The Intelligence. Next, they must realize that The Intelligence is different from our faculty of reasoning (the so-called rational principle), that reasoning implies, as it were, separate steps and movements. They must see that knowledge consists in the manifestation of the rational forms that exist in The Soul and come to The Soul from The Intelligence, the source of knowledge. After one has seen The Intelligence, which like a thing of sense is immediately perceived (but which, although it transcends the soul, is its begetter and the author of the intelligible world), one must think of it as quiet, unwavering movement; embracing all things and being all things, in its multiplicity it is both indivisible and divisible. It is not divisible as are the ingredients of discursive reason, conceived item by item. Still its content is not confused either: each element is distinct from the other, just as in science the theories form an indivisible whole and yet each theory has its own separate status. This multitude of co-existing beings, the intelligible realm, is near The One. (Its existence is necessary, as reason demonstrates, if one admits The Soul exists, to which it is superior.) It is nevertheless not the supreme because it is neither one nor simple.

The One, the source of all things, is simple. It is above even the highest in the world of being because it is above The Intelligence, which itself, not The One but like The One, would become The One. Not sundered from The One, close to The One, but to itself present, it has to a degree dared secession.

The awesome existent above, The One, is not a being for then its unity would repose in another than itself. There is no name that suits it, really. But, since name it we must, it may appropriately be called "one," on the understanding, however, that it is not a substance that possesses unity only as an attribute. So, the strictly nameless, it is difficult to know. The best approach is through its offspring, Being: we know it brings The Intelligence into existence, that it is the source of all that is best, the self-sufficing and unflagging begetter of every being, to be numbered among none of them since it is their prior.

We are necessarily led to call this "The One" in our discussions the better to designate "partlessness" while we strive to bring our minds to "oneness." But when we say that it is one and partless, it is not in the same sense that we speak of geometrical point or numerical unit, where "one" is the quantitative principle which would not exist unless substance, and that which precedes substance and being, were there first. It is not of this kind of unity that we are to think, but simply use such things here below—in their simplicity and the absence of multiplicity and division—as symbols of the higher.

6.

In what sense, then, do we call the supreme The One? How can we conceive of it?

We shall have to insist that its unity is much more perfect than that of the numerical unit or the geometrical point. For with regard to these, the soul, abstracting from magnitude and numerical plurality, stops indeed at that which is smallest and comes to rest in something indivisible. This kind of unity is found in something that is divisible and exists in a subject other than itself. But "what is not in another than itself" is not in the divisible: Nor is it indivisible in the same sense in which the smallest is indivisible. On the contrary, The One is the greatest, not physically but dynamically. Hence it is indivisible, not physically but dynamically. So also the beings that proceed from it; they are, not in mass but in might, indivisible and partless. Also, The One is infinite not as extension or a numerical series is infinite, but in its limitless power. Conceive it as intelligence or divinity; it is more than that. Compress unity within your mind, it is still more than that. Here is unity superior to any your thought lays hold of, unity that exists by itself and in itself and is without attributes.

Something of its unity can be understood from its self-sufficiency. It is necessarily the most powerful, the most self-sufficient, the most independent of all. Whatever is not one, but multiple, needs something else. Its being needs unification. But The One is already one. It does not even need itself. A being that is multiple, in order to be what it is, needs the multiplicity of things it contains. And each of the things contained is what it is by its union with the others and not by itself, and so it needs the others. Accordingly, such a being is deficient both with regard to its parts and as a whole. There must be something that is fully self-sufficient. That is The One; it alone, within and without, is without need. It needs nothing outside itself either to exist, to achieve well-being, or to be sustained in existence. As it is the cause of the other things, how could it owe its existence to them? And how could it derive its well-being from outside itself since its well-being is not something contingent but is its very nature? And, since it does not occupy space, how can it need support or foundation? What needs foundation is the material mass which, unfounded, falls. The One is the foundation of all other things and gives them, at one and the same time, existence and location; what needs locating is not self-sufficing.

Again, no principle needs others after it. The principle of all has no need of anything at all. Deficient being is deficient because it aspires to its principle. But if The One were to aspire to anything, it would evidently seek not to be The One, that is, it would aspire to that which destroys it. Everything in need needs well-being and preservation. Hence The One cannot aim at any good or desire anything: it is superior to the Good; it is the Good, not for itself, but for other things to the extent to which they can share in it.

The One is not an intellective existence. If it were, it would constitute a duality. It is motionless because it is prior to motion quite as it is prior to thinking. Anyhow, what would it think? Would it think itself? If it did, it would be in a state of ignorance before thinking, and the self-sufficient would be in need of thought. Neither should one suppose it to be in a state of ignorance on the ground that it does not know itself and does not think itself. Ignorance presupposes a dual relationship: one does not know another. But The One, in its aloneness, can neither know nor be ignorant of anything. Being with itself, it does not need to know itself. Still, we should not even attribute to it this presence with itself if we are to preserve its unity.

Excluded from it are both thinking of itself and thinking of others. It is not like that which thinks but, rather, like the activity of thinking. The activity of thinking does not itself think; it is the cause that has some other being think and cause cannot be identical with effect. This cause, therefore, of all existing things cannot be any one of them. Because it is the cause of good it cannot, then, be called the Good; yet in another sense it is the Good above all.

7.

If the mind reels at this, The One being none of the things we mentioned, a start yet can be made from them to contemplate it.

Do not let yourself be distracted by anything exterior, for The One is not in some one place, depriving all the rest of its presence. It is present to all those who can touch it and absent only to those who cannot. No man can concentrate on one thing by thinking of some other thing; so he should not connect something else with the object he is thinking of if he wishes really to grasp it. Similarly, it is impossible for a soul, impressed with something else, to conceive of The One so long as such an impression occupies its attention, just as it is impossible that a soul, at the moment when it is attentive to other things, should receive the form of what is their contrary. It is said that matter must be void of all qualities in order to be capable of receiving all forms. So must the soul, and for a stronger reason, be stripped of all forms if it would be filled and fired by the supreme without any hindrance from within itself.

Having thus freed itself of all externals, the soul must turn totally inward; not allowing itself to be wrested back towards the outer, it must forget everything, the subjective first and, finally, the objective. It must not even know that it is itself that is applying itself to contemplation of The One.

After having dwelled with it sufficiently, the soul should, if it can, reveal to others this transcendent communion. (Doubtless it was enjoyment of this communion that was the basis of calling Minos "the confidant of Zeus"; remembering, he made laws that are the image of The One, inspired to legislate by his contact with the divine.) If a man looks down on the life of the city as unworthy of him, he should, if he so wishes, remain in this world above. This does indeed happen to those who have contemplated much.

This divinity, it is said, is not outside any being but, on the contrary, is present to all beings though they may not know it. They are fugitives from the divine, or rather from themselves. What they turn from they cannot reach. Themselves lost, they can find no other. A son distraught and beside himself is not likely to recognize his father. But the man who has learned to know himself will at the same time discover whence he comes.

8.

Self-knowledge reveals to the soul that its natural motion is not, if uninterrupted, in a straight line, but circular, as around some inner object, about a center, the point to which it owes its origin. If the soul knows this, it will move around this center from which it came, will cling to it and commune with it as indeed all souls should but only divine souls do. That is the secret of their divinity, for divinity consists in being attached to the center. One who withdraws far from it becomes an ordinary man or an animal.

Is this "center" of our souls, then, the principle we are seeking? No, we must look for some other principle upon which all centers converge and to which, only by analogy to the visible circle, the word "center" is applied. The soul is not a circle as, say, a geometrical figure. Our meaning is that in the soul and around about it exists the "primordial nature," that it derives its existence from the first existence especially when entirely separate from the body. Now, however, as we have a part of our being contained in the body, we are like a man whose feet are immersed in water while the rest of his body remains above it. Raising ourselves above the body by the part of us that is not submerged, we are, by our own center, attaching ourselves to the center of all. And so we remain, just as the centers of the great circles coincide with that of the sphere that surrounds them. If these circles were material and not spiritual, center and circumference would have to occupy definite places. But since the souls are of the intelligible realm and The One is still above The Intelligence, we are forced to say that the union of the intellective thinking being with its object proceeds by different means. The intellective thinking being is in the presence of its object by virtue of its similarity and identity, and it is united with its kindred with nothing to separate it from them. Bodies are by their bodies kept from union, but the bodiless are not held by this bodily limitation. What separates bodiless beings from one another is not spatial distance but their own differences and diversities: when there is no difference between them, they are mutually present.

As The One does not contain any difference, it is always present and we are present to it when we no longer contain difference. The One does not aspire to us, to move around us; we aspire to it, to move around it. Actually, we always move around it; but we do not always look. We are like a chorus grouped about a conductor who allow their attention to be distracted by the audience. If, however, they were to turn towards their conductor, they would sing as they should and would really be with him. We are always around The One. If we were not, we would dissolve and cease to exist. Yet our gaze does not remain fixed upon The One. When we look at it, we then attain the end of our desires and find rest. Then it is that, all discord past, we dance an inspired dance around it.

9.

In this dance the soul looks upon the source of life, the source of The Intelligence, the origin of Being, the cause of the Good, the root of The Soul.

All these entities emanate from The One without any lessening for it is not a material mass. If it were, the emanants would be perishable. But they are eternal because their originating principle always stays the same; not fragmenting itself in producing them, it remains entire. So they persist as well, just as light persists as long as sun shines.

We are not separated from The One, not distant from it, even though bodily nature has closed about us and drawn us to itself. It is because of The One that we breathe and have our being: it does not bestow its gifts at one moment only to leave us again; its giving is without cessation so long as it remains what it is. As we turn towards The One, we exist to a higher degree, while to withdraw from it is to fall. Our soul is delivered from evil by rising to that place which is free of all evils. There it knows. There it is immune. There it truly lives. Life not united with the divinity is shadow and mimicry of authentic life. Life there is the native act of The Intelligence, which, motionless in its contact with The One, gives birth to gods, beauty, justice, and virtue.

With all of these The Soul, filled with divinity, is pregnant; this is its starting point and its goal. It is its starting point because it is from the world above that it proceeds. It is its goal because in the world above is the Good to which it aspires and by returning to it there its proper nature is regained. Life here below in the midst of sense objects is for the soul a degradation, an exile, a loss of wings.

Further proof that our good is in the realm above is the love innate in our souls; hence the coupling in picture and story of Eros with Psyche. The soul, different from the divinity but sprung from it, must needs love. When it is in the realm above, its love is heavenly; here below, only commonplace. The heavenly Aphrodite dwells in the realm above; here below, the vulgar, harlot Aphrodite.

Every soul is an Aphrodite, as is suggested in the myth of Aphrodite's birth at the same time as that of Eros. As long as soul stays true to itself, it loves the divinity and desires to be at one with it, as a daughter loves with a noble love a noble father. When, however, the soul has come down here to human birth, it exchanges (as if deceived by the false promises of an adulterous lover) its divine love for one that is mortal. And then, far from its begetter, the soul yields to all manner of excess.

But, when the soul begins to hate its shame and puts away evil and makes its return, it finds its peace.

How great, then, is its bliss can be conceived by those who have not tasted it if they but think of earthly unions in love, marking well the joy felt by the lover who succeeds in obtaining his desires. But this is love directed to the mortal and harmful—to shadows—and soon disappears because such is not the authentic object of our love nor the good we really seek. Only in the world beyond does the real object of our love exist, the only one with which we can unite ourselves, of which we can have a part and which we can intimately possess without being separated by the barriers of flesh.

Anyone who has had this experience will know what I am talking about. He will know that the soul lives another life as it advances towards The One, reaches it and shares in it. Thus restored, the soul recognizes the presence of the dispenser of the true life. It needs nothing more. On the contrary, it must renounce everything else and rest in it alone, become it alone, all earthiness gone, eager to be free, impatient of every fetter that binds below in order so to enbrace the real object of its love with its entire being that no part of it does not touch The One.

Then of it and of itself the soul has all the vision that may be—of itself luminous now, filled with intellectual light, become pure light, subtle and weightless. It has become divine, is part of the eternal that is beyond becoming. It is like a flame. If later it is weighted down again by the realm of sense, it is like a flame extinguished.

10.

Why does a soul that has risen to the realm above not stay there? Because it has not yet entirely detached itself from things here below. Yet a time will come when it will uninterruptedly have vision, when it will no longer be bothered by body. The part of us that sees is not troubled. It is the other part which, even when we cease from our vision, does not cease from its activity of demonstration, proof and dialectic. But the act and faculty of vision is not reason but something greater than, prior and superior to, reason. So also is the object of the vision. When the contemplative looks upon himself in the act of contemplation, he will see himself to be like its object. He feels himself to be united to himself in the way that the object is united to itself; that is to say, he will experience himself as simple, just as it is simple.

Actually, we should not say, "He will see." What he sees (in case it is still possible to distinguish here the seer and the seen, to assert that the two are one would be indeed rash) is not seen, not distinguished, not represented as a thing apart. The man who obtains the vision becomes, as it were, another being. He ceases to be himself, retains nothing of himself. Absorbed in the beyond he is one with it, like a center coincident with another center. While the centers coincide, they are one. They become two only when they separate. It is in this sense that we can speak of The One as something separate.

Therefore it is so very difficult to describe this vision, for how can we represent as different from us what seemed, while we were contemplating it, not other than ourselves but perfect at-oneness with us?

11.

This, doubtless, is what is back of the injunction of the mystery religions which prohibit revelation to the uninitiated. The divine is not expressible, so the initiate is forbidden to speak of it to anyone who has not been fortunate enough to have beheld it himself.

The vision, in any case, did not imply duality; the man who saw was identical with what he saw. Hence he did not "see" it but rather was "oned" with it. If only he could preserve the memory of what he was while thus absorbed into The One, he would possess within himself an image of what it was.

In that state he had attained unity, nothing within him or without effecting diversity. When he had made his ascent, there was within him no disturbance, no anger, emotion, desire, reason, or thought. Actually, he was no longer himself; but, swept away and filled with the divine, he was still, solitary, and at rest, not turning to this side or that or even towards himself. He was in utter rest, having, so to say, become rest itself. In this state he busied himself no longer even with the beautiful. He had risen above beauty, had passed beyond even the choir of virtues.

He was like one who, penetrating the innermost sanctuary of a temple, leaves temple images behind. They will be the first objects to strike his view upon coming out of the sanctuary, after his contemplation and communion there not with an image or statue but with what they represent. They are but lesser objects of contemplation.

Such experience is hardly a vision. It is a seeing of a quite different kind, a self-transcendence, a simplification, self-abandonment, a striving for union and a repose, an intentness upon conformation. This is the way one sees in the sanctuary. Anyone who tries to see in any other way will see nothing.

By the use of these images, the wise among the soothsayers expressed in riddles how the divinity is seen. A wise priest, reading the riddle, will, once arrived in the realm beyond, achieve the true vision of the sanctuary. One who has not yet arrived there and knows the sanctuary is invisible, is the source and principle of everything, will also know that by hypostasis is hypostasis seen, and that like alone joins like. He will leave aside nothing of the divine the soul is capable of acquiring. If his vision is not yet complete, he will attend to its completion, which, for him who has risen above all, is The One that is above all. It is not the soul's nature to attain to utter nothingness. Falling into evil it falls, in this sense, into nothingness, but still not complete nothingness. And when it reverses direction, it arrives not at something different but at itself. Thus, when it is not in anything else, it is in nothing but itself. Yet, when it is in itself alone and not in being, it is in the supreme.

We as well transcend Being by virtue of The Soul with which we are united.

Now if you look upon yourself in this state, you find yourself an image of The One.

If you rise beyond yourself, an image rising to its model, you have reached the goal of your journey.

When you fall from this vision, you will, by arousing the virtue that is within yourself and by remembering the perfection that you possess, regain your likeness and through virtue rise to The Intelligence and through wisdom to The One.

Such is the life of the divinity and of divine and blessed men: detachment from all things here below, scorn of all earthly pleasures, the flight of the lone to the Alone.

8. Charles Tart

EDITOR'S INTRODUCTION

True mystics are rare; rarer still are individuals—like Plotinus—who are intellectuals or philosophers of note, as well as mystics. But much the same could be said about the representatives of any tradition, be it rationalism, empiricism, or mysticism. Actually, many of the phenomena characteristic of the mystical experience occur quite frequently, but to a modest degree. Thus, in a national survey, Greeley[1] found that 35% of the people reported having had at least one mysticlike experience, and about 5% have had such experiences repeatedly. Maslow[2] goes even further and claims that almost everyone has had "peak" experiences, or ecstasies, which resemble the mystical experience. And with the recent widespread use of hallucinogenic and other types of drugs, many people have experienced altered states of consciousness that contain some of the more dramatic features often described by mystics.

Mysticlike experiences pose two general questions of interest to psychology. (1) How are they to be analyzed and explained within a scientific framework? and (2) Is there any validity to the mystic's claim that there are more direct (intuitive) paths to truth and reality than that afforded by ordinary discursive thought?

With regard to the first question, let us summarize briefly some features common to most mystical experiences. Perhaps the most frequently noted characteristic is a disappearance of self-identity and a sense of unity with all things. For Plotinus, this experience of undifferentiated unity is symbolized by the One. The mystical experience is also characterized by heightened consciousness or

---

[1] A. M. Greeley, *Ecstasy: A way of knowing.* Englewood Cliffs, N.J.: Prentice-Hall, 1974.

[2] A. H. Maslow, *The farther reaches of human nature.* New York: Viking, 1971.

awareness. If the experience is not complete, as in most drug-induced states, this heightened consciousness may involve especially vivid and unusual sensory impressions. The full-blown mystical experience, however, is often described as transcending all sense impressions, no matter how vivid or unusual; it is a state of heightened consciousness *simpliciter*. This is what makes the mystical experience so difficult to describe. Finally, the mystical experience is characterized by a sense of realness, not just of the state itself, but also of the ultimate reality that supposedly underlies the experience. To the mystic, the experience signifies its own truth.

Probably the most typical explanation (from the point of view of conventional psychology) for these characteristics is that the mystical experience involves the breakdown of the cognitive structures that mediate everyday experience. As was explained in Chapter 1, cognitive structures may be likened to a set of "programs" that control the flow of information through the brain. These programs mediate the normal relationship between a man and his environment and help define reality for him. Most cognitive structures are built up through a lifetime of socialization, although some may be "wired in" through natural selection. In any case, through meditation, drugs, physical trauma, or unusual stimulation, it is sometimes possible temporarily to interrupt the normal flow of information through the brain. The result is a breakup of customary distinctions (e.g., between the self and others), a heightened awareness of internal as opposed to external cues, and a transference of the sense of reality from external objects to internal experience.

This is only the bare outline of how mystical experiences might be analyzed from a psychological point of view. Such an analysis does not mean, of course, that the mystic's claim of direct and intuitive knowledge is necessarily an illusion. The mystic, in fact, would argue just the reverse, namely, that the picture of reality painted by ordinary discursive thought is the illusion. In the following selection, Charles Tart (who has had considerable first-hand experience with both altered states of consciousness and scientific research) suggests a middle course. There are alternative ways in which cognition can be structured, Tart argues, and each may require its own state-specific science. However, certain cannons of scientific method must be observed even by those who choose to view reality from the perspective of another state of consciousness.

States of Consciousness and State-Specific Sciences: the extension of scientific method to the essential phenomena of altered states of consciousness is proposed

Blackburn (1) recently noted that many of our most talented young people are "turned off" to science: as a solution, he proposed that we recognize the validity of a more sensuous-intuitive approach to nature, treating it as complementary to the classical intellectual approach.

I have seen the same rejection of science by many of the brightest students in California, and the problem is indeed serious. Blackburn's analysis is valid, but not deep enough. A more fundamental source of alienation is the widespread experience of altered states of consciousness (ASC's) by the young, coupled with the almost total rejection of the knowledge gained during the experiencing of ASC's by the scientific establishment. Blackburn himself exemplifies this rejection when he says: "Perhaps science has much to learn along this line from the disciplines, *as distinct from the content*, of Oriental religions" (my italics).

To illustrate, a recent Gallup poll (2) indicated that approximately half of American college students have tried marijuana, and a large number of them use it fairly regularly. They do this at the risk of having their careers ruined and going to jail for several years. Why? Conventional research on the nature of marijuana intoxication tells us that the primary effects are a slight increase in heart rate, reddening of the eyes, some difficulty with memory, and small decrements in performance on complex psychomotor tests.

Would you risk going to jail to experience these?

A young marijuana smoker who hears a scientist or physician talk about these findings as the basic nature of marijuana intoxication will simply sneer and have his antiscientific attitude further reinforced. It is clear to him that the scientist has no real understanding of what marijuana intoxication is all about (3).

More formally, an increasingly significant number of people are experimenting with ASC's in themselves, and finding the experiences thus gained of extreme importance in their philosophy and style of life. The conflict between experiences in these ASC's and the attitudes and intellectual-emotional systems that have evolved in our ordinary state of consciousness (SoC) is a major factor behind the increased alienation of many people from conventional science. Experiences of ecstasy, mystical union, other "dimensions," rapture, beauty, space-and-time transcendence, and transpersonal knowledge, all common in ASC's, are simply not treated adequately in conventional scientific approaches. These experiences will not "go away" if we crack down more on psychedelic drugs, for immense numbers of people now practice various non-drug techniques for producing ASC's, such as meditation (4) and yoga.

The purpose of this article is to show that it is possible to investigate and work with the important phenomena of ASC's in a manner which is perfectly compatible with the essence of scientific method. The conflict discussed above is not necessary.

STATES OF CONSCIOUSNESS

An ASC may be defined for the purposes of this article as a qualitative alteration in the overall pattern of mental functioning, such that the experiencer feels his consciousness is radically different from the way it functions ordinarily. An SoC is thus defined not in terms of any particular content of consciousness, or specific behavior or physiological change, but in terms of the overall patterning of psychological functioning.

An analogy with computer functioning can clarify this definition. A computer has a complex program of many subroutines. If we reprogram it quite differently, the same sorts of input data may be handled in quite different ways; we will be able to predict very little from our knowledge of the old program about the effects of varying the input, even though old and new programs have some subroutines in common. The new program with its input-output interactions must be studied in and of itself. An ASC is analogous to changing temporarily the program of a computer.

The ASC's experienced by almost all ordinary people are dreaming states and the hypnogogic and hypnopompic states, the transitional states between sleeping and waking. Many other people experience another ASC, alcohol intoxication.

The relatively new (to our culture) ASC's that are now having such an impact are those produced by marijuana, more powerful psychedelic drugs such as LSD, meditative states, so-called possession states, and auto-hypnotic states (5).

STATES OF CONSCIOUSNESS
AND PARADIGMS

It is useful to compare this concept of an SoC, a qualitatively distinct organization of the patterning of mental functioning, with Kuhn's (6) concept of paradigms in science. A paradigm is an intellectual achievement that underlies normal science and attracts and guides the work of an enduring number of adherents in their scientific activity. It is a kind of "super theory," a formulation of scope wide enough to affect the organization of most or all of the major known phenomena of its field. Yet it is sufficiently open-ended that there still remain important problems to be solved within that framework. Examples of important paradigms in the history of science have been Copernican astronomy and Newtonian dynamics.

Because of their tremendous success, paradigms undergo a change which, in principle, ordinary scientific theories do not undergo. An ordinary scientific theory is always subject to further questioning and testing as it is extended. A paradigm becomes an implicit framework for most scientists working within it; it is the natural way of looking at things and doing things. It does not seriously occur to the adherents of a paradigm to question it any more (we may ignore, for the moment, the occurrence of scientific revolutions). Theories become referred to as laws: people talk of the law of gravity, not the theory of gravity, for example.

A paradigm serves to concentrate the attention of a researcher on sensible problem areas and to prevent him from wasting his time on what might be trivia. On the other hand, by implicitly defining some lines of research as trivial or nonsensical; a paradigm acts like a blinder. Kuhn has discussed this blinding function as a key factor in the lack of effective communications during paradigm clashes.

The concept of a paradigm and of an SoC are quite similar. Both constitute complex, interlocking sets of rules and theories that enable a person to interact with and interpret experiences within an environment. In both cases, the rules are largely implicit. They are not recognized as tentative working hypotheses; they operate automatically and the person feels he is doing the obvious or natural thing.

PARADIGM CLASH BETWEEN
"STRAIGHT" AND "HIP"

Human beings become emotionally attached to the things which give them pleasure, and a scientist making important progress within a particular paradigm becomes emotionally attached to it. When data which make no sense in terms of the (implicit) paradigm are brought to our attention, the usual result is not a reevaluation of the paradigm, but a rejection or misperception of the data. This rejection seems rational to others sharing that paradigm and irrational or rationalizing to others committed to a different paradigm.

The conflict now existing between those who have experienced certain ASC's (whose ranks include many young scientists) and those who have not is very much a paradigmatic conflict. For example, a subject takes LSD, and tells his investigator that "You and I, we are all one, there are no separate selves." The investigator reports that his subject showed a "confused sense of identity and distorted thinking process." The subject is reporting what is obvious to him, the investigator is reporting what is obvious to him. The investigator's implicit paradigm, based on his scientific training, his cultural background, and his normal SoC, indicates that a literal interpretation of the subject's statement cannot be true, and therefore must be interpreted as mental dysfunction on the part of the subject. The subject, his paradigms radically changed for the moment by being in an ASC, not only reports what is obviously true to him, but perceives the investigator as showing mental dysfunction, by virtue of being incapable of perceiving the obvious!

Historically, paradigm clashes have been characterized by bitter emotional antagonisms, and total rejection of the opponent. Currently we are seeing the same sort of process: the respectable psychiatrist, who would not take any of those "psychotomimetic" drugs himself or sit down and experience that crazy meditation process, carries out research to show that drug takers and those who practice meditation are escapists. The drug taker or meditator views the same investigator as narrow-minded, prejudiced, and repressive, and as a result drops out of the university. Communication between the two factions is almost nil.

Must the experiencers of ASC's continue to see the scientists as concentrating on the irrelevant, and the scientists see the experiencers as confused (7) or mentally ill? Or can science deal adequately with the experiences of these people? The thesis I shall now present in detail is that we can deal with the important aspects of ASC's using the essence of scientific method, even though a variety of nonessentials, unfortunately identified with current science, hinder such an effort.

THE NATURE OF KNOWLEDGE

Basically, science (from the Latin *scire*, to know) deals with knowledge. Knowledge may be defined as an immediately given experiential feeling of congruence between two different kinds of experience, a matching. One set of experiences may be regarded as perceptions of the external world, of others, of oneself; the second set may be regarded as a theory, a scheme, a system of understanding. The feeling of congruence is something immediately given in experience, although many refinements have been worked out for judging degrees of congruence.

All knowledge, then, is basically experiential knowledge. Even my knowledge of the physical world can be reduced to this: given certain sets of experiences, which I (by assumption) attribute to the external world activating my sensory apparatus, it may be possible for me to compare them with purely internal experiences (memories, previous knowledge) and predict with a high degree of reliability other kinds of experiences, which I again attribute to the external world.

Because science has been incredibly successful in dealing with the physical world, it has been historically associated with a philosophy of physicalism, the belief that reality is all reducible to certain kinds of physical entities. The vast majority of phenomena of ASC's have no known physical manifestations: thus to physicalistic philosophy they are epiphenomena, not worthy of study. But insofar as science deals with knowledge, it need not restrict itself only to physical kinds of knowledge.

THE ESSENCE OF SCIENTIFIC METHOD

I shall discuss the essence of scientific method, and show that this essence is perfectly compatible with an enlarged study of the important phenomena of ASC's. In particular, I propose that state-specific sciences (SSS) be developed.

As satisfying as the feeling of knowing can be, we are often wrong: what seems like congruence at first later does not match, or has no generality. Man has learned that his reasoning is often faulty, his observations are often incomplete or mistaken, and that emotional and other nonconscious factors can seriously distort both reasoning and observational processes. His reliance on authorities, "rationality" or "elegance," are no sure criteria for achieving truth. The development of scientific method may be seen as a determined effort to systematize the process of acquiring knowledge in such a way as to minimize the various pitfalls of observation and reasoning.

I shall discuss four basic rules of scientific method to which an investigator is committed: (i) good observation; (ii) the public nature of observation; (iii) the necessity to theorize logically; and (iv) the testing of theory by observable consequences; all these constitute the scientific enterprise. I shall consider the wider application of each rule to ASC's and indicate how unnecessary physicalistic restrictions may be dropped. I will show that all these commitments or rules can be accommodated in the development of SSS's that I propose.

OBSERVATION

The scientist is committed to observe as well as possible the phenomena of interest and to search constantly for better ways of making these observations. But our paradigmatic commitments, our SoC's, make us likely to observe certain parts of reality and to ignore or observe with error certain other parts of it.

Many of the most important phenomena of ASC's have been observed poorly or not at all because of the physicalistic labeling of them as epiphenomena, so that they have been called "subjective," "ephemeral," "unreliable," or "unscientific." Observations of internal processes are probably much more difficult to make than those of external physical processes, because of their inherently greater complexity. The essence of science, however, is that we observe what there is to be observed whether it is difficult or not.

Furthermore, most of what we know about the phenomena of ASC's has been obtained from untrained people, almost none of whom have shared the scientists' commitment to constantly reexamine their observations in greater and greater detail. This should not imply that internal phenomena are inherently unobservable or unstable; we are comparing the first observations of internal phenomena with observations of physical sciences that have undergone centuries of refinement.

We must consider one other problem of observation. One of the traditional idols of science, the "detached observer," has no place in dealing with many internal phenomena of SoCs. Not only are the observer's perceptions selective, he may also affect the things he observes. We must try to understand the characteristics of each individual observer in order to compensate for them.

A recognition of the unreality of the detached observer in the psychological sciences is becoming widespread, under the topics of experimenter bias (8) and demand characteristics (9). A similar recognition long ago occurred in physics when it was realized that the observed was altered by the process of observation at subatomic levels. When we deal with ASC's where the observer is the experiencer of the ASC, this factor is of paramount importance. Knowing the characteristics of the observer can also confound the process of consensual validation, which I shall now consider.

PUBLIC NATURE OF OBSERVATION

Observations must be public in that they must be replicable by any properly trained observer. The experienced conditions that led to the report of certain experiences must be described in sufficient detail that others may duplicate them and consequently have experiences which meet criteria of identicality. That someone else may set up similar conditions but not have the same experiences proves that the original investigator gave an incorrect description of the conditions and observations, or that he was not aware of certain essential aspects of the conditions.

The physicalistic accretion to this rule of consensual validation is that, physical data being the only "real" data, internal phenomena must be reduced to physiological or behavioral data to become reliable or they will be ignored entirely. I believe most physical observations to be much more readily replicable by any trained observer because they are inherently simpler phenomena than internal ones. In principle, however, consensual validation of internal phenomena by a trained observer is quite possible.

The emphasis on public observations in science has had a misleading quality insofar as it implies that any intelligent man can replicate a scientist's observations. This might have been true early in the history of science, but nowadays only the trained observer can replicate many observations. I cannot go into a modern physicist's laboratory and confirm his observations. Indeed, his talk of what he has found in his experiments (physicists seem to talk about innumerable invisible entities these days) would probably seem mystical to me, just as many descriptions of internal states sound mystical to those with a background in the physical sciences.

Given the high complexity of the phenomena associated with ASC's, the need for replication by trained observers is exceptionally important. Since it generally takes 4 to 10 years of intensive training to produce a scientist in any of our conventional sciences, we should not be surprised that there has been very little reliability of observations by untrained observers of ASC phenomena.

Further, for the state-specific sciences that I propose should be established, we cannot specify the requirements that would constitute adequate training. These would only be determined after considerable trial and error. We should also recognize that very few people might complete the training successfully. Some people do not have the necessary innate characteristics to become physicists, and some probably do not have the innate characteristics to become, say, scientific investigators of meditative states.

Public observation, then, always refers to a limited, specially trained public. It is only by basic agreement among those specially trained people that data become accepted as a foundation for the development of a science. That laymen cannot replicate the observations is of little relevance.

A second problem in consensual validation arises from a phenomenon predicted by my concept of ASC's, but not yet empirically investigated, namely, state-specific communication. Given that an ASC is an overall qualitative and quantitative shift in the complex functioning of consciousness, such that there are new "logics" and perceptions (which would constitute a paradigm shift), it is quite reasonable to hypothesize that communication may take a different pattern. For two observers, both of whom, we assume, are fluent in communicating with each other in a given SoC, communication about some new observations may seem adequate to them, or may be improved or deteriorated in specific ways. To an outside observer, an observer in a different SoC, the communication between these two observers may seem "deteriorated."

Practically all investigations of communication by persons in ASC's have resulted in reports of deterioration of communication abilities. In designing their studies, however, these investigators have not taken into account the fact that the pattern of communication may have changed. If I am listening to two people speaking in English, and they suddenly begin to intersperse words and phrases in Polish, I, as an outside (that is, a non-Polish speaking) observer, will note a gross deterioration in communication. Adequacy of communication between people in the same SoC and across SoC's must be empirically determined.

Thus consensual validation may be restricted by the fact that only observers in the same ASC are able to communicate adequately with each other, and they may not be able to communicate adequately to someone in a different SoC, say normal consciousness (10).

THEORIZING

A scientist may theorize about his observations as much as he wishes to, but the theory he develops must consistently account for all that he has observed, and should have a logical structure that other scientists can comprehend (but not necessarily accept).

The requirement to theorize logically and consistently with the data is not as simple as it looks, however. Any logic consists of a basic set of assumptions and a set of rules for manipulating information, based on these assumptions. Change the assumptions, or change the rules, and there may be entirely different outcomes from the same data. A paradigm, too, is a logic: it has certain assumptions and rules for working within these assumptions. By changing the paradigm, altering the SoC, the nature of theory building may change radically. Thus a person in SoC 2 might come to very different conclusions about the nature of the same events that he observed in SoC 1. An investigator in SoC 1 may comment on the comprehensibility of the second person's ideas from the point of view (paradigm) of SoC 1, but can say nothing about their inherent validity. A scientist who could enter either SoC 1 or SoC 2, however, could pronounce on the comprehensibility of the other's theory, and the adherence of that theory to the rules and logic of SoC 2. Thus, scientists trained in the same SoC may check on the logical validity of each other's theorizing. We have then the possibility of a state-specific logic underlying theorizing in various SoC's.

OBSERVABLE CONSEQUENCES

Any theory a scientist develops must have observable consequences, and from that theory it must be possible to make predictions that can be verified by observation. If such verification is not possible, the theory must be considered invalid, regardless of its elegance, logic, or other appeal.

Ordinarily we think of empirical validation, of validation in terms of testable consequences that produce physical effects, but this is misleading. Any effect, whether interpreted as physical or nonphysical, is ultimately an experience in the observer's mind. All that is essentially required to validate a theory is that it predict that "When a certain experience (observed condition) has occurred, another (predicted) kind of experience will follow, under specified experiential conditions." Thus a perfectly scientific theory may be based on data that have no physical existence.

STATE–SPECIFIC SCIENCES

We tend to envision the practice of science like this: centered around interest in some particular range of subject matter, a small number of highly selected, talented, and rigorously trained people spend considerable time making detailed observations on the subject matter of interest. They may or may not have special places (laboratories) or instruments or methods to assist them in making finer observations. They speak to one another in a special language which they feel conveys precisely the important facts of their field. Using this language, they confirm and extend each other's knowledge of certain data basic to the field. They theorize about their basic data and construct elaborate systems. They validate these by recourse to further observation. These trained people all have a long-term commitment to the constant refinement of observation and extension of theory. Their activity is frequently incomprehensible to laymen.

This general description is equally applicable to a variety of sciences, or areas that could become sciences, whether we called such areas biology, physics, chemistry, psychology, understanding of mystical states, or drug-induced enhancement of cognitive processes. The particulars of research would look very different, but the basic scientific method running through all is the same.

More formally, I now propose the creation of various state-specific sciences. If such sciences could be created, we would have a group of highly skilled, dedicated, and trained practitioners able to achieve certain SoC's, and able to agree with one another that they have attained a common state. While in that SoC, they might then investigate other areas of interest, whether these be totally internal phenomena of that given state, the interaction of that state with external, physical reality, or people in other SoC's.

The fact that the experimenter should be able to function skillfully in the SoC itself for a state-specific science does not necessarily mean that he would always be the subject. While he might often be the subject, observer, and experimenter simultaneously, it would be quite possible for him to collect data from experimental manipulations of other subjects in the SoC, and either be in that SoC himself at the time of data collection or be in that SoC himself for data reduction and theorizing.

Examples of some observations made and theorizing done by a scientist in a specific ASC would illustrate the nature of a proposed state-specific science. But this is not possible because no state-specific sciences have yet been established (11). Also, any example that would make good sense to the readers of this article (who are, presumably, all in a normal SoC) would not really illustrate the uniqueness of a state-specific science. If it did make sense, it would be an example of a problem that could be approached adequately from both the ASC and normal SoC's, and thus it would be too easy to see the entire problem in terms of accepted scientific procedures for normal SoC's and miss the point about the necessity for developing state-specific sciences.

STATE–SPECIFIC SCIENCES
AND RELIGION

Some aspects of organized religion appear to resemble state-specific sciences. There are techniques that allow the believer to enter an ASC and then have religious experiences in that ASC which are proof of his religious belief. People who have had such experiences usually describe them as ineffable in important ways—that is, as not fully comprehensible in an ordinary SoC. Conversions at revivalistic meetings are the most common example of religious experiences occurring in various ASC's induced by an intensely emotional atmosphere.

In examining the esoteric training systems of some religions, there seems to be even more resemblance between such mystical ways and state-specific sciences, for here we often have the picture of devoted specialists, complex techniques, and repeated experiencing of the ASC's in order to further religious knowledge.

Nevertheless the proposed state-specific sciences are not simply religion in a new guise. The use of ASC's in religion may involve the kind of commitment to searching for truth that is needed for developing a state-specific science, but practically all the religions we know might be defined as state-specific technologies, operated in the service of a priori belief systems. The experiencers of ASC's in most religious contexts have already been thoroughly indoctrinated in a particular belief system. This belief system may then mold the content of the ASC's to create specific experiences which reinforce or validate the belief system.

The crucial distinction between a religion utilizing ASC's and a state-specific science is the commitment of the scientist to reexamine constantly his own belief system and to question the obvious in spite of its intellectual or emotional appeal to him. Investigators of ASC's would certainly encounter an immense variety of phenomena labeled religious experience or mystical revelation during the development of state-specific sciences, but they would have to remain committed to examining these phenomena more carefully, sharing their observations and techniques with colleagues, and subjecting the beliefs (hypotheses, theories) that result from such experiences to the requirement of leading to testable predictions. In practice, because we are aware of the immense emotional power of mystical experiences, this would be a difficult task, but it is one that will have to be undertaken by disciplined investigators if we are to understand various ASC's.

RELATIONSHIP BETWEEN STATE-SPECIFIC SCIENCES

Any state-specific science may be considered as consisting of two parts, observations and theorizations. The observations are what can be experienced relatively directly; the theories are the *inferences* about what sort of nonobservable factors account for the observations. For example, the phenomena of synesthesia (seeing colors as a result of hearing sounds) is a theoretical proposition for me in my ordinary SoC: I do not experience it, and can only generate theories about what other people report about it. If I were under the influence of a psychedelic drug such as LSD or marijuana (3), I could probably experience synesthesia directly, and my descriptions of the experience would become data.

Figure 1 demonstrates some possible relationships between three state-specific sciences. State-specific sciences 1 and 2 show considerable overlap.

The area labeled $O_1 O_2$ permits direct observation in both sciences. Area $T_1 T_2$ permits theoretical inferences about common subject matter from the two perspectives. In area $O_1 T_2$, by contrast, the theoretical propositions of state-specific science number 2 are matters of direct observation for the scientist in SoC number 1, and vice versa for the area $T_1 O_2$. State-specific science number 3 consists of a body of observation and theory exclusive to that science and has no overlap with the other two sciences: it neither confirms, denies, nor complements them.

It would be naively reductionistic to say that the work in one state-specific science *validates* or *invalidates* the work in a second

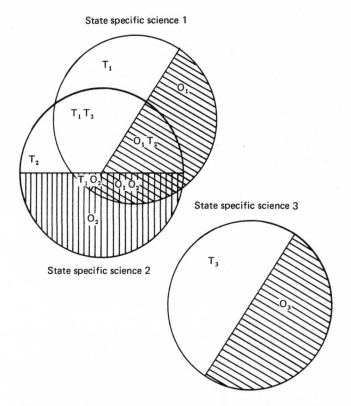

FIGURE 1 Possible relationships between three state-specific sciences. The area labeled $O_1 O_2$ is subject matter capable of direct observation in both sciences. Area $T_1 T_2$ consists of theoretical (T) inferences about subject matter overlapping the two sciences. By contrast, in area $O_1 T_2$, the theoretical propositions of state-specific science number 2 are matters of direct observation for the scientist in state of consciousness number 1, and vice versa for area $T_1 O_2$. State-specific science number 3 consists of a body of observation and theory exclusive to that science.

state-specific science; I prefer to say that two different state-specific sciences, where they overlap, provide quite different points of view with respect to certain kinds of theories and data, and thus complement (12) each other. The proposed creation of state-specific sciences neither validates nor invalidates the activities of normal consciousness sciences (NCS). The possibility of developing certain state-specific sciences means only that certain kinds of phenomena may be handled more adequately within these potential new sciences.

Interrelationships more complex than those that are illustrated in Fig. 1 are possible.

The possibility of stimulating interactions between different state-specific sciences is very real. Creative breakthroughs in NCS have frequently been made by scientists temporarily going into an ASC (13). In such instances, the scientists concerned saw quite different views of their problems and performed different kinds of reasoning, conscious or nonconsciousness, which led to results that could be tested within their NCS.

A current example of such interaction is the finding that in Zen meditation (a highly developed discipline in Japan) there are physiological correlates of meditative experiences, such as decreased frequency of alpha-rhythm, which can also be produced by means of instrumentally aided feedback-learning techniques (14). This finding might elucidate some of the processes peculiar to each discipline.

INDIVIDUAL DIFFERENCES

A widespread and misleading assumption that hinders the development of state-specific sciences and confuses their interrelationships is the assumption that because two people are normal (not certified insane), their ordinary SoC's are essentially the same. In reality I suspect that there are enormous differences between the SoC's of some normal people. Because societies train people to behave and communicate along socially approved lines, these differences are covered up.

For example, some people think in images, others in words. Some can voluntarily anesthetize parts of their body, most cannot. Some recall past events by imaging the scene and looking at the relevant details; others use complex verbal processes with no images.

This means that person A may be able to observe certain kinds of experiential data that person B cannot experience in his ordinary SoC, no matter how hard B tries. There may be several consequences. Person B may think that A is insane, too imaginative, or a liar, or he may feel inferior to A. Person A may also feel himself odd, if he takes B as a standard of normality.

In some cases, B may be able to enter an ASC and there experience the sorts of things that A has reported to him. A realm of knowledge that is ordinary for A is then specific for an ASC for B. Similarly, some of the experiences of B in his ASC may not be available for direct observation by A in his ordinary SoC.

The phenomenon of synesthesia can again serve as an example. Some individuals possess this ability in their ordinary SoC, most do not. Yet 56 percent of a sample of experienced marijuana users experienced synesthesia at least occasionally (3) while in the drug-induced ASC.

Thus we may conceive of bits of knowledge that are specific for an ASC for one individual, part of ordinary consciousness for another. Arguments over the usefulness of the concept of states of consciousness may reflect differences in the structure of the ordinary SoC of various investigators.

Another important source of individual differences, little understood at present, is the degree to which an individual may first make a particular observation or form a concept in one SoC and then be able to reexperience or comprehend it in another SoC. That is, many items of information which were state-specific when observed initially may be learned and somehow transferred (fully or partially) to another SoC. Differences across individuals, various combinations of SoC's, and types of experience will probably be enormous.

I have only outlined the complexities created by individual differences in normal SoC's and have used the normal SoC as a baseline for comparison with ASC's; but it is evident that every SoC must eventually be compared against every other SoC.

PROBLEMS, PITFALLS, AND PERSONAL PERILS

If we use the practical experience of Western man with ASC's as a guide, the development of state-specific sciences will be beset by a number of difficulties. These difficulties will be of two kinds: general methodological problems stemming from the inherent nature of some ASC's; and those concerned with personal perils to the investigator. I shall discuss state-related problems first.

The first important problem in the proposed development of state-specific sciences is the obvious perception of truth. In many ASC's, one's experience is that one is obviously and lucidly experiencing truth directly, without question. An immediate result of this may be an extinction of the desire for further questioning. Further, this experience of obvious truth, while not necessarily preventing the individual investigator from further examining his data, may not arouse his desire for consensual validation. Since one of the greatest strengths of science is its insistence on consensual validation of basic data, this can be a serious drawback. Investigators attempting to develop state-specific sciences will have to learn to distrust the obvious.

A second major problem in developing state-specific sciences is that in some ASC's one's abilities to visualize and imagine are immensely enhanced, so that whatever one imagines seems perfectly real. Thus one can imagine that something is being observed and experience it as datum. If one can essentially conjure up anything one wishes, how can we ever get at truth?

One way of looking at this problem is to consider any such vivid imaginings as potential effects: they are data, in the sense that what can be vividly imagined in a given SoC is important to know. It may not be the case that anything can be imagined with equal facility, and the relationships between what can be imagined may show a lawful pattern.

More generally, the way to approach this problem is to realize that it is not unique to ASC's. One can have all sorts of illusions, and misperceptions in our ordinary SoC. Before the rise of modern physical science, all sorts of things were imagined about the nature of the physical world that could not be directly refuted. The same techniques that eliminated these illusions in the physical sciences will also eliminate them in state-specific sciences dealing with nonphysical data—that is, all observations will have to be subjected to consensual validation and all their theoretical consequences will have to be examined. Insofar as experiences are purely arbitrary imaginings, those that do not show consistent patterns and cannot be replicated will be distinguished from those phenomena which do show general lawfulness.

The effects of this enhanced vividness of imagination in some ASC's will be complicated further by two other important problems, namely, experimenter bias (8, 9), and the fact that one person's illusion in a given ASC can sometimes be communicated to another person in the same ASC so that a kind of false consensual validation results. Again, the only long-term solution to this would be the requirement that perdictions based on concepts arising from various experiences be verified experientially.

A third major problem is that state-specific sciences probably cannot be developed for all ASC's: some ASC's may depend on or result from genuine deterioration of observational and reasoning abilities, or a deterioration of volition. Those SoC's for which state-specific sciences might well be developed will be discussed later, but it should be made clear that the development of each science should result from trial and error, and not from a priori decisions based on reasoning in our ordinary SoC's.

A fourth major problem is that of ineffability. Some experiences are ineffable in the sense that: (i) a person may experience them, but be unable to express or conceptualize them adequately to himself; (ii) while a person may be able to conceptualize an experience tc himself he may not be able to communicate it adequately to anyone else. Certain phenomena of the first type may simply be inaccessible to scientific investigation. Phenomena of the second type may be accessible to scientific investigation only insofar as we are willing to recognize that a science, in the sense of following most of the basic rules, may exist only for a single person. Insofar as such a solitary science would lack all the advantages gained by consensual validation, we could not expect it to have as much power and rigor as conventional scientific endeavor.

Many phenomena which are now considered ineffable may not be so in reality. This may be a matter of our general lack of experience with ASC's and the lack of an adequate language for communicating about ASC phenomena. In most well-developed languages the major part of the vocabulary was developed primarily in adaptation to survival in the physical world.

Finally, we should recognize the possibility that various phenomena of ASC's may be too complex for human beings to understand. The phenomena may depend on or be affected by so many variables that we shall never understand them. In the history of science, however, many phenomena which appeared too complex at first were eventually comprehensible.

PERSONAL PERILS

The personal perils that an investigator will face in attempting to develop a state-specific science are of two kinds, those associated with reactions colloquially called a bad trip and a good trip, respectively.

Bad trips, in which an extremely unpleasant, emotional reaction is experienced in an ASC, and in which there are possible long-term adverse consequences on a person's personal adjustment, often stem from the fact that our upbringing has not prepared us to undergo radical alterations in our ordinary SoC's. We are dependent on stability, we fear the unknown, and we develop personal rigidities and various kinds of personal and social taboos. It is traditional in our society to consider ASC's as signs of insanity; ASC's therefore cause great fears in those who experience them.

In many ASC's, defenses against unacceptable personal impulses may become partially or wholly ineffective, so the person feels flooded with traumatic material that he cannot handle. All these things result in fear and avoidance of ASC's, and make it difficult or impossible for some individuals to function in an ASC in a way that is consistent with the development of a state-specific science.

Maslow (15) has discussed these as pathologies of cognition that seriously interfere with the scientific enterprise in general, as well as ordinary life. In principle, adequate selection and training could minimize these hazards for at least some people.

Good trips may also endanger an investigator. A trip may produce experiences that are so rewarding that they interfere with the scientific activity of the investigator. The perception of obvious truth, and its effect of eliminating the need for further investigation or consensual validation have already been mentioned. Another peril comes from the ability to imagine or create vivid experiences. They may be so highly rewarding that the investigator does not follow the rule of investigating the obvious regardless of his personal satisfaction with results. Similarly, his attachment to good feelings, ecstasy, and the like, and his refusal to consider alternative conceptualizations of these, can seriously stifle the progress of investigation.

These personal perils again emphasize the necessity of developing adequate training programs for scientists who wish to develop state-specific sciences. Although it is difficult to envision such a training program, it is evident that much conventional scientific training is contrary to what would be needed to develop a state-specific science, because it tends to produce rigidity and avoidance of personal involvement with subject matter, rather than open-mindedness and flexibility. Much of the training program would have to be devoted to the scientist's understanding of himself so that the (unconscious) effects of his personal biases will be minimized during his investigations of an ASC.

Many of us know that there have been cases where scientists, after becoming personally involved with ASC's, have subsequently become very poor scientists or have experienced personal psychological crises. It would be premature, however, to conclude that such unfortunate consequences cannot be avoided by proper training and discipline. In the early history of the physical sciences we had many fanatics who were nonobjective about their investigations. Not all experiencers of various ASC's develop pathology as a result: indeed, many seem to become considerably more mature. Only from actual attempts to develop state-specific sciences will we be able to determine the actual SoC's that are suitable for development, and the kinds of people that are best suited to such work (16).

PROSPECTS

I believe that an examination of human history and our current situation provides the strongest argument for the necessity of developing state-specific sciences. Throughout history man has been influenced by the spiritual and mystical factors that are expressed (usually in watered-down form) in the religions that attract the masses of people. Spiritual and mystical experiences are primary phenomena of various ASC's: because of such experiences, untold numbers of both the noblest and most horrible acts of which people are capable have been committed. Yet in all the time that Western science has existed, no concerted attempt has been made to understand these ASC phenomena in scientific terms.

It was the hope of many that religions were simply a form of superstition that would be left behind in our "rational" age. Not only has this hope failed, but our own understanding of the nature of reasoning now makes it clear that it can never be fulfilled. Reason is a tool, and a tool that is wielded in the service of assumptions, beliefs, and needs which are not themselves subject to reason. The irrational, or, better yet, the arational, will not disappear from the human situation. Our immense success in the development of the physical sciences has not been particularly successful in formulating better philosophies of life, or increasing our real knowledge of ourselves. The sciences we have developed to date are not very human sciences. They tell us how to do things, but give us no scientific insights on questions of what to do, what not to do, or why to do things.

The youth of today and mature scientists in increasing numbers are turning to meditation, oriental religions, and personal use of psychedelic drugs. The phenomena encountered in these ASC's provide more satisfaction and are more relevant to the formulation of philosophies of life and deciding upon appropriate ways of living, than "pure reason" (17). My own impressions are that very large numbers of scientists are now personally exploring ASC's, but few have begun to connect this personal exploration with their scientific activities.

It is difficult to predict what the chances are of developing state-specific sciences. Our knowledge is still too diffuse and dependent on our normal SoC's. Yet I think it is probable that state-specific sciences can be developed for such SoC's as auto-hypnosis, meditative states, lucid dreaming, marijuana intoxication, LSD intoxication, self-remembering, reverie, and biofeedback-induced states (18). In all of these SoC's, volition seems to be retained, so that the observer can indeed carry out experiments on himself or others or both. Some SoC's, in which the volition to experiment during the state may disappear, but in which some experimentation can be carried out if special conditions are prepared before the state is entered, might be alcohol intoxication, ordinary dreaming, hypnogogic and hypnopompic states, and high dreams (18). It is not clear whether other ASC's would be suitable for developing state-specific sciences or whether mental deterioration would be too great. Such questions will only be answered by experiment.

I have nothing against religious and mystical groups. Yet I suspect that the vast majority of them have developed compelling belief systems rather than state-specific sciences. Will scientific method be extended to the development of state-specific sciences so as to improve our human situation? Or will the immense power of ASC's be left in the hands of many cults and sects? I hope that the development of state-specific sciences will be our goal.

REFERENCES AND NOTES

1. T. Blackburn, Science 172, 1003 (1971).
2. Newsweek, 25 January 1971, p. 52.
3. An attempt to describe the phenomena of marijuana intoxication in terms that make sense to the user, as well as the investigator, has been presented elsewhere. See C. Tart, On Being Stoned: A Psychological Study of Marijuana Intoxication (Science & Behavior Books, Palo Alto, 1971).
4. C. Naranjo and R. Ornstein, On the Psychology of Meditation (Viking, New York, 1971).
5. Note that an SoC is defined by the stable parameters of the pattern that constitute it, not by the particular technique of inducing that pattern, for some ASC's can be induced by a variety of induction methods. By analogy, to understand the altered computer program you must study what it does, not study the programmer who originally set it up.
6. T. Kuhn, The Structure of Scientific Revolutions (Univ. of Chicago Press, Chicago, 1962).
7. Note that states of confusion and impaired functioning are certainly aspects of some drug-induced SoC's, but are not of primary interest here.
8. R. Rosenthal, Experimenter Effects in Behavioral Research (Appleton-Century-Crofts, New York, 1966).
9. M. Orne, Amer. Psychol. 17, 776 (1962).
10. A state-specific scientist might find his own work somewhat incomprehensible when he was not in that SoC because of the phenomenon of state-specific memory—that is, not enough of his work would transfer to his ordinary SoC to make it comprehensible, even though it would make perfect sense when he was again in the ASC in which he did his scientific work.
11. "Ordinary consciousness science" is not a good example of a "pure" state-specific science because many important discoveries have occurred during ASC's, such as reverie, dreaming, and meditative-like states.
12. N. Bohr, in Essays, 1958-1962, on Atomic Physics and Human Knowledge (Wiley, New York, 1963).

13. B. Ghiselin, *The Creative Process* (New American Library, New York, 1952).
14. E. Green, A. Green, E. Walters, *J. Transpers. Psychol.* 2, 1 (1970).
15. A. Maslow, *The Psychology of Science: A Reconnaissance* (Harper & Row, New York, 1966).
16. The ASC's resulting from very dangerous drugs (heroin, for example) may be scientifically interesting, but the risk may be too high to warrant our developing state-specific sciences for them. The personal and social issues involved in evaluating this kind of risk are beyond the scope of this article.
17. J. Needleman, *The New Religions* (Doubleday, New York, 1970).
18. C. Tart, *Altered States of Consciousness: A Book of Readings* (Wiley, New York, 1969).

V. THE LIMITS OF REASON AND WILL

9. Augustine

EDITOR'S INTRODUCTION

One of the greatest difficulties in reading the history of science, or any history for that matter, is to be able to see the world through the eyes of people who lived and worked in another cultural epoch. The problem is analogous to that described by Kuhn (Chapt. 2) with regard to scientists operating under different paradigms. In the case of history, however, the "paradigm" is not limited to a restricted area of inquiry, but may encompass an entire world view. For the contemporary student, the medieval period presents a particularly difficult problem. Classical Greek philosophy, like modern science, tended to be secular and optimistic. The concern was with nature and society as it does—or should—exist, and there was a deeply held conviction that human betterment could be achieved through rational inquiry. When we turn to the Middle Ages, however, the dominant world view is in many respects the antithesis of that of modern science. The early Middle Ages are characterized by a rise of asceticism with regard to things of this world, pessimism about the ability of man to better his earthly condition, and burning religious convictions. We already have seen some of these attitudes expressed in the mysticism of Plotinus. But in spite of (or perhaps because of) his successful mystical endeavors, Plotinus never abandoned completely his trust in rationality and the ability of man to achieve happiness through knowledge. Granted, discursive (inductive and deductive) reasoning has its limitations, according to Plotinus, and ordinary thought processes must be transcended in the intuitive contemplation of the One. But Plotinus' own attempt to construct a rational scheme of nature without appeal to theological scriptures or dogma places him within the classical Greek tradition.

Because the intellectual tone of the Middle Ages is in so many respects antithetical to both classical Greek and modern science, the reader must approach the period with special sympathy and patience. To help foster such an attitude, it might be helpful at this point to consider four general ways in which medieval thought contributed to the ultimate development of modern science; we shall then return to make a few observations regarding Augustine and his place in the history of psychology.

Perhaps the greatest barrier to the appreciation of medieval thought is the religious fervor that permeates the writings of this period. For the medieval thinker, faith in revealed truths, rather than reason or empirical observation, was the ultimate source of knowledge. The sense of mystery and faith that characterized medieval thought was not, however, without beneficial side effects for science. Classical Greek science—mathematics, astronomy, biology, etc.—had become in many respects *too* logical and concrete. A certain "loosening up" of thought was necessary before science could enter into a period of renewed growth. This point may be illustrated with an example from mathematics.

Greek mathematicians were unable to comprehend the infinite, a notion that was quite natural to thinkers of the Middle Ages and that is central to modern mathematics. One manifestation of this inability is the failure of Greek mathematicians to develop techniques similar to the infinitesimal calculus of Newton, although the calculus is a natural extension of the "method of exhaustion" employed by Greek geometers to estimate the magnitude of curves. Thus, although the Greeks recognized that a circle could be approximated by a polygon with many sides, they could not conceive of a circle as a polygon with an *infinite* number of sides. This may be contrasted with the attitude toward infinitesimals following the medieval period, as illustrated by a controversy between Bishop Berkeley and some Postnewtonian critics of religion. The latter believed that the success of Newtonian mechanics made religion obsolete, and they criticized theologians for accepting on faith such mysteries as the Trinity. Berkeley, one of the major philosophers of the period as well as a bishop, responded to these critics by pointing out that they demanded greater rigor in theology than in science. To back up his claim he subjected Newton's use of the calculus to a critical analysis, noting many inconsistencies. Berkeley concluded that "he who can digest a second or third fluxion, a second or third difference, need not, methinks, be squeamish about any point in divinity."[1] Of course,

---

[1] G. Berkeley, The analyst. In A. C. Fraser (Ed.), *Berkeley's complete works* (Vol. 3). Oxford: Clarendon Press, 1901, p. 21.

Berkeley's argument works both ways. A person who could digest any point in divinity—as Newton and most other scientists of the period did—need not be squeamish about a second or third fluxion (the derivative of modern calculus).

Logical rigor, is of course, a desideratum of any scientific theory, but it is not an end in itself. If history teaches no other lesson, this one at least is clear: the premature demand for logical rigor can be as debilitating to the advancement of science as is the uncritical acceptance of the illogical.

The medieval emphasis on mystery and faith, it should be added, was not so much an acceptance of the illogical as an acceptance of the limitation of the human mind to know the *supremely* logical—God. Many of the Greeks, including Aristotle, had allowed that chance plays a role in the determination of events. For the medieval thinker, on the other hand, nothing occurred except for a reason. Even miracles, which seem to go against the laws of nature, are part of a divine plan. This attitude was ultimately to play a very important role in the development of science, for it meant that everything is *in principle* explicable. But more than that: by attributing to a single godhead all power and knowledge over natural events, the task of science was greatly simplified. No longer need science, or its critics, be concerned about a great number of semiautonomous and often competing deities. Indeed, one of the achievements of Christianity was the replacement of animistic sprites with saints as the objects of popular religious concern. In the words of one commentator: "The cult of the saints smashed animism and provided the cornerstone for the naturalistic (but not necessarily irreligious) view of the world which is essential to a highly developed technology."[2]

Another deeply held tenet of the medieval period—and of modern science—is that nature is at the service of man, to be used for his betterment. Thus, in one of the principal textbooks of scholastic philosophy during the late Middle Ages it is stated: "As man is made for the sake of God, namely, that he may serve him, so is the world made for the sake of man, that it may serve him."[3] This, of course, only repeats the biblical theme, found in the Book of Genesis

And God said, Let us make man in our image, after our likeness: and let them have dominion over the fish of the sea, and over the fowl of the air, and over the cattle, and over all the earth, and over every creeping thing that creepeth upon the earth.

[2] L. White, What accelerated technological progress in the Western middle ages? In A. C. Crombie (Ed.), *Scientific change*. New York: Basic Books, 1963, p. 283.
[3] Quoted by A. O. Lovejoy, *The great chain of being*. Cambridge, Mass: Harvard University Press, 1966, p. 187.

The blatant anthropocentric teleology—that everything exists for the sake of man—contained in such assertions was explicitly denied by some of the founders of modern science, especially Descartes, but only because they saw in a mechanistic universe the opportunity for even greater control. The basic conviction that nature is man's to exploit has seldom been questioned since the Middle Ages, at least not until the last few decades when the technological advances have come to seriously threaten the balance of nature.

Science advances best when speculative thought is wedded to technological innovation. For the most part, such a wedding was absent during classical antiquity. According to Plutarch, Plato once rebuked two Greeks for constructing an apparatus to help solve geometrical problems; by working with their hands they were contaminating thought. Even Archimedes, perhaps the greatest engineer of the ancient world, was supposedly ashamed of the machines he built.[4] This condescending attitude toward manual labor underwent fundamental change during the Middle Ages. Within the Judeo-Christian tradition, work is not merely a practical necessity, but an obligation to God. With the collapse of the Roman political system, learning and education passed from secular to church authorities, and especially to the monasteries (which began to appear in Western Europe after the founding of Monte Cassino by St. Benedict in 529). The monks toiled, both intellectually and manually, as a form of worship. And while few innovations in speculative thought or technology can be attributed to the early monasteries, their example was fundamental in creating an attitude toward work and craftsmanship that was conducive to the development of science.

In summary, the medieval period is characterized by a certain tolerance of mystery, together with a firm belief in the ultimate rationality of, and man's dominion over, the universe. These attitudes, together with a belief in the dignity of practical labor, are among the legacies of the medieval period that ultimately proved invaluable to the advancement of science. None of these attitudes, it should be noted, was unique to the Middle Ages; all had been expressed by one thinker or another during earlier periods. But it was not until the Middle Ages that they became integrally woven into the very fabric of Western society, and that was crucial for the long-range development of science.

Let us return now to St. Augustine, the dominant intellectual figure throughout the early Middle Ages (from about the fifth to

[4] White, p. 285.

the twelfth centuries). Like Plotinus (and Plato before him), Augustine was obsessed with a quest for certainty, inner peace, and moral rectitude. Plotinus seems to have achieved his goal, at least to an extent, and there is a certain calmness and serenity in his writings. The works of Augustine, by contrast, are filled with expressions of self-doubt and anguish. Augustine had little confidence in man's capacity to reason, or in his ability to effect his own salvation. In part, the reasons for this doubt were theological: Whatever increased man's autonomy diminished in like measure God's omnipotence. But perhaps more importantly, Augustine's personal experience seemed to mock the powers of reason and will. After a period of search in his youth, Augustine became intellectually convinced (through Neoplatonic sources) of the plausibility of Christian doctrine. Moreover, he wanted to become a Christian, something his mother (St. Monica) had longed and prayed for since he was a child. But in spite of his intellectual persuasion and sincere desire, Augustine could not embrace Christianity with emotional conviction. Unlike Plotinus, he could not achieve peace and happiness through his own study and contemplation, nor could he even will to adopt the religion of his choice. An outside agency (the grace of God) was required before his conversion could occur.

In the excerpt reprinted here, Augustine recounts the events that finally led to his conversion to Christianity. Augustine's conversion provides an instructive sequel to Plotinus' description of his mystical reunion with the One. As noted in the introduction to Chapter 8, a mystical experience involves the dismantling of cognitive structures (i.e., the breakup of customary modes of thought). This results in a disruption of the distinction between self and other, and an oceanic feeling of oneness with reality (or, if conditions are unfavorable, acute anxiety). It is, of course, not easy to dismantle cognitive structures or to operate in a state where customary modes of thought are suspended. Therefore, when cognitive dissolution does occur, restructuring is usually rapid. The result is a short circuiting of the mystical (or anxiety) experience and, in the case of religious and political conversions, a reconstitution of the self.

A Transformation of the Self

THE PIOUS OLD MAN REJOICES THAT HE READ PLATO AND THE SCRIPTURES, AND TELLS HIM OF THE RHETORICIAN VICTORINUS HAVING BEEN CONVERTED TO THE FAITH THROUGH THE READING OF THE SACRED BOOKS

To Simplicianus then I went—the father of Ambrose (at that time a bishop) in receiving Thy grace, and whom he truly loved as a father. To him I narrated the windings of my error. But when I mentioned to him that I had read certain books of the Platonists, which Victorinus, sometime Professor of Rhetoric at Rome (who died a Christian, as I had been told), had translated into Latin, he congratulated me that I had not fallen upon the writings of other philosophers, which were full of fallacies and deceit, after the rudiments of the world, whereas they, in many ways, led to the belief in God and His word. Then, to exhort me to the humility of Christ, hidden from the wise, and revealed to little ones, he spoke of Victorinus himself, whom, while he was at Rome, he had known very intimately; and of him he related that about which I will not be silent. For it contains great praise of Thy grace, which ought to be confessed unto Thee, how that most learned old man, highly skilled in all the liberal sciences, who had read, criticised, and explained so many works of the philosophers; the teacher of so many noble senators; who also, as a mark of his excellent discharge of his duties, had (which men of this world esteem a great honor) both merited and obtained a statue in the Roman Forum, he—even to that age a worshipper of idols, and a participator in the sacrilegious rites to which almost all the nobility of Rome were wedded, and had inspired the people with the love of

> The dog Anubis, and a medley crew
> Of monster gods [who] 'gainst Neptune stand in arms,
> 'Gainst Venus and Minerva, steel-clad Mars,

whom Rome once conquered, now worshipped, all which old Victorinus had with thundering eloquence defended so many years—he now blushed not to be the child of Thy Christ, and an infant at Thy fountain, submitting his neck to the yoke of

Reprinted from Augustine, *The Confessions* (Book VIII)(J. G. Pilkington, trans.) in J. W. Oates (Ed.), *Basic writings of Saint Augustine* (Vol. 1). New York: Random House, 1948.

humility, and subduing his forehead to the reproach of the Cross.

O Lord, Lord, who has bowed the heavens and come down, touched the mountains and they did smoke, by what means didst Thou convey Thyself into that bosom? He used to read, as Simplicianus said, the Holy Scripture, most studiously sought after and searched into all the Christian writings, and said to Simplicianus—not openly, but secretly, and as a friend—"Know thou that I am a Christian." To which he replied, "I will not believe it, nor will I rank you among the Christians unless I see you in the Church of Christ." Whereupon he replied derisively, "Is it then the walls that make Christians?" And this he often said, that he already was a Christian; and Simplicianus making the same answer, the conceit of the walls was by the other as often renewed. For he was fearful of offending his friends, proud demon-worshippers, from the height of whose Babylonian dignity, as from cedars of Lebanon which had not yet been broken by the Lord, he thought a storm of enmity would descend upon him. But after that, from reading and inquiry, he had derived strength, and feared lest he should be denied by Christ before the holy angels if he now was afraid to confess Him before men, and appeared to himself guilty of a great fault in being ashamed of the sacraments of the humility of Thy word, and not being ashamed of the sacrilegious rites of those proud demons, whose pride he had imitated and their rites adopted, he became bold-faced against vanity, and shame-faced toward the truth, and suddenly and unexpectedly said to Simplicianus—as he himself informed me—"Let us go to the church; I wish to be made a Christian." But he, not containing himself for joy, accompanied him. And having been admitted to the first sacraments of instruction, he not long after gave in his name, that he might be regenerated by baptism—Rome marvelling, and the Church rejoicing. The proud saw, and were enraged; they gnashed with their teeth, and melted away! But the Lord God was the hope of Thy servant, and He regarded not vanities and lying madness.

Finally, when the hour arrived for him to make profession of his faith (which at Rome they who are about to approach Thy grace are wont to deliver from an elevated place, in view of the faithful people, in a set form of words learnt by heart), the presbyters, he said, offered Victorinus to make his profession more privately, as the custom was to do to those who were likely, through bashfulness, to be afraid; but he chose rather to profess his salvation in the presence of the holy assembly. For it was not salvation that he taught in rhetoric, and yet he had publicly professed that. How much less, therefore, ought he, when pronouncing Thy word, to dread Thy meek flock, who, in the delivery of his own words, had not feared the mad multitudes! So, then, when he ascended to make his profession, all, as they recognised him, whispered his name one to the other, with a voice of congratulation. And who was there amongst them that did not know him? And there ran a low murmur through the mouths of all the rejoicing multitude, "Victorinus! Victorinus!" Sudden was the burst of exultation at the sight of him; and suddenly were they hushed, that they might hear him. He pronounced the true faith with an excellent boldness, and all desired to take him to their very heart—by their love and joy they took him thither; such were the hands with which they took him. . . .

OF THE CAUSES WHICH ALIENATE US FROM GOD

But when that man of Thine, Simplicianus, related this to me about Victorinus, I burned to imitate him; and it was for this end he had related it. But when he had added this also, that in the time of the Emperor Julian, there was a law made by which Christians were forbidden to teach grammar and oratory, and he, in obedience to this law, chose rather to abandon the wordy school than Thy word, by which Thou makest eloquent the tongues of the dumb—he appeared to me not more brave than happy, in having thus discovered an opportunity of waiting on Thee only, which thing I was sighing for, thus bound, not with the irons of another, but my own iron will. My will was the enemy master of, and thence had made a chain for me and bound me. Because of a perverse will was lust made; and lust indulged in became custom; and custom not resisted became necessity. By which links, as it were, joined together (whence I term it a "chain"), did a hard bondage hold me enthralled. But that new will which had begun to develop in me, freely to worship Thee, and to wish to enjoy Thee, O God, the only sure enjoyment, was not able as yet to overcome my former wilfulness, made strong by long indulgence. Thus did my two wills, one old and the other new, one carnal, the other spiritual, contend within me; and by their discord they unstrung my soul.

Thus came I to understand, from my own experience, what I had read, how the flesh lusteth against the Spirit, and the Spirit against the flesh. I lusted both ways; yet more in that which I approved in myself, than in that which I disapproved in myself. For this last it was now rather not "I," because in much I rather suffered against my will than did it willingly. And yet it was through me that custom became more combative against me, because I had come willingly whither I willed not. And who, then, can with any justice speak against it, when just punishment follows the sinner? Nor had I now any longer my wonted excuse, that as yet I hesitated to be above the world and serve Thee, because my perception of the truth was uncertain; for now it was certain. But I, still bound to the earth, refused to be Thy soldier; and was as much afraid of being freed from all embarrassments, as we ought to fear to be embarrassed.

Thus with the baggage of the world was I sweetly burdened, as when in slumber; and the thoughts wherein I meditated upon Thee were like the efforts of those desiring to awake, who, still overpowered with a heavy drowsiness are again steeped therein. And as no one desires to sleep always, and in the sober judgment of all waking is better, yet does a man generally defer to shake off drowsiness, when there is a heavy lethargy in all his limbs, and, though displeased, yet even after it is time to rise with pleasure yields to it, so was I assured that it were much better for me to give up myself to Thy charity, than to yield myself to my own cupidity; but the former course satisfied and vanquished me, the latter pleased me and fettered me. Nor had I aught to answer Thee calling to me, "Awake, thou that sleepest, and arise from the dead, and Christ shall give thee light." And to Thee showing me on every side, that what Thou saidst was true, I, convicted by the truth, had nothing at all to reply, but the drawling and drowsy words: "Presently, lo, presently;" "Leave me a little while." But "presently, presently," had no present; and my "leave me a little while" went on for a long while. In vain did I delight in Thy law after the inner man, when another law in my members warred against the law of my mind, and brought me into captivity to the law of sin which is in my members. For the law of sin is the violence of custom, whereby the mind is drawn and held, even against its will; deserving to be so held in that it so willingly falls into it. O wretched man that I am! who shall deliver me from the body of this death but Thy grace only, through Jesus Christ our Lord?

PONTITIANUS' ACCOUNT OF ANTONY, THE FOUNDER OF MONACHISM, AND OF SOME WHO IMITATED HIM

And how, then, Thou didst deliver me out of the bonds of carnal desire, wherewith I was most firmly fettered, and out of the drudgery of worldly business, will I now declare and confess unto Thy name, O Lord, my strength and my Redeemer. Amid increasing anxiety, I was transacting my usual affairs, and daily sighing unto Thee. I resorted as frequently to Thy church as the business, under the burden of which I groaned, left me free to do. Alypius was with me, being after the third sitting disengaged from his legal occupation, and awaiting further opportunity of selling his counsel, as I was wont to sell the power of speaking, if it can be supplied by teaching. But Nebridius had, on account of our friendship, consented to teach under Verecundus, a citizen and a grammarian of Milan, and a very intimate friend of us all; who vehemently desired, and by the right of friendship demanded from our company, the faithful aid he greatly stood in need of. Nebridius, then, was not drawn to this by any desire of gain (for he could have made much more of his learning had he been so inclined), but, as a most sweet and kindly friend, he would not be wanting in an office of friendliness and slight our request. But in this he acted very discreetly, taking care not to become known to those personages whom the world esteems great; thus avoiding distraction of mind, which he desired to have free and at leisure as many hours as possible, to search, or read, or hear something concerning wisdom.

Upon a certain day, then, Nebridius being away (why, I do not remember), there came to the house to see Alypius and me, Pontitianus, a countryman of ours, in so far as he was an African, who held high office in the emperor's court. What he wanted with us I know not, but we sat down to talk together, and it fell out that upon a table before us, used for games, he noticed a book; he took it up, opened it, and, contrary to his expectation, found it to be the Apostle Paul—for he imagined it to be one of those books which I was wearing myself out in teaching. At this he looked up at me smilingly, and expressed his delight and wonder that he had so unexpectedly found this book, and this only, before my eyes. For he was both a Christian and baptized, and often prostrated himself before Thee our God in the church, in constant and daily prayers. When, then, I had told him that I bestowed much pains upon these writings, a conversation ensued on his speaking of Antony, the Egyptian monk, whose name was in high repute among Thy servants, though up to that time not familiar to us. When he came to know this, he lingered on that topic, imparting to us a knowledge of this man so eminent, and marvelling at our ignorance. But we were amazed, hearing Thy wonderful works most fully manifested in times so recent, and almost in our own, wrought in the true faith and the Catholic Church. We all wondered—we, that they were so great, and he, that we had never heard of them.

From this his conversation turned to the companies of the monasteries, and their manners so fragrant unto Thee, and of the fruitful deserts of the wilderness, of which we knew nothing. And there was a monastery at Milan full of good brethren, without the walls of the city, under the fostering care of Ambrose, and we were ignorant of it. He went on with his relation, and we listened intently and in silence. He then related to us how on a certain afternoon, at Triers, when the emperor was taken up with seeing the Circensian games, he and three others, his comrades, went out for a walk in the gardens close to the city walls, and there, as they chanced to walk two and two, one strolled away with him, while the other two went by themselves; and these, in their rambling, came upon a certain cottage inhabited by some of Thy servants, poor in spirit, of whom is the kingdom of heaven, where they found a book in which was written the life of Antony. This one of them began to read, marvel at, and be inflamed by it; and in the reading, to meditate on embracing such a life, and giving up his worldly employments to serve Thee. And these were of the body called Agents for Public Affairs. Then, suddenly being overwhelmed with a holy love and a sober sense of shame, in anger with himself, he cast his eyes upon his friend, exclaiming, "Tell me, I entreat thee, what end we are striving for by all these labors of ours. What is our aim? What is our motive in doing service? Can our hopes in court rise higher than to be ministers of the emperor? And in such a position, what is there not brittle, and fraught with danger, and by how many dangers arrive we at greater danger? And when arrive we thither? But if I desire to become a friend of God, behold, I am even now made it." Thus he spoke, and in the pangs of the travail of the new life, he turned his eyes again upon the page and continued reading, and was inwardly changed where Thou sawest, and his mind was divested of the world, as soon became evident; for as he read, and the surging of his heart rolled along, he raged awhile, discerned and resolved on a better course, and now, having become Thine, he said to his friend, "Now have I broken loose from those hopes of ours, and am determined to serve God; and this, from this hour, in this place, I enter upon. If thou art reluctant to imitate me, hinder me not." The other replied that he would cleave to him, to share in so great a reward and so great a service. Thus both of them, being now Thine, were building a tower at the necessary cost—of forsaking all that they had and following Thee. Then Pontitianus, and he who had walked with him through other parts of the garden, came in search of them to the same place, and having found them, reminded them to return as the day had declined. But they, making known to him their resolution and purpose, and how such a resolve had sprung up and become confirmed in them, entreated them not to molest them, if they refused to join themselves to them. But the others, no whit changed from their former selves, did yet (as he said) bewail themselves, and piously congratulated them, recommending themselves to their prayers; and with their hearts inclining towards earthly things, returned to the palace. But the other two, setting their affections upon heavenly things, remained in the cottage. And both of them had affianced brides, who, when they heard of this, dedicated also their virginity to Thee.

HE DEPLORES HIS WRETCHEDNESS, THAT HAVING BEEN BORN THIRTY-TWO YEARS, HE HAD NOT YET FOUND OUT THE TRUTH

Such was the story of Pontitianus. But Thou, O Lord, whilst he was speaking, didst turn me towards myself, taking me from behind my back, where I had placed myself while unwilling to exercise self-scrutiny; and Thou didst set me face to face with myself, that I might behold how foul I was, and how crooked and sordid, bespotted and ulcerous. And I beheld and loathed myself; and whither to fly from myself I discovered not. And if I sought to turn my gaze away from myself, he continued his narrative, and Thou again opposedst me unto myself, and thrustedst me before my own eyes, that I might discover my iniquity, and hate it. I had known it, but acted as though I knew it not—winked at it, and forgot it.

But now, the more ardently I loved those whose healthful affections I heard of, that they had given up themselves wholly to Thee to be cured, the more did I abhor myself when compared with them. For many of my years (perhaps twelve) had passed away since my nineteenth, when, on the reading of Cicero's *Hortensius*, I was roused to a desire for wisdom; and still I was delaying to reject mere worldly happiness, and to devote myself to search out that of which not the finding alone, but the bare search, ought to have been preferred before the treasures and kingdoms of this world, though already found, and before the pleasures of the body, though encompassing me at my will. But I, miserable young man, supremely miserable even in the very outset of my youth, had entreated chastity of Thee, and said, "Grant me chastity and continency, but not yet." For I was afraid lest Thou shouldst hear me soon, and soon deliver me from the disease of concupiscence, which I desired to have satisfied rather than extinguished. And I had wandered through perverse ways in a sacrilegious superstition; not indeed assured thereof, but preferring that to the others, which I did not seek religiously, but opposed maliciously.

And I had thought that I delayed from day to day to reject worldly hopes and follow Thee only, because there did not appear anything certain whither to direct my course. And now had the day arrived in which I was to be laid bare to myself, and my conscience was to chide me. "Where art thou, O my tongue? Thou saidst that for an uncertain truth thou wert not willing to cast off the baggage of vanity. Behold, now it is certain, and yet doth that burden still oppress thee; whereas they who neither have so worn themselves out with searching after it, nor yet have spent ten years and more in thinking thereon, have had their shoulders unburdened, and gotten wings to fly away." Thus was I inwardly consumed and mightily confounded with a horrible shame, while Pontitianus was relating these things. And he, having finished his story, and the business he came for, went his way. And to myself, what said I not within myself? With what scourges of rebuke lashed I not my soul to make it follow me, struggling to go after Thee! Yet it drew back; it refused, and exercised not itself. All its arguments were exhausted and confuted. There remained a silent trembling; and it feared, as it would death, to be restrained from the flow of that custom whereby it was wasting away even to death.

THE CONVERSATION WITH ALYPIUS BEING ENDED, HE RETIRES TO THE GARDEN, WHITHER HIS FRIEND FOLLOWS HIM

In the midst, then, of this great strife of my inner dwelling, which I had strongly raised up against my soul in the chamber of my heart, troubled both in mind and countenance, I seized upon Alypius, and exclaimed: "What is wrong with us? What is this? What heardest thou? The unlearned start up and 'take' heaven, and we, with our learning, but wanting heart, see where we wallow in flesh and blood! Because others have preceded us, are we ashamed to follow, and not rather ashamed at not following?" Some such words I uttered, and in my excitement flung myself from him, while he gazed upon me in silent astonishment. For I spoke not in my wonted tone, and my brow, cheeks, eyes, color, tone of voice, all expressed my emotion more than the words. There was a little garden belonging to our lodging, of which we had the use, as of the whole house; for the master, our landlord, did not live there. Thither had the tempest within my breast hurried me, where no one might impede the fiery struggle in which I was engaged with myself, until it came to the issue that Thou knewest, though I did not. But I was mad that I might be whole, and dying that I might have life, knowing what evil thing I was, but not knowing what good thing I was shortly to become. Into the garden, then, I retired, Alypius following my steps. For his presence was no bar to my solitude; or how could he desert me so troubled? We sat down at as great a distance from the house as we could. I was disquieted in spirit, being most impatient with myself that I entered not into Thy will and covenant, O my God, which all my bones cried out to me to enter, extolling it to the skies. And we enter not therein by ships, or chariots, or feet, no, nor by going so far as I had come from the house to that place where we were sitting. For not to go only, but to enter there, was naught else but to will to go, but to will it resolutely and thoroughly; not to stagger and sway about this way and that, a changeable and half-wounded will, wrestling, with one part falling as another rose.

Finally, in the very fever of my irresolution, I made many of those motions with my body which men sometimes desire to do, but cannot, if either they have not the limbs, or if their limbs be bound with fetters, weakened by disease, or hindered in any other way. Thus, if I tore my hair, struck my forehead, or if, entwining my fingers, I clasped my knee, this I did because I willed it. But I might have willed and not done it, if the power of motion in my limbs had not responded. So many things, then, I did, when to have the will was not to have the power, and I did not that which both with an unequalled desire I longed more to do, and which shortly when I should will I should have the power to do; because shortly when I should will, I should will thoroughly. For in such things the power was one with the will, and to will was to do, and yet was it not done; and more readily did the body obey the slightest wish of the soul in the moving its limbs at the order of the mind, than the soul obeyed itself to accomplish in the will alone this its great will.

THAT THE MIND COMMANDS THE MIND, BUT IT WILLS NOT ENTIRELY

Whence is this monstrous thing? And why is it? Let Thy mercy shine on me, that I may inquire, if the hiding-places of man's punishment and the darkest contritions of the sons of Adam may perhaps answer me. Whence is this monstrous thing? and why is it? The mind commands the body, and it obeys forthwith; the mind commands itself, and is resisted. The mind commands the hand to be moved, and such readiness is there that the command is scarce to be distinguished from the obedience. Yet the mind is mind, and the hand is body. The mind commands the mind to will, and yet, though it be itself, it obeys not. Whence this monstrous thing? and why is it? I repeat, it commands itself to will, and would not give the command unless it willed; yet is not that done which it commands. But it wills not entirely; therefore it commands not entirely. For so far forth it commands, as it wills; and so far forth is the thing commanded not done, as it wills not. For the will commands that there be a will—not another, but itself. But it does not command entirely, therefore that is not which it commands. For were it entire, it would not even command it to be, because it would already be. It is, therefore, no monstrous thing partly to will, partly to be unwilling, but an infirmity of the mind, that it does not wholly rise, sustained by truth, pressed down by custom. And so there are two wills, because one of them is not entire; and the one is supplied with what the other needs. . . .

IN WHAT MANNER THE SPIRIT STRUGGLED WITH THE FLESH, THAT IT MIGHT BE FREED FROM THE BONDAGE OF VANITY

Thus was I sick and tormented, accusing myself far more severely than was my wont, tossing and turning me in my chain till that was utterly broken, whereby I now was but slightly, but still was held. And Thou, O Lord, pressedst upon me in my inward parts by a severe mercy, redoubling the lashes of fear and shame, lest I should again give way, and that same slender remaining tie not being broken off, it should recover strength, and enchain me the faster. For I said mentally, "Lo, let it be done now, let it be done now." And as I spoke, I all but came to a resolve. I all but did it, yet I did it not. Yet I fell not back to my old condition, but took up my position hard by, and drew breath. And I tried again, and wanted but very little of reaching it, and somewhat less, and then all but touched and grasped it; and yet came not at it, nor touched, nor grasped it, hesitating to die to death, and to live to life; and the worse, to which I had been habituated, prevailed more with me than the better, which I had not tried. And the very moment in which I was to become another man, the nearer it approached me, the greater horror did it strike into me; but it did not strike me back, nor turn me aside, but kept me in suspense.

The very toys of toys, and vanities of vanities, my old mistresses, still enthralled me; they shook my fleshly garment, and whispered softly, "Dost thou part with us? And from that moment shall we no more be with thee for ever? And from that moment shall not this or that be lawful for thee for ever?" And what did they suggest to me in the words "this or that?" What is it that they suggested, O my God? Let Thy mercy avert it from the soul of Thy servant. What impurities did they suggest! What shame! And now I far less than half heard them, not openly showing themselves and contradicting me, but muttering, as it were, behind my back, and furtively plucking me as I was departing, to make me look back upon them. Yet they did delay me, so that I hesitated to burst and shake myself free from them, and to leap over whither I was called—an unruly habit saying to me, "Dost thou think thou canst live without them?"

But now it said this very faintly; for on that side towards which I had set my face, and whither I trembled to go, did the chaste dignity of Continence appear to me, cheerful, but not dissolutely gay, honestly alluring me to come and doubt nothing, and extending her holy hands, full of a multiplicity of good examples, to receive and embrace me. There were there so many young men and maidens, a multitude of youth and every age, grave widows and ancient virgins, and Continence herself in all, not barren, but a fruitful mother of children of joys, by Thee, O Lord, her Husband. And she smiled on me with an encouraging mockery, as if to say, "Canst not thou do what these youths and maidens can? Or can one or other do it of themselves, and not rather in the Lord their God? The Lord their God gave me to them. Why standest thou in thine own strength, and so standest not? Cast thyself upon Him; fear not, He will not withdraw that thou shouldest fall; cast thyself upon Him without fear, He will receive thee, and heal thee." And I blushed beyond measure, for I still heard the muttering of those toys, and hung in suspense. And she again seemed to say, "Shut up thine ears against those unclean members of thine upon the earth, that they may be mortified. They tell thee of delights, but not as doth the law of the Lord thy God." This controversy in my heart was naught but self against self. But Alypius, sitting close by my side, awaited in silence the result of my unwonted emotion.

HAVING PRAYED TO GOD, HE POURS FORTH A SHOWER OF TEARS, AND, ADMONISHED BY A VOICE, HE OPENS THE BOOK AND READS THE WORDS IN ROM. XIII. 13; BY WHICH, BEING CHANGED IN HIS WHOLE SOUL, HE DISCLOSES THE DIVINE FAVOR TO HIS FRIEND AND HIS MOTHER

But when a profound reflection had, from the secret depths of my soul, drawn together and heaped up all my misery before the sight of my heart, there arose a mighty storm, accompanied by as mighty a shower of tears. Which, that I might pour forth fully, with its natural expressions, I stole away from Alypius; for it suggested itself to me that solitude was fitter for the business of weeping. So I retired to such a distance that even his presence could not be oppressive to me. Thus it was with me at that time, and he perceived it; for something, I believe, I had spoken, wherein the sound of my voice appeared choked with weeping, and in that state had I risen up. He then remained where we had been sitting, most completely astonished. I flung myself down, how, I know not, under a certain fig-tree, giving free course to my tears, and the streams of mine eyes gushed out, an acceptable sacrifice unto Thee. And, not indeed in these words, yet to this effect, spake I much unto Thee—"But Thou, O Lord, how long?" "How long, Lord? Wilt Thou be angry for ever? Oh, remember not against us former iniquities;" for I felt that I was enthralled by them. I sent up these sorrowful cries—"How long, how long? To-morrow, and to-morrow? Why not now? Why is there not this hour an end to my uncleanness?"

I was saying these things and weeping in the most bitter contrition of my heart, when, lo, I heard the voice as of a boy or girl, I know not which, coming from a neighboring house, chanting, and oft repeating, "Take up and read; take up and read." Immediately my countenance was changed, and I began most earnestly to consider whether it was usual for children in any kind of game to sing such words; nor could I remember ever to have heard the like. So, restraining the torrent of my tears, I rose up, interpreting it no other way than as a command to me from Heaven to open the book, and to read the first chapter I should light upon. For I had heard of Antony, that, accidentally coming in while the gospel was being read, he received the admonition as if what was read were addressed to him, "Go and sell that thou hast, and give to the poor, and thou shalt have treasure in heaven; and come and follow me." And by such oracle was he forthwith converted unto Thee. So quickly I returned to the place where Alypius was sitting; for there had I put down the volume of the apostles, when I rose thence. I grasped, opened, and in silence read that paragraph on which my eyes first fell—"Not in rioting and drunkenness, not in chambering and wantonness, not in strife and envying; but put ye on the Lord Jesus Christ, and make not provision for the flesh, to fulfill the lusts thereof." No further would I read, nor did I need; for instantly, as the sentence ended—by a light, as it were, of security infused into my heart—all the gloom of doubt vanished away.

Closing the book, then, and putting either my finger between, or some other mark, I now with a tranquil countenance made it known to Alypius. And he thus disclosed to me what was wrought in him, which I knew not. He asked to look at what I had read. I showed him; and he looked even further than I had read, and I knew not what followed. This it was, "Him that is weak in the faith, receive ye;" which he applied to himself, and discovered to me. By this admonition was he strengthened; and by a good resolution and purpose, very much in accord with his character (in which, for the better, he was always far different from me), without any restless delay he joined me. Thence we go in to my mother. We make it known to her—she rejoices. We relate how it came to pass—she leaps for joy, and triumphs, and blesses Thee, who art able to do exceeding abundantly above all that we ask or think; for she perceived Thee to have given her more for me than she used to ask by her pitiful and most doleful groanings. For Thou didst so convert me unto Thyself, that I sought neither a wife, nor any other of this world's hopes—standing in that rule of faith in which Thou, so many years before, had showed me unto her in a vision. And thou didst turn her grief into a gladness, much more plentiful than she had desired, and much dearer and chaster than she used to crave, by having grandchildren of my body.

10. Theodore R. Sarbin and Nathan Adler

EDITOR'S INTRODUCTION

In this chapter, Sarbin and Adler propose a theory to account for the radical transformations of the self that sometimes occur during psychotherapy, drug rehabilitation programs, etc. At first, it might seem like a long leap—in spirit even more than in time—from Augustine's attempt to abandon his former life style for Christianity and, say, an alcoholic's attempt to "kick the habit." Yet the underlying problem in both cases is similar; the difference is more one of degree than of kind. Like Augustine, the alcoholic may be intellectually convinced that his behavior is disadvantageous and may sincerely wish to change, yet he cannot seem to do so. The alcoholic longing for just one more drink might well empathize with Augustine's anguished plea to God: "Grant me chastity and continency, but not yet."

The dilemma faced by Augustine and the alcoholic, or anyone else who wishes to change his behavior, illustrates one aspect of a larger metatheoretical issue, namely, freedom versus determinism. Is a person free to do what he wills, or is his behavior completely determined by factors beyond his control? Augustine addressed this issue on numerous occasions and his analysis deserves brief consideration. Augustine was ambivalent and not entirely consistent in his position regarding freedom of the will. When arguing against determinists such as the Stoics, he took the position that man is basically free; if behavior were completely determined, there would be little reason to try to better oneself or one's fellow man, e.g., through religious practices. On the other hand, when arguing against those who believed in complete voluntary control, e.g., the Pelagians, Augustine took the position that human behavior is ultimately determined. This stance seemed necessary, for if man has control over his own destiny, then God cannot be omnipotent and all-knowing.

Modern psychologists find themselves in an analogous dilemma. Most psychologists are strict determinists, in the sense that they believe that all behavior is ultimately caused by antecedent conditions. However, many psychologists also are uneasy about saying that freedom of choice is a mere fiction or illusion. This is especially true in many applied settings where it may be desirable to encourage people to make decisions and to accept responsibility for their actions. But how can personal freedom be admitted, and even encouraged, without undermining the fundamental principle of determinism?

Augustine's solution to this dilemma was to point out that a willful or voluntary act is simply one that is not done under duress; hence, it is by definition free. But *free* in this sense does not mean uncaused or undetermined; rather, it means that the action is a product of the self and not of external pressures. Stated differently, a man wills what it is his character to will. An analogy might help clarify what is implied by this proposition. We are accustomed to recognizing individual differences in intellectual and physical abilities. For example, if asked what "caused" a person to solve a very difficult mathematical problem, we might point to his superior intelligence. Analogously, if asked why a person did a particularly charitable act, we might point out that he is a person "of good will." It will be recognized that these are explanations in terms of dispositional properties, or formal causes in the Aristotelian sense.

For Augustine, then, acts of will are both free (in that they are not the product of external duress) and yet determined (in that they are the product of a person's own character). This raises the question: How can a person will to do what is not in his character? How could Augustine, for example convert to Christianity while still being his old self; and how can a modern alcoholic "kick the habit" if drinking is part of his character? The answer is that one's character must be reconstituted so that the new behavior becomes part of the self. In what follows, Sarbin and Adler examine the processes by which such a reconstitution of the self occurs.

THEODORE R. SARBIN AND
NATHAN ADLER

Self-Reconstitution Processes:
a preliminary report

ABSTRACT

This paper is a preliminary excursion in an effort to formulate a general theory of conduct reorganization. Briefly put, our thesis is that significant conduct reorganization occurs when certain antecedent conditions are met, the particular species of intervention—e.g., psychotherapy, Synanon, religious conversion, etc.—being relatively incidental so long as the same basic processes occur. Conduct reorganization is achieved when the patient, client, initiate, or convert becomes actively involved in all the social and psychological stages of an indentifiable sequence of events. In keeping with the prefatory nature of this paper, we describe in a general way the components of the change process and their functional equivalents.

INTRODUCTION

At least since the middle of the nineteenth century, psychologists interested in changing the conduct of individuals have leaned heavily on rationalistic models and have consistently avoided, neglected or rejected models that included nonrationalistic components. The theories of Freud, Rogers, and Sullivan, for example, are suffused with rationalism and focused upon an almost exclusive concern with verbal transactions, i.e., talk, as the mediator of rationality.

This emphasis on rationality in the transactions that are directed toward altering behavior has been in the nature of an ideological commitment to science. Nineteenth- and twentieth-century psychological theorists, hoping to emulate the progress of their contemporaries in the natural sciences, organized their efforts toward discovering "scientific" methods that would be congruent

Reprinted from *The Psychoanalytic Review*, Vol. 57, No. 4, 1970–1971, through the courtesy of the Editors and the Publisher, National Psychological Association for Psychoanalysis, New York, N.Y., pp. 599–616.

An earlier version of this paper was presented at the meetings of the California State Psychological Association, San Diego, January 1967. We are grateful to David B. Clarke, Jr., Neil Ross, Joseph Juhasz, and Warren Gould for valuable assistance and stimulation. The Institute of Social Science (University of California) supported the present work with grants-in-aid. The present version was completed during the senior author's tenure as a Fellow of the Center for Advanced Studies, Wesleyan University, 1968–69.

with contemporary science and its rationalistic imperatives. A byproduct of the limits thus imposed was the rejection of any model of behavior change, no matter how effective, whose basic metaphors were inconsistent with the vocabulary preferred by contemporary scientists. Thus, any method of behavior change that employed theological metaphors, or exploited such procedures as ritual, dancing, isolation, fasting, prayer, and other means that departed from apparent rationality (polite talk) was declared unscientific and unworthy of serious study. Parenthetically, misled by surface appearances, we have failed to recognize or to make explicit that often our standard, official models of change masked rituals where the "irrational" quality was attenuated or disguised.

Because of this rationalistic emphasis, most systematic writers have failed to take advantage of the world literature on conduct and personality alteration, such as the writings of William James, McNeill, Loyola, Kierkegaard, and others. For example, William James' observations in his *Varieties of Religious Experience*, in spite of his own rationalism, makes use of metaphors that have not been assimilated into contemporary rationalistic models. In one essay, he posits two kinds of persons. The first are the healthy-minded who need to be born only once, and others are "sick souls" who must be twice-born in order to make some tolerable adjustment to an imperfect world. James employed a number of metaphors that were congruent with a humanistic ethos but which were ignored by most rationalistic theory-builders.

> Such unification or rebirth may come gradually or it may occur abruptly; it may come through altered powers of action: or it may come through new intellectual insights, or through experiences which we shall later have to designate as "mystical."

> In all these instances we have precisely the same psychological form of event—a firmness, stability, and equilibrium succeeding a period of storm and stress and inconsistency.[9]

Similarly, McNeill's *History of the Cure of Souls* makes use of another metaphorical system. That he is interested in conduct reorganization through reconstitution of the self can be readily inferred from the following excerpt:

> The cure of souls, then, is the sustaining and curative treatment of persons in those matters that reach beyond the requirements of the animal life. Man is a seeker after health, but not health of the body alone. Health of body may be contributory to, but it does not guarantee, health of personality. It may be possessed by man who

suffers painful disorders of mind and spirit. On the other hand, it may be destroyed by mental or emotional disease. The health that is ultimately sought is not something to be secured by material means alone: it is the well-being of the soul.[15]

McNeill traces the history of cures from the rationalistic approach of Cicero and Seneca, through the "rebirth" of Nicodemus by his faith in Jesus, to the concepts of confession and reawakening of Luther and Calvin.

The *Spiritual Exercises* of Saint Ignatius of Loyola, a system of reconstitution of the self employing the death and rebirth theme, offer a simplicity unmatched by any system of contemporary behavioral science. One must be prepared to find in the theological vocabularies and metaphors the same underlying behavioral operations and processes. The exercises of St. Ignatius are carried out during a "retreat," in which four phases are identified as "weeks" of irregular intervals. During these four "weeks" the aspirant passes through stages of reconstitution of the self (soul) reminiscent of exercises in other Eastern and Western religions, and involving processes of "Purgation" or catharsis, "Illumination" or insight, and sanctification or reorientation. Metaphors of Death, Transition and Rebirth order events familiar to us in secular programs.

The exercises in the first week require the subject to meditate on *Sin* and its consequences, to contemplate hell and to meditate upon his own death, picturing in detail his last moments and their agony. Is this dissimilar from the "anxiety" that brings the patient to therapy from the compulsive repetition and circularity of failures and injured self-esteem of the initial anamnesis? Meditations for the second week involve the Saviour as a means of salvation. The aspirant contemplates the humility, agony, poverty and love of Him. Within the theological metaphors is this other from the externalization of the ego-ideal, the aspiration level for the individual's self. The third "week" is a phase in which the exercises seek to confirm the election to Christ; i.e. working through to confirm the way of holiness. The fourth week is characterized by the setting aside of dreadful thoughts and sadness, meditating instead on the life eternal. It is not necessary to match absolutely identical events and processes to suggest that similar generic elements are involved.

When, at the turn of the century, psychology was breaking away from philosophy and attempting to affirm itself as a natural science, the human organism was construed as a passive entity inactive unless prodded by instincts or pushed by external stimuli.

To reconstruct the forces in the "mind," or to change personal habits, rationalistic psychologists and psychiatrists turned to manipulating verbal stimuli as levers. The study of myths and their effect on conduct, let alone such literary works as those of James Joyce or Dylan Thomas, makes compelling the conclusion that verbal transactions provide no automatic warrant for "rationality." An additional difficulty of this conceptual model was that it encouraged the partition of the subject who is isolated from his social milieu and regarded as a kind of solitary specimen in the laboratory, where verbal utterances could be analyzed through the use of rationalistic schemata.

Recent developments in general psychological theory make apparent the gross limitations of earlier association models and call for the construct of an active self. Psychological theory no longer finds plausible or useful the image of a passive, stimulus-bound organism; instead, contemporary theory is moving toward a conception of an intrinsically active organism whose ongoing knowledge-seeking activity leads to broader and more structured resolutions of the distal field.[22] The passive organism, waiting for the stirrings of tissue needs or the promptings of "anxiety" signals and only then looking for an external tranquilizer, is an obsolescent construct. The newer view of man as an active creature requires a metaphor that embraces the fact that he is an inveterate, ongoing decision maker, rehearsing possibilities on the basis of expectancies garnered from the environment. And such rehearsal involves not only organized beliefs about the ecology ("Moving heavy objects requires strength"), but also beliefs about the self ("I am weak"). Like all abstractions, the active self is not an ideal metaphor, but it does reflect the changing view of the human organism. For the present we restrict ourselves to the statement that to be an effective decision maker a person must locate (assign meanings to) self as object as well as other persons and things. To do this, he must be able to construct abstractions about himself as well as the behavioral environment.

A set of concepts has proved useful in our attempts to account for the kinds of changes referred to variously as the process of conversion, reconstitution of the self, transvaluation of social identity, and profound conduct reorganization. This set of concepts deals with the source of information from which persons make decisions regarding action. Two categories are posited: (1) the proximal ecology (or the proprium) which provides sensory input from posture, movement, proprioception, imaginings; (2) the distal ecologies. It has been useful to differentiate five distal ecologies:[19] the self-maintenance ecology, the spatial-temporal ecology, the normative ecology, the social ecology, and the transcendental ecology. The human organism defines a smooth course of action for himself by making sense of the data gleaned from these input sources; in other words he is able to answer ecologically relevant questions, *What am I in relation to the self-maintenance ecology?*, *Where am I?*, *Who am I?*, and so on, in terms of existing cognitive organization.[19] Although the construct of the self involves placement in all ecologies, in this paper we single out the social (or role) ecology, the source of inputs for constructing a social identity, and the transcendental ecology, the source of inputs for constructing a self as abstraction in relation to other abstractions such as God, the universe, humanity, and justice.

In this prolegomenon, we can only sketch our conceptualization of the self. The self is regarded as a set of knowings or beliefs that accumulate as the result of efforts actively to locate oneself with reference to differentiated habitats or ecologies. Such efforts are facilitated by searching behaviors, by the person asking questions of the form *Who am I?* (the self in relation to others) and *What am I?* (the self in relation to the cosmos), as well as other questions. Both the everyday object world and the transcendental world of meaning and value are included in the latter. Answers to the *Who am I?* question represents the socius, *the subjective aspect of social identity.* Answers to the *What am I?* questions, drawn from inputs generated both proximally and distally, represent the self as cosmological object—*the subjective aspect of "thingness."*

Inasmuch as the answers to these questions are directly relevant to the person's choice of actions, usually with social reference, we posit that social roles are perceived and enacted against a background of self. Self and role may be viewed as coordinates. The construct, self, refers to the inferences the person makes about the predicates for "I"; the "I" in turn is the subjective aspect of identity.

Our point of departure is this: significant conduct reorganization can be understood as the sequelae of a reconstitution of the self. Such reconstitution comes about as the result of efforts to change the conditions for locating of self in the cosmological and the social ecologies.[17] Such efforts are not recondite nor mysterious. For example, they may include such knowable antecedent operations as altering body-image boundaries through motoric activity, fasting, or hyperventilation, and altering identity supports through degradation rituals, isolation, ostracism, or aversive social reinforcements.[1]

REFERENCE CASES

We are not addressing ourselves to the discovery of the communalities in *all* systems of behavior change. For example, learning how to add and subtract or learning how to repair a tire are instances of behavior change, broadly defined. The processes involved in these forms of learning embrace different orders of concepts than those of interest to us that we have labelled *conduct reorganization*. To point specifically to the kinds of conduct change with which we are concerned, we list five reference cases illustrative of different modalities of change. Typical of the systems whose operations we are scrutinizing and analyzing, they suggest some interesting contrasts to the clients of conventional twentieth-century rationalistic models of therapy.

1. A young man recently graduated from high school, "at large" in the Standard Average American culture, decides to enter the Jesuit order and is accepted. Soon after he enters the novitiate, and having renounced all his worldly goods, he enters a thirty-day retreat from which he emerges a "new man," a Jesuit novice.

2. A degraded drunk on the skids joins Alcoholics Anonymous, and after a period of achieving "12 steps" emerges as a respectable, teetotaling citizen.

3. An American Army Major captured in Korea, despite a Top Secret clearance that characterizes him as loyal and trustworthy, after a period of "brain washing," tapes a series of broadcasts denouncing his government.

4. Cardinal Mindszenty, after a few weeks in prison, appears in court and denounces himself as a traitor and spy.

5. A life-long criminal, who has spent the better part of his 40 years in reformatories and prison, "converted" to a Fundamentalist religious sect, after release from prison establishes himself as a law-abiding citizen, marries, goes into business, and becomes a pillar of the community.

To account for these examples of conduct reorganization requires a conceptual system of considerable complexity. The notion of reconstituting the self is the keystone of such a system. The aim of the present enterprise is to sketch a social-psychological model that specifies the activities and operations of change agents and that predicts outcomes in terms of public role behavior as well as in terms of self-assessment.

Our studies share with the earlier work of Sargent,[21] Frank,[7] and Lifton,[12] the recognition that there are communalities to be found, e.g., in brainwashing and conversion and in the different schools and systems of psychotherapy. But where these investigators try to account for the communalities as instances of operant conditioning, classical conditioning or of other single-factor models, we describe a synoptic model that permits us to examine conversion models as well as traditional rationalistic models as instances of more general theory of reconstitution of the self leading to conduct reorganization. The thrust of our historical and contemporary review is to ensure that empirical investigation will not be forced into narrow parochial models.

Our model is derived from a review of the literature that has been virtually ignored and rejected by behavioral scientists. Among the sources consulted are works on spiritual exercises, conversion, enthusiasm, shamanism, ecstasy and other processes of conduct change operating in a religious setting. We have examined the procedures of Thought Reform, military indoctrination in boot camp and officer candidate schools, and other processes in the political arena; we have looked into socially oriented change conditions such as Synanon, Alcoholics Anonymous, *rites de passage*, as well as hypnosis and sensory deprivation. Examining the behavioral operations involved in profound and critical conduct reorganization, we have been able to identify a number of variables that have been ignored or scanted by theorists and expositors of one or another traditional psychotherapeutic system.

COMMON THEMES

Our initial excursion into the literature suggests that there are communalities that can be abstracted from the multiplicity of systems developed over the centuries. We have isolated a number of themes and the steps or operations that lead to the reconstruction of the self as preliminary to, or concurrent with, profound changes in conduct.

Theme I. Symbolic Death and Rebirth

One theme is recurrent in these diverse systems—the theme of symbolic death and rebirth or the annihilation and reconstruction of the self. How this is conceptualized depends upon the metaphors employed in the thought models carried by the persons involved. The theme characterizes a central feature of a number of currently voguish therapies—the encounter, confrontation, action, and Gestalt therapies. Our concepts are intended to provide a means for establishing the validity of these "therapeutic systems."

We have kept an eye open to the possibility that the recurrent and reemergent theme of symbolic death and rebirth may be more useful in establishing a generic model of conduct reorganization than the older themes of insight, shift in dynamic equilibrium, or deconditioning.

Our analysis of the literature leads to the proposition that, at first, certain personal behaviors diminish or cease altogether, at the same time being replaced by a new set of overt behaviors and corresponding self-definitions. The metaphoric use of the words dying, being reborn and saved, is well known in Catholic and Fundamentalist literature. These metaphors are used frequently in autobiographical and literary descriptions of conversions. The dual process is noted in such metaphors as "death and rebirth," "death and transfiguration," "the spiritual awakening," "degradation and renewal." In all the systems we have reviewed we have found the recurrent theme of death and rebirth, whether it takes the form of a ritualized dying ceremony, "surrendering" before one begins a new life, "hitting rock bottom," "renunciation" of worldy and bodily pleasures, penance, humiliation, or being forcibly degraded to justify a spiritual death. The specific operations by which this "death" is brought about, the point at which the "death" is reached, the "rebirth" phenomenon and the group acceptance which follow are keys to understanding the conversion process in all its forms.

C. Eric Lincoln, in his analysis of the Black Muslim religion in America,[13] discusses the initiation of an individual into the Muslim sect—a process which exemplifies the death-rebirth theme:

> To clinch the conversion of those true believers who approach the Movement in simple curiosity, Muhammad offers the lure of personal rebirth. The true believer who becomes a Muslim casts off at last his old self and takes on a new identity. He changes his name, his religion, his homeland, his "natural" language, his moral and natural values, his very purpose in living. He is no longer a Negro, so long despised by the white man that he has come almost to despise himself. Now he is a Black Man—divine, ruler of the universe, different only in degree from Allah Himself. He is no longer discontent and baffled, harried by social obloquy and a gnawing sense of personal inadequacy. Now he is a Muslim, bearing in himself the power of the Black Nation and its glorious destiny. His new life is not an easy one: it demands unquestioning faith, unrelenting self-mastery, unremitting hatred. He may have to sacrifice his family and friends, his trade or profession, if they do not serve his new-found cause. But he is not alone, and he now knows *why* his life matters. He has seen the truth, and the truth has set him free. . . . This change of name is, of course, only the most outward

token of rebirth. Perhaps the deepest change promised—and delivered—is the release of energies that had been damned or buried in the old personality. This release may account in part for the regeneration of criminals, alcoholics and narcotic addicts which is a hallmark of the Movement.

The death-rebirth theme in this context may be viewed, then, as the death or loss or relinquishment of one social identity and the rebirth or formation of another. The point of death, to use a metaphor of the social sciences, is when the individual becomes a "nonperson." The individual is treated by relevant others as not being able to meet minimal cultural expectations; he is perceived as not being able to perform actions to make good the occupancy of the most undifferentiated, granted social roles. Being a nonperson, with reference to his social ecology, it is as if he were *dead.* This symbolic death process is characterized by a mounting of high arousal and cognitive strain.[4] Restrictions are placed on the employment of adaptive techniques for reducing cognitive strain so that the nonperson, to make sense of the confusion of inputs, must change the structure of his belief system. The process may be viewed as an "assault" upon the individual's conception of self as a cosmological object and/or as a social identity. The modification, reevaluation, and/or transformation of these "knowings" is brought about by planned events so that alternative, more congruent, and more easily instantiated views of self are available. The new self (after the rebirth) is tagged with labels carrying connotations of wholeness (healed, holy) rather than fractionated (cracked, crazed, split, schizoid).

Postures and artifacts required in diverse systems of conduct change, all support the ceremonies of symbolic death and rebirth, and are instruments of change. Examples of such symbolic support are the couch, the horizontal position, the hypnotic "trance," the waiting period, the ritual fractionation of time into weeks of spiritual exercises or hours of therapy, the ritual separation of spiritual and therapeutic exercises from the routines of customary world.

Models that emphasize warmth, support, "tender-loving care," and that focus solely on the nurturant role of the therapist, fail to recognize that a therapy that aims at reorganization of the personality has other functions too. Failure to appreciate the wide range of therapeutic roles, and the extremely different phases in the ongoing process, and insisting on the passive receptive role alone may be responsible for the frequently observed stalemate in therapy. The need for the active induction of stress, of directed organismic involvement, is a central factor in all the systems we have reviewed. This is perhaps more easily recognized in radical techniques developed outside the mental health profession but as readily recognized in the classic forms of psychoanalysis. The assault on the self is brought about in numerous ways: the "meat-axe" and "hot seat" therapy of some group procedures, the Synanon "haircut," the exhaustion, toxicity, and the sensory deprivation of "marathon" therapy.

Similarities among diverse systems of change are noted in recognizing that converts or patients may avoid or delay the "death" or degradation process. Thought reform techniques in China differentiate the earlier false confession from the ultimate true confession. The addict initially comes to Synanon for reasons other than "the cure."[5] He begins with a false confession which must be exposed as a maneuver. A central myth of Synanon is the "Night of the Big Copout." The junkie is compelled to break the code of his group and "squeal" as a repudiation of his old self and the beginnings of a commitment to a new self. In the psychoanalytic idiom, Kris[10] has referred to the initial anamnesis as the "myth of the hero" that serves defensive functions and stands in the way of degradation of self. Such defensive maneuvers must be overcome before change can occur. It is often the case that patients come to psychoanalytic treatment to try by new means to achieve their goals and to avert their suffering rather than to demean the self through repudiating such goals as a step toward reorganization.

The application of the death-rebirth theme to modern psychotherapy depends upon the readiness of the mental health profession to shift metaphors, to overcome current nonutilitarian myths and to displace them with new or revived metaphors that are more continuous with observations. Angyal talked about psychotherapy in an idiom more in keeping with the death-rebirth theme. He wrote about the patient being faced with the futility of his customary ways, hopeless and degraded, who had to acknowledge his bankruptcy and confront his damaged self esteem. "The neurotic structure melts in the fire of an intensive and persuasive emotional experience. . . . There is profound despair."[2,3] Such a situation may not have to occur in the minor first aid type of therapy that is essentially "mask repair." But where fundamental unmasking and recasting of the self is the goal, this step is of central importance. "There is no other way," Angyal maintains, "than the way that leads through despair . . . a sweeping experience of bankruptcy must come if the person is to break out and take a chance on a different mode of existence."

Crucial to the process of behavior change is the involvement of self in role. It may vary from precipitously waking one morning to assume a new life to persisting experiences of terror and/or ecstasy. The greater the involvement, the greater the probability of the shift in self-conception, and the more probable the renunciation of the former self. The beliefs and values held antecedent to immersing oneself in actions characterized by high involvement becomes the "before," not completely forgotten or denied, but reorganized and reconstructed to justify and maintain the newly adopted self. The degree of conduct change necessary to meet the demands of the converted covers a wide range. At one end of the distribution we could place the ex-alcoholic in Alcoholics Anonymous who now drinks coffee with his companions; at the other end, the Yogi Guru, once a successful businessman who now literally contemplates his navel for days. In this conversion process what is *converted* is the self as social identity and/or the self as a cosmological abstraction, i.e., the complex of answers to the *Who am I?* and *What am I?* questions.

Theme II. The Group and Other

The relationship between the convert (or patient, novice, plebe, etc.) and the group varies according to the degree of involvement and specificity of role perception. At one pole this relationship may take the form of an individual who comes into contact with a particular group, such as a religious or millenial culture. The group, then, provides the setting for change. Not only does the group provide role models which specifically furnish the objects of emulation, imitation and identification, but also the conditions that *demand* certain performances from the initiate.

The individual (self) is further located in abstract ephemeral reference groups: the generalized other in a theological or transcendental reference. Locating oneself, then, with reference to God, One, Unity, Nature helps to provide answers to the individual struggling with the *"What am I?"* question. The demands imposed on the individual not only dictate which social roles he is permitted to enact but also influence self-assessment. The individual not only changes overt behavior to meet role expectations and demands, but in the process his conception of self becomes modified.

In the reconstitution of the self, the role of an Other[16] as a role model and/or source of information is required. This mandatory role, whether occupied by a group or an individual, or a symbolic surrogate (oracle, Book, icon), has been found in each of the systems we have studied. This role might best be designated as "teacher," although different systems adopt other names: sponsor, priest, therapist, shaman, doctor, guard, guru, or captor. This Other or teacher is an esteemed member of the group in which the actor desires membership, such membership being a prerequisite for the invalidation of the old self and the confirmation of the new identity.[18] What appears to be most relevant is that the role of the teacher serves to *socialize the activity*; that is, it serves the purpose of an evaluative audience for the adaptive measures the actor takes in handling the strains involved in the change process. What the actor *does* is under observation and scrutiny by the teacher who has the power (legitimate and/or coercive) to apply reinforcements for approved behavior, and also the power (expert) to guide the actor into appropriate role behavior. The presence of the therapist, even in silence, makes the activity public and shifts from exclusive concern with existential questions to concern with identity questions—a shift from proprium to socius dimension.

As we have mentioned with Alcoholics Anonymous, public testimony is a widely used method of assault that takes into account the importance of group coercion. The Salvation Army, Alcoholics Anonymous, and revivalist conversions are well known exemplars of the public testimonial. It is usual for several converts to give their testimony. More than affirmation of faith, they tell the audience their experiences, their joys and their sorrows; they speak of sins, failures and weaknesses, and of their temptations, once irresistible but now overcome through the intervention of a transcendental force, e.g., Grace of Christ. The reported experiences of members of the audience give validation to the new converts' testimony. The words of the speakers and the preachers are reaffirmed in chants and songs, recited or sung in unison. Symbolic reinforcement comes not only from the leader but from peers.

The use of drugs to facilitate conduct reorganization tends to operate at cross-purposes to the social facilitation provided by the Other or group. Drugs tend to turn the actor to his "private" experiences rather than to events with a group reference. Drugs confirm private time and idiosyncratic conceptual forms. This is not to say that under some conditions drugs may not have value. They may disrupt the relations of self to surroundings, breaking through habitual and perhaps rigid conceptualizations of self. Under such conditions, given the group control of distal inputs, the actor may become more manipulable.[1]

The group and its representative, the Other, hold a key position as a primary component in a model of conduct reorganization. It is, of course, the group or Other that manipulates sensory input from the distal ecologies, that creates situations that activate inputs from the proximal ecology (e.g., proprioceptive inputs), and holds the key to reinforcement.

Theme III. Ritual Behavior

Overlapping the death-rebirth theme and the group theme is the theme of ritual behavior. We can further divide this theme into two components: the varieties of ritualized activity *per se*, and its relationship with the changing concept of self; and the use of such activities to manipulate time into concentrated or limited spans of individual attention, i.e., time binding.

The isolation of time increases concentration and limits the span of attention. The waiting period, the postponement of the initial appointment, the setting aside of the therapeutic hour, and the use of the retreat, can be understood as the ritual manipulation of time. Such manipulation of time may be independent of the content of the time. The bracketing or isolation of time prepares the actor for the nonconfirmation of earlier specific roles and, given the absence of customary audience feedback, initiates the stripping of achieved statuses, a prerequisite for "dying." Time can be ritually manipulated so that it appears to contract to a pinpoint or to expand otiosely. The ritual manipulation of time can shift the perspectives of the ongoing present and of past and future. In such a shifting of time, attention moves from socius to proprium and back again, depending on the form of conversion. Depersonalization and fugue, as drug "trips" suggest, can be induced. Such acts as staring, closing the eyes, praying, speaking in tongues, repeating sentences monotonously, singing, chanting, dancing, jumping, regulating the breath, and other methods are used in the various systems to limit the convert's span of attention and enhance his concentration on the objects, goals, and means of conversion.

The learning and perfecting of ritual acts may also serve to neutralize arousal and reduce strain during the process of conversion. Ritual activity may be required in the performance of new roles. Incorporating various aspects of ritual into one's repertoire of instrumental acts provides for a shift from viewing oneself as *agency* to that of *agent*, from a possessed victim to one who (again) may actively cope with the distal ecologies. Prayer, for example, may be viewed as an active involvement of oneself in manipulating one's own destiny. In most of the systems of conduct reorganization we have encountered, the use of ritual has been to allow for the smooth transition from "old" to "new" lives. The repetition of sacred sentences or prayers, the strict regulation of physical habits, all are important in the reestablishing of the boundaries of the self. The performance of such tasks may serve as means of mastering basic definitions of new roles and, particularly, may initiate social ecological responses of a positive nature, i.e., reinforcement from the distal ecology. The convert, like the infant, learns to master his own behavior through elementary ritualistic and imitative activity. It is a mastery of a new and alien world, the world of the "new life."

Theme IV. Proprioceptive Stimuli

Sensory inputs from the proximal ecology play a crucial role in all systems of conduct reorganization. When the somatic components of the proximal ecology are not readily instantiated, when they "make no sense" the person actively seeks constructs or premises to help make sense out of a baffling situation. The locating and manipulating of core anchorages of the self can be managed by variations in proprioceptive stimuli. Emphasized in all of the systems we have investigated are those positions and states of the body which allow the subject or convert to shift his perception of the world, for example, kneeling, standing, lying and prostrating. Fatigue states, cramps, hunger and sleeplessness are induced and the subject's sensory dependence on external stimuli is challenged. Ritualized activity plays a role in disrupting the boundaries of the self by reorganizing stimulus inputs in the proximal ecology. Psychoanalytic procedures can be understood in this light. They establish a stimulus restriction and withdraw attention location of self on social dimensions and, instead, guide the patient to inputs that provide answers to the *What am I?* questions.

Excitement and relaxation to induce quietude and calm are specific procedures used by many systems of behavior change that intend to achieve relaxation after periods of high involvement. In this activity the self-other relations are modified. Field dependence or independence as a perceptual function is modified and, therefore, such modifications and manipulations of field dependency shift one's subjective view of "thingness." Thus, the shifts brought about by variations of stimuli within the proximal ecology provide a somatic basis for the process of symbolic death and rebirth.

The components of ritualistic time-binding and proprioceptive inputs are not mutually exclusive categories. Both components are used in the various systems of conduct reorganization to shift attention from external to internal events, to increase involvement, to emphasize the convert's passivity, and to arouse and heighten cognitive strain and physiological arousal. Also, as we have seen, the components may be used to provide sources of gratification and reinforcement, calm and serenity, support and nurturance.

Theme V. Triggers

We have found that "triggers," events whose presence is likely to produce or enhance the process of conversion, can be identified in all the reports of self change. The term "trigger" was first used by Laski in her book *Ecstasy*,[11] a lengthy investigation of the ecstatic experiences of religious converts, authors and literary characters, and lay persons. The exact function of the trigger is uncertain and possibly idiocyncratic to the convert, but the presence of the trigger or "high value stimulus" is undeniable. The usefulness of the concept is in its ability to tie together characteristics of the conversion process and the feelings and perceptions of the convert. Finding the qualities of triggers difficult to categorize, Laski emphasized the similarity of the feeling of the ecstatic subject to the quality of the trigger, that is, the *mode* of the sensory input may be related to the type of experience. Dewey[6] and Hutchinson,[8] using different metaphors, also emphasized the importance of triggers in the reorganization of thought. In the elaboration of the present model, we have found that the trigger is most effective if occurring at the point of transition (or immediately preceding that point) in the "death-rebirth" process.

SUMMARY

These themes on the self-reconstitution process are not mutually exclusive, nor do they necessarily exhaust the number of elements involved in the process. It is our concern, as we continue our study, to isolate and specify their limits. The operations necessary for the reconstitution of the self, whether found in thought reform and brainwashing, in religious conversion or in orthodox therapy, in shamanistic rites or in psychedelic cults, differ from each other, we believe with Lifton,[12] only in degree. To the prisoner of war the reform camp has a different meaning than Loyola's exercises have for the volunteer at a retreat, or than 12 Steps have for a member of Alcoholics Anonymous. However, in terms of organismic involvement, the resolution of cognitive tension in the modes of challenging central beliefs and values, the procedures used by the various systems, are functionally equivalent. In all these procedures three central processes appear to be at work: (1) a physical and/or psychological assault (symbolic death); a developing confusion about self and other beliefs (the bridge between death and rebirth); (2) surrender and despair (becoming a nonperson), and (3) a working through, active mastery, reeducation or adaptation process (the rebirth experience). We have found the forms of the process to be constant, though the metaphors vary to meet the needs and values of groups or individuals. In the West the convert seeks to uplift and raise himself, while in the East the experience may be formulated as a sinking, or deepening or descent to the material depths of nature. The West may focus on the salvation of social identity, the East on cosmological properties.

In the *Annual Reviews of Psychology*, the persistent criticism of the literature on psychotherapeutic processes notes the lack of useful units of measurement, confusion and variability in identifying the relevant interactional factors, and difficulty in establishing significant intervening variables. The paucity of meaningful parameters and of criteria for change is perennially deplored. Many take refuge in this situation in the argument that therapy is essentially a matter of art and style. This only retreats from the question.

Our formulation, we believe, offers a rationale for studying the occurrences when conduct changes. It suggests a systematic formulation of the role and operations of both the subject and of the change agent. Further, it orders the kinds of interventions and their appropriate timing and position. Our continuing investigations will, we trust, establish a theoretical framework that can account for the multifarious techniques of conduct reorganization and the various modes of psychotherapy as instances of an underlying, structured generic process.

REFERENCES

1. Adler, N. The Antinomian Personality: The Hippie Character Type. *Psychiatry*, Vol. 31, No. 4, 1968.
2. ———. The Manipulation of Body Image Sensibility and Self: The Antinomian Personality as Tuned Organ. *Proceedings, Conference on Drug Use and Drug Abuse*, Feb. 19, 1970. N.I.M.H.
3. Angyal, A. *Neurosis and Treatment: A Holistic Approach*. E. Hanforan and R. M. Jover (Eds.). New York: Wiley, 1965.

4. Cannon, W. B. Voodoo Death. *American Anthropologist.* Vol. 44, 1942. pp. 169–181.
5. Dederich, C. H. *Proceedings, California Parole Officers Association*, 1968. Mimeo.
6. Dewey, J. *How We Think.* New York: Heath, 1910.
7. Frank, J. D. *Persuasion and Healing.* Baltimore: Johns Hopkins Press, 1961.
8. Hutchinson, E. E. Varieties of Insight in Humans. *Psychiatry*, Vol. 1, 1939, pp. 323–332.
9. James, W. *Varieties of Religious Experience.* New York: Random House, 1902.
10. Kris, E. The Personal Myth, A Problem in Psychoanalytic Technique. *Journal of the American Psychoanalytic Association.* Vol. 4, 1956.
11. Laski, M. *Ecstasy: A Study of Some Secular and Religious Experiences.* London: Cresset Press, 1961.
12. Lifton, R. J. *Thought Reform and The Psychology of Totalism.* New York: Norton, 1961.
13. Lincoln, C. E. *The Black Muslims in America.* Boston: Beacon Press, 1961.
14. Loyola, I. *The Spiritual Exercises of St. Ignatius of Loyola.* London: Burns and Oates, 1963.
15. McNeill, J. T. *A History of The Cure of Souls.* New York: Harper and Row, 1951.
16. Mead, G. H. *Mind, Self, and Society.* Chicago: University of Chicago Press, 1934.
17. Nelson, B. Self-Images and Systems of Spiritual Direction in The History of European Civilization. In S. C. Klausner (Ed.), *The Quest for Self Control: Classical Philosophies and Scientific Research.* New York: Free Press, 1965.
18. Nelson, B. The Psychoanalyst as Mediator and Double Agent: An Introductory Survey. *This Review*, Vol. 52, 1965.
19. Sarbin, T. Anxiety: Reification of a Metaphor. *Journal of General Psychiatry.* Vol. 10, 1964. pp. 630–638.
20. Sarbin, T. and V. Allen. Role Theory. In Gardner Lindzey (Ed.), *Handbook of Social Psychology.* Cambridge: Addison-Wesley, 1968.
21. Sargent, W. *Battle for the Mind.* New York: Doubleday, 1957.
22. Wilden, A. Marcuse and the Freudian Model. *Salmagundi*, No. 10–11, Fall 1969–Winter 1970. pp. 196–245.

VI. THE MEANING OF EMOTION

11. Thomas Aquinas

EDITOR'S INTRODUCTION

There are many reasons for including Aquinas in a history of psychological thought. First, and perhaps most importantly, his mental and moral philosophy entitles him to rank among such notables as Plato, Aristotle, Plotinus, Augustine, and the others included in this anthology. Secondly, he was instrumental in reintroducing the works of Aristotle to the Latin West, and in synthesizing these with the intellectural traditions developed during the Middle Ages. Much of Aristotle's influence on Western thought can be traced to Aquinas. Finally, Thomistic psychology is the oldest of the contemporary schools of psychology. It is rightfully called "contemporary" because the teachings of Aquinas provided a foundation for much of the psychology taught in Catholic institutions and—to the extent that it is reasonable to speak of "national trends" in psychology—in some countries where the dominant religion is Catholicism. Perhaps the nearest comparison in this respect is the influence that Marx has exerted on psychological thought in communist countries.

The selections from Aquinas reprinted here have to do with the sensitive powers of the soul, and especially the emotions. In order to place these passages in context, it will be helpful to have a brief outline of Aquinas' view of the soul. As depicted in Table 1, Aquinas recognized three functional levels or grades of the soul—the vegetative, sensitive, and intellectual—each with an increasing superiority of operation over corporeal nature. The sensitive and intellectual levels are further subdivided into cognitive and appetitive functions, which are the manifestation of certain "powers" or capacities. The cognitive powers make possible the apprehension of knowledge or information; the appetitive powers underlie the tendency of every creature to fulfill itself, to actualize its potential.

The Meaning of Emotion

TABLE 1   Powers of the soul, according to Aquinas

Levels of the soul	Cognitive powers (*apprehensiva*)	Appetitive powers (*appetitiva*)
Intellectual	Active and passive reason	Will
Sensitive	Exterior and interior senses	Irascible and concupiscible emotions
Vegetative	Nutrition, growth, reproduction	

Considering first the sensitive level of the soul, the cognitive powers involve the five exterior senses (touch, taste, smell, hearing, and sight) and four interior senses. The latter include the common sense (the power to perceive an object as an entity and not just to sense its color, sound, etc.); imagination (the power to retain sense images in the absence of the object); memory (the association of sense images with past time); and the estimative power (the ability to appraise intuitively the functional significance of an object, e.g., as a source of danger or benefit). The appetitive powers on the sensory level are manifested in the emotions, which are tendencies to respond immediately and intuitively to what is apprehended through the exterior and interior senses.

All these powers are common to animals and man. On the intellectual level of the soul, by contrast, the powers are peculiar to man. These include, on the cognitive side, active and passive reason, the function of which will be explained shortly. On the appetitive side, the intellectual powers are manifested in deliberate acts of will.

This chapter is concerned primarily with the sensitive powers of the soul, both cognitive and appetitive. But before discussing these powers in more detail, a few comments must be made with regard to the style of exposition used by Aquinas. The *Summa Theologiae*, from which the present selections are taken, consists of a series of questions designed to explicate particular points of theology, civil law, natural philosophy, etc. After posing a particular question, Aquinas mentions a number of possible objections (usually three) to the answer he eventually will give. A brief aside is then made, often a quotation from scripture or some authority indicating the gist of the argument to follow. A detailed answer to the question is then provided and, finally, the original objections are rebutted. This style of exposition does not make for very lively reading. It is, however, well suited to the exposition of fine logical distinctions, a characteristic that was both the strength and the weakness of scholastic thought.

Four sets of questions are reprinted here. In the first set,

Aquinas examines the exterior and interior senses. In the second set, he considers in a general way the "powers of sensuality," or the sensitive appetite. There are two such powers, the irascible and concupiscible, which correspond roughly to the spirited and appetitive parts of the soul as conceived by Plato. The emotions, which are discussed in detail in the third set of questions, are a manifestation of the irascible and concupiscible powers. Finally, in the last set of questions, Aquinas sets forth a scheme for the classification of the fundamental emotions.

The manner in which Aquinas deals with these questions is, for the most part, clear and self-explanatory. However, his analysis of the cognitive processes (sensation and reason) requires some clarification, as does his classification of the emotions. Part of the difficulty is the technical vocabulary of the scholastics, which gives special meaning to such terms as *immutation, accident, intention, passion,* and the like.

Sensation, according to Aquinas, involves an *immutation* of the sense organ by the object being sensed. There are two kinds of immutation on the sensitive level—"natural" and "spiritual." In natural immutation, the sense organ actually acquires the quality or *accident* that is sensed. (In scholastic terminology, an accident is any reality, such as warmth, color, etc., that depends on another reality, the warm object, for its existence.) Thus, when the hand feels a warm object, it becomes warm in the process. In spiritual immutation, by contrast, the sense organ does not acquire the quality of the object sensed. The eye, for example, does not become green when it views a green object. What is acquired during vision is the sensible form or an *intention* of "greenness." The other exterior senses (taste, smell, and hearing) can be arranged in a hierarchy between touch and vision, depending on the relative importance of natural and spiritual immutation in their operation.

As one proceeds from the sensory to the intellectual functions of the soul, another kind of immutation is brought into operation. The passive intellect, which is the potential for knowledge, becomes actuality when it acquires the intelligible species, i.e., the universal form, of a class of objects. This is a higher type of immutation than the spiritual immutation involved in vision, for in the latter only the form of individual objects is actualized. Finally, the hierarchy is completed by the active intellect. For Aquinas, universal forms do not exist in a Platonic sense. While embedded in matter, a form is not fully actual; it is made actual when known, and this requires an active power of the soul distinct from the mere potentiality of the passive intellect.

The analysis of cognitive functions assumes that the organism (animal or man) is in direct contact with a qualitative world: accidents such as colors, sounds, tastes, odors, and all the other sensory qualities are "out there," so to speak, waiting to be actualized. As will be discussed in subsequent chapters, this is a far different conception of reality—and, implicitly, a different theory of cognition—than the one that became dominant following the Scientific Revolution.

Let us turn now to the powers of sensuality, i.e., the appetitive functions of the soul at the sensitive level. It was a fundamental "law" of scholastic psychology that all appetitive functions presuppose knowledge of the thing desired. The sense appetites are tendencies toward concrete objects apprehended by the senses as either good or evil. The intensity of such tendencies is the source of the emotions, or passions of the soul.

The analysis and classification of the emotions proved to be a fertile field of inquiry for scholastic thinkers. The scheme developed by Aquinas is depicted in Table 2. Aquinas used three criteria to distinguish among eleven basic emotions. The first

TABLE 2   The passions of the soul

Accessibility of the object	Quality of the object	Position of the person with respect to the object	Basic emotion
Concupiscible (easy to achieve or avoid)	Good	Fundamental attitude toward the object	Love
		Unhindered approach	Desire
		Possession	Joy
	Evil	Fundamental attitude toward the object	Hate
		Unhindered retreat	Aversion
		Possession	Sorrow
Irascible (difficult to achieve or avoid)	Good	Approach toward an object judged attainable	Hope
		Retreat from an object judged unattainable	Despair
	Evil	Approach toward an object judged vincible	Courage
		Retreat from an object judged invincible	Fear
		Possession of, and struggle against, the vincible	Anger

criterion is whether the object of the emotion is easy or difficult to achieve (or avoid). This is the distinction between the concupiscible and irascible appetites mentioned earlier. In a sense, it represents a kind of medieval version of the frustration-aggression hypothesis. The concupiscible emotions (love, desire, joy, aversion, and sorrow) represent unobstructed tendencies toward or away from objects appraised as good or evil. In the case of the irascible emotions, direct approach or avoidance is hindered. The result may be anger (*ira*), which gives this class of emotions its name. But, other emotions may also follow frustration (namely, hope, despair, courage, or fear), depending upon the circumstances.

The second criterion for the classification of the emotions is whether the object is suitable (good) or unsuitable (evil) to the well-being of the individual.

The third criterion is a complex one and might best be described as the position of the person relative to the object. Three possibilities exist here. First, the object might already be present and in the possession of the individual (joy, sorrow, anger). Second, the object may not be present, in which case the individual may approach it (desire, hope, courage) or retreat from in (aversion, despair, fear). Third, the individual may simply have a fundamental attitude (love, hate) toward the object that does not necessarily involve either possession, approach, or avoidance.

Aquinas' analysis of the emotions is quite sophisticated—superior, in fact, to that found in many contemporary textbooks of psychology. This is because, in the present selections at least, Aquinas is not so much trying to explain the underlying mechanisms of emotion as he is presenting a detailed account of what we mean by emotional concepts. Such conceptual analyses are the forte of scholastic thought.

The Sensitive Powers of the Soul: of the specific powers of the soul

Part 1a. Q.78.

[*Under this question there are four articles, only the last two of which are reprinted here.*]

THIRD ARTICLE

Whether the Five Exterior Senses are Properly Distinguished?

We proceed thus to the Third Article:—

Objection 1. It would seem inaccurate to distinguish five exterior senses. For sense can know accidents. But there are many kinds of accidents. Therefore, as powers are distinguished by their objects, it seems that the senses are multiplied according to the number of the kinds of accidents.

Obj. 2. Further, magnitude and shape, and other things which are called *common sensibles*, are *not sensibles by accident*, but are contradistinguished from them by the Philosopher (*De Anima* ii. 6). Now the diversity of objects, as such, diversifies the powers. Since, therefore, magnitude and shape are further from color than sound is, it seems that there is much more need for another sensitive power than can grasp magnitude or shape than for that which grasps color or sound.

Obj. 3. Further, one sense regards one contrariety; as sight regards white and black. But the sense of touch grasps several contraries; such as hot or cold, damp or dry, and suchlike. Therefore it is not a single sense but several. Therefore there are more than five senses.

Obj. 4. Further, a species is not divided against its genus. But taste is a kind of touch. Therefore it should not be classed as a distinct sense of touch.

On the contrary, The Philosopher says (*De Anima* iii. 1): *There is no other besides the five senses.*

I answer that, The reason of the distinction and number of the senses has been assigned by some to the organs in which one or other of the elements preponderate, as water, air, or the like. By

Reprinted with permission from Aquinas, T., *The Summa Theologica of St. Thomas Aquinas* (Vol. 1.). (Fathers of the Dominican Province, trans.) New York: Benzinger Brothers, Inc., 1947, pp. 392–396, 410–412, 691–697.

others it has been assigned to the medium, which is either in conjunction or extrinsic, and is either water or air, or suchlike. Others have ascribed it to the various natures of the sensible qualities, according as such quality belongs to a simple body or results from complexity. But none of these explanations is apt. For the powers are not for the organs, but the organs for the powers; wherefore there are not various powers for the reason that there are various organs; on the contrary, for this has nature provided a variety of organs, that they might be adapted to various powers. In the same way nature provided various mediums for the various senses, according to the convenience of the acts of the powers. And to be cognizant of the natures of sensible qualities does not pertain to the senses, but to the intellect.

The reason of the number and distinction of the exterior senses must therefore be ascribed to that which belongs to the senses properly and *per se*. Now, sense is a passive power, and is naturally immuted by the exterior sensible. Wherefore the exterior cause of such immutation is what is *per se* perceived by the sense, and according to the diversity of that exterior cause are the sensitive powers diversified.

Now, immutation is of two kinds, one natural, the other spiritual. Natural immutation takes place by the form of the immuter being received, according to its natural existence, into the thing immuted, as heat is received into the thing heated. Whereas spiritual immutation takes place by the form of the immuter being received, according to a spiritual mode of existence, into the thing immuted, as the form of color is received into the pupil which does not thereby become colored. Now, for the operation of the senses, a spiritual immutation is required, whereby an intention[1] of the sensible form is effected in the sensile organ. Otherwise, if a natural immutation alone sufficed for the sense's action, all natural bodies would feel when they undergo alteration.

But in some senses we find spiritual immutation only, as in *sight*: while in others we find not only a spiritual but also a natural immutation; either on the part of the object only, or likewise on the part of the organ. On the part of the object we find natural immutation, as to place, in sound which is the object of *hearing*; for sound is caused by percussion and commotion of the air: and we find natural immutation by alteration, in odor which is the object of *smelling*; for in order to exhale an odor, a body must be in a measure affected by heat. On the part of the organ, natural immutation takes place in *touch* and *taste*; for the

---

[1] [The scholastic notion of intention, although strange to the modern reader, came to play a fundamental role in the recent history of psychology—cf. F. Brentano, *Psychology from the empirical standpoint* (1874). New York: Humanities Press, 1973.]

hand that touches something hot becomes hot, while the tongue is moistened by the humidity of the flavored morsel. But the organs of smelling and hearing are not affected in their respective operations by any natural immutation unless indirectly.

Now, the sight, which is without natural immutation either in its organ or in its object, is the most spiritual, the most perfect, and the most universal of all the senses. After this comes the hearing and then the smell, which require a natural immutation on the part of the object; while local motion is more perfect than, and naturally prior to, the motion of alteration, as the Philosopher proves (*Phys.* viii. 7). Touch and taste are the most material of all: of the distinction of which we shall speak later on (*ad* 3, 4). Hence it is that the three other senses are not exercised through a medium united to them, to obviate any natural immutation in their organ; as happens as regards these two senses.

Reply Obj. 1. Not every accident has in itself a power of immutation, but only qualities of the third species, which are the principles of alteration: therefore only suchlike qualities are the objects of the senses; because *the senses are affected by the same things whereby inanimate bodies are affected,* as stated in *Phys.* vii. 2.

Reply Obj. 2. Size, shape, and the like, which are called *common sensibles*, are midway between *accidental sensibles* and *proper sensibles*, which are the objects of the senses. For the proper sensibles first, and of their very nature, affect the senses; since they are qualities that cause alteration. But the common sensibles are all reducible to quantity. As to size and number, it is clear that they are species of quantity. Shape is a quality about quantity, since the notion of shape consists in fixing the bounds of magnitude. Movement and rest are sensed according as the subject is affected in one or more ways in the magnitude of the subject or of its local distance, as in the movement of growth or of locomotion, or again, according as it is affected in some sensible qualities, as in the movement of alteration; and thus to sense movement and rest is, in a way, to sense one thing and many. Now quantity is the proximate subject of the qualities that cause alteration, as surface is of color. Therefore the common sensibles do not move the senses first and of their own nature, but by reason of the sensible quality; as the surface by reason of color. Yet they are not accidental sensibles, for they produce a certain variety in the immutation of the senses. For sense is immuted differently by a large and by a small surface: since whiteness itself is said to be great or small, and therefore it is divided according to its proper subject.

Reply Obj. 3. As the Philosopher seems to say (*De Anima*

ii. 11), the sense of touch is generically one, but is divided into several specific senses, and for this reason it extends to various contrarieties; which senses, however, are not separate from one another in their organ, but are spread throughout the whole body, so that their distinction is not evident. But taste, which perceives the sweet and the bitter, accompanies touch in the tongue, but not in the whole body; so it is easily distinguished from touch. We might also say that all those contrarieties agree, each in some proximate genus, and all in a common genus, which is the common and formal object of touch. Such common genus is, however, unnamed, just as the proximate genus of hot and cold is unnamed.

Reply Obj. 4. The sense of taste, according to a saying of the Philosopher (*De Anima* ii. 9), is a kind of touch existing in the tongue only. It is not distinct from touch in general, but only from the species of touch distributed in the body. But if touch is one sense only, on account of the common formality of its object: we must say that taste is distinguished from touch by reason of a different formality of immutation. For touch involves a natural, and not only a spiritual, immutation in its organ, by reason of the quality which is its proper object. But the organ of taste is not necessarily immuted by a natural immutation by reason of the quality which is its proper object, so that the tongue itself becomes sweet or bitter: but by reason of a quality which is a preamble to, and on which is based, the flavor, which quality is moisture, the object of touch.

FOURTH ARTICLE

Whether the Interior Senses Are Suitably Distinguished?

We proceed thus to the Fourth Article:—

Objection 1. It would seem that the interior senses are not suitably distinguished. For the common is not divided against the proper. Therefore the common sense should not be numbered among the interior sensitive powers, in addition to the proper exterior senses.

Obj. 2. Further, there is no need to assign an interior power of apprehension when the proper and exterior sense suffices. But the proper and exterior senses suffice for us to judge of sensible things; for each sense judges of its proper object. In like manner they seem to suffice for the perception of their own actions; for since the action of the sense is, in a way, between the power and its object, it seems that sight must be much more able to perceive its own vision, as being nearer to it, than the color; and in like manner with the other senses. Therefore for this there is no need to assign an interior power, called the common sense.

Obj. 3. Further, according to the Philosopher (*De Memor. et Remin.* i), the imagination and the memory are passions of the *first sensitive.* But passion is not divided against its subject. Therefore memory and imagination should not be assigned as powers distinct from the senses.

Obj. 4. Further, the intellect depends on the senses less than any power of the sensitive part. But the intellect knows nothing but what it receives from the senses; whence we read (*Poster.* i, 8), that *those who lack one sense lack one kind of knowledge.* Therefore much less should we assign to the sensitive part a power, which they call the *estimative* power, for the perception of intentions which the sense does not perceive.

Obj. 5. Further, the action of the cogitative power, which consists in comparing, adding, and dividing, and the action of the reminiscence, which consists in the use of a kind of syllogism for the sake of inquiry, is not less distant from the actions of the estimative and memorative powers, than the action of the estimative is from the action of the imagination. Therefore either we must add the cogitative and reminiscitive to the estimative and memorative powers, or the estimative and memorative powers should not be made distinct from the imagination.

Obj. 6. Further, Augustine (*Gen. ad lit.* xii. 6, 7, 24) describes three kinds of vision; namely, corporeal, which is an action of the sense; spiritual, which is an action of the imagination or phantasy; and intellectual, which is an action of the intellect. Therefore, there is no interior power between the sense and intellect, besides the imagination.

On the contrary, Avicenna (*De Anima* iv. 1) assigns five interior sensitive powers; namely, *common sense, phantasy, imagination, and the estimative and memorative powers.*

I answer that, As nature does not fail in necessary things, there must needs be as many actions of the sensitive soul as may suffice for the life of a perfect animal. If any of these actions cannot be reduced to the same one principle, they must be assigned to diverse powers; since a power of the soul is nothing else than the proximate principle of the soul's operation.

Now we must observe that for the life of a perfect animal, the animal should apprehend a thing not only at the actual time of sensation, but also when it is absent. Otherwise, since animal motion and action follow apprehension, an animal would not be moved to seek something absent: the contrary of which we may observe specially in perfect animals, which are moved by progression, for they are moved towards something apprehended and absent. Therefore an animal through the sensitive soul must not only receive the species of sensible things, when it is actually affected by them, but it must also retain and preserve them. Now to receive and retain are, in corporeal things, reduced to diverse principles; for moist things are apt to receive, but retain with difficulty, while it is the reverse with dry things. Wherefore, since the sensitive power is the act of a corporeal organ, it follows that the power which receives the species of sensible things must be distinct from the power which preserves them.

Again we must observe that if an animal were moved by pleasing and disagreeable things only as affecting the sense, there would be no need to suppose that an animal has a power besides the apprehension of those forms which the senses perceive, and in which the animal takes pleasure, or from which it shrinks with horror. But the animal needs to seek or to avoid certain things, not only because they are pleasing or otherwise to the senses, but also on account of other advantages and uses, or disadvantages: just as the sheep runs away when it sees a wolf, not on account of its color or shape, but as a natural enemy: and again a bird gathers together straws, not because they are pleasant to the sense, but because they are useful for building its nest. Animals, therefore, need to perceive such intentions, which the exterior sense does not perceive. And some distinct principle is necessary for this; since the perception of sensible forms comes by an immutation caused by the sensible, which is not the case with the perception of those intentions.

Thus, therefore, for the reception of sensible forms, the *proper sense* and the *common sense* are appointed, and of their distinction we shall speak farther on (*ad* 1, 2). But for the retention and preservation of these forms, the *phantasy* or *imagination* is appointed; which are the same, for phantasy or imagination is as it were a storehouse of forms received through the senses. Furthermore, for the apprehension of intentions which are not received through the senses, the *estimative* power is appointed: and for the preservation thereof, the *memorative* power, which is a storehouse of such-like intentions. A sign of which we have in the fact that the principle of memory in animals is found in some such intention, for instance, that something is harmful or otherwise. And the very formality of the past, which memory observes, is to be reckoned among these intentions.

Now, we must observe that as to sensible forms there is no difference between man and other animals; for they are similarly immuted by the extrinsic sensible. But there is a difference as to the above intentions: for other animals perceive these intentions only by some natural instinct, while man perceives them by means of coalition of ideas. Therefore the power which in other animals is called the natural estimative, in man is called the *cogitative*, which by some sort of collation discovers these intentions. Wherefore it is also called the *particular reason*, to which medical men assign a certain particular organ, namely, the middle part of the head: for it compares individual intentions, just as the intellectual reason compares universal intentions. As to the memorative power, man has not only memory, as other animals have in the sudden recollection of the past; but also *reminiscence* by syllogistically, as it were, seeking for a recollection of the past by the application of individual intentions. Avicenna, however, assigns between the estimative and the imaginative, a fifth power, which combines and divides imaginary forms: as when from the imaginary form of gold, and the imaginary form of a mountain, we compose the one form of a golden mountain, which we have never seen. But this operation is not to be found in animals other than man, in whom the imaginative power suffices thereto. To man also does Averroës attribute this action in his book *De sensu et sensibilibus* (viii). So there is no need to assign more than four interior powers of the sensitive part—namely, the common sense, the imagination, and the estimative and memorative powers.

Reply Obj. 1. The interior sense is called *common* not by predication, as if it were a genus; but as the common root and principle of the exterior senses.

Reply Obj. 2. The proper sense judges of the proper sensible by discerning it from other things which come under the same sense; for instance, by discerning white from black or green. But neither sight nor taste can discern white from sweet: because what discerns between two things must know both. Wherefore the discerning judgment must be assigned to the common sense; to which, as to a common term, all apprehensions of the senses must be referred: and by which, again, all the intentions of the senses are perceived; as when someone sees that he sees. For this cannot be done by the proper sense, which only knows the form of the sensible by which it is immuted, in which immutation the action of sight is completed, and from which immutation follows another in the common sense which perceives the act of vision.

Reply Obj. 3. As one power arises from the soul by means of another, as we have seen above (Q. 77, A. 7), so also the soul is the subject of one power through another. In this way the imagination and the memory are called passions of the *first sensitive*.

Reply Obj. 4. Although the operation of the intellect has its origin in the senses: yet, in the thing apprehended through the senses, the intellect knows many things which the senses cannot perceive. In like manner does the estimative power, though in a less perfect manner.

Reply Obj. 5. The cogitative and memorative powers in man owe their excellence not to that which is proper to the sensitive part; but to a certain affinity and proximity to the universal reason, which, so to speak, overflows into them. Therefore they are not distinct powers, but the same, yet more perfect than in other animals.

Reply Obj. 6. Augustine calls that vision spiritual which is effected by the images of bodies in the absence of bodies. Whence it is clear that it is common to all interior apprehensions.

Part 1a. Q.81.
of the power of sensuality

(In Three Articles)

Next we have to consider the power of sensuality, concerning which there are three points of inquiry: (1) Whether sensuality is only an appetitive power? (2) Whether it is divided into irascible and concupiscible as distinct powers? (3) Whether the irascible and the concupiscible powers obey reason?

FIRST ARTICLE

Whether Sensuality Is Only Appetitive?

We proceed thus to the First Article:—

Objection 1. It would seem that sensuality is not only appetitive, but also cognitive. For Augustine says (*De Trin.* xii. 12) that *the sensual movement of the soul which is directed to the bodily senses is common to us and beasts.* But the bodily senses belong to the apprehensive powers. Therefore sensuality is a cognitive power.

Obj. 2. Further, things which come under one division seem to be of one genus. But Augustine (*De Trin.* xii, *loc. cit.*) divides sensuality against the higher and lower reason, which belong to knowledge. Therefore sensuality also is apprehensive.

Obj. 3. Further, in man's temptations sensuality stands in the place of the *serpent*. But in the temptation of our first parents, the serpent presented himself as one giving information and proposing sin, which belong to the cognitive power. Therefore sensuality is a cognitive power.

On the contrary, Sensuality is defined as *the appetite of things belonging to the body.*

I answer that, The name sensuality seems to be taken from the sensual movement, of which Augustine speaks (*De Trin.* xii. 12, 13), just as the name of a power is taken from its act; for instance, sight from seeing. Now the sensual movement is an appetite following sensitive apprehension. For the act of the apprehensive power is not so properly called a movement as the act of the appetite: since the operation of the apprehensive power is completed in the very fact that the thing apprehended is in the one that apprehends: while the operation of the appetitive power is completed in the fact that he who desires is borne towards the thing desirable. Therefore the operation of the apprehensive power is likened to rest: whereas the operation of the appetitive power is rather likened to movement. Wherefore by sensual movement we understand the operation of the appetitive power: so that sensuality is the name of the sensitive appetite.

Reply Obj. 1. By saying that the sensual movement of the soul is directed to the bodily senses, Augustine does not give us to understand that the bodily senses are included in sensuality, but rather that the movement of sensuality is a certain inclination to the bodily senses, since we desire things which are apprehended through the bodily senses. And thus the bodily senses appertain to sensuality as a preamble.

Reply Obj. 2. Sensuality is divided against higher and lower reason, as having in common with them the act of movement: for the apprehensive power, to which belong the higher and lower reason, is a motive power; as is appetite, to which appertains sensuality.

Reply Obj. 3. The serpent not only showed and proposed sin, but also incited to the commission of sin. And in this, sensuality is signified by the serpent.

SECOND ARTICLE

Whether the Sensitive Appetite Is Divided into the Irascible and Concupiscible as Distinct Powers?

We proceed thus to the Second Article:—

Objection 1. It would seem that the sensitive appetite is not divided into the irascible and concupiscible as distinct powers. For the same power of the soul regards both sides of a contrariety, as sight regards both black and white, according to the Philosopher (*De Anima* ii. 11). But suitable and harmful are contraries. Since, then, the concupiscible power regards what is suitable, while the irascible is concerned with what is harmful, it seems that irascible and concupiscible are the same power in the soul.

Obj. 2. Further, the sensitive appetite regards only what is suitable according to the senses. But such is the object of the concupiscible power. Therefore there is no sensitive appetite differing from the concupiscible.

Obj. 3. Further, hatred is in the irascible part: for Jerome says on Matt. xiii. 33: *We ought to have the hatred of vice in the irascible power.* But hatred is contrary to love, and is in the concupiscible part. Therefore the concupiscible and irascible are the same powers.

On the contrary, Gregory of Nyssa (Nemesius, *De Natura Hominis*) and Damascene (*De Fid. Orth.* ii. 12) assign two parts of the sensitive appetite, the irascible and the concupiscible.

I answer that, The sensitive appetite is one generic power, and is called sensuality; but it is divided into two powers, which are species of the sensitive appetite—the irascible and the concupiscible. In order to make this clear, we must observe that in natural corruptible things there is needed an inclination not only to the acquisition of what is suitable and to the avoiding of what is harmful, but also to resistance against corruptive and contrary agencies which are a hindrance to the acquisition of what is suitable, and are productive of harm. For example, fire has a natural inclination, not only to rise from a lower position, which is unsuitable to it, towards a higher position which is suitable, but also to resist whatever destroys or hinders its action. Therefore, since the sensitive appetite is an inclination following sensitive apprehension, as natural appetite is an inclination following the natural form, there must needs be in the sensitive part two appetitive powers—one through which the soul is simply inclined to seek what is suitable, according to the senses, and to fly from what is hurtful, and this is called the concupiscible: and another, whereby an animal resists these attacks that hinder what is suitable, and inflict harm, and this is called the irascible. Whence we say that its object is something arduous, because its tendency is to overcome and rise above obstacles. Now these two are not to be reduced to one principle: for sometimes the soul busies itself with unpleasant things, against the inclination of the concupiscible appetite, in order that, following the impulse of the irascible appetite, it may fight against obstacles. Wherefore also the passions of the irascible appetite counteract the passions of the concupiscible appetite: since concupiscence, on being roused, diminishes anger; and anger being roused, diminishes concupiscence in many cases. This is clear also from the fact that the irascible is, as it were, the champion and defender of the concupiscible, when it rises up against what hinders the acquistion of the suitable things which the concupiscible desires, or against what inflicts harm, from which the concupiscible flies. And for this reason all the passions of the irascible appetite rise from the passions of the concupiscible appetite and terminate in them; for instance, anger rises from sadness, and having wrought vengeance, terminates in joy. For this reason also the quarrels of animals are about things concupiscible— namely, food and sex, as the Philosopher says (De Animal. viii).*

Reply Obj. 1. The concupiscible power regards both what is suitable and what is unsuitable. But the object of the irascible power is to resist the onslaught of the unsuitable.

Reply Obj. 2. As in the apprehensive powers of the sensitive part there is an estimative power, which perceives those things which do not impress the senses, as we have said above (Q. 78, A. 2); so also in the sensitive appetite there is a certain appetitive power which regards something as suitable, not because it pleases the senses, but because it is useful to the animal for self-defence: and this is the irascible power.

Reply Obj. 3. Hatred belongs simply to the concupiscible appetite: but by reason of the strife which arises from hatred, it may belong to the irascible appetite.

THIRD ARTICLE

Whether the Irascible and Concupiscible Appetites Obey Reason?

We proceed thus to the Third Article:—

Objection 1. It would seem that the irascible and concupiscible appetites do not obey reason. For irascible and concupiscible are parts of sensuality. But sensuality does not obey reason, wherefore it is signified by the serpent, as Augustine says (De Trin. xii. 12, 13). Therefore the irascible and concupiscible appetites do not obey reason.

Obj. 2. Further, what obeys a certain thing does not resist it. But the irascible and concupiscible appetites resist reason: according to the Apostle (Rom. vii. 23): *I see another law in my*

*De Animal. Histor.

members fighting against the law of my mind. Therefore the irascible and concupiscible appetites do not obey reason.

Obj. 3. Further, as the appetitive power is inferior to the rational part of the soul, so also is the sensitive power. But the sensitive part of the soul does not obey reason: for we neither hear nor see just when we wish. Therefore, in like manner, neither do the powers of the sensitive appetite, the irascible and concupiscible, obey reason.

On the contrary, Damascene says (*De Fid. Orth.* ii. 12) that *the part of the soul which is obedient and amenable to reason is divided into concupiscence and anger.*

I answer that, In two ways the irascible and concupiscible powers obey the higher part, in which are the intellect or reason, and the will; first, as to reason, secondly as to the will. They obey the reason in their own acts, because in other animals the sensitive appetite is naturally moved by the estimative power; for instance, a sheep, esteeming the wolf as an enemy, is afraid. In man the estimative power, as we have said above (Q. 78, A. 4), is replaced by the cogitative power, which is called by some *the particular reason,* because it compares individual intentions. Wherefore in man the sensitive appetite is naturally moved by this particular reason. But this same particular reason is naturally guided and moved according to the universal reason: wherefore in syllogistic matters particular conclusions are drawn from universal propositions. Therefore it is clear that the universal reason directs the sensitive appetite, which is divided into concupiscible and irascible; and this appetite obeys it. But because to draw particular conclusions from universal principles is not the work of the intellect, as such, but of the reason: hence it is that the irascible and concupiscible are said to obey the reason rather than to obey the intellect. Anyone can experience this in himself: for by applying certain universal considerations, anger or fear or the like may be modified or excited.

To the will also is the sensitive appetite subject in execution, which is accomplished by the motive power. For in other animals movement follows at once the concupiscible and irascible appetites: for instance, the sheep, fearing the wolf, flees at once, because it has no superior counteracting appetite. On the contrary, man is not moved at once, according to the irascible and concupiscible appetites: but he awaits the command of the will, which is the superior appetite. For wherever there is order among a number of motive powers, the second only moves by virtue of the first: wherefore the lower appetite is not sufficient to cause movement, unless the higher appetite consents. And this is what the Philosopher says (*De Anima*. iii. 11), that *the higher appetite moves the lower appetite, as the higher sphere moves the lower.* In this way, therefore, the irascible and concupiscible are subject to reason.

Reply Obj. 1. Sensuality is signified by the serpent, in what is proper to it as a sensitive power. But the irascible and concupiscible powers denominate the sensitive appetite rather on the part of the act, to which they are led by the reason, as we have said.

Reply Obj. 2. As the Philosopher says (*Polit.* i. 2): *We observe in an animal a despotic and a politic principle: for the soul dominates the body by a despotic power; but the intellect dominates the appetite by a politic and royal power.* For a power is called despotic whereby a man rules his slaves, who have not the right to resist in any way the orders of the one that commands them, since they have nothing of their own. But that power is called politic and royal by which a man rules over free subjects, who, though subject to the government of the ruler, have nevertheless something of their own, by reason of which they can resist the orders of him who commands. And so, the soul is said to rule the body by a despotic power, because the members of the body cannot in any way resist the sway of the soul, but at the soul's command both hand and foot, and whatever member is naturally moved by voluntary movement, are moved at once. But the intellect or reason is said to rule the irascible and concupiscible by a politic power: because the sensitive appetite has something of its own, by virtue whereof it can resist the commands of reason. For the sensitive appetite is naturally moved, not only by the estimative power in other animals, and in man by the cogitative power which the universal reason guides, but also by the imagination and sense. Whence it is that we experience that the irascible and concupiscible powers do resist reason, inasmuch as we sense or imagine something pleasant, which reason forbids, or unpleasant, which reason commands. And so from the fact that the irascible and concupiscible resist reason in something, we must not conclude that they do not obey.

Reply Obj. 3. The exterior senses require for action exterior sensible things, whereby they are affected, and the presence of which is not rules by reason. But the interior powers, both appetitive and apprehensive, do not require exterior things. Therefore they are subject to the command of reason, which can not only incite or modify the affections of the appetitive power, but can also form the phantasms of the imagination.

Part 1a2ae. Q.22.
of the subject of the soul's passions

(In Three Articles)

We must now consider the passions of the soul: first, in general; secondly, in particular. Taking them in general, there are four things to be considered: (1) Their subject: (2) The difference between them: (3) Their mutual relationship: (4) Their malice and goodness.

Under the first head there are three points of inquiry: (1) Whether there is any passion in the soul? (2) Whether passion is in the appetitive rather than in the apprehensive part? (3) Whether passion is in the sensitive appetite rather than in the intellectual appetite, which is called the will?

FIRST ARTICLE

Whether Any Passion Is in the Soul?

We proceed thus to the First Article:—

Objection 1. It would seem that there is no passion in the soul. Because passivity belongs to matter. But the soul is not composed of matter and form, as stated in the First Part (Q. 75, A. 5). Therefore there is no passion in the soul.

Obj. 2. Further, passion is movement, as is stated in *Phys.* iii. 3. But the soul is not moved, as is proved in *De Anima* i. 3. Therefore passion is not in the soul.

Obj. 3. Further, passion is the road to corruption; since *every passion, when increased, alters the substance* as is stated in *Topic.* vi. 6. But the soul is incorruptible. Therefore no passion is in the soul.

On the contrary, The Apostle says (Rom. vii. 5): *When we were in the flesh, the passions of sins which were by the law, did the work in our members.* Now sins are, properly speaking, in the soul. Therefore passions also, which are described as being *of sins*, are in the soul.

I answer that, The word *passive* is used in three ways. First, in a general way, according as whatever receives something is passive, although nothing is taken from it: thus we may say that the air is passive when it is lit up. But this is to be perfected rather than to be passive. Secondly, the word *passive* is employed in its proper sense, when something is received, while something else is taken away: and this happens in two ways. For sometimes that which is lost is unsuitable to the thing: thus when an animal's body is healed, it is said to be passive, because it receives health, and loses sickness.—At other times the contrary occurs: thus to ail is to be passive; because the ailment is received and health is lost. And here we have passion in its most proper acceptation. For a thing is said to be passive from its being drawn to the agent: and when a thing recedes from what is suitable to it, then especially does it appear to be drawn to something else. Moreover in *De Generat.* i. 3, it is stated that when a more excellent thing is generated from a less excellent, we have generation simply, and corruption in a particular respect: whereas the reverse is the case, when from a more excellent thing, a less excellent is generated. In these three ways it happens that passions are in the soul. For in the sense of mere reception, we speak of *feeling and understanding as being a kind of passion* (*De Anima* i. 5). But passion, accompanied by the loss of something, is only in respect of a bodily transmutation; wherefore passion properly so called cannot be in the soul, save accidentally, in so far, to wit, as the *composite* is passive. But here again we find a difference; because when this transmutation is for the worse, it has more of the nature of a passion, than when it is for the better: hence sorrow is more properly a passion than joy.

Reply Obj. 1. It belongs to matter to be passive in such a way as to lose something and to be transmuted: hence this happens only in those things that are composed of matter and form. But passivity, as implying mere reception, need not be in matter, but can be in anything that is in potentiality. Now, though the soul is not composed of matter and form, yet it has something of potentiality, in respect of which it is competent to receive or to be passive, according as the act of understanding is a kind of passion, as stated in *De Anima* iii. 4.

Reply Obj. 2. Although it does not belong to the soul in itself to be passive and to be moved, yet it belongs accidentally, as stated in *De Anima* i. 3.

Reply Obj. 3. This argument is true of passion accompanied by transmutation to something worse. And passion, in this sense, is not found in the soul, except accidentally: but the composite, which is corruptible, admits of it by reason of its own nature.

SECOND ARTICLE

Whether Passion Is in the Appetitive Rather Than in the Apprehensive Part?

We proceed thus to the Second Article:—

Objection 1. It would seem that passion is in the apprehensive part of the soul rather than in the appetitive. Because that which is first in any genus, seems to rank first among all things that are in that genus, and to be their cause, as is stated in *Metaph.* ii. 1. Now passion is found to be in the apprehensive, before being in the appetitive part: for the appetitive part is not affected unless there be a previous passion in the apprehensive part. Therefore passion is in the apprehensive part more than in the appetitive.

Obj. 2. Further, what is more active is less passive; for action is contrary to passion. Now the appetitive part is more active than the apprehensive. Therefore it seems that passion is more in the apprehensive part.

Obj. 3. Further, just as the sensitive appetite is the power of a corporeal organ, so is the power of sensitive apprehension. But passion in the soul occurs, properly speaking, in respect of a bodily transmutation. Therefore passion is not more in the sensitive appetitive than in the sensitive apprehensive part.

On the contrary, Augustine says (*De Civ. Dei* ix. 4) that *the movements of the soul, which the Greeks call πάθη, are styled by some of our writers, Cicero* for instance, disturbances; by some, affections or emotions; while others rendering the Greek more accurately, call them passions*. From this it is evident that the passions of the soul are the same as affections. But affections manifestly belong to the appetitive, and not to the apprehensive part. Therefore the passions are in the appetitive rather than in the apprehensive part.

I answer that, As we have already stated (A. 1) the word *passion* implies that the patient is drawn to that which belongs to the agent. Now the soul is drawn to a thing by the appetitive power rather than by the apprehensive power: because the soul has, through its appetitive power, an order to things as they are in themselves: hence the Philosopher says (*Metaph.* vi. 4) that *good and evil, i.e., the objects of the appetitive power, are in things themselves*. On the other hand the apprehensive power is not drawn to a thing, as it is in itself; but knows it by reason of an *intention* of the thing, which *intention* it has in itself, or receives in its own way. Hence we find it stated (*ibid.*) that *the true and the false*, which pertain to knowledge, *are not in things, but in the mind*. Consequently it is evident that the nature of passion is consistent with the appetitive, rather than with the apprehensive part.

Reply Obj. 1. In things relating to perfection the case is the opposite, in comparison to things that pertain to defect. Because in things relating to perfection, intensity is in proportion to the

---

**Those things which the Greeks call* πάθη, *we prefer to call disturbances rather than diseases* (Tusc. iv. 5).

approach to one first principle; to which the nearer a thing approaches, the more intense it is. Thus the intensity of a thing possessed of light depends on its approach to something endowed with light in a supreme degree, to which the nearer a thing approaches the more light it possesses. But in things that relate to defect, intensity depends, not on approach to something supreme, but in receding from that which is perfect; because therein consists the very notion of privation and defect. Wherefore the less a thing recedes from that which stands first, the less intense it is: and the result is that at first we always find some small defect, which afterwards increases as it goes on. Now passion pertains to defect, because it belongs to a thing according as it is in potentiality. Wherefore in those things that approach to the Supreme Perfection, *i.e.*, to God, there is but little potentiality and passion: while in other things, consequently, there is more. Hence also, in the supreme, *i.e.*, the apprehensive, power of the soul, passion is found less than in the other powers.

Reply Obj. 2. The appetitive power is said to be more active, because it is, more than the apprehensive power, the principle of the exterior action: and this for the same reason that it is more passive, namely, its being related to things as existing in themselves: since it is through the external action that we come into contact with things.

Reply Obj. 3. As stated in the First Part (Q. 78, A. 3), the organs of the soul can be changed in two ways. First, by a spiritual change, in respect of which the organ receives an *intention* of the object. And this is essential to the act of the sensitive apprehension: thus is the eye changed by the object visible, not by being colored, but by receiving an intention of color. But the organs are receptive of another and natural change, which affects their natural disposition; for instance, when they become hot or cold, or undergo some similar change. And whereas this kind of change is accidental to the act of the sensitive apprehension; for instance, if the eye be wearied through gazing intently at something, or be overcome by the intensity of the object: on the other hand, it is essential to the act of the sensitive appetite; wherefore the material element in the definitions of the movements of the appetitive part, is the natural change of the organ; for instance, *anger* is said to be *a kindling of the blood about the heart.* Hence it is evident that the notion of passion is more consistent with the act of the sensitive appetite, than with that of the sensitive apprehension, although both are actions of a corporeal organ.

THIRD ARTICLE

Whether Passion Is in the Sensitive Appetite Rather Than in the Intellectual Appetite, Which Is Called the Will?

We proceed thus to the Third Article:—

Objection 1. It would seem that passion is not more in the sensitive than in the intellectual appetite. For Dionysius declares (*Div. Nom.* ii) Hierotheus *to be taught by a kind of yet more Godlike instruction; not only by learning Divine things, but also by suffering (patiens) them.* But the sensitive appetite cannot *suffer* Divine things, since its object is the sensible good. Therefore passion is in the intellectual appetite, just as it is also in the sensitive appetite.

Obj. 2. Further, the more powerful the active force, the more intense the passion. But the object of the intellectual appetite, which is the universal good, is a more powerful active force than the object of the sensitive appetite, which is a particular good. Therefore passion is more consistent with the intellectual than with the sensitive appetite.

Obj. 3. Further, joy and love are said to be passions. But these are to be found in the intellectual and not only in the sensitive appetite: else they would not be ascribed by the Scriptures to God and the angels. Therefore the passions are not more in the sensitive than in the intellectual appetite.

On the contrary, Damascene says (*De Fide Orthod.* ii. 22), while describing the animal passions: *Passion is a movement of the sensitive appetite when we imagine good or evil: in other words, passion is a movement of the irrational soul, when we think of good or evil.*

I answer that, As stated above (A. 1) passion is properly to be found where there is corporeal transmutation. This corporeal transmutation is found in the act of the sensitive appetite, and is not only spiritual, as in the sensitive apprehension, but also natural. Now there is no need for corporeal transmutation in the act of the intellectual appetite: because this appetite is not exercised by means of a corporeal organ. It is therefore evident that passion is more properly in the act of the sensitive appetite, than in that of the intellectual appetite; and this is again evident from the definitions of Damascene quoted above.

Reply Obj. 1. By *suffering* Divine things is meant being well affected towards them, and united to them by love: and this takes place without any alteration in the body.

Reply Obj. 2. Intensity of passion depends not only on the power of the agent, but also on the possibility of the patient: because things that are disposed to passion, suffer much even from petty agents. Therefore although the object of the intellectual appetite has greater activity than the object of the sensitive appetite, yet the sensitive appetite is more passive.

Reply Obj. 3. When love and joy and the like are ascribed to God or the angels, or to man in respect of his intellectual appetite, they signify simple acts of the will having like effects, but without passion. Hence Augustine says (*De Civ. Dei* ix. 5): *The holy angels feel no anger while they punish . . ., no fellow-feeling with misery while they relieve the unhappy: and yet ordinary human speech is wont to ascribe to them also these passions by name, because, although they have none of our weakness, their acts bear a certain resemblance to ours.*

Part 1a2ae. Q.23.
how the passions differ
from one another
(*In Four Articles*)

We must now consider how the passions differ from one another: and under this head there are four points of inquiry: (1) Whether the passions of the concupiscible part are different from those of the irascible part? (2) Whether the contrariety of passions in the irascible part is based on the contrariety of good and evil? (3) Whether there is any passion that has no contrary? (4) Whether, in the same power, there are any passions, differing in species, but not contrary to one another?

FIRST ARTICLE

Whether the Passions of the Concupiscible Part Are Different from Those of the Irascible Part?

We proceed thus to the First Article:—

Objection 1. It would seem that the same passions are in the irascible and concupiscible parts. For the Philosopher says (*Ethic.* ii. 5) that the passions of the soul are those emotions *which are followed by joy or sorrow.* But joy and sorrow are in the concupiscible part. Therefore all the passions are in the concupiscible part, and not some in the irascible, others in the concupiscible part.

Obj. 2. Further, on the words of Matth. xiii. 33, *The kingdom of heaven is like to leaven*, etc., Jerome's gloss says: *We should have prudence in the reason; hatred of vice in the irascible faculty; desire of virtue, in the concupiscible part.* But hatred is in the concupiscible faculty, as also is love, of which it is the contrary, as is stated in *Topic.* ii. 7. Therefore the same passion is in the concupiscible and irascible faculties.

Obj. 3. Further, passions and actions differ specifically according to their objects. But the objects of the irascible and concupiscible passions are the same, viz., good and evil. Therefore the same passions are in the irascible and concupiscible faculties.

On the contrary, The acts of different powers differ in species; for instance, to see, and to hear. But the irascible and the concupiscible are two powers into which the sensitive appetite is divided, as stated in the First Part (Q. 81, A. 2). Therefore, since the passions are movements of the sensitive appetite, as stated above (Q. 22, A. 3), the passions of the irascible faculty are specifically distinct from those of the concupiscible part.

I answer that, The passions of the irascible part differ in species from those of the concupiscible faculty. For since different powers have different objects, as stated in the First Part (Q. 77, A. 3), the passions of different powers must of necessity be referred to different objects. Much more, therefore, do the passions of different faculties differ in species; since a greater difference in the object is required to diversify the species of the powers, than to diversify the species of passions or actions. For just as in the physical order, diversity of genus arises from diversity in the potentiality of matter, while diversity of species arises from diversity of form in the same matter; so in the acts of the soul, those that belong to different powers, differ not only in species but also in genus, while acts and passions regarding different specific objects, included under the one common object of a single power, differ as the species of that genus.

In order, therefore, to discern which passions are in the irascible, and which in the concupiscible, we must take the object of each of these powers. For we have stated in the First Part (Q. 81, A. 2) that the object of the concupiscible power is sensible good or evil, simply apprehended as such, which causes pleasure or pain. But, since the soul must, of necessity, experience difficulty or struggle at times, in acquiring some such good, or in avoiding some such evil, in so far as such good or evil is more than our animal nature can easily acquire or avoid; therefore this very good or evil, inasmuch as it is of an arduous or difficult nature, is the object of the irascible faculty. Therefore whatever passions regard good or evil absolutely, belong to the concupiscible power; for instance, joy, sorrow, love, hatred and such like: whereas those passions which regard good or bad as arduous, through being difficult to obtain or avoid, belong to the irascible faculty; such are daring, fear, hope and the like.

Reply Obj. 1. As stated in the First Part (*loc. cit.*), the irascible faculty is bestowed on animals, in order to remove the obstacles that hinder the concupiscible power from tending towards its object, either by making some good difficult to obtain, or by making some evil hard to avoid. The result is that all the irascible passions terminate in the concupiscible passions: and thus it is that even the passions which are in the irascible faculty are followed by joy and sadness which are in the concupiscible faculty.

Reply Obj. 2. Jerome ascribes hatred of vice to the irascible faculty, not by reason of hatred, which is properly a concupiscible passion; but on account of the struggle, which belongs to the irascible power.

Reply Obj. 3. Good, inasmuch as it is delightful, moves the concupiscible power. But if it prove difficult to obtain, from this very fact it has a certain contrariety to the concupiscible power: and hence the need of another power tending to that good. The same applies to evil. And this power is the irascible faculty. Consequently the concupiscible passions are specifically different from the irascible passions.

SECOND ARTICLE

Whether the Contrariety of the Irascible Passions Is Based on the Contrariety of Good and Evil?

We proceed thus to the Second Article:—

Objection 1. It would seem that the contrarity of the irascible passions is based on no other contrariety than that of good and evil. For the irascible passions are ordained to the concupiscible passions, as stated above (A. 1 *ad* 1). But the contrariety of the concupiscible passions is no other than that of good and evil; take, for instance, love and hatred, joy and sorrow. Therefore the same applies to the irascible passions.

Obj. 2. Further, passions differ according to their objects; just as movements differ according to their termini. But there is no other contrariety of movements, except that of the termini, as is stated in *Phys.* v. 3. Therefore there is no other contrariety of passions, save that of the objects. Now the object of the appetite is good or evil. Therefore in no appetitive power can there be contrariety of passions other than that of good and evil.

Obj. 3. Further, *every passion of the soul is by way of approach and withdrawal*, as Avicenna declares in his sixth book of *Physics.* Now approach results from the apprehension of good; withdrawal, from the apprehension of evil: since just as *good is what all desire* (*Ethic.* i. 1), so evil is what all shun. Therefore, in the passions of the soul, there can be no other contrariety than that of good and evil.

On the contrary, Fear and daring are contrary to one another, as stated in *Ethic.* iii. 7. But fear and daring do not differ in respect of good and evil: because each regards some kind of evil. Therefore not every contrariety of the irascible passions is that of good and evil.

I answer that, Passion is a kind of movement, as stated in *Phys.* iii. 3. Therefore contrariety of passions is based on contrariety of movements or changes. Now there is a twofold contrariety in changes and movements, as stated in *Phys.* v. 5. One is according to approach and withdrawal in respect of the same term: and this contrariety belongs properly to changes, *i.e.*, to generation, which is a change *to being*, and to corruption, which is change *from being*. The other contrariety is according to opposition of termini, and belongs properly to movements: thus whitening, which is movement from black to white, is contrary to blackening, which is movement from white to black.

Accordingly there is a twofold contrariety in the passions of the soul: one, according to contrariety of objects, *i.e.*, of good and evil; the other, according to approach and withdrawal in respect of the same term. In the concupiscible passions the former contrariety alone is to be found; viz., that which is based on the objects: whereas in the irascible passions, we find both forms of contrariety. The reason of this is that the object of the concupiscible faculty, as stated above (A. 1), is sensible good or evil considered absolutely. Now good, as such, cannot be a term where-from, but only a term whereto, since nothing shuns good as such; on the contrary, all things desire it. In like manner, nothing desires evil, as such; but all things shun it: wherefore evil cannot have the aspect of a term whereto, but only of a term wherefrom. Accordingly every concupiscible passion in respect of good, tends to it, as love, desire and joy; while every concupiscible passion in respect of evil, tends from it, as hatred, avoidance or dislike, and sorrow. Wherefore, in the concupiscible passions, there can be no contrariety of approach and withdrawal in respect of the same object.

On the other hand, the object of the irascible faculty is sensible good or evil, considered not absolutely, but under the aspect of difficulty or arduousness. Now the good which is difficult or arduous, considered as good, is of such a nature as to produce in us a tendency to it, which tendency pertains to the passion of *hope*; whereas, considered as arduous or difficult, it makes us turn from it; and this pertains to the passion of *despair*. In like manner the arduous evil, considered as an evil, has the aspect of something to be shunned; and this belongs to the passion of *fear*: but it also contains a reason for tending to it, as attempting something arduous, whereby to escape being subject to evil; and this tendency is called *daring*. Consequently, in the irascible passions we find contrariety in respect of good and evil (as between hope and fear): and also contrariety according to approach and withdrawal in respect of the same term (as between daring and fear).

From what has been said the replies to the objections are evident.

THIRD ARTICLE

Whether Any Passion of the Soul Has No Contrary?

We proceed thus to the Third Article:—

Objection 1. It would seem that every passion of the soul has a contrary. For every passion of the soul is either in the irascible or in the concupiscible faculty, as stated above (A. 1). But both kinds of passions have their respective modes of contrariety. Therefore every passion of the soul has its contrary.

Obj. 2. Further, every passion of the soul has either good or evil for its object; for these are the common objects of the appetitive part. But a passion having good for its object, is contrary to a passion having evil for its object. Therefore every passion has a contrary.

Obj. 3. Further, every passion of the soul is in respect of approach or withdrawal, as stated above (A. 2). But every approach has a corresponding contrary withdrawal, and vice versa. Therefore every passion of the soul has a contrary.

On the contrary, Anger is a passion of the soul. But no passion is set down as being contrary to anger, as stated in *Ethic.* iv. 5. Therefore not every passion has a contrary.

I answer that, The passion of anger is peculiar in this, that it cannot have a contrary, either according to approach and withdrawal, or according to the contrariety of good and evil. For anger is caused by a difficult evil already present: and when such an evil is present, the appetite must needs either succumb, so that it does not go beyond the limits of *sadness*, which is a concupiscible passion; or else it has a movement of attack on the hurtful evil, which movement is that of *anger*. But it cannot have a movement of withdrawal: because the evil is supposed to be already present or past. Thus no passion is contrary to anger according to contrariety of approach and withdrawal.

In like manner neither can there be according to contrariety of good and evil. Because the opposite of present evil is good obtained, which can no longer have the aspect of arduousness or difficulty. Nor, when once good is obtained, does there remain any other movement, except the appetite's repose in the good obtained; which repose belongs to joy, which is a passion of the concupiscible faculty.

Accordingly no movement of the soul can be contrary to the movement of anger, and nothing else than cessation from its movement is contrary thereto; thus the Philosopher says (*Rhetor.* ii. 3) that *calm is contrary to anger*, by opposition not of contrariety but of negation or privation.

From what has been said the replies to the objections are evident.

FOURTH ARTICLE

Whether in the Same Power, There Are Any Passions, Specifically Different, but Not Contrary to One Another?

We proceed thus to the Fourth Article:—

Objection 1. It would seem that there cannot be, in the same power, specifically different passions that are not contrary to one another. For the passions of the soul differ according to their objects. Now the objects of the soul's passions are good and evil; and on this distinction is based the contrariety of the passions. Therefore no passions of the same power, that are not contrary to one another, differ specifically.

Obj. 2. Further, difference of species implies a difference of form. But every difference of form is in respect of some contrariety, as stated in *Metaph.* x. 8. Therefore passions of the same power, that are not contrary to one another, do not differ specifically.

Obj. 3. Further, since every passion of the soul consists in approach or withdrawal in respect of good or evil, it seems that every difference in the passions of the soul must needs arise from the difference of good and evil; or from the difference of approach and withdrawal; or from degrees in approach or withdrawal. Now the first two differences cause contrariety in the passions of the soul, as stated above (A. 2): whereas the third difference does not diversify the species; else the species of the soul's passions would be infinite. Therefore it is not possible for passions of the same power to differ in species, without being contrary to one another.

On the contrary, Love and joy differ in species, and are in the concupiscible power; and yet they are not contrary to one another; rather, in fact, one causes the other. Therefore in the same power there are passions that differ in species without being contrary to one another.

I answer that, Passions differ in accordance with their active causes, which, in the case of the passions of the soul, are their objects. Now the difference in active causes may be considered in two ways: first, from the point of view of their species or nature, as fire differs from water; secondly, from the point of view of the difference in their active power. In the passions of the soul we can treat the difference of their active or motive causes in respect of their motive power, as if they were natural agents. For every mover, in a fashion, either draws the patient to itself, or repels it from itself. Now in drawing it to itself, it does three things in the patient. Because, in the first place, it gives the patient an inclination or aptitude to tend to the mover: thus a light body, which is above, bestows lightness on the body generated, so that it has an inclination or aptitude to to be above. Secondly, if the generated body be outside its proper place, the mover gives it movement towards that place.—Thirdly, it makes it to rest, when it shall have come to its proper place: since to the same cause are due, both rest in a place, and the movement to that place. The same applies to the cause of repulsion.

Now, in the movements of the appetitive faculty, good has, as it were, a force of attraction, while evil has a force of repulsion. In the first place, therefore, good causes, in the appetitive power, a certain inclination, aptitude or connaturalness in respect of good: and this belongs to the passion of *love*: the corresponding contrary of which is *hatred* in respect of evil.—Secondly, if the good be not yet possessed, it causes in the appetite a movement towards the attainment of the good beloved: and this belongs to the passion of *desire* or *concupiscence*: and contrary to it, in respect of evil, is the passion of *aversion* or *dislike*.—Thirdly, when the good is obtained, it causes the appetite to rest, as it were, in the good obtained: and this belongs to the passion of *delight* or *joy*: the contrary of which, in respect of evil, is *sorrow* or *sadness*.

On the other hand, in the irascible passions, the aptitude, or inclination to seek good, or to shun evil, is presupposed as arising from the concupiscible faculty, which regards good or evil absolutely. And in respect of good not yet obtained, we have *hope* and *despair*. In respect of evil not yet present we have *fear* and *daring*. But in respect of good obtained there is no irascible passion: because it is no longer considered in the light of something arduous, as stated above (A. 3). But evil already present gives rise to the passion of *anger*.

Accordingly it is clear that in the concupiscible faculty there are three couples of passions; viz., love and hatred, desire and aversion, joy and sadness. In like manner there are three groups in the irascible faculty; viz., hope and despair, fear and daring, and anger which has no contrary passion.

Consequently there are altogether eleven passions differing specifically; six in the concupiscible faculty, and five in the irascible; and under these all the passions of the soul are contained.

From this the replies to the objections are evident.

ɔd

12. Magda B. Arnold

EDITOR'S INTRODUCTION

Because emotions (passions) are sometimes experienced passively, i.e., as beyond our control, they often have been viewed as primitive, disruptive, and automatic responses, divorced from "higher" mental or cognitive processes. In recent years, however, there has been an upsurge of interest in the cognitive mediation of emotion. To a certain extent, this represents a rediscovery of the scholastic dictum that all appetitive functions presuppose a knowledge of the thing desired. In the case of the emotions, this dictum means that people cannot simply be angry, afraid, or proud; they must be angry *at* something, afraid *of* something, proud *of* something, and so forth. In other words, emotions have objects. The connection between an emotion and its object helps to classify the response as a particular kind of emotion. Without special explanation, for example, people cannot be angry at the good deed of another, sorrowful at their own good fortune, jealous of someone stepping on their toes, or proud of the stars. This connection between an appraised object and the resulting response provides a cognitive core to emotional reactions.

Among contemporary psychologists, Magda Arnold was one of the first to recognize the importance of cognitive appraisals for any theory of emotion. This chapter contains a brief summary of her views.

Arnold defines an emotion as "a strong appetitive tendency toward or away from something appraised as good or bad for the person here and now that urges to appropriate action and is accompanied (but not initiated) by physiological change." It will be recognized that this is a brief paraphrase of Aquinas' view. Whereas Aquinas spoke of the estimative power of the soul, Arnold speaks of intuitive appraisals whereby objects are judged (here and now) as suitable or unsuitable to the well-being of the individual. Appraisals lead, in turn, to appetitive tendencies toward or away from an object; and such appetitive tendencies are accompanied by physiological change, or in Aquinas' terminology, by a "bodily transmutation."

The influence of Aquinas on Arnold is evident in other ways as well. For example, what she calls *affective memory*—an important element in emotional appraisals—is essentially Aquinas' *memorative power*. And when it comes to the situational determinants of emotion, Arnold's analysis is mainly an expansion on the criteria used by Aquinas to classify the basic emotions, i.e., whether the object is good or bad, present or absent, easy or difficult, and whether an obstacle is surmountable or not.

It is a tribute to the insightfulness of Aquinas that his analysis of emotion is still of contemporary relevance; and it is a tribute to the wisdom of Arnold that she should recognize and expand on that relevance. If more psychologists took the time and effort to examine historical sources, perhaps psychology as a science would be subject to fewer "discoveries" and greater progress.

MAGDA B. ARNOLD

Human Emotion and Action

I. INTRODUCTION

In this paper I would like to attempt a short sketch of my theory of emotion and show how it is connected with action, motivation, and personality. Essentially, this theory starts with a phenomenological analysis of the sequence from perception to action. Granted that we do not start afresh with every perception; but by and large, we must see, hear, or otherwise experience something, know what it is, interpret its significance, decide on the best possible action, before we can do what is necessary to cope with it. We do not throw a ball before we have it in the hand, nor do we ordinarily open an umbrella before we notice that it is raining. There is a natural sequence from perception to action, and this sequence cannot be reversed. A phenomenological analysis should give us the psychological functions as they follow one another in this sequence, even though they are often so contracted as to be almost instantaneous. With this sequence as a clue, it should be possible to identify the neural structures and circuits that mediate each function and so trace the connection from sensory cortical areas to the motor area. In this way, we should be able to describe not only psychological functioning but the brain structures that make it possible.

II. PHENOMENOLOGICAL ANALYSIS

This analysis necessarily has to start with human experience. At the same time, at this point we are not concerned with the fullness of human experience but rather with the psychological functions that make such experience possible. In other words, I want to describe the "psychic apparatus," as Freud would call it, before we investigate how this apparatus is used to live a human life, to establish human goals in science, art, business, or industry. This psychic apparatus includes many functions we share with animals: animals also can see, hear, taste, smell, touch; they want food, drink, mate; go about getting them in various ways; and show considerable ingenuity when these things are not readily available. Animals, like human beings, dislike things that hurt, and avoid them; they attack what threatens them; they can and do learn

M. B. Arnold, Human emotion and action. In *Human Action, Conceptual and Empirical Issues*, T. Mischel, ed., New York: Academic, 1969, 167–185, 196–197. By permission.

when motivated by hunger, thirst, or pain. Consequently, they must be able to *remember*. Moreover, they *expect* food and expect to avoid harm by running a maze or pressing a bar in the laboratory, or by the various activities they undertake in their natural habitat.

Since these activities are common to man and animal, it will often be conventient to refer to animal experiments to demonstrate some of the points in this discussion. Just because animals have no access to the highly complex experience of a civilized human being, it is easier to show on their example what are the basic functions of the psychic apparatus.

A. Perception

In recent years, it has been the fashion to include a grab bag of functions in "perception." To listen to modern psychologists, one might think that perception is the only kind of experience and leads directly to action. Though perception is based on sense experience, many psychologists also include meaning, learning, and, at least in one theory (Leeper, 1963), emotion in it. Perhaps we have settled on this wastebasket category because we are afraid that other categories are too "mentalistic" to be respectable. But perception surely is as mentalistic as is memory, learning, or emotion; all are recognizable experiences that do not gain in precision by being taken altogether-all-at-once. If to be mentalistic is so disgraceful, perhaps we had better exclude perception also and return to Watsonian behaviorism with its aridity. On the other hand, if we have reached the point where we cannot do without perception in our theorizing, as I think we have, it surely is better to take a careful look at the kind of experience we are dealing with. For that, we need a careful phenomenological analysis.

When we look at a bear, we not only have a visual experience, we also *know* that this is a bear and *remember* that this animal is wild. We *see* that the bear is behind a fence in the zoo, we *recall* that this kind of fence is strong and *expect* that it will keep the bear from breaking out. Finally, we *assess* the bear behind the fence and his potential for us and *decide* that we are in no danger. We might even throw food to him, though we realize it is inadvisable to hold it out to him. The whole complex is a "perceptual" experience for most psychologists. But actually it includes sense experience, conceptual thinking, inference, memory, and imagination; it also includes the appraisal that the bear is not dangerous here and now.

B. Appraisal

In the human being, such an evaluation is of two kinds, deliberate and intuitive. It is deliberate because it depends on conceptual knowledge that is recalled at will: that this is a bear; that bears are dangerous; that the fence is intended to keep the bear away from the visitors to the zoo. On the basis of such knowledge, we judge that the bear cannot attack us. This deliberate judgment is accompanied by an immediate intuitive appraisal that this bear is harmless, so that we approach the fence with confidence, unafraid. That there are these two kinds of evaluation is best seen in cases where one appraisal is positive, the other negative.

For instance, a child may be told that the bear cannot break out, and may have confidence in his father who tells him so. But the bear looks very big and fierce and the child is afraid, despite his reflective judgment. An even better example is the child on the beach who is afraid to go in the water. His father may have taken the little boy by the hand or held him in his arms while he walks with him into the shallows. The child knows that nothing harmful is happening to him, but he does not stop crying as long as he is in the water and cannot be persuaded to go in again.

Another example is the fear of a man suffering from obsessive-compulsive neurosis who washes his hands incessantly whenever he has touched anything. He is afraid of contamination, but he knows that his skin will be roughened by frequent washing and so offer a more vulnerable surface. He is so afraid of germs that he feels compelled to wash his hands despite his conceptual and reflective knowledge that his fear is exaggerated and that washing will only increase the danger. It is his unconcious intuitive appraisal that produces the fear and the conscious reflective evaluation that is impotent against it. Just as we have to distinguish between sense experience of objects and conceptual knowledge, which enables us to talk about them, so must we make a distinction between intuitive appraisal (which could be called sense judgment) and deliberate judgment.

This intuitive appraisal is not an emotion, though it can give rise to an emotion; nor is it what James has called a "cold perception." Sheer perception only establishes what is there. It takes an evaluation to relate what is perceived to the perceiving subject. Something is either good for me or bad for me, and that in varying degree. If it is appraised as neither good nor bad, it is indifferent and will be disregarded.

In contrast to conscious deliberate judgment, the intuitive appraisal is not consciously experienced. It is experienced as no more than a feeling, a favorable or unfavorable attitude to this thing, a liking or disliking. Such an appraisal is possible for the animal as well as for man. Some psychologists may quarrel with this statement on the grounds that the animal cannot report his experiences. But this objection misses the point. The human being also cannot report his intuitive appraisals because he experiences them only as favorable or unfavorable attitudes. He can report that he likes and wants one thing and not another, but only by reflection can we infer that this constitutes an intuitive judgment. Liking something is not an experience of sensory qualities like seeing or hearing or touching. But it is just as immediate, it completes sensory experience and links it with action. The human being (unlike the animal) also makes deliberate judgments (practical judgments, as they are often called), which are conscious.

The animal does not have conceptual knowledge in the sense that he cannot abstract the essential feature of a thing and use a symbol to refer to it. If he had conceptual knowledge, he would have no difficulty developing or learning a conceptual language. Accordingly, the animal cannot make deliberate judgments, which are based on conceptual knowledge. But he can and does evaluate intuitively. He likes this thing and dislikes that, and so approaches the one while he avoids the other. Foods preferences in the white rat, for instance, have been painstakingly investigated by P. T. Young (1961). Thus to anyone but an adamant behaviorist, the statement that animals have likes and dislikes needs no apology. We can call this liking or disliking a feeling.

1. Appraisal for action Such an intuitive estimate, experienced as liking or disliking something, brings about an immediate urge to action. What is liked, attracts. But the type of approach will depend on another intuitive appraisal answering the question: "What is it good for?" The monkey likes a banana for eating, a female for mating. Both banana and mate have a positive valence, but the action tendency produced by each of the two appraisals is quite different. Both things are "good here and now," but there is a specific approach for each. In fact, this appraisal for action has many dimensions. The animal is aware that he sees the food, and gauges the distance he must cover before he can take it. When he can touch it, however, he simply opens his mouth and bites. Every situation requires not only an estimate of its value for the subject but also a gauging of the action required to appraoch or avoid it. The first estimate leads to an urge to approach (or escape), the second, to an urge to approach in a particular way. It is the whole appraisal complex, the thing-appraised-as-good-for-a-particular-action, that produces the desire to do something in particular, that arouses a specific appetitive tendency.

C. Appetitive Tendency, Instinct, and Emotion

Any appetitive tendency, then, is based on the appraisal of something as good for a particular action here and now. There are some appetitive tendencies, however, that seem to be based on an innate appraisal. If the cheek of a newborn infant is touched, the infant will turn its head and seek to grasp the touching finger with its mouth. In the same way, any neonate mammal will seek with its mouth until it finds something to suck, and the newly hatched chick will start to peck at something small, before mammal or chick can have acquired any experience that nipple or grain can provide satisfaction.

It is usually assumed that "instinct" provides the impulsion behind such behavior, though the mechanism of such impulsion has never been spelled out. I venture to suggest that instinct works through the same mechanism of appraisal and appetitive tendency discussed above, a mechanism that is set in motion by various hormonal changes. Apparently, hormonal changes in the composition of the blood are detected by the hypothalamus (e.g., in hunger, thirst) and bring about a sensitivity to certain objects such that at this time, and neither before nor afterward, these objects become attractive. Only the hungry infant will seek with its mouth, only the hungry chick will peck, and only the sexually mature animal will react to a female in heat. Though the hormonal change accounts for the attractiveness of the instinctive object, it must still be found and appraised as good for a particular action before it can be approached and obtained. Thus appraisal and appetitive tendency are the psychological functions that make instinctive action possible; and "instinct" becomes a species-specific sequence of activities rather than the impulsion behind each action in the sequence.

In emotion, there is no such hormonal change that sensitizes perception. Rather the object or situation is appraised as to its effect on the individual here and now. If that effect is pronounced, the appetitive tendency (toward or away from the object) develops into an emotion. Actually, an emotion is a strong appetitive tendency toward or away from something appraised as good or bad for the person here and now that urges to appropriate action and is accompanied (but not initiated) by physiological changes.

D. Memory

The neonate does not experience emotions because he is not as yet capable of an appraisal for action. He does, however, experience feelings in all gradations from pleasure to pain.* Feelings, as mentioned before, are the experiences of the beneficial or harmful effects of stimulation or, put differently, the experiences of intuitive appraisal. Pleasure and pain can be experienced immediately: colic, hunger pain, discomfort from a pinprick or a chafing diaper are the most usual pain experiences of the infant. The only pleasures he seems to feel are the pleasure of satiety and the pleasure of gentle touch. According to Watson, the newborn baby has only three "emotions": fear, when it is dropped; love, when it is stroked or handled gently; and anger, when it is restrained. None of these is an emotion. What Watson calls fear is really startle, though the newborn needs a more intense stimulus than does an older child or adult. What Watson calls love is the pleasure of touch, and what he calls anger, the simple dislike of restraint with no attempt to retaliate.

On the basis of such experiences of pleasure and pain, the infant later develops emotions. Because he remembers what has brought pleasure or pain, he hopes for the one and fears the other. Without such memory, anything that is as yet distant, anything that is merely heard or seen, could not be appraised either as beneficial or dangerous, and so could neither be approached nor avoided. Without memory, only direct somesthetic experience can bring either pleasure or pain. Only memory makes it possible to anticipate pleasure or pain and act accordingly.

The memory necessary to appraise something seen, heard, or smelled as good or bad is not merely visual, auditory, or olfactory memory. Over and above such modality-specific memories there is also what could be called "affective memory," a reliving of past likes and dislikes as soon as the same situation recurs. When something has brought pain, it is disliked on sight the second time. This dislike is a recurrence of the earlier appraisal and is experienced as a "here-and-now feeling" rather than a memory. Since this dislike is felt immediately, yet obviously cannot be aroused by something that is still in the distance, it must be the residue of previous appraisals of its effect on us as soon as it came near us: it must be *affective memory*.

---

*Pain has been considered a sensation in recent years because it is known that pain is mediated by fine somesthetic fibers that are found, together with thicker beta fibers, in somesthetic nerves. But from various reports it can be inferred that these fine fibers mediate the *intensity* of somesthetic stimulation (i.e., its effect) rather than its *quality* (like touch, stretch, etc.).

1. Affective memory Such affective memory is aroused not only by what has actually hurt us in the past. Anything similar may have the same effect. The burnt child is afraid of fire, any fire, even St. Elmo's fire or a magnesium flare. A child who has once felt pain in the dentist's chair will be afraid of the dentist, even though he may never have seen this particular dentist before. Freud suggested that a traumatic memory is repressed and goes on working underground, to explain why the emotion aroused by the traumatic experience recurs in similar situations though these have no connection with the original trauma. However, an emotion often recurs even when the traumatic experience is well remembered: A man who nearly drowned when his boat capsized may be afraid of boats ever after; a boy who was thrown by a horse may never go near a horse again. In addition, emotional experiences do not need to be traumatic to leave an affective memory. An emotional situation encountered repeatedly may have the same effect. A child who experiences repeated failure may finally refuse to try even when he is assured of success. All these cases can be explained by affective memory, that is, the spontaneous reliving of an experienced liking or dislike on encountering a similar situation, which leads to the same impulse to approach or withdraw as did the original appraisal.

What Freud has explained as the effect of a repressed traumatic memory has been explained by academic psychologists as "emotional conditioning." It has usually been assumed that emotional conditioning is based on the same association of unconditioned with conditioned stimuli that occurs in ordinary conditioning. But there are some important differences: ordinary conditioning requires repeated exposure of the unconditioned stimulus following upon the conditioned stimulus, until the CS arouses the same response as the US. But in emotional conditioning, one exposure to the unconditioned, "traumatic" stimulus may be sufficient for man or animal to react in the same way to a number of stimuli that have never been formally associated with the unconditioned stimulus. Think, for instance, of the fear developed by little Albert when he was frightened by a loud noise as soon as he streched out his hand for a white rabbit (Watson, 1929). Soon he was afraid not only of the rabbit but of his mother's white fur coat and the white beard of Santa Claus. This is usually explained as "stimulus generalization." But just what does happen in stimulus generalization?

When an animal has been trained to go through a door marked with a square rather than a door marked with a cross to find food, it will also choose a door with an octagon, polyhedron, a circle, and even a triangle, rather than the door with the cross. The animal apparently appraises anything with a white center and black outline as good, but anything with a black center as bad, provided his choice is confirmed by finding food behind one door and not the other. His response is governed by affective memory, the immediate liking for and approach to anything with a white center behind which he has found food. Thus affective memory actually takes precedence over visual memory and so determines the animal's response. Similarly, little Albert experienced an instant dislike as soon as he saw anything white and furry, anything similar enough to the white rabbit to arouse the affective memory.

2. *Motor memory versus kinesthetic memory* The appraisal for action depends not only on modality-specific and affective memory but also on motor memory. Psychologists have often identified motor memory with kinesthetic memory, that is, with the memory of the sensations experienced as a result of various movements. Though kinesthetic memory undoubtedly exists, I do not believe that it is the only or even the most important factor in learning a motor skill. Rather, kinesthetic memory seems to be involved in the "feel" of learned movements. When they are correct, they also "feel" right, so that the sensory feedback of movement seems to be a confirmation or check on learned motions rather than a template according to which movements are organized. Every golfer or baseball pitcher knows this feeling of "right" movement and knows as soon as he has made his drive or pitched his ball whether he has done well, long before the ball has landed. He also knows that the harder he tries to achieve this feeling, the worse his drive or pitch will be. But if he keeps relaxed and confident and lets his trained muscles take over, he will make the right movements and have their correctness confirmed by kinesthetic sensations that are familiar and appraised as right.

If kinesthetic memory really were the deciding factor in learned performance, patients with parietal lesions that destroy somesthetic memory should lose their motor skill. Such patients will have tactual agnosia, that is, they can no longer recognize an object by touch alone, but they are still able to write, play tennis or golf, and engage in other skilled performances. Motor skills (particularly speaking and writing, which depend exclusively on motor memory) are severely impaired by lesions of the lateral prefrontal cortex (e.g., Broca's area). This is consonant with the notion that the prefrontal area is a motor association area and that skilled performance depends on motor memories registered in this region.

By motor memory I mean the disposition to move in a particular pattern, which is strengthened by every correct movement. As such a pattern is repeated, it is executed more smoothly, more speedily, and becomes a fluid effortless performance that proceeds almost automatically. The small child has great difficulty formulating speech sounds but within a very few years he becomes so proficient that he can direct his attention exclusively to what he wants to say, confident that his pronunciation will take care of itself. Though we experience such increased facility in performance, we do not immediately recognize this facilitation as motor memory. Indeed, the only memories we immediately recognize as such are visual and auditory memories because we are able to recall visual images and auditory patterns at will. We remember something we have seen as a memory *picture*, and remember something we have heard as an auditory pattern, a sentence or a melody. It is much more difficult to recall a fragrance or a taste, though we may recognize it without difficulty. Similarly, we easily recognize the touch of velvet or sandpaper, but when we try to recall it, we find ourselves visualizing velvet or sandpaper rather than recalling the touch experience directly.

Motor memory does allow recall, but usually only in its complete temporal pattern, just as visual recall is not of one feature but of the complete picture. We can recall a dance step by making it, a poem by saying it, a word or letter by writing it, either actually or in imagination, though visual recall is often involved as well. We usually have to repeat the whole poem, however, though we can easily recognize any line that is quoted from it. Motor memory, like auditory memory, has a temporal pattern. Motor imagination (to imagine doing, saying, or singing something) is just as vivid as visual imagination. The very fact that motor imagination is possible proves the existence of motor memory; indeed, Jacobson has found that motor imagination activates the muscles actually used in the imagined action, while visual imagination activates the eye muscles. Motor imagination, like visual imagination, depends on the appropriate memories and can, in the case of motor imagination, even improve motor learning. For instance, it has been reported that imagining throwing a dart at a bull's-eye, and practicing such imaginary throwing, is as effective as actual practice in dart throwing (Beattie, 1949); and Gasson (1967) found that basketball players increased their scores at the free-throw line by shooting with their eyes closed (during practice session) and simply imagining the flight of the ball.

In fact, motor memory and motor imagination are necessary

for action, whether in man or animal. Unless an individual knows what actions have been successful before, in similar situations, and unless he imagines what to do in the situation here and now, he cannot act appropriately. Without motor memory, he could not acquire his daily habits or cherished skills; and without motor imagination he could not change his habits when a changing situation requires it. Of course, the human being does not depend on motor memory to quite the same extent the animal does because he can often use concepts to guide his action. Instead of depending on an acquired habit of turning to one side or the other in a maze, he can remember to "turn once left, twice right" and learn the maze in this way; and such self-instruction can be recalled as a visual or auditory pattern as easily as by speaking the words (which would again be a motor pattern). After Goldstein insisted that brain-injured patients had lost the "abstract attitude" because they were unable to pretend to drink a glass of water or to comb their hair, later investigation disclosed that these patients could use and recognize concepts as well as normal people. They were still able to make abstractions and use abstract concepts, but they were apparently unable to *imagine* what to do. When they saw the actual glass or the actual comb, the objects recalled their use without further difficulty.

3. Feedback versus motor memory Cyberneticists insist that organismic movement follows the procedure of the feedback apparatus; that is, we aim, begin to move, and predict a miss upon sensory feedback information, and so correct our aim. This makes a chopped-up and jerky zigzag out of what is in practice a fluid movement. Actually, modern tracking mechanisms need a computer to do the tracking effectively. The aim has to be corrected by computing the direction in which an airplane or ship travels, its speed, and that of the missile, so that the missile is dispatched to the point the vessel will have reached at the exact time the missile will arrive. To aim by such feedback information requires the lightening speed of a computer. Our mental processes of computing speed and direction are considerably slower.

Yet the Western gunman could draw and shoot practically in one movement without loss of accuracy. The new technique of "quick kill" in the Vietnam war has revived this method of using the weapon as an extension of the arm in pointing because this method of aiming gives the only assurance of hitting the enemy before being hit. Obviously, this technique does not employ feedback information for aiming. Since it is far more accurate and speedy than deliberate aiming, feedback cannot be the sole or even the best method for hitting the target. Imaginary practice, as described above, also dispenses with feedback information, yet markedly improves the learner's aim. What holds for aiming applies to other movements as well. Any movement that depends on feedback information is necessarily slower than a movement that is executed by focusing on the goal and letting the muscles do the rest. The quick draw, like any other practiced motion, depends on motor memory that is activated as the movement is started; if correct, it "feels right" without any attempt to modify it.

4. Emotion and motor memory Emotion as a felt appetitive tendency partakes of the nature of movement, at least to some extent. There is "facilitation" in emotion as in movement. Not only will someone who is apprehensive appraise a new situation as dangerous more easily than his more courageous fellow, (affective memory), his tendency to withdraw will become a habit if he never tries to go against his fear, so that he will find it more and more difficult to act courageously. This is true not only for the felt urge to keep away from danger but also for the physiological changes that go with it: such a man will feel more "nervous" as time goes on, will tremble more easily, feel a greater malaise, have a fast heart rate even in trivial situations.

I noticed in one of my classes that one student sometimes seemed to be completely abstracted, was very pale, and kept grimacing as if in pain. When I finally asked him what was the matter, he explained that he was afraid he had heart disease because he noticed that his pulse began to race as soon as he started counting it. He had done this for a few weeks and found his pulse faster every day. When I pointed out that it was his increasing fear that produced the acceleration, he did not believe it. However, he did agree to leave his pulse alone for a while. When he took it again some days later, he found it had slowed down considerably. Now he was ready to admit that his lessened fear had something to do with the improvement.

5. Memory and imagination Appraisal is not based on spontaneous recall alone. If it were, the reaction to a situation would be completely stereotyped and would repeat the original response as dictated by the original appraisal. Actually, we not only recall what has happened and what we have done, and relive the appropriate feeling and emotion; we also take account of various differences in the present situation, gauge their possible effect, and then estimate whether the situation as it is here and now is good or bad for us. Similarly, we plan our action to fit the present circumstances, that is, we imagine it and appraise its possible effects. Memory and imagination together make it possible to learn from past experience and to adapt our performance to present requirements.

III. APPETITIVE TENDENCIES AND ACTION

An appetitive tendency produced by appraisal will lead to action unless a new round of appraisal, based on different aspects of the situation, produces a different or even contrary response tendency. If that happens, there is a conflict, which has to be resolved by one or more reappraisals until the strongest response tendency wins. In the animal, appetitive tendencies (toward both instinctive and emotional actions) are the only available response tendencies. There is no conflict between two such tendencies urging toward different *instinctive* objects: an animal that is hungry and thirsty will drink until its thirst is slaked sufficiently to start eating, and vice versa. Buridan's ass would first eat the one bundle of hay and then turn to the other. The only conflict possible is between a positive (instinctive) and a negative (emotional) tendency. An animal that is hungry wants to approach the food box. But if it has been given an electric shock on beginning to eat, it may hang back the next time—make a few steps and then stop, or not approach at all, depending on the intensity of pain he has experienced before. Since pain is more urgent than hunger, the fear of pain, if intensive enough, usually wins out over instinctive tendencies.

With human beings, more is involved in a conflict than two kinds of appetitive tendencies. The diabetic may want sweets but refrain from indulging because he knows what the consequences will be. The smoker knows the long-range effects of smoking but he may take a chance and hope that he will be one of the lucky ones. In both cases, there is an appetitive tendency that urges one course of action and sober reflection that urges another. There is conflict only when both alternatives are as desirable in some way as they are undesirable in another. The final decision may not necessarily be the most attractive alternative, nor is it always the most prudent choice. Because we know from personal experience that it is possible though difficult to choose the unattractive but useful course of action, it has been maintained that man is free to act in one way or the other, to act or not to act. What this means is that a man is able to choose something that he knows at the moment of choice is less than the absolute best for him. By his choice he just "shuts his eyes" to the other alternative, refuses to consider it further, so that only one "good" course of action is left for him to take. It is the choice that makes the chosen action the better one at the moment.

At any rate, it will be generally admitted that human evaluation and judgment is not only intuitive but can be deliberate or reflective. Man has sources of information the animal lacks. Is it too much to suggest that therefore the impulse to action that is produced by an intuitive appraisal will be different from the impulse to action produced by a deliberate or reflective appraisal? Granted that even the deliberate appraisal must have a modicum of attraction or we would never judge anything as good for us here and now, or feel urged to approach it. But that admixture of appetition is so slight that it does not carry us into action unquestioningly, as is the case with a strong emotion. It may be necessary again and again to call to mind the reason for an unattractive course of action to persevere in it. On the other hand, if there is a strong conviction in favor of an unpopular course of action, there will be enough emotional appeal to carry it through. What I am trying to say is that without an appetitive tendency there could be no action; but the strength of this tendency does not determine what action a man will take.

Because human beings must often act against strong emotional desires, I cannot fully agree with Lazarus (1966), who speaks of emotion only as *coping* processes. True, emotional or appetitive tendencies are indispensable for actions, including coping actions. But the actions to which strong emotions urge us are not always those that will really cope with the situation. Indeed, they often defeat the purpose for which they are done. The alcoholic or drug addict has a strong desire, yet he can, with help, resist it. Only by subduing his desire will he cope with the difficulties his addiction has created for him. If emotions are so intense that they must be obeyed (as in obsessive-compulsive and anxiety neuroses), coping becomes impossible—and this is not merely a semantic quibble.

A. Neural Mediation

A phenomenological analysis of the chain of psychological activities from sense experience to appetitive tendency and action should give us some hints as to the brain structures and circuits that make them possible. What has always prevented a genuine theory of brain function is the difficulty of finding the connections between the cortical receptor areas, which, as we know, mediate sense experience, and the cortical motor areas, which produce muscular contractions. We know that such a circuit must go through the subcortex because cutting around any sensory area has no effect, while undercutting it prevents sensory discrimination in this particular modality. Our analysis would indicate that the connection is not a simple neural linkage from receptor to motor areas but consists of several circuits corresponding to recall, imagination, appraisal, and appetitive tendency, including emotion.

First of all, the appraisal of an object or situation as good or bad (which, as I have indicated, completes perception and initiates a response tendency that leads to action) seems to be mediated by the limbic system. Olds (1955, 1956) has called this a "reward system" because self-stimulation in this area may be kept up indefinitely without any other reward; and "reward" is an objective term for the subjective experience of pleasure or satisfaction. The limbic system consists of a simple three-layer type of cortex (in contrast to the six layers of sensory and motor cortex) and borders on all the sensory and motor areas in the cortex. Accordingly, the appraisal of things seen, heard, touched, smelled, tasted, and the appraisal of movements seem to be mediated by connections to the neighboring limbic cortex.

Since most situations require memory and imagination before they can be fully appraised for action, there should be connecting circuits that make recall and planning possible. It is curious that scientists have expended much thought on the problem how various sense impressions are preserved, but none on the question how these "engrams" could be revived. For psychologists, at any rate, the latter is the more urgent problem: since we can test learning and memory only through performance, we are primarily interested in recall and anything that influences it. There is general agreement that the registration of sense impressions implies a modification of nervous tissue. It also seems that the tissue amenable to such modification is in the so-called association cortex. From many research reports we can infer that the visual association cortex serves the registration of visual memories, the auditory cortex that of auditory memories, and so on. It stands to reason that recall should require a reactivation of the modified cells in the same pattern (spatial and temporal) that occurred during the original registration. In contrast, in imagining something, we reorganize remembered experiences in new spatial and temporal patterns. Consequently, the circuits activating sense impressions in recall must be different from the circuits activating them during imagination.

Since we are looking for the connection from sensory to motor areas, using the clues from our phenomenological analysis, we would expect that the circuit mediating recall would start from the structures mediating appraisal, that is, from the limbic system. Integrated sense experience seems to be registered in sensory association areas and is recalled, I suggest, via a memory circuit that runs from the limbic system via the hippocampal circuit to fornix, midbrain, sensory thalamic nuclei, and back to the sensory association areas (*sensory recall circuit*). An *affective memory circuit* can be found to go from limbic cortex via cingulum, postcommissural fornix, mamillary bodies, and anterior thalamic nuclei back to the limbic system. An *imagination circuit* carrying visual, auditory, and other sensory patterns can be found to run from limbic cortex via amygdala and thalamic association nuclei to the cortical association areas.

Bodily movement seems to be initiated via the *action circuit* from the limbic system via the hippocampal system to fornix, midbrain, cerebellum, and ventral thalamus to the frontal lobe; *motor memory* seems to be registered in the prefrontal area and reactivated during movement via the action circuit. *Motor imagination*, finally, seems to employ relay stations in the amygdala, connecting with the dorsomedial thalamic nuclei and prefrontal area. All appetitive tendencies, including emotions, seem to be mediated via the action circuit and registered in the prefrontal area. They would be experienced when the relay of nerve impulses over the action circuit arrives in the premotor area. Since the action circuit activates not only voluntary muscles but also glands and involuntary muscles, particularly those of the blood vessel walls, the influence of emotion on muscular tension, glandular secretion, blood pressure, and heart rate can easily be accounted for. So can the fact that these emotional effects are cumulative, for they are preserved as dispositional changes in the prefrontal cortex. With every new emotion, the motor effect of similar past emotions is revived, which accounts, for instance, for the increasing muscular tension in chronic fear.

The (now abandoned) surgical operation of prefrontal lobotomy, which separates the prefrontal cortex from the thalamus and hypothalamus and so interrupts the action circuit, markedly reduced severe anxiety and intractable pain. The patients reported that they were still afraid or in pain, but it did not bother them any longer. I would say that they still felt fear (the premotor area and its connections with the thalamus were largely untouched) but the distressing physiological symptoms of fear were considerably reduced because the new danger no longer revived past fears and their physiological accompaniment. Interestingly enough, when relief from anxiety was insufficient or temporary, and the lobotomy was extended farther back to encroach upon thalamic connections to the premotor area, the patient was permanently relieved of fear but did not feel much impulse to action, either. He might sit for hours doing nothing at all. This would indicate that the premotor area does mediate impulses to action, including emotional response tendencies.

I would like to emphasize that this sketch of various circuits is not just unsupported speculation. It is based on thousands of actual research studies reported in the literature and is extensively documented in Volume 2 of *Emotion and Personality* (Arnold, 1960). The theory may be wrong in some details, but I am convinced that an approach like this is essential if we want to unravel the complex cat's cradle that is the brain.

B. Emotion and Motive

As we have seen, experienced emotions are tendencies to action but do not always lead to action. Accordingly, I would like to define a motive as a "want that leads to action." A want could be described as a goal, or a course of action leading to a goal, appraised as desirable. A want will entice or impel to action, provided there are no contrary wants, no subsequent appraisals that interdict action. Human wants are based on deliberate as well as intuitive appraisals, and lead to voluntary decisions as well as emotional impulses to action. "Decision making" really consists in refusing to reappraise the matter further so that the last appraisal stands and now flows into action.

If motives stem from appraisal, they must be at least partly conscious. A man may want to make a trip and is quite aware of the reasons that speak for it. He may not be too aware at the moment that his deeper reason for the trip is the chance he may see that slick chick he had met there before. The conscious motives do not become spurious because an unconscious motive is also present. In fact, it has been argued that unconscious motives are far less important in well-integrated people than in neurotics (Allport, 1953), who almost by definition are helpless in the face of their emotions. I need hardly say that in my opinion such "unconscious motives" are the affective memories that are touched off at this moment so that we experience desire or anxiety without remembering the original situation that gave rise to such emotions.

C. Conditions of Appraisal

I have said that the first appraisal (that something is good or bad for me here and now) is experienced as liking or dislike and will flow into an action impulse, which is the appetitive tendency. Now the second appraisal, of the action to be taken, will refer to the conditions that determine the emotion. If what we perceive and like is "a bird in the hand," we feel *joy* or *delight*. If what we like is unobtainable, or if it is lost to us, we keep thinking of it, keep wanting it, and feel *sorrow* or *sadness.*

What we like may not be at hand but relatively within reach: our tending toward it is *desire.* If we dislike something and can easily get out of its way, we feel *aversion* or *repulsion.* There will be times when the action to be taken has to be strenuous. Then the simple impulse toward or away from a thing is intensified into an urge that is the mark of *contending* emotions. For instance, something we like may require effort though it is attainable: we *hope* for it. If, however, we are convinced that it is utterly out of reach, we fall into *hopelessness* and *despair.*

If something bad, hence disliked, is on its way to us but we realize that it can be met and overcome, though with some difficulty, we feel an urge to face it *bravely.* But if we appraise it as something to avoid, at whatever cost, we feel the urge to flee because we are *afraid.* On the other hand, if something harmful is upon us but is evaluated as something we can overcome, though with some effort, we feel *anger.* But if we judge that we cannot get away from it at all, no matter how much we want to, we fall into *dejection.*

Accordingly, an intuitive appraisal confronts various conditions on which the resulting emotion depends: the goodness or badness of the object, its attainability or unattainability, whether it is at hand or at a distance; and finally, whether something bad can be overcome or is to be avoided, no matter what the cost. These polarities of appraisal produce the polarities of emotion. Of course, a given situation may be appraised in many different ways, one after another. For this reason, emotions are chameleonlike and change with every new aspect that is evaluated. However, certain appraisals become habitual. The resulting emotions become more intense and are more quickly aroused because of affective and motor memory (see Section II, D). They become emotional attitudes. When emotions are acted out repeatedly, they soon become what could be called emotional habits.

D. Physiological Accompaniment of Emotion

All action tendencies result in the activation of a whole pattern of voluntary and involuntary muscles, of glands of internal and external secretion. But only in the case of emotion is the activation of the autonomic nervous system and the organs it innervates really conspicuous. This pattern of activation depends on the appraisal for action, or on the sequence of appraisals that comes before the final decision to act. We know that some emotions, notably fear, result in sympathetic nervous system excitation with adrenaline secretion, which produces pallor, fatigue, fast and shallow heartbeat, and eventually exhaustion. (The spurt of energy on sudden fright, which makes it possible to escape danger, is the result of the activation of the neural action circuit that occurs before adrenaline has diffused into the blood stream. The longer the fear lasts, the more the exhausting adrenaline effects become noticeable; see Arnold, 1960 Vol. 2.) Anger, on the other hand, is accompanied by sympathetic excitation with noradrenaline secretion, which does not have the enervating effects of adrenaline but favors vasodilation and a sudden access of muscular energy. Sorrow, hoplessness, and dejection seem to have some of the effects of fear (pallor, shallow heartbeat) but are also characterized by a general slowing of respiration, heartbeat, and metabolic functions, which soon produces a picture of powerlessness as well as hopelessness. In contrast to these enervating emotions, positive emotions like love seem to be accompanied by parasympathetic excitation producing muscular relaxation, soft voice, vasodilation, wide pupils, moderately rapid respiration and heartbeat, secretion of sex hormones, moist conjunctiva, salivation, and a feeling of warmth (Cobb, 1950). As soon as the action tendency becomes stronger, and love becomes desire (or hope for the presence of the beloved), muscular relaxation is replaced by muscular activation. It is obvious that such positive emotions produce the conditions that are most favorable for organismic well-being, while negative emotions, like fear, sorrow, hopelessness, and dejection, interfere with physical well-being.

These effects are temporary as long as the corresponding emotions are transitory. But when emotions become attitudes and habits, their physiological effects become cumulative and can greatly influence an individual's health. The happy and contented man or woman is usually healthy. The fear-ridden neurotic has innumerable physical complaints that are not imaginary but are the result of physical changes during fear. A person in a deep depression, completely hopeless, can neither work nor do anything to help himself. . . .

REFERENCES

Allport, G. W. The trend in motivational theory. *American Journal of Orthopsychiatry*, 1953, 23, 107-119.

Arnold, M. B. *Emotion and personality*. New York: Columbia Univer. Press, 1960. 2 vols.

Beattie, D. M. The effect of imaginary practice on the acquisition of a motor skill. Unpublished master's thesis, Univer. of Toronto, 1949.

Cobb, S. *Emotions and clinical medicine*. New York: Norton, 1950.

Gasson, J. A. Personal communication. 1967.

Lazarus, R. S. *Psychological stress and the coping process*. New York: McGraw-Hill, 1966.

Leeper, R. The motivational theory of emotion. In C. L. Stacey and M. F. DeMartino (Eds.), *Understanding human motivation*. Cleveland, Ohio: Howard Allen, 1963.

Olds, J. Physiological mechanisms of reward. In M. R. Jones (Ed.), *Nebraska symposium on motivation*. Lincoln, Neb.: Univer. of Nebraska Press, 1955.

Olds, J. A Preliminary mapping of electrical reinforcing effects in the rat brain. *Journal of Comparative and Physiological Psychology*, 1956, **49**, 281-285.

Watson, J. B. *Psychology from the standpoint of a behaviorist*. (3rd ed.) Philadelphia, Penn.: Lippincott, 1929.

Young, P. T. *Motivation and emotion*. New York: Wiley, 1961.

VII. THE MENTAL AND THE PHYSICAL

13. René Descartes

EDITOR'S INTRODUCTION

The history of Western thought can be divided roughly into three periods: ancient, medieval, and modern. This is not a trivial division, connoting little more than a beginning, middle, and current state; rather, it represents a real division based on deep-seated shifts in cultural outlook. Some idea of the change from the classical Greek to the early medieval period can be seen by comparing the chapters by Plato and Aristotle with those by Plotinus and Augustine. The latter are characterized by a kind of emotionalism—ecstasy, despair, guilt, suffering, contempt for this world, and burning faith in another. In a phrase, the early medieval period is marked by what one commentator called a "failure of nerve."[1]

By the late Middle Ages, however, a philosophical, religious, and social synthesis had been achieved that was both intellectually sophisticated and emotionally satisfying. Everything in the universe had its place, and within the "great chain of being," the place of man was among the most exalted. The earth, his habitat, was at the center of the universe, and the creatures of the earth were there for his benefit and use. And as befitted man's station, the world over which he held domain was immediately present and intelligible to him (cf. Aquinas). The burning faith remained, but there was a return of optimism and self-confidence: No one suffered in vain—all is part of a divine plan, the ulitmate outcome of which can only be good.

The intellectual foundations of the medieval synthesis were greatly undermined, if not totally destroyed, during the course of the scientific revolution, with its concurrent social and economic

---

[1] G. Murray, *Five stages of Greek religion*. New York: Doubleday, 1955. p. 119.

changes. Within the world view painted by modern science, the earth is but one planet among many, and a rather insignificant one at that; essential nature is nothing but matter (invisible atoms) in motion; the world of sense experience is "secondary," a function of the perceiving organism and not an essential part of nature; and the physical universe is a vast machine that responds only to efficient causes. The place of man in this mechanistic universe has been poignantly described by Bertrand Russell:

> Amid such a world, if anywhere, our ideals henceforward must find a home. That man is the product of causes which had no prevision of the end they were achieving; that his origin, his growth, his hopes and fears, his loves and his beliefs, are but the outcome of accidental collocations of atoms; that no fire, no heroism, no intensity of thought and feeling, can preserve an individual life beyond the grave; that all the labours of the ages, all the devotion, all the inspirations, all the noonday brightness of human genius, are destined to extinction in the vast death of the solar system, and that the whole temple of Man's achievement must inevitably be buried beneath the debris of a universe in ruins—all these things, if not quite beyond dispute, are yet so nearly certain, that no philosophy which rejects them can hope to stand. . . . Blind to good and evil, reckless of destruction, omnipotent matter rolls on its relentless way; for Man, condemned to-day to lose his dearest, tomorrow himself to pass through the gate of darkness, it remains only to cherish, ere yet the blow of darkness, the lofty thoughts that ennoble his little day; disdaining the terror of the slave of Fate, to worship at the shrine that his own hands have built; undismayed by the empire of chance, to preserve a mind free from the wanton tyranny that rules his outward life; proudly defiant of the irresistible forces that tolerate, for a moment, his knowledge and his condemnation, to sustain alone, a weary but unyielding Atlas, the world that his own ideals have fashioned despite the trampling march of unconscious power.[2]

The cultural revolution wrought by science has been so vast that few thinkers of the Middle Ages could sympathize with, or even understand, the sentiments expressed by Russell. This does not mean, of course, that everyone today would agree with him. The picture painted by modern science is by no means uniform, and others have interpreted it differently than Russell. Yet, there are probably few people of any persuasion who have not experienced the kind of pride and despair that Russell so eloquently describes; while science has made man more powerful

[2] B. Russell, A free man's worship. In *Mysticism and Logic.* © George Allen & Unwin Ltd., 1963 (By permission of Harper & Row, Publishers, Inc., Barnes & Noble Books; and of George Allen & Unwin Ltd.) pp. 45–46.

than many of the gods of mythology, it also has vastly reduced his significance within the realm of "omnipotent matter."

René Descartes is generally considered the first major philosopher of the modern period, because he was the first to incorporate *the* scientific world view into a philosophical system that purported to encompass all aspects of knowledge. To reconstruct philosophy along new lines, Descartes believed that he literally had to start afresh, casting doubt on all traditionally held truths. This meant not only the teachings of ancient and medieval philosophers, but also the knowledge derived from sense experience and even mathematics. The idea that sense experience does not provide a firm foundation for knowledge is, of course, nothing new (cf. Plato). But mathematical propositions, according to Descartes, are also subject to doubt, for it can be imagined that an evil genius (a kind of anti-God) implanted false propositions in our minds. If this kind of doubting seems far-fetched, it must be remembered that Descartes was not arguing that ordinary experience or mathematics are always false, but only that it is conceivable that they might be. In essence, Descartes was simply asking for a provisional suspension of judgment regarding commonly held beliefs so that the criteria of truth might be examined more critically.

Like Augustine before him, Descartes ultimately found certainty in his own mental activity. The one thing that he could not doubt was that he was doubting. This fact established, or so it seemed to Descartes, the existence of a mental substance—a thing that thinks. By arguments that need not concern us here, Descartes then proceeded to establish, first the existence of God (rather than a deceiving evil genius) and, second, the existence of material objects. After establishing these axioms or principles, largely on intuitive grounds, Descartes attempted to deduce propositions with observable consequences. In this fashion he conceptually reconstructed the universe, but it was a fundamentally different universe than that conceived by ancient or medieval philosophers. It was a world divided into two realities, the mental and the physical, each with its own distinct nature and subject to its own laws. In addition to its philosophical appeal, this division of the world into autonomous realms also had definite pragmatic advantages for Descartes, who was a devout Christian as well as an advocate of the new science. Within Descartes' scheme, theology need have nothing to fear from science, for science does not pertain to spiritual truths: Minds are not determined, as are bodies, by antecedent events; and free will, moral responsibility, etc., are not mere illusions in a mechanistic universe. By the same token, science may proceed unmolested by theology: Physics does not investigate final causes or the forms of things, only matter and motion.

Descartes' arrival at his fundamental principle, "I think, therefore I am," is set forth in the first two *Meditations* included in this chapter. Having established the existence of mental and material substances (his arguments for the latter are not reprinted here), Descartes was faced with the obvious question of the relationship between the two. How can an unextended thinking substance interact with an extended material substance? As far as inanimate objects and lower forms of life (plants and animals) are concerned, this posed no great difficulty for Descartes. All are automata—machines of various grades of complexity. Indeed, the universe itself may be pictured as a vast machine that, once created by God, proceeds on its way with little tinkering or divine intervention. In the case of man, however, the question of the interaction between the mental and the physical could not be avoided, for man is a composite of soul (that which thinks) and body.

In the *Passions of the Soul*, selections from which also appear here, Descartes describes the respective functions of the human soul and body, and proposes a mechanism for their interaction. Briefly, a very fine-grained substance called animal spirits produces movement in the body much like steam produces movement in an engine. The soul can influence the flow of these animal spirits through the nerves (hollow tubules) of the body, causing movements in the pineal gland (a small organ located at the center of the brain). Such "self-induced" movements are actions of the soul. Passions of the soul result from the reverse process, i.e., actions of the body that are transmitted to the soul via movement of the pineal gland.

It takes little perspicacity to recognize that Descartes' solution to the problem of interaction is no real solution at all. Simply localizing a function in some bodily structure does not explain that function; it merely substitutes the easier question, "Where?" for the more difficult question, "How?" With regard to the latter question, Descartes was ultimately forced to make an appeal to common sense:

Metaphysical reflections, which exercise the pure intellect, are what make us familiar with the notion of the soul; the study of mathematics, which chiefly exercises the imagination in considering figures and movements, accustoms us to form very distinct notions of body; finally, it is just by means of ordinary life and conversation, by abstaining from meditating and from studying things that exercise the imagination, that one learns to conceive the union of soul and body.[3]

Descartes' appeal to "ordinary life and conversation" did not prove very convincing, and alternative solutions to the mind–body relationship were soon offered, e.g., the parallelism of Leibnitz. But these alternatives need not detain us here. Our primary concern is with Descartes' conception of the mental and the physical, and with its influence on contemporary psychology. We shall therefore conclude these introductory remarks with an attempt to show how even 20th-century behaviorism is a stepchild of Cartesian dualism. (The implications of more specific aspects of Descartes' philosophy, e.g., regarding language and emotion, will be discussed in the next chapter.)

Cartesian dualism, it will be noted, is not simply the postulation of distinct substances, mind and body; it also is a proposed definition for "mental" and "physical" phenomena. Mental events include all conscious activity, but more particularly, thinking and acts of will. Everything else is a physical event, including the behavior of animals and also a good part of human behavior. Underlying this distinction is the assumption that *in principle* there is no difference between the behavior (nonmental) of living organisms and the behavior of inanimate objects—both are explicable in the same mechanistic terms. Modern behaviorism accepts Descartes' assumption but extends the domain of behavior to include perception, language, thinking, decision making, and the like (in short, everything that Descartes took to be "mental").

Any concept, if it is to have meaning, must stand in opposition to some other concept. For example, if we were to eliminate "goodness," then "badness" also would lose meaning; similarly, if there were no use for a concept of "light," then there also would be no use for a concept of "dark." Stated differently, within a given domain of discourse, a concept that applies to everything is not informative about anything. But we have just noted that the concept of behavior (as used by most behaviorists) originally derived its meaning from a contrast with mental phenomena in a Cartesian sense. It follows that we cannot simply discard the notion of the mental, or extend the concept of behavior to include all mental events, without also rendering the notion of behavior meaningless.

---

[3] R. Descartes, Correspondence with Princess Elizabeth (1643). In E. Anscombe and P. T. Geach (Eds.), *Descartes: Philosophical writings.* London: Nelson, 1954, p. 280, with permission.

In summary, if we are to eliminate Cartesian dualism from psychology, it is not enough simply to eliminate one of its terms (the mental) without also reanalyzing the other (the physical). Contemporary behaviorism has taken the first step, but not the second. And what might a non-Cartesian definition of behavior entail? There have been numerous suggestions along these lines in recent years, most relying in some way or another on the notion of purposive behavior (but often couched in the highly technical language of control theory[4]). Ironically, Descartes' conception of the mental—but without his emphasis on consciousness—is in many respects closer to recent definitions of psychological phenomena than is his conception of the physical. This will be dealt with in more detail later.

[4] W. T. Powers. Feedback: Beyond behaviorism. *Science*, 1973, *179*, 351-356.

The Primacy of the Mind

MEDITATION I

Of the things which may be brought within the sphere of the doubtful.

It is now some years since I detected how many were the false beliefs that I had from my earliest youth admitted as true, and how doubtful was everything I had since constructed on this basis; and from that time I was convinced that I must once for all seriously undertake to rid myself of all the opinions which I had formerly accepted, and commence to build anew from the foundation, if I wanted to establish any firm and permanent structure in the sciences. But as this enterprise appeared to be a very great one, I waited until I had attained an age so mature that I could not hope that at any later date I should be better fitted to execute my design. This reason caused me to delay so long that I should feel that I was doing wrong were I to occupy in deliberation the time that yet remains to me for action. To-day, then, since very opportunely for the plan I have in view I have delivered my mind from every care [and am happily agitated by no passions] and since I have procured for myself an assured leisure in a peaceable retirement, I shall at last seriously and freely address myself to the general upheaval of all my former opinions.

Of the things as to which we may doubt.

Now for this object it is not necessary that I should show that all of these are false—I shall perhaps never arrive at this end. But inasmuch as reason already persuades me that I ought no less carefully to withhold my assent from matters which are not entirely certain and indubitable than from those which appear to me manifestly to be false, if I am able to find in each one some reason to doubt, this will suffice to justify my rejecting the whole. And for that end it will not be requisite that I should examine each in particular, which would be an endless undertaking; for owing to the fact that the destruction of the foundations of necessity brings with it the downfall of the rest of the edifice, I shall only in the first place attack those principles upon which all my former opinions rested.

All that up to the present time I have accepted as most true and certain I have learned either from the senses or through the

R. Descartes, Meditations on the first philosophy in which the existence of God and the distinction between mind and body are demonstrated, (I and II), E. S. Haldane and G. R. Ross, (trans.) In *The philosophical works of Descartes.* Cambridge: The University Press, 1968, pp. 144–146, 147–148, 149–152,153–157. By permission.

senses; but it is sometimes proved to me that these senses are deceptive, and it is wiser not to trust entirely to any thing by which we have once been deceived.

But it may be that although the senses sometimes deceive us concerning things which are hardly perceptible, or very far away, there are yet many others to be met with as to which we cannot reasonably have any doubt, although we recognise them by their means. For example, there is the fact that I am here, seated by the fire, attired in a dressing gown, having this paper in my hands and other similar matters. And how could I deny that these hands and this body are mine, were it not perhaps that I compare myself to certain persons, devoid of sense, whose cerebella are so troubled and clouded by the violent vapours of black bile, that they constantly assure us that they think they are kings when they are really quite poor, or that they are clothed in purple when they are really without covering, or who imagine that they have an earthenware head or are nothing but pumpkins or are made of glass. But they are mad, and I should not be any the less insane were I to follow examples so extravagant.

At the same time I must remember that I am a man, and that consequently I am in the habit of sleeping, and in my dreams representing to myself the same things or sometimes even less probable things, than do those who are insane in their waking moments. How often has it happened to me that in the night I dreamt that I found myself in this particular place, that I was dressed and seated near the fire, whilst in reality I was lying undressed in bed! At this moment it does indeed seem to me that it is with eyes awake that I am looking at this paper; that this head which I move is not asleep, that it is deliberately and of set purpose that I extend by hand and perceive it; what happens in sleep does not appear so clear nor so distinct as does all this. But in thinking over this I remind myself that on many occasions I have in sleep been deceived by similar illusions, and in dwelling carefully on this reflection I see so manifestly that there are no certain indications by which we may clearly distinguish wakefulness from sleep that I am lost in astonishment. And my astonishment is such that it is almost capable of persuading me that I now dream. . . . [But] whether I am awake or asleep, two and three together always form five, and the square can never have more than four sides, and it does not seem possible that truths so clear and apparent can be suspected of any falsity [or uncertainty].

Nevertheless I have long had fixed in my mind the belief that an all-powerful God existed by whom I have been created such as I am. But how do I know that He has not brought it to pass that there is no earth, no heaven, no extended body, no magnitude, no place, and that nevertheless [I possess the perceptions of all these things and that] they seem to me to exist just exactly as I now see them? And, besides, as I sometimes imagine that others deceive themselves in the things which they think they know best, how do I know that I am not deceived every time that I add two and three, or count the sides of a square, or judge of things yet simpler, if anything simpler can be imagined? But possibly God has not desired that I should be thus deceived, for He is said to be supremely good. If, however, it is contrary to His goodness to have made me such that I constantly deceive myself, it would also appear to be contrary to His goodness to permit me to be sometimes deceived, and nevertheless I cannot doubt that He does permit this.

There may indeed be those who would prefer to deny the existence of a God so powerful, rather than believe that all other things are uncertain. But let us not oppose them for the present, and grant that all that is here said of a God is a fable; nevertheless in whatever way they suppose that I have arrived at the state of being that I have reached—whether they attribute it to fate or to accident, or make out that it is by a continual succession of antecedents, or by some other method—since to err and deceive oneself is a defect, it is clear that the greater will be the probability of my being so imperfect as to deceive myself ever, as is the Author to whom they assign my origin the less powerful. To these reasons I have certainly nothing to reply, but at the end I feel constrained to confess that there is nothing in all that I formerly believed to be true, of which I cannot in some measure doubt, and that not merely through want of thought or through levity, but for reasons which are very powerful and maturely considered; so that henceforth I ought not the less carefully to refrain from giving credence to these opinions than to that which is manifestly false, if I desire to arrive at any certainty [in the sciences] . . . .

I shall then suppose, not that God who is supremely good and the fountain of truth, but some evil genius not less powerful than deceitful, has employed his whole energies in deceiving me; I shall consider that the heavens, the earth, colours, figures, sound, and all other external things are nought but the illusions and dreams of which this genius has availed himself in order to lay traps for my credulity; I shall consider myself as having no hands, no eyes, no flesh, no blood, nor any senses, yet falsely believing myself to possess all these things; I shall remain obstinately attached to this idea, and if by this means it is not in my power to arrive at the

knowledge of any truth, I may at least do what is in my power
[i.e. suspend my judgment], and with firm purpose avoid giving
credence to any false thing, or being imposed upon by this arch
deceiver, however powerful and deceptive he may be. . . .

MEDITATION II

*Of the Nature of the Human Mind; and that it is more easily
known than the Body.*

The Meditation of yesterday filled my mind with so many
doubts that it is no longer in my power to forget them. And yet I
do not see in what manner I can resolve them; and, just as if I had
all of a sudden fallen into very deep water, I am so disconcerted
that I can neither make certain of setting my feet on the bottom,
nor can I swim and so support myself on the surface. I shall
nevertheless make an effort and follow anew the same path as that
on which I yesterday entered, i.e. I shall proceed by setting aside
all that in which the least doubt could be supposed to exist, just as
if I had discovered that it was absolutely false; and I shall ever
follow in this road until I have met with something which is
certain, or at least, if I can do nothing else, until I have learned for
certain that there is nothing in the world that is certain.
Archimedes, in order that he might draw the terrestrial globe out
of its place, and transport it elsewhere, demanded only that one
point should be fixed and immoveable; in the same way I shall
have the right to conceive high hopes if I am happy enough to
discover one thing only which is certain and indubitable.

I suppose, then, that all the things that I see are false; I
persuade myself that nothing has ever existed of all that my
fallacious memory represents to me. I consider that I possess no
senses; I imagine that body, figure, extension, movement and place
are but the fictions of my mind. What, then, can be esteemed as
true? Perhaps nothing at all, unless that there is nothing in the
world that is certain.

But how can I know there is not something different from
those things that I have just considered, of which one cannot have
the slightest doubt? Is there not some God, or some other being
by whatever name we call it, who puts these reflections into my
mind? That is not necessary, for is it not possible that I am
capable of producing them myself? I myself, am I not at least
something? But I have already denied that I had senses and body.
Yet I hesitate, for what follows from that? Am I so dependent on
body and senses that I cannot exist without these? But I was
persuaded that there was nothing in all the world, that there was

no heaven, no earth, that there were no minds, nor any bodies: was I not then likewise persuaded that I did not exist? Not at all; of a surety I myself did exist since I persuaded myself of something [or merely because I thought of something]. But there is some deceiver or other, very powerful and very cunning, who ever employs his ingenuity in deceiving me. Then without doubt I exist also if he deceives me, and let him deceive me as much as he will, he can never cause me to be nothing so long as I think that I am something. So that after having reflected well and carefully examined all things, we must come to the definite conclusion that this proposition: I am, I exist, is necessarily true each time that I pronounce it, or that I mentally conceive it.

But I do not yet know clearly enough what I am, I who am certain that I am; and hence I must be careful to see that I do not imprudently take some other object in place of myself, and thus that I do not go astray in respect of this knowledge that I hold to be the most certain and most evident of all that I have formerly learned. That is why I shall now consider anew what I believed myself to be before I embarked upon these last reflections; and of my former opinions I shall withdraw all that might even in a small degree be invalidated by the reasons which I have just brought forward, in order that there may be nothing at all left beyond what is absolutely certain and indubitable.

What then did I formerly believe myself to be? Undoubtedly I believed myself to be a man. But what is a man? Shall I say a reasonable animal? Certainly not; for then I should have to inquire what an animal is, and what is reasonable; and thus from a single question I should insensibly fall into an infinitude of others more difficult; and I should not wish to waste the little time and leisure remaining to me in trying to unravel subtleties like these. But I shall rather stop here to consider the thoughts which of themselves spring up in my mind, and which were not inspired by anything beyond my own nature alone when I applied myself to the consideration of my being. In the first place, then, I considered myself as having a face, hands, arms, and all that system of members composed of bones and flesh as seen in a corpse which I designated by the name of body. In addition to this I considered that I was nourished, that I walked, that I felt, and that I thought, and I referred all these actions to the soul: but I did not stop to consider what the soul was, or if I did stop, I imagined that it was something extremely rare and subtle like a wind, a flame, or an ether, which was spread throughout my grosser parts. As to body I had no manner of doubt about its nature, but thought I had a very clear knowledge of it; and if I had desired to explain it according to the notions that I had then formed of it, I should have described it thus: By the body I understand all that which can be defined by a certain figure: something which can be confined in a certain place, and which can fill a given space in such a way that every other body will be excluded from it; which can be perceived either by touch, or by sight, or by hearing, or by taste, or by smell: which can be moved in many ways not, in truth, by itself, but by something which is foreign to it, by which it is touched [and from which it receives impressions]: for to have the power of self-movement, as also of feeling or of thinking, I did not consider to appertain to the nature of body: on the contrary, I was rather astonished to find that faculties similar to them existed in some bodies.

But what am I, now that I suppose that there is a certain genius which is extremely powerful, and, if I may say so, malicious, who employs all his powers in deceiving me? Can I affirm that I possess the least of all those things which I have just said pertain to the nature of body? I pause to consider, I revolve all these things in my mind, and I find none of which I can say that it pertains to me. It would be tedious to stop to enumerate them. Let us pass to the attributes of soul and see if there is any one which is in me? What of nutrition or walking [the first mentioned]? But if it is so that I have no body it is also true that I can neither walk nor take nourishment. Another attribute is sensation. But one cannot feel without body, and besides I have thought I perceived many things during sleep that I recognised in my waking moments as not having been experienced at all. What of thinking? I find here that thought is an attribute that belongs to me; it alone cannot be separated from me. I am, I exist, that is certain. But how often? Just when I think; for it might possibly be the case if I ceased entirely to think, that I should likewise cease altogether to exist. . . .

But what then am I? A thing which thinks. What is a thing which thinks? It is a thing which doubts, understands, [conceives], affirms, denies, wills, refuses, which also imagines and feels.

Certainly it is no small matter if all these things pertain to my nature. But why should they not so pertain? Am I not that being who now doubts nearly everything, who nevertheless understands certain things, who affirms that one only is true, who denies all the others, who desires to know more, is averse from being deceived, who imagines many things, sometimes indeed despite his will, and who perceives many likewise, as by the intervention of the bodily organs? Is there nothing in all this which is as true as it is certain that I exist, even though I should always sleep and though he who has given me being employed all his ingenuity in deceiving me? Is there likewise any one of these attributes which can be distinguished from my thought, or which might be said to be separated from myself? For it is so evident of itself that it is I who doubts, who understands, and who desires, that there is no reason here to add anything to explain it. And I have certainly the power of imagining likewise; for although it may happen (as I formerly supposed) that none of the things which I imagine are true, nevertheless this power of imagining does not cease to be really in use, and it forms part of my thought. Finally, I am the same who feels, that is to say, who perceives certain things, as by the organs of sense, since in truth I see light, I hear noise, I feel heat. But it will be said that these phenomena are false and that I am dreaming. Let it be so; still it is at least quite certain that it seems to me that I see light, that I hear noise and that I feel heat. That cannot be false; properly speaking it is what is in me called feeling; and used in this precise sense that is no other thing than thinking.

From this time I begin to know what I am with a little more clearness and distinction than before; but nevertheless it still seems to me, and I cannot prevent myself from thinking, that corporeal things, whose images are framed by thought, which are tested by the senses, are much more distinctly known than that obscure part of me which does not come under the imagination. Although really it is very strange to say that I know and understand more distinctly these things whose existence seems to me dubious, which are unknown to me, and which do not belong to me, than others of the truth of which I am convinced, which are known to me and which pertain to my real nature, in a word, than myself. But I see clearly how the case stands: my mind loves to wander, and cannot yet suffer itself to be retained within the just limits of truth. Very good, let us once more give it the freest rein, so that, when afterwards we seize the proper occasion for pulling up, it may the more easily be regulated and controlled.

Let us begin by considering the commonest matters, those which we believe to be the most distinctly comprehended, to wit, the bodies which we touch and see; not indeed bodies in general, for these general ideas are usually a little more confused, but let us consider one body in particular. Let us take, for example, this piece of wax: it has been taken quite freshly from the hive, and it has not yet lost the sweetness of the honey which it contains: it still retains somewhat of the odour of the flowers from which it has been culled; its colour, its figure, its size are apparent; it is hard, cold, easily handled, and if you strike it with the finger, it

will emit a sound. Finally all the things which are requisite to
cause us distinctly to recognise a body, are met with in it. But
notice that while I speak and approach the fire what remained of
the taste is exhaled, the smell evaporates, the colour alters, the
figure is destroyed, the size increases, it becomes liquid, it heats,
scarcely can one handle it, and when one strikes it, no sound is
emitted. Does the same wax remain after this change? We must
confess that it remains; none would judge otherwise. What then did
I know so distinctly in this piece of wax? It could certainly be
nothing of all that the senses brought to my notice, since all these
things which fall under taste, smell, sight, touch, and hearing, are
found to be changed, and yet the same wax remains.

Perhaps it was what I now think, viz. that this wax was not
that sweetness of honey, nor that agreeable scent of flowers, nor
that particular whiteness, nor that figure, nor that sound, but
simply a body which a little while before appeared to me as
perceptible under these forms, and which is now perceptible under
others. But what, precisely, is it that I imagine when I form such
conceptions? Let us attentively consider this, and, abstracting from
all that does not belong to the wax, let us see what remains.
Certainly nothing remains excepting a certain extended thing which
is flexible and movable. But what is the meaning of flexible and
movable? Is it not that I imagine that this piece of wax being
round is capable of becoming square and of passing from a square
to a triangular figure? No, certainly it is not that, since I imagine it
admits of an infinitude of similar changes, and I nevertheless do
not know how to compass the infinitude by my imagination, and
consequently this conception which I have of the wax is not
brought about by the faculty of imagination. What now is this
extension? Is it not also unknown? For it becomes greater when
the wax is melted, greater when it is boiled, and greater still when
the heat increases; and I should not conceive [clearly] according to
truth what wax is, if I did not think that even this piece that we
are considering is capable of receiving more variations in extension
than I have ever imagined. We must then grant that I could not
even understand through the imagination what this piece of wax is,
and that it is my mind alone which perceives it. I say this piece of
wax in particular, for as to wax in general it is yet clearer. But
what is this piece of wax which cannot be understood excepting
by the [understanding or] mind? It is certainly the same that I
see, touch, imagine, and finally it is the same which I have always
believed it to be from the beginning. But what must particularly be
observed is that its perception is neither an act of vision, nor of
touch, nor of imagination, and has never been such although it

may have appeared formerly to be so, but only an intuition of the mind, which may be imperfect and confused as it was formerly, or clear and distinct as it is at present, according as my attention is more or less directed to the elements which are found in it, and of which it is composed.

Yet in the meantime I am greatly astonished when I consider [the great feebleness of mind] and its proneness to fall [insensibly] into error; for although without giving expression to my thoughts I consider all this in my own mind, words often impede me and I am almost deceived by the terms of ordinary language. For we say that we see the same wax, if it is present, and not that we simply judge that it is the same from its having the same colour and figure. From this I should conclude that I knew the wax by means of vision and not simply by the intuition of the mind; unless by chance I remember that, when looking from a window and saying I see men who pass in the street, I really do not see them, but infer that what I see is men, just as I say that I see wax. And yet what do I see from the window but hats and coats which may cover automatic machines? Yet I judge these to be men. And similarly solely by the faculty of judgment which rests in my mind, I comprehend that which I believed I saw with my eyes.

A man who makes it his aim to raise his knowledge above the common should be ashamed to derive the occasion for doubting from the forms of speech invented by the vulgar; I prefer to pass on and consider whether I had a more evident and perfect conception of what the wax was when I first perceived it, and when I believed I knew it by means of the external senses or at least by the common sense as it is called, that is to say by the imaginative faculty, or whether my present conception is clearer now that I have most carefully examined what it is, and in what way it can be known. It would certainly be absurd to doubt as to this. For what was there in this first perception which was distinct? What was there which might not as well have been perceived by any of the animals? But when I distinguish the wax from its external forms, and when, just as if I had taken from it its vestments, I consider it quite naked, it is certain that although some error may still be found in my judgment, I can nevertheless not perceive it thus without a human mind.

But finally what shall I say of this mind, that is, of myself, for up to this point I do not admit in myself anything but mind? What then, I who seem to perceive this piece of wax so distinctly, do I not know myself, not only with much more truth and certainty, but also with much more distinctness and clearness? For if I judge that the wax is or exists from the fact that I see it, it certainly follows much more clearly that I am or that I exist myself from the fact that I see it. For it may be that what I see is not really wax, it may also be that I do not possess eyes with which to see anything; but it cannot be that when I see, or (for I no longer take account of the distinction) when I think I see, that I myself who think am nought. So if I judge that the wax exists from the fact that I touch it, the same thing will follow, to wit, that I am; and if I judge that my imagination, or some other cause, whatever it is, persuades me that the wax exists, I shall still conclude the same. And what I have here remarked of wax may be applied to all other things which are external to me [and which are met with outside of me]. And further, if the [notion or] perception of wax has seemed to me clearer and more distinct, not only after the sight or the touch, but also after many other causes have rendered it quite manifest to me, with how much more [evidence] and distinctness must it be said that I now know myself, since all the reasons which contribute to the knowledge of wax, or any other body whatever, are yet better proofs of the nature of my mind! And there are so many other things in the mind itself which may contribute to the elucidation of its nature, that those which depend on body such as these just mentioned, hardly merit being taken into account.

But finally here I am, having insensibly reverted to the point I desired, for, since it is now manifest to me that even bodies are not properly speaking known by the senses or by the faculty of imagination, but by the understanding only, and since they are not known from the fact that they are seen or touched, but only because they are understood, I see clearly that there is nothing which is easier for me to know than my mind. But because it is difficult to rid oneself so promptly of an opinion to which one was accustomed for so long, it will be well that I should halt a little at this point, so that by the length of my meditation I may more deeply imprint on my memory this new knowledge. . . .

Of the Passions in General, and Incidentally of the Whole Nature of Man

ARTICLE I

That what in respect of a subject is passion, is in some other regard always action.

There is nothing in which the defective nature of the sciences which we have received from the ancients appears more clearly than in what they have written on the passions; for, although this is a matter which has at all times been the object of much investigation, and though it would not appear to be one of the most difficult, inasmuch as since every one has experience of the passions within himself, there is no necessity to borrow one's observations from elsewhere in order to discover their nature; yet that which the ancients have taught regarding them is both so slight, and for the most part so far from credible, that I am unable to entertain any hope of approximating to the truth excepting by shunning the paths which they have followed. This is why I shall be here obliged to write just as though I were treating of a matter which no one had ever touched on before me; and, to begin with, I consider that all that which occurs or that happens anew, is by the philosophers, generally speaking, termed a passion, in as far as the subject to which it occurs is concerned, and an action in respect of him who causes it to occur. Thus although the agent and the recipient [patient] are frequently very different, the action and the passion are always one and the same thing, although having different names, because of the two diverse subjects to which it may be related.

ARTICLE II

That in order to understand the passions of the soul its functions must be distinguished from those of body.

Next I note also that we do not observe the existence of any subject which more immediately acts upon our soul than the body

R. Descartes, The passions of the soul, E. S. Haldane and G. R. Ross, trans. In the *Philosophical works of Descartes*, Cambridge: The University Press, 1968, pp. 331–333, 340, 342–345, 345–346, 347–350, 352–354.

to which it is joined, and that we must consequently consider that what in the soul is a passion is in the body commonly speaking an action; so that there is no better means of arriving at a knowledge of our passions than to examine the difference which exists between soul and body in order to know to which of the two we must attribute each one of the functions which are within us.

ARTICLE III

What rule we must follow to bring about this result.

As to this we shall not find much difficulty if we realise that all that we experience as being in us, and that to observation may exist in wholly inanimate bodies, must be attributed to our body alone; and, on the other hand, that all that which is in us and which we cannot in any way conceive as possibly pertaining to a body, must be attributed to our soul.

ARTICLE IV

That the heat and movement of the members proceed from the body, the thoughts from the soul.

Thus because we have no conception of the body as thinking in any way, we have reason to believe that every kind of thought which exists in us belongs to the soul; and because we do not doubt there being inanimate bodies which can move in as many as or in more diverse modes than can ours, and which have as much heat or more (experience demonstrates this to us in flame, which of itself has much more heat and movement than any of our members), we must believe that all the heat and all the movements which are in us pertain only to body, inasmuch as they do not depend on thought at all.

ARTICLE V

That it is an error to believe that the soul supplies the movement and heat to body.

By this means we shall avoid a very considerable error into which many have fallen; so much so that I am of opinion that this is the primary cause which has prevented our being able hitherto satisfactorily to explain the passions and the other properties of the soul. It arises from the fact that from observing that all dead bodies are devoid of heat and consequently of movement, it has been thought that it was the absence of soul which caused these movements and this heat to cease; and thus, without any reason, it was thought that our natural heat and all the movements of our body depend on the soul: while in fact we ought on the contrary to believe that the soul quits us on death only because this heat ceases, and the organs which serve to move the body disintegrate.

ARTICLE VI

The difference that exists between a living body and a dead body.

In order, then, that we may avoid this error, let us consider that death never comes to pass by reason of the soul, but only because some one of the principal parts of the body decays; and we may judge that the body of a living man differs from that of a dead man just as does a watch or other automaton (i.e. a machine that moves of itself), when it is wound up and contains in itself the corporeal principle of those movements for which it is designed along with all that is requisite for its action, from the same watch or other machine when it is broken and when the principle of its movement ceases to act. . . .

ARTICLE XVII

What the functions of the soul are.

After having thus considered all the functions which pertain to the body alone, it is easy to recognise that there is nothing in us which we ought to attribute to our soul excepting our thoughts, which are mainly of two sorts, the one being the actions of the soul, and the other its passions. Those which I call its actions are all our desires, because we find by experience that they proceed directly from our soul, and appear to depend on it alone: while, on the other hand, we may usually term one's passions all those kinds of perception or forms of knowledge which are found in us, because it is often not our soul which makes them what they are, and because it always receives them from the things which are represented by them. . . .

ARTICLE XXIII

Of the perceptions which we relate to objects which are without us.

Those which we relate to the things which are without us, to wit to the objects of our senses, are caused, at least when our opinion is not false, by these objects which, exciting certain movements in the organs of the external senses, excite them also in the brain by the intermission of the nerves, which cause the soul to perceive them. Thus when we see the light of a torch, and hear the sound of a bell, this sound and this light are two different actions which, simply by the fact that they excite two different movements in certain of our nerves, and by these means in the brain, give two different sensations to the soul, which sensations we relate to the subjects which we suppose to be their causes in such a way that we think we see the torch itself and hear the bell, and do not perceive just the movements which proceed from them.

ARTICLE XXIV

Of the perceptions which we relate to our body.

The perceptions which we relate to our body, or to some of its parts, are those which we have of hunger, thirst, and other natural appetites, to which we may unite pain, heat, and the other affections which we perceive as though they were in our members, and not as in objects which are outside us; we may thus perceive at the same time and by the intermission of the same nerves, the cold of our hand and the heat of the flame to which it approaches; or, on the other hand, the heat of the hand and the cold of the air to which it is exposed, without there being any difference between the actions which cause us to feel the heat or the cold which is in our hand, and those which make us perceive that which is without us, excepting that from the one of these actions following upon the other, we judge that the first is already in us, and what supervenes is not so yet, but is in the object which causes it.

ARTICLE XXV

Of the perceptions which we relate to our soul.

The perceptions which we relate solely to the soul are those whose effects we feel as though they were in the soul itself, and as to which we do not usually know any proximate cause to which we may relate them: such are the feelings of joy, anger, and other such sensations, which are sometimes excited in us by the objects which move our nerves and sometimes also by other causes. But, although all our perceptions, both those which we relate to objects which are outside us, and those which we relate to the diverse affections of our body, are truly passions in respect of our soul, when we use this word in its most general significance, yet we are in the habit of restricting it to the signification of those alone which are related to soul itself; and it is only these last which I have here undertaken to explain under the name of the passions of the soul.

ARTICLE XXVI

That the imaginations which only depend on the fortuitous movements of the spirits, may be passions just as truly as the perceptions which depend on the nerves.

It remains for us to notice here that all the same things which the soul perceives by the intermission of the nerves, may also be represented by the fortuitous course of the animal spirits, without there being any other difference excepting that the impressions which come into the brain by the nerves are usually more lively or definite than those excited there by the spirits, which caused me to say in Article XXI that the former resemble the shadow or picture of the latter. We must also notice that it sometimes happens that this picture is so similar to the thing which it represents that we may be mistaken therein regarding the perceptions which relate to objects which are outside us, or at least those which relate to certain parts of our body, but that we cannot be so deceived regarding the passions, inasmuch as they are so close to, and so entirely within our soul, that it is impossible for it to feel them without their being actually such as it feels them to be. Thus often when we sleep, and sometimes even when we are awake, we imagine certain things so forcibly, that we think we see them before us, or feel them in our body, although they do not exist at all; but although we may be asleep, or dream, we cannot feel sad or moved by any other passion without its being very true that the soul actually has this passion within it.

ARTICLE XXVII

The definition of the passions of the soul.

After having considered in what the passions of the soul differ from all its other thoughts, it seems to me that we may define them generally as the perceptions, feelings, or emotions of the soul which we relate specially to it, and which are caused, maintained, and fortified by some movement of the spirits.

ARTICLE XXVIII

Explanation of the first part of this definition.

We may call them perceptions when we make use of this word generally to signify all the thoughts which are not actions of the soul, or desires, but not when the term is used only to signify clear cognition; for experience shows us that those who are the most agitated by their passions, are not those who know them best; and that they are of the number of perceptions which the close alliance which exists between the soul and the body, renders confused and obscure. We may also call them feelings because they are received into the soul in the same way as are the objects of our outside senses, and are not otherwise known by it; but we can yet more accurately call them emotions of the soul, not only because the name may be attributed to all the changes which occur in it—that is, in all the diverse thoughts which come to it, but more especially because of all the kinds of thought which it may have, there are no others which so powerfully agitate and disturb it as do these passions.

ARTICLE XXIX

Explanation of the second part.

I add that they particularly relate to the soul, in order to distinguish them from the other feelings which are related, the one to outside objects such as scents, sounds, and colours; the others to our body such as hunger, thirst, and pain. I also add that they are caused, maintained, and fortified by some movement of the spirits, in order to distinguish them from our desires, which we may call emotions of the soul which relate to it, but which are caused by itself; and also in order to explain their ultimate and most proximate cause, which plainly distinguishes them from the other feelings. . . .

ARTICLE XXXI

That there is a small gland in the brain in which the soul exercises its functions more particularly than in the other parts.

It is likewise necessary to know that although the soul is joined to the whole body, there is yet in that a certain part in which it exercises its functions more particularly than in all the others; and it is usually believed that this part is the brain, or possibly the heart: the brain, because it is with it that the organs of sense are connected, and the heart because it is apparently in it that we experience the passions. But, in examining the matter with care, it seems as though I had clearly ascertained that the part of the body in which the soul exercises its functions immediately is in nowise the heart, nor the whole of the brain, but merely the most inward of all its parts, to wit, a certain very small gland which is situated in the middle of its substance and so suspended above the duct whereby the animal spirits in its anterior cavities have communication with those in the posterior, that the slightest movements which take place in it may alter very greatly the course of these spirits; and reciprocally that the smallest changes which occur in the course of the spirits may do much to change the movements of this gland.

ARTICLE XXXII

How we know that this gland is the main seat of the soul.

The reason which persuades me that the soul cannot have any other seat in all the body than this gland wherein to exercise its functions immediately, is that I reflect that the other parts of our brain are all of them double, just as we have two eyes, two hands, two ears, and finally all the organs of our outside senses are double; and inasmuch as we have but one solitary and simple thought of one particular thing at one and the same moment, it must necessarily be the case that there must somewhere be a place where the two images which come to us by the two eyes, where the two other impressions which proceed from a single object by means of the double organs of the other senses, can unite before arriving at the soul, in order that they may not represent to it two objects instead of one. And it is easy to apprehend how these images or other impressions might unite in this gland by the intermission of the spirits which fill the cavities of the brain: but there is no other place in the body where they can be thus united unless they are so in this gland. . . .

ARTICLE XXXIV

How the soul and the body act on one another.

Let us then conceive here that the soul has its principal seat in the little gland which exists in the middle of the brain, from whence it radiates forth through all the remainder of the body by means of the animal spirits, nerves, and even the blood, which, participating in the impressions of the spirits, can carry them by the arteries into all the members. And recollecting what has been said above about the machine of our body, i.e. that the little filaments of our nerves are so distributed in all its parts, that on the occasion of the diverse movements which are there excited by sensible objects, they open in diverse ways the pores of the brain, which causes the animal spirits contained in these cavities to enter in diverse ways into the muscles, by which means they can move the members in all the different ways in which they are capable of being moved; and also that all the other causes which are capable of moving the spirits in diverse ways suffice to conduct them into diverse muscles; let us here add that the small gland which is the main seat of the soul is so suspended between the cavities which contain the spirits that it can be moved by them in as many different ways as there are sensible diversities in the object, but that it may also be moved in diverse ways by the soul, whose nature is such that it receives in itself as many diverse impressions, that is to say, that it possesses as many diverse perceptions as there are diverse movements in this gland. Reciprocally, likewise, the machine of the body is so formed that from the simple fact that this gland is diversely moved by the soul, or by such other cause, whatever it is, it thrusts the spirits which surround it towards the pores of the brain, which conduct them by the nerves into the muscles, by which means it causes them to move the limbs.

ARTICLE XXXV

Example of the mode in which the impressions of the objects unite in the gland which is in the middle of the brain.

Thus, for example, if we see some animal approach us, the light reflected from its body depicts two images of it, one in each of our eyes, and these two images form two others, by means of the optic nerves, in the interior surface of the brain which faces its cavities; then from there, by means of the animal spirits with which its cavities are filled, these images so radiate towards the little gland which is surrounded by these spirits, that the movement which forms each point of one of the images tends towards the same point of the gland towards which tends the movement which forms the point of the other image, which represents the same part of this animal. By this means the two images which are in the brain form but one upon the gland, which, acting immediately upon the soul, causes it to see the form of this animal.

ARTICLE XXXVI

Example of the way in which the passions are excited in the soul.

And, besides that, if this figure is very strange and frightful—that is, if it has a close relationship with the things which have been formerly hurtful to the body, that excites the passion of apprehension in the soul and then that of courage, or else that of fear and consternation according to the particular temperament of the body or the strength of the soul, and according as we have to begin with been secured by defence or by flight against the hurtful things to which the present impression is related. For in certain persons that disposes the brain in such a way that the spirits reflected from the image thus formed on the gland, proceed thence to take their places partly in the nerves which serve to turn the back and dispose the legs for flight, and partly in those which so increase or diminish the orifices of the heart, or at least which so agitate the other parts from whence the blood is sent to it, that this blood being there rarefied in a different manner from usual, sends to the brain the spirits which are adapted for the maintenance and strengthening of the passion of fear, i.e. which are adapted to the holding open, or at least reopening, of the pores of the brain which conduct them into the same nerves. For from the fact alone that these spirits enter into these pores, they excite a particular movement in this gland which is instituted by nature in order to cause the soul to be sensible of this passion; and because these pores are principally in relation with the little nerves which serve to contract or enlarge the orifices of the heart, that causes the soul to be sensible of it for the most part as in the heart.

ARTICLE XXXVII

How it seems as though they are all caused by some movement of the spirits.

And because the same occurs in all the other passions, to wit, that they are principally caused by the spirits which are contained in the cavities of the brain, inasmuch as they take their course towards the nerves which serve to enlarge or contract the orifices of the heart, or to drive in various ways to it the blood which is in the other parts, or, in whatever other fashion it may be, to carry on the same passion, we may from this clearly understand why I have placed in my definition of them above, that they are caused by some particular movement of the animal spirits.

ARTICLE XXXVIII

Example of the movements of the body which accompany the passions and do not depend on the soul.

For the rest, in the same way as the course which these spirits take towards the nerves of the heart suffices to give the movement to the gland by which fear is placed in the soul, so, too, by the simple fact that certain spirits at the same time proceed towards the nerves which serve to move the legs in order to take flight, they cause another movement in the same gland, by means of which the soul is sensible of and perceives this flight, which in this way may be excited in the body by the disposition of the organs alone, and without the soul's contributing thereto.

ARTICLE XXXIX

How one and the same cause may excite different passions in different men.

The same impression which a terrifying object makes on the gland, and which causes fear in certain men, may excite in others courage and confidence; the reason of this is that all brains are not constituted in the same way, and that the same movement of the gland which in some excites fear, in others causes the spirits to enter into the pores of the brain which conduct them partly into the nerves which serve to move the hands for purposes of self-defence, and partly into those which agitate and drive the blood towards the heart in the manner requisite to produce the spirits proper for the continuance of this defence, and to retain the desire of it.

ARTICLE XL

The principal effect of the passions.

For it is requisite to notice that the principal effect of all the passions in men is that they incite and dispose their soul to desire those things for which they prepare their body, so that the feeling of fear incites it to desire to fly, that of courage to desire to fight, and so on.

ARTICLE XLI

The power of the soul in regard to the body.

But the will is so free in its nature, that it can never be constrained; and of the two sorts of thoughs which I have distinguished in the soul (of which the first are its actions, i.e. its desires, the others its passions, taking this word in its most general significance, which comprises all kinds of perceptions), the former are absolutely in its power, and can only be indirectly changed by the body, while on the other hand the latter depend absolutely on the actions which govern and direct them, and they can only indirectly be altered by the soul, excepting when it is itself their cause. And the whole action of the soul consists in this, that solely because it desires something, it causes the little gland to which it is closely united to move in the way requisite to produce the effect which relates to this desire. . . .

ARTICLE XLVII

In what the strife consists which we imagine to exist between the lower and higher part of the soul.

And it is only in the repugnance which exists between the movements which the body by its animal spirits, and the soul by its will, tend to excite in the gland at the same time, that all the strife which we are in the habit of conceiving to exist between the inferior part of the soul, which we call the sensuous, and the superior which is rational, or as we may say, between the natural appetites and the will, consists. For there is within us but one soul, and this soul has not in itself any diversity of parts; the same part that is subject to sense impressions is rational, and all the soul's appetites are acts of will. The error which has been committed in making it play the part of various personages, usually in opposition one to another, only proceeds from the fact that we have not properly distinguished its functions from those of the body, to which alone we must attribute every thing which can be observed in us that is opposed to our reason; so that there is here no strife, excepting that the small gland which exists in the middle of the brain, being capable of being thrust to one side by the soul, and to the other by the animal spirits, which are mere bodies, as I have said above, it often happens that these two impulses are contrary, and that the stronger prevents the other from taking effect. We may, however, distinguish two sorts of movement excited by the animal spirits in the gland—the one sort represents to the soul the objects which move the senses, or the impressions which are met with in the brain, and makes no attempt to affect its will; the others do make an effort to do so—i.e. those which cause the passions or the movements of the body which accompany the passions. And as to the first, although they often hinder the actions of the soul, or else are hindered by them, yet, because they are not directly contrary to them, we do not notice any strife between them. We only notice the strife between the latter and the acts of will which conflict with them: e.g. between the effort with which the spirits impel the gland in order to cause a desire for something in the soul, and that with which the soul repels it again by the desire which it has to avoid the very same thing. And what causes this strife to come into evidence for the most part is that the will, not having the power to excite the passions directly, as has just been said, is constrained to use its best endeavours, and to apply itself to consider successively several things as to which, though it happens that one has the power to change for a moment the course taken by the spirits, it may come to pass that that which succeeds does not have it, and that they immediately afterwards revert to that same course because the disposition which has before held its place in the nerves, heart, and blood has not changed, and thus it comes about that the soul feels itself almost at the same time impelled to desire and not to desire the same thing. It is from this that occasion has been taken to imagine in the soul two powers which strive one with the other. At the same time we may still conceive a sort of strife to exist, inasmuch as often the same cause which excites some passion in the soul, also excites certain movements in the body to which the soul does not contribute, and which it stops, or tries to stop, directly it perceives them; as we see when what excites fear also causes the spirits to enter into the muscles which serve to move the legs with the object of flight, and when the wish which we have to be brave stops them from doing so.

14. Noam Chomsky

EDITOR'S INTRODUCTION

Descartes' brand of dualism had a profound effect, both beneficial and pernicious, on subsequent thought. On the beneficial side, it gave impetus to physiological psychology, because within the Cartesian framework the machinery of the body could be interpreted in the same terms as other physical events. On the pernicious side, Cartesian dualism seemed to place higher mental processes outside the realm of science, and it raised the difficult issue of the interaction between mind and body. In most contemporary psychology textbooks, it is the pernicious effects of Cartesian dualism that are emphasized. Often, however, this negative emphasis is superficial and misleading. Certainly, most psychologists today would agree that the notion of an incorporeal soul is an unnecessary hindrance to psychological theory. But the postulation of an independent mental substance—a "ghost in the machine"—is not the real significance of Descartes' dualism.

Many philosophers before and after Descartes have postulated some immaterial aspect (*Nous*, soul) of man. There is certainly nothing unique about Descartes in this respect. In order to understand the significance of Descartes' formulation, it will be helpful to contrast his form of dualism with that of, say, Aquinas. For Aquinas, the distinction between soul and body was as much one of degree as of kind: the universe consists of a continuum from the potential (matter) to the actual (soul), with no sharp division between the two. This rather unitary view of the universe had important ramifications, for it meant that the same type of explanation was applicable to both animate and inanimate objects. The type of explanation adopted by Aquinas (as by Aristotle) was based on a functional or organismic model, i.e., one that emphasized organized wholes, end states, and (in the case of humans) purposeful behavior. One of the major outcomes of the scientific revolution was the replacement of the organismic with a mechanistic model as the accepted paradigm of scientific explanation.

By the time of Descartes, the success of mechanistic principles in explaining physical phenomena could not be denied. But what about psychological events? Could these too be explained in strictly mechanistic terms? Descartes did not think so, and herein lies the real significance of Cartesian dualism. Descartes was not just postulating two distinct substances; he also was arguing that the system of concepts being developed to explain the physical universe and man-made machines was not adequate to explain mental events. This assertion is still very much an open issue, the resolution of which has nothing to do with the postulation of distinct kinds of substances—the mental and the physical.

Most modern psychologists, especially those of the behaviorist persuasion, believe that Descartes was mistaken and that a basically mechanistic form of explanation (e.g., one couched in stimulus-response terms) is sufficient for psychology. In this chapter, Noam Chomsky takes issue with this view, and argues instead that Descartes was perhaps more right than wrong. Chomsky's starting point is the analysis of language, or more specifically, the system of rules that underlies linguistic competence.

Chomsky may be classified as a Cartesian not only because he believes that higher mental processes are not explicable in strictly mechanistic terms, but also because of his emphasis on the innate determinants of knowledge. Descartes had spoken as though the mind came equipped with certain ready-made, innate ideas. Under criticism, he modified this view and argued that innate ideas reflect the mind's potentiality for certain kinds of thought, a potentiality that requires experience to be actualized (cf. Plato's account of reminiscence). Chomsky also believes that the human mind has an innate potentiality for the acquisition of linguistic rules, and perhaps for the development of other specific kinds of knowledge. In his Russell Lectures, for example, Chomsky notes that

... our mental constitution permits us to arrive at knowledge of the world insofar as our innate capacity to create theories happens to match some aspect of the structure of the world. By exploring various faculties of the mind, we might, in principle come to understand what theories are more readily accessible to us than others, or what potential theories are accessible to us at all, what forms of scientific knowledge can be attained, if the world is kind enough to have the required properties. Where it does not, we may be able to develop a kind of "intellectual technology"—say, a technique of prediction that will, for some reason, work within limits—but not to attain what might properly be called scientific understanding or common-sense knowledge. Another organism, following different principles, might develop other sciences, or lack some of ours.[1]

The relationship between cognitive structures (whether innate or culturally determined) and the structure of reality is one of the most fundamental questions that can be addressed by psychology, for it has to do with the limits of human understanding.

[1] N. Chomsky. *Problems of knowledge and freedom: The Russell lectures.* New York: Pantheon Books, a division of Random House, 1971, pp. 20–21, with permission.

Linguistic Contributions
to the Study of Mind

I would like to focus attention on the question, What contribution can the study of language make to our understanding of human nature? In one or another manifestation, this question threads its way through modern Western thought. In an age that was less self-conscious and less compartmentalized than ours, the nature of language, the respects in which language mirrors human mental processes or shapes the flow and character of thought— these were topics for study and speculation by scholars and gifted amateurs with a wide variety of interests, points of view, and intellectual backgrounds. And in the nineteenth and twentieth centuries, as linguistics, philosophy, and psychology have uneasily tried to go their separate ways, the classical problems of language and mind have inevitably reappeared and have served to link these diverging fields and to give direction and significance to their efforts. There have been signs in the past decade that the rather artificial separation of disciplines may be coming to an end. It is no longer a point of honor for each to demonstrate its absolute independence of the others, and new interests have emerged that permit the classical problems to be formulated in novel and occasionally suggestive ways—for example, in terms of the new perspectives provided by cybernetics and the communication sciences, and against the background of developments in comparative and physiological psychology that challenge long-standing convictions and free the scientific imagination from certain shackles that had become so familiar a part of our intellectual environment as to be almost beyond awareness. All of this is highly encouraging. I think there is more of a healthy ferment in cognitive psychology—and in the particular branch of cognitive psychology known as linguistics—than there has been for many years. And one of the most encouraging signs is that skepticism with regard to the orthodoxies of the recent past is coupled with an awareness of the temptations and the dangers of premature orthodoxy, an awareness that, if it can persist, may prevent the rise of new and stultifying dogma.

From *Language and mind* (pp. 1–14, 103–108, 109–114), Enlarged Edition, by Noam Chomsky, © 1968, 1972 by Harcourt Brace Jovanovich, Inc. and reprinted with their permission.

It is easy to be misled in an assessment of the current scene; nevertheless, it seems to me that the decline of dogmatism and the accompanying search for new approaches to old and often still intractable problems are quite unmistakable, not only in linguistics but in all of the disciplines concerned with the study of mind. I remember quite clearly my own feeling of uneasiness as a student at the fact that, so it seemed, the basic problems of the field were solved, and that what remained was to sharpen and improve techniques of linguistic analysis that were reasonably well understood and to apply them to a wider range of linguistic materials. In the postwar years, this was a dominant attitude in most active centers of research. I recall being told by a distinguished anthropological linguist, in 1953, that he had no intention of working through a vast collection of materials that he had assembled because within a few years it would surely be possible to program a computer to construct a grammar from a large corpus of data by the use of techniques that were already fairly well formalized. At the time, this did not seem an unreasonable attitude, though the prospect was saddening for anyone who felt, or at least hoped, that the resources of human intelligence were somewhat deeper than these procedures and techniques might reveal. Correspondingly, there was a striking decline in studies of linguistic method in the early 1950's as the most active theoretical minds turned to the problem of how an essentially closed body of technique could be applied to some new domain—say, to analysis of connected discourse, or to other cultural phenomena beyond language. I arrived at Harvard as a graduate student shortly after B. F. Skinner had delivered his William James Lectures, later to be published in his book *Verbal Behavior*. Among those active in research in the philosophy or psychology of language, there was then little doubt that although details were missing, and although matters could not really be quite that simple, nevertheless a behavioristic framework of the sort Skinner had outlined would prove quite adequate to accommodate the full range of language use. There was now little reason to question the conviction of Leonard Bloomfield, Bertrand Russell, and positivistic linguists, psychologists, and philosophers in general that the framework of stimulus-response psychology would soon be extended to the point where it would provide a satisfying explanation for the most mysterious of human abilities. The most radical souls felt that perhaps, in order to do full justice to these abilities, one must postulate little s's and r's inside the brain alongside the capital S's and R's that were open to immediate inspection, but this extension was not inconsistent with the general picture.

Critical voices, even those that commanded considerable prestige, were simply unheard. For example, Karl Lashley gave a brilliant critique of the prevailing framework of ideas in 1948, arguing that underlying language use—and all organized behavior—there must be abstract mechanisms of some sort that are not analyzable in terms of association and that could not have been developed by any such simple means. But his arguments and proposals, though sound and perceptive, had absolutely no effect on the development of the field and went by unnoticed even at his own university (Harvard), then the leading center of psycholinguistic research. Ten years later Lashley's contribution began to be appreciated, but only after his insights had been independently achieved in another context.

The technological advances of the 1940's simply reinforced the general euphoria. Computers were on the horizon, and their imminent availability reinforced the belief that it would suffice to gain a theoretical understanding of only the simplest and most superficially obvious of phenomena—everything else would merely prove to be "more of the same," an apparent complexity that would be disentangled by the electronic marvels. The sound spectrograph, developed during the war, offered similar promise for the physical analysis of speech sounds. The interdisciplinary conferences on speech analysis of the early 1950's make interesting reading today. There were few so benighted as to question the possibility, in fact the immediacy, of a final solution to the problem of converting speech into writing by available engineering technique. And just a few years later, it was jubilantly discovered that machine translation and automatic abstracting were also just around the corner. For those who sought a more mathematical formulation of the basic processes, there was the newly developed mathematical theory of communication, which, it was widely believed in the early 1950's, had provided a fundamental concept—the concept of "information"—that would unify the social and behavioral sciences and permit the development of a solid and satisfactory mathematical theory of human behavior on a probabilistic base. At about the same time, the theory of automata developed as an independent study, making use of closely related mathematical notions. And it was linked at once, and quite properly, to earlier explorations of the theory of neural nets. There were those—John von Neumann, for example—who felt that the entire development was dubious and shaky at best, and probably quite misconceived, but such qualms did not go far to dispel the feeling that mathematics, technology, and behavioristic linguistics and psychology were converging on a point of view that was very simple, very clear, and fully adequate to provide a basic understanding of what tradition had left shrouded in mystery.

In the United States at least, there is little trace today of the illusions of the early postwar years. If we consider the current status of structural linguistic methodology, stimulus-response psycholinguistics (whether or not extended to "mediation theory"), or probabilistic or automata-theoretic models for language use, we find that in each case a parallel development has taken place: A careful analysis has shown that insofar as the system of concepts and principles that was advanced can be made precise, it can be demonstrated to be inadequate in a fundamental way. The kinds of structures that are realizable in terms of these theories are simply not those that must be postulated to underlie the use of language, if empirical conditions of adequacy are to be satisfied. What is more, the character of the failure and inadequacy is such as to give little reason to believe that these approaches are on the right track. That is, in each case it has been argued—quite persuasively, in my opinion—that the approach is not only inadequate but misguided in basic and important ways. It has, I believe, become quite clear that if we are ever to understand how language is used or acquired, then we must abstract for separate and independent study a cognitive system, a system of knowledge and belief, that develops in early childhood and that interacts with many other factors to determine the kinds of behavior that we observe; to introduce a technical term, we must isolate and study the system of *linguistic competence* that underlies behavior but that is not realized in any direct or simple way in behavior. And this system of linguistic competence is qualitatively different from anything that can be described in terms of the taxonomic methods of structural linguistics, the concepts of S-R psychology, or the notions developed within the mathematical theory of communication or the theory of simple automata. The theories and models that were developed to describe simple and immediately given phenomena cannot incorporate the real system of linguistic competence; "extrapolation" for simple descriptions cannot approach the reality of linguistic competence; mental structures are not simply "more of the same" but are qualitatively different from the complex networks and structures that can be developed by elaboration of the concepts that seemed so promising to many scientists just a few years ago. What is involved is not a matter of degree of complexity but rather a quality of complexity. Correspondingly, there is no reason to expect that the available technology can provide significant insight or understanding or useful achievements; it has noticeably failed to do so, and, in fact, an appreciable investment of time, energy, and money in the use of computers for linguistic research—appreciable by the standards of a small field like linguistics—has not provided any significant advance in our understanding of the use or nature of language. These judgments are harsh, but I think they are defensible. They are, furthermore, hardly debated by active linguistic or psycholinguistic researchers.

At the same time there have been significant advances, I believe, in our understanding of the nature of linguistic competence and some of the ways in which it is put to use, but these advances, such as they are, have proceeded from assumptions very different from those that were so enthusiastically put forth in the period I have been discussing. What is more, these advances have not narrowed the gap between what is known and what can be seen to lie beyond the scope of present understanding and technique; rather, each advance has made it clear that these intellectual horizons are far more remote than was heretofore imagined. Finally, it has become fairly clear, it seems to me, that the assumptions and approaches that appear to be productive today have a distinctly traditional flavor to them; in general, a much despised tradition has been largely revitalized in recent years and its contributions given some serious and, I believe, well-deserved attention. From the recognition of these facts flows the general and quite healthy attitude of skepticism that I spoke of earlier.

In short, it seems to me quite appropriate, at this moment in the development of linguistics and psychology in general, to turn again to classical questions and to ask what new insights have been achieved that bear on them, and how the classical issues may provide direction for contemporary research and study.

When we turn to the history of study and speculation concerning the nature of mind and, more specifically, the nature of human language, our attention quite naturally comes to focus on the seventeenth century, "the century of genius," in which the foundations of modern science were firmly established and the problems that still confound us were formulated with remarkable clarity and perspicuity. There are many far from superficial respects in which the intellectual climate of today resembles that of seventeenth-century Western Europe. One, particularly crucial in the present context, is the very great interest in the potentialities and capacities of automata, a problem that intrigued the seventeenth-century mind as fully as it does our own. I mentioned above that there is a slowly dawning realization that a significant gap—more accurately, a yawning chasm—separates the system of concepts of which we have a fairly clear grasp, on the one hand, and the nature of human intelligence, on the other. A similar realization lies at the base of Cartesian philosophy. Descartes also arrived, quite early in his investigations, at the conclusion that the study of mind faces us with a problem of quality of complexity, not merely degree of complexity. He felt that he had demonstrated that understanding and will, the two fundamental properties of the human mind, involved capacities and principles that are not realizable by even the most complex of automata.

It is particularly interesting to trace the development of this argument in the works of the minor and now quite forgotten Cartesian philosophers, like Cordemoy, who wrote a fascinating treatise extending Descartes' few remarks about language, or La Forge, who produced a long and detailed *Traité de l'esprit de l'homme* expressing, so he claimed with some reason, what Descartes would likely have said about this subject had he lived to extend his theory of man beyond physiology. One may question the details of this argument, and one can show how it was impeded and distorted by certain remnants of scholastic doctrine—the framework of substance and mode, for example. But the general structure of the argument is not unreasonable; it is, in fact, rather analogous to the argument against the framework of ideas of the early postwar years, which I mentioned at the outset of this lecture. The Cartesians tried to show that when the theory of corporeal body is sharpened and clarified and extended to its limits, it is still incapable of accounting for facts that are obvious to introspection and that are also confirmed by our observation of the actions of other humans. In particular, it cannot account for the normal use of human language, just as it cannot explain the basic properties of thought. Consequently, it becomes necessary to invoke an entirely new principle—in Cartesian terms, to postulate a second substance whose essence is thought, alongside of body, with its essential properties of extension and motion. This new principle has a "creative aspect," which is evidenced most clearly in what we may refer to as "the creative aspect of language use," the distinctively human ability to express new thoughts and to understand entirely new expressions of thought, within the framework of an "instituted language," a language that is a cultural product subject to laws and principles partially unique to it and partially reflections of general properties of mind. These laws and principles, it is maintained, are not formulable in terms of even the most elaborate extension of the concepts proper to the analysis of behavior and interaction of physical bodies, and they are not realizable by even the most complex automaton. In fact, Descartes argued that the only sure indication that another body possesses a human mind, that it is not a mere automaton, is its ability to use language in the normal way; and he argued that this ability cannot be detected in an animal or an automaton which, in other respects, shows signs of apparent intelligence exceeding those of a human, even though such an organism or machine might be as fully endowed as a human with the physiological organs necessary to produce speech.

I will return to this argument and the ways in which it was developed. But I think it is important to stress that, with all its gaps and deficiencies, it is an argument that must be taken seriously. There is nothing at all absurd in the conclusion. It seems to me quite possible that at that particular moment in the development of Western thought there was the possibility for the birth of a science of psychology of a sort that still does not exist, a psychology that begins with the problem of characterizing various systems of human knowledge and belief, the concepts in terms of which they are organized and the principles that underlie them, and that only then turns to the study of how these systems might have developed through some combination of innate structure and organism-environment interaction. Such a psychology would contrast rather sharply with the approach to human intelligence that begins by postulating, on a priori grounds, certain specific mechanisms that, it is claimed, *must* be those underlying the acquisition of all knowledge and belief. The distinction is one to which I will return in a subsequent lecture. For the moment, I want merely to stress the reasonableness of the rejected alternative and, what is more, its consistency with the approach that proved so successful in the seventeenth-century revolution in physics.

There are methodological parallels that have perhaps been inadequately appreciated between the Cartesian postulation of a substance whose essence was thought and the post-Newtonian acceptance of a principle of attraction as an innate property of the ultimate corpuscles of matter, an active principle that governs the motions of bodies. Perhaps the most far-reaching contribution of Cartesian philosophy to modern thought was its rejection of the scholastic notion of substantial forms and real qualities, of all those "little images fluttering through the air" to which Descartes referred with derision. With the exorcism of these occult qualities, the stage was set for the rise of a physics of matter in motion and a psychology that explored the properties of mind. But Newton argued that Descartes' mechanical physics wouldn't work—the second book of the *Principia* is largely devoted to this demonstration—and that it is necessary to postulate a new force to account for the motion of bodies. The postulate of an attractive force acting at a distance was inconsistent with the clear and distinct ideas of common sense and could not be tolerated by an orthodox Cartesian—such a force was merely another occult quality. Newton quite agreed, and he attempted repeatedly to find a mechanical explanation of the cause of gravity. He rejected the view that gravity is "essential and inherent to matter" and maintained that "to tell us that every species of things is endowed with an occult specific property (such as gravity) by which it acts and produces manifest effects, is to tell us nothing." Some historians of science have suggested that Newton hoped, like Descartes, to write a *Principles of Philosophy* but that his failure to explain the cause of gravity on mechanical grounds restricted him to a *Mathematical Principles of Natural Philosophy*. Thus, to the common sense of Newton as well as the Cartesians, physics was still not adequately grounded, because it postulated a mystical force capable of action at a distance. Similarly, Descartes' postulation of mind as an explanatory principle was unacceptable to the empiricist temper. But the astonishing success of mathematical physics carried the day against these common-sense objections, and the prestige of the new physics was so high that the speculative psychology of the Enlightenment took for granted the necessity of working within the Newtonian framework, rather than on the Newtonian analogy—a very different matter. The occult force of gravity was accepted as an obvious element of the physical world, requiring no explanation, and it became inconceivable that one might have to postulate entirely new principles of functioning and organization outside the framework of what soon became the new "common sense." Partly for this reason, the search for an analogous scientific psychology that would explore the principles of mind, whatever they might be, was not undertaken with the thoroughness that was then, as now, quite possible.

I do not want to overlook a fundamental distinction between the postulation of gravity and the postulation of a *res cogitans*, namely the enormous disparity in the power of the explanatory theories that were developed. Nevertheless, I think it is instructive to note that the reasons for the dissatisfaction of Newton, Leibnitz, and the orthodox Cartesians with the new physics are strikingly similar to the grounds on which a dualistic rationalist psychology was soon to be rejected. I think it is correct to say that the study of properties and organization of mind was prematurely abandoned, in part on quite spurious grounds, and also to point out that there is a certain irony in the common view that its abandonment was caused by the gradual spread of a more general "scientific" attitude.

I have tried to call attention to some similarities between the intellectual climate of the seventeenth century and that of today. It is illuminating, I think, to trace in somewhat greater detail the specific course of development of linguistic theory during the modern period, in the context of the study of mind and of behavior in general.[1]

A good place to begin is with the writings of the Spanish physician Juan Huarte, who in the late sixteenth century published a widely translated study on the nature of human intelligence. In the course of his investigations, Huarte came to wonder at the fact that the word for "intelligence," *ingenio*, seems to have the same Latin root as various words meaning "engender" or "generate." This, he argued, gives a clue to the nature of mind. Thus, "One may discern two generative powers in man, one common with the beasts and the plants, and the other participating of spiritual substance. Wit (Ingenio) is a generative power. The understanding is a generative faculty." Huarte's etymology is actually not very good; the insight, however, is quite substantial.

Huarte goes on to distinguish three levels of intelligence. The lowest of these is the "docile wit," which satisfies the maxim that he, along with Leibnitz and many others, wrongly attributes to Aristotle, namely that there is nothing in the mind that is not simply transmitted to it by the senses. The next higher level, normal human intelligence, goes well beyond the empiricist limitation: It is able to "engender within itself, by its own power, the principles on which knowledge rests." Normal human minds are such that "assisted by the subject alone, without the help of anybody, they will produce a thousand conceits they never heard spoke of . . . inventing and saying such things as they never heard from their masters, nor any mouth." Thus, normal human intelligence is capable of acquiring knowledge through its own internal resources, perhaps making use of the data of sense but going on to construct a cognitive system in terms of concepts and principles that are developed on independent grounds; and it is capable of generating new thoughts and of finding appropriate and novel ways of expressing them, in ways that entirely transcend any training or experience.

[1] For additional details and discussion, see my *Cartesian Linguistics* (New York: Harper & Row, 1966) and the references cited there.

Huarte postulates a third kind of wit, "by means of which some, without art or study, speak such subtle and surprising things, yet true, that were never before seen, heard, or writ, no, nor ever so much as thought of." The reference here is to true creativity, an exercise of the creative imagination in ways that go beyond normal intelligence and may, he felt, involve "a mixture of madness."

Huarte maintains that the distinction between docile wit, which meets the empiricist maxim, and normal intelligence, with its full generative capacities, is the distinction between beast and man. As a physician, Huarte was much interested in pathology. In particular, he notes that the most severe disability of wit that can afflict a human is a restriction to the lowest of the three levels, to the docile wit that conforms to empiricist principles. This disability, says Huarte, "resembles that of Eunuchs, incapable of generation." Under these sad circumstances, in which the intelligence can only receive stimuli transmitted by sense and associate them with one another, true education is of course impossible, since the ideas and principles that permit the growth of knowledge and understanding are lacking. In this case, then, "neither the lash of the rod, nor cries, nor method, nor examples, nor time, nor experience, nor anything in nature can sufficiently excite him to bring forth anything."

Huarte's framework is useful for discussing "psychological theory" in the ensuing period. Typical of later thought is his reference to use of language as an index of human intelligence, of what distinguishes man from animals, and, specifically, his emphasis on the creative capacity of normal intelligence. These concerns dominated rationalist psychology and linguistics. With the rise of romanticism, attention shifted to the third type of wit, to true creativity, although the rationalist assumption that normal human intelligence is uniquely free and creative and beyond the bounds of mechanical explanation was not abandoned and played an important role in the psychology of romanticism, and even in its social philosophy.

As I have already mentioned, the rationalist theory of language, which was to prove extremely rich in insight and achievement, developed in part out of a concern with the problem of other minds. A fair amount of effort was devoted to a consideration of the ability of animals to follow spoken commands, to express their emotional states, to communicate with one another, and even apparently to cooperate for a common goal; all of this, it was argued, could be accounted for on "mechanical grounds," as this notion was then understood—that is, through the functioning of physiological mechanisms in terms of which one could formulate the properties of reflexes, conditioning and reinforcement, association, and so on. Animals do not lack appropriate organs of communication, nor are they simply lower along some scale of "general intelligence."

In fact, as Descartes himself quite correctly observed, language is a species-specific human possession, and even at low levels of intelligence, at pathological levels, we find a command of language that is totally unattainable by an ape that may, in other respects, surpass a human imbecile in problem-solving ability and other adaptive behavior. I will return later to the status of this observation, in the light of what is now known about animal communication. There is a basic element lacking in animals, Descartes argued, as it is lacking in even the most complex automaton that develops its "intellectual structures" completely in terms of conditioning and association—namely Huarte's second type of wit, the generative ability that is revealed in the normal human use of language as a free instrument of thought. If by experiment we convince ourselves that another organism gives evidence of the normal, creative use of language, we must suppose that it, like us, has a mind and that what it does lies beyond the bounds of mechanical explanation, outside the framework of the stimulus-response psychology of the time, which in relevant essentials is not significantly different from that of today, though it falls short in sharpness of technique and scope and reliability of information.

It should not be thought, incidentally, that the only Cartesian arguments for the beast-machine hypothesis were those derived from the apparent inability of animals to manifest the creative aspect of language use. There were also many others—for example, the natural fear of population explosion in the domains of the spirit if every gnat had a soul. Or the argument of Cardinal Melchior de Polignac, who argued that the beast-machine hypothesis followed from the assumption of the goodness of God, since, as he pointed out, one can see "how much more humane is the doctrine that animals suffer no pain."[2] Or there is the argument of Louis Racine, son of the dramatist, who was struck by the following insight: "If beasts had souls and were capable of feelings, would they show themselves insensible to the affront and injustice done them by Descartes? Would they not rather have risen up in wrath against the leader and the sect which so degraded

---

[2] These examples are taken from the excellent study by Leonora Cohen Rosenfield, *From Beast-Machine to Man-Machine* (New York: Oxford University Press, 1941). The quotes are her paraphrases of the original.

them?" One should add, I suppose, that Louis Racine was regarded by his contemporaries as the living proof that a brilliant father could not have a brilliant son. But the fact is that the discussion of the existence of other minds, and, in contrast, the mechanical nature of animals, continually returned to the creative aspect of language use, to the claim that—as formulated by another minor seventeenth-century figure—"if beasts reasoned, they would be capable of true speech with its infinite variety."

It is important to understand just what properties of language were most striking to Descartes and his followers. The discussion of what I have been calling "the creative aspect of language use" turns on three important observations. The first is that the normal use of language is innovative, in the sense that much of what we say in the course of normal language use is entirely new, not a repetition of anything that we have heard before and not even similar in pattern—in any useful sense of the terms "similar" and "pattern"—to sentences or discourse that we have heard in the past. This is a truism, but an important one, often overlooked and not infrequently denied in the behaviorist period of linguistics to which I referred earlier, when it was almost universally claimed that a person's knowledge of language is representable as a stored set of patterns, overlearned through constant repetition and detailed training, with innovation being at most a matter of "analogy." The fact surely is, however, that the number of sentences in one's native language that one will immediately understand with no feeling of difficulty or strangeness is astronomical; and that the number of patterns underlying our normal use of language and corresponding to meaningful and easily comprehensible sentences in our language is orders of magnitude greater than the number of seconds in a lifetime. It is in this sense that the normal use of language is innovative.

However, in the Cartesian view even animal behavior is potentially infinite in its variety, in the special sense in which the readings of a speedometer can be said, with an obvious idealization, to be potentially infinite in variety. That is, if animal behavior is controlled by external stimuli or internal states (the latter including those established by conditioning), then as the stimuli vary over an indefinite range, so may the behavior of the animal. But the normal use of language is not only innovative and potentially infinite in scope, but also free from the control of detectable stimuli, either external or internal. It is because of this freedom from stimulus control that language can serve as an instrument of thought and self-expression, as it does not only for the exceptionally gifted and talented, but also, in fact, for every normal human.

Still, the properties of being unbounded and free from stimulus control do not, in themselves, exceed the bounds of mechanical explanation. And Cartesian discussion of the limits of mechanical explanation therefore took note of a third property of the normal use of language, namely its coherence and its "appropriateness to the situation"—which of course is an entirely different matter from control by external stimuli. Just what "appropriateness" and "coherence" may consist in we cannot say in any clear or definite way, but there is no doubt that these are meaningful concepts. We can distinguish normal use of language from the ravings of a maniac or the output of a computer with a random element.

Honesty forces us to admit that we are as far today as Descartes was three centuries ago from understanding just what enables a human to speak in a way that is innovative, free from stimulus control, and also appropriate and coherent. This is a serious problem that the psychologist and biologist must ultimately face and that cannot be talked out of existence by invoking "habit" or "conditioning" or "natural selection."

The Cartesian analysis of the problem of other minds, in terms of the creative aspect of language use and similar indications of the limits of mechanical explanation, was not entirely satisfying to contemporary opinion—Bayle's *Dictionary*, for example, cites the inability to give a satisfactory proof of the existence of other minds as the weakest element in the Cartesian philosophy—and there was a long and intriguing series of discussions and polemics regarding the problems that Descartes raised. From the vantage point of several centuries, we can see that the debate was inconclusive. The properties of human thought and human language emphasized by the Cartesians are real enough; they were then, as they are now, beyond the bounds of any well-understood kind of physical explanation. Neither physics nor biology nor psychology gives us any clue as to how to deal with these matters.

As in the case of other intractable problems, it is tempting to try another approach, one that might show the problem to be misconceived, the result of some conceptual confusion. This is a line of argument that has been followed in contemporary philosophy, but, it seems to me, without success. It is clear that the Cartesians understood, as well as Gilbert Ryle and other contemporary critics understand, the difference between providing criteria for intelligent behavior, on the one hand, and providing an explanation for the possibility of such behavior, on the other; but, as distinct from Ryle, they were interested in the latter problem as well as the former. As scientists, they were not satisfied with the formulation of experimental tests that would show the behavior of another organism to be creative, in the special sense just outlined; they were also troubled, and quite rightly so, by the fact that the abilities indicated by such tests and observational criteria transcended the capacities of corporeal bodies as they understood them, just as they are beyond the scope of physical explanation as we understand it today. There is surely nothing illegitimate in an attempt to go beyond elaboration of observational tests and collection of evidence to the construction of some theoretical explanation for what is observed, and this just what was at stake in the Cartesian approach to the problem of mind. As La Forge and others insisted, it is necessary to go beyond what one can perceive or "imagine" (in the technical, classical sense of this term) if one hopes to understand the nature of "l'esprit de l'homme," just as Newton did—successfully—in trying to understand the nature of planetary motion. On the other hand, the proposals of the Cartesians were themselves of no real substance; the phenomena in question are not explained satisfactorily by attributing them to an "active principle" called "mind," the properties of which are not developed in any coherent or comprehensive way.

It seems to me that the most hopeful approach today is to describe the phenomena of language and of mental activity as accurately as possible, to try to develop an abstract theoretical apparatus that will as far as possible account for these phenomena and reveal the principles of their organization and functioning, without attempting, for the present, to relate the postulated mental structures and processes to any physiological mechanisms or to interpret mental function in terms of "physical causes." We can only leave open for the future the question of how these abstract structures and processes are realized or accounted for in some concrete terms, conceivably in terms that are not within the range of physical processes as presently understood—a conclusion that, if correct, should surprise no one. . . .

I think it is now possible to make some fairly definite proposals about the organization of human language and to put them to empirical test. The theory of transformational-generative grammar, as it is evolving along diverse and sometimes conflicting paths, has put forth such proposals; and there has been, in the past few years, some very productive and suggestive work that attempts to refine and reconstruct these formulations of the processes and structures that underlie human language.

The theory of grammar is concerned with the question, What is the nature of a person's knowledge of his language, the knowledge that enables him to make use of language in the normal, creative fashion? A person who knows a language has mastered a system of rules that assigns sound and meaning in a definite way for an infinite class of possible sentences. Each language thus consists (in part) of a certain pairing of sound and meaning over an infinite domain. Of course, the person who knows the language has no consciousness of having mastered these rules or of putting them to use, nor is there any reason to suppose that this knowledge of the rules of language can be brought to consciousness. Through introspection, a person may accumulate various kinds of evidence about the sound-meaning relation determined by the rules of the language that he has mastered; there is no reason to suppose that he can go much beyond this surface level of data so as to discover, through introspection, the underlying rules and principles that determine the relation of sound and meaning. Rather, to discover these rules and principles is a typical problem of science. We have a collection of data regarding sound-meaning correspondence, the form and interpretation of linguistic expressions, in various languages. We try to determine, for each language, a system of rules that will account for such data. More deeply, we try to establish the principles that govern the formation of such systems of rules for any human language.

The system of rules that specifies the sound-meaning relation for a given language can be called the "grammar"—or, to use a more technical term, the "generative grammar"—of this language. To say that a grammar "generates" a certain set of structures is simply to say that it specifies this set in a precise way. In this sense, we may say that the grammar of a language generates an infinite set of "structural descriptions," each structural description being an abstract object of some sort that determines a particular sound, a particular meaning, and whatever formal properties and configurations serve to mediate the relation between sound and meaning. For example, the grammar of English generates structural descriptions for the sentences I am now speaking; or to take a simpler case for purposes of illustration, the grammar of English would generate a structural description for each of these sentences:

1. John is certain that Bill will leave.
2. John is certain to leave.

Each of us has mastered and internally represented a system of grammar that assigns structural descriptions to these sentences; we use this knowledge, totally without awareness or even the possibility of awareness, in producing these sentences or understanding them when they are produced by others. The structural descriptions include a phonetic representation of the sentences and a specification of their meaning. In the case of the cited examples 1 and 2, the structural descriptions must convey roughly the following information: They must indicate that in the case of 1, a given psychological state (namely, being certain that Bill will leave) is attributed to John; whereas in the case of 2, a given logical property (namely, the property of being certain) is attributed to the proposition that John will leave. Despite the superficial similarity of form of these two sentences, the structural descriptions generated by the grammar must indicate that their meanings are very different: One attributes a psychological state to John, the other attributes a logical property to an abstract proposition. The second sentence might be paraphrased in a very different form:

3. That John will leave is certain.

For the first there is no such paraphrase. In the paraphrase 3 the "logical form" of 2 is expressed more directly, one might say. The grammatical relations in 2 and 3 are very similar, despite the difference of surface form; the grammatical relations in 1 and 2 are very different, despite the similarity of surface form. Such facts as these provide the starting point for an investigation of the grammatical structure of English—and more generally, for the investigation of the general properties of human language.

To carry the discussion of properties of language further, let me introduce the term "surface structure" to refer to a representation of the phrases that constitute a linguistic expression and the categories to which these phrases belong. In sentence 1, the phrases of the surface structure include: "that Bill will leave," which is a full proposition; the noun phrases "Bill" and "John"; the verb phrases "will leave" and "is certain that Bill will leave," and so on. In sentence 2, the surface structure includes the verb phrases "to leave" and "is certain to leave"; but the surface structure of 2 includes no proposition of the form "John will leave," even though this proposition expresses part of the meaning of "John is certain to leave," and appears as a phrase in the surface structure of its paraphrase, "that John will leave is certain." In this sense, surface structure does not necessarily provide an accurate indication of the structures and relations that determine the meaning of a sentence; in the case of sentence 2, "John is certain to leave," the surface structure fails to indicate that the proposition "John will leave" expresses a part of the meaning of the sentence—although in the other two examples that I gave the surface structure comes rather close to indicating the semantically significant relations.

Continuing, let me introduce the further technical term "deep structure" to refer to a representation of the phrases that play a more central role in the semantic interpretation of a sentence. In the case of 1 and 3, the deep structure might not be very different from the surface structure. In the case of 2, the deep structure will be very different from the surface structure, in that it will include some such proposition as "John will leave" and the predicate "is certain" applied to this proposition, though nothing of the sort appears in the surface structure. In general, apart from the simplest examples, the surface structures of sentences are very different from their deep structures.

The grammar of English will generate, for each sentence, a deep structure, and will contain rules showing how this deep structure is related to a surface structure. The rules expressing the relation of deep and surface structure are called "grammatical transformations." Hence the term "transformational-generative grammar." In addition to rules defining deep structures, surface structures, and the relation between them, the grammar of English contains further rules that relate these "syntactic objects" (namely, paired deep and surface structures) to phonetic representations on the one hand, and to representations of meaning on the other. A person who has acquired knowledge of English has internalized these rules and makes use of them when he understands or produces the sentences just given as examples, and an indefinite range of others.

Evidence in support of this approach is provided by the observation that interesting properties of English sentences can be explained directly in terms of the deep structures assigned to them. Thus consider once again the two sentences 1 ("John is certain that Bill will leave") and 2 ("John is certain to leave"). Recall that in the case of the first, the deep structure and surface structure are virtually identical, whereas in the case of the second, they are very different. Observe also that in the case of the first, there is a corresponding nominal phrase, namely, "John's certainty that Bill will leave (surprised me)"; but in the case of the second, there is no corresponding nominal phrase. We cannot say "John's certainty to leave surprised me." The latter nominal phrase is intelligible, I suppose, but is not well formed in English. The speaker of English can easily make himself aware of this fact, though the reason for it will very likely escape him. This fact is a special case of a very general property of English: Namely, nominal phrases exist corresponding to sentences that are very close in surface form to deep structure, but not corresponding to such sentences that are remote in surface form from deep structure. Thus "John is certain that Bill will leave," being close in surface form to its deep structure, corresponds to the nominal phrase "John's certainty that Bill will leave"; but there is no such phrase as "John's certainty to leave" corresponding to "John is certain to leave," which is remote from its deep structure.

The notions of "closeness" and "remoteness" can be made quite precise. When we have made them precise, we have an explanation for the fact that nominalizations exist in certain cases but not in others—though were they to exist in these other cases, they would often be perfectly intelligible. The explanation turns on the notion of deep structure: In effect, it states that nominalizations must reflect the properties of deep structure. There are many examples that illustrate this phenomenon. What is important is the evidence it provides in support of the view that deep structures which are often quite abstract exist and play a central role in the grammatical processes that we use in producing and interpreting sentences. Such facts, then, support the hypothesis that deep structures of the sort postulated in transformational-generative grammar are real mental structures. These deep structures, along with the transformation rules that relate them to surface structure and the rules relating deep and surface structures to representations of sound and meaning, are the rules that have been mastered by the person who has learned a language. They constitute his knowledge of the language; they are put to use when he speaks and understands.

The examples I have given so far illustrate the role of deep structure in determining meaning, and show that even in very simple cases, the deep structure may be remote from the surface form. There is a great deal of evidence indicating that the phonetic form of a sentence is determined by its surface structure, by principles of an extremely interesting and intricate sort that I will not try to discuss here. From such evidence it is fair to conclude that surface structure determines phonetic form, and that the grammatical relations represented in deep structure are those that determine meaning. Furthermore, as already noted, there are certain grammatical processes, such as the process of nominalization, that can be stated only in terms of abstract deep structures.

The situation is complicated, however, by the fact that surface structure also plays a role in determining semantic interpretation.[3] The study of this question is one of the most controversial aspects

[3] I discuss this matter in some detail in "Deep Structure and Semantic Interpretation," in R. Jakobson, and S. Kawamoto, eds., *Studies in General and Oriental Linguistics*, commemorative volume for Shiro Hattori, TEC Corporation for Language and Educational Research, Tokyo, 1970.

of current work, and, in my opinion, likely to be one of the most fruitful. As an illustration, consider some of the properties of the present perfect aspect in English—for example, such sentences as "John has lived in Princeton." An interesting and rarely noted feature of this aspect is that in such cases it carries the presupposition that the subject is alive. Thus it is proper for me to say "I have lived in Princeton" but, knowing that Einstein is dead, I would not say "Einstein has lived in Princeton." Rather, I would say "Einstein lived in Princeton." (As always, there are complications, but this is accurate as a first approximation.) But now consider active and passive forms with present perfect aspect. Knowing that John is dead and Bill alive, I can say "Bill has often been visited by John," but not "John has often visited Bill"; rather, "John often visited Bill." I can say "I have been taught physics by Einstein" but not "Einstein has taught me physics"; rather, "Einstein taught me physics." In general, active and passive are synonymous and have essentially the same deep structures. But in these cases, active and passive forms differ in the presuppositions they express; put simply, the presupposition is that the person denoted by the surface subject is alive. In this respect, the surface structure contributes to the meaning of the sentence in that it is relevant to determining what is presupposed in the use of a sentence. . . .

The role of surface structure in determining meaning is illustrated once again by the phenomenon of pronominalization.[4] Thus if I say "Each of the men hates his brothers," the word "his" may refer to one of the men; but if I say "The men each hate his brothers," the word "his" must refer to some other person, not otherwise referred to in the sentence. However, the evidence is strong that "each of the men" and "the men each" derive from the same deep structure. Similarly, it has been noted that placement of stress plays an important role in determining pronominal reference. Consider the following discourse: "John washed the car; I was afraid someone *else* would do it." The sentence implies that I hoped that John would wash the car, and I'm happy that he did. But now consider the following: "John washed the car; I was *afraid* someone else would do it." With stress on "afraid," the sentence implies that I hoped that John would not wash the car. The reference of "someone else" is different in the two cases. There are many other examples that

[4] The examples that follow are due to Ray Dougherty, Adrian Akmajian, and Ray Jackendoff. See my article in Jakobson and Kawamoto, eds., *Studies in General and Oriental Linguistics*, for references.

illustrate the role of surface structure in determining pronominal reference.

To complicate matters still further, deep structure too plays a role in determining pronominal reference. Thus consider the sentence "John appeared to Bill to like him." Here, the pronoun "him" may refer to Bill but not John. Compare "John appealed to Bill to like him." Here, the pronoun may refer to John but not Bill. Thus we can say "John appealed to Mary to like him," but not "John appeared to Mary to like him," where "him" refers to "John"; on the other hand, we can say "John appeared to Mary to like her," but not "John appealed to Mary to like her," where "her" refers to Mary. Similarly, in "John appealed to Bill to like himself," the reflexive refers to Bill; but in "John appeared to Bill to like himself," it refers to John. These sentences are approximately the same in surface structure; it is the differences in deep structure that determine the pronominal reference.

Hence pronominal reference depends on both deep and surface structure. A person who knows English has mastered a system of rules which make use of properties of deep and surface structure in determining pronominal reference. Again, he cannot discover these rules by introspection. In fact, these rules are still unknown, though some of their properties are clear.

To summarize: The generative grammar of a language specifies an infinite set of structural descriptions, each of which contains a deep structure, a surface structure, a phonetic representation, a semantic representation, and other formal structures. The rules relating deep and surface structure—the so-called "grammatical transformations"—have been investigated in some detail, and are fairly well understood. The rules that relate surface structure and phonetic representation are also reasonably well understood (though I do not want to imply that the matter is beyond dispute; far from it). It seems that both deep and surface structure enter into the determination of meaning. Deep structure provides the grammatical relations of prediction, modification, and so on, that enter into the determination of meaning. On the other hand, it appears that matters of focus and presupposition, topic and comment, the scope of logical elements, and pronominal reference are determined, in part at least, by surface structure. The rules that relate syntactic structures to representations of meaning are not at all well understood. In fact, the notion "representation of meaning" or "semantic representation" is itself highly controversial. It is not clear at all that it is possible to distinguish sharply between the contribution of grammar to the determination of meaning, and the contribution of so-called "pragmatic considerations," questions of fact and belief and context of utterance. It is perhaps worth mentioning that rather similar questions can be raised about the notion "phonetic representation." Although the latter is one of the best established and least controversial notions of linguistic theory, we can, nevertheless, raise the question whether or not it is a legitimate abstraction, whether a deeper understanding of the use of language might not show that factors that go beyond grammatical structure enter into the determination of perceptual representations and physical form in an inextricable fashion, and cannot be separated, without distortion, from the formal rules that interpret surface structure as phonetic form.

So far, the study of language has progressed on the basis of a certain abstraction: Namely, we abstract away from conditions of use of language and consider formal structures and the formal operations that relate them. Among these formal structures are those of syntax, namely, deep and surface structures; and also the phonetic and semantic representations, which we take to be certain formal objects related to syntactic structures by certain well-defined operations. This process of abstraction is in no way illegitimate, but one must understand that it expresses a point of view, a hypothesis about the nature of mind, that is not a priori obvious. It expresses the working hypothesis that we can proceed with the study of "knowledge of language"—what is often called "linguistic competence"—in abstraction from the problems of how language is used. The working hypothesis is justified by the success that is achieved when it is adopted. A great deal has been learned about the mechanisms of language, and, I would say, about the nature of mind, on the basis of this hypothesis. But we must be aware that in part, at least, this approach to language is forced upon us by the fact that our concepts fail us when we try to study the use of language. We are reduced to platitudes, or to observations which, though perhaps quite interesting, do not lend themselves to systematic study by means of the intellectual tools presently available to us. On the other hand, we can bring to the study of formal structures and their relations a wealth of experience and understanding. It may be that at this point we are facing a problem of conflict between significance and feasibility, a conflict of the sort that I mentioned earlier in this paper. I do not believe that this is the case, but it is possible. I feel fairly confident that the abstraction to the study of formal mechanisms of language is appropriate; my confidence arises from the fact that many quite elegant results have been achieved on the basis of this abstraction. Still, caution is in order. It may be that the next great advance in the study of language will require the forging of new intellectual tools that permit us to bring into consideration a variety of questions that have been cast into the waste-bin of "pragmatics," so that we could proceed to study questions that we know how to formulate in an intelligible fashion.

As noted, I think that the abstraction to linguistic competence is legitimate. To go further, I believe that the inability of modern psychology to come to grips with the problems of human intelligence is in part, at least, a result of its unwillingness to undertake the study of abstract structures and mechanisms of mind. Notice that the approach to linguistic structure that I have been outlining has a highly traditional flavor to it. I think it is no distortion to say that this approach makes precise a point of view that was inherent in the very important work of the seventeenth- and eighteenth-century universal grammarians, and that was developed, in various ways, in rationalist and romantic philosophy of language and mind. The approach deviates in many ways from a more modern, and in my opinion quite erroneous conception that knowledge of language can be accounted for as a system of habits, or in terms of stimulus-response connections, principles of "analogy" and "generalization," and other notions that have been explored in twentieth-century linguistics and psychology, and that develop from traditional empiricist speculation. The fatal inadequacy of all such approaches, I believe, results from their unwillingness to undertake the abstract study of linguistic competence. Had the physical sciences limited themselves by similar methodological strictures, we would still be in the era of Babylonian astronomy.

One traditional concept that has reemerged in current work is that of "universal grammar," and I want to conclude by saying just a word about this topic. There are two kinds of evidence suggesting that deep-seated formal conditions are satisfied by the grammars of all languages. The first kind of evidence is provided by the study of a wide range of languages. In attempting to construct generative grammars for languages of widely varied kinds, investigators have repeatedly been led to rather similar assumptions as to the form and organization of such generative systems. But a more persuasive kind of evidence bearing on universal grammar is provided by the study of a single language. It may at first seem paradoxical that the intensive study of a single language should provide evidence regarding universal grammar, but a little thought about the matter shows that this is a very natural consequence.

To see this, consider the problem of determining the mental capacities that make language acquisition possible. If the study of grammar—of linguistic competence—involves an abstraction from language use, then the study of the mental capacities that make acquisition of grammar possible involves a further, second-order abstraction. I see no fault in this. We may formulate the problem of determining the intrinsic characteristics of a device of unknown properties that accepts as "input" the kind of data available to the child learning his first language, and produces as "output" the generative grammar of that language. The "output," in this case, is the internally represented grammar, mastery of which constitutes knowledge of the language. If we undertake to study the intrinsic structure of a language-acquisition device without dogma or prejudice, we arrive at conclusions which, though of course only tentative, still seem to me both significant and reasonably well-founded. We must attribute to this device enough structure so that the grammar can be constructed within the empirically given constraints of time and available data, and we must meet the empirical condition that different speakers of the same language, with somewhat different experience and training, nevertheless acquire grammars that are remarkably similar, as we can determine from the ease with which they communicate and the correspondences among them in the interpretation of new sentences. It is immediately obvious that the data available to the child is quite limited—the number of seconds in his lifetime is trivially small as compared with the range of sentences that he can immediately understand and can produce in the appropriate manner. Having some knowledge of the characteristics of the acquired grammars and the limitations on the available data, we can formulate quite reasonable and fairly strong empirical hypotheses regarding the internal structure of the language-acquisition device that constructs the postulated grammars from the given data. When we study this question in detail, we are, I believe, led to attribute to the device a very rich system of constraints on the form of a possible grammar; otherwise, it is impossible to explain how children come to construct grammars of the kind that seem empirically adequate under the given conditions of time and access to data. But if we assume, furthermore, that children are not genetically predisposed to learn one rather than another language, then the conclusions we reach regarding the language-acquisition device are conclusions regarding universal grammar. These conclusions can be falsified by showing that they fail to account for the construction of grammars of other languages, for example. And these conclusions are further verified if they serve to explain facts about other languages. This line of argument seems to me very reasonable in a general way, and when pursued in detail it leads us to strong empirical hypotheses concerning universal grammar, even from the study of a particular language.

I have discussed an approach to the study of language that takes this study to be a branch of theoretical human psychology. Its goal is to exhibit and clarify the mental capacities that make it possible for a human to learn and use a language. As far as we know, these capacities are unique to man, and have no significant analogue in any other organism. If the conclusions of this research are anywhere near correct, then humans must be endowed with a very rich and explicit set of mental attributes that determine a specific form of language on the basis of very slight and rather degenerate data. Furthermore, they make use of the mentally represented language in a highly creative way, constrained by its rules but free to express new thoughts that relate to past experience or present sensations only in a remote and abstract fashion. If this is correct, there is no hope in the study of the "control" of human behavior by stimulus conditions, schedules of reinforcement, establishment of habit structures, patterns of behavior, and so on. Of course, one can design a restricted environment in which such control and such patterns can be demonstrated, but there is no reason to suppose that any more is learned about the range of human potentialities by such methods than would be learned by observing humans in a prison or an army—or in many a schoolroom. The essential properties of the human mind will always escape such investigation. And if I can be pardoned a final "nonprofessional" comment, I am very happy with this outcome.

VIII. EMPIRICISM AND THE ILLUSION OF KNOWLEDGE

15. David Hume

EDITOR'S INTRODUCTION

In Chapter 1, a contrast was made between what William James called tender-minded and tough-minded philosophers. Of the thinkers examined thus far, Plato, Augustine, and Descartes could be classified as tender-minded (rationalists), while Aristotle and Aquinas could be considered tough-minded (empiricists). On an extended scale, however, even Aristotle and Aquinas would be considered tender-minded. It is not until the British philosophers—Bacon, Hobbes, Locke, Berkeley, and Hume—that empiricism receives its most thorough test. David Hume, especially, took the basic assumption of empiricism—that all factual knowledge is based on sense experience—and pursued it to its logical conclusions. This chapter is devoted to two aspects of Hume's thought, namely, his analysis of causation and of the self.

As a preface to Hume's analysis of causation, let us review briefly the vicissitudes that the notion of causality underwent since the time of Aristotle. It will be recalled that Aristotle (Chapt. 5) distinguished among formal, final, and efficient causes. The way each of these was conceived underwent considerable transformation during the course of the Scientific Revolution. At the hands of Copernicus and Kepler, for example, the notion of formal cause became a mystical faith in the mathematical nature of the universe. This sentiment was expressed by Kepler: "I feel carried away and possessed by an unutterable rapture over the divine spectacle of the heavenly harmony."[1] The explanation of, say, planetary motion meant for Kepler the discovery of underlying mathematical relationships or "harmonies." Although this Platonic point of view was an important force in shaping the Scientific Revolution, it

[1] Cited by H. Kearney, *Science and change: 1500-1700.* New York: McGraw-Hill, 1971, p. 138.

ultimately gave way to a more "realistic" emphasis on mathematics as an intellectual tool or device, not as an ultimate explanatory principle with mystical overtones.

The notion of final cause also was influential in the work of some scientists during the Scientific Revolution (e.g., the physiologist Harvey). For the most part, however, Aristotelian philosophy with its emphasis on teleology was part of the orthodoxy, the overthrow of which made the Scientific Revolution a revolution. And in the new orthodoxy, there was no room for such things as purposes and goals. At best, these were aspects of Descartes' *res cogitans*; at worst, they were mere illusions in a completely mechanical universe.

In short, during the course of the Scientific Revolution, formal and final causes came to be viewed as mental or subjective phenomena, not as real constituents of the physical universe. Yet, for most theorists of the period the very possibility of science seemed to rest on the supposition that every event has a cause. The only possibility that remained, then, was the efficient cause (disregarding for the moment the notion of material cause). Efficient causes, at least, were considered to be real and "out there," an essential part of the mechanical universe. But what allows one object to effect a change in another? Is it some power or force inherent in the first?

These are the questions Hume asks in the first several selections reprinted in this chapter. According to Hume, there are three conditions for inferring that event A caused event B: (1) A and B are contiguous; (2) A is antecedent to B; and (3) any event similar to A is contiguous and antecedent to any event similar to B. But condition (3) can never be known with certainty, Hume argued, for it can always be contradicted at some future time. Nevertheless, when events obeying conditions (1) and (2) are so related that they give rise to the *belief* that condition (3) is also true, then we may speak of "a natural cause" between them. The specification of the conditions that lead to belief in (3) is a psychological problem that Hume did not pursue, except to state that it is a belief based on repeated past occurrences of (1) and (2). That is, if A and B have always occurred together in the past in the requisite manner, we come to *feel* that there is a necessary connection between them—the "necessity" here being psychological and not logical.

Hume's analysis of causation is deceptively simple, but its implications are profound. One implication, for example, is an extreme skepticism regarding knowledge of matters of fact (i.e., empirical as opposed to logical or mathematical truths). According to Hume, all reasoning concerning matters of fact is based on the relation of cause and effect. But if that is true, and if Hume's analysis of causation is correct, then there is never any possibility of gaining more than a "natural belief," a feeling of psychological certainty, about empirical facts. The search for absolute truths about the world that so motivated thinkers such as Plato, Augustine, and Descartes is misguided and doomed to failure. Scientific laws can never be more than (to use Plato's term) opinions, justifiable, if at all, on pragmatic grounds. Or, stated differently, scientific laws are not to be judged on the basis of truth or falsity, but by their usefulness.

Now let us turn to Hume's analysis of the self or personal identity. By way of introduction, it may be pointed out that the concept of self is an instance of the general class of concepts known as universals. A universal refers to that which can be predicated of many particular instances of a more general phenomenon or class of objects. For example, the concept *dog* is applicable to a great number of individual animals. In the case of the concept of self, the particular instances are the anatomical structures, behaviors, and experiences that collectively and over time an individual labels as *I* or *me*. Thus, I am the same self that nearly 40 years ago was a screeching, crying infant, and who 40 years from now will be (if at all) an old man of quite different structure and habits. What thread, if any, ties the various manifestations of an individual together, from infancy to old age, allowing each to be referred to as an instance of the same self?

The problem of universals is one of the most vexing in the history of philosophy. Consider for a moment the concept of dog, which is a simpler case than the concept of self. To what does the term *dog* refer? One answer is that *dog* refers to the essence of all dogs, i.e., that which makes a dog a dog and not a cat or a skunk. But this does not get us very far, for we must then ask: What is an essence?

There are, roughly speaking, three possible answers to this question: (1) essences have a real existence or actuality separable from the particular objects of which they are predicated; (2) essences are actual in their own right but are not separable from particular objects; and (3) essences have no actuality in their own right, but are merely names for observable likenesses among particular objects. Plato's theory of Forms is representative of the first type of answer; Aristotle's conception of matter as potentiality and form as actuality exemplifies the second type of answer; Hume illustrates the third type of answer, namely, that universals exist in name only. This latter position is known as *nominalism*. It follows from a consistently applied empiricism: if all knowledge is derived from sense experience, then all knowledge must ultimately be of particulars. For example, no one has ever seen or patted "dogginess" per se, only particular dogs such as old Rover. Similarly, when Hume attempted to observe a substantive self by looking inward, he saw nothing but particular sensations and feelings. And since Hume could not detect anything that would correspond to the "self" per se, he concluded that the belief in personal identity was philosophically untenable.

Why, then, it might be asked, do people generally believe in a continuous thread that ties the experiences of their lives together? This belief, Hume argued, is due to a kind of mental laziness. Strictly speaking, change destroys identity; and since the experiences (as well as the bodily characteristics) of a person continuously change with time, there can be no such thing as personal identity. This fact is overlooked by most people because they confuse the idea of an object that remains invariant over time with the idea of a succession of closely related but different objects. The latter is what actually characterizes a person. However, when the confusion is pointed out, the force of custom or habit is so strong that an underlying substratum (e.g., soul) is *invented* in order to lend substance to the notion of personal identity. But this is a vacuous solution, for no such substratum can be empirically observed.

As in his analysis of causation, Hume offers no alternative solution to the confusion he believes he has exposed. Philosophical analyses can raise skeptical doubts concerning human understanding, but it cannot wholly replace the "natural beliefs" supported by custom.

Skepticism Regarding Matters of Fact

SKEPTICAL DOUBTS CONCERNING THE
OPERATIONS OF THE UNDERSTANDING

All the objects of human reason or enquiry may naturally be divided into two kinds, to wit, *Relations of Ideas*, and *Matters of Fact*. Of the first kind are the sciences of Geometry, Algebra, and Arithmetic; and in short, every affirmation which is either intuitively or demonstratively certain. *That the square of the hypothenuse is equal to the square of the two sides*, is a proposition which expresses a relation between these figures. *That three times five is equal to the half of thirty*, expresses a relation between these numbers. Propositions of this kind are discoverable by the mere operation of thought, without dependence on what is anywhere existent in the universe. Though there never were a circle or triangle in nature, the truths demonstrated by Euclid would for ever retain their certainty and evidence.

Matters of fact, which are the second objects of human reason, are not ascertained in the same manner; nor is our evidence of their truth, however great, of a like nature with the foregoing. The contrary of every matter of fact is still possible; because it can never imply a contradiction, and is conceived by the mind with the same facility and distinctness, as if ever so conformable to reality. *That the sun will not rise to-morrow* is no less intelligible a proposition, and implies no more contradiction than the affirmation, *that it will rise*. We should in vain, therefore, attempt to demonstrate its falsehood. Were it demonstratively false, it would imply a contradiction, and could never be distinctly conceived by the mind.

It may, therefore, be a subject worthy of curiosity, to enquire what is the nature of that evidence which assures us of any real existence and matter of fact, beyond the present testimony of our senses, or the records of our memory. This part of philosophy, it is observable, has been little cultivated, either by the ancients or moderns; and therefore our doubts and errors, in the prosecution of so important an enquiry, may be the more excusable; while we march through such difficult paths without any guide or direction. They may even prove useful, by exciting curiosity, and destroying

D. Hume, *Enquiries concerning human understanding.* (L. A. Selby-Bigge, Ed.,) 3rd ed., with notes and text revised by P. H. Nidditch, 1975, by permission of the Oxford University Press, Oxford.

that implicit faith and security, which is the bane of all reasoning and free enquiry. The discovery of defects in the common philosophy, if any such there be, will not, I presume, be a discouragement, but rather an incitement, as is usual, to attempt something more full and satisfactory than has yet been proposed to the public.

All reasonings concerning matter of fact seem to be founded on the relation of *Cause and Effect*. By means of that relation alone we can go beyond the evidence of our memory and senses. If you were to ask a man, why he believes any matter of fact, which is absent; for instance, that his friend is in the country, or in France; he would give you a reason; and this reason would be some other fact; as a letter received from him, or the knowledge of his former resolutions and promises. A man finding a watch or any other machine in a desert island, would conclude that there had once been men in that island. All our reasonings concerning fact are of the same nature. And here it is constantly supposed that there is a connexion between the present fact and that which is inferred from it. Were there nothing to bind them together, the inference would be entirely precarious. The hearing of an articulate voice and rational discourse in the dark assures us of the presence of some person: Why? because these are the effects of the human make and fabric, and closely connected with it. If we anatomize all the other reasonings of this nature, we shall find that they are founded on the relation of cause and effect, and that this relation is either near or remote, direct or collateral. Heat and light are collateral effects of fire, and the one effect may justly be inferred from the other.

If we would satisfy ourselves, therefore, concerning the nature of that evidence, which assures us of matters of fact, we must enquire how we arrive at the knowldege of cause and effect.

I shall venture to affirm, as a general proposition, which admits of no exception, that the knowledge of this relation is not, in any instance, attained by reasonings *a priori*; but arises entirely from experience, when we find that any particular objects are constantly conjoined with each other. Let an object be presented to a man of ever so strong natural reason and abilities; if that object be entirely new to him, he will not be able, by the most accurate examination of its sensible qualities, to discover any of its causes or effects. Adam, though his rational faculties be supposed, at the very first, entirely perfect, could not have inferred from the fluidity and transparency of water that it would suffocate him, or from the light and warmth of fire that it would consume him. No object ever discovers, by the qualities which appear to the senses, either the causes which produced it, or the effects which will arise from it; nor can our reason, unassisted by experience, ever draw any inference concerning real existence and matter of fact.

This proposition, *that causes and effects are discoverable, not by reason but by experience*, will readily be admitted with regard to such objects, as we remember to have once been altogether unknown to us; since we must be conscious of the utter inability, which we then lay under, of foretelling what would arise from them. Present two smooth pieces of marble to a man who has no tincture of natural philosophy; he will never discover that they will adhere together in such a manner as to require great force to separate them in a direct line, while they make so small a resistance to a lateral pressure. Such events, as bear little analogy to the common course of nature, are also readily confessed to be known only by experience; nor does any man imagine that the explosion of gunpowder, or the attraction of a loadstone, could ever be discovered by arguments *a priori*. In like manner, when an effect is supposed to depend upon an intricate machinery or secret structure of parts, we make no difficulty in attributing all our knowledge of it to experience. Who will assert that he can give the ultimate reason, why milk or bread is proper nourishment for a man, not for a lion or a tiger?

But the same truth may not appear, at first sight, to have the same evidence with regard to events, which have become familiar to us from our first appearance in the world, which bear a close analogy to the whole course of nature, and which are supposed to depend on the simple qualities of objects, without any secret structure of parts. We are apt to imagine that we could discover these effects by the mere operation of our reason, without experience. We fancy, that were we brought on a sudden into this world, we could at first have inferred that one Billiard-ball would communicate motion to another upon impulse; and that we needed not to have waited for the event, in order to pronounce with certainty concerning it. Such is the influence of custom, that, where it is strongest, it not only covers our natural ignorance, but even conceals itself, and seems not to take place, merely because it is found in the highest degree.

But to convince us that all the laws of nature, and all the operations of bodies without exception, are known only by experience, the following reflections may, perhaps, suffice. Were any object presented to us, and were we required to pronounce concerning the effect, which will result from it, without consulting past observation; after what manner, I beseech you, must the mind proceed in this operation? It must invent or imagine some event, which it ascribes to the object as its effect; and it is plain that this invention must be entirely arbitrary. The mind can never possibly find the effect in the supposed cause, by the most accurate scrutiny and examination. For the effect is totally different from the cause, and consequently can never be discovered in it. Motion in the second Billiard-ball is a quite distinct event from motion in the first; nor is there anything in the one to suggest the smallest hint of the other. A stone or piece of metal raised into the air, and left without any support, immediately falls: but to consider the matter *a priori*, is there anything we discover in this situation which can beget the idea of a downward, rather than an upward, or any other motion, in the stone or metal?

And as the first imagination or invention of a particular effect, in all natural operations, is arbitrary, where we consult not experience; so must we also esteem the supposed tie or connexion between the cause and effect, which binds them together, and renders it impossible that any other effect could result from the operation of that cause. When I see, for instance, a Billiard-ball moving in a straight line towards another; even suppose motion in the second ball should by accident be suggested to me, as the result of their contact or impulse; may I not conceive, that a hundred different events might as well follow from that cause? May not both these balls remain at absolute rest? May not the first ball return in a straight line, or leap off from the second in any line or direction? All these suppositions are consistent and conceivable. Why then should we give the preference to one, which is no more consistent or conceivable than the rest? All our reasonings *a priori* will never be able to show us any foundation for this preference. . . .

OF THE IDEA OF NECESSARY CONNEXION

The great advantage of the mathematical sciences above the moral consists in this, that the ideas of the former, being sensible, are always clear and determinate, the smallest distinction between them is immediately perceptible, and the same terms are still expressive of the same ideas, without ambiguity or variation. An oval is never mistaken for a circle, nor an hyperbola for an ellipsis. The isosceles and scalenum are distinguished by boundaries more exact than vice and virtue, right and wrong. If any term be defined in geometry, the mind readily, of itself, substitutes, on all occasions, the definition for the term defined: Or even when no definition is employed, the object itself may be presented to the senses, and by that means be steadily and clearly apprehended. But the finer sentiments of the mind, the operations of the understanding, the various agitations of the passions, though really in themselves distinct, easily escape us, when surveyed by reflection; nor is it in our power to recall the original object, as often as we have occasion to contemplate it. Ambiguity, by this means, is gradually introduced into our reasonings: Similar objects are readily taken to be the same: And the conclusion becomes at last very wide of the premises. . . .

There are no ideas, which occur in metaphysics, more obscure and uncertain, than those of *power, force, energy* or *necessary connexion*, of which it is every moment necessary for us to treat in all our disquisitions. We shall, therefore, endeavour, in this section, to fix, if possible, the precise meaning of these terms, and thereby remove some part of that obscurity, which is so much complained of in this species of philosophy.

It seems a proposition, which will not admit of much dispute, that all our ideas are nothing but copies of our impressions, or, in other words, that it is impossible for us to *think* of any thing, which we have not antecedently *felt*, either by our external or internal senses. . . .

To be fully acquainted, therefore, with the idea of power or necessary connexion, let us examine its impression; and in order to find the impression with greater certainty, let us search for it in all the sources, from which it may possibly be derived.

When we look about us towards external objects, and consider the operation of causes, we are never able, in a single instance, to discover any power or necessary connexion; any quality, which binds the effect to the cause, and renders the one an infallible consequence of the other. We only find, that the one does actually, in fact, follow the other. The impulse of one billiard-ball is attended with motion in the second. This is the whole that appears to the *outward* senses. The mind feels no sentiment or *inward* impression from this succession of objects: Consequently, there is not, in any single, particular instance of cause and effect, any thing which can suggest the idea of power or necessary connexion.

From the first appearance of an object, we never can conjecture what effect will result from it. But were the power or energy of any cause discoverable by the mind, we could foresee the effect, even without experience; and might, at first, pronounce with certainty concerning it, by mere dint of thought and reasoning.

In reality, there is no part of matter, that does ever, by its sensible qualities, discover any power or energy, or give us ground to imagine, that it could produce any thing, or be followed by any other object, which we could denominate its effect. Solidity, extension, motion; these qualities are all complete in themselves, and never point out any other event which may result from them. The scenes of the universe are continually shifting, and one object follows another in an uninterrupted succession; but the power of force, which actuates the whole machine, is entirely concealed from us, and never discovers itself in any of the sensible qualities of body. We know, that, in fact, heat is a constant attendant of flame; but what is the connexion between them, we have no room so much as to conjecture or imagine. It is impossible, therefore, that the idea of power can be derived from the contemplation of bodies, in single instances of their operation; because no bodies ever discover any power, which can be the original of this ideal.[1]

Since, therefore, external objects as they appear to the senses, give us no idea of power or necessary connexion, by their operation in particular instances, let us see, whether this idea be derived from reflection on the operations of our own minds, and be copied from any internal impression. It may be said, that we are every moment conscious of internal power; while we feel, that, by the simple command of our will, we can move the organs of our body, or direct the faculties of our mind. An act of volition produces motion in our limbs, or raises a new idea in our imagination. This influence of the will we know by consciousness. Hence we acquire the idea of power or energy; and are certain, that we ourselves and all other intelligent beings are possessed of power. This idea, then, is an idea of reflection, since it arises from reflecting on the operations of our own mind, and on the command which is exercised by will, both over the organs of the body and faculties of the soul.

We shall proceed to examine this pretension; and first with regard to the influence of volition over the organs of the body. This influence, we may observe, is a fact, which, like all other natural events, can be known only by experience, and can never be foreseen from any apparent energy or power in the cause, which connects it with the effect, and renders the one an infallible consequence of the other. The motion of our body follows upon the command of our will. Of this we are every moment conscious.

[1] Mr. Locke, in his chapter of power, says that, finding from experience, that there are several new productions in nature, and concluding that there must somewhere be a power capable of producing them, we arrive at last by this reasoning at the idea of power. But no reasoning can ever give us a new, original, simple idea; as this philosopher himself confesses. This, therefore, can never be the origin of that idea.

But the means, by which this is effected; the energy, by which the will performs so extraordinary an operation; of this we are so far from being immediately conscious, that it must for ever escape our most diligent enquiry.

For *first*; is there any principle in all nature more mysterious than the union of soul with body; by which a supposed spiritual substance acquires such an influence over a material one, that the most refined thought is able to actuate the grossest matter? Were we empowered, by a secret wish, to remove mountains, or control the planets in their orbit; this extensive authority would not be more extraordinary, nor more beyond our comprehension. But if by consciousness we perceived any power or energy in the will, we must know this power; we must know its connexion with the effect; we must know the secret union of soul and body, and the nature of both these substances; by which the one is able to operate, in so many instances, upon the other.

Secondly, We are not able to move all the organs of the body with a like authority; though we cannot assign any reason besides experience, for so remarkable a difference between one and the other. Why has the will an influence over the tongue and fingers, not over the heart or liver? This question would never embarrass us, were we conscious of a power in the former case, not in the latter. We should then perceive, independent of experience, why the authority of will over the organs of the body is circumscribed within such particular limits. Being in that case fully acquainted with the power or force, by which it operates, we should also know, why its influence reaches precisely to such boundaries and no farther.

A man, suddenly struck with palsy in the leg or arm, or who had newly lost those members, frequently endeavours, at first to move them, and employ them in their ususal offices. Here he is as much conscious of power to command such limbs, as a man in perfect health is conscious of power to actuate any member which remains in its natural state and condition. But consciousness never deceives. Consequently, neither in the one case nor in the other, are we ever conscious of any power. We learn the influence of our will from experience alone. And experience only teaches us, how one event constantly follows another; without instructing us in the secret connexion, which binds them together, and renders them inseparable.

Thirdly, We learn from anatomy, that the immediate object of power in voluntary motion, is not the member itself which is moved, but certain muscles, and nerves, and animal spirits, and, perhaps, something still more minute and more unknown, through which the motion is successively propagated, ere it reach the member itself whose motion is the immediate object of volition. Can there be a more certain proof, that the power, by which this whole operation is performed, so far from being directly and fully known by an inward sentiment or consciousness, is, to the last degree mysterious and unintelligible? Here the mind wills a certain event: Immediately another event, unknown to ourselves, and totally different from the one intended, is produced: This event produces another, equally unknown: Till at last, through a long succession, the desired event is produced. But if the original power were felt, it must be known: Were it known, its effect also must be known; since all power is relative to its effect. And *vice versa*, if the effect be not known, the power cannot be known nor felt. How indeed can we be conscious of a power to move our limbs, when we have no such power; but only that to move certain animal spirits, which, though they produce at last the motion of our limbs, yet operate in such a manner as is wholly beyond our comprehension?

We may, therefore, conclude from the whole, I hope, without any temerity, though with assurance; that our idea of power is not copied from any sentiment or consciousness of power within ourselves, when we give rise to animal motion, or apply our limbs to their proper use and office. That their motion follows the command of the will is a matter of common experience, like other natural events: But the power or energy by which this is effected, like that in other natural events, is unknown and inconceivable.[2] . . .

But to hasten to a conclusion of this argument, which is already drawn out to too great a length: We have sought in vain for an idea of power or necessary connexion in all the sources from which we could suppose it to be derived. It appears that, in single instances of the operation of bodies, we never can, by our

---

[2] It may be pretended, that the resistance which we meet with in bodies, obliging us frequently to exert our force, and call up all our power, this gives us the idea of force and power. This is *nisus*, or strong endeavour, of which we are conscious, that is the original impression from which this idea is copied. But, first, we attribute power to a vast number of objects, where we never can suppose this resistance or exertion of force to take place; to the Supreme Being, who never meets with any resistance; to the mind in its command over its ideas and limbs, in common thinking and motion, where the effect follows immediately upon the will, without any exertion or summoning up of force; to inanimate matter, which is not capable of this sentiment. *Secondly*, This sentiment of an endeavour to overcome resistance has no known connexion with any event: What follows it, we know by experience; but could not know it *a priori*. It must, however, be confessed, that the animal *nisus*, which we experience, though it can afford no accurate precise idea of power, enters very much into that vulgar, inaccurate idea, which is formed of it.

utmost scrutiny, discover any thing but one event following another, without being able to comprehend any force or power by which the cause operates, or any connexion between it and its supposed effect. The same difficulty occurs in contemplating the operations of mind on body—where we observe the motion of the latter to follow upon the volition of the former, but are not able to observe or conceive the tie which binds together the motion and volition, or the energy by which the mind produces this effect. The authority of the will over its own faculties and ideas is not a whit more comprehensible: So that, upon the whole, there appears not, throughout all nature, any one instance of connexion which is conceivable by us. All events seem entirely loose and separate. One event follows another; but we never can observe any tie between them. They seem *conjoined*, but never *connected*. And as we can have no idea of any thing which never appeared to our outward sense or inward sentiment, the necessary conclusion *seems* to be that we have no idea of connexion or power at all, and that these words are absolutely without any meaning, when employed either in philosophical reasonings or common life.

But there still remains one method of avoiding this conclusion, and one source which we have not yet examined. When any natural object or event is presented, it is impossible for us, by any sagacity or penetration, to discover, or even conjecture, without experience, what event will result from it, or to carry our foresight beyond that object which is immediately present to the memory and senses. Even after one instance or experiment where we have observed a particular event to follow upon another, we are not entitled to form a general rule, or foretell what will happen in like cases; it being justly esteemed in unpardonable temerity to judge of the whole course of nature from one single experiment, however accurate or certain. But when one particular species of event has always, in all instances, been conjoined with another, we make no longer any scruple of foretelling one upon the appearance of the other, and of employing that reasoning, which can alone assure us of any matter of fact or existence. We then call the one object, *Cause*; the other, *Effect*. We suppose that there is some connexion between them; some power in the one, by which it infallibly produces the other, and operates with the greatest certainty and strongest necessity.

It appears, then, that this idea of a necessary connexion among events arises from a number of similar instances which occur of the constant conjunction of these events; nor can that idea ever be suggested by any one of these instances, surveyed in all possible lights and positions. But there is nothing in a number of instances, different from every single instance, which is supposed to be exactly similar; except only, that after a repetition of similar instances, the mind is carried by habit, upon the appearance of one event, to expect its usual attendant, and to believe that it will exist. This connexion, therefore, which we *feel* in the mind, this customary transition of the imagination from one object to its usual attendant, is the sentiment or impression from which we form the idea of power or necessary connexion. Nothing farther is in the case. Contemplate the subject on all sides; you will never find any other origin of that idea. This is the sole difference between one instance, from which we can never receive the idea of connexion, and a number of similar instances, by which it is suggested. The first time a man saw the communication of motion by impulse, as by the shock of two billiard balls, he could not pronounce that the one event was *connected*: but only that it was *conjoined* with the other. After he has observed several instances of this nature, he then pronounces them to be *connected*. What alteration has happened to give rise to this new idea of *connexion*? Nothing but that he now *feels* these events to be *connected* in his imagination, and can readily foretell the existence of one from the appearance of the other. When we say, therefore, that one object is connected with another, we mean only that they have acquired a connexion in our thought, and give rise to this inference, by which they become proofs of each other's existence: A conclusion which is somewhat extraordinary, but which seems founded on sufficient evidence. Nor will its evidence be weakened by any general diffidence of the understanding, or sceptical suspicion concerning every conclusion which is new and extraordinary. No conclusions can be more agreeable to scepticism than such as make discoveries concerning the weakness and narrow limits of human reason and capacity.

And what stronger instance can be produced of the surprising ignorance and weakness of the understanding than the present? For surely, if there be any relation among objects which it imports to us to know perfectly, it is that of cause and effect. On this are founded all our reasonings concerning matter of fact or existence. By means of it alone we attain any assurance concerning objects which are removed from the present testimony of our memory and senses. The only immediate utility of all sciences, is to teach us, how to control and regulate future events by their causes. Our thoughts and enquiries are, therefore, every moment, employed about this relation: Yet so imperfect are the ideas which we form concerning it, that it is impossible to give any just definition of cause, except what is drawn from something extraneous and foreign to it. Similar objects are always conjoined with similar. Of this we have experience. Suitably to this experience, therefore, we may define a cause to be *an object, followed by another, and where all the objects similar to the first are followed by objects similar to the second.* Or in other words *where, if the first object had not been, the second never had existed.* The appearance of a cause always conveys the mind, by a customary transition, to the idea of the effect. Of this also we have experience. We may, therefore, suitably to this experience, form another definition of cause, and call it, *an object followed by another, and whose appearance always conveys the thought to that other.* But though both these definitions be drawn from circumstances foreign to the cause, we cannot remedy this inconvenience, or attain any more perfect definition, which may point out that circumstance in the cause, which gives it a connexion with its effect. We have no idea of this connexion, nor even any distinct notion what it is we desire to know, when we endeavour at a conception of it. We say, for instance, that the vibration of this string is the cause of this particular sound. But what do we mean by that affirmation? We either mean *that this vibration is followed by this sound, and that all similar vibrations have been followed by similar sounds*: Or, *that this vibration is followed by this sound, and that upon the appearance of one the mind anticipates the senses, and forms immediately an idea of the other.* We may consider the relation of cause and effect in either of these two lights; but beyond these, we have no idea of it. . . .

Skepticism Regarding Personal Identity

OF PERSONAL IDENTITY

There are some philosophers, who imagine we are every moment intimately conscious of what we call our *Self*; that we feel its existence and its continuance in existence; and are certain, beyond the evidence of a demonstration, both of its perfect identity and simplicity. The strongest sensation, the most violent

D. Hume, Of personal identity. In L. A. Selby-Bigge (Ed.), *Treatise of human nature* Book 1, *Of the understanding.* Oxford: Clarendon Press, 1888, by permission of Oxford University Press, Oxford.

passion, say they, instead of distracting us from this view, only fix it the more intensely, and make us consider their influence on *self* either by their pain or pleasure. To attempt a farther proof of this were to weaken its evidence; since no proof can be deriv'd from any fact, of which we are so intimately conscious; nor is there any thing, of which we can be certain, if we doubt of this.

Unluckily all these positive assertions are contrary to that very experience, which is pleaded for them, nor have we any idea of *self*, after the manner it is here explain'd. For from what impression cou'd this idea be deriv'd? This question 'tis impossible to answer without a manifest contradiction and absurdity; and yet 'tis a question, which must necessarily be answer'd, if we wou'd have the idea of self pass for clear and intelligible. It must be some one impression, that gives rise to every real idea. But self or person is not any one impression, but that to which our several impressions and ideas are suppos'd to have a reference. If any impression gives rise to the idea of self, that impression must continue invariably the same, thro' the whole course of our lives; since self is suppos'd to exist after that manner. But there is no impression constant and invariable. Pain and pleasure, grief and joy, passions and sensations succeed each other, and never all exist at the same time. It cannot, therefore, be from any of these impressions, or from any other, that the idea of self is deriv'd; and consequently there is no such idea.

But farther, what must become of all our particular perceptions upon this hypothesis? All these are different, and distinguishable, and separable from each other, and may be separately consider'd, and may exist separately, and have no need of any thing to support their existence. After what manner, therefore, do they belong to self; and how are they connected with it? For my part, when I enter most intimately into what I call *myself*, I always stumble on some particular perception or other, of heat or cold, light or shade, love or hatred, pain or pleasure. I never can catch *myself* at any time without a perception, and never can observe any thing but the perception. When my perceptions are remov'd for any time, as by sound sleep; so long am I insensible of *myself*, and may truly be said not to exist. And were all my perceptions remov'd by death, and cou'd I neither think, nor feel, nor see, nor love, nor hate after the dissolution of my body, I shou'd be entirely annihilated, nor do I conceive what is farther requisite to make me a perfect non-entity. If any one upon serious and unprejudic'd reflection, thinks he has a different notion of *himself*, I must confess I can reason no longer with him. All I can allow him is, that he may be in the right as well as I, and that we are essentially different in this particular. He may, perhaps, perceive something simple and continu'd, which he calls *himself*; tho' I am certain there is no such principle in me.

But setting aside some metaphysicians of this kind, I may venture to affirm of the rest of mankind, that they are nothing but a bundle or collection of different perceptions, which succeed each other with an inconceivable rapidity, and are in a perpetual flux and movement. Our eyes cannot turn in their sockets without varying our perceptions. Our thought is still more variable than our sight; and all our other senses and faculties contribute to this change; nor is there any single power of the soul, which remains unalterably the same, perhaps for one moment. The mind is a kind of theatre, where several perceptions successively make their appearance; pass, re-pass, glide away, and mingle in an infinite variety of postures and situations. There is properly no *simplicity* in it at one time, nor *identity* in different; whatever natural propension we may have to imagine that simplicity and identity. The comparison of the theatre must not mislead us. They are the successive perceptions only, that constitute the mind; nor have we the most distant notion of the place, where these scenes are represented, or of the materials, of which it is compos'd.

What then gives us so great a propension to ascribe an identity to these successive perceptions, and to suppose ourselves possest of an invariable and uninterrupted existence thro' the whole course of our lives? In order to answer this question, we must distinguish betwixt personal identity, as it regards our thought or imagination, and as it regards our passions or the concern we take in ourselves. The first is our present subject; and to explain it perfectly we must take the matter pretty deep, and account for that identity, which we attribute to plants and animals; there being a great analogy betwixt it, and the identity of a self or person.

We have a distinct idea of an object, that remains invariable and uninterrupted thro' a suppos'd variation of time; and this idea we call that of *identity* or *sameness*. We have also a distinct idea of several different objects existing in succession, and connected together by a close relation; and this to an accurate view affords as perfect a notion of *diversity*, as if there was no manner of relation among the objects. But tho' these two ideas of identity, and a succession of related objects be in themselves perfectly distinct, and even contrary, yet 'tis certain, that in our common way of thinking they are generally confounded with each other. That action of the imagination, by which we consider the uninterrupted and invariable object, and that by which we reflect on the succession of related objects, are almost the same to the feeling, nor is there much more effort of thought requir'd in the latter case than in the former. The relation facilitates the transition of the mind from one object to another, and renders its passage as smooth as if it contemplated one continu'd object. This resemblance is the cause of the confusion and mistake, and makes us substitute the notion of identity, instead of that of related objects. However at one instant we may consider the related succession as variable or interrupted, we are sure the next to ascribe to it a perfect identity, and regard it as invariable and uninterrupted. Our propensity to this mistake is so great from the resemblance above-mention'd, that we fall into it before we are aware; and tho' we incessantly correct ourselves by reflection, and return to a more accurate method of thinking, yet we cannot long sustain our philosophy, or take off this bias from the imagination. Our last resource is to yield to it, and boldly assert that these different related objects are in effect the same, however interrupted and variable. In order to justify to ourselves this absurdity, we often feign some new and unintelligible principle, that connects the objects together, and prevents their interruption or variation. Thus we feign the continu'd existence of the perceptions of our senses, to remove the interruption; and run into the notion of a *soul*, and *self*, and *substance*, to disguise the variation. But we may farther observe, that where we do not give rise to such a fiction, our propension to confound identity with relation is so great, that we are apt to imagine something unknown and mysterious, connecting the parts, beside their relation; and this I take to be the case with regard to the identity we ascribe to plants and vegetables. And even when this does not take place, we still feel a propensity to confound these ideas, tho' we are not able fully to satisfy ourselves in that particular, nor find any thing invariable and uninterrupted to justify our notion of identity.

Thus the controversy concerning identity is not merely a dispute of words. For when we attribute identity, in an improper sense, to variable or interrupted objects, our mistake is not confin'd to the expression, but is commonly attended with a fiction, either of something invariable and uninterrupted, or of something mysterious and inexplicable, or at least with a propensity to such fictions. What will suffice to prove this hypothesis to the satisfaction of every fair enquirer, is to shew from daily experience and observation, that the objects, which are variable or interrupted, and yet are suppos'd to continue the same, are such only as consist of a succession of parts, connected together by resemblance, contiguity, or causation. For as such a succession answers evidently to our notion of diversity, it can only be by mistake we ascribe to it an identity; and as the relation of parts, which leads us into this mistake, is really nothing but a quality, which produces an association of ideas, and an easy transition of the imagination from one to another, it can only be from the resemblance, which this act of the mind bears to that, by which we contemplate one continu'd object, that the error arises. Our chief business, then, must be to prove, that all objects, to which we ascribe identity, without observing their invariableness and uninterruptedness, are such as consist of a succession of related objects.

In order to this, suppose any mass of matter, of which the parts are contiguous and connected, to be plac'd before us; 'tis plain we must attribute a perfect identity to this mass, provided all the parts continue uninterruptedly and invariably the same, whatever motion or change of place we may observe either in the whole or in any of the parts. But supposing some very *small* or *inconsiderable* part to be added to the mass, or substracted from it; tho' this absolutely destroys the identity of the whole, strictly speaking; yet as we seldom think so accurately, we scruple not to pronounce a mass of matter the same, where we find so trivial an alteration. The passage of the thought from the object before the change to the object after it, is so smooth and easy, that we scarce perceive the transition, and are apt to imagine, that 'tis nothing but a continu'd survey of the same object.

There is a very remarkable circumstance, that attends this experiment; which is, that tho' the change of any considerable part in a mass of matter destroys the identity of the whole, yet we must measure the greatness of the part, not absolutely, but by its *proportion* to the whole. The addition or diminution of a mountain wou'd not be sufficient to produce a diversity in a planet; tho' the change of a very few inches wou'd be able to destroy the identity of some bodies. 'Twill be impossible to account for this, but by reflecting that objects operate upon the mind, and break or interrupt the continuity of its actions not according to their real greatness, but according to their proportion to each other: And therefore, since this interruption makes an object cease to appear the same, it must be the uninterrupted progress of the thought, which constitutes the [perfect?] [imperfect] identity.

This may be confirm'd by another phaenomenon. A change in any considerable part of a body destroys its identity; but 'tis remarkable, that where the change is produc'd *gradually* and *insensibly* we are less apt to ascribe to it the same effect. The reason can plainly be no other, than that the mind, in following the successive changes of the body, feels an easy passage from the surveying its condition in one moment to the viewing of it in another, and at no particular time perceives any interruption in its actions. From which continu'd perception, it ascribes a continu'd existence and identity to the object.

But whatever precaution we may use in introducing the changes gradually, and making them proportionable to the whole, 'tis certain, that where the changes are at last observ'd to become considerable, we make a scruple of ascribing identity to such different objects. There is, however, another artifice, by which we may induce the imagination to advance a step farther; and that is, by producing a reference of the parts to each other, and a combination to some *common end* or purpose. A ship, of which a considerable part has been chang'd by frequent reparations, is still consider'd as the same; nor does the difference of the materials hinder us from ascribing an identity to it. The common end, in which the parts conspire, the same under all their variations, and affords an easy transition of the imagination from one situation of the body to another.

But this is still more remarkable, when we add a *sympathy* of parts to their *common end*, and suppose that they bear to each other, the reciprocal relation of cause and effect in all their actions and operations. This is the case with all animals and vegetables; where not only the several parts have a reference to some general purpose, but also a mutual dependance on, and connexion with each other. The effect of so strong a relation is, that tho' every one must allow, that in a very few years both vegetables and animals endure a *total* change, yet we still attribute identity to them, while their form, size, and substance are entirely alter'd. An oak, that grows from a small plant to a large tree, is still the same oak; tho' there be not one particle of matter, or figure of its parts the same. An infant becomes a man, and is sometimes fat, sometimes lean, without any change in his identity.

We may also consider the two following phaenomena, which are remarkable in their kind. The first is, that tho' we commonly be able to distinguish pretty exactly betwixt numerical and specific identity, yet it sometimes happens, that we confound them, and in our thinking and reasoning employ the one for the other. Thus a man, who hears a noise, that is frequently interrupted and renew'd, says, it is still the same noise; tho' 'tis evident the sounds have only a specific identity or resemblance, and there is nothing numerically the same, but the cause, which produc'd them. In like manner it may be said without breach of the propriety of language, that such a church, which was formerly of brick, fell to ruin, and that the parish rebuilt the same church of free-stone, and according to modern architecture. Here neither the form nor materials are the same, nor is there any thing common to the two objects, but their relation to the inhabitants of the parish; and yet this alone is sufficient to make us denominate them the same. But we must observe, that in these cases the first object is in a manner annihilated before the second comes into existence; by which means, we are never presented in any one point of time with the idea of difference and multiplicity; and for that reason are less scrupulous in calling them the same.

Secondly, We may remark, that tho' in a succession of related objects, it be in a manner requisite, that the change of parts be not sudden nor entire, in order to preserve the identity, yet where the objects are in their nature changeable and inconstant, we admit of a more sudden transition, than wou'd otherwise be consistent with that relation. Thus as the nature of a river consists in the motion and change of parts; tho' in less than four and twenty hours these be totally alter'd; this hinders not the river from continuing the same during several ages. What is natural and essential to any thing is, in a manner, expected; and what is expected makes less impression, and appears of less moment, than what is unusual and extraordinary. A considerable change of the former kind seems really less to the imagination, than the most trivial alteration of the latter; and by breaking less the continuity of the thought, has less influence in destroying the identity.

We now proceed to explain the nature of *personal identity*, which has become so great a question in philosophy, especially of late years in *England*, where all the abstruser sciences are study'd with a peculiar ardour and application. And here 'tis evident, the same method of reasoning must be continu'd, which has so successfully explain'd the identity of plants, and animals, and ships, and houses, and of all the compounded and changeable productions either of art or nature. The identity, which we ascribe to the mind of man, is only a fictitious one, and of a like kind with that which we ascribe to vegetables and animal bodies. It cannot, therefore, have a different origin, but must proceed from a like operation of the imagination upon like objects.

But lest this argument shou'd not convince the reader; tho' in my opinion perfectly decisive; let him weigh the following reasoning, which is still closer and more immediate. 'Tis evident, that the identity, which we attribute to the human mind, however perfect we may imagine it to be, is not able to run the several different perceptions into one, and make them lose their characters of distinction and difference, which are essential to them. 'Tis still true, that every distinct perception, which enters into the composition of the mind, is a distinct existence, and is different, and distinguishable, and separable from every other perception, either contemporary or successive. But, as, notwithstanding this distinction and separability, we suppose the whole train of perceptions to be united by identity, a question naturally arises concerning this relation of identity; whether it be something that really binds our several perceptions together, or only associates their ideas in the imagination. That is, in other words, whether in pronouncing concerning the identity of a person, we observe some real bond among his perceptions, or only feel one among the ideas we form of them. This question we might easily decide, if we wou'd recollect what has been already prov'd at large, that the understanding never observes any real connexion among objects, and that even the union of cause and effect, when strictly examin'd, resolves itself into a customary association of ideas. For from thence it evidently follows, that identity is nothing really belonging to these different perceptions, and uniting them together; but is merely a quality, which we attribute to them, because of the union of their ideas in the imagination, when we reflect upon them. Now the only qualities, which can give ideas an union in the imagination, are these three relations above-mention'd. These are the uniting principles in the ideal world, and without them every distinct object is separable by the mind, and may be separately consider'd, and appears not to have any more connexion with any other object, than if disjoin'd by the greatest difference and remoteness. 'Tis, therefore, on some of these three relations of resemblance, contiguity and causation, that identity depends; and as the very essence of these relations consists in their producing an easy transition of ideas; it follows, that our notions of personal identity, proceed entirely from the smooth and uninterrupted progress of the thought along a train of connected ideas, according to the principles above-explain'd.

The only question, therefore, which remains, is, by what relations this uninterrupted progress of our thought is produc'd, when we consider the successive existence of a mind or thinking person. And here 'tis evident we must confine ourselves to resemblance and causation, and must drop contiguity, which has little or no influence in the present case.

To begin with resemblance; suppose we cou'd see clearly into the breast of another, and observe that succession of perceptions, which constitutes his mind or thinking principle and suppose that he always preserves the memory of a considerable part of past perceptions; 'tis evident that nothing cou'd more contribute to the bestowing a relation on this succession amidst all its variations. For what is the memory but a faculty, by which we raise up the images of past perceptions? And as an image necessarily resembles its object, must not the frequent placing of these resembling perceptions in the chain of thought, convey the imagination more easily from one link to another, and make the whole seem like the continuance of one object? In this particular, then, the memory not only discovers the identity, but also contributes to its production, by producing the relation of resemblance among the perceptions. The case is the same whether we consider ourselves or others.

As to *causation*; we may observe, that the true idea of the human mind, is to consider it as a system of different perceptions or different existences, which are link'd together by the relation of cause and effect, and mutually produce, destroy, influence, and modify each other. Our impressions give rise to their correspondent ideas; and these ideas in their turn produce other impressions. One thought chaces another, and draws after it a third, by which it is expell'd in its turn. In this respect, I cannot compare the soul more properly to any thing than to a republic or commonwealth, in which the several members are united by the reciprocal ties of government and subordination, and give rise to other persons, who propagate the same republic in the incessant changes of its parts. And as the same individual republic may not only change its members, but also its laws and constitutions; in like manner the same person may vary his character and disposition, as well as his impressions and ideas, without losing his identity. Whatever changes he endures, his several parts are still connected by the relation of causation. And in this view our identity with regard to the passions serves to corroborate that with regard to the imagination, by the making our distant perceptions influence each other, and by giving us a present concern for our past or future pains or pleasures.

As memory alone acquaints us with the continuance and extent of this succession of perceptions, 'tis to be consider'd, upon that account chiefly, as the source of personal identity. Had we no memory, we never shou'd have any notion of causation, nor consequently of that chain of causes and effects, which constitute our self or person. But having once acquir'd this notion of causation from the memory, we can extend the same chain of causes, and consequently the identity of our persons beyond our memory, and can comprehend times, and circumstances, and actions, which we have entirely forgot, but suppose in general to have existed. For how few of our past actions are there, of which we have any memory? Who can tell me, for instance, what were his thoughts and actions on the first of *January* 1715, the 11th of *March* 1719, and the 3d of *August* 1733? Or will he affirm, because he has entirely forgot the incidents of these days, that the present self is not the same person with the self of that time; and by that means overturn all the most establish'd notions of personal identity? In this view, therefore, memory does not so much *produce* as *discover* personal identity, by shewing us the relation of cause and effect among our different perceptions. 'Twill be incumbent on those, who affirm that memory produces entirely our personal identity, to give a reason why we can thus extend our identity beyond our memory.

The whole of this doctrine leads us to a conclusion, which is of great importance in the present affair, *viz.* that all the nice and subtile questions concerning personal identity can never possibly be decided, and are to be regarded rather as grammatical than as philosophical difficulties. Identity depends on the relations of ideas; and these relations produce identity, by means of that easy transition they occasion. But as the relations, and the easiness of the transition may diminish by insensible degrees, we have no just standard, by which we can decide any dispute concerning the time, when they acquire or lose a title to the name of identity. All the disputes concerning the identity of connected objects are merely verbal, except so far as the relation of parts gives rise to some fiction or imaginary principle of union, as we have already observ'd.

16. Gordon W. Allport

EDITOR'S INTRODUCTION

Hume's assumption that causal relations imply nothing more than "constant conjunction" is accepted today by many psychologists, especially those working within the behaviorist tradition.[1] However, several refinements are typically added to Hume's account. For example, cause is generally identified as a stimulus event, and effect as a response to that stimulus. In this way, a stimulus-response analysis becomes assimilated into a causal analysis. A second refinement is a distinction between correlation and causation. Even if two events are constantly conjoined, it may be that both are covarying as a function of some third variable. The laboratory experiment is the preferred method for disentangling such relationships. By manipulating stimulus events (the independent variable), and observing changes in behavior (the dependent variable), causal relations can presumably be distinguished from simple correlations.

Although oversimplified, this account shows the close conceptual link between cause and effect (in the Humean sense), stimulus and response (in the behaviorist sense), and independent and dependent variables (in the experimental sense). This conceptual trilogy contributed to a profound suspicion among many psychologists of explanations of behavior that refer to personality variables (e.g., traits or dispositions). A trait such as hostility is not a stimulus event and hence cannot serve as an efficient cause. (As explained in the Editor's Introduction to Chapt. 6, traits can be conceptualized as formal causes in the Aristotelian sense, but there is no place for formal causes within the Humean scheme.) For similar reasons, personality traits are not

[1] J. E. R. Staddon, On the notion of cause, with applications to behaviorism. *Behaviorism*, 1973, *1*, 25–63.

treated as independent variables within a laboratory context. Rather, in most experiments, individual differences are considered to be a source of "error variance" and an attempt is made to minimize their influence.

In this chapter, Gordon Allport argues for the reality and importance of personality variables in psychological theory and research. In a sense, he is arguing against Hume and the contemporary offshoots of Hume's position. Or perhaps it would be more accurate to say that Allport is taking up the challenge posed by Hume, who was never completely satisfied with the implications of his own argument. In an appendix to his analysis of the self, for example, Hume considered the obvious fact that our thoughts cohere in such a manner that we have a *feeling* of personal identity. But he was not able to discover any principle that would account for this unity of experience. Instead, he pleaded "the privilege of a skeptic," namely, "that this difficulty is too hard for my understanding."[2] Nevertheless, Hume expressed the hope that others, or perhaps himself after more mature reflection, would discover a hypothesis to reconcile the contradictions that he felt were implicit in his analysis.

The reprinted material by Allport is divided into five sections. Each section contains selections from a different chapter in Allport's major text, *Pattern and Growth in Personality*. In the first section, Allport analyzes the experience of the self into various components, e.g., bodily sensations, self-esteem, and social and material possessions. In the second section, Allport addresses one of the most fundamental questions in psychology: What is the proper unit of analysis? Allport believes that for the study of personality, at least, the proper unit of analysis is the trait or disposition. Two kinds of personality traits—those that are common to many persons and those that are idiosyncratic to a single individual—are examined in the third and fourth sections, respectively. Finally, in the fifth section, Allport returns to the experience of the self. As will be explained more fully later, Allport argues that it is a person's own sense of self that lends unity and organization to personality.

It is evident that Allport is dealing with two different but related topics—the self and personality traits. In contemporary psychological usage, the notion of *self* typically refers to the way one experiences and conceptualizes one's own behavior. Self-theorists, therefore, often use a phenomenological approach to the study of personality. The notion of *personality trait*, on the other

[2] D. Hume, *A Treatise on human nature*. L. A. Selby-Bigge (Ed.), Oxford: Clarendon Press, 1888, pp. 633 ff.

hand, refers to supposedly objective personal characteristics—intelligence, honesty, anxiety, and the like. Trait theorists tend to prefer psychometric (statistical) approaches to personality research. In this chapter, Allport attempts to integrate these two approaches within a single framework.

Of course, the notions of self and personality trait overlap in many respects. Honesty, for example, may be part of a person's self-image and also an objectively measurable characteristic (trait) of the individual. Indeed, one's image of oneself as honest may help account for the trait of honesty. Because of this overlap, it is not surprising that many of the same issues arise in the analysis of both the self and personality traits. One of these issues concerns the proper unit of analysis. As noted previously, Allport discusses this issue primarily in connection with personality traits. At this point it may be helpful to discuss briefly how the same issue also arises in connection with the self, using Hume's analysis as an example. Within the empiricist tradition, there is a tendency to analyze complex structures into elementary particles, assuming that the whole is nothing more than the sum of its parts. In Hume's case, the elementary units of analysis were sense impressions. But, as we have seen, after analyzing the self into elementary perceptions, Hume was never able to reconstruct the whole from its parts. Among more behavioristically oriented empiricists, the search for elements has typically led to a form of stimulus-response unit; but within this context, too, it has proven difficult to reconstruct the whole of personality.

Faced with this difficulty, Allport adopts the personality trait as his unit of analysis. He defines a trait as a neuropsychic structure that renders diverse stimuli and responses as functionally equivalent. Stated more simply, traits are dispositions to perceive and respond in a characteristic manner. Each individual represents a unique and dynamic organization of such dispositions. And here we return to the problem that so puzzled Hume: What accounts for the organization and continuity of personality? It is, according to Allport, one's sense of self, particularly the image of what one ideally would like to be. For Allport, the self—as a principle of organization and continuity—is less a matter of what one is than of what one is striving to become.

Pattern and Growth in Personality
1. the evolving sense of self

The psychology of personality harbors an awesome enigma—the problem of the self. The self is something of which we are immediately aware. We think of it as the warm, central, private region of our life. As such it plays a crucial part in our consciousness (a concept broader than self), in our personality (a concept broader than consciousness), and in our organism (a concept broader than personality). Thus it is some kind of core in our being. And yet it is not a constant core. Sometimes the core expands and seems to take command of all our behavior and consciousness; sometimes it seems to go completely offstage, leaving us with no awareness whatsoever of self.

A complete theory of personality cannot shelve this difficult problem of the subjective (felt) nature of the self, but must face up to it. Let us ask first why the problem is so difficult and elusive. There seem to be three principal reasons. (1) The term *self* is used in a great many ways by a great many theorists. Often the term *ego* is employed instead. And since no clear and consistent distinction has been made between *ego* and *self*, we shall need to treat them as equivalent. (2) Although each of us has an acute awareness of self, we cannot tell just what we are aware of. Some thoughts and acts *seem* to us more "self-relevant" than others, but there is no sharp dividing line. Therefore it is impossible to fix boundaries to assist our definition. (3) The subject opens up profound philosophical dilemmas concerning the nature of man, of "soul," of freedom and immortality. It is easy to see why many psychological discussions of personality avoid the problem altogether.

But evasion is not allowable. Again there are three reasons. (1) The one and only sure criterion of our personal existence and identity lies in our sense of self. To leave out this subjective pivot of personality is to keep the rim but discard the hub of our problem. (2) As we have already seen, our theories of learning, motivation, development cannot be complete or correct without distinguishing what is "self-relevant" in personality from what is not. (3) Although psychology cannot hope to solve the ultimate dilemmas of philosophy, it is obligated to provide a careful factual account of the evolving sense of self in order to assist philosophy in its task.

The present chapter, therefore, considers the factual aspects of the problem. The most helpful approach is to trace the developing sense of self from infancy onward.

EARLY INFANCY

We do not know what an infant's conscious experience may be like. Years ago William James called it a "big, blooming, buzzing, confusion," and he may be right. One thing is quite certain: the young infant is not aware of himself as a *self*. He does not separate the "me" from the rest of the world. And it is precisely this separation that is the pivot of later life. Consciousness and self-consciousness are not the same, neither for the infant nor for the adult. The infant, though presumably conscious, lacks self-consciousness completely; the adult has both, but they are not identical.

Self-consciousness, as we shall see, is a gradual acquisition during the first five or six years of life, making most rapid strides with the coming of language in the second year. Although the process is gradual, it is no doubt the most important development that occurs during a person's entire life. . . .

BODILY SELF

Probably the first aspect of selfhood to evolve is the sense of a bodily me. The infant receives a constant stream of organic sensations from the internal organs of the body, from muscles, joints, tendons. There is a continuous postural strain; especially the head region feels the strain because of its anatomical position. . . .

The sense of the bodily me grows not only from recurrent organic sensation but from frustrations arising "out there." A child who cannot eat when he wants to, who bumps his head, soon learns the limitations of his too, too solid flesh. . . .

The bodily sense remains a lifelong anchor for our self-awareness. It is true that in health the normal stream of sensations is often unnoticed, while in a state of ill-health or pain or deprivation, the bodily sense is keenly configurated. But at all times the underlying support of the bodily me is there. How very intimate it is can be seen if you imagine the following situation. Think first of swallowing the saliva in your mouth, or do so. Then imagine spitting it into a tumbler and drinking it. What seemed natural and "mine" suddenly becomes disgusting and alien. Or, to continue this unpleasant line of thought for a moment, picture yourself sucking the blood from a prick in your finger; then imagine sucking blood from a bandage around your finger. What you perceive as belonging intimately to your body is warm and welcome; what you perceive as separate becomes instantly cold and foreign.

Important as bodily sense is, it is not the whole of one's self. Those who have suffered extreme torture report that while feeling pain, they also feel a detachment. "This," they say, "is happening to my body, not to *me*." "I shall come through this somehow, and continue to be the same self I have always been." And so the sense of self depends on more than the bodily me.

SELF-IDENTITY

Today I remember some of my thoughts of yesterday, and tomorrow I shall remember some of my thoughts of both yesterday and today; and I am certain that they are the thoughts of the same person—of myself. Even an oldster of eighty is sure that he is the same "I" as at the age of three, although everything about him—including the cells of his body and his environment—has changed many times over. This sense of self-identity is a striking phenomenon, since change is otherwise the invincible rule of growth. Every experience we have modifies our brain, so it is impossible for the identical experience to occur a second time. For this reason every thought, every act is altered with time. Yet the self-identity continues, even though we know that the rest of our personality has changed. . . .

[W]e can point to one very important psychological factor in establishing the sense of identity in the second year of life, and to its continuation—the factor of language. When the child can speak and think in terms of toys, or his shoes or daddy, he has tools for relating the it to the I. By sometimes leaving and sometimes returning to the object and speaking its name, the inference grows that the I is the continuing factor in these intermittent relationships. . . .

SELF-ESTEEM

Before the age of two a child wants to push his stroller, wants to control his world, wants to make things *do* things. He has a fierce passion to manipulate objects. What does ink do? paint? lipstick? a razor blade? What can one do with cupboards, bureau drawers, matches, electric switches, cats, dogs, grandma's wig? Within a few minutes the curious two-year-old can wreck the house.

This passion, the bane of every parent, is not a direct reflection of selfhood. It is simply the normal adient relation between child and environment—the "exploratory drive," if you wish. The sense of self enters when these activities are thwarted.

> A two-year-old went to the bathroom with his father to have his face washed. Saying, "Let me," he struggled to turn on the faucet. He persisted without success. For a time the father waited patiently, but finally "helped" the child. Bursting into screams of protest the child ran from the bathroom and refused to be washed. His father had spoiled everything.

Such incidents are common at this age. When the exploratory bent is frustrated the child feels it a blow to his self-esteem. The ego is thwarted, resulting in humiliation and anger. The child becomes acutely aware of himself as a self. So conspicuous is this behavior that some psychologists say that the *need for autonomy* is the outstanding mark of selfhood in the second and third year of life.[1] . . .

THE EARLY SELF: SUMMARY

We have been saying that three aspects of self-awareness gradually evolve during the first three years of life:

Aspect 1: Sense of bodily self
Aspect 2: Sense of continuing self-identity
Aspect 3: Self-esteem, pride

Contributing to the development are many influences: maturation (anatomical and physiological), recurrent bodily sensations, memory aided by verbal concepts, one's proper name as an anchorage point, frustrations during the process of exploring and manipulating the environment, a period of negativism where the child practices his emerging sense of self. At this stage the child begins to feel himself autonomous and separate from others. But even now he can easily "depersonalize" in play, and feel himself to be an object, an animal, or another person. . . .

[1] For example, E. H. Erikson, Identity and the life cycle, *Psychol. Issues*, 1959, 1, No. 1. (New York: Int. Univ. Press.)

FOUR TO SIX

During this period we may date the appearance of two aspects of selfhood in addition to the three we have previously discussed.

Aspect 4: The extension of self
Aspect 5: The self-image

We have said that the sense of competition starts only after the age of three. With it comes the sense of possession. This ball is *mine. I* own the tricycle. My daddy, my brother, my dog, my house are felt to be warm parts of one's self. The child cannot yet, of course, extend himself to embrace his country, his church, or his career. But the foundations are laid for this important extension of selfhood. At the adult level we sometimes say, "A man is what he loves.". . . By this statement we mean that we know personality best by knowing what the extended-self embraces. But the young child has only the rudiments of such self-extension.

Rudimentary, too, is the *self-image.* The child begins to know that his parents want him to be a "good" boy, and also that at times he is "naughty." By the interaction process he comes to know what his parents expect of him, and to compare this expectation with his own behavior. Of course, as yet, he has no clearly developed conscience, nor any image of himself as he would like to be in adulthood. He is, however, laying the foundations for the intentions, goals, sense of moral responsibility, and self-knowledge that will later play a prominent part in his personality. In childhood the capacity to think of oneself as one is, as one wants to be, and as one ought to be is merely germinal.

SIX TO TWELVE

The child's sense of identity, his self-image, and his capacity for self-extension are greatly enhanced by his entrance into school. His classmates are frank and brutal regarding his weaknesses or idiosyncrasies. They call him "Four-eyes" or "Fatso." Such critical nicknames may hurt, but they also help establish an identity and render more acute the inner sense of selfhood.

The child soon learns that what is expected of him outside the home is very different from parental standards. Tribal (peer) standards of clothing and of speech are something new. A boy must soon learn to shift rapidly from the harsh and obscene talk of his peers to the politer world of his parents, and somehow to incorporate both worlds into his own being. When children enter their peer society they have a sharp lesson in "reality testing." They learn in effect to say, "Now I must do this. Now I must do that. Now I must be careful. Now I can do as I please." Such shifts intensify the sense of self.

It is well known that children of this age become moralistic and legalistic. Rules of the game must be followed rigidly. Parental rules are important, but the rules of the gang are utterly binding. The child does not yet trust himself to be an independent moral agent. His sense of self is comfortable only if he adapts to outer rules, extends himself into the gang, and develops a self-image of a safe conformer. The child fiercely believes that his family, his religion, and also his peer-group are right. While he may feel conflict between parent and peer standards, he is firmly loyal to these particular extensions of himself. In this period "identification" becomes an important principle of learning.

All the while the child's intellectual life is developing. Early in the school years he becomes addicted to riddles and puns, and a little later to codes, cryptograms, and foreign words. Objective knowledge fascinates him, and the question "Why?" is always on his lips. He begins to sense a new power, a new aspect of his selfhood:

Aspect 6: The self as rational coper

It is true that from early months the child has been able to solve single problems, but only now does he fully realize that he has a rational capacity to bring to bear upon them. Previously he *thought*, but now he *thinks* about thinking.

The self as a "coper" coincides fairly well with Freud's definition of the ego. For Freud the ego is the conscious portion of personality whose duty it is to find a solution to the problems created by impulses (the id), by the outer environment, and by the prohibitions taken over from one's parents and from society (the superego). Like a horseback rider the rational self tries to pick his way to avoid the traps laid by these three "tyrants." The ego, of course, is not always fully rational. It is often merely "defensive." Its duty includes the inventing of excuses and "rationalizations" to prevent injury to self-esteem. It may deny that obstacles exist and invent escapes and strategies that are mere fake solutions to life's problems.

It is, we admit, somewhat arbitrary to date the evolution of this aspect of selfhood as late as the period six to twelve, but we do so because it is during this period that children begin to engage in reflective and formal thought. They now fully know that the self is a thinker, and this function becomes for them warm and central, like all other aspects of selfhood.

ADOLESCENCE

Erikson points out that the chief feature of adolescence is the renewed search for self-identity.[2] The two-year-old, we recall, has already gone through the preliminary stage. But later he has lost himself again, so to speak, in his family and gang loyalties. Now in adolescence the problem once more becomes acute. The central teenage problem becomes "Just who am I?" . . .

The core of the identity problem for the adolescent is the selecting of an occupation or other life-goal. The future, he knows, must follow a *plan*, and in this respect his sense of selfhood takes on a dimension entirely lacking in childhood. Often youth aims too high. Idealism is a frequent, and lovable, quality. Many adolescent ideals are so high that a bad tumble is in store. Perhaps during the late twenties the youth will discover that he has less talent than he thought, that he will make less of a mark on the world, and that his marriage is less perfect than he had hoped. Paring down the self-image and aspirations to life-size is a task for his adult years.

But the important point is that in adolescence long-range purposes and distant goals add a new dimension to the sense of selfhood. We shall speak therefore of

Aspect 7: Propriate striving

Various writers maintain that the cement holding a life together is its "directedness" or "intentionality." In order to be normal an adolescent, and especially an adult, needs a defining objective, a line of promise. It is not necessary that the goals be rigidly focused, but only that a central theme of striving be present.[3]

This important aspect of self is not present in earlier life. The young child, to be sure, "wants" to be a fireman or a pilot when he grows up, but at this time there is no integrated effort. Until youth begins to plan, the sense of self is not complete. Some

[2] See Note 1, above.
[3] W. McDougall, *The energies of men* (London: Methuen, 1932). Also, C. Bühler, *Der menschliche Lebenslauf als psychologisches Problem* (Leipzig: Hirzel, 1933; rev. ed., Bonn: Hogrefe, 1959).

adolescents, it is true, drift into adulthood without any appreciable sense of purpose. When this is so, we can say that their personalities are of an "opportunistic" and immature order. Their sense of selfhood is still rudimentary.

William James once defined the self as a "fighter for ends." He was here accenting the propriate (central striving) aspect of selfhood. James, however, was well aware of additional aspects we have described. With his rubrics of "bodily," "material," and "spiritual" selves, he anticipated our present more detailed analysis in terms of bodily sense, self-identity, self-esteem, self-image, self-extension, and propriate striving.[4]

THE PROPRIUM

Is there no way to unite these seven aspects of selfhood? They are all states of self-relevance that we *feel*. Each in its way is an intimate region of personality involved in matters of importance to the organized emotional life of the individual. Together they compose the me as felt and known.

So it seems reasonable to unite these aspects (even though they are phenomenologically different, i.e., differently experienced) under a single name. Let us choose the term *proprium*. Why not simply the term *self*? There are two reasons: (1) Most writers, as we have seen, use *self* or *ego* for only one or two of the limited aspects we have treated. We prefer a fresher and broader label. (2) There is one remaining philosophical problem pertaining to the self to which we now turn, the question of "the knower." Since this aspect of selfhood is also properly termed *self*, we suggest using *proprium* to cover the self "as object" of knowledge and feeling. We are directly aware of the proprium in a sense that we are never directly aware of the "knower." . . .

It is important to point out that the proprium is not at all moments conscious. True, we *derive* the concept from experiences of self of which we are fully aware. But the traces of these experiences are effective even when we are not observing them. In propriate striving, for example, we characteristically "lose ourselves," because we are deeply absorbed in what we are doing. But it is nonetheless true that ego-involved interest is still playing a persistent role. And as we earlier pointed out, we are not constantly aware of the bodily me, perhaps hardly at all until pain or sensory deprivation forces such awareness upon us. Yet all seven propriate functions play a part, an important part,

[4] W. James, *Principles of psychology* (New York: Holt, Rinehart and Winston, 1890), Vol. I, Chap. 10.

in the "go" of personality, sometimes consciously, but often unconsciously.

THE PROBLEM OF THE KNOWER

This puzzling problem arises when we ask, "Who is the I who knows the bodily me, who has an image of myself and sense of identity over time, who knows that I have propriate strivings?" I know all these things and, what is more, I know that I know them. But who is it who has this perspectival grasp?

Philosophers beyond count have racked their brains with this problem. It is beyond our present scope to enter into the argument. Let us be content with a brief statement of two contrary views.

The philosopher Immanuel Kant argued that we never experience the knowing self in the same way we experience the object-self (proprium). The knowing self is just there; a transcendental or pure ego. The knower apprehends but is not itself apprehended. We catch bare glimpses of its shadow, but nothing more.

The opposite solution, offered by William James and John Dewey among others, holds that there is no substantive knower apart from the process of knowing. Each moment of consciousness overlaps with the previous moment, and the knower is somehow embedded in what is known. It is only when we stop the normal process of knowing, and grow reflective about the matter, that we imagine the problem to exist. The knower is nothing more than the organism itself.

We shall not here presume to choose between these two solutions, or others that have been offered.[5] There is, for example, the view that holds the self to be a central *agency* within personality. It knows, it wants, it strives, it wills. The self is the center of personal energy. This so-called self-psychology takes various forms, but the general position is the same.[6]

It has the merit of focusing, as we have done, on the unity and coherence that mark the propriate functions of personality, and of setting them off to some extent from the large balance of mere organismic and nonego-relevant functions.

---

[5] For a fuller discussion of the problem see G. W. Allport, *Becoming: basic considerations for a psychology of personality* (New Haven, Conn.: Yale Univ. Press, 1955), pp. 36–62.

[6] Cf. P. A. Bertocci, The psychological self, the ego, and personality, *Psychol. Rev.*, 1945, 52, 91–99; J. Macmurray, *The self as agent* (London: Faber & Faber, 1957); and M. B. Arnold and J. A. Gasson, *The human person: an approach to an integral theory of personality* (New York: Ronald, 1954).

It has, however, one serious danger from the scientific point of view. If we admit the self as a separate agent that knows, wills, wants, and so on, are we not in danger of creating a personality within a personality? We seem to be postulating "a little man within the breast." If we ask why Jim works hard, it explains nothing to say that "his self wills it." If we ask why this hospital patient is depressed, it is not helpful to say that "the self has a wrong self-image." To say that the self does this or that, wants this or that, wills this or that, is to beg a series of difficult questions. The psychologist does not like to pass the buck to a self-agent.

It is my position that in the structure of *personality*, if rightly understood—including, of course, the propriate structure—we shall find the explanations we seek. It is unwise to assign our problems to an inner agent who pulls the strings. . . .

2. search for elements

Man's nature, like all of nature, is composed of relatively stable structures. The success of psychological science, therefore, as of any science, depends in large part upon its ability to identify the significant units of which its assigned portion of the cosmos is composed. Without its table of elements chemistry could not exist. Where would physics be without its quanta, or biology without the cell? All science is analytic, and *analysis* means "to loosen or unbind."

PSYCHOLOGY'S PECULIAR PROBLEM

It is often said that psychology is "far behind" other sciences because psychology cannot discover its fundamental units. Within the past century many have been proposed (among them, *faculties, ideas, instincts, reflex arcs, sensations, images, feelings, drives, habits, factors, attitudes, sentiments, event-structures*). No fundamental agreement has been reached.

The lack of agreement comes from the fact that psychologists have different purposes in view. Wundt and Titchener, whose interest lay only in conscious mental life, thought *sensations, images, feelings* were the ultimate units. Experimenters with animals favor stimulus-response units (*drive, habit*); physiological psychologists speak of *cell assemblies*; statistical workers of *clusters* or *factors*; clinical psychologists lean toward *need*; others concerned with personality favor *traits*, *attitudes*, or *sentiments*. . . .

STIMULUS-RESPONSE UNITS

At this point we must tackle a fundamental issue in personality theory. Let us call it the issue of *specificity*. This point of view, though less common than it was two decades ago, is still widespread in America. It holds that "personality is made up of thousands of independent and specific habits." In other words, there is no organization at higher levels, such as is suggested in the ordinary usage of the term *trait*. The essential element is the specific habit. The only unit is a "specific behavior tendency which must be defined in terms of a particular stimulus and a particular response."[7] . . .

In spite of its manifest weaknesses, the doctrine of specificity has considerable appeal to American theories (not at all to the European). It fits the tradition of William James and E. L. Thorndike, who placed heavy emphasis upon the habit unit of conduct. It is congenial to stimulus-response doctrines that look for one measurable response to follow one measurable stimulus (a situation sometimes approximated in animal research). It is congenial to some sociologists who place heavy emphasis upon the situation. They like to think of recurrent situations (culture patterns) as causing whatever stability there is in man's conduct, rather than think of man as having stable traits that determine his behavior without marked dependence on the situation. Stated more broadly, the analytic tradition is strong in American thought; we like to reduce behavior to the smallest possible components. . . .

IDENTICAL ELEMENTS

If one views personality as composed of "countless specific habits," one must answer the question, How do you account for the considerable consistency people show in their conduct? A traditional answer has been in terms of *identical elements*.

Let us see how the theory works. We may say of a certain boy that he is *courteous*. The theory of specificity (identical elements) says, "No, he has no general trait of courtesy." Rather, he "learns

[7] Statements of this point of view may be found in H. Hartshorne, M. A. May, and F. K. Shuttleworth, *Studies in the organization of character* (New York: Macmillan, 1930); P. M. Symonds, *Diagnosing personality and conduct* (New York: Appleton-Century-Crofts, 1931), Chap. 9; W. Coutu, *Emergent human nature* (New York: Knopf, 1949).

to take off a specific cap when coming in a specific door and in the presence of his mother. But in time he may take off his cap or hat or whatever he has on his head when entering any door, in any house whatsoever, whether or not in the presence of a person."[8] Courtesy, then, is nothing more than the repetition of the same habits over and over again when provoked by stimuli previously associated with these habits, or when the habits themselves have some threadlike connection. . . .

The tradition of specificity and identical elements has prevailed in Anglo-American psychology from the time of the British empiricists in the eighteenth century (e.g., Locke, Hume) down to modern stimulus-response theories. To summarize this view we may say that it first posits very small units (Locke's *simple idea*, Hume's *sensation*, the behaviorists' *reflex arc* or *habit*). It then seeks to account for higher-level structures by positing connections or associations between these small elements.

The whole matter comes to focus when we ask the question, What is *similarity*? In Goethe's line, "Green is life's golden tree," we do somehow feel the poet's meaning but where is there an identical element uniting life with golden tree and simultaneously with green? Similarity, yes; identical elements, no. In a metaphor once used to describe a popular but sentimentally trashy poet—"a purple-plushed exuder of poetic cheese pies"—where is the common element to unite the unfortunate poet with this withering image? This metaphor and others may strike us as apt expressions of similarity—and yet the tracing of a specific common element (whether sensation, habit, nerve tract, or any other identical bond) is impossible.

Now to bring the issue back to personality. A certain superpatriot (shall we call him McCarley?) has, let us say, a phobia against communism. This seems to be his leading trait. To him Russians, most college professors, all liberals, all peace organizations, the United Nations itself, antisegregationists, and Jews—all are "communist" and he hates them. It seems unreasonable to suppose that such diverse stimuli have elements in common. But to him they compose an organized concept (a similarity). Anything new or strange or foreign is likely to be included in this very general attitude (or trait).

Look for a moment at his behavior. Sometimes McCarley will give vent to his hatred by writing a letter to the local newspaper, sometimes by growing red in the face and blustering, or again by joining rioters and stoning the house of some Negro or other

[8] P. M. Symonds, *The nature of conduct* (New York: Macmillan, 1928), p. 294.

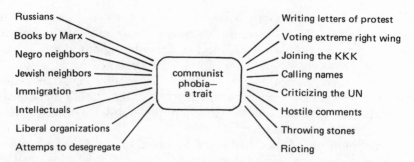

FIGURE 1 Generality of a trait. The range of a trait is determined by the equivalence of stimuli that arouse it and by the equivalence of responses that it provokes.

"communist." The behavior from situation to situation is similar, yes, but in no intelligible sense does it involve identical elements (in each case wholly different muscle groups may be involved).

What we are saying is that our personal traits (like our thought-life) are organized on the basis of similarities and that similarities cannot be reduced to identical elements. The term *similarity*, of course, has a subjective flavor. We *perceive* similarities. But we may, if we prefer, employ a more objective concept, and speak of *equivalence of stimuli* and *equivalence of response*. Many situations may arouse a generalized trait (or concept) and many forms of behavior may be equivalent in giving expression of the trait (or concept). The lad who takes off his hat and wipes his shoes on entering a house is not doing so just because elements in the two acts are mechanically tied, but because to him they have the same essential social meaning. He is generally "housebroken," and, as more equivalent acts are included in the system, we say he has a trait of courtesy, which means that many situations evoke the disposition of thoughtfulness-of-others, and lead to many varied forms of behavior, all having equivalent meaning.

There are several difficulties with the doctrine of identical elements. One is that the theory is unable to specify just what an element is, or just how identical an identity must be. But chiefly the theory runs afoul of much negative experimental evidence.[9] In the educational process we do not find that children learn new material in proportion to the number of identical elements in it

[9] The whole problem of identical elements and relevant evidence is reviewed at greater length in G. W. Allport, *Personality: a psychological interpretation* (New York: Holt, Rinehart and Winston, 1937), Chap. 10.

and in old material; but they learn in proportion to their understanding of *principles* (i.e., seeing the wide sweep of similarity in cases).[10]

Evidence favors a theory of the opposite order, one in which integration and generalization play the leading part. Here transfer effects depend chiefly upon the equivalence of meaning to the individual of the fields that confront him. If they are similar, transfer takes place. Equivalence and similarity are not uniform for all; they are a personal matter, and hence it is impossible to predict for people en masse the transfer value of a single experience, or to arrange a program of school studies that will secure uniform transfer effects for *all* children.

So swiftly and so subtly do we group our experiences and form our own concepts and attitudes and traits that the process is admittedly baffling. The whys and wherefores of similarity and equivalence are beyond our present comprehension. We may borrow a phrase from William James and say that all human beings have "an electric aptitude for analogies." At present we cannot predict with exactness what stimuli and what responses will be equivalent for a person—though we can often do so with some success. We can be fairly safe in saying that our Mr. McCarley will react negatively to anything "foreign." Or that our courteous boy will be thoughtful in almost any situation. But we may make mistakes. . . .

3. the theory of common traits

Scarcely anyone questions the existence of traits as the fundamental units of personality. Common speech presupposes them. This man, we say, is *gruff* and *shy*, but a *hard worker*; that woman is *fastidious*, *talkative*, and *stingy*. Psychologists, too, talk in these terms. One psychologist recently wrote a letter of recommendation for a former student characterizing him as *ambitious*, *friendly*, an *enthusiastic teacher*, but having a *quick temper*. Even in their technical research in personality most investigators have some kind of trait-doctrine (as the preceding chapter has shown). At the same time psychologists know that common sense is sometimes a faulty guide, and the issue of traits

---

[10] See, for example, R. C. Craig, *The transfer value of guided learning* (New York: Columbia Univ., Teachers College, Bureau of Publications, 1953).

is one of the areas where common sense, even if fundamentally correct, needs to be critically examined and refined. . . .

ARE TRAITS VERIDICAL OR FICTIONAL?

A metaphysical question arises at the outset of any discussion of traits, and if allowed to do so bedevils the whole problem. The sooner we can dispose of it the better. The question in brief is this: Are traits genuine, veridical dispositions? (The term *veridical* in philosophy means that the object under discussion is really *there*.) Thus a trait, if veridical, corresponds to some neurophysiological system. Or, on the other hand, are traits nothing more than nominal fictions, mere words, convenient groupings, of a plurality of unrelated acts?

As examples of the veridical view of traits we cite two definitions:

> A trait is a constant directing psychic force which determines the active and reactive behavior of the individual.[11]
>
> A trait is a dimension or aspect of personality, consisting of a group of consistent and related reactions that characterize a person's typical adjustments.[12]

The nominalistic view was expressed more than a century ago by Jeremy Bentham, who was ever on his guard against substituting fictitious entities for real ones:

> Now disposition [trait] is a kind of fictitious entity, feigned for the convenience of discourse, in order to express what there is supposed to be permanent in a man's frame of mind.[13]

A more recent statement of the same point of view is the following:

> Traits are only convenient names given to types or qualities of behavior which have elements in common. They are not psychological entities but rather categories for the classification of habits.[14] . . .

---

[11] F. Baumgarten, Character qualities, *Brit. J. Psychol.*, 1936, 26, 290.

[12] L. F. Shaffer and E. J. Shoben, *The psychology of adjustment* (Rev. ed.; Boston: Houghton Mifflin, 1956), p. 317.

[13] J. Bentham, *Principles of morals and legislation* (Oxford: Clarendon, 1879), Chap. 9, p. 131.

[14] M. May, Problems of measuring character and personality, *J. soc. Psychol.*, 1932, 3, 133. In the previous chapter the specificist argument was examined and reasons for rejecting it were given.

Briefly stated, the arguments for the nominalistic position are as follows: (1) No one ever *saw* a trait of any person; nor can we prove that a trait corresponds to neurophysiological structure. (2) All language, including the names we give to traits, is nominal. Words designate *social* and not *natural* categories. As we shall see later in the chapter, there are about 18,000 terms in the English language descriptive of alleged human traits, but these terms are classificatory tags; they have social utility but cannot be proved to derive from the cleavages in nature. (3) Everyone likes to oversimplify his perceptions and judgments of people. One may hold, for example, that Negroes (all Negroes) are *lazy*, *ignorant*, and *superstitious*. In this case the overgeneralization is obviously nonsensical.[15] Ascribing traits in such a coarse fashion always lands us in trouble. And yet we do tend to pigeonhole people (individuals as well as groups) with the aid of a few linguistic tags. No one is as simple and firmly structured as our labels imply.

Now all these arguments are sound, but they do not prove that persons are devoid of traits. They prove only that we should guard against our tendency to oversimplify the structure of *alter's* (the other fellow's) personality. We are warned not to assume that the words we use correspond precisely to the psychological unit we are attempting to name. Finally, the argument tells us that we need sound methods for establishing the existence of *alter's* traits since we can never observe them directly. . . .

THE NATURE OF COMMON TRAITS

We have voted in favor of the veridical view of traits. We believe that a trait is a broad system of similar action tendencies existing in the person we are studying. "Similar action tendencies" are those that an observer, looking at them from the actor's point of view, can categorize together under one rubric of meaning.

But we take this veridical view with certain qualifications. First, we know that the verbal or mathematical tags we give are derived from our own perceptions of another's behavior, and that the act of characterizing our perceptions is bedeviled by the evil of simplification. We know, too, that we are forcing what we observe into the social or mathematical rubrics available to us (rubrics such as *aggressive* or *ardent*, or Factors A, B, or C). . . .

Now there is good logic for assuming the existence of *common traits* and for measuring a given personality on a common dimensional scale along with other people. The logic is this:

[15] Cf. G. W. Allport, *The nature of prejudice* (Cambridge, Mass.: Addison-Wesley, 1954), Chaps. 10 and 11.

Normal people in a given culture-area necessarily tend to develop somewhat roughly comparable modes of adjustment. For example, people who live in English-speaking countries all develop more or less proficiency in the use of English, and it is entirely reasonable to give uniform tests of language achievement to see whether a person's mastery of English is at, above, or below average.

Or take the common trait *ascendance-submission.* In a competitive society, such as ours, every individual tends to find a level of assertiveness or ascendance that is congenial to his own way of life. One person may live quite comfortably (and charmingly) by being a "yielder." Another (by temperament or training) finds that dominance is a more congenial style of adjusting to, and mastering, his environment. Some people evolve a style of extreme aggressiveness; others, of extreme passivity. The point is that in our society people can be compared (roughly) in the way they have solved this problem of relating to the environment and to other people. . . .

Logical as it may be to evolve a uniform scale for ascendance-submission, the procedure is at best *approximate.* After all, there are endless varieties of dominators, leaders, aggressors, followers, yielders, and timid souls. The scale does not and cannot recognize the subtle shadings of traits in individuals. In the following chapter we shall examine more closely the problem of individual or personal traits.

Meanwhile let us restate the case for common traits. There are many aspects of personality in respect to which all people in a given culture may reasonably be compared. Besides ascendence-submission we may mention talkativeness, radicalism, money-mindedness, seclusion, anxiety, need for achievement, race prejudice, and hundreds of additional dimensions. *Common traits are, then, those aspects of personality in respect to which most people within a given culture can be profitably compared.*

As for veridicality, it should now be clear that we do rather more violence to the structure of John's personality if we *force* him into uniform trait categories than if we look at him as an individual in his own right and try to discover the actual internal systems of his own personal life.

To conclude the matter, common traits do not depart entirely from the natural cleavages of personality, because similarly constructed mortals in similar environments *would* develop similar goals and similar methods of obtaining them. At the same time, common traits are to some extent artifacts of our method of *forcing* categories upon individual persons. Common traits are therefore more nominal and less veridical than personal traits

(Chapter 15). We might say, then, that they are only semiveridical, but are nonetheless indispensable whenever we undertake to study personality by scales, tests, ratings, or any other comparative method. . . .

NAMING COMMON TRAITS

There are approximately 18,000 words (chiefly adjectives) in the English language designating distinctive forms of personal behavior.[16] At first sight this array seems like a semantic nightmare. Yet it is obvious that trait-names bear some relation to the underlying structural units of personality, and it is our duty to discover, if we can, what this relation is.

These thousands of terms have originated from two separate kinds of interest. First of all, we can be sure that men experience a desire to label what is truly present in human nature. If our fellow mortals did not *have* capacities and dispositions, we would be unlikely to name them. What is more, names are to some extent self-correcting, for there is no gain in preserving through names an erroneous belief in fabulous entities; there is everything to gain by using terms that designate true psychic structures. This is one reason we have trait names; if it were the only reason, the correspondence between our dictionary and psychological truth would be close, much closer than it is.

A second influence upon our lexicon of trait-names is wholly different; it comes via fads and fashions in cultural interest. Very early, thanks to the persistence of Galenian medicine, English used such trait-names as *sanguine, choleric, melancholic, phlegmatic, good-humored, bad-humored,* as well as *cold-blooded, hearty, heartless,* and *cordial* (derived from the belief that the heart is the seat of intellect and feeling). The Protestant Reformation, with its emphasis on inwardness and introspection, brought many useful trait-adjectives, among them *sincere, pious, bigoted, precise, fanatic,* also many of the compounds of *self: self-regard, self-assurance, self-love, self-confidence, self-esteem. Selfish* is a term coined by the Presbyterians about 1640. The growing subjectivity of literature in the eighteenth century brought *apathy, chagrin, depression, daydream.* Courtly circles added *demure, gawky, interesting, boresome.* To recent years belong many expressions, some still regarded as slang: *booster, climber, beatnik, hoodlum, yes-man, four-flusher, sad-sack, jitter-bug, chiseler, gigolo, ex-urbanite.* To this ever-increasing vocabulary of human

[16] G. W. Allport and H. S. Odbert, *Trait-names: a psycho-lexical study, Psychol. Monogr.*, 1936, No. 211. The present section quotes freely from this source.

characteristics psychology has contributed *introverted, neurotic, regressive, psychopathic, somatotonic, schizoid*, and many more. Although some symbols become extinct, the tendency is for trait-names to multiply—a reflection no doubt of ever-rising interest in human nature.

We conclude, therefore, that in part our available trait-names point to common characteristics in respect to which people may be compared. In other words, many terms strive to designate truly veridical endowments of men. About 25 percent of the terms are of this order.

But language is tricky. It also serves an evaluative purpose. When we say a woman is *attractive*, we are talking not about a disposition "inside the skin," but about her effect on other people. About 30 percent of our trait-names have this predominantly evaluative flavor: among them, *adorable, angelic, boresome, disgusting, enviable, evil, magnificent, trying, winning*.

The line between veridical and evaluative terms is often hard to draw. For one thing, a term of praise or blame, such as *honest, law-abiding*, or *unselfish*, may come to represent a desired self-image, and a person may strive (that is, develop a trait) to correspond to the social ideal.

There are two additional classes of terms. We designate temporary states of mind, mood, emotion, or present activity; for example, *abashed, gibbering, rejoicing, frantic*. Although such terms describe conduct, they do not refer to permanent "preferred patterns." About 25 percent of the 18,000 words are of this sort. Finally, we have to admit a large array (20 percent of the total) that seems metaphorical or questionable, such terms as *alive, amorphous, roly-poly, prolific. . . .*

To sum up, our theory of trait-names holds that the labels offered by the lexicon are symbols socially devised from a mixture of psychological, cultural, and ethical concerns. Terms that are evaluative and censorious have little relevance to the study of the structure of personality, however useful they may be in studying the social impact of one individual upon others. Perhaps the number of single, nonjudgmental terms pointed clearly to the designation of permanent (nontemporary) traits is between 4,000 and 5,000. Yet so many combinations of words are possible that the number of accessible trait-designations is far, far greater. . . .

4. personal dispositions

For a moment we shall continue our discussion of trait-names. Some of these, we find, are derived from individual historical or fictional characters: *quixotic*, *narcistic* (originally Narcissusistic, then narcissistic, now narcistic), *chauvinistic*, *sadistic*, *pukish*, a *quisling*. Some are spelled with capital letters, *Boswellian*, *Lesbian*, *Chesterfieldian*, *Rabelaisian*, *Pickwickian*, *Emersonian*, *Falstaffian*, *Homeric*, *Faustian*. We say a person is *Christlike*, a *Don Juan*, a *Beau Brummell*, a *Xantippe*. In all these cases, and many more like them, we note that some particular outstanding characteristic of a single person gave us a new label to apply occasionally (not often) to other people.

In such instances we are not dealing with a common trait. It would be absurd to try to compare all people—or any large number of them—on a scale designed to measure the peculiar *fastidious exhibitionism* of a Beau Brummell or the *sexual cruelty* of a Marquis de Sade. Yet the very fact that we now name the characteristic shows that we have abstracted it from the individual life with the intention of applying it to other lives to which it may fit. Words are general. Even if we say "this boy," we are using two abstract words to point to a particular. Only a proper name, such as Franklin Roosevelt, comes near to designating one unique personal event in nature.

THE UNIQUENESS OF PERSONAL DISPOSITIONS

We come again to the proposition that seems so shocking to science. Franklin Roosevelt was a unique historical event in nature, and the fabulously complex organization of his mental processes and nervous system was likewise unique. It could not be otherwise considering the individuality of his inheritance, the individuality of his life experience. . . . Even the subsystems of his personality were ultimately unique. When confronted with this unassailable logic, one outraged psychologist exclaimed, "I think it is nonsense to say that no two men ever have the same trait. I mean, of course it is true, but it is one of those truths that can't be accepted." We reply: Unfortunately, this is one truth that the study of personality *must* accept, however great the difficulties it creates.

In order to keep the problem distinct from that of common traits, we shall adopt a different terminology. We could with propriety speak of *individual* (or of *personal*) traits as distinct from *common* traits, for there is similarity between the two conceptions (both, for example, refer to a complex level of organization). Yet for purposes of clarity we shall designate the individual unit not as a trait, but as a *personal disposition* (and shall occasionally use the abbreviation *p.d.*)[17]

Much that we have said concerning common traits applies also to personal dispositions. Both are broad (generalized) determining tendencies; both differ in the same way from habits, attitudes, and types; both refer to the level of analysis most suitable to the study of personality; the existence of both is inferred by the occurrence of activities having "functional equivalence."

But there are differences. It makes no sense to speak of the "normal distribution" of p.d.'s, since each is unique to one person. Trait-names fit common traits better than they fit p.d.'s. (Generally several words are needed to designate a disposition, as when we say, "Little Susan has a peculiar anxious helpfulness all her own"; or, "He will do anything for you if it doesn't cost him any effort.")

Our contention is that, if correctly diagnosed, p.d.'s reflect the personality structure accurately, whereas common traits are categories into which the individual is forced.

For example, by common trait methods, we find that Peter stands high in *esthetic interest* and *anxiety*, but low in *leadership* and *need-achievement*. The truth is that all these common traits have a special coloring in his life, and—still more important—they interact with one another. Thus it might be more accurate to say that his personal disposition is a kind of *artistic and self-sufficient solitude*. His separate scores on common traits do not fully reflect this pattern. . . .

5. the unity of personality

Personality is many things in one—a *unitas multiplex*. In the preceding [section] we have considered the multiplex in terms of

---

[17] Another possible label for the unit I have in mind is *morphogenic trait*. This term properly suggests a unit that carries the "form" of the personality structure, and helps to maintain this form over considerable periods of time.

Morphogenesis is a branch of biology that tries to account for the patterned properties of a whole organism. It is a relatively neglected area of biology, where major effort is expended on finding the ultimate elements that are common to all life. Molecular biology has demonstrated that these ultimate units, in terms of nucleic acids, proteins, genetic principles, are remarkably alike in all organisms whatever their form. This discovery, of course, makes it more imperative (not less imperative) that the forces accounting for the patterned integrity of individual organisms be sought. The parallel with psychology is almost perfect. With analytical zeal we have sought uniform units of all personalities (common traits, needs, factors, and so on), but have lost sight of internal morphogenic patterning along the way. . . .

traits and dispositions. We come now to the problem of unity. For two reasons it is a perplexing problem: first, because there are many senses in which the term *unity* may be applied to personality; and second, because it is questionable whether unity is ever achieved. Such unification as exists seems to be only a matter of degree. The German writer Von Herder said, "Man is never complete; his existence lies in becoming." . . .

[O]ur discussion of the evolving sense of *self* [section 1] forms a prelude to our present discussion of unity. The very term *self* implies unity. After discarding the concept for some decades psychologists have returned to it, for they now recognize that without it there is no adequate way to speak of some of the morphogenic aspects of personality.

PHILOSOPHICAL VIEWS

Many philosophers tell us that everything we do, say, or are presupposes unity. Even a simple and common experience, such as *disappointment*, does so. One cannot feel disappointed unless there are a series of previous stages: desire, expectation, lack of fulfillment, all being stages belonging to one continuing actor. The fact that we have conflicts and clashes of purpose within our breasts is proof of unity. A present conflict could not be known except in terms of prior unity, or a hoped-for unity in the future. Hence conflict, dissociation, even the disintegration of personality have no meaning apart from the supposition that the person—first, last, and all the time—is a fundamental and continuing unit.[18]

This issue has worried many, perhaps most, philosophers, but not all of them reach the same conclusion. The philosopher Hume, for example, concluded reluctantly and with no strong sense of conviction, that a continuing agent (a self) was more of an illusion than a fundamental fact. He decided that men are made up of discrete bits of experience. William James—wrestling with the same problem—concluded that there is no single cementing principle but that unity lies in the overlap of successive states and acts, much as the unity of a shingled roof consists of the overlay of shingles.

The opposite conclusion, as we saw in [section 1], is reached by Kant, who argues that since we know our separate acts to be *ours*, there must be a "pure ego" continuing to guarantee personal unity throughout life. Philosophers who follow Kant may take one of two views. Either they hold that the self is a passive guarantor of unity—a "continuing ground" without active participation and

---

[18] Cf. W. Stern, *General psychology from the personalistic standpoint* (Transl. by H. D. Spoerl; New York: Macmillan, 1938), p. 449. See also E. S. Brightman, *Person and reality* (New York: Ronald, 1958), Chap. 14.

"intervention"; or else they hold that the self is an *agent* that wills, directs, steers, selects conduct, and thus actively forges unity.

Extending this latter point of view, Thomistic psychologists say that the unifying self has one objective and inevitable goal. It is the nature of self to strive (not always successfully) for a higher degree of perfection than now exists. Even the feeblest life manifests a basic tendency for enrichment, for progress beyond its present limits. The direction of the goal is the ideal of a perfect person as the individual conceives him to be. Since man is made in the image of God, there is then a norm of perfection (of man as he ought to be) that guides, however imperfectly, the unifying activity of the self. Man glimpses the road toward ultimate unity, and insofar as he follows it, by reason and by choice, he will achieve a factual unification of his personality.[19] This line of thought calls attention to the conviction of some writers that the question of unity cannot be considered at all without at the same time considering the problem of the ultimate nature and destiny of man.

Other philosophers avoid the assumption that the self is a unifying agent. They see unity in the essential "systematic" nature of personality. They postulate a "tendency to stability" (Fechner), a "systematic relevance" (Whitehead), or a "conatus" (Spinoza). In human beings, according to Spinoza, the conatus takes the form of a tendency to grow into one's own perfected form. These philosophers admit that lower forms of life achieve unity more easily than do human beings, who have so many more diversified potentialities claiming fulfillment. As Keyserling points out, a kingfisher alertly catching food on the shores of a pond, is a more perfect, if less intricate, unity than is a human being in quest of his daily bread.

If these various philosophical solutions seem confusing, the reason is that they require far deeper study than we can here offer. Our purpose in calling attention to them is to show that philosophical sophistication is needed in order to reach a completely satisfactory theory of the nature of unification in the personal life.

UNITY AS STRIVING

One line of philosophical thinking is especially close to the psychologist's stock in trade. The so-called romantic philosophers of the nineteenth century were fond of saying, "A man is what he

[19] Cf. Magda B. Arnold and J. A. Gasson (Eds.), *The human person: an approach to an integral theory of personality* (New York: Ronald, 1954).

loves." We never fully attain what we love; we simply keep on loving it and wanting more and more of it. Love of learning, to take an example, is a unifying force; but possession of learning is not.

What integrates our energies is the pursuit of some goal. When the goal is attained, the energy is dispersed. A person centered on becoming what he wants to become is far more integrated than one who has reached his goal—and has no place to go. To reach a goal we have to overcome distractions, discords, and obstacles. The effort involved welds unity.

Goethe saw that it was Faust's relentless search for objectives, particularly for the life-goal he set himself ("a free people on a free soil"), that was his salvation. Mephisto made a wager with Faust that he could so beguile him that Faust would no longer struggle for completeness but would surrender to some tempting state of self-satisfaction along the way. Had Faust yielded to the illusion that he had found his objective, he would have been damned. In the end he was saved because he ceaselessly strove for the goal he never attained.

Like all great epics, Goethe's Faust gives us a profound insight into human nature; in this case into the conditions under which unification of personality is achieved. The psychologist Jung recognizes the same situation in his definition of *self*. According to Jung the *self* is not something we have, but something we are throughout our life span endeavoring to achieve. It is in this special sense that "self" confers unity. . . .

UNITY AND THE SELF-IMAGE

Implied in the doctrine of striving is the presence of a cognitive factor—a self-image (page 416). One psychologist, Lecky, defines personality as "an organization of ideas which are felt to be consistent with one another." He adds that the one overpowering motivation in life is to maintain the unity of this system:

> Behavior expresses the effort to maintain integrity and unity of the organization. . . . In order to be immediately assimilated, the idea formed as the result of a new experience must be felt to be consistent with the ideas already present in the system. On the other hand, ideas whose inconsistency is recognized as the personality develops must be expelled from the system. There is thus a constant assimilation of new ideas and the expulsion of old ideas throughout life.[20] . . .

[20] P. Lecky, *Self-consistency: a theory of personality* (New York: Island, 1945), p. 135.

Another author, Carl Rogers, is concerned with the importance of helping people attain a self-image that is accurate and complete. Many people fail to achieve healthy unity in their personalities because of self-deception.

> It would appear that when all of the ways in which the individual perceives himself—all perceptions of the qualities, abilities, impulses, and attitudes of the person, all perceptions of himself in relation to others—are accepted into the organized conscious concept of the self, then this achievement is accompanied by feelings of comfort and freedom from tension.[21] . . .

This line of thought identifies health in personality with a complete and unified self-image. The self-image includes not only a view of "what I am," but also "what I want to be" and "what I ought to be." By bringing these aspects of the self-image together one approaches unification. . . .

PROPRIATE FUNCTIONS AND UNITY

Both striving and the self-image are *propriate* aspects of personality [section 1]. We may then venture a generalization: *unity in personality is to be sought primarily in propriate (and not in opportunistic or peripheral) functions.*

We recall the story of G. B. Shaw's *Pygmalion*, where the heroine, an ignorant flower girl, is taken up by Professor Higgins for speech training. He teaches her to speak in an educated way, and finds that she readily obeys his order. If he tells her to act like a servant, she does so; like a lady, and she does. Outwardly it would seem that Eliza Doolittle has no consistency at all in her personality. But underneath there is one unifying explanation of her conduct: she is in love with her teacher. Her love is a propriate factor. And it is propriate factors that explain such unity as is found in personality.

Let us refer to an experimental study.

Klein and Schoenfeld wished to study *confidence* as an attribute of personality. They gave a group of subjects a series of intelligence tests under two experimental conditions. In the first, the atmosphere was neutral, dull, not ego-involved. The subjects were merely laboratory guinea pigs going through routine motions. After each of the six tests they were asked to state the degree of confidence they felt in the accuracy of their performances. Among the six tests there was little consistency in these ratings of

---

[21] C. R. Rogers, Some observations on the organization of personality, *Amer. Psychologist*, 1947, 2, 358–368.

confidence. After an interval of time, a second equivalent set of tests was given and the atmosphere markedly changed. The subjects were placed under greater strain, were told to try hard since the results of these intelligence tests would be entered on their college records. The shift was effective. The confidence ratings became sharply consistent. A student who felt assured that he had done well (or poorly) on one test felt assured he had done well (or poorly) on the other five. The authors conclude that *confidence* is a consistent personality trait *when the ego is involved*, but that it is variable and inconsistent when the subject has no propriate interest at stake.[22]

Ego-involvement in any situation seems to bring greater consistency. Public-opinion polls show that people who feel strongly about an issue will be quite consistent (unified) in endorsing all the propositions that are related to this issue. If they feel less strongly (less ego-involved) they are variable and inconsistent.[23]

To generalize our point: thoughts and behavior have greater consistency when they relate to what we consider to be warm, central, and important in our lives than they have when they are not so related. Or, to put the matter more briefly: propriate functions tend to unify personality.

CORRESPONDENCE VERSUS CONGRUENCE

A corollary follows. We must expect greater unification to be evident in personal dispositions than in common traits. Common traits are merely variables on which we compare a large population of people, whether or not these variables have a central importance in their lives.

Now it is true that statistical studies of common traits can give us *some* evidence of the consistency or unity of personality. When we say, for example, that a certain trait test (e.g., ascendance-submission) has a coefficient of reliability of .85, we are saying that most people respond in the same meaningful way from item to item and from time to time. And so most people, we conclude, hold to a fairly constant level of dominant, submissive, or average adjustment.[24]

[22] G. S. Klein and W. Shoenfeld, The influence of ego-involvement on confidence, *J. abnorm. soc. Psychol.*, 1941, 36, 249-258.

[23] H. Cantril, *Gauging public opinion* (Princeton, N.J.: Princeton Univ. Press, 1943), Chap. 5.

[24] One may go further and study the amount of "integratedness" shown by single individuals in many traits. Do they answer questions day after day in the same way, or are they variable? Such a device for measuring the common trait of over-all "integratedness" is proposed by R. B. Cattell, Fluctuation of sentiments and attitudes as a measure of character integration and of temperament, *Amer. J. Psychol.*, 1943, 56, 195-216.

Evidence for unity that comes from the correlation of measures in a general population we shall call evidence of *correspondence*. By this term we mean that subjects' scores on a common trait scale are fairly constant. . . .

It is easier to be "objective" in studying the correspondence of measures than in studying congruence. Standard operations are prescribed for statistical studies of correspondence, but to detect congruence we often have to make a clinical interpretation—the rightness of which is harder to prove. It is probably for this reason that the investigators in the field of personality tend to overlook the geno-typical dispositions in the individual life that help to resolve the apparent contradictions in personal behavior. We admit, however, that it is not easy to establish with certainty our insightful diagnoses of congruence. Often we can be in error. Nor should we say that, if only we knew the root congruences, everything in personality would prove to be consistent with everything else. The following statement presses the point too far:

> The unity of a person can be traced in each instant of his life. There is nothing in character that contradicts itself. If a person who is known to us seems to be incongruous with himself, that is only an indication of the inadequacy and superficiality of our previous observations.[25]

After all, unity in personality is only a matter of *degree*, and we should avoid exaggerating it.

It is difficult to keep a balanced footing. On the one hand, there is no doubt that experimental and statistical studies tend to underestimate the unity of personality simply because their techniques fail to focus upon the propriate regions of the individual life. On the other hand, it is easy to read into discordant behavior some mythical unity, thereby substituting arbitrary interpretation for fact.

[25] R. Franke, Gang and Charakter (Ed. by H. Bogen and O. Lipmann), Z. f. angew. Psychol., 1931, No. 58, p. 45.

IX. THE PROBLEM OF KNOWLEDGE REFORMULATED

17. Immanuel Kant

EDITOR'S INTRODUCTION

The selection by Hume (Chapt. 15) began with a distinction between "relations of ideas" (e.g., mathematical theorems) and "matters of fact" (e.g., empirical observations). The former are, according to Hume, "discoverable by the mere operation of thought, without dependence on what is anywhere existent in the universe." Reasoning concerning matters of fact, on the other hand, is founded on the relation of cause and effect. But this relation, Hume argued, is itself based on experience; hence, matters of fact can never be known with certainty. Stated differently, relations of ideas are necessarily true but they also are uninformative, since their validity depends only on the analysis of concepts and not on the observation of what actually exists in the universe. Matters of fact, on the other hand, are informative about the world, being based on observation, but their truth can never be demonstrated with certainty. Where does this leave the laws of science, which, at least in Hume's time, were considered to be necessarily true (like relations of ideas) and also informative (like matters of fact)? This is the problem that awoke Kant from his "dogmatic slumbers."

Kant could not refute the logic of Hume's argument, but neither could he accept the skeptical conclusion to which that argument led. The alternative, then, was to question the premises on which the argument was based. Perhaps the central premise—central not only to Hume, but to most theories of knowledge prior to Kant—was that true knowledge must conform to the nature of reality. That is, an idea is true to the extent that it correctly represents some independent reality, however that reality might be conceived. In what he called his Copernican revolution in epistemology, Kant turned this relationship around. He argued that the structure of reality, insofar as it can be the object of knowledge, must conform to the structure of thought, rather than vice versa.

Kant's elaboration of this thesis is intricate and difficult to follow, and only a portion of it can be reprinted here. Because of this, these introductory remarks will sketch in broad outline the nature of Kant's argument.

Kant begins with a distinction between pure (a priori) and empirical (a posteriori) judgments or propositions. Pure judgments, which include the laws of mathematics and science, are universally and necessarily true. Any proposition that fulfills these two criteria (universality and necessity) cannot be derived from sense experience; hence, it must be a priori. Empirical judgments, on the other hand, are derived from experience (are a posteriori), and thus are always open to refutation on the basis of further evidence. At first, this appears similar to Hume's distinction between relations of ideas and matters of fact, and to Plato's distinction between knowledge and opinion (see Chapt. 3). But both the rationalist, Plato, and the empiricist, Hume, had only part of the truth (albeit different parts).

According to Kant, much of the work of reason consists of the analysis of concepts that we already possess, and this gives a kind of knowledge that is universally and necessarily true. Both Plato and Hume also recognized this fact, but they drew quite different conclusions from it. The success of conceptual analysis led Plato and other rationalists to abandon the world of sense experience in order to erect intellectual edifices based on reason alone. What they did not recognize was that their edifices lacked foundation; reason alone, divorced from experience, can yield no knowledge. Hume clearly recognized this fact, which led to his skeptical doubts concerning human understanding. He assumed that because some—perhaps most—a priori judgments are based on the analysis of concepts (relations of ideas), then all a priori propositions must be so based; in this case, they cannot refer to anything that "is anywhere existent in the universe."

To salvage the insights of both the rationalists and empiricists, Kant introduced a further distinction, between analytic and synthetic propositions. In an analytic proposition (e.g., all dogs are mammals), the predicate is contained within the subject term (e.g., part of the definition of *dog* is that it refers to a mammal). All analytic propositions are also a priori, since the predicate cannot be denied of the subject without self-contradiction. By contrast, in synthetic propositions (e.g., some dogs bite) the predicate enlarges upon the conception of the subject (e.g., that some such animals should bite is not part of the definition of *dog*).

The question now arises: Are there any synthetic propositions that are also a priori? Hume had denied this, and Kant set out to prove that Hume was wrong, that the laws of mathematics and science are in fact synthetic a priori propositions.

Synthetic a priori judgments are possible, Kant reasoned, only if experience contributes one element (the synthetic) while mind contributes the other element (the a priori). But before proceeding to the details of this argument, one further distinction introduced by Kant must be noted. Today, when referring to mental events, we quite naturally distinguish between sensations, perceptions, and conceptions, each representing a more complex level of operation. Before the time of Hume and Kant, such a division was not made, and mental events were generally referred to simply as *ideas*. Hume distinguished *impressions* from other ideas on the basis of their vivacity, and with some modification this led to the modern notion of sensation. Kant introduced a further distinction between perceptions and conceptions. For Kant, sensations are the simple affectation or stimulation of the sense organs; perception involves the ordering of the sensory impressions in conformity with the "forms of intuition" (space and time); and, finally, conception involves the synthesis of percepts according to certain rules of thought or "categories of judgment." The forms of intuition and the categories of judgment are the a priori elements contributed by the mind.

With these distinctions in mind, we are in a position to outline very briefly some of the main features of Kant's argument. First, synthetic propositions must contain a sensory element, for all knowledge that is not strictly analytic has to begin with experience. However, propositions derived from particular sense experiences can never be judged as universally and necessarily true, as Hume demonstrated. Therefore, synthetic a priori propositions must be based on general conditions common to all experience, and these general conditions can be contributed only by the mind. Thus, one way to demonstrate the existence of synthetic a priori propositions is to show that, if such propositions were not true of objects, then objects could not be experienced at all.

For anything to be perceived, it must be perceived in space (external experience) and time (internal experience). Hence, space and time are universal and necessary conditions for perception. But we not only perceive, say, patches of red, in a spatiotemporal order, we also make judgments (e.g., that this object is red).

Moreover, these judgments fall into certain logical types related to substance, causality, and the like, which comprise the categories of judgment.

Perhaps an example will help clarify the nature of Kant's argument. Imagine that you are a native of some remote tribe that has never had contact with modern industrialized society. One day, as you are walking through the forest, a helicopter hovers over a nearby clearing and a group of men leap out. What do you "see"? Not having any concept of *helicopter*, or of any other complex man-made machine, you might see a giant insect disgorging men; or perhaps you would see some other object that fits the categories developed by your culture to make experience meaningful. That is, whether you see a helicopter, a giant insect, or whatever, depends on whether or not you have the appropriate concepts. But what about the fact that you see a *thing* at all, as opposed to a mere concatenation and succession of colors and sounds? Might that not also be based on a concept and, moreover, a concept that is a priori? Let us (after Kant) call such a concept a *substance*. Substance, then, is a rule of thought, innately given, by which a sensory manifold is experienced as a permanent pattern or object. Without such a concept, no one would experience perceptions as representing *things*, not to mention such particular things as helicopters or giant insects.

The reader may have noted that this discussion began with a question regarding the status of scientific laws and quickly progressed to statements about cognition in general. This progression requires comment. According to Kant, sensation provides the "matter" for perception, while space and time provide the form. Both in terminology and conception, this hierarchical process bears a close resembalnce to the dialectical type of analysis offered by Aristotle (Chapt. 5) for psyche, in general, and by Aquinas (Chapt. 11) for the cognitive powers of the soul, in particular. This highlights an important feature of Kant's analysis. Raw sensations (pure matter) do not exist in actuality. All sensations are subject to the forms of intuition (space and/or time) in order to be experienced at all. Similarly, all perceptions are *informed* (in the etymological sense of the word) by the categories of judgment. This means that not even the simplest phenomenal experience exists independently of the categories. Kant sometimes spoke as though there were some judgments that are strictly synthetic a posteriori; in the final analysis, however, *all* experience has a priori elements contributed by the mind. His analysis of the synthetic a priori is thus not limited to scientific judgments, but pertains to the operation of the human mind in general.

The Cognitive Construction of Reality:
preface to "The Critique of Pure Reason"

This may well be called the age of criticism, a criticism from which nothing need hope to escape. When religion seeks to shelter itself behind its sanctity, and the law behind its majesty, they justly awaken suspicion against themselves, and lose all claim to the sincere respect which reason yields only to that which has been able to bear the test of its free and open scrutiny.

Metaphysic has been the battlefield of endless conflicts. Dogmatism at first held despotic sway; but . . . from time to time scepticism destroyed all settled order of society; . . . and now a widespread indifferentism prevails. Never has metaphysic been so fortunate as to strike into the sure path of science, but has kept groping about, and groping, too, among mere ideas. What can be the reason of this failure? Is a science of metaphysic impossible? Then, why should nature disquiet us with a restless longing after it, as if it were one of our most important concerns? Nay more, how can we put any faith in human reason, if in one of the very things that we most desire to know, it not merely forsakes us, but lures us on by false hopes only to cheat us in the end? Or are there any indications that the true path has hitherto been missed, and that by starting afresh we may yet succeed where others have failed?

It seems to me that the intellectual revolution, by which at a bound mathematics and physics became what they now are, is so remarkable, that we are called upon to ask what was the essential feature of the change that proved so advantageous to them, and to try at least to apply to metaphysic as far as possible a method that has been successful in other sciences of reason. In mathematics I believe that, after a long period of groping, the true path was disclosed in the happy inspiration of a single man. If that man was Thales, things must suddenly have appeared to him in a new light, the moment he saw how the properties of the isosceles triangle could be demonstrated. The true method, as he found, was not to inspect the visible figure of the triangle, or to analyze the bare conception of it, and from this, as it were, to read off its properties, but to bring out what was necessarily implied in the conception that he had himself formed *a priori*, and put into the figure, in the construction by which he presented it to himself.

From I. Kant, The critique of pure reason, in J. Watson, Ed. and trans., *The Philosophy of Kant*. Glasgow: Jackson, Wylie, & Co., 1934. Pp. 1–17 *passim*, 19, 20, 22–25, 26–29, 40–43.

Physics took a much longer time than mathematics to enter on the highway of science, but here, too, a sudden revolution in the way of looking at things took place. When Galileo caused balls which he had carefully weighed to roll down an inclined plane, or Torricelli made the air bear up a weight which he knew beforehand to be equal to a standard column of water, a new light broke on the mind of the scientific discoverer. It was seen that reason has insight only into that which it produces after a plan of its own, and that it must itself lead the way with principles of judgment based upon fixed laws, and force nature to answer its questions. Even experimental physics, therefore, owes the beneficial revolution in its point of view entirely to the idea, that, while reason can know nothing purely of itself, yet that which it has itself put into nature must be its guide to the discovery of all that it can learn from nature.

In metaphysical speculations it has always been assumed that all our knowledge must conform to objects; but every attempt from this point of view to extend our knowledge of objects *a priori* by means of conceptions has ended in failure. The time has now come to ask, whether better progress may not be made by supposing that objects must conform to our knowledge. Plainly this would better agree with the avowed aim of metaphysic, to determine the nature of objects *a priori*, or before they are actually presented. Our suggestion is similar to that of Copernicus in astronomy, who, finding it impossible to explain the movements of the heavenly bodies on the supposition that they turned round the spectator, tried whether he might not succeed better by supposing the spectator to revolve and the stars to remain at rest. Let us make a similar experiment in metaphysic with *perception*. If it were really necessary for our perception to conform to the nature of objects, I do not see how we could know anything of it *a priori*; but if the sensible object must conform to the constitution of our faculty of perception, I see no difficulty in the matter. Perception, however, can become knowledge only if it is related in some way to the object which it determines. Now here again I may suppose, either that the *conceptions* through which I effect that determination conform to the objects, or that the objects, in other words the experience in which alone the objects are known, conform to conceptions. In the former case, I fall into the same perplexity as before, and fail to explain how such conceptions can be known *a priori*. In the latter case, the outlook is more hopeful. For, experience is itself a mode of knowledge which implies intelligence, and intelligence has a rule of its own, which must be an *a priori* condition of all knowledge of objects presented to it. To this rule, as expressed in *a priori* conceptions, all objects of experience must necessarily conform, and with it they must agree.

Our experiment succeeds as well as we could wish, and gives promise that metaphysic may enter upon the sure course of a science, at least in its first part, where it is occupied with those *a priori* conceptions to which the corresponding objects can be given. The new point of view enables us to explain how there can be *a priori* knowledge, and what is more, to furnish satisfactory proofs of the laws that lie at the basis of nature as a totality of objects of experience. But the consequences that flow from this deduction of our faculty of *a priori* knowledge, which constitutes the first part of our inquiry, are unexpected, and at first sight seem to be fatal to the aims of metaphysic, with which we have to deal in the second part of it. For we are brought to the conclusion that we never can transcend the limits of possible experience, and therefore never can realize the object with which metaphysic is primarily concerned. In truth, however, no better indirect proof could be given that we were correct in holding, as the result of our first estimate of the *a priori* knowledge of reason, that such knowledge relates not at all to the thing as it exists in itself, but only to phenomena. For that which necessarily forces us to go beyond the limits of experience and of all phenomena is the *unconditioned*, which reason demands of things in themselves, and by right and necessity seeks in the complete series of conditions for everything conditioned. If, then, we find that we cannot think the unconditioned without contradiction, on the supposition of our experience conforming to objects as things in themselves; while, on the contrary, the contradiction disappears, on the supposition that our knowledge does not conform to things in themselves, but that objects as they are given to us as phenomena conform to our knowledge; we are entitled to conclude that what we at first assumed as an hypothesis is now established as a truth.

It may seem from this that the result of our critical investigation is purely *negative*, and merely warns us not to venture with speculative reason beyond the limits of experience. And no doubt this is its first use; but a *positive* result is obtained when it is seen that the principles with which speculative reason ventures beyond its proper limits, in reality do not *extend* the province of reason, but inevitably *narrow* it. For in seeking to go altogether beyond its true limits, the limits of sensibility, those principles threaten to supplant pure reason in its practical aspect. Let us suppose that the necessary distinction which our criticism shows to exist between things as objects of experience and the same things as they are in themselves, had not been made. Then the principle of causality, and with it the mechanical conception of nature as determined by it, would apply to all things in general as efficient causes. Hence I could not, without palpable contradiction, say of the same being, for instance the human soul, that its will is free, and yet is subject to the necessity of nature, that is, is not free. But, if our criticism is sound and the object may be taken in two distinct senses, on the one hand as a phenomenon, and on the other hand as a thing in itself; there is no contradiction in supposing that the very same will, in its visible acts as a phenomenon, is *not free*, but necessarily subject to the law of nature, while yet, as belonging to a thing in itself, it is not subject to that law, but is *free*. . . .

introduction

1. DISTINCTION OF PURE AND EMPIRICAL KNOWLEDGE

There can be no doubt whatever that all our knowledge begins with experience. By what means should the faculty of knowledge be aroused to activity but by objects, which, acting upon our senses, partly of themselves produce ideas in us, and partly set our understanding at work to compare these ideas with one another, and, by combining or separating them, to convert the raw material of our sensible impressions into that knowledge of objects which is called experience? In the order of time, therefore, we have no knowledge prior to experience, and with experience all our knowledge begins.

But, although all our knowledge begins *with* experience, it by no means follows that it all originates *from* experience. For it may well be that experience is itself made up of two elements, one received through impressions of sense, and the other supplied from itself by our faculty of knowledge on occasion of those impressions. If that be so, it may take long practice before our attention is drawn to the element added by the mind, and we learn to distinguish and separate it from the material to which it is applied.

It is, therefore, a question which cannot be lightly put aside, but can be answered only after careful investigation, whether there is any knowledge that is independent of experience, and even of all impressions of sense. Such knowledge is said to be *a priori*, to distinguish it from *empirical* knowledge, which has its sources *a posteriori*, or in experience.

The term *a priori* must, however, be defined more precisely, in order that the full meaning of our question may be understood. We say of a man who undermines the foundations of his house, that he might have known *a priori* that it would fall; by which we mean, that he might have known it would fall, without waiting for the event to take place in his experience. But he could not know it completely *a priori*; for it is only from experience that he could learn that bodies are heavy, and must fall by their own weight when there is nothing to support them.

By *a priori* knowledge we shall, therefore, in what follows understand, not such knowledge as is independent of this or that experience, but such as is *absolutely* independent of all experience. Opposed to it is empirical knowledge, or that which is possible only *a posteriori*, that is, by experience. *A priori* knowledge is *pure*, when it is unmixed with anything empirical. . . .

2. SCIENCE AND COMMON SENSE CONTAIN A PRIORI KNOWLEDGE

Evidently what we need is a criterion by which to distinguish with certainty between pure and empirical knowledge. Now, experience can tell us that a thing is so and so, but not that it cannot be otherwise. Firstly, then, if we find a proposition that, in being thought, is thought as necessary, it is an *a priori* judgment; and if, further, it is not derived from any proposition except which is itself necessary, it is absolutely *a priori*. Secondly, experience never bestows on its judgments true or strict universality, but only the assumed or comparative universality of induction: so that, properly speaking, it merely says, that so far as our observation has gone, there is no exception to this or that rule. If, therefore, a judgment is thought with strict universality, so that there can be no possible exception to it, it is not derived from experience, but is absolutely *a priori*. Necessity and strict universality are, therefore, sure criteria of *a priori* knowledge, and are also inseparably connected with each other.

Now, it is easy to show that in human knowledge there actually are judgments, that in the strictest sense are universal, and therefore pure *a priori*. If an example from the sciences is desired, we have but to think of any proposition in mathematics; if an instance from common sense is preferred, it is enough to cite the proposition, that there can be no change without a cause. To take the latter case, the very idea of cause so manifestly implies the idea of necessary connection with an effect, that it would be completely lost, were we to derive it, with Hume, from the repeated association of one event with another that precedes it, and were we to reduce it to the subjective necessity arising from the habit of passing from one idea to another. Even without appealing to such examples to show that as a matter of fact there are in our knowledge pure *a priori* principles, we might prove *a priori* that without such principles there could be no experience whatever. For, whence could experience derive the certainty it has, if all the rules that it follows were merely empirical and therefore contingent? Surely such rules could not be dignified with the name of first principles. . . .

3. A SCIENCE IS NEEDED TO DETERMINE THE POSSIBILITY, THE PRINCIPLES, AND THE EXTENT OF ALL A PRIORI KNOWLEDGE

A far more important consideration remains than anything that has yet been stated. There is a sort of knowledge that even quits the field of all possible experience, and claims to extend the range of our judgments beyond its limits by means of conceptions to which no corresponding object can be presented in experience. Now, it is just in the province of this sort of knowledge, where experience can neither show us the true path nor put us right when we go astray, that reason carries on those high investigations, the results of which we regard as more important than all that understanding can discover within the domain of phenomena. Nay, we are even willing to stake our all, and to run the risk of being completely deluded, rather than consent to forego inquiries of such moment, either from uncertainty or from carelessness and indifference. These unavoidable problems, set by pure reason itself, are *God, freedom*, and *immortality*, and the science which brings all its resources to bear on the one single task of solving them is *metaphysic.*

Now, one might think that men would hesitate to leave the solid ground of experience, and to build an edifice of truth upon knowledge that has come to them they know not how, and in blind dependence upon principles of which they cannot tell the origin, without taking the greatest pains to see that the foundation was secure. One might think it only natural, that they would long ago have raised the question, how we have come into possession of all this *a priori* knowledge, and what may be its extent, its import and its value. But the fact is, that a part of this knowledge—

mathematical knowledge, for instance—has so long been established as certain, that we are less ready to suspect the evidence for other parts, although these may be of a totally different nature. Besides, when we are once outside the circle of experience, we are sure not to be contradicted by experience; and so strong is the impulse to enlarge our knowledge, that nothing short of a clear contradiction will avail to arrest our footsteps. Now, such contradiction may easily be avoided, even where we are dealing with objects that are merely imaginary, if we are only careful in putting our fictions together. Mathematics shows us by a splendid instance, how far a science may advance *a priori* without the aid of experience. It is true that by it objects and conceptions are considered only in so far as they can be presented in perception; but it is easy to overlook the limitation, because the perception in this case can itself be given *a priori*, and is therefore hard to distinguish from a mere idea. Deceived by this proof of the power of reason, we can see no limits to the extension of knowledge. So Plato forsook the world of sense, chafing at the narrow limits it set to our knowledge, and, on the wings of pure ideas, launched out into the empty space of the pure understanding. He did not see that with all his efforts he was making no real progress. But it is no unusual thing for human reason to complete its speculative edifice in such haste, that it forgets to look to the stability of the foundation. The reason why we have no fear or anxiety while the work of construction is going on, but take it for granted that the foundation stands firm, is, that much of the work of reason, perhaps the greater part, consists in the *analysis* of conceptions which we already possess. This analysis really gives us a kind of *a priori* knowledge that is safe and useful. But, misled by this success, reason interpolates propositions of quite a different character, which but superficially resemble the others. I shall therefore at the very outset point out the distinction between these two kinds of knowledge.

4. THE DISTINCTION BETWEEN ANALYTIC AND SYNTHETIC JUDGMENTS

There are two ways in which the predicate of an affirmative judgment may be related to the subject. Either the predicate B is already tacitly contained in the subject A, or B lies entirely outside of A, although it is in some way connected with it. In the one case I call the judgment *analytic*, in the other case *synthetic*. Analytic judgments are those in which the predicate is related to the subject in the way of identity, while in synthetic judgments the predicate is not thought as identical with the subject. The former class might also be called *explicative*, because the predicate adds nothing to the subject, but merely breaks it up into its logical elements, and brings to clear consciousness what was already obscurely thought in it. The latter class we may call *ampliative*, as adding in the predicate something that was in no sense thought in the subject, and that no amount of analysis could possibly extract from it. "Body is extended," for instance, is an analytic judgment. For, to be conscious that extension is involved in the conception signified by the term body, it is not necessary to go outside that conception, but merely to analyze it into the various logical elements that are always thought in it. But in the proposition "Body has weight," the predicate is not implied in the very conception of body, but is a perfectly new idea. The addition of such a predicate, therefore, yields a synthetic judgment.

Judgments of experience are all by their very nature synthetic. To say that I must have recourse to experience for an analytic judgment is absurd, because I can frame the judgment without going beyond the conception I already possess. I have, for instance, the conception of body, and by mere analysis I become aware of the attributes extension, impenetrability, figure, etc., which the thought of it involves. To enlarge my conception, I turn again to experience, from which the conception was originally derived, and, finding weight to be invariably connected with those attributes, I attach it to them by synthesis as a new attribute. The possibility of this synthesis of the attribute weight with the conception body therefore rests upon experience. The two ideas are quite distinct, but they yet are parts of the same experience, and experience is itself a whole in which a number of perceptions are synthetically though only contingently combined.

In *a priori* synthetic judgments, on the other hand, I can get no aid whatever from experience. But, if it is here vain to look to experience for aid, on what other support am I to rely, when I seek to go beyond a certain conception A, and to connect B synthetically with it? Take the proposition, that every event must have its cause. No doubt I cannot have the conception of an event without thinking of something as having a moment of time before it, and from this certain analytic judgments may be derived. But the conception of a cause lies entirely outside the conception of an event, and introduces an idea not contained in it. By what right, then, do I pass from the conception of an event to the totally different conception of a cause? How do I know that there is a necessary connection between the two conceptions, when I can perfectly well think the one without the other? What is here the unknown x, which gives support to the understanding, when it seems to have discovered an entirely new predicate B to belong necessarily to the subject A? Experience it cannot be, because the principle has a degree of universality that experience can never supply, as it is supposed to connect the new conception with the old in the way of necessity, and must do so entirely *a priori*, and on the basis of mere conceptions. And yet our speculative *a priori* knowledge must rest upon such synthetic or ampliative propositions.

5. THE PRINCIPLES OF ALL THEORETICAL SCIENCES OF REASON ARE A PRIORI SYNTHETIC JUDGMENTS

(1) All *mathematical* judgments, without exception, are synthetic. No doubt the mathematician, in his demonstrations, proceeds on the principle of contradiction, but it is a mistake to suppose that the propositions on which his demonstrations rest can be known to be true by that principle. The mistake arises from not observing that, while a synthetic proposition may certainly be seen to be true by the principle of contradiction, its truth is in that case evident, not from itself, but only because it is seen to follow from another proposition that has been previously obtained by synthesis.

The first thing to notice is, that no truly mathematical judgments are empirical, but always are *a priori*. They carry necessity on their very face, and therefore cannot be derived from experience. Should any one demur to this, I am willing to limit my assertion to the propositions of *pure mathematics*, which, as everybody will admit, are not empirical judgments, but perfectly pure *a priori* knowledge.

At first sight it may seem that the proposition $7 + 5 = 12$ is purely analytic, and follows, by the principle of contradiction, from the conception of a sum of 7 and 5. But, when we look more closely we see that the conception of the sum of 7 and 5 is merely the idea of the union of the two numbers, and in no way enables us to tell what may be the single number that forms their sum. To think that 7 and 5 are to be united is not to have the conception 12, and I may analyze the idea of the possible sum as long as I please, without finding the 12 in it. To get beyond the separate ideas of 7 and 5, I must call in the aid of perception, referring to my five fingers, or to five points, and, starting with the conception 7, go on to add to it, unit by unit, the 5 so presented to me in perception. The propositions of arithmetic are therefore all synthetic. This is even more manifest if I take larger numbers, when it becomes at once obvious that without the aid of perception no mere analysis of my conceptions, turn and twist them as I may, could ever yield the sum.

Nor is any proposition of pure geometry analytic. That the straight line between any two points is the shortest, is a synthetic proposition. My idea of straight is purely an idea of quality, not of quantity. From no analysis of the conception of a straight line can the knowledge that it is the shortest be derived. Perception has to be called in to enable me to make the synthesis.

(2) The principles on which *physics* rests are *a priori* synthetic judgments. I shall content myself with citing two such judgments: first, that in all changes of the material world the quantity of matter remains the same; and, secondly, that in the communication of motion, action and reaction are always equal. Both propositions, it is plain, are not only necessary, and therefore in their origin *a priori*, but they are also synthetic. The conception of matter does not include the idea of permanence, but merely signifies its presence in the space which it occupies. When, therefore, I say that matter is permanent in quantity, I add *to* the conception of matter an attribute which was not at first thought *in* it. Accordingly, the proposition is not analytic, but at once *a priori* and synthetic; and so with the other propositions of pure physics. . . .

6. THE PROBLEM OF PURE REASON

It is of very great advantage, to others as well as to one self, to be able to bring together various topics of investigation in a single problem. Now, the true problem of pure reason may be put in this way—*How are a priori synthetic judgments possible?*

Should this question be answered in a satisfactory way, we shall at the same time learn what part reason plays in the foundation and completion of those sciences which contain a theoretical *a priori* knowledge of objects. Thus we shall be able to answer the questions—*How is pure mathematics possible? How is pure physics possible?* As these sciences actually exist, we may fairly ask *how* they are possible; for that they must be possible is proved by the fact that they exist. . . .

7. IDEA AND DIVISION OF THE CRITIQUE OF PURE REASON

From all that has been said we get the idea of a unique science, which may be called the Critique of Pure Reason. It is not a *doctrine*, but a *criticism* of pure reason, and its speculative value is entirely negative, because it does not enlarge our knowledge, but only casts light upon the nature of our reason and enables us to keep it free from error. By *transcendental* knowledge I mean all knowledge that is occupied, not with objects, but with the way in which a knowledge of objects may be gained, so far as that is possible *a priori*. What we propose is not a doctrine of pure reason, but a transcendental criticism, the purpose of which is not to extend knowledge, but to rectify it, and to supply a touchstone of the value of all *a priori* knowledge. . . .

transcendental aesthetic

1.

Sensation is the actual affection of our sensibility, or capacity of receiving impressions, by an object. The perception which refers itself to an object through sensation, is *empirical perception*. The undetermined object of such a perception is a *phenomenon* (Erscheinung).

That element in the phenomenon which corresponds to sensation I call the *matter*, while that element which makes it possible that the various determinations of the phenomenon should be arranged in certain ways relatively to one another is its *form*. Now, that without which sensations can have no order or form, cannot itself be sensation. The matter of a phenomenon is given to us entirely *a posteriori*, but its form must lie *a priori* in the mind, and hence it must be capable of being considered by itself apart from sensation.

This pure form of sensibility is also called *pure perception*. Thus, if from the consciousness of a body, I separate all that the understanding has thought into it, as substance, force, divisibility, etc., and all that is due to sensation, as impenetrability, hardness, colour, etc.; what is left over are extension and figure. These, therefore, belong to pure perception, which exists in the mind *a priori*, as a mere form of sensibility, even when no sensation or object of sense is actually present.

The science of all the *a priori* principles of sensibility I call *Transcendental Aesthetic*, in contradistinction from the science of the principles of pure thought, which I call *Transcendental Logic*.

In Transcendental Aesthetic we shall first of all isolate sensibility, abstracting from all that the understanding contributes through its conceptions, so that we may have nothing before us but empirical perception. In the next place, we shall separate from empirical perception all that belongs to sensation; when there will remain only pure perception, or the mere form of phenomena, the sole element that sensibility can yield *a priori*. If this is done, it will be found that there are two pure forms of sensible perception, which constitute principles of *a priori* knowledge, namely, Space and Time. With these it will now be our business to deal.

SECTION I.—SPACE

2. Metaphysical Exposition of Space.

In external sense we are conscious of objects as outside of ourselves, and as all without exception in space. In space their shape, size, and relative position are marked out, or are capable of being marked out. Inner sense, in which we are conscious of ourselves, or rather of our own state, gives us, it is true, no direct perception of the soul itself as an object; but it nevertheless is the one single form in which our own state comes before us as a definite object of perception; and hence all inner determinations appear to us as related to one another in time. We cannot be conscious of time as external, any more than we can be conscious of space as something within us. What, then, are space and time? Are they in themselves real things? Are they only determinations, or perhaps merely relations of things, which yet would belong to things in themselves even if those things were not perceived by us? Or, finally, have space and time no meaning except as forms of perception, belonging to the subjective constitution of our own mind, apart from which they cannot be predicated of anything whatever? To answer these questions I shall begin with a metaphysical exposition of space. An *exposition* I call it, because it gives a distinct although not a detailed, statement of what is implied in the idea of space; and the exposition is *metaphysical*, because it brings forward the reasons we have for regarding space as given *a priori*.

(1) Space is not an empirical conception, which has been derived from external experiences. For I could not be conscious that certain of my sensations are relative to something outside of me, that is, to something in a different part of space from that in which I myself am; nor could I be conscious of them as outside of and beside one another, were I not at the same time conscious that they not only are different in content, but are in different places. The consciousness of space is, therefore, necessarily presupposed in

external perception. No experience of the external relations of sensible things could yield the idea of space, because without the consciousness of space there would be no external experience whatever.

(2) Space is a necessary *a priori* idea, which is presupposed in all external perceptions. By no effort can we think space to be away, although we can quite readily think of space as empty of objects. Space we therefore regard as a condition of the possibility of phenomena, and not as a determination dependent on phenomena. It is thus *a priori*, and is necessarily presupposed in external phenomena. . . .

3. Transcendental Exposition of Space.

A transcendental exposition seeks to show how, from a certain principle, the possibility of other *a priori* synthetic knowledge may be explained. To be successful, it must prove (1) that there really are synthetic propositions which can be derived from the principle in question, (2) that they can be so derived only if a certain explanation of that principle is adopted.

Now, geometry is a science that determines the properties of space synthetically, and yet *a priori*. What, then, must be the nature of space, in order that such knowledge of it may be possible? Our original consciousness of it must be perception, for no new truth, such as we have in the propositions of geometry, can be obtained from the mere analysis of a given conception (Introduction, 5). And this perception must be *a priori*, or, in other words, must be found in us before we actually observe an object, and hence it must be pure, not empirical perception. For all geometrical propositions, as, for instance, that space has but three dimensions, are of demonstrative certainty, or present themselves in consciousness as necessary; and such propositions cannot be empirical, nor can they be derived from judgments of experience (Introduction, 2).

How, then, can there be in the mind an external perception, which is antecedent to objects themselves, and in which the conception of those objects may be determined *a priori*? Manifestly, only if that perception has its seat in the subject, that is, if it belongs to the formal constitution of the subject, in virtue of which it is so affected by objects as to have a direct consciousness or perception of them; therefore, only if perception is the universal *form* of outer sense.

Our explanation is, therefore, the only one that makes the possibility of geometry intelligible, as a mode of *a priori* synthetic knowledge. All other explanations fail to do so, and, although they may have an external resemblance to ours, may readily be distinguished from it by this criterion.

Inferences.

(*a*) Space is in no sense a property of things in themselves, nor is it a relation of things in themselves to one another. It is not a determination that still belongs to objects even when abstraction has been made from all the subjective conditions of perception. For we never could perceive *a priori* any determination of things, whether belonging to them individually or in relation to one another, antecedently to our perception of those things themselves.

(*b*) Space is nothing but the form of all the phenomena of outer sense. It is the subjective condition without which no external perception is possible for us. The receptivity of the subject, or its capability of being affected by objects, necessarily exists before there is any perception of objects. Hence it is easy to understand, how the form of all phenomena may exist in the mind *a priori*, antecedently to actual observation, and how, as a pure perception in which all objects must be determined, it may contain the principles that determine beforehand the relations of objects when they are met with in experience.

It is, therefore, purely from our human point of view that we can speak of space, of extended things, etc. Suppose the subjective conditions to be taken away, without which we cannot have any external perception, or be affected by objects, and the idea of space ceases to have any meaning. We cannot predicate spatial dimensions of things, except in so far as they appear in our consciousness. The unalterable form of this receptivity, which we call sensibility, is a necessary condition of all the relations in which objects are perceived as outside of us, and this form, when it is viewed in abstraction from objects, is the pure perception that is known by the name of space. We are not entitled to regard the conditions that are proper to our sensibility as conditions of the possibility of things, but only of things as they appear to us. Hence, while it is correct to say, that space embraces all things that are capable of appearing to us as external, we cannot say, that it embraces all things as they are in themselves, no matter what subject may perceive them, and, indeed, whether they are perceived or not. For we have no means of judging whether other thinking beings are in their perceptions bound down by the same conditions as ourselves, and which for us hold universally. If we state the limitations under which a judgment holds of a given subject, the judgment is then unconditionally true. The proposition, that all things are side by side in space, is true only under the limitation that we are speaking of our own sensible perception. But, if we more exactly define the subject of the proposition by saying, that all things as external phenomena are side by side in space, it will be true universally and without any exception. Our exposition, therefore, establishes the *reality*, or objective truth of space, as a determination of every object that can possibly come before us as external; but, at the same time, it proves the *ideality* of space, when space is considered by reason relatively to things in themselves, that is, without regard to the constitution of our sensibility. We, therefore, affirm the *empirical reality* of space, as regards all possible external experience; but we also maintain its *transcendental ideality*, or, in other words, we hold that space is nothing at all, if its limitation to possible experience is ignored, and it is treated as a necessary condition of things in themselves. . . .

transcendental logic

1. GENERAL LOGIC

There are two ultimate sources from which knowledge comes to us: either we receive ideas in the form of impressions, or, by our spontaneous faculty of conception, we know an object by means of those ideas. In the former case, the object is *given* to us; in the latter case, it is *thought* in relation to the impressions that arise in our consciousness. Perception and conception, therefore, are the two elements that enter into all our knowledge. To every conception some form of perception corresponds, and no perception yields knowledge without conception. Both may be either pure or empirical; *empirical*, if sensation, which occurs only in the actual presence of an object, is implied; *pure*, if there is no intermixture of sensation. We may call sensation the matter of sensuous knowledge. Hence pure perception contains only the form under which a something is perceived, and pure conception the form in which an object in general is thought. Pure perceptions or pure conceptions alone are possible *a priori*, while empirical perceptions or empirical conceptions are possible only *a posteriori*.

If *sensibility* is the *receptivity* of the mind in the actual apprehension of some impression, *understanding* is the *spontaneity* of knowledge, or the faculty that of itself produces ideas. We are so constituted that our *perception* always is sensuous; or it shows merely the manner in which we are affected by objects. But, we have also *understanding*, or the faculty of thinking the object of sensuous perception. Neither of these is to be regarded as superior to the other. Without sensibility no object would be given to us, without understanding none would be thought. Thoughts without content are empty, perceptions without conceptions are blind. It is therefore just as necessary to make our conceptions sensuous, that is, to add the object to them in perception, as it is to make our perceptions intelligible, that is, to bring them under conceptions. Neither of these faculties or capacities can do the work of the other. Understanding can perceive nothing, the senses can think nothing. Knowledge arises only from their united action. But this is no reason for confusing the function of either with that of the other; it is rather a strong reason for carefully separating and distinguishing the one from the other. Hence it is, that we distinguish Aesthetic, as the science of the universal rules of sensibility, from Logic, which is the science of the universal rules of understanding.

General logic, as distinguished from the special logic or organon of a particular science, is either pure or applied; but only the former is in the strict sense a science. There are two rules that must ever be kept in mind in pure general logic. (1) As *general* logic, it abstracts from all content of thought, and from all distinction of objects, and deals only with the pure form of thought. (2) As *pure* logic, it has no empirical principles. Psychology has no influence on the canon of the understanding, and therefore it does not, as has sometimes been supposed, contribute anything to pure logic. Logic is a demonstrative science, and whatever it contains must be certain entirely *a priori.*

2. TRANSCENDENTAL LOGIC

Pure general logic, then, abstracts from all the content of knowledge, or what is the same thing, from all relation of knowledge to its objects, and considers merely the logical form implied in the relation of one element of knowledge to another, or the universal form of thought. Now, we have learned from the Transcendental Aesthetic that there are pure as well as empirical perceptions, and it may well be, that a similar distinction obtains between the pure and the empirical thought of objects. In that case, there will be a logic that does not abstract from all the content of knowledge. Containing merely the rules of the pure thought of an object, it will exclude all knowledge, the content of which is empirical. It will also refer our knowledge of objects to its origin, in so far as that origin cannot be ascribed to objects themselves.

Let us suppose, then, that there are conceptions which relate to objects *a priori*, but which, as mere functions of pure thought, stand to objects in quite a different relation from that in which perceptions stand to them, whether these are pure or sensuous. As these conceptions will be of neither empirical nor aesthetic origin, we get the idea of a science of pure understanding and pure reason, the aim of which is to examine into the knowledge which we obtain by thinking objects completely *a priori*. Such a science, as setting forth the origin, the limits, and the objective validity of pure conceptions, we must call *Transcendental Logic*.

18. Konrad Lorenz

EDITOR'S INTRODUCTION

Kant devoted a great deal of effort to demonstrating that there are only 2 forms of intuition (space and time) and 12 categories of judgment (of which substance and causality are perhaps the most important). It is now generally agreed that the specific modes of thought that Kant took to be fundamental and a priori are actually a reflection of the scientific world view prevalent during the latter part of the 18th century. This recognition, rather than destroying Kant's basic insight into the relationship between knowledge and reality, has stimulated further research into the origins of the a priori. The reading by Konrad Lorenz presented here deals with one phase of that research, namely, the biological determinants of thought. To outline briefly, Lorenz argues that each species has evolved its own categories of thought. These species-characteristic categories are a priori in the sense that they are prior to, and necessary for, the experience of any given individual; they are, however, a posteriori in the sense that they are dependent on the collective experience of the species during the course of evolution.

When a priori categories of thought are interpreted within a biological perspective, new light is thrown on Kant's distinction between objects of experience (phenomena) and things as they are in themselves (noumena). According to Kant, "physical" objects (substance) exist only in experience; moreover, it is only in experience that principles such as cause and effect have meaning. We thus cannot *know* what things in themselves are "really" like. However, we can *think* and have beliefs about things in themselves. Such beliefs are not based on theoretical knowledge but are the result of practical considerations. This distinction between theoretical knowledge of phenomena and practical beliefs about things in themselves can be illustrated by Kant's solution to the perennial issue of freedom versus determinism. Kant thought it necessary to moral conduct to believe in freedom of the will. But this belief, he maintained, is not incompatible with a deterministic philosophy of science, for the will is an aspect of the noumenal self. Observable behavior, on the other hand, is a part of the phenomenal world and hence is subject to the principle of causality.

There is thus a wide gulf between phenomena and noumena within Kant's system. In some respects, an interpretation of the a priori in biological terms widens this gulf even further. Not only can't we know things in themselves, but what we do know (objects of experience) is made dependent on the peculiar evolutionary history of the species. It is easy to envision, for example, another species of animals that was equal in intelligence to human beings but that had undergone a very different course of evolution. Members of such a species might experience the world very differently than we now do, and they might also develop a very different (though equally valid) "species-specific" science.

In another respect, however, an evolutionary perspective helps to bridge the gap between the phenomenal and noumenal worlds. This is because thought processes, being biological adaptations, must reflect the way things are in themselves. Lorenz illustrates this point by considering such morphological features as the hoof of a horse or the fin of a fish. These are biological adaptations to certain environments; and, in a sense, the hoof does reflect a "knowledge" of the terrain, and the fin a "knowledge" of the sea. It is this fact that allows paleontologists to reconstruct the environment of an extinct species from its skeletal remains.

What can be said of the skeletal apparatus can be said even more appropriately of the "apparatus of thought." That is, our ways of experiencing nature are intimately related to, and reflect a knowledge of, things in themselves. This knowledge is, of course, limited and only partial. As mystics are wont to emphasize, there are ways of experiencing nature other than through the senses and by means of ordinary discursive thought. But although mystics may be right in this regard, theirs is not the only way of transcending the limitations imposed by evolution on human cognition. Through the development of sophisticated scientific instruments, it is now possible to experience events (from subatomic particles to intergalactic spaces) that are unlike anything experienced by our evolutionary ancestors. These experiences demand, in turn, new conceptual schemes that transcend biologically conditioned categories of thought. In short, biological evolution has set certain constraints on the way we as human beings think and perceive; on the other hand, cultural evolution has provided the means by which those constraints can be overcome, at least to a limited degree.

Kant's Doctrine of the A Priori
in the Light of Contemporary Biology

For Kant, the categories of space, time, causality, etc., are givens established a priori, determining the form of all of our experience, and indeed making experience possible. For Kant, the validity of these primary principles of reason is absolute. This validity is fundamentally independent of the laws of the real nature which lies behind appearances. This validity is not to be thought of as arising from these laws. The a priori categories and forms of intuition cannot be related to the laws inherent in the "thing-in-itself" by abstraction or any other means. The only thing we can assert about the thing-in-itself, according to Kant, is the reality of its existence. The relationship which exists between it and the form in which it affects our senses and appears in our world of experience is, for Kant, alogical (to somewhat overstate it). For Kant, the thing-in-itself is on principle unknowable, because the form of its appearance is determined by the purely ideal forms and categories of intuition, so that its appearance has no connection with its essence. This is the viewpoint of Kantian "transcendental" or "critical" idealism, restated in a condensed version.

Kant's orientation has been transformed very liberally by various natural philosophers. In particular, the ever more urgent questionings of the theory of evolution have led to conceptions of the a priori which are perhaps not so far removed from those of Kant himself as from those of the Kantian philosopher tied to the exact terms of Kant's definition of his concepts.

Reprinted with permission from *General Systems Yearbook*, 1962, 7, 23–30.

Translated from: Kant's Lehre vom apriorischen im Lichte geganwärtiger Biologie. *Blätter für Deutsche Philosophie*, 1941, 15, 94–125. This rough translation has been prepared by Charlotte Ghurye and edited by Donald T. Campbell with the assistance of Professor Lorenz and William A. Reupke. Ghurye, Lorenz, and Reupke have not had an opportunity to see the translation in its present form. While the translation is still very uneven, there is one naiveté of wording which represents a deliberate avoiding of some more sophisticated usages. The hyphenated phrase "thing-in-itself" has been used as a translation for the Kantian phrases "Ding an sich," "An sich Seienden," "An sich Bestehended," "An sich der Dinge," "An sich extenden Natur," etc. This has seemed preferable here to the usual usages of leaving the phrase untranslated, or of translating it into the Greek "noumena." To preserve some Kantian distinctions even at the expense of awkward renditions, these equivalents have been used: Wahrnehmung = perception; Anschauung = intuition; Realität = reality; Wirklichkeit = actuality; Gegenstand = object; Ding = thing.

The biologist convinced of the fact of the great creative events of evolution asks of Kant these questions: Is not human reason with all its categories and forms of intuition something that has organically evolved in a continuous cause-effect relationship with the laws of the immediate nature, just as has the human brain? Would not the laws of reason necessary for a priori thought be entirely different if they had undergone an entirely different historical mode of origin, and if consequently we had been equipped with an entirely different kind of central nervous system? Is it at all probable that the laws of our cognitive apparatus should be disconnected with those of real external world? Can an organ that has evolved in the process of a continuous coping with the laws of nature have remained so uninfluenced that the theory of appearances can be pursued independently of the existence of the thing-in-itself, as if the two were totally independent of each other? In answering these questions the biologist takes a sharply circumscribed point of view. The exposition of this point of view is the subject of the present paper. We are not just concerned with special discussions of space, time and causality. The latter are for our study simply examples of the Kantian theory of the a priori, and are treated incidentally to our comparison of the views of the a priori taken by transcendental idealism and the biologist.

It is the duty of the natural scientist to attempt a natural explanation before he contents himself with drawing upon factors extraneous to nature. This is an important duty for the psychologist who has to cope with the fact that something like Kant's a priori forms of thought do exist. One familiar with the innate modes of reaction of subhuman organisms can readily hypothesize that the a priori is due to hereditary differentiations of the central nervous system which have become characteristic of the species, producing hereditary dispositions to think in certain forms. One must realize that this conception of the "a priori" as an organ means the destruction of the concept: something that has evolved in evolutionary adaptation to the laws of the natural external world has evolved a posteriori in a certain sense, even if in a way entirely different from that of abstraction or deduction from previous experience. The functional similarities which have led many researchers to Lamarckian views about the origin of hereditary modes of reaction from previous "species experience" today are recognized as completely misleading.

The essential character of the natural sciences of today signifies such an abandonment of transcendental idealism that a rift has developed between the scientist and the Kantian philosopher. The rift is caused by the fundamental change of the concepts of the thing-in-itself and the transcendental, a change which results from the redefinition of the concept of the a priori. If the "a priori" apparatus of possible experience with all its forms of intuition and categories is not something immutably determined by factors extraneous to nature but rather something that mirrors the natural laws in contact with which it has evolved in the closest reciprocal interaction, then the boundaries of the transcendental begin to shift. Many aspects of the thing-in-itself which completely escape being experienced by our present-day apparatus of thought and perception may lie within the boundaries of possible experience in the near future, geologically speaking. Many of those aspects which today are within the sphere of the imminent may have still been beyond these boundaries in the recent past of mankind. It is obvious that the question of the extent to which the absolutely existent can be experienced by one *particular* organism has the slightest influence on the fundamental question. However, such consideration alters something in the definition which we have to make of the thing-in-itself behind the phenomena. For Kant (who in all his speculations took into consideration only mature civilized man, representing an immutable system created by God) no obstacle presented itself to defining the thing-in-itself as basically uncognizable. In his static way of looking at it, he could include the limit of possible experience in the definition of the thing-in-itself. This limit would be the same for man and amoeba—infinitely far from the thing-in-itself. In view of the indubitable fact of evolution this is no longer tenable. Even if we recognize that the absolutely existent will never be completely knowable (even for the highest imaginable living beings there will be a limit set by the necessity of categorical forms of thought), the boundary separating the experienceable from the transcendental must vary for each individual type of organism. The location of the boundary has to be investigated separately for each type of organism. It would mean an unjustifiable anthropomorphism to include the purely accidental present-day location of this boundary for the human species in the definition of the thing-in-itself. If, in spite of the indubitable evolutionary modifiability of our apparatus of experience one nevertheless wanted to continue to define the thing-in-itself as that which is uncognizable for this very apparatus, the definition of the absolute would thereby be held to be relative, obviously an absurdity. Rather, every natural silence urgently needs a concept of the absolutely real which is as little anthropomorphic and as independent as possible of the accidental, present-day location of the limits of the humanly experienceable. The absolutely actual can in no way be a matter of the degree to which it is reflected in the brain of a human, or any other temporary form. On the other hand, it is the object of a most important branch of comparative science to investigate the type of this reflection, and to find out the extent to which it is in the form of crudely simplifying symbols which are only superficially analogous or to what extent it reproduces details, i.e., how far its exactness goes. By this investigation of prehuman forms of knowledge we hope to gain clues to the mode of functioning and historical origin of our own knowledge, and in this manner to push ahead the critique of knowledge further than was possible without such comparisons.

I assert that nearly all natural scientists of today, at least all biologists, consciously or unconsciously assume in their daily work a real relationship between the thing-in-itself and the phenomena of our subjective experience, but a relationship that is by no means a "purely" ideal one in the Kantian sense. I even would like to assert that Kant himself assumed this in all the results of his own empirical research. In our opinion, the real relationship between the thing-in-itself and the specific a priori form of its appearance has been determined by the fact that the form of appearance has developed as an adaptation to the laws of the thing-in-itself in the coping negotiation with these continuously present laws during the evolutionary history of mankind, lasting hundreds of millenia. This adaptation has provided our thought with an innate structuralization which corresponds to a considerable degree to the reality of the external world. "Adaptation" is a word already loaded with meaning and easily misunderstood. It should not, in the present condition, denote more than that our forms of intuition and categories "fit" to that which really exists in the manner in which our foot fits the floor or the fin of the fish suits the water. The a priori which determines the forms of appearance of the real things in our world is, in short, an organ, or more precisely the functioning of an organ. We come closer to understanding the a priori if we confront it with the questions asked of everything organic: "What for," "where from," and "why." These questions are, first, how does it preserve the species; second, what is its genealogical origin; third, what natural causes make it possible. We are convinced that the a priori is based on central nervous systems which are entirely as real as the things of the external world whose phenomenal form they determine for us. This central nervous apparatus does not prescribe the laws of nature any more than the hoof of the horse prescribes the form of the ground. Just as the hoof of the horse, this central nervous apparatus stumbles over unforeseen changes in its task. But just as the hoof of the horse is adapted to the ground of the steppe which it copes with, so our central nervous apparatus for organizing the image of the world is adapted to the real world with which man has to cope. Just like any organ, this apparatus has attained its expedient species-preserving form through this coping of real with the real during its genealogical evolution, lasting many eons.

Our view of the origin of the "a priori" (an origin which in a certain sense is "a posteriori") answers very fittingly Kant's question as to whether the forms of perception of space and time, which we do not derive from experience (as Kant, contrary to Hume, emphasizes quite correctly) but which are a priori in our representation "were not mere chimeras of the brain made by us to which no object corresponds, at least not adequately."[1] If we conceive our intellect as the function of an organ (and there is no valid argument against this) our obvious answer to the question why its form of function is adapted to the real world is simply the following: Our categories and forms of perception, fixed prior to individual experience, are adapted to the external world for exactly the same reasons as the hoof of the horse is already adapted to the ground of the steppe before the horse is born and the fin of the fish is adapted to the water before the fish hatches. No sensible person believes that in any of these cases the form of the organ "prescribes" its properties to the object. To everyone it is self-evident that water possesses its properties independently of whether the fins of the fish are biologically adapted to these properties or not. Quite evidently some properties of the thing-in-itself which is at the bottom of the phenomenon "water" have led to the specific form of adaptation of the fins which have been evolved independently of one another by fishes, reptiles, birds, mammals, cephalopods, snails, crayfish, arrow worms, etc. It is obviously the properties of water that have prescribed to these different organisms the corresponding form and function of their organ of locomotion. But when reckoning in regard to structure and mode of function of his own brain the transcendental philosopher assumes something fundamentally different. In paragraph 11 of the Prolegomena Kant says: "If anyone were to have the slightest doubt that both [the forms of intuition of space and time] are not determinations of the thing in itself but mere determinations of their relation to sensibility, I should like to know how it could be found possible to know a priori and thus prior to all acquaintance with things, namely before they are given

---

[1] Prolegomena, First Part, Note III. The present translators have used here the translation of Kant provided by P. G. Lucas, Manchester University Press, 1953.

to us, what their intuition must be like, which is the case here with space and time."[2] This question clarifies two very important facts. First, it shows that Kant, no more than Hume, thought of the possibility of a formal adaptation between thought and reality other than through abstracting from previous experience. Second, it shows that he assumed the impossibility of any different form of origin. Furthermore, it shows the great and fundamentally new discovery of Kant, i.e., that human thought and perception have certain functional structures prior to every individual experience.

Most certainly Hume was wrong when he wanted to derive all that is a priori from that which the senses supply to experience, just as wrong as Wundt or Helmholtz who simply explain it as an abstraction from preceding experience. Adaptation of the a priori to the real world has no more originated from "experience" than has adaptation of the fin of the fish to the properties of water. Just as the form of the fin is given a priori, prior to any individual coping of the young fish with the water, and just as it is this form that makes possible this coping: so is it also the case with our forms of perception and categories in their relationship to our coping with the real external world by means of experience. For animals there are specific limitations to the forms of experience which are possible. We believe we can demonstrate the closest functional and probably genetic relationship between these animal a priori's and our human a priori.

Contrary to Hume, we believe as did Kant in the possibility of a "pure" science of the innate forms of human thought independent of all experience. This "pure" science, however, would be able to convey only a very one-sided understanding of the essence of a priori forms of thought because it neglects the organic nature of these structures and does not pose the basic biological question concerning their species-preserving meaning. Bluntly speaking, it is just as if someone wanted to write a "pure" theory on the characteristics of a modern photographic camera, a Leica for example, without taking into consideration that this is an apparatus for photographing the external world, and without consulting the pictures the camera produces which enable one to understand its function and the essential meaning of its existence. As far as the produced pictures (just as experiences) are concerned, the Leica is entirely a priori. It exists prior to and independently of every picture; indeed, it determines the form of the pictures, nay, makes them possible in the first place. Now I assert: To separate "pure Leicology" from the theory of the pictures it

---

[2] Translation of P. G. Lucas, Manchester University Press, 1953.

produces is just as meaningless as to separate the theory of the a priori from the theory of the external world, of phenomenology from the theory of the thing-in-itself. All the lawfulnesses of our intellect which we find to be there a priori are not freaks of nature. We live off them! And we can get insight into their essential meaning only if we take into consideration their function. Just as the Leica could not originate without the activity of photography, carried out long before the Leica was constructed, just as the completed Leica with all its incredibly well-conceived and "fitting" constructional details has not dropped from the heavens, so neither has our infinitely more wonderful "pure reason." This, too, has arrived at its relative perfection from out of its activity, from its negotiation with the thing-in-itself.

Although for the transcendental idealist the relationship between the thing-in-itself and its appearance is extraneous to nature and alogical, it is entirely real for us. It is certain that not only does the thing-in-itself "affect" our receptors, but also vice versa, our effectors on their part "affect" absolute reality. The word "actually" comes from the verb "to act." [Wirklichkeit kommt von Wirker!] What appears in our world is by no means only our experience one-sidedly influenced by real external things as they work on us as through the lenses of the ideal possibilities of experience. What we witness as experience is always a coping of the real in us with the real outside of us. Therefore the relationship between the events in and outside of us is not alogical and does not basically prohibit drawing conclusions about the lawfulness of the external world from the lawfulness of the internal events. Rather, this relationship is the one which exists between image and object, between a simplified model and the real thing. It is the relationship of an analogy of greater or less remoteness. The degree of this analogy is fundamentally open to comparative investigation. That is, it is possible to make statements as to whether agreement between appearance and actuality is more exact or less exact in comparing one human being to another, or one living organism to another.

On these premises also depends the self-evident fact that there are more and less correct judgments about the external world! The relationship between the world of phenomena and things-in-themselves is thus not fixed once-and-for-all by ideal laws of form which are extraneous to nature and in principle inaccessible to investigation. Neither do the judgments made on the basis of these "necessities of thought" have an independent and absolute validity. Rather, all our forms of intuition and categories are thoroughly natural. Like every other organ, they are evolutionarily developed receptacles for the reception and retroactive utilization of those lawful consequences of the thing-in-itself with which we have to cope if we want to remain alive and preserve our species. The special form of these organic receptacles has the properties of the thing-in-itself a relationship grown entirely out of real natural connections. The organic receptacles are adapted to these properties in a manner that has a practical biological sufficiency, but which is by no means absolute nor even so precise that one could say their form equals that of the thing-in-itself. Even if we as natural scientists are in a certain sense naive realists, we still do not take the appearance for the thing-in-itself nor the experienced reality for the absolutely existent! Thus we are not surprised to find the laws of "pure reason" entangled in the most serious contradictions not only with one another, but also with the empirical facts whenever research demands greater precision. This happens particularly where physics and chemistry enter the nuclear phase. There not only does the intuition-form of space-perception break down, but also the categories of causality, or substantiality, and in a certain sense even quantity (even though quantity otherwise appears to have the most unconditional validity except for the intuition-form of time-perception). "Necessary for thought" in no way means "absolutely valid" in view of these empirical facts, highly essential in nuclear physics, quantum mechanics and wave theory.

The realization that all laws of "pure reason" are based on highly physical or mechanical structures of the human central nervous system which have developed through many eons like any other organ, on the one hand shakes our confidence in the laws of pure reason and on the other hand substantially raises our confidence in them. Kant's statement that the laws of pure reason have absolute validity, nay, that every imaginable rational being, even if it were an angle, must obey the same laws of thought, appears as an anthropocentric presumption. Surely the "keyboard" provided by the forms of intuition and categories—Kant himself calls it that—is something definitely located on the physico-structural side of the psychophysical unity of the human organism. The forms of intuition and categories relate to the "freedom" of the mind (if there is such a thing) as physical structures are usually related to the possible degrees of freedom of the psychic, namely by both supporting and restraining at the same time. But surely these clumsy categorical boxes into which we have to pack our external world "in order to be able to spell them as experiences" (Kant) can claim no autonomous and absolute validity whatsoever. This is certain for us the moment we conceive them as evolutionary adaptations—and I would indeed like to know what scientific argument could be brought against this conception. At the same time, however, the nature of their adaptation shows that the categorical forms of intuition and categories have proved themselves as working hypotheses in the coping of our species with the absolute reality of the environment (in spite of their validity being only approximate and relative). This has clarified the paradoxical fact that the laws of "pure reason" which break down at every step in modern theoretical science, nonetheless have stood (and still stand) the test in the practical biological matters of the struggle for the preservation of the species.

The "dots" produced by the coarse "screens" used in the reproductions of photographs in our daily papers are satisfactory representations when looked at superficially, but cannot stand closer inspection with a magnifying glass. So, too, the reproductions of the world by our forms of intuition and categories break down as soon as they are required to give a somewhat closer representation of their objects, as is the case in wave mechanics and nuclear physics. All the knowledge an individual can wrest from the empirical reality of the "physical world-picture" is essentially only a working hypothesis. And as far as their species-preserving function goes, all those innate structures of the mind which we call "a priori" are likewise only working hypotheses. Nothing is absolute except that which hides in and behind the phenomena. Nothing that our brain can think has absolute a priori validity in the true sense of the word, not even mathematics with all its laws. The laws of mathematics are but an organ for the quantification of external things, and what is more, an organ exceedingly important for man's life, without which he never could play his role in dominating the earth, and which thus has amply proved itself biologically, as have all the other "necessary" structures of thought. Of course, "pure" mathematics is not only possible, it is, as a theory of the internal laws of this miraculous organ of quantification, of an importance that can hardly be overestimated. But this does not justify us in making it absolute. Counting and mathematical number affect reality in approximately the same manner as do a dredging-machine and its shovels. Regarded statistically, in a large number of individual cases each shovel dredges up roughly the same amount but actually not even two can ever have exactly the same content. The pure mathematical equation is a tautology: I state that if my dredging-machine brings in such and such a number of shovels, then such and such a number are brought in. Two shovels of my machine are absolutely equal to each other because strictly speaking it is the same shovel each time, namely the number one.

But only the empty sentence always has this validity. Two shovels filled with something or other are never equal to each other, the number one applied to a real object will never find its equal in the whole universe. It is true that two plus two equals four, but two apples, rams or atoms plus two more never equal four others because no equal apples, rams or atoms exist! In this sense we arrive at the paradoxical fact that the equation two plus two equals four in its application to real units, such as apples or atoms, has a much smaller degree of approximation to reality than the equation two million plus two million equal four million because the individual dissimilarities of the counted units level out statistically in the case of a large number. Regarded as a working hypothesis or as a functional organ, the form of thought of numerical quantification is and remains one of the most miraculous apparatuses that nature has ever created; it evokes the admiration of the biologist, particularly by the incredible breadth of its sphere of application even if one does not consider its sphere of validity absolute.

It would be entirely conceivable to imagine a rational being that does not quantify by means of the mathematical number (that does not use 1, 2, 3, 4, 5, the number of individuals approximately equal among themselves, such as rams, atoms or milestones, to mark the quantity at hand) but grasps these immediately in some other way. Instead of quantifying water by the number of the filled liter vessels, one could, for example, conclude from the tension of a rubber balloon of a certain size how much water it contains. It can very well be purely coincidental, in other words brought about by purely historical causes, that our brain happens to be able to quantify extensive quantities more readily than intensive ones. It is by no means a necessity of thought and it would be entirely conceivable that the ability to quantify intensively according to the method indicated by the example of measuring the tension in the rubber balloon could be developed up to the point where it would become equally valuable and replace numerical mathematics. Indeed, the ability to estimate quantities immediately, present in man and in a number of animals, is probably due to such an intensive process of quantification. A mind quantifying in a purely intensive manner would carry out some operations more simply and immediately than our mathematics of the "dredging-scoop" variety. For example, it might be able to calculate curves immediately, which is possible in our extensive mathematics only by means of the detour of integral and differential calculus, a detour which tides us over the limitations of the numerical steps, but still clings to them conceptually. An intellect quantifying purely by intensity would not be able to grasp that two times two equals four. Since it would have no understanding for the number one, for our empty numerical box, it would also not comprehend our postulate of the equality of two such boxes and would reply to our arrangement of an equation that it is incorrect because no equal boxes, rams or atoms exist. And in regard to its system, it would be just as correct in its statement as we would be in ours. Certainly an intensive quantification system would perform many operations more poorly, that is, in a more involved manner, than does numerical mathematics. The fact that the latter has developed so much further than the ability of intensive quantitative estimation speaks for its being the more "practical" one. But even so it is and remains only an organ, an evolutionarily acquired, "innate working hypothesis" which basically is only approximately adapted to the data of the thing-in-itself.

If a biologist attempts to grasp the relationship of hereditary structure to the regulated plasticity of all that is organic, he arrives at a universal law holding both for physical and intellectual structures and as valid for the plastic protoplasm and the skeletal elements of a protozoan as for the categorical forms of thought and the creative plasticity of the human mind. From its simplest beginnings in the domain of the protozoa, solid structure is just as much a condition for any higher evolution as is organic plasticity. In this sense, solid structure is just as indispensable and as consistent a property of living matter as is its plastic freedom. However, every solid structure, although indispensable as a support for the organic system, carries with it an undesired side effect: it makes for rigidness, and takes away a certain degree of freedom from the system. Every enlistment of a mechanical structure means in some sense to bind oneself. Von Uexkuell has said aptly: "The amoeba is less of a machine than the horse," thinking mainly about physical properties. Nietzsche has expressed poetically the same relationship between structure and plasticity in human thought: ". . . a thought—Now still hot liquid lava, but all lava builds a castle around itself. Every thought finally crushes itself with 'laws.'" This simile of a structure crystallizing out of the liquid state goes much deeper than Nietzsche sensed: It is not entirely impossible that all that becomes solid, in the intellectual-psychic as well as in the physical, is bound to be a transition from the liquid state of certain plasma parts to the solid state.

But Nietzsche's simile and Uexkuell's statement overlook something. The horse is a higher animal than the amoeba not despite, but to a large extent because of its being richer in solid differentiated structures. Organisms with as few structures as possible must remain amoebae, whether they like it or not, for without any solid structure all higher organization is inconceivable. One could symbolize organisms with a maximum of highly differentiated fixed structures as lobsters, stiffly armored creatures which could move only in certain joints with precisely allowed degrees of freedom or as railroad cars which could only move along a prescribed track having very few switching points. For every living being, increasing mental and physical differentiation is always a compromise between these two extremes, neither one representing the highest realization of the possibilities of organic creation. Always and everywhere differentiation to a higher level of mechanical structure has the dangerous tendency to fetter the mind, whose servant it was just a moment ago, and to prevent its further evolution. The hard exoskeleton of the arthropods is such an obstruction in evolution, as is also the fixed instinctual movements of many higher organisms and the industrial machinery of man.

Indeed, every system of thought that commits itself to a nonplastic "absolute" has this same fettering effect. The moment such a system is finished, when it has disciples who believe in its perfection, it is already "false." Only in the state of becoming is the philosopher a human being in the most proper meaning of the word. I am reminded of the beautiful definition of man which we owe to the pragmatist and which probably is given in its clearest formulation in Gehlen's book *Der Mensch*. Man is defined as the permanently unfinished being, permanently unadapted and poor in structure, but continuously open to the world, continuously in the state of becoming.

When the human thinker, be it even the greatest, has finished his system, he has in a fundamental way taken on something of the properties of the lobster or the railroad car. However, ingeniously his disciples may manipulate the prescribed and permitted degrees of freedom of his lobster-armor, his system will only be a blessing for the progress of human thought and knowledge when he finds followers who break it apart and, using new, not "built in," degrees of freedom, turn its pieces into a new construction. If, however, a system of thought is so well joined together that for a long time no one appears who has the power and the courage to burst it asunder, it can obstruct progress for centuries: "There lies the stone, one has to let it be, and everyone limps on his crutch of faith to devil's stone, to devil's bridge!" (Goethe *Faust*).

And just as a system of thought created by the individual human being enslaves its creator, so also do the evolutionarily developed supra-individual forms of thought of the a priori: They, too, are held to be absolute! The machine whose species-preserving meaning was originally in quantifying real external things, the machine that was created for "counting rams" suddenly pretends to be absolute and buzzes with an admirable absence of internal friction and contradiction, but only as long as it runs empty, counting its own shovels. If one lets a dredging machine, an engine, a band saw, a theory, or an a priori function of thought run empty in this way, then its function proceeds ipso facto without noticeable friction, heat, or noise; for the parts in such a system do not, of course, contradict one another and so fit together intelligibly and in a well-tuned manner. When empty they are indeed "absolute," but absolutely empty. Only when the system is expected to work, that is, to achieve something in relation to the external world in which the real and species-preserving meaning of its whole existence does indeed consist, then the thing starts to groan and crack: when the shovels of the dredging-machine dig into the soil, the teeth of the band saw dig into the wood, or the assumptions of the theory dig into the material of empirical facts which is to be classified, then develop the undesirable side-noises that come from the inevitable imperfection of every naturally developed system: *and no other systems exist for the natural scientist.* But these noises are just what does indeed represent the coping of the system with the real external world. In this sense they are the door through which the thing-in-itself peeps into our world of phenomena, the door through which the road to further knowledge continues to lead. They, and not the unresisting empty humming of the apparatus are "reality." They, are indeed, what we have to place under the magnifying glass if we want to get to know the imperfections of our apparatus of thought and experience and if we want to gain knowledge beyond these imperfections. The side-noises have to be considered methodically if the machine is to be improved. The fundamentals of pure reason are just as imperfect and down to earth as the band saw, but also just as real.

Our working hypothesis should read as follows: Everything is a working hypothesis. This holds true not only for the natural laws which we gain through individual abstraction a posteriori from the facts of our experience, but also for the laws of pure reason. The faculty of understanding does not in itself constitute an explanation of phenomena, but the fact that it projects phenomena for us in a practically usable form on to the projection-screen of our experiencing is due to its formulation of working hypotheses; developed in evolution and tested through millions of years!

Santayana says: "Faith in the intellect is the only faith that has justified itself by the fruit it has borne. But the one who clings forever to the form of faith is a Don Quixote, rattling with outmoded armor. I am a decided materialist with regard to natural philosophy, but I do not claim to know what matter is. I am waiting for the men of science to tell me that."

Our view that all human thought is only a working hypothesis must not be interpreted as lowering the value of the knowledge secured by mankind. It is true that this knowledge is only a working hypothesis for us, it is true that we are ready at any moment to throw overboard our favorite theories when new facts demand this. But even if nothing is "absolutely true," every new piece of knowledge, every new truth, is nevertheless a step forward in a very definite, definable direction: the absolutely existent is apprehended from a new, up to this point unknown, aspect; it is covered in a new characteristic. For us that working hypothesis is true which paves the way for the next step in knowledge or which at least does not obstruct the way. Human science must act like a scaffolding for reaching the greatest possible height, without its absolute extent being foreseeable at the start of the construction. At the moment when such a construction is committed to a permanently-set supporting pillar, the latter fits only a building of a certain form and size. Once these are reached and the building is to continue, the supporting-pillar has to be demolished and rebuilt, a process which can become the more dangerous for the entire structure, the more deeply that which is to be rebuilt is set in its foundation. Since it is a constituent property of all true science that its structure should continue to grow into the boundless, all that is mechanically systematic, all that corresponds to solid structures and scaffolding, must always be something provisional, alterable at anytime. The tendency to secure one's own building for the future by declaring it absolute leads to the opposite of the intended success: Just that "truth" which is dogmatically believed in, sooner or later leads to a revolution in which the actual truth-content and value of the old theory are all too easily demolished and forgotten along with the obsolete obstructions to progress. The heavy cultural losses which may accompany revolutions are special cases of this phenomenon. The character of all truths as working hypotheses must always be kept in mind, in order to prevent the necessity of demolishing the established structure, and in order to preserve for the "established" truths, that eternal value which they potentially deserve.

Our conception that a priori forms of thought and intuition have to be understood just as any other organic adaptation carries with it the fact that they are for us "inherited working hypotheses," so to speak, whose truth-content is related to the absolutely existent in the same manner as that of ordinary working hypotheses which have proven themselves just as splendidly adequate in coping with the external world. This conception, it is true, destroys our faith in the absolute truth of any a priori thesis necessary for thought. On the other hand it gives the conviction that something actual "adequately corresponds" to every phenomenon in our world. Even the smallest detail of the world of phenomena "mirrored" for us by the innate working hypotheses of our forms of intuition and thought is in fact pre-formed to the phenomenon it reproduces, having a relationship corresponding to the one existing between organic structures and the external world in general (e.g., the analogy of the fin of the fish and the hoof of the horse, above). It is true that the a priori is only a box whose form unpretentiously fits that of the actuality to be portrayed. This box, however, is accessible to our investigation even if we cannot comprehend the thing-in-itself except by means of the box. But access to the laws of the box, i.e., of the instrument, makes the thing-in-itself relatively comprehensible. . . .

X. THE EVOLUTION OF BEHAVIOR

19. Charles Darwin

EDITOR'S INTRODUCTION

Ernst Mayr, a prominent contemporary biologist, described the Darwinian revolution as "perhaps the most fundamental of all intellectual revolutions in the history of mankind."[1] A similar statement could be made—and undoubtedly has been—by the enthusiastic supporters of any of the historical figures represented in this volume. Partisan enthusiasm aside, Darwin does hold a special place in the history of psychological thought. The theory of evolution initiated by Darwin, and refined by many others over the last century, is the only theory in the life sciences that bears comparison in scope and explanatory power to the major theories of the physical sciences (e.g., Newtonian physics and Einstein's theory of relativity).

Darwin's contribution to the theory of evolution is often depicted as twofold. First, through careful observation and argument, he established beyond reasonable doubt the existence of biological evolution; and, second, he proposed a specific mechanism, natural selection, to explain how such evolution might occur. Both these points are in a sense correct, but they do not convey the full impact of Darwin's work. As was pointed out in Chapter 1, an evolutionary way of thinking was becoming common during the 19th century and was by no means limited to biological evolution. But even if we limit consideration to biology, many of Darwin's predecessors, including his own grandfather, had advanced evolutionary hypotheses in order to explain the similarity and diversity among species. Moreover, there was sufficient empirical evidence before Darwin to make a theory of evolution more plausible than the then-current theories of special creation. Still,

---

[1] E. Mayr, The nature of the Darwinian revolution. *Science*, 1972, *176*, 981.

most leading biologists before Darwin rejected the notion of evolution, and many remained unconvinced by his arguments. Why?

Opposition to the theory of evolution generally has been ascribed to theological and emotional factors. Certainly, these factors were an important source of opposition—and they remain so today. In 1973, for example, the Tennessee legislature passed a law that read in part:

> Any biology textbook used for teaching in the public schools which expresses an opinion of, or relates to a theory about the origins or creation of man and his world shall be prohibited from being used as a textbook in such system unless it specially states that it is a theory as to the origin and creation of man and his world and is not represented to be scientific fact. Any textbook so used in the public education system which expresses an opinion or relates to a theory or theories shall give in the same textbook and under the same subject commensurate attention to, and equal amount of emphasis on, the origins and creation of man and his world as the same is recorded in other theories including, but not limited to, the Genesis account in the Bible.[2]

It would be a mistake, however, to attribute all opposition to Darwin to religious dogmatism, or to political and social ideology. Mayr[3] has suggested that the truly revolutionary aspect of Darwin's theory—and the source of much of the original opposition among biologists—lay not in its threat to religious orthodoxy, but in its fundamentally new way of thinking about species. Prior to Darwin, most biologists were what might be called *essentialists.* That is, they believed that all members of a species must share some essential characteristic that differentiates them from members of other species, and, moreover, that these essential characteristics are in some sense "real." There are several varieties of the essentialist thesis, reflecting either the Platonic or Aristotelian traditions regarding substantial forms. In either case, essentialism attributes greater reality to what is common to members of a group than to individual differences. The latter are treated as "noise" in the system or as imperfect reflections of reality. Ghiselin has summarized the essentialist nature of pre-Darwinian biology as follows:

> What was real was the essence and the differentae, and the peculiarities of individuals were overlooked. An implication, of enormous historical

---

[2] This law was declared unconstitutional in 1975 by the Tennessee Supreme Court.
[3] Op. cit.

importance, was that it became very difficult to classify things which change, or which grade into one another, and even to conceive of or to discuss them. Indeed, the very attempt of reason in terms of essences forces one to ignore everything dynamic or transitory. One could hardly design a philosophy better suited to predispose one toward dogmatic reasoning and static concepts. The Darwinian revolution thus depended upon the collapse of the Western intellectual tradition.[4]

The Darwinian conception of a species is that of a *population* of potentially interacting (in this case, interbreeding) individuals. From such a populational viewpoint, individual differences represent reality while common characteristics become mental fictions (cf. the "average" American). The essentialist thesis is thus turned inside out.

Like many intellectual innovations, a populational viewpoint appears quite simple. But the simplicity is deceptive. Even today, most people find it very difficult to think in populational terms. Take, for example, popular treatments of race (subspecies). All members of a particular race, it is often implied, share some common characteristic that sets them apart from members of other races. The "sophisticated" student is liable to scoff at such an assertion, recognizing in it one of the roots of racial prejudice. It is one thing, however, to recognize the fallacy of an assertion when we disagree with its implications; it is another thing to recognize a similar fallacy when it forms part of an argument with which we basically agree. Consider, therefore, the following line of reasoning embedded in an argument against racial prejudice:

> If you spend your time concentrating upon variations, aren't you likely to forget about the nature of what you are studying and why it is there in the first place? For instance, if you set about accounting for variations in prejudice, won't you tend to ignore the nature and meaning of prejudice as a social phenomenon and what this might tell us about why there is prejudice at all?[5]

With the substitution of only a few words (namely, *species* for *prejudice* and *biological phenomenon* for *social phenomenon*), it is easy to imagine this argument being raised against Darwin's *Origin of Species*.

But let us return for a moment to Ghiselin's contention, quoted previously, that the Darwinian revolution "depended upon

[4] M. T. Ghiselin, *The triumph of the Darwinian method.* Berkeley: University of California Press, 1969, p. 52. Copyright © 1969 by The Regents of the University of California, reprinted by permission of the University of California Press.

[5] N. Armistead, Introduction. In M. N. Armistead (Ed.), *Reconstructing Social Psychology.* Baltimore: Penguin Books, 1974, p. 19, with permission.

the collapse of the Western intellectual tradition." This appears to be an overstatement, to say the least, because the repudiation of essentialism was by no means novel to Darwin. In philosophical terms, the antithesis of essentialism is *nominalism*, the view that only particulars are real, and that the only thing shared by all members of a group is their common name. Nominalism is the natural outgrowth of a consistently applied empiricism, because only particulars—not universals—can be the direct objects of sense perception.

Although the nominalist thesis has considerable intuitive appeal, if carried to an extreme it can lead to absurdities. We have seen, for example, how Hume's nominalism led him to claim that the concept of self refers to nothing but a bundle of disparate sensations, hardly a fruitful starting point for the analysis of personality. And to many, nominalism per se also did not seem to be a very fruitful starting point for a theory of biological evolution. If a species is nothing more than a name applied to a collection of individuals, then the evolution of species becomes terminological. Nevertheless, by providing a counterpoint to the essentialist thesis, nominalism helped pave the way for Darwin's conception of a species as a population or system of interrelated members. In Darwin's own words, "I look at the term species, as one arbitrarily given for the sake of convenience to a set of individuals closely resembling each other." But Darwin did not conclude from this, as a thoroughgoing nominalist might, that species do not exist *in any sense* but name only. Nominalism and essentialism represent two extreme positions, to which Darwin offered a creative synthesis.

It does not detract from Darwin's originality to say that his populational model represents an evolutionary step in, and not a collapse of, the Western intellectual tradition.

Notes on Writing
the "Origin of Species"

From September 1854 I devoted my whole time to arranging my huge pile of notes, to observing, and to experimenting in relation to the transmutation of species. During the voyage of the *Beagle* I had been deeply impressed by discovering in the Pampean formation great fossil animals covered with armour like that on the existing armadillos; secondly, by the manner in which closely allied animals replace one another in proceeding southwards over the Continent; and thirdly, by the South American character of most of the productions of the Galapagos archipelago, and more especially by the manner in which they differ slightly on each island of the group; none of the islands appearing to be very ancient in a geological sense.

It was evident that such facts as these, as well as many others, could only be explained on the supposition that species gradually become modified; and the subject haunted me. But it was equally evident that neither the action of the surrounding conditions, nor the will of the organisms (especially in the case of plants) could account for the innumerable cases in which organisms of every kind are beautifully adapted to their habits of life—for instance, a woodpecker or a tree-frog to climb trees, or a seed for dispersal by hooks or plumes. I had always been much struck by such adaptations, and until these could be explained it seemed to me almost useless to endeavour to prove by indirect evidence that species have been modified.

After my return to England it appeared to me that by following the example of Lyell in Geology, and by collecting all facts which bore in any way on the variation of animals and plants under domestication and nature, some light might perhaps be thrown on the whole subject. My first note-book was opened in July 1837. I worked on true Baconian principles, and without any theory collected facts on a wholesale scale, more especially with respect to domesticated productions, by printed enquiries, by conversation with skilful breeders and gardeners, and by extensive reading. When I see the list of books of all kinds which I read and abstracted, including whole series of Journals and Transactions, I am surprised at my industry. I soon perceived that selection was

From *The autobiography of Charles Darwin and selected papers*, Francis Darwin, Ed., New York: Dover, 1958. (Originally published, 1892). Pp. 41–44, 45, 46–47, 52–56, 57–58.

the keystone of man's success in making useful races of animals and plants. But how selection could be applied to organisms living in a state of nature remained for some time a mystery to me.

In October 1838, that is, fifteen months after I had begun my systematic enquiry, I happened to read for amusement Malthus on *Population*, and being well prepared to appreciate the struggle for existence which everywhere goes on from long-continued observation of the habits of animals and plants, it at once struck me that under these circumstances favourable variations would tend to be preserved and unfavourable ones to be destroyed. The result of this would be the formation of new species. Here, then, I had at last got a theory by which to work; but I was so anxious to avoid prejudice, that I determined not for some time to write even the briefest sketch of it. In June 1842 I first allowed myself the satisfaction of writing a very brief abstract of my theory in pencil in 35 pages; and this was enlarged during the summer of 1844 into one of 230 pages, which I had fairly copied out and still possess.

But at that time I overlooked one problem of great importance; and it is astonishing to me, except on the principle of Columbus and his egg, how I could have overlooked it and its solution. This problem is the tendency in organic beings descended from the same stock to diverge in character as they become modified. That they have diverged greatly is obvious from the manner in which species of all kinds can be classed under genera, genera under families, families under sub-orders, and so forth; and I can remember the very spot in the road, whilst in my carriage, when to my joy the solution occurred to me; and this was long after I had come to Down. The solution, as I believe, is that the modified offspring of all dominant and increasing forms tend to become adapted to many and highly diversified places in the economy of nature.

Early in 1856 Lyell advised me to write out my views pretty fully, and I began at once to do so on a scale three or four times as extensive as that which was afterwards followed in my *Origin of Species*; yet it was only an abstract of the materials which I had collected, and I got through about half the work on this scale. But my plans were overthrown, for early in the summer of 1858 Mr. Wallace, who was then in the Malay archipelago, sent me an essay *On the Tendency of Varieties to depart indefinitely from the Original Type*; and this essay contained exactly the same theory as mine. Mr. Wallace expressed the wish that if I thought well of his essay, I should send it to Lyell for perusal.

The circumstances under which I consented at the request of Lyell and Hooker to allow of an abstract from my MS., together with a letter to Asa Gray, dated September 5, 1857, to be published at the same time with Wallace's Essay, are given in the *Journal of the Proceedings of the Linnean Society*, 1858, p. 45. I was at first very unwilling to consent, as I thought Mr. Wallace might consider my doing so unjustifiable, for I did not then know how generous and noble was his disposition. The extract from my MS. and the letter to Asa Gray had neither been intended for publication, and were badly written. Mr. Wallace's essay, on the other hand, was admirably expressed and quite clear. Nevertheless, our joint productions excited very little attention, and the only published notice of them which I can remember was by Professor Haughton of Dublin, whose verdict was that all that was new in them was false, and what was true was old. This shows how necessary it is that any new view should be explained at considerable length in order to arouse public attention.

In September 1858 I set to work by the strong advice of Lyell and Hooker to prepare a volume on the transmutation of species, but was often interrupted by ill-health, and short visits to Dr. Lane's delightful hydropathic establishment at Moor Park. I abstracted the MS. begun on a much larger scale in 1856, and completed the volume on the same reduced scale. It cost me thirteen months and ten days' hard labour. It was published under the title of the *Origin of Species*, in November 1859. Though considerably added to and corrected in the later editions, it has remained substantially the same book.

It is no doubt the chief work of my life. It was from the first highly successful. The first small edition of 1250 copies was sold on the day of publication, and a second edition of 3000 copies soon afterwards. Sixteen thousand copies have now (1876) been sold in England; and considering how stiff a book it is, this is a large sale. It has been translated into almost every European tongue, even into such languages as Spanish, Bohemian, Polish, and Russian. . . .

The success of the *Origin* may, I think, be attributed in large part to my having long before written two condensed sketches, and to my having finally abstracted a much larger manuscript, which was itself an abstract. By this means I was enabled to select the more striking facts and conclusions. I had, also, during many years, followed a golden rule, namely, that whenever a published fact, a new observation or thought came across me, which was opposed to my general results, to make a memorandum of it without fail and at once: for I had found by experience that such facts and thoughts were far more apt to escape from the memory than favourable ones. Owing to this habit, very few objections were raised against my views which I had not at least noticed and attempted to answer.

It has sometimes been said that the success of the *Origin* proved "that the subject was in the air," or "that men's minds were prepared for it." I do not think that this is strictly true, for I occasionally sounded not a few naturalists, and never happened to come across a single one who seemed to doubt about the permanence of species. Even Lyell and Hooker, though they would listen with interest to me, never seemed to agree. I tried once or twice to explain to able men what I meant by Natural selection, but signally failed. What I believe was strictly true is that innumerable well-observed facts were stored in the minds of naturalists ready to take their proper places as soon as any theory which would receive them was sufficiently explained. Another element in the success of the book was its moderate size; and this I owe to the appearance of Mr. Wallace's essay; had I published on the scale in which I began to write in 1856, the book would have been four or five times as large as the *Origin*, and very few would have had the patience to read it. . . .

I have almost always been treated honestly by my reviewers, passing over those without scientific knowledge as not worthy of notice. My views have often been grossly misrepresented, bitterly opposed and ridiculed, but this had been generally done, as I believe, in good faith. On the whole I do not doubt that my works have been over and over again greatly overpraised. I rejoice that I have avoided controversies, and this I owe to Lyell, who many years ago, in reference to my geological works, strongly advised me never to get entangled in a controversy, as it rarely did any good and caused a miserable loss of time and temper.

Whenever I have found out that I have blundered, or that my work has been imperfect, and when I have been contemptuously criticised, and even when I have been overpraised, so that I have felt mortified, it has been my greatest comfort to say hundreds of times to myself that "I have worked as hard and as well as I could, and no man can do more than this." I remember when in Good Success Bay, in Tierra del Fuego, thinking (and I believe that I wrote home to the effect) that I could not employ my life better than in adding a little to Natural Science. This I have done to the best of my abilities, and critics may say what they like, but they cannot destroy this conviction. . . .

I am not conscious of any change in my mind during the last thirty years, excepting in one point presently to be mentioned; nor, indeed, could any change have been expected unless one of general deterioration. But my father lived to his eighty-third year with his mind as lively as ever it was, and all his faculties undimmed; and I hope that I may die before my mind fails to a sensible extent. I think that I have become a little more skilful in guessing right explanations and in devising experimental tests; but this may probably be the result of mere practice, and of a larger store of knowledge. I have as much difficulty as ever in expressing myself clearly and concisely; and this difficulty has caused me a very great loss of time; but it has had the compensating advantage of forcing me to think long and intently about every sentence, and thus I have been led to see errors in reasoning and in my own observations or those of others.

There seems to be a sort of fatality in my mind leading me to put at first my statement or proposition in a wrong or awkward form. Formerly I used to think about my sentences before writing them down; but for several years I have found that it saves time to scribble in a vile hand, whole pages as quickly as I possibly can, contracting half the words; and then correct deliberately. Sentences thus scribbled down are often better ones than I could have written deliberately.

Having said thus much about my manner of writing, I will add that with my large books I spend a good deal of time over the general arrangement of the matter. I first make the rudest outline in two or three pages, and then a larger one in several pages, a few words or one word standing for a whole discussion or series of facts. Each one of these headings is again enlarged and often transferred before I begin to write *in extenso*. As in several of my books facts observed by others have been very extensively used, and as I have always had several quite distinct subjects in hand at the same time, I may mention that I keep from thirty to forty large portfolios, in cabinets with labelled shelves, into which I can at once put a detached reference or memorandum. I have bought many books, and at their ends I make an index of all the facts that concern my work; or, if the book is not my own, write out a separate abstract, and of such abstracts I have a large drawer full. Before beginning on any subject I look to all the short indexes and make a general and classified index, and by taking the one or more proper portfolios I have all the information collected during my life ready for use.

I have said that in one respect my mind has changed during the last twenty or thirty years. Up to the age of thirty, or beyond it, poetry of many kinds, such as the works of Milton, Gray, Byron, Wordsworth, Coleridge, and Shelley, gave me great pleasure, and even as a schoolboy I took intense delight in Shakespeare, especially in the historical plays. I have also said that formerly pictures gave me considerable, and music very great delight. But now for many years I cannot endure to read a line of poetry; I have tried lately to read Shakespeare, and found it so intolerably dull that it nauseated me. I have also almost lost my taste for pictures or music. Music generally sets me thinking too energetically on what I have been at work on, instead of giving me pleasure. I retain some taste for fine scenery, but it does not cause me the exquisite delight which it formerly did. On the other hand, novels, which are works of the imagination, though not of a very high order, have been for years a wonderful relief and pleasure to me, and I often bless all novelists. A surprising number have been read aloud to me, and I like all if moderately good, and if they do not end unhappily—against which a law ought to be passed. A novel, according to my taste, does not come into the first class unless it contains some person whom one can thoroughly love, and if a pretty woman all the better.

This curious and lamentable loss of the higher aesthetic tastes is all the odder, as books on history, biographies, and travels (independently of any scientific facts which they may contain), and essays on all sorts of subjects interest me as much as ever they did. My mind seems to have become a kind of machine for grinding general laws out of large collections of facts, but why this should have caused the atrophy of that part of the brain alone, on which the higher tastes depend, I cannot conceive. A man with a mind more highly organised or better constituted than mine, would not, I suppose, have thus suffered; and if I had to live my life again, I would have made a rule to read some poetry and listen to some music at least once every week; for perhaps the parts of my brain now atrophied would thus have been kept active through use. The loss of these tastes is a loss of happiness, and may possibly be injurious to the intellect, and more probably to the moral character, by enfeebling the emotional part of our nature.

My books have sold largely in England, have been translated into many languages, and passed through several editions in foreign countries. I have heard it said that the success of a work abroad is the best test of its enduring value. I doubt whether this is at all trustworthy; but judged by this standard my name ought to last for a few years. Therefore it may be worth while to try to analyse the mental qualities and the conditions on which my success has depended; though I am aware that no man can do this correctly.

I have no great quickness of apprehension or wit which is so remarkable in some clever men, for instance, Huxley. I am therefore a poor critic: a paper or book, when first read, generally excites my admiration, and it is only after considerable reflection that I perceive the weak points. My power to follow a long and purely abstract train of thought is very limited; and therefore I could never have succeeded with metaphysics or mathematics. My memory is extensive, yet hazy: it suffices to make me cautious by vaguely telling me that I have observed or read something opposed to the conclusion which I am drawing, or on the other hand in favour of it; and after a time I can generally recollect where to search for my authority. So poor in one sense is my memory, that I have never been able to remember for more than a few days a single date or a line of poetry.

Some of my critics have said, "Oh, he is a good observer, but he has no power of reasoning!" I do not think that this can be true, for the *Origin of Species* is one long argument from the beginning to the end, and it has convinced not a few able men. No one could have written it without having some power of reasoning. I have a fair share of invention, and of common sense or judgment, such as every fairly successful lawyer or doctor must have, but not, I believe, in any higher degree.

On the favourable side of the balance, I think that I am superior to the common run of men in noticing things which easily escape attention, and in observing them carefully. My industry has been nearly as great as it could have been in the observation and collection of facts. What is far more important, my love of natural science has been steady and ardent.

This pure love has, however, been much aided by the ambition to be esteemed by my fellow naturalists. From my early youth I have had the strongest desire to understand or explain whatever I observed,—that is, to group all facts under some general laws. These causes combined have given me the patience to reflect or ponder for any number of years over any unexplained problem. As far as I can judge, I am not apt to follow blindly the lead of other men. I have steadily endeavoured to keep my mind free so as to give up any hypothesis, however much beloved (and I cannot resist forming one on every subject), as soon as facts are shown to be opposed to it. Indeed, I have had no choice but to act in this manner, for with the exception of the Coral Reefs, I cannot remember a single first-formed hypothesis which had not after a time to be given up or greatly modified. This has naturally led me to distrust greatly, deductive reasoning in the mixed sciences. On the other hand, I am not very sceptical,—a frame of mind which I believe to be injurious to the progress of science. A good deal of scepticism in a scientific man is advisable to avoid much loss of time, [but] I have met with not a few men, who, I feel sure, have often thus been deterred from experiment or observations, which would have proved directly or indirectly serviceable. . . .

My habits are methodical, and this has been of not a little use for my particular line of work. Lastly, I have had ample leisure from not having to earn my own bread. Even ill-health, though it has annihilated several years of my life, has saved me from the distractions of society and amusement.

Therefore, my success as a man of sicence, whatever this may have amounted to, has been determined, as far as I can judge, by complex and diversified mental qualities and conditions. Of these, the most important have been—the love of science—unbounded patience in long reflecting over any subject—industry in observing and collecting facts—and a fair share of invention as well as of common-sense. With such moderate abilities as I possess, it is truly surprising that I should have influenced to a considerable extent the belief of scientific men on some important points. . . .

A Variation and Selection Model of Evolution

VARIATION UNDER NATURE

To treat this subject at all properly, a long catalogue of dry facts should be given; but these I shall reserve for my future work. Nor shall I here discuss the various definitions which have been given of the term species. No one definition has as yet satisfied all naturalists; yet every naturalist knows vaguely what he means when he speaks of a species. Generally the term includes the unknown element of a distinct act of creation. The term "variety" is almost equally difficult to define; but here community of descent is almost universally implied, though it can rarely be proved. We have also what are called monstrosities; but they graduate into varieties. By a monstrosity I presume is meant some considerable deviation of structure in one part, either injurious to or not useful to the species, and not generally propagated. Some authors use the term "variation" in a technical sense, as implying a modification directly due to the physical conditions of life; and "variations" in this sense are supposed not to be inherited: but who can say that the dwarfed condition of shells in the brackish waters of the Baltic, or dwarfed plants on Alpine summits, or the thicker fur of an animal

From Charles Darwin, *On the origin of species: A facsimile of the first edition.* Cambridge: Harvard University Press, 1964. (Originally published, 1859). Pp. 44–45, 51–52, 62–67, 80–85, 87–90, 199–203.

from far northwards, would not in some cases be inherited for at least some few generations? and in this case I presume that the form would be called a variety.

Again, we have many slight differences which may be called individual differences, such as are known frequently to appear in the offspring from the same parents, or which may be presumed to have thus arisen, from being frequently observed in the individuals of the same species inhabiting the same confined locality. No one supposes that all the individuals of the same species are cast in the very same mould. These individual differences are highly important for us, as they afford materials for natural selection to accumulate, in the same manner as man can accumulate in any given direction individual differences in his domesticated productions. . . .

Hence I look at individual differences, though of small interest to the systematist, as of high importance for us, as being the first step towards such slight varieties as are barely thought worth recording in works on natural history. And I look at varieties which are in any degree more distinct and permanent, as steps leading to more strongly marked and more permanent varieties; and at these latter, as leading to sub-species, and to species. The passage from one stage of difference to another and higher stage may be, in some cases, due merely to the long-continued action of different physical conditions in two different regions; but I have not much faith in this view; and I attribute the passage of a variety, from a state in which it differs very slightly from its parent to one in which it differs more, to the action of natural selection in accumulating (as will hereafter be more fully explained) differences of structure in certain definite directions. Hence I believe a well-marked variety may be justly called an incipient species; but whether this belief be justifiable must be judged of by the general weight of the several facts and views given throughout this work. . . .

From these remarks it will be seen that I look at the term species, as one arbitrarily given for the sake of convenience to a set of individuals closely resembling each other, and that it does not essentially differ from the term variety, which is given to less distinct and more fluctuating forms. The term variety, again, in comparison with mere individual differences, is also applied arbitrarily, and for mere convenience sake. . . .

STRUGGLE FOR EXISTENCE

I should premise that I use the term Struggle for Existence in a large and metaphorical sense, including dependence of one being on another, and including (which is more important) not only the life of the individual, but success in leaving progeny. Two canine animals in a time of dearth, may be truly said to struggle with each other which shall get food and live. But a plant on the edge of a desert is said to struggle for life against the drought, though more properly it should be said to be dependent on the moisture. A plant which annually produces a thousand seeds, of which on an average only one comes to maturity, may be more truly said to struggle with the plants of the same and other kinds which already clothe the ground. The missletoe is dependent on the apple and a few other trees, but can only in a far-fetched sense be said to struggle with these trees, for if too many of these parasites grow on the same tree, it will languish and die. But several seedling missletoes, growing close together on the same branch, may more truly be said to struggle with each other. As the missletoe is disseminated by birds, its existence depends on birds; and it may metaphorically be said to struggle with other fruit-bearing plants, in order to tempt birds to devour and thus disseminate its seeds rather than those of other plants. In these several senses, which pass into each other, I use for convenience sake the general term of struggle for existence.

A struggle for existence inevitably follows from the high rate at which all organic beings tend to increase. Every being, which during its natural lifetime produces several eggs or seeds, must suffer destruction during some period of its life, and during some season or occasional year, otherwise, on the principle of geometrical increase, its numbers would quickly become so inordinately great that no country could support the product. Hence, as more individuals are produced than can possibly survive, there must in every case be a struggle for existence, either one individual with another of the same species, or with the individuals of distinct species, or with the physical conditions of life. It is the doctrine of Malthus applied with manifold force to the whole animal and vegetable kingdoms; for in this case there can be no artificial increase of food, and no prudential restraint from marriage. Although some species may be now increasing, more or less rapidly, in numbers, all cannot do so, for the world would not hold them.

There is no exception to the rule that every organic being naturally increases at so high a rate, that if not destroyed, the earth would soon be covered by the progeny of a single pair. Even slow-breeding man has doubled in twenty-five years, and at this rate, in a few thousand years, there would literally not be standing room for his progeny. Linnaeus has calculated that if an annual plant produced only two seeds—and there is no plant so unproductive as this—and their seedlings next year produced two, and so on, then in twenty years there would be a million plants. The elephant is reckoned to be the slowest breeder of all known animals, and I have taken some pains to estimate its probable minimum rate of natural increase: it will be under the mark to assume that it breeds when thirty years old, and goes on breeding til ninety years old, bringing forth three pair of young in this interval; if this be so, at the end of the fifth century there would be alive fifteen million elephants, descended from the first pair.

But we have better evidence on this subject than mere theoretical calculations, namely, the numerous recorded cases of the astonishingly rapid increase of various animals in a state of nature, when circumstances have been favourable to them during two or three following seasons. Still more striking is the evidence from our domestic animals of many kinds which have run wild in several parts of the world: if the statements of the rate of increase of slow-breeding cattle and horses in South-America, and latterly in Australia, had not been well authenticated, they would have been quite incredible. So it is with plants: cases could be given of introduced plants which have become common throughout whole islands in a period of less than ten years. Several of the plants now most numerous over the wide plains of La Plata, clothing square leagues of surface almost to the exclusion of all other plants, have been introduced from Europe; and there are plants which now range in India, as I hear from Dr. Falconer, from Cape Comorin to the Himalaya, which have been imported from America since its discovery. In such cases, and endless instances could be given, no one supposes that the fertility of these animals or plants has been suddenly and temporarily increased in any sensible degree. The obvious explanation is that the conditions of life have been very favourable, and that there has consequently been less destruction of the old and young, and that nearly all the young have been enabled to breed. In such cases the geometrical ratio of increase, the result of which never fails to be surprising, simply explains the extraordinarily rapid increase and wide diffusion of naturalised productions in their new homes.

In a state of nature almost every plant produces seed, and amongst animals there are very few which do not annually pair. Hence we may confidently assert, that all plants and animals are tending to increase at a geometrical ratio, that all would most rapidly stock every station in which they could any how exist, and that the geometrical tendency to increase must be checked by destruction at some period of life. Our familiarity with the larger domestic animals tends, I think, to mislead us: we see no great destruction falling on them, and we forget that thousands are annually slaughtered for food, and that in a state of nature an equal number would have somehow to be disposed of.

The only difference between organisms which annually produce eggs or seeds by the thousand, and those which produce extremely few, is, that the slow-breeders would require a few more years to people, under favourable conditions, a whole district, let it be ever so large. The condor lays a couple of eggs and the ostrich a score, and yet in the same country the condor may be the more numerous of the two: the Fulmar petrel lays but one egg, yet it is believed to be the most numerous bird in the world. One fly deposits hundreds of eggs, and another, like the hippobosca, a single one; but this difference does not determine how many individuals of the two species can be supported in a district. A large number of eggs is of some importance to those species, which depend on a rapidly fluctuating amount of food, for it allows them rapidly to increase in number. But the real importance of a large number of eggs or seeds is to make up for much destruction at some period of life; and this period in the great majority of cases is an early one. If an animal can in any way protect its own eggs or young, a small number may be produced, and yet the average stock be fully kept up; but if many eggs or young are destroyed, many must be produced, or the species will become extinct. It would suffice to keep up the full number of a tree, which lived on an average for a thousand years, if a single seed were produced once in a thousand years, supposing that this seed were never destroyed, and could be ensured to germinate in a fitting place. So that in all cases, the average number of any animal or plant depends only indirectly on the number of its eggs or seeds.

In looking at Nature, it is most necessary to keep the foregoing considerations always in mind—never to forget that every single organic being around us may be said to be striving to the utmost to increase in numbers; that each lives by a struggle at some period of its life; that heavy destruction inevitably falls either on the young or old, during each generation or at recurrent intervals. Lighten any check, mitigate the destruction ever so little, and the number of the species will almost instantaneously increase to any amount. . . .

NATURAL SELECTION

How will the struggle for existence, discussed too briefly in the last [section], act in regard to variation? Can the principle of selection, which we have seen is so potent in the hands of man, apply in nature? I think we shall see that it can act most effectually. Let it be borne in mind in what an endless number of strange peculiarities our domestic productions, and, in a lesser degree, those under nature, vary; and how strong the hereditary tendency is. Under domestication, it may be truly said that the whole organisation becomes in some degree plastic. Let it be borne in mind how infinitely complex and close-fitting are the mutual relations of all organic beings to each other and to their physical conditions of life. Can it, then, be thought improbable, seeing that variations useful to man have undoubtedly occurred, that other variations useful in some way to each being in the great and complex battle of life, should sometimes occur in the course of thousands of generations? If such do occur, can we doubt (remembering that many more individuals are born than can possibly survive) that individuals having any advantage, however slight, over others, would have the best chance of surviving and of procreating their kind? On the other hand, we may feel sure that any variation in the least degree injurious would be rigidly destroyed. This preservation of favourable variations and the rejection of injurious variations, I call Natural Selection. Variations neither useful nor injurious would not be affected by natural selection, and would be left a fluctuating element, as perhaps we see in the species called polymorphic.

We shall best understand the probable course of natural selection by taking the case of a country undergoing some physical change, for instance, of climate. The proportional numbers of its inhabitants would almost immediately undergo a change, and some species might become extinct. We may conclude, from what we have seen of the intimate and complex manner in which the inhabitants of each country are bound together, that any change in the numerical proportions of some of the inhabitants, independently of the change of climate itself, would most seriously affect many of the others. If the country were open on its borders, new forms would certainly immigrate, and this also would seriously disturb the relations of some of the former inhabitants. Let it be remembered how powerful the influence of a single introduced tree or mammal has been shown to be. But in the case of an island, or of a country partly surrounded by barriers, into which new and better adapted forms could not freely enter, we should then have places in the economy of nature which would assuredly be better filled up, if some of the original inhabitants were in some manner modified; for, had the area been open to immigration, these same places would have been seized on by intruders. In such case, every slight modification, which in the course of ages chanced to arise, and which in any way favoured the individuals of any of the species, by better adapting them to their altered conditions, would tend to be preserved; and natural selection would thus have free scope for the work of improvement.

We have reason to believe, as stated in the first chapter, that a change in the conditions of life, by specially acting on the reproductive system, causes or increases variability; and in the foregoing case the conditions of life are supposed to have undergone a change, and this would manifestly be favourable to natural selection, by giving a better chance of profitable variations occurring; and unless profitable variations do occur, natural selection can do nothing. Not that, as I believe, any extreme amount of variability is necessary; as man can certainly produce great results by adding up in any given direction mere individual differences, so could Nature, but far more easily, from having incomparably longer time at her disposal. Nor do I believe that any great physical change, as of climate, or any unusual degree of isolation to check immigration, is actually necessary to produce new and unoccupied places for natural selection to fill up by modifying and improving some of the varying inhabitants. For as all the inhabitants of each country are struggling together with nicely balanced forces, extremely slight modifications in the structure or habits of one inhabitant would often give it an advantage over others; and still further modifications of the same kind would often still further increase the advantage. No country can be named in which all the native inhabitants are now so perfectly adapted to each other and to the physical conditions under which they live, that none of them could anyhow be improved; for in all countries, the natives have been so far conquered by naturalised productions, that they have allowed foreigners to take firm possession of the land. And as foreigners have thus everywhere beaten some of the natives, we may safely conclude that the natives might have been modified with advantage, so as to have better resisted such intruders.

As man can produce and certainly has produced a great result by his methodical and unconscious means of selection, what may not nature effect? Man can act only on external and visible characters: nature cares nothing for appearances, except in so far as they may be useful to any being. She can act on every internal organ, on every shade of constitutional difference, on the whole machinery of life. Man selects only for his own good; Nature only for that of the being which she tends. Every selected character is fully exercised by her; and the being is placed under well-suited conditions of life. Man keeps the natives of many climates in the same country; he seldom exercises each selected character in some peculiar and fitting manner; he feeds a long and a short beaked pigeon on the same food; he does not exercise a long-backed or long-legged quadruped in any peculiar manner; he exposes sheep with long and short wool to the same climate. He does not allow the most vigorous males to struggle for the females. He does not rigidly destroy all inferior animals, but protects during each varying season, as far as lies in his power, all his productions. He often begins his selection by some half-monstrous form; or at least by some modification prominent enough to catch his eye, or to be plainly useful to him. Under nature, the slightest difference of structure or constitution may well turn the nicely-balanced scale in the struggle for life, and so be preserved. How fleeting are the wishes and efforts of man! how short his time! and consequently how poor will his products be, compared with those accumulated by nature during whole geological periods. Can we wonder, then, that nature's productions should be far "truer" in character than man's productions; that they should be infinitely better adapted to the most complex conditions of life, and should plainly bear the stamp of far higher workmanship?

It may be said that natural selection is daily and hourly scrutinising, throughout the world, every variation, even the slightest; rejecting that which is bad, preserving and adding up all that is good; silently and insensibly working, whenever and wherever opportunity offers, at the improvement of each organic being in relation to its organic and inorganic conditions of life. We see nothing of these slow changes in progress, until the hand of time has marked the long lapse of ages, and then so imperfect is our view into long past geological ages, that we only see that the forms of life are now different from what they formerly were.

Although natural selection can act only through and for the good of each being, yet characters and structures, which we are apt to consider as of very trifling importance, may thus be acted on. We we see leaf-eating insects green, and bark-feeders mottled-grey; the alpine ptarmigan white in winter, the red-grouse the colour of heather, and the black-grouse that of peaty earth, we must believe that these tints are of service to these birds and insects in preserving them from danger. Grouse, if not destroyed at some period of their lives, would increase in countless numbers; they are known to suffer largely from birds of prey; and hawks are guided by eyesight to their prey,—so much so, that on parts of the Continent persons are warned not to keep white pigeons, as being the most liable to destruction. Hence I can see no reason to doubt that natural selection might be most effective in giving the proper colour to each kind of grouse, and in keeping that colour, when once acquired, true and constant. Nor ought we to think that the occasional destruction of an animal of any particular colour would produce little effect: we should remember how essential it is in a flock of white sheep to destroy every lamb with the faintest trace of black. In plants the down on the fruit and the colour of the flesh are considered by botanists as characters of the most trifling importance: yet we hear from an excellent horticulturist, Downing, that in the United States smooth-skinned fruits suffer far more from a beetle, a curculio, than those with down; that purple plums suffer far more from a certain disease than yellow plums; whereas another disease attacks yellow-fleshed peaches far more than those with other coloured flesh. If, with all the aids of art, these slight differences make a great difference in cultivating the several varieties, assuredly, in a state of nature, where the trees would have to struggle with other trees and with a host of enemies, such differences would effectually settle which variety, whether a smooth or downy, a yellow or purple fleshed fruit, should succeed. . . .

Sexual Selection

Inasmuch as pecularities often appear under domestication in one sex and become hereditarily attached to that sex, the same fact probably occurs under nature, and if so, natural selection will be able to modify one sex in its functional relations to the other sex, or in relation to wholly different habits of life in the two sexes, as is sometimes the case with insects. And this leads me to say a few words on what I call Sexual Selection. This depends, not on a struggle for existence, but on a struggle between the males for possession of the females; the result is not death to the unsuccessful competitor, but few or no offspring. Sexual selection is, therefore, less rigorous than natural selection. Generally, the most vigorous males, those which are best fitted for their places in nature, will leave most progeny. But in many cases, victory will depend not on general vigour, but on having special weapons, confined to the male sex. A hornless stag or spurless cock would have a poor chance of leaving offspring. Sexual selection by always allowing the victor to breed might surely give indomitable courage, length to the spur, and strength to the wing to strike in the spurred leg, as well as the brutal cockfighter, who knows well that he can improve his breed by careful selection of the best cocks. How low in the scale of nature this law of battle descends, I know not; male alligators have been described as fighting, bellowing, and whirling round, like Indians in a war-dance, for the possession of the females; male salmons have been seen fighting all day long; male stag-beetles often bear wounds from the huge mandibles of other males. The war is, perhaps, severest between the males of polygamous animals, and these seem oftenest provided with special weapons. The males of carnivorous animals are already well armed; though to them and to others, special means of defence may be given through means of sexual selection, as the mane to the lion, the shoulder-pad to the boar, and the hooked jaw to the male salmon; for the shield may be as important for victory, as the sword or spear.

Amongst birds, the contest is often of a more peaceful character. All those who have attended to the subject, believe that there is the severest rivalry between the males of many species to attract by singing the females. The rock-thrush of Guiana, birds of Paradise, and some others, congregate; and successive males display their gorgeous plumage and perform strange antics before the females, which standing by as spectators, at last choose the most attractive partner. Those who have closely attended to birds in confinement well know that they often take individual preferences and dislikes: thus Sir R. Heron has described how one pied peacock was eminently attractive to all his hen birds. It may appear childish to attribute any effect to such apparently weak means: I cannot here enter on the details necessary to support this view; but if man can in a short time give elegant carriage and beauty to his bantams, according to his standard of beauty, I can see no good reason to doubt that female birds, by selecting, during thousands of generations, the most melodious or beautiful males, according to their standard of beauty, might produce a marked effect. I strongly suspect that some well-known laws with respect to the plumage of male and female birds, in comparison with the plumage of the young, can be explained on the view of plumage having been chiefly modified by sexual selection, acting when the birds have come to the breeding age or during the breeding season; the modifications thus produced being inherited at corresponding ages or seasons, either by the males alone, or by the males and females; but I have not space here to enter on this subject.

Thus it is, as I believe, that when the males and females of any animal have the same general habits of life, but differ in structure, colour, or ornament, such differences have been mainly caused by sexual selection; that is, individual males have had, in successive generations, some slight advantage over other males, in their weapons, means of defence, or charms; and have transmitted these advantages to their male offspring. Yet, I would not wish to attribute all such sexual differences to this agency: for we see peculiarities arising and becoming attached to the male sex in our domestic animals (as the wattle in male carriers, horn-like protuberances in the cocks of certain fowls, &c.), which we cannot believe to be either useful to the males in battle, or attractive to the females. We see analogous cases under nature, for instance, the tuft of hair on the breast of the turkey-cock, which can hardly be either useful or ornamental to this bird;—indeed, had the tuft appeared under domestication, it would have been called a monstrosity. . . .

DIFFICULTIES ON THEORY

The foregoing remarks lead me to say a few words on the protest lately made by some naturalists, against the utilitarian doctrine that every detail of structure has been produced for the good of its possessor. They believe that very many structures have been created for beauty in the eyes of man, or for mere variety. This doctrine, if true, would be absolutely fatal to my theory. Yet I fully admit that many structures are of no direct use to their possessors. Physical conditions probably have had some little effect on structure, quite independently of any good thus gained. Correlation of growth has no doubt played a most important part, and a useful modification of one part will often have entailed on other parts diversified changes of no direct use. So again characters which formerly were useful, or which formerly had arisen from correlation of growth, or from other unknown cause, may reappear from the law of reversion, though now of no direct use. The effects of sexual selection, when displayed in beauty to charm the females, can be called useful only in rather a forced sense. But by far the most important consideration is that the chief part of the organisation of every being is simply due to inheritance; and consequently, though each being assuredly is well fitted for its place in nature, many structures now have no direct relation to the habits of life of each species. Thus, we can hardly believe that the webbed feet of the upland goose or of the frigate-bird are of special use to these birds; we cannot believe that the same bones in the arm of the monkey, in the fore leg of the horse, in the wing of the bat, and in the flipper of the seal, are of special use to these animals. We may safely attribute these structures to inheritance. But to the progenitor of the upland goose and of the frigate-bird, webbed feet no doubt were as useful as they now are to the most aquatic of existing birds. So we may believe that the progenitor of the seal had not a flipper, but a foot with five toes fitted for walking or grasping; and we may further venture to believe that the several bones in the limbs of the monkey, horse, and bat, which have been inherited from a common progenitor, were formerly of more special use to that progenitor, or its progenitors, than they now are to these animals having such widely diversified habits. Therefore we may infer that these several bones might have been acquired through natural selection, subjected formerly, as now, to the several laws of inheritance, reversion, correlation of growth, &c. Hence every detail of structure in every living creature (making some little allowance for the direct action of physical conditions) may be viewed, either as having been of special use to some ancestral form, or as being now of special use to the descendants of this form—either directly, or indirectly through the complex laws of growth.

Natural selection cannot possibly produce any modification in any one species exclusively for the good of another species; though throughout nature one species incessantly takes advantage of, and profits by, the structure of another. But natural selection can and does often produce structures for the direct injury of other species, as we see in the fang of the adder, and in the ovipositor of the ichneumon, by which its eggs are deposited in the living bodies of other insects. If it could be proved that any part of the structure of any one species had been formed for the exclusive good of another species, it would annihilate my theory, for such could not have been produced through natural selection. Although many statements may be found in works on natural history to this effect, I cannot find even one which seems to me of any weight. It is admitted that the rattlesnake has a poison-fang for its own defence and for the destruction of its prey; but some authors suppose that at the same time this snake is furnished with a rattle for its own injury, namely, to warn its prey to escape. I would almost as soon believe that the cat curls the end of its tail when preparing to spring, in order to warn the doomed mouse. But I have not space here to enter on this and other such cases.

Natural selection will never produce in a being anything injurious to itself, for natural selection acts solely by and for the good of each. No organ will be formed, as Paley has remarked, for the purpose of causing pain or for doing an injury to its possessor. If a fair balance be struck between the good and evil caused by each part, each will be found on the whole advantageous. After the lapse of time, under changing conditions of life, if any part comes to be injurious, it will be modified; or if it be not so, the being will become extinct, as myriads have become extinct.

Natural selection tends only to make each organic being as

perfect as, or slightly more perfect than, the other inhabitants of the same country with which it has to struggle for existence. And we see that this is the degree of perfection attained under nature. The endemic productions of New Zealand, for instance, are perfect one compared with another; but they are now rapidly yielding before the advancing legions of plants and animals introduced from Europe. Natural selection will not produce absolute perfection, nor do we always meet, as far as we can judge, with this high standard under nature. The correction for the aberration of light is said, on high authority, not to be perfect even in that most perfect organ, the eye. If our reason leads us to admire with enthusiasm a multitude of inimitable contrivances in nature, this same reason tells us, though we may easily err on both sides, that some other contrivances are less perfect. Can we consider the sting of the wasp or of the bee as perfect, which, when used against many attacking animals, cannot be withdrawn, owing to the backward serratures, and so inevitably causes the death of the insect by tearing out its viscera?

If we look at the sting of the bee, as having originally existed in a remote progenitor as a boring and serrated instrument, like that in so many members of the same great order, and which has been modified but not perfected for its present purpose, with the poison originally adapted to cause galls subsequently intensified, we can perhaps understand how it is that the use of the sting should so often cause the insect's own death: for if on the whole the power of stinging be useful to the community, it will fulfill all the requirements of natural selection, though it may cause the death of some few members. If we admire the truly wonderful power of scent by which the males of many insects find their females, can we admire the production for this single purpose of thousands of drones, which are utterly useless to the community for any other end, and which are ultimately slaughtered by their industrious and sterile sisters? It may be difficult, but we ought to admire the savage instinctive hatred of the queen-bee, which urges her instantly to destroy the young queens her daughters as soon as born, or to perish herself in the combat; for undoubtedly this is for the good of the community; and maternal love or maternal hatred, though the latter fortunately is most rare, is all the same to the inexorable principle of natural selection. . . .

20. B. F. Skinner

EDITOR'S INTRODUCTION

To use an evolutionary metaphor, some features of Darwin's theory were well suited to the American social and intellectual environment, and these features flourished. Other features, which were not so well suited, have had to struggle continually for existence. To be more specific, American society during the last half of the 19th century tended to be (1) individualistic, (2) pragmatic, (3) agrarian, and (4) environmentalistic. For its part, Darwinian theory emphasized (1) individual differences, (2) adaptation, (3) the continuity between animals and man, and (4) nativism, or the innate determinants of behavior. There is an affinity between the first three features of American society and the corresponding features of Darwinian theory; only with regard to the fourth feature—environmentalism, on the one hand, and nativism, on the other—are the two in basic conflict. The present chapter deals with that conflict, and a recommendation for its resolution by a psychologist whose name is often (though somewhat erroneously) associated with an extreme environmentalist position, B. F. Skinner. But before turning to Skinner's contribution, let us consider very briefly the aforementioned affinities between Darwinian theory and the American environment.

We have seen the central importance that Darwin placed on variations within species. Variations are reality, while common properties ("essences") are abstractions. This emphasis on individual differences led Francis Galton, Darwin's cousin, to study the distribution of human intellectual abilities. Although the specific tests developed by Galton to measure mental functioning did not prove effective, the spirit of his inquiry found ready acceptance in America, with its emphasis on individuality. Today, mental measurement and the study of individual differences are among the largest and most flourishing areas of American psychology.

The Darwinian emphasis on adaptation was also compatible with American social thought. Perhaps America's most original contribution to intellectual history is philosophical pragmatism, which posits "workability," or the functional significance of an idea, as a criterion of truth. The philosophers who conceived of and developed pragmatism—Charles Sanders Peirce, William James, and John Dewey—also were instrumental in the establishment of American psychology. Dewey, especially, combined philosophical pragmatism with evolutionary biology, giving impetus to America's first "school" of psychology—functionalism. And although functionalism is no longer a self-conscious school, most contemporary American psychologists would probably consider themselves to be functionalists in one sense or another.

As illustrated by many of the preceding chapters in this book, the historic preoccupation of psychology has been the human mind, and especially rational thought. By emphasizing the continuity between humans and animals, Darwin helped shatter this preoccupation and legitimize the study of animals. In America, animals quickly became the favored subjects for experimental research. This trend was facilitated by the fact that during the formative years of American psychology, the United States was still predominantly an agrarian society. Many of the early experimental psychologists were from rural areas, and they found it not only convenient but also comfortable to work with animals.[1] One illustration of this is John Watson, the founder of American behaviorism. Raised in the rural South, Watson was quite explicit in his preference for animals: "I never wanted to use human subjects. I hated to serve as a subject. . . . I was always uncomfortable and acted unnaturally. With animals I was at home."[2]

But in spite of a bias toward animal subjects, a true comparative psychology did not develop in the United States. This rather anomalous state of affairs can be attributed, in part, to the antipathy shown by American psychologists to the notion of innate characteristics. Even today, if one suggests that socially important psychological traits (e.g., intelligence or aggression) are partly determined by genetic factors, the response is liable to be professional silence, or even outright condemnation. For the most

---

[1] D. Bakan, Behaviorism and American urbanization. *Journal of the History of the Behaviorial Sciences*, 1966, *2*, 5–28.

[2] J. B. Watson, Autobiography. In C. Murchison (Ed.), *A history of psychology in autobiography* Vol. 3. Worcester, Mass.: Clark University Press, 1966, p. 276.

part, American psychologists have preferred explanations of behavior that invoke ontogenic as opposed to phylogenic mechanisms, i.e., learning as opposed to heredity.

There is, however, no basic conflict between the ontogeny and phylogeny of behavior, as this chapter illustrates. Skinner's analysis proceeds along two lines, one substantive and the other analogical. On the substantive side, he shows how learning itself is a biological adaptation. With regard to intelligence, for example, "what has been selected (during evolution) appears to be a susceptibility to ontogenic contingencies, leading particularly to a greater speed of conditioning and the capacity to maintain a larger repertoire without confusion." It should go without saying that any complex behavior is bound to be a product of both phylogenic (natural selection) and ontogenic (reinforcement) contingencies. And simply classifying a response as intelligent, say, does not tell us anything about which set of contingencies was the more important in its development. Two responses that are superficially alike, each being equally "intelligent," might in one case be primarily the result of favorable heredity and in another case the result of favorable learning experiences.

While exploring the implications of such facts, Skinner also develops an analogy between natural selection and operant conditioning. Darwin, it will be recalled, assumed that within any species there are large individual differences in the ability to compete successfully for limited resources. Natural selection is a kind of "weeding out" process whereby the less successful are eliminated from competition. Darwin could not explain adequately how individual differences arose in the first place, or how successful characteristics were passed from one generation to the next; the science of genetics came after Darwin's time. However, the idea of natural selection does not derive its meaning from any specific hereditary mechanism. Indeed, as a general concept, it may even be divorced entirely from the theory of biological evolution and applied to a wide variety of other developmental phenomena, including learned behavior.

As Skinner points out, the behavior of an organism varies continuously over time. If some of these variations in response are selectively reinforced, the probability of their occurrence increases. And through the combination of many small changes in behavior, complex responses may emerge that are well adapted to the environment.

For Skinner, then, operant conditioning is logically analogous to natural selection. The analogy does, of course, have its limitations, as Skinner is careful to note. In one respect, however, he is perhaps too careful in not carrying the analogy far enough. Skinner seems to imply that operant conditioning "stamps in" successful (reinforced) responses; natural selection, by contrast, "weeds out" unsuccessful characteristics. Staddon and Simmelhag[3] have argued cogently that a number of problems in learning theory could be avoided if the effects of reinforcement also were viewed as the result of a weeding-out rather than a stamping-in process.

[3] J. E. R. Staddon & V. L. Simmelhag, The "superstition" experiment: A reexamination of its implications for the principles of adaptive behavior. *Psychological Review*, 1971, *78*, 3–43.

The Phylogeny and Ontogeny of Behavior: contingencies of reinforcement throw light on contingencies of survival in the evolution of behavior

Parts of the behavior of an organism concerned with the internal economy, as in respiration or digestion, have always been accepted as "inherited," and there is no reason why some responses to the external environment should not also come ready-made in the same sense. It is widely believed that many students of behavior disagree. The classical reference is to John B. Watson(1):

> I should like to go one step further now and say, "Give me a dozen healthy infants, well-formed, and my own specified world to bring them up in and I'll guarantee to take any one at random and train him to become any type of specialist I might select—doctor, lawyer, artist, merchant-chief and, yes, even beggarman and thief, regardless of his talents, penchants, tendencies, abilities, vocations, and race of his ancestors." I am going beyond my facts and I admit it, but so have the advocates of the contrary and they have been doing it for many thousands of years.

Watson was not denying that a substantial part of behavior is inherited. His challenge appears in the first of four chapters describing "how man is equipped to behave at birth." As an enthusiastic specialist in the psychology of learning he went beyond his facts to emphasize what could be done in spite of genetic limitations. He was actually, as Gray (2) has pointed out, "one of the earliest and one of the most careful workers in the area of animal ethology." Yet he is probably responsible for the persistent myth of what has been called "behaviorism's counter-factual dogma" (3). And it is a myth. No reputable student of animal behavior has ever taken the position "that the animal comes to the laboratory as a virtual *tabula rasa*, that species' differences are insignificant, and that all responses are about equally conditionable to all stimuli" (4).

Reprinted with permission from *Science*, 1966, *153*, 1205–1213, Copyright 1966 by the American Association for the Advancement of Science.

The author is Edgar Pierce Professor of psychology at Harvard University, Cambridge, Massachusetts. This article is adapted from a paper presented 11 November 1965 at a symposium celebrating the centennial of the founding of the University of Kentucky, Lexington.

But what does it mean to say that behavior is inherited? Lorenz (5) has noted that ethologists are not agreed on "the concept of 'what we formerly called innate.' " Insofar as the behavior of an organism is simply the physiology of an anatomy, the inheritance of behavior is the inheritance of certain bodily features, and there should be no problem concerning the meaning of "innate" that is not raised by any genetic trait. Perhaps we must qualify the statement that an organism inherits a visual reflex, but we must also qualify the statement that it inherits its eye color.

If the anatomical features underlying behavior were as conspicuous as the wings of *Drosophila*, we should describe them directly and deal with their inheritance in the same way, but at the moment we must be content with so-called behavioral manifestations. We describe the behaving organism in terms of its gross anatomy, and we shall no doubt eventually describe the behavior of its finer structures in much the same way, but until then we analyze behavior without referring to fine structures and are constrained to do so even when we wish to make inferences about them.

What features of behavior will eventually yield a satisfactory genetic account? Some kind of inheritance is implied by such concepts as "racial memory" or "death instinct," but a sharper specification is obviously needed. The behavior observed in mazes and similar apparatuses may be "objective," but it is not described in dimensions which yield a meaningful genetic picture. Tropisms and taxes are somewhat more readily quantified, but not all behavior can be thus formulated, and organisms selected for breeding according to tropistic or taxic performances may still differ in other ways (6).

The experimental analysis of behavior has emphasized another property. The probability that an organism will behave in a given way is a more valuable datum than the mere fact that it does so behave. Probability may be inferred from frequency of emission. It is a basic datum, in a theoretical sense, because it is related to the question: Why does an organism behave in a given way at a given time? It is basic in a practical sense because frequency has been found to vary in an orderly way with many independent variables. Probability of response is important in examining the inheritance, not only of specific forms of behavior but of behavioral processes and characteristics often described as traits. Very little has been done in studying the genetics of behavior in this sense. Modes of inheritance are not, however, the only issue. Recent advances in the formulation of learned behavior throw considerable light on other genetic and evolutionary problems.

THE PROVENANCE OF BEHAVIOR

Upon a given occasion we observe that an animal displays a certain kind of behavior—learned or unlearned. We describe its topography and evaluate its probability. We discover variables, genetic or environmental, of which the probability is a function. We then undertake to predict or control the behavior. All this concerns a current state of the organism. We have still to ask where the behavior (or the structures which thus behave) came from.

The provenance of learned behavior has been thoroughly analyzed. Certain kinds of events function as "reinforcers," and, when such an event follows a response, similar responses are more likely to occur. This is operant conditioning. By manipulating the ways in which reinforcing consequences are contingent upon behavior, we generate complex forms of response and bring them under the control of subtle features of the environment. What we may call the ontogeny of behavior is thus traced to contingencies of reinforcement.

In a famous passage Pascal (7) suggested that ontogeny and phylogeny have something in common. "Habit," he said, "is a second nature which destroys the first. But what is this nature? Why is habit not natural? I am very much afraid that nature is itself only first habit as habit is second nature." The provenance of "first habit" has an important place in theories of the evolution of behavior. A given response is in a sense strengthened by consequences which have to do with the survival of the individual and species. A given form of behavior leads not to reinforcement but to procreation. (Sheer reproductive activity does not, of course, always contribute to the survival of a species, as the problems of overpopulation remind us. A few well-fed breeders presumably enjoy an advantage over a larger but impoverished population. The advantage may also be selective. It has recently been suggested (8) that some forms of behavior such as the defense of a territory have an important effect in restricting breeding.) Several practical problems raised by what may be called contingencies of selection are remarkably similar to problems which have already been approached experimentally with respect to contingencies of reinforcement.

An identifiable unit. A behavioral process, as a change in frequency of response, can be followed only if it is possible to count responses. The topography of an operant need not be completely fixed, but some defining property must be available to identify instances. An emphasis upon the occurrence of a repeatable unit distinguishes an experimental analysis of behavior from historical or anecdotal accounts. A similar requirement is recognized in ethology. As Julian Huxley has said, "This concept . . . of unit releasers which act as specific key stimuli unlocking genetically determined unit behavior patterns . . . is probably the most important single contribution of Lorenzian ethology to the science of behavior" (9).

The action of stimuli. Operant reinforcement not only strengthens a given response; it brings the response under the control of a stimulus. But the stimulus does not elicit the response as in a reflex; it merely sets the occasion upon which the response is more likely to occur. The ethologists' "releaser" also simply sets an occasion. Like the discriminative stimulus, it increases the probability of occurrence of a unit of behavior but does not force it. The principal difference between a reflex and an instinct is not in the complexity of the response but in, respectively, the eliciting and releasing actions of the stimulus.

Origins of variations. Ontogenic contingencies remain ineffective until a response has occurred. In a familiar experimental arrangement, the rat must press the lever at least once "for other reasons" before it presses it "for food." There is a similar limitation in phylogenic contingencies. An animal must emit a cry at least once for other reasons before the cry can be selected as a warning because of the advantage to the species. It follows that the entire repertoire of an individual or species must exist prior to ontogenic or phylogenic selection, but only in the form of minimal units. Both phylogenic and ontogenic contingencies "shape" complex forms of behavior from relatively undifferentiated material. Both processes are favored if the organism shows an extensive, undifferentiated repertoire.

Programmed contingencies. It is usually not practical to condition a complex operant by waiting for an instance to occur and then reinforcing it. A terminal performance must be reached through intermediate contingencies (perhaps best exemplified by programmed instruction). In a demonstration experiment a rat pulled a chain to obtain a marble from a rack, picked up the marble with its forepaws, carried it to a tube projecting two inches above the floor of its cage, lifted it to the top of the tube, and dropped it inside. "Every step in the process had to be worked out through a series of approximations since the component responses were not in the original repertoire of the rat" (10). The "program" was as follows. The rat was reinforced for any movement which caused a marble to roll over any edge of the floor of its cage, then only over the edge on one side of the cage, then over only a small section of the edge, then over only that section slightly raised, and so on. The raised edge became a tube of gradually diminishing diameter and increasing height. The earlier member of the chain, release of the marble from the rack, was added later. Other kinds of programming have been used to establish subtle stimulus control (11), to sustain behavior in spite of infrequent reinforcement (12), and so on.

A similar programming of complex phylogenic contingencies is familiar in evolutionary theory. The environment may change, demanding that behavior which contributes to survival for a given reason become more complex. Quite different advantages may be responsible for different stages. To take a familiar example the electric organ of the eel could have become useful in stunning prey only after developing something like its present power. Must we attribute the completed organ to a single complex mutation, or were intermediate stages developed because of other advantages? Much weaker currents, for example, may have permitted the eel to detect the nature of objects with which it was in contact. The same question may be asked about behavior. Pascal's "first habit" must often have been the product of "programmed instruction." Many of the complex phylogenic contingencies which now seem to sustain behavior must have been reached through intermediate stages in which less complex forms had lesser but still effective consequences.

The need for programming is a special case of a more general principle. We do not explain any system of behavior simply by demonstrating that it works to the advantage of, or has "net utility" for, the individual or species. It is necessary to show that a given advantage is contingent upon behavior in such a way as to alter its probability.

Adventitious contingencies. It is not true, as Lorenz (5) has asserted, that "adaptiveness is always the irrefutable proof that this process [of adaptation] has taken place." Behavior may have advantages which have played no role in its selection. The converse is also true. Events which follow behavior but are not necessarily produced by it may have a selective effect. A hungry pigeon placed in an apparatus in which a food dispenser operates every 20 seconds regardless of what the pigeon is doing acquires a stereotyped response which is shaped and sustained by wholly coincidental reinforcement (13). The behavior is often "ritualistic;"

we call it superstitious. There is presumably a phylogenic parallel. All current characteristics of an organism do not necessarily contribute to its survival and procreation, yet they are all nevertheless "selected." Useless structures with associated useless functions are as inevitable as superstitious behavior. Both become more likely as organisms become more sensitive to contingencies. It should occasion no surprise that behavior has not perfectly adjusted to either ontogenic or phylogenic contingencies.

Unstable and intermittent contingencies. Both phylogenic and ontogenic contingencies are effective even though intermittent. Different schedules of reinforcement generate different patterns of changing probabilities. If there is a phylogenic parallel, it is obscure. A form of behavior generated by intermittent selective contingencies is presumably likely to survive a protracted period in which the contingencies are not in force, because it has already proved powerful enough to survive briefer periods, but this is only roughly parallel with the explanation of the greater resistance to extinction of intermittently reinforced operants.

Contingencies also change, and the behaviors for which they are responsible then change too. When ontogenic contingencies specifying topography of response are relaxed, the topography usually deteriorates, and when reinforcements are no longer forthcoming the operant undergoes extinction. Darwin discussed phylogenic parallels in *The Expression of Emotions in Man and Animals.* His "serviceable associated habits" were apparently both learned and unlearned and he seems to have assumed that ontogenic contingencies contribute to the inheritance of behavior, at least in generating responses which may then have phylogenic consequences. The behavior of the domestic dog in turning around before lying down on a smooth surface may have been selected by contingencies under which the behavior made a useful bed in grass or brush. If dogs now show this behavior less frequently, it is presumably because a sort of phylogenic extinction has set in. The domestic cat shows a complex response of covering feces which must once have had survival value with respect to predation or disease. The dog has been more responsive to the relaxed contingencies arising from domestication or some other change in predation or disease, and shows the behavior in vestigial form.

Multiple contingencies. An operant may be affected by more than one kind of reinforcement, and a given form of behavior may be traced to more than one advantage to the individual or the species. Two phylogenic or ontogenic consequences may work together or oppose each other in the development of a given response and presumably show "algebraic summation" when opposed.

Social contingencies. The contingencies responsible for social behavior raise special problems in both phylogeny and ontogeny. In the development of a language the behavior of a speaker can become more elaborate only as listeners become sensitive to elaborated speech. A similarly coordinated development must be assumed in the phylogeny of social behavior. The dance of the bee returning from a successful foray can have advantageous effects for the species only when other bees behave appropriately with respect to it, but they cannot develop the behavior until the dance appears. The terminal system must have required a kind of subtle programming in which the behaviors of both "speaker" and "listener" passed through increasingly complex stages. A bee returning from a successful foray may behave in a special way because it is excited or fatigued, and it may show phototropic responses related to recent visual stimulation. If the strength of the behavior varies with the quantity or quality of food the bee has discovered and with the distance and direction it has flown, then the behavior may serve as an important stimulus to other bees, even though its characteristics have not yet been affected by such consequences. If different bees behave in different ways, then more effective versions should be selected. If the behavior of a successful bee evokes the behavior on the part of "listeners" which is reinforcing to the "speaker," then the "speaker's" behavior should be ontogenically intensified. The phylogenic development of responsive behavior in the "listener" should contribute to the final system by providing for immediate reinforcement of conspicuous forms of the dance.

The speaker's behavior may become less elaborate if the listener continues to respond to less elaborate forms. We stop someone who is approaching us by pressing our palm against his chest, but he eventually learns to stop upon seeing our outstretched palm. The practical response becomes a gesture. A similar shift in phylogenic contingencies may account for the "intentional movements" of the ethologists.

Behavior may be intensified or elaborated under differential reinforcement involving the stimulation either of the behaving organism or of others. The more conspicuous a superstitious response, for example, the more effective the adventitious contingencies. Behavior is especially likely to become more conspicuous when reinforcement is contingent on the response of another organism. Some ontogenic instances, called "ritualization," are easily demonstrated. Many elaborate rituals of primarily phylogenic origin have been described by ethologists.

SOME PROBLEMS RAISED BY
PHYLOGENIC CONTINGENCIES

Lorenz has recently argued that "our absolute ignorance of the physiological mechanisms underlying learning makes our knowledge of the causation of phyletic adaptation seem quite considerable by comparison" (5). But genetic and behavioral processes are studied and formulated in a rigorous way without reference to the underlying biochemistry. With respect to the provenance of behavior we know much more about ontogenic contingencies than phylogenic. Moreover, phylogenic contingencies raise some very difficult problems which have no ontogenic parallels.

The contingencies responsible for unlearned behavior acted a very long time ago. The natural selection of a given form of behavior, no matter how plausibly argued, remains an inference. We can set up phylogenic contingencies under which a given property of behavior arbitrarily selects individuals for breeding, and thus demonstrate modes of behavioral inheritance, but the experimenter who makes the selection is performing a function of the natural environment which also needs to be studied. Just as the reinforcements arranged in an experimental analysis must be shown to have parallels in "real life" if the results of the analysis are to be significant or useful, so the contingencies which select a given behavioral trait in a genetic experiment must be shown to play a plausible role in natural selection.

Although ontogenic contingencies are easily subjected to an experimental analysis, phylogenic contingencies are not. When the experimenter has shaped a complex response, such as dropping a marble into a tube, the provenance of the behavior raises no problem. The performance may puzzle anyone seeing it for the first time, but it is easily traced to recent, possibly recorded, events. No comparable history can be invoked when a spider is observed to spin a web. We have not seen the phylogenic contingencies at work. All we know is that spiders of a given kind build more or less the same kind of web. Our ignorance often adds a touch of mystery. We are likely to view inherited behavior with a kind of awe not inspired by acquired behavior of similar complexity.

The remoteness of phylogenic contingencies affects our scientific methods, both experimental and conceptual. Until we have identified the variables of which an event is a function, we tend to invent causes. Learned behavior was once commonly attributed to "habit," but an analysis of contingencies of reinforcement has made the term unnecessary. "Instinct," as a hypothetical cause of phylogenic behavior, has had a longer life. We no longer say that our rat possesses a marble-dropping habit, but we are still likely to say that our spider has a web-spinning instinct. The concept of instinct has been severely criticized and is now used with caution or altogether avoided, but explanatory entities serving a similar function still survive in the writings of many ethologists.

A "mental apparatus," for example, no longer finds a useful place in the experimental analysis of behavior, but it survives in discussions of phylogenic contingencies. Here are a few sentences from the writings of prominent ethologists which refer to consciousness or awareness: "The young gosling . . . gets imprinted upon its mind the image of the first moving object it sees" (W. H. Thorpe, 14); "the infant expresses the inner state of contentment by smiling" (Julian Huxley, 9); "[herring gulls show a] lack of insight into the ends served by their activities" (Tinbergen, 15); "[chimpanzees were unable] to communicate to others the unseen things in their minds" (Kortlandt, 16).

In some mental activities awareness may not be critical, but other cognitive activities are invoked. Thorpe (14) speaks of a disposition "which leads the animal to pay particular attention to objects of a certain kind." What we observe is simply that objects of a certain kind are especially effective stimuli. We know how ontogenic contingencies work to produce such an effect. The ontogenic contingencies which generate the behavior called "paying attention" also presumably have phylogenic parallels. Other mental activities frequently mentioned by ethologists include "organizing experience" and "discovering relations." Expressions of all these sorts show that we have not yet accounted for behavior in terms of contingencies, phylogenic or ontogenic. Unable to show how the organism can behave effectively under complex circumstances, we endow it with a special cognitive ability which permits it to do so. Once the contingencies are understood, we no longer need to appeal to mentalistic explanations.

Other concepts replaced by a more effective analysis included "need" or "drive" and "emotion." In ontogenic behavior we no longer say that a given set of environmental conditions first gives rise to an inner state which the organism then expresses or resolves by behaving in a given way. We no longer represent relations among emotional and motivational variables as relations among such states, as in saying that hunger overcomes fear. We no longer use dynamic analogies or metaphors, as in explaining sudden action as the overflow or bursting out of dammed-up needs or drives. If these are common practices in ethology, it is evidently because the functional relations they attempt to formulate are not clearly understood.

Another kind of innate endowment, particularly likely to appear in explanations of human behavior, takes the form of "traits" or "abilities." Though often measured quantitatively, their dimensions are meaningful only in placing the individual with respect to a population. The behavior measured is almost always obviously learned. To say that intelligence is inherited is not to say that specific forms of behavior are inherited. Phylogenic contingencies conceivably responsible for "the selection of intelligence" do not specify responses. What has been selected appears to be a susceptibility to ontogenic contingencies, leading particularly to a greater speed of conditioning and the capacity to maintain a larger repertoire without confusion.

It is often said that an analysis of behavior in terms of ontogenic contingencies "leaves something out of account," and this is true. It leaves out of account habits, ideas, cognitive processes, needs, drives, traits, and so on. But it does not neglect the facts upon which these concepts are based. It seeks a more effective formulation of the very contingencies to which those who use such concepts must eventually turn to explain their explanations. The strategy has been highly successful at the ontogenic level, where the contingencies are relatively clear. As the nature and mode of operation of phylogenic contingencies come to be better understood, a similar strategy should yield comparable advantages.

IDENTIFYING PHYLOGENIC AND ONTOGENIC VARIABLES

The significance of ontogenic variables may be assessed by holding genetic conditions as constant as possible—for example, by studying "pure" strains or identical twins. The technique has a long history. According to Plutarch (*De Puerorum Educatione*) Licurgus, a Spartan, demonstrated the importance of environment by raising two puppies from the same litter so that one became a good hunter while the other preferred food from a plate. On the other hand, genetic variables may be assessed either by studying organisms upon which the environment has had little opportunity to act (because thay are newborn or have been reared in a controlled environment) or by comparing groups subject to extensive, but on the average probably similar, environmental histories. The technique also has a long history. In his journal for the 24th of January 1805, Stendahl refers to an experiment in which two birds taken from the nest after hatching and raised by hand exhibited their genetic endowment by eventually mating and building a nest two weeks before the female laid eggs. Behavior exhibited by most of the members of a species is often accepted as inherited if it is unlikely that all the members could have been exposed to relevant ontogenic contingencies.

When contingencies are not obvious, it is perhaps unwise to call any behavior either inherited or acquired. Field observations, in particular, will often not permit a distinction. Friedmann (17) has described the behavior of the African honey guide as follows:

> When the bird is ready to begin guiding, it either comes to a person and starts a repetitive series of churring notes or it stays where it is and begins calling. . . .
>
> As the person comes to within 15 or 20 feet, . . . the bird flies off with an initial conspicuous downward dip, and then goes off to another tree, not necessarily in sight of the follower, in fact more often out of sight than not. Then it waits there, churring loudly until the follower again nears it, when the action is repeated. This goes on until the vicinity of the bees' nest is reached. Here the bird suddenly ceases calling and perches quietly in a tree nearby. It waits there for the follower to open the hive, and it usually remains there until the person has departed with his loot of honey-comb, when it comes down to the plundered bees' nest and begins to feed on the bits of comb left strewn about.

The author is quoted as saying that the behavior is "purely instinctive," but it is possible to explain almost all of it in other ways. If we assume that honey guides eat broken bees' nests and cannot eat unbroken nests, that men (not to mention baboons and ratels) break bees' nests, and that birds more easily discover unbroken nests, then only one other assumption is needed to explain the behavior in ontogenic terms. We must assume that the response which produces the churring note is elicited either (i) by any stimulus which frequently precedes the receipt of food (comparable behavior is shown by a hungry dog jumping about when food is being prepared for it) or (ii) when food, ordinarily available, is missing (the dog jumps about when food is not being prepared for it on schedule). An unconditioned honey guide occasionally sees men breaking nests. It waits until they have gone, and then eats the remaining scraps. Later it sees men near but not breaking nests, either because they have not yet found the nests or have not yet reached them. The sight of a man near a nest, or the sight of man when the buzzing of bees around a nest can be heard, begins to function in either of the ways just noted to elicit the churring response. The first step in the construction of the final pattern is thus taken by the honey guide. The second step is taken by the man (or baboon or ratel, as the case may be). The churring sound becomes a conditioned stimulus in the presence of which a search for bees' nests is frequently successful. The buzzing of bees would have the same effect if the man could hear it.

The next change occurs in the honey guide. When a man approaches and breaks up a nest, his behavior begins to function as a conditioned reinforcer which, together with the fragments which he leaves behind, reinforces churring, which then becomes more probable under the circumstances and emerges primarily as an operant rather than as an emotional response. When this has happened, the geographical arrangements work themselves out naturally. Men learn to move toward the churring sound, and they break nests more often after walking toward nests than after walking in other directions. The honey guide is therefore differentially reinforced when it takes a position which induces men to walk toward a nest. The contingencies may be subtle, but the final topography is often far from perfect.

As we have seen, contingencies which involve two or more organisms raise special problems. The churring of the honey guide is useless until men respond to it, but men will not respond in an appropriate way until the churring is related to the location of bees' nests. The conditions just described compose a sort of program which could lead to the terminal performance. It may be that the conditions will not often arise, but another characteristic of social contingencies quickly takes over. When one honey guide and one man have entered into this symbiotic arrangement, conditions prevail under which other honey guides and other men will be much more rapidly conditioned. A second man will more quickly learn to go in the direction of the churring sound because the sound is already spatially related to bees' nests. A second honey guide will more readily learn to churr in the right places because men respond in a way which reinforces that behavior. When a large number of birds have learned to guide and a large number of men have learned to be guided, conditions are highly favorable for maintaining the system. (It is said that, where men no longer bother to break bees' nests, they no longer comprise an occasion for churring, and the honey guide turns to the ratel or baboon. The change in contingencies has occurred too rapidly to work through natural selection. Possibly an instinctive response has been unlearned, but the effect is more plausibly interpreted as the extinction of an operant.)

Imprinting is another phenomenon which shows how hard it is to detect the nature and effect of phylogenic contingencies. In Thomas More's *Utopia*, eggs were incubated. The chicks "are no sooner out of the shell, and able to stir about, but they seem to consider those that feed them as their mothers, and follow them as other chickens do the hen that hatched them." Later accounts of imprinting have been reviewed by Gray (2). Various facts suggest phylogenic origins: the response of following an imprinted object appears at a certain age; if it cannot appear then, it may not appear at all; and so on. Some experiments by Peterson (18), however, suggest that what is inherited is not necessarily the behavior of following but a susceptibility to reinforcement by proximity to the mother or mother surrogate. A distress call reduces the distance between mother and chick when the mother responds appropriately, and walking toward the mother has the same effect. Both behaviors may therefore be reinforced (19), but they appear before these ontogenic contingencies come into play and are, therefore, in part at least phylogenic. In the laboratory, however, other behaviors can be made effective which phylogenic contingencies are unlikely to have strengthened. A chick can be conditioned to peck a key, for example, by moving an imprinted object toward it when it pecks or to walk away from the object if, through a mechanical arrangement, this behavior actually brings the object closer. To the extent that chicks follow an imprinted object simply because they thus bring the object closer or prevent it from becoming more distant, the behavior could be said to be "species-specific" in the unusual sense that it is the product of *ontogenic* contingencies which prevail for most members of the species.

Ontogenic and phylogenic behaviors are not distinguished by any essence or character. Form of response seldom if ever yields useful classifications. The verbal response *Fire!* may be a command to a firing squad, a call for help, or an answer to the question, *What do you see?* The topography tells us little, but the controlling variables permit us to distinguish three very different verbal operants (20). The sheer forms of instinctive and learned behaviors also tell us little. Animals court, mate, fight, hunt, and rear their young, and they use the same effectors in much the same way in all sorts of learned behavior. Behavior is behavior whether learned or unlearned; it is only the controlling variables which make a difference. The difference is not always important. We might show that a honey guide is controlled by the buzzing of bees rather than by the sight of a nest, for example, without prejudice to the question of whether the behavior is innate or acquired.

Nevertheless the distinction is important if we are to undertake to predict or control the behavior. Implications for human affairs have often affected the design of research and the conclusions drawn from it. A classical example concerns the practice of exogamy. Popper (21) writes:

> Mill and his psychologistic school of sociology . . . would try to explain [rules of exogamy] by an appeal to 'human nature,' for instance to some sort of instinctive aversion against incest (developed perhaps through natural selection . . .); and something like this would also be the naive or popular explanation. [From Marx's] point of view . . . however, one could ask whether it is not the other way round, that is to say, whether the apparent instinct is not rather a product of education, the effect rather than the cause of the social rules and traditions demanding exogamy and forbidding incest. It is clear that these two approaches correspond exactly to the very ancient problem whether social laws are 'natural' or 'conventions.' . . .

Much earlier, in his *Supplement to the Voyage of Bougainville*, Diderot (22) considered the question of whether there is a natural basis for sexual modesty or shame (*pudeur*). Though he was writing nearly a hundred years before Darwin, he pointed to a possible basis for natural selection. "The pleasures of love are followed by a weakness which puts one at the mercy of his enemies. That is the only natural thing about modesty; the rest is convention." Those who are preoccupied with sex are exposed to attack (indeed, may be stimulating attack); hence, those who engage in sexual behavior under cover are more likely to breed successfully. Here are phylogenic contingencies which either make sexual behavior under cover stronger than sexual behavior in the open or reinforce the taking of cover when sexual behavior is strong. Ontogenic contingencies through which organisms seek cover to avoid disturbances during sexual activity are also plausible.

The issue has little to do with the character of incestuous or sexual behavior, or with the way people "feel" about it. The basic distinction is between provenances. And provenance is important because it tells us something about how behavior can be supported or changed. Most of the controversy concerning heredity and environment has arisen in connection with the practical control of behavior through the manipulation of relevant variables.

INTERRELATIONS AMONG PHYLOGENIC
AND ONTOGENIC VARIABLES

The ways in which animals behave compose a sort of taxonomy of behavior comparable to other taxonomic parts of biology. Only a very small percentage of existing species has as yet been investigated. (A taxonomy of behavior may indeed be losing ground as new species are discovered.) Moreover, only a small part of the repertoire of any species is ever studied. Nothing approaching a fair sampling of species-specific behavior is therefore ever likely to be made.

Specialists in phylogenic contingencies often complain that those who study learned behavior neglect the genetic limitations of their subjects, as the comparative anatomist might object to conclusions drawn from the intensive study of a single species. Beach, for example, has written (23): "Many . . . appear to believe that in studying the rat they are studying all or nearly all that is important in behavior. . . . How else are we to interpret . . . [a] 457-page opus which is based exclusively upon the performance of rats in bar-pressing situations but is entitled simply *The Behavior of Organisms*?" There are many precedents for concentrating on one species (or at most a very few species) in biological investigations. Mendel discovered the basic laws of genetics—in the garden pea. Morgan worked out the theory of the gene—for the fruitfly. Sherrington investigated the integrative action of the nervous system—in the dog and cat. Pavlov studied the physiological activity of the cerebral cortex—in the dog.

In the experimental analysis of behavior many species differences are minimized. Stimuli are chosen to which the species under investigation can respond and which do not elicit or release disrupting responses: visual stimuli are not used if the organism is blind, nor very bright lights if they evoke evasive action. A response is chosen which may be emitted at a high rate without fatigue and which will operate recording and controlling equipment: we do not reinforce a monkey when it pecks a disk with its nose or a pigeon when it trips a toggle switch—though we might do so if we wished. Reinforcers are chosen which are indeed reinforcing, either positively or negatively. In this way species differences in sensory equipment, in effector systems, in susceptibility to reinforcement, and in possible disruptive repertoires are minimized. The data then show an extraordinary uniformity over a wide range of species. For example, the processes of extinction, discrimination, and generalization, and the performances generated by various schedules of reinforcement are reassuringly similar. (Those who are interested in fine structure may interpret these practices as minimizing the importance of sensory and motor areas in the cortex and emotional and motivational areas in the brain stem, leaving for study the processes associated with nerve tissue as such, rather than with gross anatomy.) Although species differences exist and should be studied, an exhaustive analysis of the behavior of a single species is as easily justified as the study of the chemistry or microanatomy of nerve tissue in one species.

A rather similar objection has been lodged against the extensive use of domesticated animals in laboratory research (24). Domesticated animals offer many advantages. They are more easily handled, they thrive and breed in captivity, they are resistant to the infections encountered in association with men, and so on. Moreover, we are primarily interested in the most domesticated of all animals—man. Wild animals are, of course, different—possibly as different from domesticated varieties as some species are from others, but both kinds of differences may be treated in the same way in the study of basic processes.

The behavioral taxonomist may also argue that the contrived environment of the laboratory is defective since it does not evoke characteristic phylogenic behavior. A pigeon in a small enclosed space pecking a disk which operates a mechanical food dispenser is behaving very differently from pigeons at large. But in what sense is this behavior not "natural"? If there is a natural phylogenic environment, it must be the environment in which a given kind of behavior evolved. But the phylogenic contingencies responsible for current behavior lie in the distant past. Within a few thousand years—a period much too short for genetic changes of any great magnitude—all current species have been subjected to drastic changes in climate, predation, food supply, shelter, and so on. Certainly no land mammal is now living in the environment which selected its principle genetic features, behavioral or otherwise. Current environments are almost as "unnatural" as a laboratory. In any case, behavior in a natural habitat would have no special claim to genuineness. What an organism does is a fact about that organism regardless of the conditions under which it does it. A behavioral process is none the less real for being exhibited in an arbitrary setting.

The relative importance of phylogenic and ontogenic contingencies cannot be argued from instances in which unlearned or learned behavior intrudes or dominates. Breland and Breland (4) have used operant conditioning and programming to train performing animals. They conditioned a pig to deposit large wooden coins in a "piggy bank." "The coins were placed several feet from the bank and the pig required to carry them to the bank and deposit them. . . . At first the pig would eagerly pick up one dollar, carry it to the bank, run back, get another, carry it rapidly and neatly, and so on. . . . Thereafter, over a period of weeks the behavior would become slower and slower. He might run over eagerly for each dollar, but on the way back, instead of carrying the dollar and depositing it simply and cleanly, he would repeatedly drop it, root it, drop it again, root it along the way, pick it up, toss it up in the air, drop it, root it some more, and so on." They also conditioned a chicken to deliver plastic capsules containing small toys by moving them toward the purchaser with one or two sharp straight pecks. The chickens began to grab at the capsules and "pound them up and down on the floor of the cage," perhaps as if they were breaking seed pods or pieces of food too large to be swallowed. Since other reinforcers were not used, we cannot be sure that these phylogenic forms of food-getting behavior appeared because the objects were manipulated under food-reinforcement. The conclusion is plausible, however, and not disturbing. A shift in controlling variables is often observed. Under reinforcement on a so-called "fixed-interval schedule," competing behavior emerges at predictable points (25). The intruding behavior may be learned or unlearned. It may disrupt a performance or, as Kelleher (26) has shown, it may not. The facts do not show an inherently greater power of phylogenic contingencies in general. Indeed, the intrusions may occur in the other direction. A hungry pigeon which was being trained to guide missiles (27) was reinforced with food on a schedule which generated a high rate of pecking at a target projected on a plastic disk. It began to peck at the food as rapidly as at the target. The rate was too high to permit it to take grains into its mouth, and it began to starve. A product of ontogenic contingencies had suppressed one of the most powerful phylogenic activities. The behavior of civilized man shows the extent to which environmental variables may mask an inherited endowment.

MISLEADING SIMILARITIES

Since phylogenic and ontogenic contingencies act at different times and shape and maintain behavior in different ways, it is dangerous to try to arrange their products on a single continuum or to describe them with a single set of terms.

An apparent resemblance concerns intention or purpose. Behavior which is influenced by its consequences seems to be directed toward the future. We say that spiders spin webs in order to catch flies and that men set nets in order to catch fish. The "order" is temporal. No account of either form of behavior would be complete if it did not make some reference to its effects. But flies or fish which have not yet been caught cannot affect behavior. Only past effects are relevant. Spiders which have built effective webs have been more likely to leave offspring, and a way of setting a net that has effectively caught fish has been reinforced. Both forms of behavior are therefore more likely to occur again, but for very different reasons.

The concept of purpose has had, of course, an important place in evolutionary theory. It is still sometimes said to be needed to explain the variations upon which natural selection operates. In human behavior a "felt intention" or "sense of purpose" which precedes action is sometimes proposed as a current surrogate for future events. Men who set nets "know why they are doing so," and something of the same sort may have produced the spider's web-spinning behavior which then became subject to natural selection. But men behave because of operant reinforcement even though they cannot "state their purpose"; and, when they can, they may simply be describing their behavior and the contingencies responsible for its strength. Self-knowledge is at best a by-product of contingencies, it is not a cause of the behavior generated by them. Even if we could discover a spider's felt intention or sense of purpose, we could not offer it as a cause of the behavior.

Both phylogenic and ontogenic contingencies may seem to "build purpose into" an organism. It has been said that one of the achievements of cybernetics has been to demonstrate that machines may show purpose. But we must look to the construction of the machine, as we look to the phylogeny and ontogeny of behavior, to account for the fact that an ongoing system acts as if it had a purpose.

Another apparent characteristic in common is "adaptation." Both kinds of contingencies change the organism so that it adjusts to its environment in the sense of behaving in it more effectively. With respect to phylogenic contingencies, this is what is meant by natural selection. With respect to ontogeny, it is what is meant by operant conditioning. Successful responses are selected in both cases, and the result is adaptation. But the processes of selection are very different, and we cannot tell from the mere fact that behavior is adaptive which kind of process has been responsible for it.

More specific characteristics of behavior seem to be common products of phylogenic and ontogenic contingencies. Imitation is an example. If we define imitation as behaving in a way which resembles the observed behavior of another organism, the term will describe both phylogenic and ontogenic behavior. But important distinctions need to be made. Phylogenic contingencies are presumably responsible for well-defined responses released by similar behavior (or its products) on the part of others. A warning cry is taken up and passed along by others; one bird in a flock flies off, and the others fly off; one member of a herd starts to run, and the others start to run. A stimulus acting upon only one member of a group thus quickly affects other members, with plausible phylogenic advantages.

The parrot displays a different kind of imitative behavior. Its vocal repertoire is not composed of inherited responses, each of which, like a warning cry, is released by the sound of a similar response in others. It acquires its imitative behavior ontogenically, but only through an apparently inherited capacity to be reinforced by hearing itself produce familiar sounds. Its responses need not be released by immediately preceding stimuli (the parrot speaks when not spoken to); but an echoic stimulus is often effective, and the response is then a sort of imitation.

A third type of imitative contingency does not presuppose an inherited tendency to be reinforced by behaving as others behave. When other organisms are behaving in a given way, similar behavior is likely to be reinforced, since they would not be behaving in that way if it were not. Quite apart from any instinct of imitation, we learn to do what others are doing because we are then likely to receive the reinforcement they are receiving. We must not overlook distinctions of this sort if we are to use or cope with imitation in a technology of behavior.

Aggression is another term which conceals differences in provenance. Inherited repertoires of aggressive responses are elicited or released by specific stimuli. Azrin, for example, has studied the stereotyped, mutually aggressive behavior evoked when two organisms receive brief electric shocks. But he and his associates have also demonstrated that the opportunity to engage in such behavior functions as a reinforcer and, as such, may be used to shape an indefinite number of "aggressive" operants of arbitrary topographies (28). Evidence of damage to others may be reinforcing for phylogenic reasons because it is associated with competitive survival. Competition in the current environment may make it reinforcing for ontogenic reasons. To deal successfully with any specific aggressive act we must respect its provenance. (Emotional responses, the bodily changes we feel when we are aggressive, like sexual modesty or aversion to incest, may conceivably be the same whether of phylogenic or ontogenic origin; the importance of the distinction is not thereby reduced.) Konrad Lorenz's recent book *On Aggression* (29) could be seriously misleading if it diverts our attention from relevant manipulable variables in the current environment to phylogenic contingencies which, in their sheer remoteness, encourage a nothing-can-be-done-about-it attitude.

The concept of territoriality also often conceals basic differences. Relatively stereotyped behavior displayed in defending a territory, as a special case of phylogenic aggression, has presumably been generated by contingencies involving food supplies, breeding, population density, and so on. But cleared territory, associated with these and other advantages, becomes a conditioned reinforcer and as such generates behavior much more specifically adapted to clearing a given territory. Territorial behavior may also be primarily ontogenic. Whether the territory defended is as small as a spot on a crowded beach or as large as a sphere of influence in international politics, we shall not get far in analyzing the behavior if we recognize nothing more than "a primary passion for a place of one's own" (30) or insist that "animal behavior provides prototypes of the lust for political power" (31).

Several other concepts involving social structure also neglect important distinctions. A hierarchical "pecking order" is inevitable if the members of a group differ with respect to aggressive behavior in any of the forms just mentioned. There are therefore several kinds of pecking orders, differing in their provenances. Some dominant and submissive behaviors are presumably phylogenic stereotypes; the underdog turns on its back to escape further attack, but it does not follow that the vassal prostrating himself before king or priest is behaving for the same reasons. The ontogenic contingencies which shape the organization of a large company or governmental administration show little in common with the phylogenic contingencies responsible for the hierarchy in the poultry yard. Some forms of human society may resemble the anthill or beehive, but not because they exemplify the same behavioral processes (32).

Basic differences between phylogenic and ontogenic contingencies are particularly neglected in theories of communication. In the inherited signal systems of animals the behavior of a "speaker" furthers the survival of the species when it affects a "listener." The distress call of a chick evokes appropriate behavior in the hen; mating calls and displays evoke appropriate responses in the opposite sex; and so on. De Laguna (33) suggested that animal calls could be classified as declarations, commands, predictions, and so on, and Sebeok (34) has recently attempted a similar synthesis in modern linguistic terms, arguing for the importance of a science of zoosemiotics.

The phylogenic and ontogenic contingencies leading, respectively, to instinctive signal systems and to verbal behavior are quite different. One is not an early version of the other. Cries, displays, and other forms of communication arising from phylogenic contingencies are particularly insensitive to operant reinforcement. Like phylogenic repertoires in general, they are restricted to situations which elicit or release them and hence lack the variety and flexibility which favor operant conditioning. Vocal responses which at least closely resemble instinctive cries have been conditioned, but much less easily than responses using other parts of the skeletal nervous system. The vocal responses in the human child which are so easily shaped by operant reinforcement are not controlled by specific releasers. It was the development of an undifferentiated vocal repertoire which brought a new and important system of behavior within range of operant reinforcement through the mediation of other organisms (20).

Many efforts have been made to represent the products of both sets of contingencies in a single formulation. An utterance, gesture, or display, whether phylogenic or ontogenic, is said to have a referent which is its meaning, the referent or meaning being inferred by a listener. Information theory offers a more elaborate version: the communicating organism selects a message from the environment, reads our relevant information from storage, encodes the message, and emits it; the receiving organism decodes the message, relates it to other stored information, and acts upon it effectively. All these activities, together with the storage of material, may be either phylogenic or ontogenic. The principal terms in such analyses (input, output, sign, referent, and so on) are objective enough, but they do not adequately describe the actual behavior of the speaker or the behavior of the listener as he responds to the speaker. The important differences between phylogenic and ontogenic contingencies must be taken into account in an adequate analysis. It is not true, as Sebeok contends, that "any viable hypothesis about the origin and nature of language will have to incorporate the findings of zoosemiotics." Just as we can analyze and teach imitative behavior without analyzing the phylogenic contingencies responsible for animal mimicry, or study and construct human social systems without analyzing the phylogenic contingencies which lead to the social life of insects, so we can analyze the verbal behavior of man without taking into account the signal systems of other species.

Purpose, adaptation, imitation, aggression, territoriality, social structure, and communication—concepts of this sort have, at first sight, an engaging generality. They appear to be useful in describing both ontogenic and phylogenic behavior and to identify important common properties. Their very generality limits their usefulness, however. A more specific analysis is needed if we are to deal effectively with the two kinds of contingencies and their products.

REFERENCES AND NOTES

1. J. B. Watson, *Behaviorism* (W. W. Norton, New York, 1924).
2. P. H. Gray, *J. Gen. Psychol.* **68**, 333 (1963).
3. J. Hirsch, *Science* **142**, 1436 (1963).
4. K. Breland and M. Breland, *Amer. Psychologist* **16**, 681 (1961).
5. K. Lorenz, *Evolution and Modification of Behavior* (Univ. of Chicago Press, Chicago, 1965).
6. E. Erlenmeyer-Kimling, J. Hirsch, J. M. Weiss, *J. Comp. Physiol. Psychol.* **55**, 722 (1962).
7. B. Pascal, *Pensées* (1670).
8. V. C. Wynne-Edwards, *Science* **147**, 1543 (1965).
9. J. Huxley, *Perspectives Biol. Med.* **7**, 4 (1964).
10. B. F. Skinner, *The Behavior of Organisms* (Appleton-Century-Crofts, New York, 1938).
11. H. S. Terrace, *J. Exp. Anal. Behavior* **6**, 223 (1963).
12. C. B. Ferster and B. F. Skinner, *Schedules of Reinforcement* (Appleton-Century-Crofts, New York, 1957).
13. B. F. Skinner, *J. Exp. Psychol.* **38**, 168 (1948).
14. W. H. Thorpe, *Ibis* **93**, 1 (1951).
15. N. Tinbergen, *The Herring-Gull's World* (Collins, London, 1953).
16. A. Kortlandt, *Current Anthropol.* **6**, 320 (1965).
17. H. Friedmann quoted in *Science* **123**, 55 (1956).
18. N. Peterson, *Science* **132** 1395 (1960).
19. H. S. Hoffman, D. Schiff, J. Adams, J. L. Searle, *ibid.* **151**, 352 (1966).
20. B. F. Skinner, *Verbal Behavior* (Appleton-Century-Crofts, New York, 1957).
21. K. R. Popper, *The Open Society and Its Enemies* (Routledge & Kegan Paul, London, 1957).
22. D. Diderot, *Supplement au Voyage de Bougainville* (written in 1774, published in 1796).
23. F. Beach, *Amer. Psychologist* **5**, 115 (1950).
24. J. L. Kavanau, *Science* **143**, 490 (1964).
25. W. H. Morse and B. F. Skinner, *J. Comp. Physiol. Psychol.* **50**, 279 (1957).
26. R. T. Kelleher, *Amer. Psychologist* **17**, 659 (1962).
27. B. F. Skinner, *ibid.* **15**, 28 (1960).

28. N. H. Azrin, R. R. Hutchinson, R. McLaughlin, *J. Exp. Anal. Behav.* 8, 171 (1965).
29. K. Lorenz, *On Aggression* (Harcourt, Brace & World, New York, 1966, German ed. 1963).
30. R. Ardrey, *African Genesis* (Atheneum, New York, 1961).
31. R. Dubos, *Amer. Scientist* 53, 4 (1965).
32. W. C. Allee, *Cooperation Among Animals* (Abelard-Schuman, New York, 1938).
33. G. DeLaguna, *Speech: Its Function and Development* (Yale University Press, New Haven, 1927).
34. T. A. Sebeok, *Science* 147, 1006 (1965).
35. This article was prepared with the help of the NIH grant K6-MH-21, 775 and the Aaron E. Norman Fund.

XI. THE INSTITUTIONALIZATION OF BEHAVIOR

21. Karl Marx

EDITOR'S INTRODUCTION

Speaking at Marx's grave, Frederick Engels referred to his former colleague as the Darwin of sociology. There are, in fact, many similarities between the works of Marx and Darwin. In 1859 Marx, an exile in England for ten years, published his *Contribution to the Critique of Political Economy*. This was the same year that Darwin published *On the Origin of Species*. In the introduction to the *Critique*, reprinted here, Marx characterized political economy (i.e., the production and distribution of goods) as the anatomy of society. And, as the anatomy of a species may undergo evolutionary changes, so too does the political economy of a society. Specifically, a given mode of production achieves ascendency because it meets the needs of people at a particular locale and at a particular stage of technological development. However, any mode of production necessarily creates new material conditions with which it may not be able to cope. These new conditions necessitate the development of still other modes of production. The result is a developmental sequence, with later stages resolving conflicts initiated by earlier adaptations. Historically, in the West, this evolutionary process can be seen in the progression from ancient, to feudal, to capitalist societies. The culmination of this process is, according to Marx, the communist state, which supposedly does not contain within itself the seeds of its own destruction (since ideally it is free of class conflict).

Although both were evolutionists, it would be misleading to push the analogy between Marx and Darwin too far. Marx's theory differed fundamentally from Darwin's in that the latter was neutral about the overall direction of change. That is, Darwin was not concerned with *progressive* evolution, but with the alteration in populations (species) as a function of immediate environmental demands. Furthermore, Marx was more vague than Darwin concerning the mechanism of evolution, i.e., there is nothing within Marxist theory comparable in precision to natural selection. And, finally, Marx and Darwin represent basically different philosophical traditions. Marx could be characterized as an empiricist by conviction and a rationalist by temperament, whereas the opposite description might be applied to Darwin.

Marx's empiricism is evidenced in such propositions as "Science is only *genuine* science when it proceeds from sense experience" and "It is not the consciousness of men that determines their existence, but, on the contrary, their social existence determines their consciousness." Marx did not, however, view the human mind as a blank slate upon which experience is free to write. The metaphor of a blank slate implies a kind of passivity or subjugation to external events that was foreign to Marx's thinking. According to the Marxist thesis, man is not only a product of his environment, but the environment is also a human product. In a sense, it might be said that man produces himself through his environment.

In order to illustrate the rationalist elements in Marx's philosophy, it is necessary to review very briefly some of the changes that occurred in this tradition from Plato to Kant and Hegel, especially concerning such questions as the immediate source of knowledge and the nature of reality. As we have seen, Plato, Plotinus, Augustine, and, most especially, Descartes treated the mind and external objects as distinct substances, mind being able to comprehend external objects through reason. Kant went a long way in destroying this dichotomy by making phenomena—events within the spatiotemporal manifold—dependent on the forms of intuition and categories of judgment. Kant did not deny the existence of objects independent of mind (*noumena*), but he did place these beyond the pale of rational knowledge.

The postulation of an independent but unknowable noumena was unacceptable to many post-Kantian philosophers. Hegel, in particular, denied the distinction between phenomena and noumena, and thus the independence of subject and object. According to Hegel, mind and external reality are not distinct *substances*; rather, both are reflections of an underlying evolutionary *process*. Stated differently, both subject (mind) and object (external reality) stand in a dialectic relationship, each producing the other.

Hegel's substitution of process for substance offers an interesting contrast to the views of Plato and other early rationalists. Plato greatly distrusted change and saw truth in the imutable Forms; Hegel, by contrast, seemed to distrust permanence. For him, there are no immutable truths in the Platonic sense, only change. Yet Hegel was no skeptic. Knowledge is possible because the type of change that Hegel envisioned involves a rational, logical progression from lower to higher forms. Knowledge, then, is not the apprehension of some unchanging truth; rather, it is the recognition that the state of affairs at one moment of time is a necessary outcome of processes occurring at earlier stages of development. The seeds of this Hegelian view were, of course, sown by Kant when he elevated time to an equal status with space as a form of intuition, and degraded substance—the notion of permanent being—to merely one of twelve categories of judgment.

If in this synopsis of Hegel's philosophy, we substitute *man* for *mind* and *social existence* for *external reality*, then we have a basic tenet of Marxism: Man and society are the mutual products of an underlying dialectic process that tends toward a foreordained conclusion—the classless society and "new man" of communist ideology.

The readings in this chapter illustrate two of the central themes of Marxist thought: the nature of man as a social being and the problem of alienation. As we shall see, these themes are closely related. There are two senses in which Marx viewed man as a social being. The first is summarized in his statement, one of the *Theses on Feuerbach*, that "The essence of man is no abstraction inherent in each separate individual. In its reality it is the ensemble of social relations." The human infant is, to borrow a phrase from Aristotle, sheer potentiality. It does not yet have an essence, except as a striving, active organism. The infant achieves actualization when it incorporates as its own the "ensemble of social relations" handed down by previous generations. In this sense, the society into which one is born becomes an essential part of one's makeup, and each person becomes a product of social evolution.

Society, however, does not completely preempt an individual's potential, and this bring us to the second way in which people are dependent on society for their "essences." As we have already noted, people are basically doers. They not only incorporate societal relations passed on by prior generations, they further build upon these relations to produce individual selves. If it were not for society, each person would be so preoccupied with survival that there would be no opportunity to engage in truly creative (human) activities. It is only through communal effort that people achieve the means and the freedom to express themselves in art, literature, recreation, and other forms of productive "labor." And, in Marx's own words, "As individuals express their life, so they are." Ultimately, then, it is through communion with others that a person achieves individuality.

We are now in a position to outline briefly Marx's notion of alienation. Through actions or labor, people produce objects. These objects are *externalizations* and *objectifications* of themselves. For example, if I write a poem, in creating the poem I am also creating myself, for I am a product of my actions. But the poem also is an object that can be manipulated independently of myself (e.g., it can be copyrighted, bought, and sold).

Alienation begins when people lose control over the products of their own labor. This could occur, for example, when the products belong to another, or when they are controlled by impersonal economic "laws" that the producers do not understand and over which they have no control. But the product of labor is only the tail that wags the dog, so to speak. If the product is alienated, then the labor itself can no longer be a free and spontaneous expression of the individual. At best, labor becomes a means to satisfy other (extrinsic) needs. Thus, if I write a poem, not for self-expression, but in order to buy goods, leisure time, etc., then the act of writing as well as the poem itself have become alienated. And as labor becomes tied to extrinsic goals, people come to view each other, not as fellow human beings, but as objects whose value is determined by the marketplace. This destroys the social relationships that are necessary if people are to actualize themselves. The end result of the entire sequence is, then, one's alienation from one's true nature as a "species-being," i.e., as a self-conscious member of the human species.

The concept of alienation has become very popular in contemporary psychological literature, where it often is used to refer to subjective feelings of distress, powerlessness, and estrangement. This, however, was not Marx's conception. For Marx, alienation stands for a disparity between what one actually is and what one is capable of becoming; people need never be subjectively aware of their alienation.

By focusing too closely on the subjective manifestations of alienation, it is easy to lose sight of the major thrust of Marx's analysis, which concerns the power of social institutions to shape human nature. Unfortunately, Marx shared with other Romantics of the mid-19th century the view that social (or at least state) institutions are primarily detrimental to human development. Therefore, in contrast to his often incisive critique of prevailing social institutions, he was less insightful regarding the kinds of institutions that might preclude conditions such as alienation in a modern industrial society.

Autobiographical Sketch

[S]ome remarks as to the course of my own politico-economic studies may be in place here.

The subject of my professional studies was jurisprudence, which I pursued, however, in connection with and as secondary to the studies of philosophy and history. In 1842-43, as editor of the "Rheinische Zeitung," I found myself embarassed at first when I had to take part in discussions concerning so-called material interests. The proceedings of the Rhine Diet in connection with forest thefts and the extreme subdivision of landed property; the official controversy about the condition of the Mosel peasants into which Herr von Schaper, at that time president of the Rhine Province, entered with the "Rheinische Zeitung;" finally, the debates on free trade and protection, gave me the first impulse to take up the study of economic questions. At the same time a weak, quasi-philosophic echo of French socialism and communism made itself heard in the "Rheinische Zeitung" in those days when the good intentions "to go ahead" greatly outweighed knowledge of facts. I declared myself against such botching, but had to admit at once in a controversy with the "Allgemeine Augsburger Zeitung" that my previous studies did not allow me to hazard an independent judgment as to the merits of the French schools. When, therefore, the publishers of the "Rheinische Zeitung" conceived the illusion that by a less aggressive policy the paper could be saved from the death sentence pronounced upon it, I was glad to grasp that opportunity to retire to my study room from public life.

The first work undertaken for the solution of the question that troubled me, was a critical revision of Hegel's "Philosophy of Law"; the introduction to that work appeared in the "Deutsche-Französische Jahrbücher," published in Paris in 1844. I was led by my studies to the conclusion that legal relations as well as forms of state could neither be understood by themselves nor explained by the so-called general progress of the human mind, but that they are rooted in the material conditions of life, which are summed up by Hegel after the fashion of the English and French of the eighteenth century under the name "civic society;" the anatomy of that civic society is to be sought in political economy. The study of the latter which I had taken up in Paris, I continued at Brussels whither I emigrated on account of an order of expulsion issued by

Marx, Karl, *A Contribution to the Critique of Political Economy* (N. I. Stone, trans.) Chicago: Charles H. Kerr and Company, 1904. Pp. 10–15.

Mr. Guizot. The general conclusion at which I arrived and which, once reached, continued to serve as the leading thread in my studies, may be briefly summed up as follows: In the social production which men carry on they enter into definite relations that are indispensable and independent of their will; these relations of production correspond to a definite stage of development of their material powers of production. The sum total of these relations of production constitutes the economic structure of society—the real foundation, on which rise legal and political superstructures and to which correspond definite forms of social consciousness. The mode of production in material life determines the general character of the social, political and spiritual processes of life. It is not the consciousness of men that determines their existence, but, on the contrary, their social existence determines their consciousness. At a certain stage of their development, the material forces of production in society come in conflict with the existing relations of production, or—what is but a legal expression for the same thing—with the property relations within which they had been at work before. From forms of development of the forces of production these relations turn into their fetters. Then comes the period of social revolution. With the change of the economic foundation the entire immense superstructure is more or less rapidly transformed. In considering such transformations the distinction should always be made between the material trans-formation of the economic conditions of production which can be determined with the precision of natural science, and the legal, political, religious, aesthetic or philosophic—in short ideological forms in which men become conscious of this conflict and fight it out. Just as our opinion of an individual is not based on what he thinks of himself, so can we not judge of such a period of transformation by its own consciousness; on the contrary, this consciousness must rather be explained from the contradictions of material life, from the existing conflict between the social forces of production and the relations of production. No social order ever disappears before all the productive forces, for which there is room in it, have been developed; and new higher relations of production never appear before the material conditions of their existence have matured in the womb of the old society. Therefore, mankind always takes up only such problems as it can solve; since, looking at the matter more closely, we will always find that the problem itself arises only when the material conditions necessary for its solution already exist or are at least in the process of formation. In broad outlines we can designate the Asiatic, the ancient, the feudal, and the modern bourgeois methods of production as so many epochs in the progress of the economic formation of society. The bourgeois relations of production are the last antagonistic form of the social process of production—antagonistic not in the sense of individual antagonism, but of one arising from conditions surrounding the life of individuals in society; at the same time the productive forces developing in the womb of bourgeois society create the material conditions for the solution of that antagonism. This social formation constitutes, therefore, the closing chapter of the prehistoric stage of human society.

Frederick Engels, with whom I was continually corresponding and exchanging ideas since the appearance of his ingenious critical essay on economic categories (in the "Deutsche-Französische Jahrbücher"), came by a different road to the same conclusions as myself (see his "Condition of the Working Classes in England"). When he, too, settled in Brussels in the spring of 1845, we decided to work out together the contrast between our view and the idealism of the German philosophy, in fact to settle our accounts with our former philosophic conscience. The plan was carried out in the form of a criticism of the post-Hegelian philosophy. The manuscript in two solid octavo volumes had long reached the publisher in Westphalia, when we received information that conditions had so changed as not to allow of its publication. We abandoned the manuscript to the stinging criticism of the mice the more readily since we had accomplished our main purpose—the clearing up of the question to ourselves. Of the scattered writings on various subjects in which we presented our views to the public at that time, I recall only the "Manifesto of the Communist Party" written by Engels and myself, and the "Discourse on Free Trade" written by myself. The leading points of our theory were first presented scientifically, though in a polemic form, in my "Misère de la Philosophie, etc." directed against Proudhon and published in 1847. An essay on "Wage Labor," written by me in German, and in which I put together my lectures on the subject delivered before the German Workmen's Club at Brussels, was prevented from leaving the hands of the printer by the February revolution and my expulsion from Belgium which followed it as a consequence.

The publication of the "Neue Rheinische Zeitung" in 1848 and 1849, and the events which took place later on, interrupted my economic studies which I could not resume before 1850 in London. The enormous material on the history of political economy which is accumulated in the British Museum; the favorable view which London offers for the observation of bourgeois society; finally, the new stage of development upon which the latter seemed to have entered with the discovery of gold in California and Australia, led me to the decision to resume my studies from the very beginning and work up critically the new material. These studies partly led to what might seem side questions, over which I nevertheless had to stop for longer or shorter periods of time. Especially was the time at my disposal cut down by the imperative necessity of working for a living. My work as contributor on the leading Anglo-American newspaper, the "New York Tribune," at which I have now been engaged for eight years, has caused very great interruption in my studies, since I engage in newspaper work proper only occasionally. Yet articles on important economic events in England and on the continent have formed so large a part of my contributions that I have been obliged to make myself familiar with practical details which lie outside the proper sphere of political economy.

This account of the course of my studies in political economy is simply to prove that my views, whatever one may think of them, and no matter how little they agree with the interested prejudices of the ruling classes, are the result of many years of conscientious research. At the entrance to science, however, the same requirement must be put as at the entrance to hell:

Qui si convien lasciare ogni sospetto
Ogni viltà convien che qui sia morta.

Here must all distrust be left
All cowardice must here be dead
    Dante, *The Divine Comedy*

Alienation of the Self:
alienated labour

We have begun from the presuppositions of political economy. We have accepted its terminology and its laws. We presupposed private property; the separation of labour, capital and land, as also of wages, profit and rent; the division of labour; competition; the concept of exchange value, etc. From political economy itself, in its own words, we have shown that the worker sinks to the level of a commodity, and to a most miserable commodity; that the misery

From "The economic and philosophical manuscripts of 1844," in *Karl Marx: Early Writings* translated and edited by T. B. Bottomore (London, 1963, C. A. Watts: New York, 1963, McGraw-Hill), pp. 120–131, 157–167. Reprinted by permission of the publishers.

of the worker increases with the power and volume of his production; that the necessary result of competition is the accumulation of capital in a few hands, and thus a restoration of monopoly in a more terrible form; and finally that the distinction between capitalist and landlord, and between agricultural labourer and industrial worker, must disappear, and the whole of society divide into the two classes of property *owners* and *propertyless* workers.

Political economy begins with the fact of private property; it does not explain it. It conceives the *material* process of private property, as this occurs in reality, in general and abstract formulas which then serve it as laws. It does not *comprehend* these laws; that is, it does not show how they arise out of the nature of private property. Political economy provides no explanation of the basis for the distinction of labour from capital, of capital from land. When, for example, the relation of wages to profits is defined, this is explained in terms of the interests of capitalists; in other words, what should be explained is assumed. Similarly, competition is referred to at every point and is explained in terms of external conditions. Political economy tells us nothing about the extent to which these external and apparently accidental conditions are simply the expression of a necessary development. We have seen how exchange itself seems an accidental fact. The only motive forces which political economy recognizes are *avarice* and the *war between the avaricious, competition.*

Just because political economy fails to understand the interconnexions within this movement it was possible to oppose the doctrine of competition to that of monopoly, the doctrine of freedom of the crafts to that of the guilds, the doctrine of the division of landed property to that of the great estates; for competition, freedom of crafts, and the division of landed property were conceived only as accidental consequences brought about by will and force, rather than as necessary, inevitable and natural consequences of monopoly, the guild system and feudal property.

Thus we have now to grasp the real connexion between this whole system of alienation—private property, acquisitiveness, the separation of labour, capital and land, exchange and competition, value and the devaluation of man, monopoly and competition—and the system of *money.*

Let us not begin our explanation, as does the economist, from a legendary primordial condition. Such a primordial condition does not explain anything; it merely removes the question into a grey and nebulous distance. It asserts as a fact or event what it should deduce, namely, the necessary relation between two things; for example, between the division of labour and exchange. In the same way theology explains the origin of evil by the fall of man; that is, it asserts as a historical fact what it should explain.

We shall begin from a *contemporary* economic fact. The worker becomes poorer the more wealth he produces and the more his production increases in power and extent. The worker becomes an ever cheaper commodity the more goods he creates. The *devaluation* of the human world increases in direct relation with the *increase in value* of the world of things. Labour does not only create goods; it also produces itself and the worker as a *commodity*, and indeed in the same proportion as it produces goods.

This fact simply implies that the object produced by labour, its product, now stands opposed to it as an *alien being*, as a *power independent* of the producer. The product of labour is labour which has been embodied in an object and turned into a physical thing; this product is an *objectification* of labour. The performance of work is at the same time its objectification. The performance of work appears in the sphere of political economy as a *vitiation* of the worker, objectification as a *loss* and as *servitude to the object*, and appropriation as *alienation*.

So much does the performance of work appear as vitiation that the worker is vitiated to the point of starvation. So much does objectification appear as loss of the object that the worker is deprived of the most essential things not only of life but also of work. Labour itself becomes an object which he can acquire only by the greatest effort and with unpredictable interruptions. So much does the appropriation of the object appear as alienation that the more objects the worker produces the fewer he can possess and the more he falls under the domination of his product, of capital.

All these consequences follow from the fact that the worker is related to the *product of his labour* as to an *alien* object. For it is clear on this presupposition that the more the worker expends himself in work the more powerful becomes the world of objects which he creates in face of himself, the poorer he becomes in his inner life, and the less he belongs to himself. It is just the same as in religion. The more of himself man attributes to God the less he has left in himself. The worker puts his life into the object, and his life then belongs no longer to himself but to the object. The greater his activity, therefore, the less he possesses. What is embodied in the product of his labour is no longer his own. The greater this product is, therefore, the more he is diminished. The *alienation* of the worker in his product means not only that his labour becomes an object, assumes an *external* existence, but that it exists independently, *outside himself*, and alien to him, and that it stands opposed to him as an autonomous power. The life which he has given to the object sets itself against him as an alien and hostile force.

Let us now examine more closely the phenomenon of *objectification*; the worker's production and the *alienation* and *loss* of the object it produces, which is involved in it. The worker can create nothing without *nature*, without the *sensuous external world*. The latter is the material in which his labour is realized, in which it is active, out of which and through which it produces things.

But just as nature affords the *mean of existence* of labour, in the sense that labour cannot *live* without objects upon which it can be exercised, so also it provides the *means of existence* in a narrower sense; namely the means of physical existence for the *worker* himself. Thus, the more the worker *appropriates* the external world of sensuous nature by his labour the more he deprives himself of *means of existence*, in two respects: first, that the sensuous external world becomes progressively less an object belonging to his labour or a means of existence of his labour, and secondly, that it becomes progressively less a means of existence in the direct sense, a means for the physical subsistence of the worker.

In both respects, therefore, the worker becomes a slave of the object; first, in that he receives an *object of work*, i.e. receives *work*, and secondly, in that he receives *means of subsistence*. Thus the object enables him to exist, first as a *worker* and secondly, as a *physical subject*. The culmination of this enslavement is that he can only maintain himself as a *physical subject* so far as he is a *worker*, and that it is only as a *physical subject* that he is a worker.

(The alienation of the worker in his object is expressed as follows in the laws of political economy: the more the worker produces the less he has to consume; the more value he creates the more worthless he becomes; the more refined his product the more crude and misshapen the worker; the more civilized the product the more barbarous the worker; the more powerful the work the more feeble the worker; the more the work manifests intelligence the more the worker declines in intelligence and becomes a slave of nature.)

Political economy conceals the alienation in the nature of labour in so far as it does not examine the direct relationship between the worker (work) and production. Labour certainly produces marvels for the rich but it produces privation for the worker. It produces palaces, but hovels for the worker. It produces beauty, but deformity for the worker. It replaces labour by machinery, but it casts some of the workers back into a barbarous kind of work and turns the others into machines. It produces intelligence, but also stupidity and cretinism for the workers.

The direct relationship of labour to its products is the relationship of the worker to the objects of his production. The relationship of property owners to the objects of production and to production itself is merely a *consequence* of this first relationship and confirms it. We shall consider this second aspect later.

Thus, when we ask what is the important relationship of labour, we are concerned with the relationship of the *worker* to production.

So far we have considered the alienation of the worker only from one aspect; namely, *his relationship with the products of his labour.* However, alienation appears not merely in the result but also in the *process* of *production*, within *productive activity* itself. How could the worker stand in an alien relationship to the product of his activity if he did not alienate himself in the act of production itself? The product is indeed only the *résumé* of activity, of production. Consequently, if the product of labour is alienation, production itself must be active alienation—the alienation of activity and the activity of alienation. The alienation of the object of labour merely summarizes the alienation in the work activity itself.

What constitutes the alienation of labour? First, that the work is *external* to the worker, that it is not part of his nature; and that, consequently, he does not fulfil himself in his work but denies himself, has a feeling of misery rather than well-being, does not develop freely his mental and physical energies but is physically exhausted and mentally debased. The worker, therefore, feels himself at home only during his leisure time, whereas at work he feels homeless. His work is not voluntary but imposed, *forced labour.* It is not the satisfaction of a need, but only a *means* for satisfying other needs. Its alien character is clearly shown by the fact that as soon as there is no physical or other compulsion it is avoided like the plague. External labour, labour in which man alienates himself, is a labour of self-sacrifice, of mortification. Finally, the external character of work for the worker is shown by the fact that it is not his own work but work for someone else, that in work he does not belong to himself but to another person.

Just as in religion the spontaneous activity of human fantasy, of the human brain and heart, reacts independently as an alien activity of gods or devils upon the individual, so the activity of the worker is not his own spontaneous activity. It is another's activity and a loss of his own spontaneity.

We arrive at the result that man (the worker) feels himself to be freely active only in his animal functions—eating, drinking and procreating, or at most also in his dwelling and in personal adornment—while in his human functions he is reduced to an animal. The animal becomes human and the human becomes animal.

Eating, drinking and procreating are of course also genuine human functions. But abstractly considered, apart from the environment of human activities, and turned into final and sole ends, they are animal functions.

We have now considered the act of alienation of practical human activity, labour, from two aspects: (1) the relationship of the worker to the *product of labour* as an alien object which dominates him. This relationship is at the same time the relationship to the sensuous external world, to natural objects, as an alien and hostile world; (2) the relationship of labour to the *act of production* within *labour*. This is the relationship of the worker to his own activity as something alien and not belonging to him, activity as suffering (passivity), strength as powerlessness, creation as emasculation, the *personal* physical and mental energy of the worker, his personal life (for what is life but activity?), as an activity which is directed against himself, independent of him and not belonging to him. This is *self-alienation* as against the above-mentioned alienation of the *thing*.

We have now to infer a third characteristic of *alienated labour* from the two we have considered.

Man is a species-being not only in the sense that he makes the community (his own as well as those of other things) his object both practically and theoretically, but also (and this is simply another expression for the same thing) in the sense that he treats himself as the present, living species, as a *universal* and consequently free being.

Species-life, for man as for animals, has its physical basis in the fact that man (like animals) lives from inorganic nature, and since man is more universal than an animal so the range of inorganic nature from which he lives is more universal. Plants, animals, minerals, air, light, etc. constitute, from the theoretical aspect, a part of human consciousness as objects of natural science and art; they are man's spiritual inorganic nature, his intellectual means of life, which he must first prepare for enjoyment and perpetuation.

So also, from the practical aspect, they form a part of human life and activity. In practice man lives only from these natural products, whether in the form of food, heating, clothing, housing, etc. The universality of man appears in practice in the universality which makes the whole of nature into his inorganic body: (1) as a direct means of life; and equally (2) as the material object and instrument of his life activity. Nature is the inorganic body of man; that is to say nature, excluding the human body itself. To say that man *lives* from nature means that nature is his *body* with which he must remain in a continuous interchange in order not to die. The statement that the physical and mental life of man, and nature, are interdependent means simply that nature is interdependent with itself, for man is a part of nature.

Since alienated labour: (1) alienates nature from man; and (2) alienates man from himself, from his own active function, his life activity; so it alienates him from the species. It makes *species-life* into a means of individual life. In the first place it alienates species-life and individual life, and secondly, it turns the latter, as an abstraction, into the purpose of the former, also in its abstract and alienated form.

For labour, *life activity*, *productive life*, now appear to man only as *means* for the satisfaction of a need, the need to maintain his physical existence. Productive life is, however, species-life. It is life creating life. In the type of life activity resides the whole character of a species, its species-character; and free, conscious activity is the species-character of human beings. Life itself appears only as a *means of life*.

The animal is one with its life activity. It does not distinguish the activity from itself. It is *its activity*. But man makes his life activity itself an object of his will and consciousness. He has a conscious life activity. It is not a determination with which he is completely identified. Conscious life activity distinguishes man from the life activity of animals. Only for this reason is he a species-being. Or rather, he is only a self-conscious being, i.e. his own life is an object for him, because he is a species-being. Only for this reason is his activity free activity. Alienated labour reverses the relationship, in that man because he is a self-conscious being makes his life activity, his *being*, only a means for his *existence*.

The practical construction of an *objective world*, the *manipulation* of inorganic nature, is the confirmation of man as a conscious species-being, i.e. a being who treats the species as his own being or himself as a species-being. Of course, animals also produce. They construct nests, dwellings, as in the case of bees, beavers, ants, etc. But they only produce what is strictly necessary for themselves or their young. They produce only in a single direction, while man produces universally. They produce only under the compulsion of direct physical needs, while man produces when he is free from physical need and only truly produces in freedom from such need. Animals produce only themselves, while man reproduces the whole of nature. The products of animal production belong directly to their physical bodies, while man is free in face of his product. Animals construct only in accordance with the standards and needs of the species to which they belong, while man knows how to produce in accordance with the standards of every species and knows how to apply the appropriate standard to the object. Thus man constructs also in accordance with the laws of beauty.

It is just in his work upon the objective world that man really proves himself as a *species-being*. This production is his active species-life. By means of it nature appears as *his* work and his reality. The object of labour is, therefore, the *objectification of man's species-life*; for he no longer reproduces himself merely intellectually, as in consciousness, but actively and in a real sense, and he sees his own reflection in a world which he has constructed. While, therefore, alienated labour takes away the object of production from man, it also takes away his *species-life*, his real objectivity as a species-being, and changes his advantage over animals into a disadvantage in so far as his inorganic body, nature, is taken from him.

Just as alienated labour transforms free and self-directed activity into a means, so it transforms the species-life of man into a means of physical existence.

Consciousness, which man has from his species, is transformed through alienation so that species-life becomes only a means for him. (3) Thus alienated labour turns the *species-life of man*, and also nature as his mental species-property, into an *alien* being and into a *means* for his *individual existence*. It alienates from man his own body, external nature, his mental life and his *human* life. (4) A direct consequence of the alienation of man from the product of his labour, from his life activity and from his species-life, is that *man* is *alienated* from other *men*. When man confronts himself he also confronts *other* men. What is true of man's relationship to his work, to the product of his work and to himself, is also true of his relationship to other men, to their labour and to the objects of their labour.

In general, the statement that man is alienated from his species-life means that each man is alienated from others, and that each of the others is likewise alienated from human life.

Human alienation, and above all the relation of man to himself, is first realized and expressed in the relationship between each man and other men. Thus in the relationship of alienated labour every man regards other men according to the standards and relationships in which he finds himself placed as a worker.

We began with an economic fact, the alienation of the worker and his production. We have expressed this fact in conceptual terms as *alienated labour*, and in analysing the concept we have merely analysed an economic fact.

Let us now examine further how this concept of alienated labour must express and reveal itself in reality. If the product of labour is alien to me and confronts me as an alien power, to whom does it belong? If my own activity does not belong to me but is an alien, forced activity, to whom does it belong? To a being *other* than myself. And who is this being? The *gods*? It is apparent in the earliest stages of advanced production, e.g. temple building, etc. in Egypt, India, Mexico, and in the service rendered to gods, that the product belonged to the gods. But the gods alone were never the lords of labour. And no more was *nature*. What a contradiction it would be if the more man subjugates nature by his labour, and the more the marvels of the gods are rendered superfluous by the marvels of industry, the more he should abstain from his joy in producing and his enjoyment of the product for love of these powers.

The *alien* being to whom labour and the product of labour belong, to whose service labour is devoted, and to whose enjoyment the product of labour goes, can only be *man* himself. If the product of labour does not belong to the worker, but confronts him as an alien power, this can only be because it belongs to *a man other than the worker*. If his activity is a torment to him it must be a source of *enjoyment* and pleasure to another. Not the gods, nor nature, but only man himself can be this alien power over men.

Consider the earlier statement that the relation of man to himself is first *realized, objectified*, through his relation to other men. If he is related to the product of his labour, his objectified labour, as to an *alien*, hostile, powerful and independent object, he is related in such a way that another alien, hostile, powerful and independent man is the lord of this object. If he is related to his own activity as to unfree activity, then he is related to it as activity in the service, and under the domination, coercion and yoke, of another man.

Every self-alienation of man, from himself and from nature, appears in the relation which he postulates between other men and himself and nature. Thus religious self-alienation is necessarily exemplified in the relation between laity and priest, or, since it is here a question of the spiritual world, between the laity and a mediator. In the real world of practice this self-alienation can only be expressed in the real, practical relation of man to his fellow men. The medium through which alienation occurs is itself a *practical* one. Through alienated labour, therefore, man not only produces his relation to the object and to the process of production as to alien and hostile men; he also produces the relation of other men to his production and his product, and the relation between himself and other men. Just as he creates his own production as a vitiation, a punishment, and his own product as a loss, as a product which does not belong to him, so he creates the domination of the non-producer over production and its product. As he alienates his own activity, so he bestows upon the stranger an activity which is not his own. . . .

Thus, through alienated labour the worker creates the relation of another man, who does not work and is outside the work process, to this labour. The relation of the worker to work also produces the relation of the capitalist (or whatever one likes to call the lord of labour) to work. *Private property* is, therefore, the product, the necessary result, of *alienated labour*, of the external relation of the worker to nature and to himself.

Private property is thus derived from the analysis of the concept of *alienated labour*; that is, alienated man, alienated labour, alienated life, and estranged man.

We have, of course, derived the concept of *alienated labour* (*alienated life*) from political economy, from an analysis of the *movement of private property*. But the analysis of this concept shows that although private property appears to be the basis and cause of alienated labour, it is rather a consequence of the latter, just as the gods are *fundamentally* not the cause but the product of confusions of human reason. At a later stage, however, there is a reciprocal influence.

Only in the final stage of the development of private property is its secret revealed, namely, that it is on one hand the *product* of alienated labour, and on the other hand the *means* by which labour is alienated, *the realization of this alienation*. . . .

private property and communism

We have seen how, on the assumption that private property has been positively superseded, man produces man, himself and then other men; how the object which is the direct activity of his personality is at the same time his existence for other men and their existence for him. Similarly, the material of labour and man himself as a subject are the starting-point as well as the result of this movement (and because there must be this starting-point private property is a historical necessity). Therefore, the *social* character is the universal character of the whole movement; *as* society itself produces *man* as *man*, so it is *produced* by him. Activity and mind are social in their content as well as in their *origin*; they are *social* activity and social mind. The *human* significance of nature only exists for *social* man, because only in this case is nature a *bond* with other *men*, the basis of his existence for others and of their existence for him. Only then is nature the *basis* of his own *human* experience and a vital element of human reality. The *natural* existence of man has here become his *human* existence and nature itself has become human for him. Thus *society* is the accomplished union of man with nature, the veritable resurrection of nature, the realized naturalism of man and the realized humanism of nature.

Social activity and social mind by no means exist *only* in the form of activity or mind which is directly communal. Nevertheless, communal activity and mind, i.e. activity and mind which express and confirm themselves directly in a *real association* with other men, occur everywhere where this direct expression of sociability arises from the content of the activity or corresponds to the nature of mind.

Even when I carry out *scientific* work, etc., an activity which I can seldom conduct in direct association with other men, I perform a *social*, because *human*, act. It is not only the material of my activity—such as the language itself which the thinker uses—which is given to me as a social product. My *own existence* is a social activity. For this reason, what I myself produce I produce for society, and with the consciousness of acting as a social being.

My universal consciousness is only the *theoretical* form of that whose *living* form is the real community, the social entity, although at the present day this universal consciousness is an abstraction from real life and is opposed to it as an enemy. That is why the *activity* of my universal consciousness as such is my *theoretical* existence as a social being.

It is above all necessary to avoid postulating "society" once again as an abstraction confronting the individual. The individual *is* the *social being*. The manifestation of his life—even when it does not appear directly in the form of a communal manifestation, accomplished in association with other men—is, therefore, a manifestation and affirmation of *social life*. Individual human life and species-life are not different things, even though the mode of existence of individual life is necessarily either a more *specific* or a more *general* mode of species-life, or that of species-life a *specific* or more *general* mode of individual life.

In his *species-consciousness* man confirms his real *social life*, and reproduces his real existence in thought; while conversely, species-life confirms itself in species-consciousness and exists for itself in its universality as a thinking being. Though man is a unique individual—and it is just his particularity which makes him an individual, a really *individual* communal being—he is equally the *whole*, the ideal whole, the subjective existence of society as thought and experienced. He exists in reality as the representation and the real mind of social existence, and as the sum of human manifestations of life.

Thought and being are indeed *distinct* but they also form a unity. *Death* seems to be a harsh victory of the species over the individual and to contradict their unity; but the particular individual is only a *determinate species-being* and as such he is mortal.

4. Just as *private property* is only the sensuous expression of the fact that man is at the same time an *objective* fact for himself and becomes an alien and non-human object for himself; just as his manifestation of life is also his alienation of life and his self-realization a loss of reality, the emergence of an *alien* reality; so the positive supersession of private property, i.e. the *sensuous* appropriation of the human essence and of human life, of objective man and of human *creations*, by and for man, should not be taken only in the sense of *immediate*, exclusive *enjoyment*, or only in the sense of *possession* or *having*. Man appropriates his manifold being in an all-inclusive way, and thus as a whole man. All his *human* relations to the world—seeing, hearing, smelling, tasting, touching, thinking, observing, feeling, desiring, acting, loving—in short, all the organs of his individuality, like the organs which are directly communal in form, are in their objective action (their *action in relation to the object*) the appropriation of this object, the appropriation of human reality. The way in which they react to the object is the confirmation of *human reality*.[1] It is human effectiveness and human *suffering*, for suffering humanly considered is an enjoyment of the self for man.

Private property has made us so stupid and partial that an object is only *ours* when we have it, when it exists for us as capital or when it is directly eaten, drunk, worn, inhabited, etc., in short,

[1] It is, therefore, just as varied as the determinations of human nature and activities are diverse.

utilized in some way. But private property itself only conceives these various forms of possession as *means of life*, and the life for which they serve as means is the *life* of *private property*—labour and creation of capital.

Thus *all* the physical and intellectual senses have been replaced by the simple alienation of *all* these senses; the sense of *having.* The human being had to be reduced to this absolute poverty in order to be able to give birth to all his inner wealth. (On the category of *having* see Hess in *Einundzwanzig Bogen.*)

The supersession of private property is, therefore, the complete *emancipation* of all the human qualities and senses. It is such an emancipation because these qualities and senses have become *human,* from the subjective as well as the objective point of view. The eye has become a *human* eye when its *object* has become a *human,* social object, created by man and destined for him. The senses have, therefore, become directly theoreticians in practice. They relate themselves to the thing for the sake of the thing, but the thing itself is an *objective human* relation to itself and to man, and vice versa.[2] Need and enjoyment have thus lost their *egoistic* character and nature has lost its mere *utility* by the fact that its utilization has become *human* utilization.

Similarly, the senses and minds of other men have become my *own* appropriation. Thus besides these direct organs, *social* organs are constituted, in the form of society; for example, activity in direct association with others has become an organ for the manifestation of life and a mode of appropriation of *human* life.

It is evident that the human eye appreciates things in a different way from the crude, non-human eye, the human *ear* differently from the crude ear. As we have seen, it is only when the object becomes a *human* object, or objective *humanity,* that man does not become lost in it. This is only possible when man himself becomes a *social* object; when he himself becomes a social being and society becomes a being for him in this object.

On the one hand, it is only when objective reality everywhere becomes for man in society the reality of human faculties, human reality, and thus the reality of his own faculties, that all *objects* become for him the *objectification of himself.* The objects then confirm and realize his individuality, they are *his own* objects, i.e. man himself becomes the object. *The manner in which these objects* become his own depends upon the *nature of the object* and the nature of the corresponding faculty; for it is precisely the *determinate character* of this relation which constitutes the specific

---

[2] In practice I can only relate myself in a human way to a thing when the thing is related in a human way to man.

real mode of affirmation. The object is not the same for the *eye* as for the *ear*, for the ear as for the eye. The *distinctive character* of each faculty is precisely its *characteristic* essence and thus also the characteristic mode of its objectification, of its *objectively real*, living *being*. It is therefore not only in thought, but through *all* the senses that man is affirmed in the objective world.

Let us next consider the subjective aspect. Man's musical sense is only awakened by music. The most beautiful music has no meaning for the non-musical ear, is not an object for it, because my object can only be the confirmation of one of my own faculties. It can only be so for me in so far as my faculty exists for itself as a subjective capacity, because the meaning of an object for me extends only as far as the sense extends (only makes sense for an appropriate sense). For this reason, the *senses* of social man are *different* from those of non-social man. It is only through the objectively deployed wealth of the human being that the wealth of subjective *human* sensibility (a musical ear, an eye which is sensitive to the beauty of form, in short, senses which are capable of human satisfaction and which confirm themselves as human faculties) is cultivated or created. For it is not only the five senses, but also the so-called spiritual senses, the practical senses (desiring, loving, etc.), in brief, human sensibility and the human character of the senses, which can only come into being through the existence of *its* object, through humanized nature. The cultivation of the five senses is the work of all previous history. Sense which is subservient to crude needs has only a restricted meaning. For a starving man the human form of food does not exist, but only its abstract character as food. It could just as well exist in the most crude form, and it is impossible to say in what way this feeding-activity would differ from that of animals. The needy man, burdened with cares, has no appreciation of the most beautiful spectacle. The dealer in minerals sees only their commercial value, not their beauty or their particular characteristics; he has no mineralogical sense. Thus, the objectification of the human essence, both theoretically and practically, is necessary in order to *humanize* man's senses, and also to create the *human senses* corresponding to all the wealth of human and natural being.

Just as society at its beginnings finds, through the development of *private property* with its wealth and poverty (both intellectual and material), the materials necessary for this *cultural development*, so the fully constituted society produces man in all the plenitude of his being, the wealthy man endowed with all the senses, as an enduring reality. It is only in a social context that subjectivism and objectivism, spiritualism and materialism, activity and passivity, cease to be antinomies and thus cease to exist as such antinomies. The resolution of the *theoretical* contradictions is possible *only* through practical means, only through the *practical* energy of man. Their resolution is not by any means, therefore, only a problem of knowledge, but is a *real* problem of life which philosophy was unable to solve precisely because it saw there a purely theoretical problem.

It can be seen that the history of *industry* and industry as it *objectively* exists is an *open* book of the *human faculties*, and a human *psychology* which can be sensuously apprehended. This history has not so far been conceived in relation to human *nature*, but only from a superficial utilitarian point of view, since in the condition of alienation it was only possible to conceive real human faculties and *human* species-action in the form of general human existence, as religion, or as history in its abstract, general aspect as politics, art and literature, etc. *Everyday material industry* (which can be conceived as part of that general development; or equally, the general development can be conceived as a specific part of industry since all human activity up to the present has been labour, i.e. industry, self-alienated activity) shows us, in the form of *sensuous useful objects*, in an alienated form, the *essential human faculties* transformed into objects. No psychology for which this book, i.e. the most tangible and accessible part of history, remains closed, can become a *real* science with a genuine content. What is to be thought of a science which stays aloof from this enormous field of human labour, and which does not feel its own inadequacy even though this great wealth of human activity means nothing to it except perhaps what can be expressed in the single phrase—"need," "common need"?

The *natural sciences* have developed a tremendous activity and have assembled an ever-growing mass of data. But philosophy has remained alien to these sciences just as they have remained alien to philosophy. Their momentary *rapprochement* was only a *fantastic* illusion. There was a desire for union but the power to effect it was lacking. Historiography itself only takes natural science into account incidentally, regarding it as a factor making for enlightenment, for practical utility and for particular great discoveries. But natural science has penetrated all the more *practically* into human life through industry. It has transformed human life and prepared the emancipation of humanity, even though its immediate effect was to accentuate the dehumanization of man. *Industry* is the actual historical relationship of nature, and thus of natural science, to man. If industry is conceived as the *exoteric* manifestation of the essential human *faculties*, the *human* essence of nature and the *natural* essence of man can also be understood. Natural science will then abandon its abstract materialist, or rather idealist, orientation, and will become the basis of a *human* science, just as it has already become—though in an alienated form—the basis of actual human life. One basis for life and another for science is *a priori* a falsehood. Nature, as it develops in human history, in the act of genesis of human society, is the *actual* nature of man; thus nature, as it develops through industry, though in an *alienated* form, is truly *anthropological* nature.

Sense experience (*see* Feuerbach) must be the basis of all science. Science is only genuine science when it proceeds from sense experience, in the two forms of *sense perception* and *sensuous* need; i.e. only when it proceeds from nature. The whole of history is a preparation for "man" to become an object of *sense* perception, and for the development of human needs (the needs of man as such). History itself is a *real* part of *natural history*, of the development of nature into man. Natural science will one day incorporate the science of man, just as the science of man will incorporate natural science; there will be a *single* science.

Man is the direct object of natural science, because directly *perceptible nature* is for man directly human sense experience (an identical expression) in the form of the *other person* who is directly presented to him in a sensuous way. His own sense experience only exists as human sense experience for himself through the *other person*. But *nature* is the direct object of the *science of man*. The first object for man—man himself—is nature, sense experience; and the particular sensuous human faculties, which can only find objective realization in *natural* objects, can only attain self-knowledge in the science of natural being. The element of thought itself, the element of the living manifestation of thought, language, is sensuous in character. The *social* reality of nature and *human* natural science, or the *natural science of man*, are identical expressions.

It will be seen from this how, in place of the *wealth* and *poverty* of political economy, we have the *wealthy* man and the plenitude of *human* need. The wealthy man is at the same time one who *needs* a complex of human manifestations of life, and whose own self-realization exists as an inner necessity, a *need*. Not only the wealth but also the *poverty* of man acquires, in a socialist perspective, a *human* and thus a social meaning. Poverty is the passive bond which leads man to experience a need for the greatest wealth, the *other* person. The sway of the objective entity within me, the sensuous eruption of my life-activity, is the passion which here becomes the *activity* of my being.

A being does not regard himself as independent unless he is his own master, and he is only his own master when he owes his existence to himself. A man who lives by the favour of another considers himself a dependent being. But I live completely by another person's favour when I owe to him not only the continuance of my life but also *its creation*; when he is its *source*. My life has necessarily such a cause outside itself if it is not my own creation. The idea of *creation* is thus one which it is difficult to eliminate from popular consciousness. This consciousness is *unable to conceive* that nature and man exist on their own account, because such an existence contradicts all the tangible facts of practical life.

The idea of the creation of the *earth* has received a severe blow from the science of geogeny, i.e. from the science which portrays the formation and development of the earth as a process of spontaneous generation. *Generatio aequivoca* (spontaneous generation) is the only practical refutation of the theory of creation.

But it is easy indeed to say to the particular individual what Aristotle said: You are engendered by your father and mother, and consequently it is the coitus of two human beings, a human species-act, which has produced the human being. You see, therefore, that even in a physical sense man owes his existence to man. Consequently, it is not enough to keep in view only one of the two aspects, the *infinite* progression, and to ask further: who engendered my father and my grandfather? You must also keep in mind the *circular movement* which is perceptible in that progression, according to which man, in the act of generation reproduces himself; thus *man* always remains the subject. But you will reply: I grant you this circular movement, but you must in turn concede the progression, which leads ever further to the point where I ask; who created the first man and nature as a whole? I can only reply: your question is itself a product of abstraction. Ask yourself how you arrive at that question. Ask yourself whether your question does not arise from a point of view to which I cannot reply because it is a perverted one. Ask yourself whether that progression exists as such for rational thought. If you ask a question about the creation of nature and man you abstract from nature and man. You suppose them *non-existent* and you want me to demonstrate that they *exist*. I reply: give up your abstraction and at the same time you abandon your question. Or else, if you want to maintain your abstraction, be consistent, and if you think of man and nature as non-existent, think of yourself too as non-existent, for you are also man and nature. Do not think, do not ask me any questions, for as soon as you think and ask questions your abstraction from the existence of nature and man becomes meaningless. Or are you such an egoist that you conceive everything as non-existent and yet want to exist yourself?

You may reply: I do not want to conceive the nothingness of nature, etc.; I only ask you about the act of its creation, just as I ask the anatomist about the formation of bones, etc.

Since, however, for socialist man, the *whole of what is called world history* is nothing but the creation of man by human labour, and the emergence of nature for man, he, therefore, has the evident and irrefutable proof of his *self-creation*, of his own *origins*. Once the essence of man and of nature, man as a natural being and nature as a human reality, has become evident in practical life, in sense experience, the quest for an *alien* being, a being above man and nature (a quest which is an avowal of the unreality of man and nature) becomes impossible in practice. *Atheism*, as a denial of this unreality, is no longer meaningful, for atheism is a *negation of God* and seeks to assert by this negation the *existence of man*. Socialism no longer requires such a roundabout method; it begins from the *theoretical* and *practical sense perception* of man and nature as essential beings. It is positive human *self-consciousness*, no longer a self-consciousness attained through the negation of religion; just as the *real life* of man is positive and no longer attained through the negation of private property, through *communism*. Communism is the phase of negation of the negation and is, consequently, for the next stage of historical development, a real and necessary factor in the emancipation and rehabilitation of man. Communism is the necessary form and the dynamic principle of the immediate future, but communism is not itself the goal of human development—the form of human society.

22. Alexander R. Luria

EDITOR'S INTRODUCTION

Alienation is among the most vogue (and vague) concepts in contemporary social science. Its current usage in American psychology can be traced rather directly to Marx's "Economic and Philosophical Manuscripts," excerpts from which are reprinted in Chapter 21. Although these manuscripts were originally written in 1844, when Marx was only 26, they were not published in complete and accurate form until 1932; it is with their publication that the concept of alienation began to receive wide currency. However, the popularity of this concept cannot be attributed just to Marx. Loosely defined, *alienation* is often used to refer to a wide range of phenomena discussed under different rubrics by psychoanalytic and existentialist writers. Indeed, the concept of alienation is sometimes viewed as a potential meeting ground for representatives of these conflicting traditions.[1]

One reason the concept of alienation did not gain wide currency until recently is that Marx, in his later, more widely known works, did not emphasize the notion. In fact, he sometimes even ridiculed those who wrote about alienation, accusing them of engaging in philosophical nonsense. Perhaps Marx recognized that the concept could be used so loosely and vaguely that it might obfuscate rather than clarify the basic issues involved. But, in spite of these later attitudes, the theory of alienation put forward in the "Economic and Philosophical Manuscripts" does reflect the same basic assumptions that underlie Marx's more mature view of man.[2]

[1] See, for example, E. Fromm, *The sane society*. New York: Holt, 1955; H. Marcuse, *One-dimensional man*. Boston: Beacon, 1964; J. P. Sartre, *Search for a method*. New York: Knopf, 1963.

[2] B. Ollman, *Alienation: Marx's conception of man in capitalist society*. Cambridge: Cambridge University Press, 1971.

It is these assumptions, not Marx's conception of alienation per se, that are important and that form the subject matter of this chapter.

Perhaps the most basic assumption made by Marx is that man is an active, creative being who, in communion with others, determines his own nature. One implication of this assumption is that such higher mental processes as perception, attention, memory, and reasoning do not reflect invariant properties of the human organism. Rather, they are the product of the social conditions under which an individual lives. But social conditions are also a product of human activity or labor. This means that psychological and social processes stand in a dialectic relationship, each helping to determine the other.

In this chapter, Alexander Luria describes experiments designed to test the influence of changing social conditions on supposedly invariant psychological processes. The subjects of these studies were peasant farmers living in isolated villages in Soviet Central Asia. These villages underwent considerable social change following the Soviet revolution and, as Luria reports, there were corresponding changes in the way the villagers came to form abstract concepts and in how they reached conclusions based on syllogistic reasoning.

In order to appreciate the implications of Luria's analysis, it is important to note that he is not simply claiming that the content of thought changes with changing social conditions. That would be a rather trivial assertion. He is arguing that fundamental psychological processes (i.e., the *way* we think) are the product of social conditions. To help make this distinction clear, consider the case of language. The content of the English language—its vocabulary and grammar—is very different from the content of the Russian language. But are there certain underlying features common to both (indeed, to all) languages? Chomsky (cf. Chapt. 14) believes there are, although the issue is far from settled. But even if there are invariant linguistic rules, or "deep structures," language itself is only one element in most complex thought processes. Thinking also includes such nonlinguistic factors as selective attention, memory, and judgment. One might ask of each of these in turn, "Does it possess invariant properties?" The answer, in almost every case, is that none has been found to date.[3] And as we combine these lower-order processes into more complex functions, such as concept formation and deductive reasoning, the argument for invariance becomes even more problematic.

[3] W. Thorngate, Process invariance: Another red herring. *Personality and Social Psychology Bulletin.* 1975, *1*, 485–488.

Ever since psychology was founded as a science, one of its major goals has been the discovery of laws that could be true regardless of the person or the situation. The failure to find such laws has generally been attributed to the fact that psychology is still a young science (although what is meant by "young" in this context is seldom made explicit). Luria's analysis suggests that the source of the "problem" may lie elsewhere; namely, universal psychological laws have not been found because they do not exist.

This last assertion requires some qualification. The existence of universal laws in psychology depends, in part, on the level of analysis. On a very abstract level, for example, the assertion that psycholgical processes are a function of social and historical conditions might itself be interpreted (if true) as a universal law. At the other extreme of abstractness, invariant processes might also be found at the level of neuronal functioning. But most psychological research falls between these extremes; and, at this in-between level of analysis, the issue of invariant psychological processes can only be settled by further research of the kind reported by Luria.

ALEXANDER R. LURIA

Towards the Problem of the Historical Nature
of Psychological Processes

INTRODUCTION

Over the course of centuries, classical psychology arrived at the idea that there is a unitary, unchanging structure to human psychological processes. This structure is thought to operate on a series of sharply delimited psychological processes: sensation and perception, attention and memory, association and logical relation, judgement and reasoning. The structure of these processes was said not to depend on social-historical conditions and to remain the same at any particular point in history.

These concepts are accepted by almost any school of classical psychology. While one school might believe that the nature of psychological processes should be interpreted as the manifestation of the general catagory of spiritual life, and another believes that psychological processes are the natural function of brain tissue, an ahistorical conception of the nature of psychological processes is commonly shared.

Although the idea that the structure of fundamental psychological processes is unchanging has been accepted by classical psychology, more and more facts have been gathered in the course of concrete psychological experimentation which clearly indicate that the structure of psychological processes changes as a function of history; consciousness does not have a constant, unchanging structure. As a function of the development of the child and as a result of transitions from one social-historical stage to another, not only the contents of psychological life, but its structure change. In other words, the facts more and more clearly indicate that we must consider the historical nature of man's

Reprinted from the *International Journal of Psychology*, 1971, Vol. 6, no. 4, pp. 259-272, by permission of the International Union of Psychological Science and Dunod Editeur, Paris.

This paper was translated from Russian into English by M. Cole.

This paper includes the first published account of research carried out by Professor Luria during two expeditions to Tadzhikistan and Uzbekhistan in the early 1930's. On the basis of early discussions with Professor Luria, my colleagues and I have been able to replicate certain of his observations, particularly those having to do with syllogistic reasoning. This work, carried out in Liberia, replicated in all important respects the work described in Sections 4 and 5, of this paper. (See M. Cole, J. Gay, J. Glick and D. Sharp, *The cultural context of learning and thinking*. New York: Basic Books, 1971). A great many topics investigated by Professor Luria and his colleagues are not reported in this paper, because Professor Luria believes that his thinking on the problems posed by his cross-cultural work is still at preliminary state of development. *(Translator's note)*.

psychological processes. This position will be the subject of the present article.[1]

I

As early as the end of the 1920's, the great Soviet psychologist, L. S. Vygotskii, put forward the view that while such elementary psycho-physiological processes as sensation, movement, elementary forms of attention, and memory, are undoubtedly natural functions of the nervous tissue, the higher psychological functions (voluntary memory, active attention, abstract thought, voluntary memory, active attention, abstract thought, and voluntary movement) cannot be understood as a direct function of the brain. He adopted the position, which was truly significant for that period, that in order to understand the substance of higher psychological processes in man, it is necessary to go beyond the limits of the organism and to search for the roots of these complex processes in the historically formed environment, in the communication of the child with adults, in the objective relations among objects, tools and language which have been laid down in the course of social history. In short, we must seek the roots or such higher psychological functions in the mastery of general, human, historically formed experience.

L. S. Vygotskii was convinced that mastery of socially determined experience changes not only the contents of psychological life (the range of ideas and knowledge), but also creates new forms of psychological processes, which take the form of higher psychological functions, which distinguish men from animals, and which create a more solid structure for the conscious activity of man.

Using the historically laid-down system of language, the mother shows the child an object and names it by the corresponding word; in so doing, she changes the environment perceived by the child, separating out the named object and turning the child's attention to it. This serves as the beginning of a most important evolutionary change in the psychological processes of the child. Initially under the control of the mother's instruction, the child then begins to use speech, naming objects which interest him, separating them from his environment and concentrating his attention on actively tying them to him. The process of communication between two

[1] In the work which we are going to describe, several people in addition to the author participated: L. I. Leventuev, F. I. Shemyakin, A. Bogoutdinov, K. H. Kakhimov, L. S. Zakhrbyants, E. Beinurova, and others.

people turns into a new form for organization of psychological processes in the growing individual. The function of calling attention to something, which was shared between two people, and which was initially of a reflex character, turns into internally organized activity; a new category, *higher psychological processes*, is created. These processes are social in their origin, mediated in their structure, and voluntarily directed in their functioning.

The roots of higher psychological processes turn out to lie outside of the organism in social-historical forms of activity. This external source of development which was never seen by classical psychology as of fundamental significance for the formation of psychological processes, becomes decisive for a scientific under-standing of higher psychological processes. Psychology can no longer be interpreted in the light of natural science positivism; psychology is becoming a social-historical science.

The greatest value of L. S. Vygotskii's ideas consists of the fact that while preserving the natural laws of the brain's organization and work, he showed the new properties which these laws take on, including a system of social-historical relations. Also important is the fact that he traced the fundamental characteristics of social-historical evolution of man's higher psychological processes which, prior to his time, had either been ignored by natural science and psychology or only described, but never explained, by idealistic psychology which called itself "the psychology of the soul". New phenomena, which had never before been the subject of scientific psychological investigation were introduced into psychology. For example, Vygotskii considered such behavior as certain people's habit of making notches in a branch or tying knots in a rope to serve as a means for organizing attention, codes in language on the basis of which abstraction and generalization occur, and the historical process by which written language and arithmetic were formed. These phenomena began to be looked at, not only as a subject for ethnology and linguistics, but also as a substantial component of psychology.

The work of L. S. Vygotskii using the experience of progressive foreign psychological movements (the French sociological school, investigations of English and German ethnologists), but filtering the data through the prism of a materialist understanding of history, became a starting point for the formation of psychology as an historical science.

II

What kinds of facts can illustrate the productivity of this approach to psychological processes as a product of social-historical development? We will turn our attention first to the problem of the historical development of the processes of speech and thinking which even now continue to be among the most important problems of psychology.

In associationistic psychology (and to some extent in contemporary American behaviorism) one often encounters the opinion that the process of the development of thought can be reduced to a simple accumulation of new ideas, to a quantitative enrichment of the vocabulary, and to a mastery of abstract concepts. Classical psychology cannot deal with such problems as the following: How does word meaning, which helps the child to direct his own behavior, develop? How does the *structure* of his intellectual processes change during ontogenesis in the deepest sense of that word? There is nothing further from the truth than the position that ontogenesis represents a mere accumulation of new elements.

As early as the 1920's, Soviet psychological science and primarily L. S. Vygotskii demonstrated that the meaning of words which the child uses, and the psychological composition of those ideational operations which he carries out with their help, represent a path of significant development. They demonstrated as well that the structure of these processes is deeply changed during the transition from pre-school to the early school age and from early school age to adolescence. Discovery of the fact that the significance of words develops and that as the child grows, the psychological structure of cognitive processes and interfunctional relations which carry out cognitive functions deeply change, represents one of the most important attainments of Soviet psychology and the results of this discovery are of great significance for the future evolution of this area of science. For this reason, we have to take a brief look at the problem.

The cognitive processes of the child receive a strong boost at the moment when the child masters his first word; they are infinitely enriched and increase in potential when they begin to be based on the system of complex codes which are part of the language. However, it would be deeply in error to think that the mastery of language, which is the most important means of social-historical organization of consciousness, can be understood as the acquisition of new ideas and that underlying the word are simple images or representations evoked with its aid.

It is well known that the semantics of a word are extremely complex and that the word potentially evokes not a single image but a whole system of possible associations. Underlying the word "oak" may be hidden both the image of a powerful tree and the wooded area on which it grows, as well as a sign of hardness (and sometimes a sign of stubbornness, as in the expression "that one—why, he's an oak"), hard material or a bench, etc. Sometimes the word evokes a natural system of abstract ties and "oak" becomes part of the same set as "birch", "pine", etc. and is included in a general category "tree", which along with the group "shrubbery" and "grass" form a category of "growing things", which in turn can be contrasted with another category, "animal".

The work of a developed consciousness consists in choosing from this set of equally probable associations those which are important for a given situation in order to replace the ambiguity of the set of associations as a whole with a definition which increases the probability of ties which are important for the given situation, and which form the basis of thought. The transition to verbal thought, therefore, constitutes a "leap from the sensory to the rational" and it guarantees an infinite variety of possible ties within which thought may move, allowing us to go beyond the limits of our immediately obtained sense data. It is exactly this property of language which led the great linguists of the last century to interpret language as a "weapon of freedom".

There is nothing more mistaken, however, than to assume that the significance of a word which is first mastered by the child immediately introduces into his consciousness the rich system of ties which we have just discussed and that it immediately allows him to complete that "leap from the world of necessity to the world of freedom". Such a view, and it has often been encountered in psychology, which was not at that time historical science, is incorrect.

Observations of the natural development of speech in a child show that the lack of differentiation among words which appear at early stages of development [*kub* instead of *kuritsa* (chicken), *av* instead of *sobochka* (dog)] to a certain extent does not match in its content with the developed forms of these words. *Kub* indicates only one of several possible *surface features* of "cat" and in one situation may indicate fuzziness or softness and in another pain or scratching, and in a third, the cat itself which fell into a mousetrap. The early words of the child still do not have a strong concrete meaning and indicate that component of a situation (most often emotional) which is noticed by the child in that particular situation. The factor which determines the significance of a word at this stage is the impression of the child. In the early period of mastering speech, the definitional role is played not by the word and its historically determined logical ties, but the child's impressions with respect to the immediate situation. This is why certain psychologists, with good reason, say that at the early stage of the development of language, the subjective idea of the word is dominant over its objective significance. A significant process occupying the two first years of a child's life is the mastery and differentiation of the language system and the transformation of the word into a carrier of the structure of an objective code.

One can observe, as I have had the opportunity to do (see Luria and Yudovich, 1955) how a diffuse word such as *tpru* begins by meaning in equal measure, a "horse" and "stop" and "let's go", but then acquires a suffix and turns into the word *tprun'ka.* In so doing, it also acquires the clear significance of a *name* and the designation "horse" no longer indicates "stop" or "let's go". The process of mastering the concrete significance of language is one of the most important periods in the psychological development of the child and it is exactly this process which is a stage in the formation of a *stable concrete picture of the world.* The naming of a concrete object by a word separates out its essential quality (watch, wood, store) and perception of the object acquires a stable, constant character. Howerver, it does not follow that this process, which ends around 6 and 7 years of age, leads to the final stage of complete mastery of the developed significance of words.

Experiments which were begun by L. S. Vygotskii and continued by his co-workers, showed that the word mastered and used by a 5–6 year old child first brings to life visual-motor, concrete, situational ties and still to only a small degree leads to inclusion of those abstract relations which stand behind the developed significance of the word. For a long period the word "wood" evokes an idea of a particular tree, a particular area of woods, a bench, or that it floats and does not sink. But the word still does not evoke an idea which is never evoked in that situation such as "palm" or "iron" (according to the principle "organic-inorganic"). The same applies to the word *lavka* in the sense of a store, which evokes a whole complex of visual images and experience (bread, scale, sack, salesperson), but still does not evoke an abstract conception (*factory*—system of production; *store*—system of distribution).

At this stage, the logical system of ties standing behind the word still does not attain a leading character and the significance of the word in many respects still has traces of a visual-motor memory, and does not have ties based on the code of logical thought. The entire system of speech/thinking in the child continues to be determined by this fundamental fact. It is necessary for the child (now he is already a school-child) to carry out substantial internal work, occupying an entire large period in order to be in a position where the situation is changed and he can respond to the words in terms of the system of logical codes formed in the process of social life. As observations have shown, only in his later periods does the child who defined horse as "she is carrying" (in other words, who replaced an abstract operation of behavior by a concrete situation), begin to give an answer such as "horse—that is an animal". That is, he begins to replace an immediate visual image by a generally accepted, abstract, logical category.

In the 1920's, L. S. Vygotskii and L. S. Sakharov carried out experiments with geometrical figures (*e.g.*, a flat green triangle and a flat red circle), using children as subjects. Each of the figures was named by an artificial word (*e.g.*, the two figures named above were called *ras*). The subject was given the task of finding what other figures were named in the same way as the two that were shown. At first, the young children select a figure more or less at random or because it belongs to the group according to a single attribute (*e.g.*, one because it is green, another because it is a triangle, a third because it is flat). Only toward late childhood does the child begin the difficult work of discovering the abstract code according to which the group of objects had been formed. Only at this later period does he show ability to use complex word meaning as a basis for an abstract "categorical" kind of thinking.[2]

The importance of this investigation consists also in the fact that it was simultaneously realized that the history of the mastery of the significance of words (which is the fundamental channel for the social formation of individual consciousness) was at the same time a reflection of the historical development of consciousness of the child, the history of the transition from visual-motor thinking directed at immediate impressions and concrete memory to a verbal-logical form of consciousness, during which the leading role is played by the logical codes laid down in the course of social history. Thanks to this series of psychological investigations, the intimate mechanisms of the social formation of individual consciousness became a subject for scientific investigations and the thesis of the social-historical nature of cognitive processes of man received its full recognition.

III

We have shown that psychological processes in childhood do not remain unchanging, but develop, changing their structure and even their nature in this process and that they possess a

[2] Details of this experiment may be found in L. S. Vygotskii, 1962 *(Translator's note).*

social-historical character. However, we are able to judge the social-historical character of this development only indirectly according to the decisive role which communication with adults plays and the significance which language plays as means for the formation of psychological processes.

A substantial barrier to a decisive judgement concerning the character of psychological development in ontogenesis derives from the fact that, during this process, maturation of the child's brain must be considered as a factor in development. It is necessary, therefore, to carry out the next step and to study a form of development of psychological processes in which maturation no longer is a factor and in which the formation of new types of psychological activity carries an unambiguously social character.

With this purpose, we will move to a consideration of the problem of a comparative study of the formation of psychological processes in different social-historical conditions and we will try to determine what changes are evoked in the structure of psychological processes by mass social-historical events. Two difficulties immediately come to mind when we consider this problem.

A theoretical difficulty consists of the fact that nowhere is the idea of the unchangingness and the unchangeableness of psychological processes so strong as in historical psychology in the narrow sense of the word. If we take as an axiom the position that the laws of perception and memory, speech and thinking, cognitive activity and emotional life are identical in all areas, we have implicitly accepted a position held by all but a few investigators, and it must be stated that in its time, this position played a progressive role in science because it acted against the reactionary position that certain races are biologically inferior and thereby psychologically inferior. Psychological changes, taking place in social history, have usually been viewed as an enrichment in knowledge, as a widening of the circle of ideas, and if we exclude such investigators as Levy-Bruhl, the idea that the process of historical development changes not only the content of con-sciousness, but its psychological structure was, specific to that still underdeveloped branch of psychology which took as its task the study of wide psychological changes in the course of history.

The second practical barrier consisted in the fact that historical advances which could reflect on the forms of psychological processes ordinarily take place over a very long period of time and this condition made it impossible to introduce psychological investigation using exact experimental methods. Investigation of psychological processes of greatly underdeveloped people was necessarily unable to study the consequence of such rapid changes and turning to the material provided by linguistics and folklore permitted access to these problems only indirectly.

Soviet investigators who approached the problem of the historical formation of psychological processes of man had two advantages over foreign investigators. On the one hand, they had accepted the propositions that—1) the fundamental categories of conscious life do not have an *a priori*, spiritual character, but are the product of historical development; and—2) that as a function of the transition from one historical form to another, not only the *contents* of consciousness, but the *structure* of higher mental processes, underlying concrete forms of psychological activity, change. On the other hand, the epoch in which they lived was one in which extraordinarily deep and rapid restructuring of historical forms was occurring, providing a unique opportunity, to trace the restructuring of psychological processes which followed the social, economic and cultural revolution. Changes in exactly the form experienced in the USSR had never occurred before.

These conditions explain why we wanted to trace directly the psychological results of the great social historical changes which occurred in our country in the 1930's. Consequently, it was decided that a group of Soviet psychologists, including myself and several co-workers would go to Soviet Central Asia. This work was carried out under the direct leadership and with the participation of L. S. Vygotskii. The starting point for our observations was the assumption that separate psychological, and, in particular, cognitive processes (such as perception and memory, abstraction and generalization, reasoning, and problem-solving) are not independent and unchanging "abilities" or "functions" of human consciousness; they are processes occuring in concrete, practical activities and are formed within the limits of this activity. Not only the content, but the structure of cognitive processes depends on the activity of which it is a part. Such a conception of the close ties between separate psychological processes and concrete forms of activity calls for a rejection of the non-scientific idea that "psychological functions" are *a priori* data, independent of historical forms; it stands in complete correspondence with the fundamental ideas of Marxist philosophy and with the fundamental pre-suppositions of Soviet psychology.

This initial position forces us to assume that different forms of practical life, which correspond to different historical periods or different social, psychological levels of development, determine the formation of psychological processes which differ according to their structure. Men living in conditions of different historical circumstances are distinguishable not only according to different forms of practical activity and different contents to their consciousness, but also to different structures of their fundamental psychological processes. Our initial position also forces us to assume that significant social-historical advances connected with a change of social-historical forms, and their accompanying fundamental cultural changes, lead also to fundamental changes in the structure of psychological processes along with the fundamental restructuring of activity. This psychological restructuring includes not only the use of new codes, organizations of new kinds of cognitive activity, but also substantial changes in the relation among psychological processes with the aide of which the new forms of cognitive activity begin to exist.

The subjects of our study were the residents of isolated villages in Central Asia whose life during the 1930's experienced a radical change in connection with the rapid socio-economic restructuring (collectivization) and cultural revolution (liquidation of illiteracy) which occurred at that time. The population of these villages live in a rural culture; however, this culture was comprised of a rather narrow social class and did not deeply affect the remaining population of the country. The population of these little villages, in the same manner as population of pre-revolutionary Russian villages, continued to live in conditions of a natural economy and remained completely non-literate. The religious ideas which were formally dominant, in practice had little influence on the ideas and cognitive processes of these people, whose thought rarely went beyond the sphere of practical activity which was determined by the demands of the natural economy. The socio-economic restructuring which began in the 1930's introduced fundamental changes into the life of the people in these areas.

The non-technological economy (gardening, cotton-raising, animal husbandry) was replaced by more complex economic systems; there was a sharp increase in the communication with the cities; new people appeared in the villages; collective economy with joint planning and with joint organization of production radically changed the previous economic activity; extensive educational and propaganda work intruded on those traditional views which previously had been determined by the simpler life of the village; a large network of schools designed to liquidate illiteracy was introduced to a large portion of the population and, in the course of a few years, the residents of these villages were included in a system of educational institutions and at the same time were introduced to a kind of theoretical activity which had previously not existed in those areas.

It seems unquestionable that a radical restructuring of concepts and a decisive widening of the circle of ideas resulted from this socio-economic and cultural revolution. All of these events placed before psychology a fundamental question. Did these changes lead only to changes in the contents of conscious life or did they change the *forms* of consciousness as well? Was the structure of psychological processes changed and were new kinds of conscious functioning produced by these socio-economic changes? The answers to these questions would define a fundamental position in psychology as an historical science. Let us now turn to the facts we obtained.

IV

Psychologists have long been of the belief that the operation of subordination to a particular category, in other words, the operation of logical generalization and the formation of concepts is not only a fundamental logical process, but also must be understood as a fundamental form of the working of the mind, equivalent in all people independent of the surrounding conditions.

However, such an approach, which we can term an ahistorical approach to logical categories as a fundamental means of thinking, is contrary to our initial assumption. We were much more inclined to believe that abstraction and generalization, the formation of abstract concepts and the relating of an object to a particular category is a product of historical development. These processes become prominent as we know them only at a certain stage of historical development when the leading role of practical life gives way to new forms of theoretical activity and when similar abstract operations begin to make sense in terms of people's activity. Our initial pre-supposition led us to believe that in less complex socio-economic conditions such abstract operations would still not play a leading role and that their role should be played by somewhat different, more concrete forms of cognitive activity, reflecting characteristic kinds of practical life required by the corresponding socio-economic condition.

In order to determine exactly what kinds of ties dominate in consciousness at different stages of historical development, we conducted a simple experiment: subjects were presented four cards on which were drawn representations of objects, three of which were members of well-defined categories (*e.g.*, saw, ax, shovel). The fourth object clearly did not belong to that category (*e.g.*, a piece of wood); and the subject was asked to select three cards which depicted "objects that go together" or objects that could be named by a single word (tool, in this case) and to place the fourth card to the side (that is, the card that did not enter into the category). Solution of this task provides no difficulties for subjects for whom the operations of inclusion of concrete objects under abstract categories (or logical operation of "categorical thought") constitutes a well-structured, dominant system of logical operations.

The picture was completely different for the residents of these isolated areas who were still at a level of relatively simple socio-economic organization and literacy. Not one of these subjects produced an abstract category in response to the task; they did not select the three pictures which belonged to the category of tools, and they did not select the abstract attributes which would relate these objects to an abstract category. Their operations were completely different; they thought of a concrete practical situation in which the three objects could be included, and they placed to the side that object which did not enter into the practical situation. "It is clear", they said, "here's a log, a saw and an ax, they go together"; "it is necessary to fell the tree, then to cut it up, and the shovel does not relate to that, it is just needed in the garden". Attempts to hint at the correct solution were not accepted by our subjects: they were told that it was possible to divide the pictures into a different group, that "one man said that the ax, the saw and the shovel had to be placed together because they are similar to each other; that it is possible to name them with one word; and that the log was not a tool and therefore did not belong." Our subjects did not accept these solutions, and considered them incorrect, often saying things such as "No, that man was not correct; he does not know his business; he is a fool. Look, the saw and the ax, what could you do with them if you did not have the log? And the shovel? We just don't need it here".

In this way, from all the possible associations evoked during the operation of comparing these pictures, our subjects selected only concrete, practical associations, while the abstract "categorical" associations, if they were evoked (which happened very rarely), were considered insignificant and non-adaptable to practice. In those situations where we used abstraction and generalization, our subjects began by thinking of concrete, practical situations in which the three objects could participate. The leading place in the psychological operation involved in comparison of objects was occupied not by verbal-logical associations (or bonds), but by processes of thought involving the concrete situation. The psychological structure of the process turned out to be completely different than we might have expected.

No less significant is the fact that when we introduced a generalizaing word into the problem, it did not lead, as a rule, to any change in the process. When we asked the subjects: "Is it true that the objects you selected are similar?", they nodded their heads and said that "of course, they were similar"; their word for "similar" was used in our sense of "suitable for each other". Although the Uzbekh language has a completely different designation (*mos keldi*) which can be used.[3] When we directly introduced the generalizing concept called "tool" (*asbob* in Uzbekhi), they formally agreed that it could be used, but they said that it is not important and that in this situation about which we were speaking, the saw, the ax, and the log in equal degree could be designated by the word *asbob*, because "they work together" and that the shovel remains as before, beside the point. Exactly the same results were obtained in attempts to classify other groups of objects (*e.g.*, a stock of wheat, a flower, a tree, and a sickle or, a plate, a knife, a cup and bread). In all these cases, the subjects from this group related the objects to a particular, practical situation and did not relate them to a well-defined category.

Completely different results were obtained when we studied the behavior of residents of the same village who had gone through a brief literacy course and who had participated as activists in the newly-formed collective farms. None of these poeple substituted concrete-visual practice for the required abstract operation, and they easily mastered the process of abstract-logical generalization; one-third of these subjects manifested the presence of both kinds of thought (situational and categorical), two-thirds of the subjects completed the abstract operations relating the objects to the known categories without any difficulties. Experiments carried out with young people from the same village who had completed one or two years of school, yielded results which could scarcely be distinguished from those which we had obtained under more technological cultural situations.

These facts lead us to make the following conclusions. Logical operations for finding relations such as "species-genus", the comparison of objects according to logical attributes and generalization of them to well-known logical categories are clearly not universal operations, occupying a leading place in the cognitive activity of people who find themselves at different levels of social-historical development. The cognitive processes of people living in less complex social-historical conditions, are constructed significantly differently than the cognitive activities known to us by our own experience. These differences rest not only in the different content of

[3] The Russian term is difficult to translate in this context, but the term "suitable" is used in the sense of "a person is suitable for the work", "he's the right man for the job" (*Translator's note*).

cognitive processes, but are significantly different according to their structure. Not the abstract significance of words, but concrete-practical ties reproduced from the experience of the subject play a directing role; not abstract thought, but visual-motor recollection determines the course of thinking. All of these facts have nothing in common with the biological feature of the people that we have studied. They are a completely social-historical feature of psychological activity; it is only necessary for the social-historical conditions to change in order for these features of cognitive activity to change and disappear.

V

The fact that a fundamental process of cognition—the formation of concepts—is different under different historical conditions, determines other differences in cognitive processes, among which are the operations of drawing conclusions and reasoning. Philosophers, just as psychologists, have never doubted that the operation of forming a syllogism and syllogistic reasoning are of a universal character and identical at all stages of development. They have accepted the position that the relation of the major and minor premises ("precious metals do not rust", "gold is precious metal",...) automatically carry with them the logical conclusion and that the necessity of this conclusion is equivalent at all stages of social-historical development. This position is bound to be completely unwarranted in view of the data from our psychological investigation.

The presence of the two initial parts of the syllogism (the major and minor premises) is said to be necessary and sufficient for the appearance of "a logical feeling" of the incompleteness of the judgement, and for the operation of the logical conclusion at that stage of historical development where the formation of the concept consists of the abstraction of the important attribute and the logical relating of the object to its corresponding category, in other words, at that stage where the thought processes are completed in a verbal-logical way. However, presence of the two first parts of the syllogism is certainly *not* sufficient for the appearance of "a logical feeling of the incompleteness of the judgement" and for the automatic completion of the operation of the logical conclusion at those historical stages when thinking carries a practical, visual-motor character and when the decisive role in reasoning is played, not by logical pre-suppositions, but by the presence of some corresponding practical experience. This is why the presentation of the two first premises of a syllogism to people living in different, simpler, socio-economic conditions, clearly does not lead to an automatic appearance of a logical conclusion. A complete logical conclusion may be made only from immediate practical experience, and cannot be made from the comparison of two verbal-logical parts of the syllogism.

In order to obtain data on this problem, we conducted a special series of experiments. We asked subjects, in our isolated villages, two kinds of unfinished syllogisms: the contents of some were taken from the concrete, practical experience of the villagers; the contents of others bore no relation to familiar, practical life. If the logical conditions of the major and minor premises played a decisive role in the operation of reasoning and were sufficient in order to make the corresponding logical conclusion, in both cases the subjects would give the necessary conclusion from the syllogism with equal ease; if the leading role in the reasoning operation is played not so much by verbal-logical relations as by the immediate practical experience of the subject, then the conclusion in the first kind of syllogism should be clear while conclusion for the second kind should turn out to be impossible. The facts obtained in this investigation completely bore out the latter assumption on our part.

For syllogisms connected with immediate practical life, we provided our subjects with the following sorts of problems: "Cotton grows where it is hot and humid. In the village it is hot and humid. Does cotton grow there or not?" For syllogisms not connected with the immediate experience, we gave such logical problems as "In the north where there is snow all year, the bears are white. Town X is there in the north. Are the bears white in that town or not?" Deciding the first type of syllogism evoked no difficulty in our subjects. They said: "Well, if the village is warm and humid, then cotton certainly must grow there, of course, if there aren't any hills nearby". And they added: "And that's the way it is, I know myself". The characteristic addition, "and I know it myself" uncovers the psychological nature of the way in which the conclusion was made. It shows that while the relation of the major and minor premises plays some role in the conclusion, the fundamental role, nevertheless, is played by the actual practical experience of the subject, and that in the given case we are dealing not so much with a conclusion from the syllogism, as conclusion from the subject's own practical experience.

This assumption is confirmed if we consider the responses to the second kind of syllogism. One interesting feature of the second kind of syllogism consisted of the fact that the assumptions of the syllogism were often repeated not as a system of logical relations, but as two isolated questions not having a definite content. For example, when they were told about a particular village in the north, where there is snow all year and all the bears are white and when they were given the second premise (such and such a place X is in the north, and there is snow all year), the subject repeated the question by saying: "In the north where there is snow all year, are the bears white or not" or they repeated the problem as: "In such and such a place X, are the bears white or not?" The omissions clearly indicate that the major premise was not accepted by them as an initial, generalizing position and that the real syllogism was not evoked by these conditions. It is therefore completely natural that our subjects, who easily reached a conclusion on the basis of the syllogism that was related to their practical life, refused to make a conclusion from the syllogism which was not connected with their practical experience. To a question formulated after the presentation of the two premises of this problem, they answered: "But I don't know what kind of bears are there. I have not been there and I don't know. Look, why don't you ask old man X, he was there and he knows, he will tell you". Sometimes these same subjects answered: "No, I don't know what kind of bears are there. I have not been there and I don't want to lie".

The refusal to accept the system of logical assumptions and to draw conclusions from them, the idea that to draw a logical conclusion not having experienced the situation oneself, means to "lie", were all typical phenomena for the vast majority of the basic group of subjects whose cognitive processes are determined in infinitely larger degree by personal, practical experience than by a system of verbal-logical ties. Just the opposite occurs in subjects who had completed a small amount of schooling, who were included in the active activity of the collective farm, and who worked along with other people to plan the production of the farm and collectively drew conclusions about the future of their farm's economy. All these people easily accepted the generalized character of the judgement, included in the major premises and without any difficulty related the two premises to obtain the necessary, logical conclusion.

These facts indicate that the operation of reaching a logical conclusion from the syllogism is certainly not of a universal character as one might have thought and that different socio-economic conditions with their corresponding special features of cultural life, create conditions in which the dominant role in cognitive processes is played by personal, practical experience. In such conditions, the necessary belief in logical premises has still not been accepted; a system of verbal-logical relations is not evoked and operations of drawing a conclusion from the syllogism have still not obtained that significance for the acquisition of new knowledge which will be the case in more complex socio-economic conditions, which lead to the development of new kinds of theoretical activity.

CONCLUSION

We have completed a brief review of our material and now we will consider a few of the conclusions.

The idea that the fundamental processes of psychological life are of a universal, ahistorical nature and must be viewed either as a category of the soul or as a natural function of the brain, independent of social-historical conditions turned out during the course of our investigations to be incorrect. Psychological processes, and most of all, higher, specifically human, forms of psychological activity, such as voluntary attention, active memory, and abstract thought, must be understood as a social phenomenon in origin, and as processes formed during the course of mastery of general human experiences. These processes are social-historical in their origin, mediated in their structure, and consciously and wilfully directed in their functioning.

Our position concerning the historical nature of psychological processes is not restricted to the facts of ontogenesis. It has been supported by the investigations of those changes which psychological processes undergo during the transition from one social-historical formation to another. Our facts indicate that the development of psychological processes during social history really cannot be interpreted as the result of more experience or the enrichment of one's circle of ideas. The origin of new forms of practical activity, the transition from visual-motor kinds of practice to complex forms of theoretical activity, is one of the most important facts of historical development, leading to a radical restructuring of cognitive processes and to the appearance of new kinds of psychological activity which did not exist previously. The facts obtained in our investigation show that even such processes as the formation of concepts, logical conclusions and reasoning cannot be understood as an historical category, they are formed in concrete social-historical conditions and are different in principle in conditions of simpler social-historical life where the role of immediate practice dominates.

Our belief that the fundamental categories of psychological processes in man are of an historical character and that psychology must be understood as an historical science is still a new idea and has not been sufficiently well understood. It was first formulated in the philosophy of Marxism, but is only presently being mastered by psychological science. There is every reason to think that it will become an organic part of psychology only in the future and that the coming generation of psychologists will have new and important prospects for the study of fundamental psychological processes in man as a function of his historical development.

REFERENCES

Leontiev, A. N. *Problems in the development of the mind.* Moscow: Publishing House of the Academy of Pedagogical Sciences, 1968.

Luria, A. R. On changes in psychological functions during the course of child development. *Problems of Psychology*, 1962, No. 3.

Luria, A. R. & Yudovich, F. Y. *Speech and development of psychological processes in the child.* Moscow: Publishing House of the Academy of Pedagogical Sciences, 1956.

Vygotskii, L. S. *Selected psychological investigations.* Moscow: Publishing House of the Academy of Pedagogical Sciences, 1956.

Vygotskii, L. S. *The development of higher psychological functions.* Moscow: Publishing House of the Academy of Pedagogical Sciences, 1960.

Vygotskii, L. S. *Thought and language.* Cambridge, Mass.: MIT Press, 1962.

Vygotskii, L. S. & Luria, A. R. *Studies in the history of behavior.* Moscow: OGIZ, 1930.

Zaporozhets, A. V. *The development of voluntary movement.* Moscow: Publishing House of the Academy of Pedagogical Sciences, 1959.

Epilog

Darwin and Marx are the last historical figures represented in this volume. The question naturally arises: Why stop there? As stated in the preface, we have been concerned with psychology's long past, rather than with its short history. The division between these two periods is, of course, arbitrary. But 1859, the year of Darwin's *On the Origin of Species* and Marx's *A Contribution to the Critique of Political Economy*, represents as good a dividing point as any. In the following year (1860), Gustav Fechner published his *Elemente der Psychophysik*. This work did much to break the prejudice against psychology as a scientific discipline. The actual founding of the first psychological laboratory by Wilhelm Wundt was still a few years off (1879), but events were beginning to move rapidly—too rapidly to be followed in a book such as this.

In this brief epilog, no attempt will be made to summarize or review the contents of the preceding chapters. The reader who wishes such a review can refer to the General Introduction (Chapt. 1). There, four themes were outlined that unite the present set of readings: (1) patterns of explanation, (2) the self and human nature, (3) the nature of emotion, and (4) the logic of evolution. A few additional comments on the first of these themes, i.e., patterns of explanation, will serve as a conclusion to this volume.

To recapitulate briefly, different patterns of explanation can be distinguished in terms of a matrix of presuppositions (see Chapt. 1, p. 7). These presuppositions involve assumptions regarding models of explanation (formalistic, mechanistic, and organismic), sources of knowledge (rationalism, empiricism, and mysticism), and types of inference (deductive, inductive, and intuitive). As a starting point for discussion, let us ask: Which of these presuppositions (or combination thereof) is most appropriate for psychology? This question is largely rhetorical, for as the preceding chapters indicate, each presupposition has its advantages and limitations. Hence, there is no *one* pattern of explanation that is the most appropriate for psychology. But this conclusion, however correct, is deceptively simple and perhaps even misleading. It therefore requires additional consideration. In particular, we must consider the manner in which conceptual diversity and the competition among ideas contribute to the advancement of science.

For the sake of brevity, discussion will be limited to the set of presuppositions concerning models of explanation. (Similar considerations apply *mutatis mutandis* to presuppositions regarding sources of knowledge and types of inference.) We will begin with a brief review of the vicissitudes the mechanistic model has undergone from ancient to modern times.

In pre-Socratic Greek philosophy, a mechanistic model was advocated by Anaxagoras and the atomists (e.g., Democritus). This model was rejected by Plato and Aristotle; yet it enjoyed a revival during the Hellenistic period (after Alexander the Great) at the hands of Archimedes and also the later Epicureans (e.g., Lucretius). With the ascendency of Neoplatonism and Christianity (Plotinus and Augustine), and the subsequent reintroduction of Aristotelian thought into the Latin West by Aquinas, the mechanistic model was all but eclipsed throughout most of the Middle Ages. However, it was again revived at the start of the 15th century and ultimately gained predominance during the Scientific Revolution (16th and 17th centuries). According to Wheeler,[1] the influence of the mechanistic model reached additional peaks approximately during the years 1775 and 1860, and (writing in 1936) he predicted that its influence would crest again around 1960.

Among American psychologists, at least, Wheeler's prediction has been largely fulfilled. During the 1950s and early 1960s, the mechanistic model was widely accepted as the best approach to scientific explanation. Recently, however, mechanistic approaches have come under mounting criticism (cf. Taylor, Chapt. 6), while interest in formalistic and organismic models has been increasing (cf. Chomsky, Chapt. 14, and Luria, Chapt. 22, respectively). But these latter approaches also have had their cycles. For example, Wheeler identified peaks in the organismic approach approximately during the years 1250, 1650, 1820, and again in 1935. (What Wheeler termed an organismic approach represents an amalgam of what we have described as formalistic and organismic models, and he was concerned primarily with the physical rather than the life sciences, but that is not particularly important from the point of view of the present discussion.)

---

[1] R. H. Wheeler, Organismic logic in the history of science. *Philosophy of Science*, 1936, *3*, 26–61.

Some more ardent critics have implied that the mechanistic model is—or should be—dead as far as psychology is concerned. This contention has been met largely with disdain from the mechanists, as though the critics were trying to strip psychology of its scientific credentials. The above considerations regarding the cyclic influence of explanatory models indicate that some temperance is needed on both sides of this sometimes acrimonious debate. On the one side, history indicates that it would be premature to write a final obituary for the mechanistic model. Even if this model should become eclipsed in the near future, it is safe to predict that it will be revived in a more sophisticated version at some subsequent time. And, on the other side, to dismiss nonmechanistic approaches as unscientific would be to ignore the contribution made by formalistic and organismic models to the past—and undoubtedly to the future—advancement of science.

This last point perhaps deserves additional comment or documentation. The Scientific Revolution is often depicted as a triumph of the mechanistic approach over alternative models of explanation. But this is more myth than fact. As Kearney[2] has recently shown, both Copernicus and Kepler worked within a formalistic[3] tradition, the origins of which can be traced back to Plato and Plotinus. And individuals such as Harvey, who worked within the organismic tradition stemming from Aristotle, also made important discoveries. Thus, the mechanistic model advocated by Galileo, Descartes, and others was simply one train of thought that contributed to the success of the Scientific Revolution. In the competition among ideas, however, the mechanistic model ultimately gained ascendency. By the end of the 17th century, Christian Huygens, the great Dutch physicist, could observe that

> In true phylosophy one conceives the cause of all natural effects in terms of mechanical motions. This, in my opinion, we must necessarily do, or else renounce all hopes of comprehending anything in physics.[4]

As the opinion expressed by Huygens became widespread, the contributions of those who worked under different presuppositions tended to be downplayed or reinterpreted to fit the newly dominant mechanistic model. Even Newton did not escape this fate. Thus today his contributions are often used to illustrate the

[2] H. Kearney, *Science and change: 1500-1700*. New York: World University Library, 1971.

[3] Kearney refers to the formalistic tradition as "magical" because of its frequently mystical overtones. Mysticism, however, is not an essential feature of formalistic models.

[4] C. Huygens. *Treatise on light*. Chicago: University of Chicago Press, 1950, p. 3.

advantages of the mechanistic approach. In his own day, however, Newton came under rather severe criticism from the more extreme mechanists (such as Huygens) for some of his ideas, especially his law of gravity describing the attraction between bodies. In a completely mechanical universe, there is no place for seemingly mysterious forces (gravity) acting at a distance. But Newton was working as much within the formalistic as within the mechanistic tradition, and that provided him the latitude to make the contributions he did.[5]

It would be interesting at this point to examine why the various models of explanation have undergone such vicissitudes in their influence, but that would be beyond the scope of this brief epilog. Therefore, we will only note in passing some of the more important reasons. These include the state of knowledge at any given time, i.e., whether the potentials of a particular model (or that version of it then prevalent) have been exhausted and its limitations exposed. Also important is the aspect of the subject matter being emphasized. This is particularly well illustrated by Descartes' adoption of a mechanistic model only with regard to physiological processes and "passions of the soul," but not with regard to "actions of the soul" (i.e., deliberate behavior). Advances in related disciplines, especially those considered more "basic," also have influenced the choice of models among psychologists. Thus, when field theories became prevalent in physics, some psychologists turned from a mechanistic to a more formalistic approach.[6]

In addition to these disciplinary factors, there are broader personal and social conditions that help determine the choice of explanatory models. At the risk of oversimplification, it may be said that when an individual or society emphasizes the practical application of science, i.e., prediction and control, then a mechanistic approach is fostered, for it is through machines that man exerts his greatest influence over nature. When, however, a humanistic orientation (in its narrow sense) is emphasized, then an organismic model may be encouraged, for such a model can better accommodate the facts of growth and change, as well as purposeful behavior. Finally, a formalistic model—with its emphasis on internal consistency and elegance—may be found most compatible by those who believe that aesthetic and intellectual achievements are worthy goals in their own right.

These relationships are, of course, very loose, and the factors

---

[5] Cf. Kearney, op. cit.

[6] See, for example, W. Köhler, *The task of Gestalt psychology.* Princeton, N.J.: Princeton University Press, 1969.

mentioned do not exhaust the list of possible influences on the choice of explanatory models (cf. Kuhn, Chapt. 2). But this is not the place to pursue the matter further.

The discussion thus far may be summarized with the observation that conceptual diversity is a necessary condition for scientific progress. This observation can not be accepted, however, without some qualification. Recalling Kuhn's analysis (Chapt. 2), it might be maintained that diversity is advantageous primarily during periods of scientific revolution and not during periods of "normal" science. According to Kuhn, normal science is marked by the widespread adoption of a single paradigm. Competition among fundamentally different patterns of thought is thus held to a minimum, and scientific investigation is directed along well-defined channels toward predetermined goals. But as was pointed out in the editor's introduction to Chapter 2, the difference between normal and revolutionary science is more a matter of degree than of kind. During scientific revolutions, normal processes are simply accelerated and accentuated. Or, stated conversely, the conceptual diversity that characterizes scientific revolutions is also present during periods of normal science, albeit to a lesser degree.

Still, it must be admitted that if conceptual diversity becomes too great, then the result may resemble intellectual anarchy rather than science (whether normal or revolutionary). That is the state of affairs that characterizes much of the social sciences today. But a solution to the problems facing the social sciences is not to be found in the premature adoption of some universal paradigm; the result in that case would not be science, but a new scholasticism in the name of science. What is needed, rather, is a recognition of the potential advantages of alternative points of view, combined with constructive criticism of all views. The latter is especially important, because it provides a selection mechanism without which progress would be impossible.

In conclusion then, what is being suggested here is an application of the variation-and-selection model of evolution (see Chapt. 1, pp. 39 ff.) to the development of science. This is not a novel suggestion, and some of its implications already have been explored in the introductory chapter. Therefore, we may bring this epilog to a close with the observation that if the present set of readings has helped to foster diversity while at the same time encouraging a critical attitude, then it has served its major purpose.

Name Index

Subject Index